Building Cisco Remote Access Networks

Catherine Paquet

Cisco Press
201 W 103rd Street
Indianapolis, IN 46290

Building Cisco Remote Access Networks

Catherine Paquet

Copyright© 1999 Cisco Press

Cisco Press logo is a trademark of Cisco Systems, Inc.

Published by:
Cisco Press
201 West 103rd Street
Indianapolis, IN 46290 USA

Printed in the United States of America 6 7 8 9 0

6th Printing January 2001

Library of Congress Cataloging-in-Publication Number: 98-86494

ISBN: 1-57870-091-4

Warning and Disclaimer

This book is designed to provide information about building Cisco remote access networks. Every effort has been made to make this book as complete and as accurate as possible, but no warranty or fitness is implied.

The information is provided on an "as is" basis. The author, Cisco Press, and Cisco Systems, Inc. shall have neither liability nor responsibility to any person or entity with respect to any loss or damages arising from the information contained in this book or from the use of the discs or programs that may accompany it.

The opinions expressed in this book belong to the author and are not necessarily those of Cisco Systems, Inc.

Trademark Acknowledgments

All terms mentioned in this book that are known to be trademarks or service marks have been appropriately capitalized. Cisco Press or Cisco Systems, Inc. cannot attest to the accuracy of this information. Use of a term in this book should not be regarded as affecting the validity of any trademark or service mark.

Feedback Information

At Cisco Press, our goal is to create in-depth technical books of the highest quality and value. Each book is crafted with care and precision, undergoing rigorous development that involves the unique expertise of members from the professional technical community.

Readers' feedback is a natural continuation of this process. If you have any comments regarding how we could improve the quality of this book, or otherwise alter it to better suit your needs, you can contact us through email at cisco-press@mcp.com. Please make sure to include the book title and ISBN in your message.

We greatly appreciate your assistance.

Publisher	J. Carter Shanklin
Executive Editor	John Kane
Cisco Systems Program Manager	Jim LeValley
Managing Editor	Patrick Kanouse
Acquisitions Editor	Brett Bartow
Development Editor	Andrew Cupp
Project Editor	Nancy Sixsmith
Technical Editor	Karen Bagwell
Team Coordinator	Amy Lewis
Cover Designer	Karen Ruggles
Indexer	Craig Small
Proofreader	Lisa Stumpf
Production Team	Wil Cruz and Eric S. Miller

CISCO SYSTEMS

CISCO PRESS

Corporate Headquarters
Cisco Systems, Inc.
170 West Tasman Drive
San Jose, CA 95134-1706
USA
http://www.cisco.com
Tel. 408 526 4000
      800 553-NETS (6387)
Fax: 408 526-4100

European Headquarters
Cisco Systems Europe s.a.r.l.
Parc Evolic, Batiment L1/L2
16 Avenue du Quebec
Villebon, BP 706
91961 Courtaboeuf Cedex
France
http://www-europe.cisco.com
Tel: 33 1 69 18 61 00
Fax: 33 1 69 28 83 26

Americas Headquarters
Cisco Systems, Inc.
170 West Tasman Drive
San Jose, CA 95134-1706
USA
http://www.cisco.com
Tel: 408 526-7660
Fax: 408 527-0883

Asia Headquarters
Nihon Cisco Systems K.K.
Fuji Building, 9th Floor
3-2-3 Marunouchi
Chiyoda-ku, Tokyo 100
Japan
http://www.cisco.com
Tel: 81 3 5219 6250
Fax: 81 3 5219 6001

Cisco Systems has more than 200 offices in the following countries. Addresses, phone numbers, and fax numbers are listed on the Cisco Connection Online Web site at http://www.cisco.com/offices.

Argentina • Australia • Austria • Belgium • Brazil • Canada • Chile • China • Colombia • Costa Rica • Croatia • Czech Republic • Denmark • Dubai, UAE Finland • France • Germany • Greece • Hong Kong • Hungary • India • Indonesia • Ireland • Israel • Italy • Japan • Korea • Luxembourg • Malaysia Mexico • The Netherlands • New Zealand • Norway • Peru • Philippines • Poland • Portugal • Puerto Rico • Romania • Russia • Saudi Arabia • Singapore Slovakia • Slovenia • South Africa • Spain • Sweden • Switzerland • Taiwan • Thailand • Turkey • Ukraine • United Kingdom • United States • Venezuela

About the Author

Catherine Paquet is a Senior Network Architect with GeoTrain Corporation, Cisco's largest worldwide training partner. She provides consulting and training services in North America and Europe. Catherine is a Cisco Certified Systems Instructor and master instructor for CMTD and BCRAN courses. She has in-depth knowledge of routing technologies and access services, mainly in the area of Frame Relay, ISDN, and asynchronous connections. Catherine's internetworking career started as a LAN manager, she was then promoted to MAN manager, and she eventually became the nation-wide WAN Manager for a federal department. Catherine has a Masters in Business Administration with a major in Management Information Systems.

About the Technical Reviewer

Karen M. Bagwell (CCIE # 3662, CCSI) is a Senior Instructor for GeoTrain Corporation. She is an established industry consultant and trainer with more than a decade of experience in networking technologies. Known best for her dynamic teaching, Karen also has extensive network design and implementation experience with a wide variety of network technologies and products. Karen lives in the beautiful state of Wisconsin with her husband, two daughters, and four dogs.

Dedications

To Pierre, Laurence, and Simon

"Destiny is not a matter of chance, it is a matter of choice; it is not a thing to be waited for, it is a thing to be achieved."

—William Jennings Bryan

Acknowledgments

There are many people I would like to thank for helping me put this book together:

The Cisco Press team. Brett Bartow was the catalyst of this project. He coordinated the efforts of all parties and ensured that sufficient resources were available for the completion of the book. Amy Lewis was instrumental in organizing the logistics and administration. Drew Cupp, development editor, has been invaluable in producing a high-quality manuscript through his perspicacity and thoroughness. Not only did he improve the presentation, but he also caught some technical errors. Nancy Sixsmith, project and copy editor, was instrumental in improving the language and consistency of this book. Many thanks also to Karen Bagwell, CCIE and Certified Cisco Systems Instructor, for her technical review and comments for every chapter and appendix.

The Cisco Systems team. Many thanks to the original developers of the BCRAN course, Joe Baggs and Keith Serrao, for their inexhaustible patience with my numerous questions and comments. Thanks also to Kevin Calkins, Certified Cisco Systems Instructor and course monitor, for his technical insight.

The GeoTrain Corporation team. Many thanks to Richard Gordon, General Manager, and Dan O'Brien, Director of Operations, for providing me with the time and appropriate tools to complete this book. Also, special thanks to Eric Dragowski, technician, for providing me with the proper equipment when I needed to run some tests.

My family. To my parents, Florence and Maurice, for your love, trust, and sacrifices to ensure that your daughters would get a proper education, thank you. To my children, princess Laurence and champion Simon, for your understanding and patience with Mommy's grumpiness during this project and for reminding me of what is important in life, thank you. And finally, to Pierre Rivard, my soulmate and husband, the source of my motivation and inspiration, I can only express my feelings to you by quoting the French poet De Ronsard: *"Deux corps mais une seule âme"* – *"Two bodies but one soul."*

God bless you all.

Contents at a Glance

Contents

Preface

The World Wide Web, electronic commerce, intranets, extranets, and client/server networked applications are part of the business revolution. One of the most important capabilities that the business revolution must deliver is *access*. Remote access is about connecting people and businesses to the enterprise.

The enterprise must provide remote connectivity for individuals who need access to corporate resources while outside the corporate site—mobile users, telecommuters, even customers and suppliers. End-to-end remote access extends the power of the LAN through dedicated, leased, and regular phone lines out to the most remote users.

Building Cisco Remote Access Networks is based on the Cisco instructor-led course of the same name. This book is one of several published by Cisco Press in support of the Cisco Career Certifications.

This book focuses on using available WAN technologies, such as ISDN and Frame Relay, to connect the enterprise to branch offices and telecommuters. You will learn different types of connectivity, software commands, configurations, and the hardware related to establishing permanent and dial connections. This book also covers the scaling of remote networks through technologies such as address translation and access control.

The book includes case studies that provide comprehensive accounts of concepts and configurations presented in different sections. Also, review questions at the end of each chapter give you an opportunity to test your conceptual and technical comprehension of the material.

This book can be used by anyone looking for extensive information on remote access and wide-area network communications. The book details dial-up concepts and technologies, access equipment, data-link protocols, routing, authentication, and traffic control and management. This book provides in-depth information to Cisco Certification candidates preparing for the BCRAN exam.

This book is based on the Cisco course called Building Cisco Remote Access Networks. Information and configurations in the course are based on the Cisco Internetwork Operating System (IOS) 11.3.

Introduction to Remote Access Networks

Introduction

The **Building Cisco Remote Access Networks** coursebook teaches readers how to build a remote access network to interconnect Central sites to branch offices and home offices for telecommuters. Once the network is built, the course further teaches students how to control access to the Central site and how to maximize bandwidth utilization over the remote links.

From this book's concisely presented information, multiple configuration examples, and in-depth case studies, you will learn how to do the following:

- Identify the Cisco products that best meet the WAN connection requirements
- Assemble and configure Cisco equipment to establish appropriate WAN network connections
- Enable protocols and technologies that allow traffic flow between each site
- Implement quality-of-service capabilities
- Implement access-control measures

By the end of this book, you will be able to connect, configure, and troubleshoot the various elements of a remote network in a WAN environment.

The book is separated into six parts. An overview of each part follows.

Part I: Introduction to Remote Access Networks

Chapter 1, "Introduction," defines the objectives and conventions of the book, provides an outline of the book, and covers the symbols of remote access networks.

Part II: Identifying Cisco Solutions to Remote Access Needs

This part provides an introduction to WAN, and to dial-up principles and concepts. It explains networking considerations to connect various company sites. You will learn about Cisco products and solutions that satisfy the wide range of requirements on a remote network. You also will learn about and see the specific physical setup used in the book for the case studies.

Chapter 2, "Selecting Cisco Products for Remote Connections," presents various remote access technologies, such as ISDN and Frame Relay, and considerations for an enterprise when building its corporate network. The chapter also discusses Cisco product selection and available tools to assist with this task.

Chapter 3, "Assembling and Cabling the WAN Components," presents the equipment used at the Central site, the branch office, and the telecommuter's location. The chapter also discusses the assembling, cabling, and verification of the network installation.

Part III: Enabling On-Demand Connections to the Central Site

This part teaches you how to complete a remote, on-demand asynchronous connection. This section introduces the use of routers as remote access tools, notably with asynchronous connections. A significant portion of the section is devoted to the Point-to-Point Protocol and the use of Windows 95 for remote access networking.

Chapter 4, "Configuring Asynchronous Connections with Modems," explains modem operation, signaling, configuration, and troubleshooting. The chapter also presents the different types of lines and Cisco equipment configuration for asynchronous communication.

Chapter 5, "Configuring Point-to-Point Protocol and Controlling Network Access," talks about PPP architecture and its main components, such as compression and multilink. The chapter extensively discusses network access control using authentication and callback.

Chapter 6, "Accessing the Central Site with Windows 95," explains how to use Windows 95 Dial-Up Networking for remote access.

Part IV: Enhancing On-Demand Connectivity

This part discusses how you can enhance your on-demand connectivity with ISDN technology. You will learn the advantages that ISDN has over asynchronous connections. You will then see how to configure an ISDN BRI and ISDN PRI connection. You will also configure DDR parameters to place an ISDN call.

Chapter 7, "Using ISDN and DDR to Enhance Remote Connectivity," presents ISDN architecture, equipment, and technologies—such as Basic Rate Interface and Primary Rate Interface.

Chapter 8, "Optimizing the Use of DDR Interface—Dialer Profiles and Rotary Groups," explains the use of virtual interfaces in remote access, particularly the operation of rotary groups and dialer profiles.

Chapter 9, "Configuring a Cisco 700 Series Router," explains the configuration of a small office, home office (SOHO) Cisco router connecting to a Central site router.

Part V: Enabling Permanent Connections to the Central Site

This part presents you with a tutorial on dedicated serial X.25 and Frame Relay connections. You will learn to enable each protocol on an interface, and monitor the traffic flow with various queuing and flow-control features. You will also learn how to configure an on-demand, dial-up backup if the permanent connection fails or is overutilized.

Chapter 10, "Establishing an X.25 Connection," covers X.25 routing. It presents an overview of the X.25 protocol, explains how packets are addressed and encapsulated in X.25, and describes how to configure X.25 routing.

Chapter 11, "Establishing a Dedicated Frame Relay Connection and Controlling Traffic Flow," reviews Frame Relay operation and configuration. It also covers traffic-shaping principles. You will then learn how to configure Frame Relay traffic shaping on a Cisco router.

Chapter 12, "Enabling Backup to a Permanent Connection," describes how to configure a backup connection for a primary connection, such as a Frame Relay serial connection, if the link goes down or is overutilized.

Chapter 13, "Managing Network Performance with Queuing and Compression," covers why you may need to implement queuing technologies on your WAN connection. It also describes how to implement the queuing technologies available by Cisco IOS software so you can prioritize traffic over your WAN connection. It then explains how you can use compression to optimize WAN utilization.

Part VI: Scaling Remote Access Networks

This part presents you with additional design options that allow you to better manage your WAN services as the network expands. Now that you have established a remote network, this module discusses how you can control your corporate network access and costs with AAA, and how to manage a depleting number of IP addresses with network address translation.

Chapter 14, "Scaling IP Addresses with Network Address Translation," introduces readers to the IP address-depletion problem.

Chapter 15, "Using AAA to Scale Access Control in an Expanding Network," provides an overview of Cisco access-control solutions. It then explains the authentication, authorization, and accounting (AAA) model, and provides explanations of active AAA on a Cisco access server.

NOTE	The term **access server** is used to describe any routers to which you can configure dial-up access. Thus, the term **access server** is synonymous with the term **router** for the purposes of this book.

Appendixes

The appendixes contain additional information and reference material related to remote access. The following is a list and brief description of each appendix:

Appendix A, "Summary of BCRAN Commands," contains a comprehensive list of the commands found in this book.

Appendix B, "Summary of ICRC Commands," contains a comprehensive list of the commands presented in the *Introduction to Cisco Router Configuration* book.

Appendix C, "OSI Model," is a brief overview of the Open System Interconnection.

Appendix D, "AT Commands for Modems and Chat-Scripts," contains a list of basic modem-configuration commands.

Appendix E, "RFC List," contains all of the Request for Comments that are referred to in this book.

Appendix F, "Emerging and Complementary Technologies," includes brief descriptions of related technologies.

Appendix G, "X.25 and Frame Relay Switching," contains commands to configure a Cisco router into a X.25 or Frame Relay switch.

Appendix H, "Answers to Review Questions," has all of the answers to the review questions included at the end of the chapters.

Appendix I, "BCRAN Case Study Addresses and Dial-up Phone Numbers," provides the addresses and phone numbers used in the case studies found in this book.

Appendix J, "Glossary," is a glossary of the terms found in this book.

Case Studies and Review Questions

At the end of most chapters, you will have a chance to review concepts and commands that you learned by performing a case study related to the material covered in the chapter.

In these case studies, you will practice building the network depicted in Figure 1-1. To accomplish this task, you will learn how to connect and configure the following:

- Cisco WAN equipment and interfaces
- Asynchronous on-demand connections using modems
- Integrated Services Digital Network (ISDN), Basic Rate Interface (BRI), and ISDN Primary Rate Interface (PRI) connectivity
- Dial-on-demand routing (DDR)—such as Legacy DDR, dialer profiles, and rotary groups
- Serial connections, such as Point-to-Point Protocol (PPP), X.25, and Frame Relay
- Traffic flow control and queuing features
- Password Authentication Protocol (PAP); Challenge Handshake Authentication Protocol (CHAP); and authentication, authorization, and accounting (AAA) to enhance access control into the network
- Network address translation to better utilize the limited number of IP addresses

Figure 1-1   *Enterprise Wide Area Network Studied through the Chapters and Case Studies*

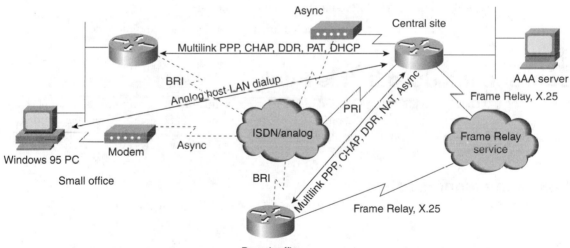

At the end of each chapter, you will also have an opportunity to test your knowledge by answering review questions on the subjects covered in the chapter. You can compare your answers to the correct answers provided in Appendix H, "Answers to Review Questions," to find out how you did and what material you might need to study further.

Who Should Read this Book?

This book is intended for network administrators who are responsible for implementing and troubleshooting enterprise WAN backbones. It is also for anyone who is interested in learning remote access concepts. You can use this book to complement the Building Cisco Remote Access Networks (BCRAN) course. If you feel that you have an extensive amount of equivalent on-the-job experience and are not going to take the BCRAN course, you'll find this book an invaluable tool for filling in any knowledge gaps.

This book focuses on introducing techniques and technology for enabling WAN solutions. To fully benefit from this book, you should be familiar with general networking terms and concepts, and have basic knowledge of the following:

- General Cisco router operation and configuration
- TCP/IP operation and configuration
- Routing protocols (RIP, IGRP, and so on)
- Routed protocols (IP, IPX, and so on)
- Standard and extended access lists
- PPP operation and PPP configuration over serial links
- Frame Relay operation and configuration on interfaces and subinterfaces

Conventions Used in this Book

This book contains several helpful elements such as illustrations, configuration examples, and sidenotes to help you learn about remote access networks. This section covers the standard conventions that you will encounter in this book.

Illustration Iconography

The icons displayed in Figure 1-2 are used in the figures presented throughout this book.

NOTE The addressing schemes and telephone numbers used in this book are reserved; they are not to be used in the public network. They are used in this book only as examples to facilitate learning. When building your network, use only the addresses and telephone numbers assigned by your service provider.

Figure 1-2   *Network Topology Icons Used in this Book*

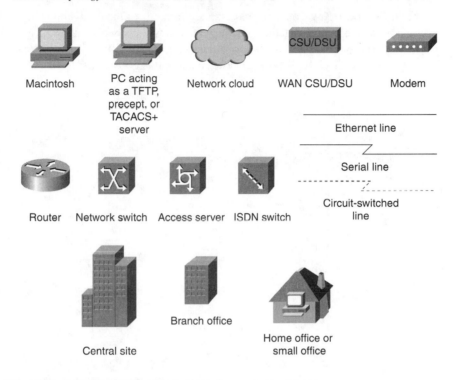

Macintosh   PC acting as a TFTP, precept, or TACACS+ server   Network cloud   WAN CSU/DSU   Modem

Ethernet line

Serial line

Circuit-switched line

Router   Network switch   Access server   ISDN switch

Central site   Branch office   Home office or small office

Command Syntax Conventions

The conventions used to present command syntax in this book are the same conventions used in the IOS Command Reference. The Command Reference describes these conventions as follows:

- Vertical bars (|) separate alternative, mutually exclusive elements.
- Square brackets [ ] indicate optional elements.
- Braces { } indicate a required choice.
- Braces within brackets [{ }] indicate a required choice within an optional element.
- **Boldface** indicates commands and keywords that are entered literally as shown. In actual examples (not syntax), boldface indicates user input (such as a **show** command).
- *Italics* indicate arguments for which you supply actual values.

Author's Notes, Key Concepts, Notes, and Warnings

The Author's Notes, Key Concepts, Notes, and Warnings found in this book are included to provide you with extra information on a subject. You will probably find these asides to be very beneficial in real-world implementation, but these notes are not subject to the exam (if you decide to take the Cisco BCRAN exam after reading this book).

PART II

Identifying Cisco Solutions to Remote Access Needs

CHAPTER 2

Selecting Cisco Products for Remote Connections

This chapter discusses various remote access technologies and considerations that face an enterprise when it builds its corporate network. This chapter also addresses Cisco product selection information.

In this chapter, you will learn about the advantages and disadvantages of different WAN connection types. You will then be provided with a list of site connection considerations. You will learn how to select the appropriate WAN connections, depending on the specific consideration of your organization.

You will also see how to interconnect your company's sites—the Central site, branch offices, home offices, and mobile users—using Cisco equipment.

Finally, you will learn about the tools provided by Cisco to help you select the appropriate equipment.

Remote Access Overview

A **WAN** is a data communications network covering a relatively broad geographic area, often using transmission facilities generally provided by service providers and telephone companies. Unlike LANs, a WAN connection is generally rented from the service provider.

WANs are used to connect various sites at different geographic regions so people at each site can exchange information.

The connection requirements vary considerably. Two sites, for example, may require a dedicated connection because they exchange much real-time data. On the other hand, a mobile user may need to connect to a site only to periodically check e-mail throughout the day.

A network administrator building a remote network must weigh such issues as user needs, bandwidth requirements, and costs of the various available technologies. The network administrator must then select the technologies that best suit the corporation's needs and budget.

Circuit-Switched Connections

Circuit switching is a WAN-switching method, in which a dedicated physical circuit through a carrier network is established, maintained, and terminated for each communication session. Initial signaling at the setup stage determines the endpoints and the connection between the two endpoints.

NOTE   **Circuit switching** requires call setup and call teardown. Circuit switching is used in the telephone company networks and works like a telephone call.

Typical circuit-switched connections are as follows:

* Asynchronous serial

* Integrated Service Digital Network (ISDN), Basic Rate Interface (BRI), and ISDN Primary Rate Interface (PRI)

Asynchronous Serial Connections

Asynchronous serial connections, as seen in Figure 2-2, require minimal cost and use the existing telephone network. It is easy for users to access a Central site from anywhere that has a telephone connection into the telephone network.

Figure 2-2   *Connections Are Made Only When Traffic Dictates a Need*

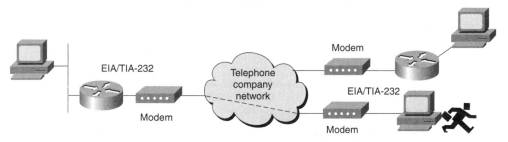

The nature of asynchronous serial circuit-switched connections allows you to configure your connection to be enabled only when you need the service by using dial-on-demand routing (DDR). DDR is ideal when you need only short-term access.

Enable DDR on your asynchronous interface under the following circumstances:

* Traffic patterns are low-volume or periodic—calls are placed and connections are established only when the router detects traffic marked as "interesting." Periodic broadcasts, such as routing protocol updates, should be prevented from triggering a call.

- When you need a backup connection for redundancy or load sharing, DDR can be used to provide backup load sharing and interface failure backup.

A router acts as an **access server**, which is a concentration point for dial-in and dial-out calls. Mobile users, for example, can call into an access server at a Central site to access their e-mail messages.

Asynchronous connections are useful in the following situations:

- A backup connection is required
- A small site
- Short-term on-demand access

Asynchronous serial connections require modems at each end of the connection to convert digital data signals to analog signals that can be transported over the telephone network. Modem speeds typically vary from 28 Kbps to 56 Kbps. The slower bandwidth speeds limit the amount of traffic that you may want to send over an asynchronous line. To place or receive an asynchronous serial call, a Cisco router should have an asynchronous serial interface. The serial standard to attach to an external modem is the EIA/TIA-232 standard. The interface to the telephone company varies by country. In the United States, a standard RJ-11 adapter connects the modem to the telephone outlet.

ISDN Connections

ISDN connections are typically circuit-switched connections that (like asynchronous connections) provide WAN access when needed, rather than requiring a dedicated link. ISDN offers increased bandwidth over a typical dial-up connection; it is intended to carry data, voice, and other traffic across a telephone network. ISDN comprises Basic Rate Interface (BRI) and Primary Rate Interface (PRI), which are illustrated in Figure 2-3.

Figure 2-3   *Circuit-Switched Connection with ISDN*

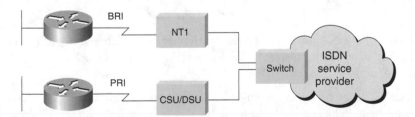

Link Access Procedure on the D channel (LAPD) is the ISDN data link layer protocol for the D channel. It was designed primarily to satisfy the signaling requirements of ISDN basic access.

To place an ISDN BRI call, your router should be equipped with a BRI interface. You will also need an ISDN terminal adapter, which is a device used to connect ISDN BRI connections to other interfaces, such as EIA/TIA-232. A terminal adapter is essentially an ISDN modem. You should also consult your telephone company for information specific to your connection.

NOTE   In Europe, the service provider generally supplies the NT1. In North America, the customer supplies it.

ISDN PRI is generally configured over connections such as T1 and E1 technologies. To place an ISDN call, your router should be equipped with either connection. TI is used in the United States and E1 is common in Europe.

As with asynchronous connections, you can also configure DDR to control access for specific periods of time.

Packet-Switched Connections

Packet switching is a WAN-switching method, in which network devices share a single point-to-point link to transport packets from a source to a destination across a carrier network. Packet-switched networks use **virtual circuits** (VCs) that provide end-to-end connectivity, as shown in Figure 2-4. Physical connections are accomplished by statistically programmed switching devices. Packet headers generally identify the destination.

Figure 2-4   *VCs—Interconnect Sites*

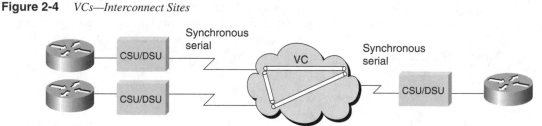

Packet-switched networks can be either privately or publicly managed. The underlying switching fabric is transparent to the user, and the switches are only responsible for the internal delivery of data.

Packet-switched networks offer an administrator less control than a point-to-point connection, and the bandwidth is shared. However, the cost is generally less than a leased line. With WAN speeds comparable to those of leased lines, packet-switched networks are generally suitable links between two large sites that require high link utilization.

Like dedicated lines, packet-switched networks are also typically employed over synchronous serial connections. The connection standards that are supported on Cisco routers are listed in Figure 2-1.

As a general rule, packet-switched connections are most cost-effective when the following situations occur:

- Long connect times
- Large geographic differences

NOTE   Packet-switched networks generally share bandwidth, but the cost is cheaper than a leased line.

Defining WAN Encapsulation Protocols

Each WAN connection uses an encapsulation protocol to encapsulate traffic while it is crossing the WAN link. To ensure that the correct encapsulation protocol is used, you need to configure the Layer 2 encapsulation type to use. The choice of encapsulation protocol depends on the WAN technology and the communicating equipment. Typical WAN protocols include the following:

- Point-to-Point Protocol (PPP)
- Serial Line Internet Protocol (SLIP)—SLIP is a standard protocol for point-to-point serial connections using a variation of TCP/IP. SLIP is the predecessor of PPP.
- High-Level Data Link Control (HDLC)—HDLC is the default encapsulation type on point-to-point, dedicated links. It is used typically when communicating between two Cisco devices. It is a bit-oriented synchronous data link layer protocol. HDLC specifies a data-encapsulation method on synchronous serial links using frame characters and checksums. If communicating with a non-Cisco device, synchronous PPP is a more viable option.
- X.25/Link Access Procedure, Balanced (LAPB)
- Frame Relay
- Asynchronous Transfer Mode (ATM)—ATM is the international standard for cell relay, in which multiple service types (such as voice, video, or data) are conveyed in fixed-length (53-byte) cells. Fixed-length cells allow processing to occur in hardware, thereby reducing transit delays. ATM is designed to take advantage of high-speed transmission media such as E3, Synchronous Optical Network (SONET), and T3.

NOTE   SLIP, HDLC, and ATM are not covered in the BCRAN course, and thus are not discussed further in this book.

PPP Encapsulation

PPP is an international standard encapsulation used for the following types of connections:

- Asynchronous serial
- ISDN
- Synchronous serial

Because it is standardized, PPP supports vendor interoperability. PPP uses its Network Control Protocol (NCP) component to encapsulate multiple protocols, as shown in Figure 2-5. This use of NCPs surpasses the limits of SLIP, the predecessor of PPP, which could only set up transport for IP packets.

Figure 2-5 *Overview of PPP Components*

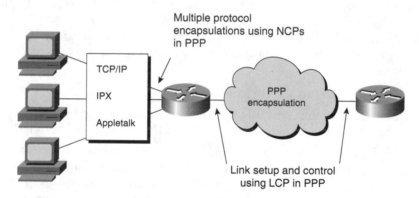

PPP uses another of its major components, the Link Control Protocol (LCP), to negotiate and set up control options on the WAN data link. Some of the PPP LCP features covered in this course follow:

- Authentication
- Compression
- Multilink

X.25 and Frame Encapsulations

X.25 encapsulation is typically seen in a packet-switched environment. In X.25 packet-switched networks, the LAPB protocol is the Data Link layer, Layer 2 protocol used to encapsulate X.25 packets. X.25 evolved in the days of analog circuits when error rates were much higher than today, so reliability was built into the X.25 framework.

Like X.25, Frame Relay is an industry-standard Data Link layer protocol that is commonly used in packet-switched networks. Frame Relay supports technological advances such as fiber-optic cabling and digital transmission. Frame Relay can eliminate time-consuming processes (such as error correction and flow control) that are necessary when using older, less reliable WAN media and protocols.

Because you are using a public network, you must consult with your service provider and obtain information specific to your link.

Determining the WAN Type to Use

When you design internetworks, you need to make several key decisions concerning connectivity between different users or groups of users in your WAN environment.

When selecting a WAN connection, you should also consider the following:

- **Availability**   Each method of connectivity has characteristics inherent in its design, usage, and implementation. For example, Frame Relay is not available in all geographic regions.

- **Bandwidth**   WAN bandwidth is expensive, and organizations cannot afford to pay for more bandwidth than they need. Determining usage over the WAN is a necessary step toward evaluating the most cost-effective WAN services for your needs.

- **Cost**   WAN usage costs are typically 80 percent of the entire Information Services budget. When different WAN services and different service providers are evaluated, cost is a major consideration. If, for example, you use the line for only one hour a day, you may want to select a dial-on-demand connection, such as an asynchronous or ISDN connection.

- **Ease of management**   Network designers are often concerned about the degree of difficulty associated with managing connections. Connection management includes both the configuration at initial startup and the outgoing configuration tasks of normal operation. Traffic management is the connection's capability to adjust to different rates of traffic, regardless of whether the traffic is steady-state or bursty in nature. Dedicated lines are often easier to manage than shared lines.

- **Application traffic**   The application traffic may be many small packets, such as during a terminal session; or very large packets, such as during file transfer.

- **Quality of service and reliability**   How critical is the traffic intended to travel over the link? A backup connection may be necessary.

- **Access control**   A dedicated connection may help control access, but electric commerce cannot occur on a wide scale unless consumers access some portion of your network.

Selecting WAN Configuration Types

Figure 2-6 illustrates bandwidth and time-selection considerations (which increase cost) when determining the best WAN technology to use. (The source of the figure is a 1995 study done by the Forrester Research firm.) The network administrator must determine the best WAN technology to implement, based on the amount of bandwidth and the time a user requires on the network. As the time of use increases, WAN services associated with a variable cost, such as dial-up, tend to be less advantageous. Likewise, as time of use decreases, WAN services associated with a fixed cost become more advantageous.

Figure 2-6 *Selection Considerations: Bandwidth and Connection Duration*

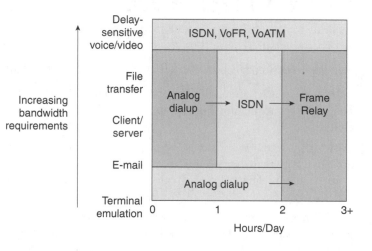

WAN Connections—Speed Comparison

Figure 2-7 illustrates the WAN speeds for typical technologies. This helps a network administrator select a WAN option, based on the amount of required bandwidth.

Figure 2-7 *Typical WAN Speeds*

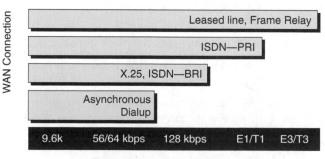

The speeds, costs, and availability vary internationally. For example, in North America, high-bandwidth speeds such as T1 are easily available at reasonable prices. Europe offers comparable speeds like E1, but the prices tend to be higher.

WAN Connections Summary

Each WAN connection has advantages and disadvantages. For example, setting up a dial-up asynchronous connection offers only limited bandwidth, but a user can call into the office from anywhere over the existing telephone network. Table 2-1 compares considerations for various types of WAN connections.

Table 2-1   *Summarized Comparison of WAN Connections*

Connection Type	Applications
Leased lines	High control, full bandwidth, high-cost enterprise networks, and last-mile access
Frame Relay	Medium control, shared bandwidth, medium-cost enterprise backbones; branch sites
ISDN	Low control, shared bandwidth, more bandwidth than dial-up
Asynchronous dial-up	Low control, shared bandwidth, variably cost-effective; for limited use connections like DDR
X.25	Low control, shared bandwidth, variably cost-effective; for limited use connections, high reliability

Identifying Site Requirements

Considerations vary, depending on the requirements of various company sites. This section discusses the WAN considerations that a network administrator must evaluate for a Central site, a branch office, and a telecommuter site.

A company may have multiple sites that vary in size, as shown in Figure 2-8. A remote network is necessary to connect the various locations in a company. Typical site locations include the following:

- **Central site**   The **Central site** is a large company site that is often the corporate headquarters or a major office. This is the site that most other regional offices and telecommuters connect into for data and information. Because users may access this site via multiple WAN technologies, it is important that your Central site be designed to accommodate many different types of WAN connections coming in from remote locations. The Central site is often termed **headquarters**, **the enterprise**, or **corporate**.

- **Remote site (branch office)**   The **remote site** is a smaller office that generally houses employees who have a compelling reason to be located in a specific region. A remote site is generally established to give a company local regional presence. A typical employee at a remote site may be a regional salesperson. Remote site users must be able to connect to the company site to access company information. Remote sites are sometimes termed **branch offices**, **remote office/branch offices (ROBOs)**, or **sales offices**.

- **Telecommuter site**   The **telecommuter site** is a small office with one to a few employees. It can also be a telecommuter's home office. Telecommuters may also be mobile users who travel. Depending on the amount of use and the WAN services available, telecommuters tend to use dial-up services. Other terms that refer to a telecommuter site are **small office**, **home office**, and **small office/home office (SOHO)**. **Mobile users** are specific telecommuters who do not work at a fixed company site. Because their locations vary, mobile users tend to access the company network via an asynchronous dial-up connection through the telephone company.

The WAN requirements may be different at each site, depending on the needs of the users at the sites.

Figure 2-8   *Company Sites*

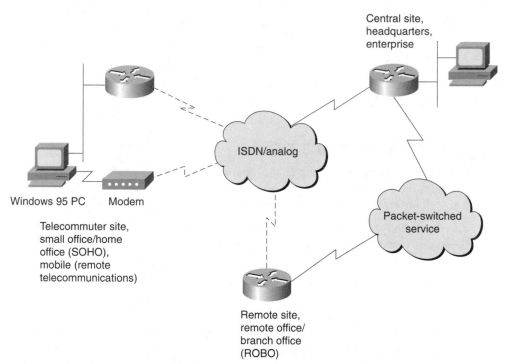

Central site,
headquarters,
enterprise

ISDN/analog

Windows 95 PC   Modem

Telecommuter site,
small office/home
office (SOHO),
mobile (remote
telecommunications)

Packet-switched
service

Remote site,
remote office/
branch office
(ROBO)

Central Site Considerations

The Central site WAN connection is a critical focal point for a company. Other sites and users access this site for information. Because many users access this site in a variety of ways, it is important that your Central site solution has a modular design that can accommodate many different types of WAN connections coming in from remote locations, as shown in Figure 2-8.

The technologies and features that are used to connect company campuses over a WAN are developed to optimize the WAN bandwidth, minimize the cost, and maximize the effective service to the end users. You should choose the WAN architecture that provides the most cost-effective bandwidth and a technology that optimizes service to end users. With that in mind, Central site considerations include the following:

- **Multiple access connections**   Multiple users connect to the Central site by using different media. So, Central site considerations must include multiple media options and simultaneous access from multiple users.

- **Cost**   Keep the costs low while maintaining an adequate level of service. For example, because some WAN charges are based on usage, such as ISDN, it is important that companies have a solution that can implement features that will optimize bandwidth and minimize WAN costs. Features such as DDR and compression ensure that WAN costs are kept to a minimum. In another example, because leased lines are generally charged on a fixed basis, you may want to consider this service only if the line can sustain a certain link-utilization level.

- **Access control**   Company information must be restricted, allowing users access only to areas in the network that they are authorized to access. For example, access-lists can filter out unauthorized data flow between offices and PPP network links, whereas Password Authentication Protocol (PAP) and Challenge Handshake Authentication Protocol (CHAP) can identify the remote entity to prevent unauthorized network connection.

- **Quality of service**   It is important to prioritize traffic over the link and manage traffic flow so that bursty traffic does not slow mission-critical traffic.

- **Redundancy and backup**   Because a link may fail or high link utilization may occur at certain peak usage times during the day, it is important to back up the connection to the central office. Avoid backing up links using the same service provider.

- **Scalability**   Build a network that will grow with the company.

NOTE   The primary considerations for the Central site are to provide access to multiple users and control the network costs.

Branch Office Considerations

A remote site is a small-site connection to a campus over a WAN. Remote is characterized by having fewer users than the Central site, so it needs a smaller-size WAN connection.

Remote sites connect to the Central site and to some other remote site offices. Telecommuters may also require access to the remote site. A remote site can use the same or different media. Remote site traffic can vary, but it is typically sporadic. The network designer must determine whether it is more cost-effective to offer a permanent or dial-up solution.

The remote site must have a mix of equipment, but not as much as the Central site requires. Typical WAN solutions that a remote site uses to connect to the Central site are as follows:

- Leased line
- Frame Relay
- X.25
- ISDN

Typical considerations for a remote site WAN connection follow:

- **Multiple access connections**   Multiple users connect to the Central site by using different media. Therefore, Central site considerations must include multiple media options and simultaneous access from multiple users.

- **Cost**   Keep the costs low while maintaining an adequate level of service. For example, because some WAN charges are based on usage, such as ISDN, it is important that companies have a solution that can implement features that will optimize bandwidth and minimize WAN costs. Features such as DDR and compression ensure that WAN costs are kept to a minimum. In another example, because leased lines are generally charged on a fixed basis, you may want to consider this service only if the line can sustain a certain link utilization level.

- **Access control**   Company information must be restricted, allowing users access only to areas in the network that they are authorized to access. For example, access-lists can filter out unauthorized data flow between offices and PPP network links, whereas Password Authentication Protocol (PAP) and Challenge Handshake Authentication Protocol (CHAP) can identify the remote entity to prevent unauthorized network connection.

- **Quality of service**   It is important to prioritize traffic over the link and manage traffic flow so that bursty traffic does not slow mission-critical traffic.

- **Redundancy and backup**   Because a link may fail or high link utilization may occur at certain peak usage times during the day, it is important to back up the connection to the central office. Avoid backing up links by using the same service provider.

- **Authentication**   The remote site must be able to authenticate itself to the Central site.

- **Availability**   Service providers may not offer certain WAN services in some regions. This consideration generally becomes more critical as sites are set up in more remote locations

---

NOTE   The primary consideration for the branch office is that it be able to access the Central site.

Telecommuter Site Considerations

As WAN technologies improve, allowing many employees to do their jobs almost anywhere, the growth in the number of telecommuter and small company sites has exploded. Like that of the other two sites, the telecommuter site must determine its WAN solution by weighing cost and bandwidth requirements.

An asynchronous dial-up solution using the existing telephony network and an analog modem is often the solution for telecommuters because it is easy to set up and the telephone facilities are already installed. As usage and bandwidth requirements increase, other remote access technologies should be considered.

The nonstationary characteristics of a mobile user make an asynchronous dial-up connection the remote solution. Employees on the road can use their PCs with modems and the existing telephone network to connect to the company.

Typical WAN connections employed at telecommuter sites are as follows:

- Asynchronous dial-up
- ISDN BRI
- Frame Relay (if the user utilizes the link for an extended time, such as half of a day)

Typical considerations for a telecommuter site WAN connection include cost, authentication, and availability.

NOTE   The primary consideration for the telecommuter site is to be able to access the company information on demand from various remote locations.

Selecting Cisco Remote Access Solutions

Cisco offers access servers, routers, and other equipment that allow connection to the WAN service. Figure 2-9 highlights some of the products that are suited for the various company sites. (Refer to Cisco Connection Online (CCO) at www.cisco.com for the latest product information.)

Figure 2-9   *Cisco Access Servers and the Sites for Which They Are Suited*

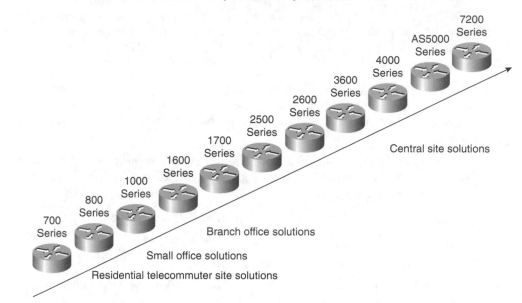

The Cisco 700 series, designed for telecommuters, is a low-cost, easy-to-manage, multiprotocol ISDN router. The 700 router has been optimized for interoperability with Cisco core networks, although these routers can connect to any network that supports the relevant standards for ISDN and IP/Internetwork Packet Exchange (IPX) routing.

The Cisco 800 series routers are Cisco's lowest-priced routers that are based on Cisco IOS software. The 800 series ISDN access routers provide big-business networking benefits to small offices and corporate telecommuters. The Cisco 800 series offers secure, manageable, high-performance solutions for Internet and corporate LAN access.

The Cisco 1000 series router is intended for remote office networking where Cisco IOS software, higher performance, and WAN options beyond ISDN are important.

The Cisco 1600 series routers are similar to the Cisco 1000 series routers, but they have a slot that accepts a WAN interface card. These cards are shared with the 1700, 2600, and 3600 series, and will be shared in future modular branch office-type products.

The Cisco 1720 access router delivers optimized security, integration, and flexibility in a desktop form factor for small- and medium-sized businesses, and for small branch offices that want to deploy Internet/intranet access or Virtual Private Networks (VPNs). The Cisco 1720 access router features two modular WAN slots that support 1600, 2600, and 3600 data WAN interface cards; and an autosensing 10/100-Mbps Fast Ethernet LAN port to provide investment protection and flexibility for growth.

The Cisco 2500 series routers provide a variety of models that are designed for branch office and remote site environments. These routers are typically fixed configuration, with at least two of the following interfaces: Ethernet, Token Ring, synchronous serial, asynchronous serial, ISDN BRI, and a hub.

The Cisco 2600 series features single or dual fixed LAN interfaces. A network module slot and two WAN interface card slots are available for WAN connections.

The 3600 series multiservice access servers/routers also offer a modular solution for dial-up and permanent connectivity over asynchronous, synchronous, and ISDN lines. Up to four network module slots are available for LAN and WAN requirements.

The Cisco 4500 and 4700 series access routers are high-performance modular Central site routers with support for a wide range of LAN and WAN technologies. The 4500 and 4700 are intended for large regional offices that do not require the density of the 7200 series. Their modular design allows easy reconfiguration as needs change.

The Cisco AS5000 series is Cisco's line of universal integrated access servers. The AS5000 series is extremely popular because it integrates the functions of standalone CSUs, channel banks, modems, communication servers, switches, and routers in a single chassis. The AS5000 series contains synchronous serial, digital ISDN, and asynchronous modem access server functionality, which are ideal for the mixed-media requirements that are becoming more prevalent every day.

The Cisco 7200 routers are also very high-performance, modular Central site routers that support a variety of LAN and WAN technologies. The 7200 is targeted for large regional offices that require high-density solutions.

Table 2-2 highlights some of the features and WAN options for each series of routers.

Table 2-2   *Remote Access Options for Each Series of Router*

Router Platform	Remote Access Options
700 series	ISDN BRI, basic telephone service ports
800 series	ISDN BRI, basic telephone service ports, entry-level Cisco IOS software
1000 series	ISDN BRI, serial (1005 router)
1600 series	ISDN BRI, 1 WAN interface card slot
1700 series	Two WAN interface card slots
2500 series	Family of routers that offers various ISDN BRI, serial, and WAN interfaces
2600 series	Various fixed LAN interface configurations, one network module slot, two WAN interface card slots
3600 series	Two and four network module slots on the 3620 and 3640, respectively
4000 series	T1/E1 ISDN PRI
AS5000 series	Access server with multiple T1/E1 ISDN PRI and modem capabilities
7200 series	Supports a wide range of WAN services, with the required high port density necessary for a scalable enterprise WAN

Determining the Appropriate Interfaces—Fixed Interfaces

The router that you select for your WAN connection must offer the interfaces that will support your WAN connection.

Typical interfaces that are found on a Cisco router and the typical WAN connections supported are as follows:

- **Asynchronous serial**   Used with a modem, it supports asynchronous dial-up connections.

- **Synchronous serial**   It supports connections such as leased lines, Frame Relay, and X.25.

- **BRI**   It supports ISDN BRI connections.

- **Channelized T1 or E1**   It supports connections such as leased lines, dial-up, ISDN PRI, and Frame Relay.

Routers such as the 2500 series can have fixed configurations. Fixed-configuration routers are available with predetermined fixed LAN and WAN interface options. Fixed-configuration routers do not require additional WAN interface cards or network modules. However, once purchased, the interfaces available are limited only to those that are factory-installed. Figure 2-10 shows a Cisco 2500 series router with a fixed configuration.

Figure 2-10 *Cisco 2500 Series Fixed-Configuration Router*

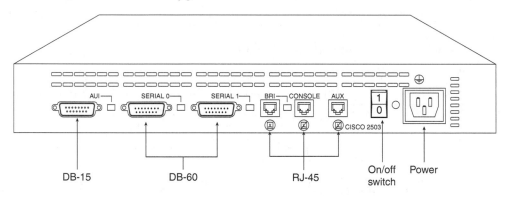

Determining the Appropriate Interfaces—Modular Interfaces

If you select a fixed-configuration router, you receive the router with the interfaces on the box. However, you cannot add or change interfaces on a fixed-configuration router.

Modular routers and access servers such as the 3600 are built with one or more slots that allow you to customize the box. You can determine the types of interfaces on the router by selecting various feature cards, network modules, or WAN interfaces, such as those shown in Figure 2-11. Although modular routers require more equipment than the physical router, they are more scalable as your network grows and your needs change.

Figure 2-11 *Modular Configuration Router*

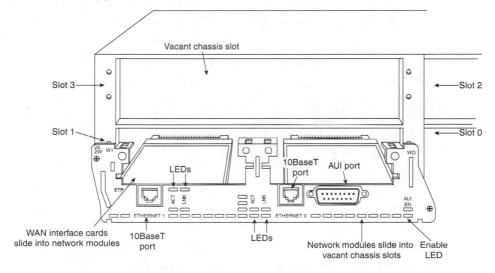

Selecting Products with Cisco Product-Selection Tools

To assist you with product selection, Cisco has extensive documentation and product-specific information on its Web site at www.cisco.com. You will also find product selection and configuration tools. These tools are designed to help you determine and configure the router that best suits your requirements.

One such tool that you will see on the Cisco Web site is a product selection tool, which is shown in Figure 2-12. The product selection tool allows you to identify your requirements. From the specifications that you highlight, the product selection tool will identify the routers available to suit the requirements.

Figure 2-12 *Cisco Product Selection Tool—Main Menu*

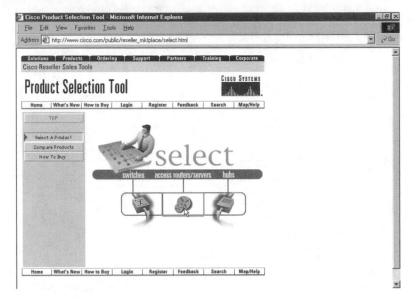

To use the tool, select from switches, access routers/servers, or hubs.

To learn about available access routers and servers, select that icon and perform the following steps:

1 Select the features that you require in the router by clicking the boxes next to the required features.

2 As you make your selections, the Product List box changes to list only the routers that meet your requirements. Once you have selected all the required features, the remaining routers on the tool are listed in the Product List box. You can also click the router name that you are interested in to display a detailed description of the product you selected.

Product Selection Tool Example

If you want to view available telecommuter routers that support ISDN, select the ISDN and telecommuter boxes. The product list section will show the available 700, 800, and 1000 series routers. Figure 2-13 illustrates this example.

Figure 2-13 *Selecting the Proper Router for a Telecommuter*

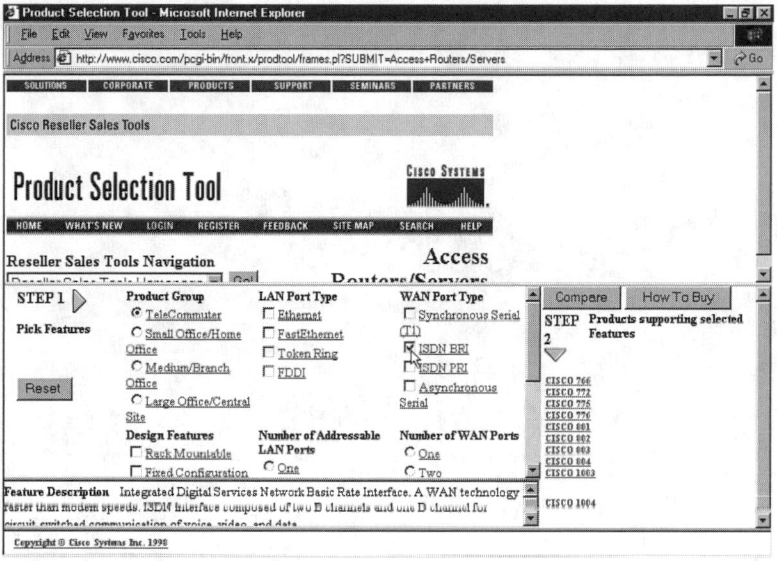

Summary

In this chapter, you learned how to determine whether a site is a Central site, branch office, or telecommuter site. You also learned how to select Cisco products to suit the specific needs of each site and how to utilize Cisco tools to select the proper equipment.

Review Questions

Answer the following questions, and then refer to Appendix H, "Answers to Review Questions," for answers and explanations.

1 Identify the types of WAN connections discussed in this chapter and the appropriate protocols used on each connection.

2 Describe the considerations when implementing a WAN connection at a Central site, branch office, and telecommuter site.

3 Identify available Cisco equipment designed for a telecommuter site, a branch office, and a Central site.

CHAPTER 3

Assembling and Cabling the WAN Components

This chapter teaches you how to connect remote sites via WAN connections. You will learn what router platform to install and how to cable it, depending on the environment. Figure 3-1 illustrates common remote solutions that are used to build a remote access network.

Figure 3-1 *Typical Network Topology*

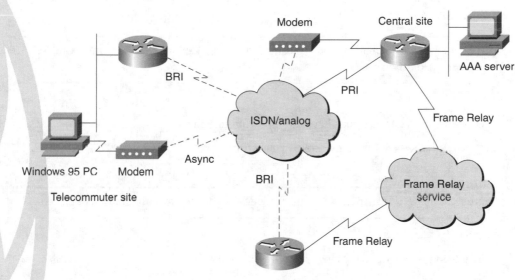

When dealing with the Central site, you will learn how to connect necessary components to allow WAN connections such as Frame Relay, and Integrated Services Digital Network (ISDN) Primary Rate Interface (PRI) connections to the branch office. You will also see ISDN PRI and asynchronous connections to the telecommuter site.

When installing a branch office router such as a 1600 series router, you will learn how to identify and connect the necessary components to allow WAN connections such as Frame Relay and ISDN Basic Rate Interface (BRI) connections to the Central site router.

When providing for a telecommuter site using routers such as a Cisco 700 series, you will learn how to identify and connect the necessary components to allow a WAN connection such as ISDN BRI to the Central site router. You will also learn how to configure a mobile user with a PC and a modem to allow an asynchronous connection to a company site router.

Network Overview

To build the network, you must select equipment for various company sites. Equipment needs vary by site. Typical site router considerations and their needs follow.

The Central site router must have the following interfaces:

- PRI interface for ISDN PRI and asynchronous calls Service Unit (CSU/DSU)
- Modem for asynchronous calls
- Serial interface for Frame Relay connections
- Ethernet connection to connect to the Authentication, Authorization, and Accounting (AAA) server

NOTE   If you are in North America, you typically provide the Channel Service Unit/Data. Service providers also offer rentals.

The branch office router must have the following interface:

- Serial interface for Frame Relay connections

NOTE   If you are in North America, you must provide the network termination 1 (NT1).

The telecommuter site must have the following interfaces:

- PC and modem for asynchronous dial-up calls
- BRI interface for ISDN BRI

You also need to work with your service provider to make the proper connections into the provider's network. Your lab will connect to equipment that will simulate a service provider's network.

Identifying Company Site Equipment

This section will show you router assembly examples for the various company sites.

Central Site Router Equipment

Choose the router that supports the WAN protocols that you will use. The 3600 series router and network modules will support the interfaces in the network topology illustrated in the "Network Overview" section.

When selecting a Central site router, typical Cisco solutions include the following:

- Cisco 3600 series
- Cisco 4000 series
- Cisco AS5x00 series
- Cisco 7000 series

Cisco 3600 series

The Cisco 3600 series is a multifunction platform that combines dial access, routing, and LAN-to-LAN services and multiservice integration of voice, video, and data in the same device. The Cisco 3600 series includes the Cisco 3640 and Cisco 3620 access servers/routers.

Cisco 4000 series

The Cisco 4000 series models provide a configurable modular router platform by using network processor modules—individual removable cards used for external network connections. Because the router's modules support many variations of protocols, line speeds, and transmission media, the Cisco 4000 series can accommodate all types of network-computing environments.

Cisco AS5x00 series

The Cisco AS5X00 family of access servers provides carrier class scalability, and multiprotocol capabilities for both Internet Service Providers and enterprises. The Cisco AS5X00 product series supports universal dial access by providing both analog modem and Integrated Services Digital Network (ISDN) support over the same bearer line, and world wide dial access by providing multiple trunk-line signaling protocols.

Cisco 7000 series

The Cisco 7000 series routers combine proven software technology with reliability, availability, serviceability, and exceptional performance features. With Cisco 7000 series, Port and Service adapters provide connection to external networks. The 7200 series supports any combination of Ethernet, Fast Ethernet, Token Ring, FDDI, ATM, serial, ISDN, and HSSI interfaces.

Branch Office Router Equipment

Choose the router that supports the WAN protocols and interfaces you will use. For example, the 1600 series router and the respective WAN interface card is an example of a branch office router that will support the interfaces required in the network topology illustrated in the "Network Overview" section.

When selecting a branch office router, typical Cisco solutions include the following:

- Cisco 1600 series
- Cisco 1700 series
- Cisco 2500 series
- Cisco 2600 series

Cisco 1600 Series

The Cisco 1600 series routers connect small offices with Ethernet LANs to the public Internet, and to a company's internal intranet or corporate LAN through several WAN connections such as ISDN, asynchronous serial, and synchronous serial. All Cisco 1600 series models include one or two Ethernet ports, and one WAN interface card expansion slot for additional connectivity and flexibility.

Cisco 1700 Series

The Cisco 1700 router is a small, modular desktop router that links small- to medium-size remote Ethernet and FastEthernet LANs over one to four WAN connections to regional and central offices.

Cisco 2500 Series

The Cisco 2500 series routers provide a variety of models that are designed for branch office and remote site environments. These routers are typically fixed-configuration with at least two of the following interfaces: Ethernet, Token Ring, synchronous serial, ISDN BRI, and Hub.

Cisco 2600 Series

The Cisco 2600 series is a family of modular access routers that offers network managers and service providers an attractively priced remote branch office solution, providing the versatility needed to adapt to changes in network technology as new services and applications become available. With full support of the Cisco IOS software, the Cisco 2600 series modular architecture provides the power to support the advanced Quality of Service (QoS), security, and network-integration features that are required in today's evolving enterprise and service provider networks.

Telecommuter Site Router Equipment

Choose the router that supports the WAN protocols and interfaces that you will use. When selecting a branch office router, typical Cisco solutions include the following:

- Cisco 700 series (760 or 770)
- Cisco 800 series
- Cisco 1000 series

Cisco 700 Series (760 or 770)

The Cisco 700M family products are low-cost, easy-to-manage multiprotocol ISDN access routers. These devices provide small professional offices, home offices, and telecommuters with high-speed remote access to enterprise networks and the Internet.

Cisco 800 Series

The Cisco 800 Series router is the entry-level platform that contains Cisco IOS technology. Ideal for use as customer premises equipment (CPE), service providers can lease or sell Cisco 800 series routers to small offices with Ethernet LANs for Internet access using Integrated Services Digital Network (ISDN) connections.

Cisco 1000 Series

The Cisco 1000 series LAN extenders and routers are easy-to-install, inexpensive, multiprotocol access products, designed for small offices and other remote sites.

Assembling and Cabling the Network

Figure 3-2 illustrates the cable connections available for the various WAN types.

Figure 3-2 *Assembling the Network*

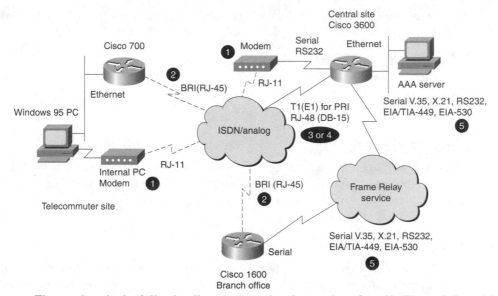

The numbers in the following list correspond to the numbers found in Figure 3-2, and the items explain the cable connections necessary for the various WAN types:

- **Asynchronous Connections (1)**   Asynchronous connections require RJ-11 cables that are attached from the modem's line port to the telephone company jack. If you are using an external modem attached to a Cisco router, you must also use a Cisco EIA/TIA-232 cable to attach the modem to the router's serial interface. The DB-60 end of the cable connects to the router. The DB-25 end attaches to the modem.

- **ISDN BRI (2)**   ISDN BRI connection interfaces require RJ-45 cables to connect the BRI interface to the ISDN network. The BRI modules and BRI WAN interface cards are available with either an S/T interface that requires an external NT1 or a U interface that has a built-in NT1.

- **ISDN PRI (North America) (3)**   Channelized T1 (CT1)/PRI modules are available with or without a built-in CSU. If you use an external CSU, attach a female DB-15 cable to the router's interface. The other end of the straight-through cable attaches to the CSU, which in turn attaches to the ISDN network. Routers with internal CSU modules attach directly to the ISDN network with a standard RJ-48 connector.

- **ISDN PRI (Europe) (4)**   Channelized E1 (CE1)/PRI modules are available with balanced and unbalanced interfaces. CE1/PRI-balanced modules provide a 120-ohm E1 interface for network connections. The unbalanced modules provide a 75-ohm E1 interface for network connections. Four serial cables are available from Cisco for the CE1/PRI module. All four cables have DB-15 connectors on the router end; they have DNC, DB-15, Twinax, or RJ-45 connectors on the network end.

- **Frame Relay (5)**—If you must establish a Frame Relay serial connection, Cisco routers support the following signaling standards: EIA/TIA-232, EIA/TIA-449, V.35, X.21, and EIA-530. Cisco supplies a DB-60 shielded serial transition cable that has the appropriate connector for the standard you specify. The router end of the shielded serial transition cable has a DB-60 connector, which connects to the DB-60 port on the router's serial interface.

The other end of the serial transition cable is available with the connector that is appropriate for the standard you specify. For specific cabling information, refer to the installation and configuration guide that came with your router. For information regarding cable pinouts, refer to the cable specification documentation. It is available on the Cisco Web site, and in the installation and configuration guide that came with your router.

Verifying Network Installation

This section contains information about how you can use the LEDs on your Cisco equipment to verify proper installation.

Verifying Central Site Installation

Each Central site router has LED displays that allow you to verify that the router components are installed and functioning properly.

NOTE	For LED information that is specific to your router, refer to the installation and configuration guide that accompanied your router.

On the Cisco 3600 router, the LEDs on the front of the router enable you to determine router performance and operation, as shown in Figure 3-3. The ready LED indicates that a functional module has been installed in the indicated slot. If the LED is off, the slot is empty or the module is not functional. The active LED blinks to indicate network activity on the module installed in the indicated slot.

Figure 3-3   *Cisco 3600 Router LEDs*

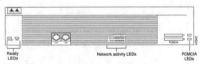

All network modules have an enable (EN) LED. The enable LED indicates that the module has passed its self-tests and is available to the router.

Each Ethernet port has two LEDs, as shown in Figure 3-4. The activity (ACT) LED indicates that the router is sending or receiving Ethernet transmissions. The link LED indicates that the Ethernet port is receiving the link integrity signal from the hub (10BaseT only).

Figure 3-4   *Ethernet Module*

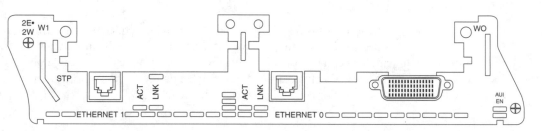

Each PRI network module has four LEDs in addition to the enable LED, as shown in Figure 3-5. The LEDs and their descriptions follow:

- REMOTE ALARM   Designates a remote alarm condition.
- LOCAL ALARM   Designates a local alarm condition.
- LOOPBACK   Designates a loopback condition.
- CARRIER DETECT   Specifies that you received the carrier on the telephone company link.

Figure 3-5   *T1/PRI CSU Network Module*

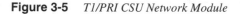
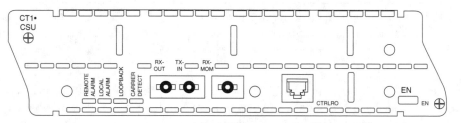

Digital modem module, shown in Figure 3-6, has five LEDs in addition to the enable LED—one for each MICA module bank. The LEDs blink during initialization. After the enable LED comes on, the MICA module LEDs indicate that the corresponding MICA module is functioning. If a MICA module fails its diagnostics or if no MICA module is installed in a position, its LED remains off.

Figure 3-6   *Digital Modem Network Module*

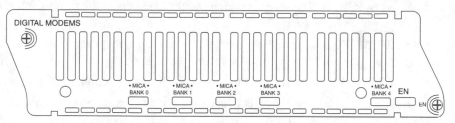

Each port on the serial network module has the additional LEDs, as shown in Figure 3-7. Descriptions of the LEDs follow:

- CN/LP   Connect when green; loopback when Yellow
- RXC   Receive clock
- RXD   Receive activity
- TXC   Transmit clock
- TXD   Transmit activity

Figure 3-7   *Serial WAN Interface Card*

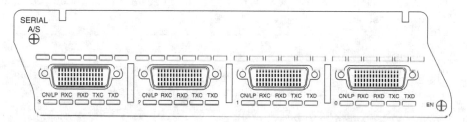

Verifying Branch Office Installation

Each branch office router has LED displays that allow you to verify that the router components are installed and functioning properly.

On the 1603 or 1604, you can use the LEDs on the front of the router to determine router performance and operation, as shown in Figure 3-8.

Figure 3-8   *Cisco 1600 LEDs*

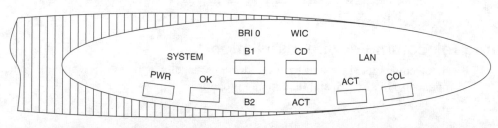

The LEDs and their descriptions follow:

- **SYSTEM PWR**   The green system power LED indicates that the router is turned on and DC power is being supplied.
- **SYSTEM OK**   The green system OK LED indicates that the router has successfully booted. It blinks while in the boot cycle.
- **BRI 0 B1**   The green B1 LED indicates an ISDN connection on B channel 1.
- **BRI 0 B2**   The green B2 LED indicates an ISDN connection on B channel 2.
- **WIC CD**   The green WAN interface card connection LED indicates an active connection on the WAN interface card serial port.
- **WIC ACT**   The green WAN interface card activity LED indicates an active connection on the WAN interface card serial port.
- **LAN ACT**   The green LAN activity LED indicates that data is being sent to or received from the local Ethernet LAN.
- **LAN COL**   A flashing yellow LAN collision LED indicates frame collisions on the local Ethernet LAN.

NOTE   For a Cisco 1600, the system power and OK LEDs indicate that the router is on and has successfully booted.

The one-port serial WAN interface card has one LED (CONN), indicating that data is being sent over the WAN interface card serial port, as shown in Figure 3-9.

Figure 3-9   *Cisco 1600—Serial WAN Interface Card*

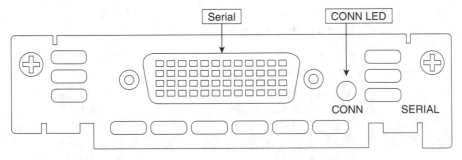

Verifying Telecommuter Site Installation

Each telecommuter site router has LED displays that allow you to verify that the router components are installed and functioning properly.

On the 766 router, you can use the LEDs on the front of the router to determine router performance and operation, as shown in Figure 3-10.

Figure 3-10 *Cisco 700 LEDs*

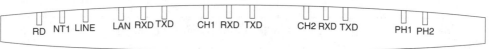

The 700 series LEDs and their descriptions are as follows:

- RD   The ready LED indicates the router operating status. This LED is on when power is supplied to the router, the router passes the self-test, and it is operating normally.

- NT1   On 700 series routers that have an internal NT1, the on LED indicates that the NT1 and ISDN switch have synchronized over the ISDN line. When blinking five blinks per second, the internal NT1 is attempting to synchronize with the telephone switch. When blinking one blink per second, the internal NT1 is attempting to synchronize with the ISDN terminal devices.

- LINE   An online LED indicates synchronization between the NT1 S interface and the ISDN terminal device(s). It also indicates framing between the router and the ISDN switch.

- LAN   An on LAN LED indicates that frames have been sent to or received from the Ethernet within the last minute.

- LAN RXD   The receive LAN LED blinks when frames are received from the Ethernet.

- LAN TXD   The transmit LAN LED blinks when frames are sent to the Ethernet.

- CH1   The channel 1 LED blinks when a call is connected on the first ISDN B channel. After the call is established, the LED remains on.

- CH1 RXD   The channel 1 received LED blinks when packets are received from the first ISDN B channel.

- CH1 TXD   The channel 1 transmitted LED blinks when packets are sent on the first ISDN B channel.

- CH2   The channel 2 LED blinks when a call is connected on the second ISDN B channel. After the call is established, the LED remains on.

- CH2 RXD   The channel 2 received LED blinks when packets are received from the second ISDN B channel.

- CH2 TXD   The channel 2 transmitted LED blinks when packets are sent on the second ISDN B channel.

- PH1, PH2   Plain Old Telephone System (POTS) ports are on when a telephone, fax, or modem is in use.

There is also one LED on the rear panel, the LINK LED. The LINK LED remains lit when the router is configured as an Ethernet hub, connected to an Ethernet hub, or configured as a node, and a valid physical connection to another Ethernet device is established.

NOTE   For a Cisco 766, the ready LED indicates the router is on and has passed its self-tests.

Summary

In this chapter, you learned how to identify and connect the necessary components to Central site, branch office, and small office routers.

In Part III, "Enabling On-Demand Connections to the Central Site," you will learn to configure the equipment to provide remote access to your users.

Review Questions

Answer the following questions and then refer to Appendix H, "Answers to Review Questions," for answers and explanations.

1 Which cables are necessary to make the proper physical asynchronous serial, ISDN, and synchronous serial connections?

2 How can you verify that you properly installed a network module in a modular router?

PART III

Enabling On-Demand Connections to the Central Site

CHAPTER 4

Configuring Asynchronous Connections with Modems

In the first three chapters, you learned how to identify your communication needs and how to select the equipment. This chapter teaches you how to establish remote connections from a home office or telecommuter to a central site, as shown in Figure 4-1.

Figure 4-1 *Small Office or Telecommuter Calling the Central Site*

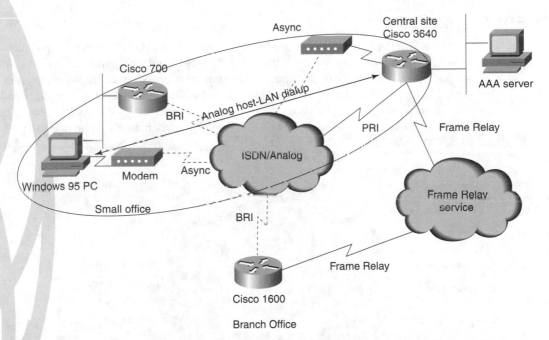

You will learn how to configure an access server for modem connectivity so that telecommuters can access the Central site by using asynchronous connection. To do this, you will learn how to perform a reverse Telnet session to the modem, how to configure it for basic asynchronous operations, and how to use the modem autoconfiguration.

Dial-Up Terminology

Following are the definitions of two terms (taken from the Cisco Web site) that you will frequently encounter in this chapter:

Analog An electrical circuit that is represented by means of continuous, variable physical quantities (such as voltages and frequencies), as opposed to discrete representations (such as the 0/1, off/on representation of digital circuits). Signal transmission over wires or through the air in which information is conveyed through variation of some combination of signal amplitude, frequency, and phase.

Asynchronous Term describing digital signals that are transmitted without precise clocking. Such signals generally have different frequencies and phase relationships. Asynchronous transmissions usually encapsulate individual characters in control bits (called start and stop bits) that designate the beginning and end of each character.

Modem Overview

Regular phone lines, also known as Plain Old Telephone Service (POTS), were designed to carry voice traffic and are analog by definition. On the other hand, computers are digital and communicate digitally. For the digital equipment to communicate over an analog connection, its current (digital) needs to be transformed into a tone (analog). A *modem* (modulator/demodulator) converts digital signals to analog, and vice versa. It converts digital to analog, only to be converted back to digital, as seen in Figure 4-2. The typical maximum data rate is usually limited to 28.8 to 56 Kbps. Multiple analog to digital conversions introduce noise.

Figure 4-2 *Typical Modem Connection*

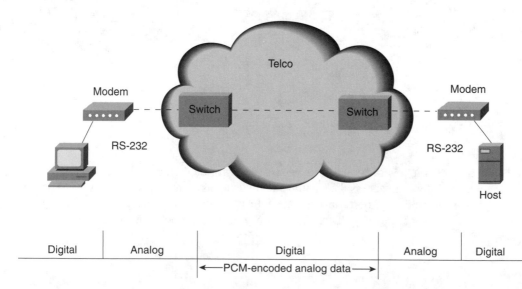

Digital	Analog	Digital	Analog	Digital
		←——PCM-encoded analog data——→		

Universal Asynchronous Receiver/Transmitter (UART)

Transmission speed can also be limited by a workstation's UART type. The UART is a computer component that handles asynchronous serial communication. Every computer contains an UART to manage serial ports, such as those used for a mouse or an external modem. Every internal modems has its own UART.

UARTs are controlled by a clock usually running at 1.84 MHz and have a maximum throughput of 115 Kbps. UARTs have a buffer to temporarily hold incoming data. This buffer varies by the model, but it is usually quite small.

Type of UARTs: 16C450

16450

16550 uses a 16-byte buffer

16550af

16750 uses a 64-byte transmit buffer and a 56-byte receive buffer

Within the telco cloud and between switches, the analog data is pulse code modulation (PCM)-encoded for transmission over telco facilities. The recovery and amplification of the digital signals reduce and eliminate the noise that would be created by subjecting analog signals to the same process. Amplifying an analog signal amplifies any noise in the signal. Amplifying a digital signal means re-creating only the on or off state of the signal.

Data terminal equipment (DTE) are end devices such as PCs, workstations, and mainframe computers. End devices communicate with each other through data communications equipment (DCE) such as modems, channel service units (CSUs), and data service units (DSUs). Figure 4-3 displays the DTE-DCE interface. DCE can also be expanded to mean data circuit-terminating equipment, which is the International Telecommunication Union-Telecommunications Standardization Sector (ITU-TSS, or simply ITU-T), formerly known as CCITT. The Electronic Industries Association (EIA) defines the DCE acronym as *data communications equipment*.

Figure 4-3   *The DTE-DCE Interface*

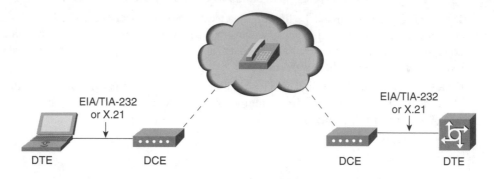

• DTE = Data terminal equipment
• DCE = Data communications equipment

The EIA/TIA-232 standard defines the interface between DTE and DCE. TIA stands for Telecommunications Industries Association.

The end-to-end communication path between two DTEs consists of three segments (as illustrated in Figure 4-3): DTE-DCE, DCE-DCE, and DCE-DTE. You must administer a set of cabling and configuration elements for each segment.

NOTE   The EIA/TIA-232-C (formerly known as RS-232-C) standard is the most commonly used asynchronous interface for data communications in North America. The RS-232 standard was first issued in 1962, and its third revision, RS-232-C, was issued in August 1969. Although the ubiquitous D-shaped 25-pin connector (DB-25) has become the market norm for EIA/TIA-232-C interfaces, it was not specified in the original RS-232-C standard. Many EIA/TIA-232-C devices use other connectors, such as the DB-9 or RJ-11/RJ-45 modular connectors. X.21 is a European standard that defines the DCE-DTE interface. For more information on these and other standards, refer to Cisco Connection Online (CCO) or another data communications reference text.

Modem Signaling and Cabling

A number of different standards define the signaling over a serial cable, including EIA/TIA-232, X.21, V.35, EIA/TIA-449, EIA-530, and EIA-613 HSSI. Each standard defines the signals on the cable and specifies the connector at the end of the cable.

With the 25-pin connector of EIA/TIA-232 standard, only eight pins are actually used for connecting a DTE (such as an access server) to a DCE (such as a modem). The other 17 signals are not interesting and are ignored. The eight interesting signals (pins) can be grouped into three categories by their functionality:

- Data transfer group
- Hardware flow control group
- Modem control group

Figure 4-4 illustrates these three groups.

Data Transfer Group

The data transfer group signals and pin designation, also known as *pinout*, for the EIA/TIA-232 specification in Figure 4-4 are explained in Table 4-1.

Figure 4-4   *Data, Flow Control, and Modem Signaling*

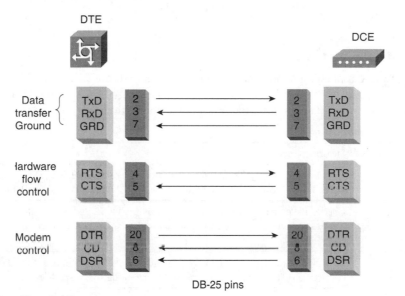

DB-25 pins

Table 4-1   *Data Transfer Group*

Signal	Description
TxD	Transmit Data. The DTE transmits data to the DCE.
RxD	Receive Data. The DTE receives data from the DCE.
GRD	Ground (pin 7). Provides the ground reference for voltage measurements.

Flow Control Group

Pins 4 and 5 form the hardware flow control group, as shown in Figure 4-4. These signals are activated between the DCE and the DTE when the equipment is ready to accept data. Table 4-2 explains the different flow control signals.

Table 4-2 *Flow Control Group*

Signal	Description
RTS	Request To Send. The DTE has buffers available to receive from the DCE. Originally intended for the DTE to request to send data during a half duplex operation (in which data can only be sent in one direction at a time), this signal is now used for full duplex communication to indicate to the DCE that the DTE is ready to receive data. This is a signal from the computer or router telling the modem when to send data.
CTS	Clear To Send. The DCE has buffers that are available to take data from the DTE. Initially used by the DCE to indicate that the DTE could transmit in half duplex mode in response to RTS. It is still used to indicate that the DTE may transmit for hardware flow control under full duplex operation. This signal is used by the modem to tell the computer when to send data.

Modem Control Group

Finally, the remaining interesting signals between a DTE device and a DCE form the modem control group, covered in Table 4-3. These signals are used between the DTE and DCE to initiate, terminate, and monitor the status of the connection.

Table 4-3 *Modem Control Group*

Signal	Description
DTR	Data terminal ready. This signal is controlled by the DTE. The DTE indicates to the DCE that the equipment (computer or router) is connected and available to receive data.
CD	Carrier Detect. This signal is controlled by the DCE, and it indicates that it has established an acceptable carrier signal with a remote DCE (there is a DCE-to-DCE connection).
DSR	Data Set Ready (pin 6). The DCE is ready for use. This pin is not used on modem connections. The DSR is active as soon as a modem is turned on.

TIP   In the teletype days, flow control was done with inband signaling using Xon/Xoff. With higher DTE speeds and faster workstations, modems and computers were not always able to exchange this inband signaling in a timely fashion. Therefore, a set of electrical signals was developed to manage the flow control and the modem control.

Communication Termination

Either the DTE device or the DCE device may signal for the connection to be terminated. The signals that are used for this function are DTR from the DTE or the modem recognizing the loss of the CD signal. Therefore, a modem connection can be terminated in two ways:

- **DTE initiated**—The access server or computer can drop the DTR signal. The modem must be programmed to terminate the connection on loss of DTR and restore to saved settings in its NVRAM.

- **DCE initiated**—The access server detects Carrier Detect low and terminates the connection. The modem must be programmed so that the CD reflects the state of the carrier.

When modem control is not configured properly, the following symptoms might occur:

- The modem does not hang up when you quit your session. This means the DTR is not dropped or recognized, so the modem is not aware that it should break the connection.

- You end up in someone else's session, which means that the CD is not dropped or recognized. This scenario happens when Caller A terminates its dial-up session, and the modem does not pass the true state of the CD to the DTE. The access server is not aware that Caller A terminated its session, so it maintains the line for Caller A. When a new caller, Caller B, comes in by the same line (interface), the access server continues with the session previously initiated by Caller A, instead of starting a new one. Thus, Caller B ends up in Caller A's session without having to authenticate. It is, therefore, very important that the true state of CD be always passed back to the DTE, so the access server terminates sessions when callers hang up.

Modem Operation

Modems perform their basic operations as follows (in one direction) and as seen in Figure 4-5:

1 Outgoing data from an originating DTE comes into the sending modem via the TxD pin.

2 If the sending modem's buffer is nearly full, the modem can control flow (via hardware) by lowering the CTS signal, thus instructing the DTE to not use TxD.

3 The data is compressed by using a proper algorithm (MNP 5 or V.42bis) that is mutually agreed upon between the two communicating modems.

4 The data is then packetized, where windowing, checksum, error control (using MNP 4 or LAP-M), and retransmission are performed.

NOTE   Here, the term *packetized* is not referring to an IP packet or layer-3 PDU. Rather, it refers to the preparation of the data by the modem.

---

5 The digital data is modulated into analog signals and sent out through the telephone network.

6 When the data reaches the receiving modem, it goes through the same steps in reverse
order. The signal will be demodulated; and the data will be depacketized, decompressed,
and delivered to the destination DTE. The DTE can use RTS to indicate that it is unable
to receive data on RxD.

Figure 4-5   *Modem Operation*

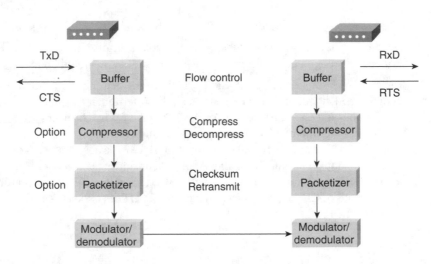

Communication Wiring and Cabling

Depending on the type of connections, the cable used can be straight-through, cross-over, or
rolled; and it can have a DB-25 or RJ-45 connector.

DTE-to-DTE Wiring—Null Modem

When two DTE devices (for example, an access server and a terminal) are near each other, it
makes sense to connect them directly without going through a telephone network and two
modems. An ordinary EIA/TIA-232 cable does not work in this case because both DTE devices
transmit on the TxD lead (pin 2), and both expect input on the RxD lead (pin 3). A *null modem
cable* is required for the DTE-to-DTE connection.

Null modems crisscross DB-25 pins 2, 3, and other corresponding pins so that the two DTE
devices can communicate, as shown in Figure 4-6. Some devices can be configured to operate
either like a DTE or a DCE. Configuring a device as a DCE usually means that it receives data
on pin 2 and transmits data on pin 3.

Figure 4-6   *Null Modem Cable Pinout*

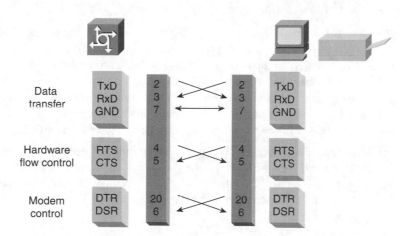

For example, many serial printers are configured as DCE devices so they can be connected directly to a DTE (for example, a PC or a terminal server) with an ordinary EIA/TIA-232 cable, eliminating the need for a null modem connection.

NOTE   On null modem cable, as seen in Figure 4-6, the CD signal is on the same pin as DSR.

RJ-45 Wiring

Cisco uses RJ-45 ports and connectors for console, auxiliary, and asynchronous port connections. The specific pinout to be used on a RJ-45 interface for EIA-232 is not defined by any standards. As such, Cisco defines the RJ-45 as a DTE pinout, as shown in Figure 4-7.

Figure 4-7   *RJ-45 Pinout*

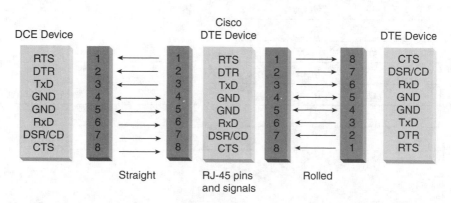

Cabling from the access server port (RJ-45) to an external device (such as a modem or terminal) requires the use of two cabling components:

- **RJ-45 to RJ-45 cable**—This can be either a rolled cable (reverse pins 1–8, 2–7, 3–6, 4–5) or a straight-through cable (1–1, 2–2, and so forth). To check whether a cable is straight or rolled, hold the two connectors (the two ends of the cable) side by side—with the keys at the back and the pins up—and compare them by inspecting the color-coded wires inside the connector. If the wires use the same colors on the same pins, it is a straight cable; if the wires are a mirror image of each other, it is a rolled cable. The octal cable used to connect to the asynchronous ports performs the equivalent of a rolled cable.

- **RJ-45 to DB-25 adapter**—This can also be straight-through or rolled. A male or female DTE adapter (MDTE or FDTE) is straight. A male or female DCE adapter (MDCE or FDCE) is rolled. An MMOD adapter is rolled. Only an MMOD adapter supports modems (modified from MDCE connectors by wiring DB-25 pin 8 to DSR, instead of pin 6).

Difference between Console and Auxiliary Ports

The console port does not entertain pin 1 (RTS) and pin 8 (CTS), as shown in the following Console Port table. Therefore, hardware flow control is nonexistent. By limiting the speed to 9600 baud, the risk of overflowing the buffer is quasi null. The Auxiliary port uses pins 1 and 8, as shown in the following table, and therefore can accommodate a modem. The source of this information is the Cisco Web site (www.cisco.com). In the following tables, any pin that is not referenced is not connected.

Console Port (DTE)		
Pin	Signal	Input/Output
1	-	-
2	DTR	Output
3	TxD	Output
4	GND	-
5	GND	-
6	RxD	Input
7	DSR	Input
8	-	-

Auxiliary Port (DTE)		
Pin	Signal	Input/Output
1	RTS	Output
2	DTR	Output
3	TxD	Output
4	GND	-
5	GND	-
6	RxD	Input
7	DSR	Input
8	CTS	Input

Cisco-Specific Connections

The auxiliary and console ports are configured as DTE devices on Cisco access servers. Terminals are also DTE devices. As noted earlier, two DTE devices cannot be directly connected unless the signals are rolled exactly once. So, you must either roll the pins in the cable or in the DB-25 adapters, but not both. The formula for a successful DTE to DTE connection is one of the following:

- DTE to a rolled RJ-45 cable to a straight DB-25 adapter to DTE
- DTE to a straight RJ-45 cable to a rolled DB-25 adapter to DTE

When connecting a DTE to a DCE, however, you should have either no rolls, or two rolls in the cable and the connector. The formula for a successful DTE to DCE connection is one of the following:

- DTE to a rolled RJ-45 cable to a rolled DB-25 adapter to DCE
- DTE to a straight RJ-45 cable to a straight DB-25 adapter to DCE

Figure 4-8 shows some possible working connections between an access server and various types of end devices.

Figure 4-8   *Cisco Working Connections*

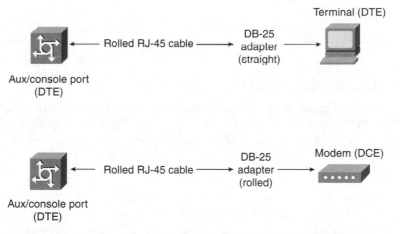

The part number for the rolled RJ-45 to RJ-45 cable is CAB-500RJ.

When you order access servers with async ports, you need to order the corresponding cable accessories. Order one CAB-OCTAL-KIT (eight-lead octal cable and eight male DB-25 modem connectors) for each 68-pin async connector that you have on the access server. If the modem uses an RJ-45 connector, you can order one CAB-OCTAL-ASYNC (a rolled eight-lead octal cable with RJ-45 connectors); special adapters might be required.

NOTE   Connecting a modem to the console port of a router is a security risk because it initially has no protection or security features enabled.

Cisco routers ship with a console and auxiliary port cabling kit that includes the following components:

- RJ-45 to RJ-45 rolled cable
- RJ-45 to DB-9 female DTE adapter (labeled TERMINAL)—typically used to connect to a PC being used as a console terminal
- RJ-45 to DB-25 female DTE adapter (labeled TERMINAL)—used to connect a terminal to the console or auxiliary port
- RJ-45 to DB-25 male DCE adapter (labeled MODEM)—used to connect the auxiliary port to a modem

Table 4-4 presents the port types for console and auxiliary ports on Cisco routers and switches.

Table 4-4   *Console and Auxiliary Port Types*

Router	Console Port	Auxiliary Port
DB-25	DCE	DTE
RJ-45	DTE (DCE on the 1700 series)	DTE

Modem Modulation Standards

The function of a modem is to convert digital signals (DTE-to-DCE) into analog signals (DCE-to-DCE), and vice versa. The ITU-T has defined and introduced several modem modulation standards over the years. Various modem manufacturers, however, have also marketed their own proprietary versions of modems. Interoperability among various types of modems, and sometimes even from the same vendor's modems, can be a challenge.

With proper configuration, V.34 modems can intelligently adapt to line conditions during a transition. Two communicating modems will initially attempt to set up a call at 28.8 Kbps. If line conditions do not allow a transmission at this speed, the modems fall back to the next highest speed in steps of 2.4 Kbps (possibly down to 2.4 Kbps, if necessary). Alternatively, if line conditions improve, the modems can increase the speed.

Older modems negotiate a fixed transmission rate during handshaking, but communications continue at the same speed after that. If line quality deteriorates below a certain threshold, the connection is lost. Older modems cannot take advantage of any increased bandwidth later, when the line quality improves. The V.32bis standard was finalized in July 1991; V.34 standards were finished in June 1994.

The V.34 annex 12 standard supports a 33.6 Kbps transmit and receive operation. When compression is used, up to 133.8 Kbps is possible if the PC can handle this speed.

The newest standard is the V.90, 56 Kbps standard. Most modem manufacturers have a V.90 product, even though the actual maximum data rate allowed is 53 Kbps within the United States.

The access server is unaware of modulations because it is directly involved with DTE-to-DCE communication only. However, the access server-to-modem speed must account for modulation speed and compression ratio for optimal end-to-end performance.

The following are some common international and proprietary modem standards:

ITU Standards   *Proprietary Methods*

V.22: 1200 Bps   V.32 terbo: 19.2 Kbps
V.22 bis: 2400 Bps   V.fast: 28.8 Kbps
V.32: 9600 Bps   V.FC: 28.8 Kbps
V.32 bis: 14.4 Kbps   K56Flex: 56 Kbps
V.34: 28.8 Kbps   X2: 56 Kbps
V.34 annex 1201H: 33.6 Kbps
V.90: 56 Kbps

Error Control and Data Compression

Error-detection and error-correction methods were developed to ensure data integrity at any speed. Some widely used methods include Microcom Networking Protocol (MNP) and Link Access Procedure for Modems (LAPM).

Compression algorithms typically require error-correction algorithms, so V.42bis and MNP 5 compression usually run over LAPM or MNP 4 correction. V.42 and V.42bis are not limited to V.32 and V.34 modems. They can also be implemented in lower speed equipment. The 4:1 compression ratio provided by V.42bis is theoretical and is rarely achieved.

The modern data-compression technique is analogous to the video-compression or disk-packing algorithms used in computers. The compression efficiency is highly dependent on data content. Some data (such as ASCII files) compress readily, whereas others can be compressed only a little.

Although some applications' software supports data compression, it is usually better to let the modem compress transmitted data. Data-compression algorithms that run in modem hardware are faster than those performed by host software. If two modems have agreed on V.42bis compression, you need to turn off your application's compression capability. This means transferring data at a higher speed on the interface between the DTE and the DCE.

Confusion often arises between the DCE-to-DCE modulation speed and DTE-to-DCE speed. The former represents how fast the modems communicate with each other across the telephone network. The latter represents how fast your computer communicates with the attached modem.

To gain full benefits from compression in an ideal situation, the DTE (for example, a PC) must send to the DCE (for example, a modem) at speeds matching the potential compression ratio (as shown in Figure 4-9). However, the EIA/TIA-232 serial interface (COM port) that is widely found on PCs and some Macintosh computers might operate considerably slower than the full potential of V.34. The problem is that some PCs and Macs use the EIA/TIA-232 serial interface with a combination of Universal Asynchronous Receiver/Transmitters (UARTs) and character-oriented communications software packages, which are not reliable at higher data rates. In a PC, DTE should be set to clock the modem at its fastest rate to take advantage of compression.

Figure 4-9   *The Speed and Compression Shown Here and Advertised By Modem Manufacturers, Assuming Ideal Conditions*

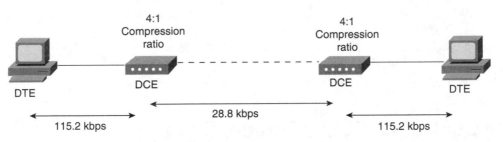

An improperly configured modem might automatically adjust DTE-DCE speeds to match the established DCE-DCE speeds. This is often called *speed mismatch*. To avoid speed mismatch, you must lock the DTE-DCE speed so it remains constant, as originally configured. This speed-locking mechanism is called *speed conversion* (also known as *port-rate adjustment* or *buffered mode*).

Figure 4-10 shows the maximum theoretical speeds that are possible for selected modem-modulation standards. Also shown are the possible speeds if V.42bis compression is used with the same standards.

Figure 4-10 *Theoretical Speeds for Selected Modem-Modulation Standards*

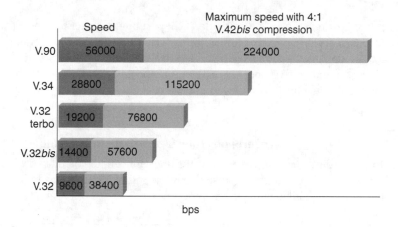

Configuration for Asynchronous Connections

Cisco access servers support both incoming asynchronous line connections (forward connections) and outgoing asynchronous line connections (reverse connections), as shown in Figure 4-11. For example, a remote terminal user that dials into the access server through an asynchronous line makes a forward connection; a user connects through an access server (reverse connection) to an attached modem to configure the modem.

Figure 4-11 *Forward Connection and Reverse Telnet*

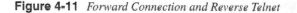
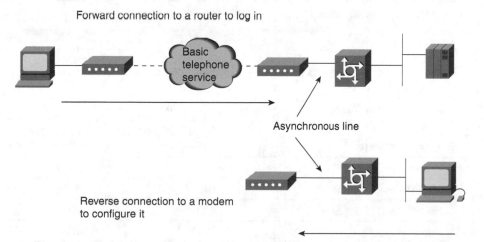

A host can make reverse Telnet connections to various types of devices attached to a Cisco access server. Different port numbers (20xx, 40xx, and 60xx) are used because different data type and protocol negotiations will take place for different types of devices attached to the access server.

The remote host must specify a particular TCP port on the router to connect with individual lines or to a rotary group. For example, if you wish to configure a modem connected to the interface Asycn 7, you will make a reverse Telnet connection using port address 2007. Note that TCP port number 2007 specifies a Telnet protocol connection (TCP port 2000) to line 7. The individual line number is added to the end of the port number type.

Asynchronous Interfaces—Line Numbering

Refer to your Router's manual to see how the lines are counted on that specific platform. As an example, the Cisco 3640 that is represented in the following table has four slots and each of those has preassigned line numbers, as follows:

97-128	65-96
33-64	1-32

The interface number of a port in a Cisco 3600 is determined by using the following formula:

Interface number = $(32 \times \text{slot number})$ + unit number + 1

For example, asynchronous port 12 in slot 1 corresponds to interface number 45 $((32 \times 1) + 12 + 1 = 45)$. This is also the line number for the port. Port 12 in slot 1 is always assigned interface number 45, regardless of whether the module in slot 0 is a 16-port asynchronous module, a 32-port asynchronous module, or some other type of module entirely; or even whether there is a network module in slot 0 at all. If you move the module in slot 1 to a different slot, however, its interface numbers change.

Table 4-5 shows the services provided, and the TCP port numbers for individual lines and rotary groups.

Table 4-5 *Services and Port Numbers for Lines and Rotary Groups101*

Services Provided	Base TCP Port for Individual Lines	Base TCP Port for Rotary Groups
Telnet protocol	2000	3000
Raw TCP protocol (no Telnet)	4000	5000
Telnet protocol, binary mode	6000	7000
Xremote protocol	9000	10000

Use the **transport input protocol** command to specify which protocol to use when connecting to a line using reverse Telnet. For example, **transport input all** allows all of the following protocols to be used for the connection: lat, mop, nasi, none, pad, rlogin, Telnet, and v120. Each of these protocols can be specified individually as a command option.

Reverse Telnet—Minimum Configuration

To successfully reverse Telnet to the modem attached to your router, the line interface must have been configured with the **transport input all** and **modem inout** commands.

EXEC Connection Commands

Use the EXEC commands in this section to initiate and control a reverse Telnet terminal session to a modem.

To make a connection with Telnet protocol:

```
Router>Telnet host [port] [/debug]
```

To disconnect the specified session or all sessions:

```
Router>disconnect [session-number]
```

To suspend a session:

```
Router>ctrl-shift-6 x
```

EXEC Command	Description
Telnet *host* [*port*] [*/debug*]	Makes a Telnet connection to a host (and optionally to a certain port). The target host can be specified, either by a host name or an IP address. The optional debug switch provides useful information about the connection by displaying the informational level of logging messages. Additionally, you can simply type the name of the host to which you wish to make the connection; by default, an attempt to establish a Telnet session is started. The interface through which the connection is made provides the source IP address for that connection.
disconnect [*session-number*]	Disconnects the specified connection, or disconnects the most recent connection if not specified.
ctrl-shift-6 x	To suspend the current session, simultaneously press the Ctrl, Shift, and 6 keys, followed by the x key.

Line Types and Numbering

Cisco devices have the following four types of lines:

- **CON: Console line**—Typically used to log in to the router for configuration purposes. This line is also referred to as CTY.

- **AUX: Auxiliary line**—RS-232 DTE port used as a backup asynchronous port (TTY). Cannot be used as a second console port.

- **TTY: Asynchronous line**—Same as asynchronous interface. Available on access server models only (Cisco 2509, 10, 11, 12, AS5100, and Cisco 1001). Used typically for remote-node, dial-in sessions that use such protocols as SLIP, PPP, and XRemote.

- **VTY: Virtual terminal line**—Used for incoming Telnet, LAT, X.25 PAD, and protocol-translation connections into synchronous ports (such as Ethernet and serial interfaces) on the router.

Different routers have different numbers of these line types. Figure 4-12 shows the Cisco line-numbering rules, where *n* represents the first physical line after the Console line, and *m* refers to the number of the vty line. For example, the vty 4 line corresponds to line 14 on a router with eight TTY ports. Because line 0 is for the Console, lines 1 to 8 are the TTY lines, line 9 is for the Auxiliary port, and lines 10 to 14 are for VTY 0 to 4.

Figure 4-12 *Cisco Line Numbering*

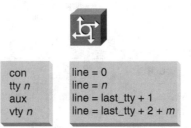

TTY lines correspond to asynchronous interfaces on a one-to-one basis, and vty lines are virtual lines that are dynamically assigned to the synchronous interfaces. Usually, you would associate vty lines with incoming Telnet sessions.

NOTE   Enter the **interface line tty ?** command to view the maximum number of TTY lines supported.

Connections to an individual line are most useful when a dial-out modem, parallel printer, or serial printer is attached to that access server line. To connect to an individual line, the remote host or terminal must specify a particular Transmission Control Protocol (TCP) port on the access server. If the Telnet protocol is used, that port is 2000 plus the line number. For example:

```
Router#Telnet 131.108.30.40 2001
```

This command indicates a Telnet connection to line 1 (2000 + 1).

Line Numbering On Cisco 1600

Some routers don't have AUX ports, and the Cisco 1600 is one of them. The following shows the way the relative and absolute line numbers are presented with the **show line** command:

```
Router#show line
Tty Typ Tx/Rx A Modem Roty AccO AccI Uses Noise Overruns
* 0 CTY - - - - - 0 1 0/0
  2 VTY - - - - - 0 0 0/0
  3 VTY - - - - - 0 0 0/0
  4 VTY - - - - - 0 0 0/0
  5 VTY - - - - - 0 0 0/0
  6 VTY - - - - - 0 0 0/0
  Line(s) not in async mode -or- with no hardware support: 1
```

The CTY port is the Console. As shown in Figure 4-12, the AUX port receives the number TTY + 1. Because this Cisco 1600 router has no Async interface (no TTY), the AUX port, if present, would have received 1 line number 1. The VTY lines are always as follows: Last_TTY + 2. Using the formula shown on Figure 4-12 to find the first VTY line number, calculate 0 TTY + 2 = 2, which is the starting number of VTY lines. By default, the router provides five virtual connections; in this case, these are numbered 2, 3, 4, 5, and 6.

You can use the **show line** command to display all types of lines and the status of each line, as exhibited in Figure 4-13. It also provides useful information about modem control and asynchronous port configuration. The **show line** *line-number* command displays more detailed information on the specified line, which includes some useful data such as baud rate, modem state (idle or ready), and modem hardware state (CTS, DSR, DTR, and RTS for hardware flow control and session control). Table 4-6 explains the output fields displayed in Figure 4-13. Figure 4-13 emphasizes concepts previously discussed in this book, with the exception of Access Class.

Filtering Traffic on VTY Lines—Access Class

If you wish to restrict incoming and outgoing connections between a particular virtual terminal line (into a Cisco device), you can use the **access-class** command on a line. The **access-class** command makes a standard access-list decide whether it should accept or reject a connection.

Remember to set identical restrictions on all the virtual terminal lines because a user can connect to any of them.

Figure 4-13 *Sample Output of the* **show line** *Command*

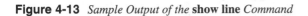

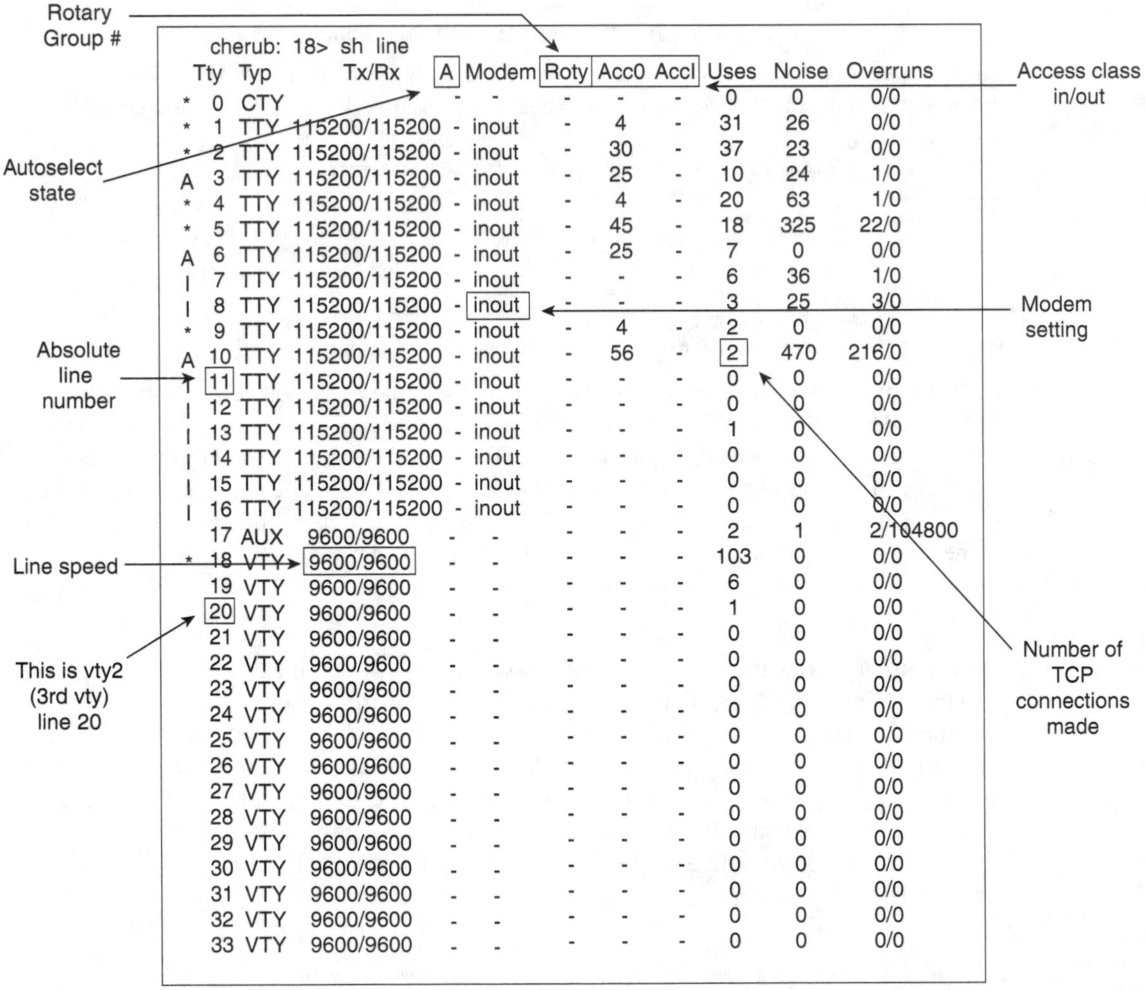

```
                 cherub: 18>  sh  line
          Tty  Typ          Tx/Rx     A  Modem  Roty  Acc0  Accl   Uses  Noise  Overruns
        *  0  CTY                      -    -      -    -     -      0     0     0/0
        *  1  TTY  115200/115200  -  inout    -    4     -     31    26    0/0
        *  2  TTY  115200/115200  -  inout    -    30    -     37    23    0/0
        A  3  TTY  115200/115200  -  inout    -    25    -     10    24    1/0
        *  4  TTY  115200/115200  -  inout    -    4     -     20    63    1/0
        *  5  TTY  115200/115200  -  inout    -    45    -     18   325    22/0
        *  6  TTY  115200/115200  -  inout    -    25    -     7     0     0/0
        A  6  TTY  115200/115200  -  inout    -    25    -     7     0     0/0
        I  7  TTY  115200/115200  -  inout    -    -     -     6     36    1/0
        I  8  TTY  115200/115200  -  inout    -    -     -     3     25    3/0
        *  9  TTY  115200/115200  -  inout    -    4     -     2     0     0/0
        A 10  TTY  115200/115200  -  inout    -    56    -     2    470   216/0
        I 11  TTY  115200/115200  -  inout    -    -     -     0     0     0/0
        I 12  TTY  115200/115200  -  inout    -    -     -     0     0     0/0
        I 13  TTY  115200/115200  -  inout    -    -     -     1     0     0/0
        I 14  TTY  115200/115200  -  inout    -    -     -     0     0     0/0
        I 15  TTY  115200/115200  -  inout    -    -     -     0     0     0/0
        I 16  TTY  115200/115200  -  inout    -    -     -     0     0     0/0
          17  AUX  9600/9600      -    -      -    -     -     2     1     2/104800
        * 18  VTY  9600/9600      -    -      -    -     -    103    0     0/0
          19  VTY  9600/9600      -    -      -    -     -     6     0     0/0
          20  VTY  9600/9600      -    -      -    -     -     1     0     0/0
          21  VTY  9600/9600      -    -      -    -     -     0     0     0/0
          22  VTY  9600/9600      -    -      -    -     -     0     0     0/0
          23  VTY  9600/9600      -    -      -    -     -     0     0     0/0
          24  VTY  9600/9600      -    -      -    -     -     0     0     0/0
          25  VTY  9600/9600      -    -      -    -     -     0     0     0/0
          26  VTY  9600/9600      -    -      -    -     -     0     0     0/0
          27  VTY  9600/9600      -    -      -    -     -     0     0     0/0
          28  VTY  9600/9600      -    -      -    -     -     0     0     0/0
          29  VTY  9600/9600      -    -      -    -     -     0     0     0/0
          30  VTY  9600/9600      -    -      -    -     -     0     0     0/0
          31  VTY  9600/9600      -    -      -    -     -     0     0     0/0
          32  VTY  9600/9600      -    -      -    -     -     0     0     0/0
          33  VTY  9600/9600      -    -      -    -     -     0     0     0/0
```

Labels around the figure:

- Rotary Group #
- Autoselect state
- Absolute line number
- Line speed
- This is vty2 (3rd vty) line 20
- Access class in/out
- Modem setting
- Number of TCP connections made

Table 4-6   **show line** *Field Descriptions*

Field	Description
Tty	Line number. An asterisk (*) preceding the number in the Tty field means that the line is currently active, running a terminal-oriented protocol.
	An "A" preceding the number indicates that the line is currently active in asynchronous mode.
	An "I" preceding the number indicates that the line is configured, but is inactive.
Typ	Type of line. Possible values are CTY-console, AUX-auxiliary port, TTY-asynchronous terminal port, and lpt-parallel printer.
Tx/Rx	Transmit rate/receive rate of the line.
A	Indicates whether autobaud is configured for the line. A value of F indicates that autobaud has been configured; a hyphen indicates that it is not configured.
Modem	Type of modem signal that has been configured for the line. Possible values include callin, callout, cts-req, DTR-Act, inout, and RIisCD.
Roty	Rotary group configured for the line.
AccO, AccI	Output or input access-list number configured for the line.
Uses	Number of connections established to or from the line since the system was restarted.
Noise	Number of times noise has been detected on the line since the system was restarted.
Overruns	Hardware (UART) overruns or software buffer overflows, both defined as the number of overruns or overflows that have occurred on the specified line since the system was restarted. Hardware overruns are buffer overruns; the UART chip has received bits from the software faster than it can process them. A software overflow occurs when the software receives bits from the hardware faster than it can process them.

Router Configuration

Some configuration is required on a router so it can place and receive asynchronous calls.

Interface Async and Line Configuration

There is often confusion between the **interface async** and **line** commands. The major difference is that the **interface async** command lets you configure the protocol (logical) aspects of an asynchronous port, as follows:

```
Router(config)#interface async 8
Router(config-if)#encapsulation ppp
```

```
Router(config-if)#async dynamic address
Router(config-if)#async mode interactive
Router(config-if)#ppp authentication chap
```

The **line** command lets you configure the physical aspects of the same port, such as the modem attached to it:

```
Router(config)#line 8
Router(config-line)#login local
Router(config-line)#modem inout
Router(config-line)#speed 115200
Router(config-line)#flowcontrol hardware
Router(config-line)#rotary 33
Router(config-line)#autoselect ppp
```

The **async** commands can be thought of as internal configuration; the **line** commands configure external characteristics of the configuration. For example, you configure the basic modem-related parameters on an access server using the **line** command, but you configure the protocol encapsulation and authentication schemes with the interface **async** command.

Basic Async Configuration—Router Preparation

To make a successful asynchronous connection, you need to configure the modem and the access server properly.

On the access server (router) use the following commands to configure the line to which the modem is attached:

```
(config)#line x
(config-line)#login
(config-line)#password password
(config-line)#flowcontrol hardware
(config-line)#speed 115200
(config-line)#transport input all
(config-line)#stopbits 1
(config-line)#modem inout
```

OR

```
(config-line)#modem dialin
```

Command	Description
line *x*	Used to identify a specific line for configuration and to start the line configuration command collection mode.
exec	Allows the EXEC process on this line. The EXEC process is activated automatically on all lines. Therefore, because this command is the default, it does not appear in the configuration.
login	Sets a login password on this line. Without the password, no connection is allowed.

Command	Description
password *password*	Sets the password to be used when logging in to this line.
flowcontrol hardware	Uses RTS/CTS for flow control.
speed 115200	Sets the maximum speed (in bits-per-second) between the modem and the access server. The **speed** command sets both the transmit and receive speed.
transport input all	Allows all protocols to be passed to the access server through this line.
stopbits 1	Sets the number of stop bits transmitted per byte.
modem inout	Uses the modem for both incoming and outgoing calls.
modem dialin	For incoming calls only. This is the default.

WARNING   Software flow control (xon and xoff characters) is not recommended with modems and Cisco routers.

Basic Async Configuration—Modem Preparation

A modem can be configured in many different ways to work with a router.

Figure 4-14 shows that you can manually configure a modem by sending AT commands. You may want to have the router automatically discover and configure the modem, or you may wish to specify to the router which configuration commands to send to the modem.

Figure 4-14 *Modem Configuration Can Be Done Manually or Automatically*

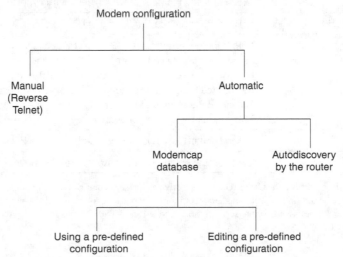

All these configuration methods are explored in greater detail in the following sections.

Manual Configuration of Modems

You can elect to manually configure the modem instead of having the router force a configuration on it.

Standard Commands

On the modem side, you can use the standard configuration commands to do the following:

- Perform hardware flow control.
- Lock DTE speed to ensure that the modem will always communicate with the access server at the specified speed. As an example, when you use an async interface, you lock the speed to its theoretical maximum of 115.2 kbps. The router speed command sets both transmit and receive speeds.
- Hang up when you quit a session.
- Have the Carrier Detect signal truthfully reflect the carrier state.

To manually configure your modem, you most likely reverse Telnet to your modem and apply some AT commands. AT stands for *attention commands* for the modem. In general, each modem vendor has its own modem command set that differs from other vendors' command sets. However, the following modem commands are common among most vendors:

Command	Description
AT&F	Loads the factory default settings (read-only).
ATS0=1	Sets the modem to automatically answer all incoming calls on the first ring. (Recommended to be set to 2 for lines with caller ID.)[1]
AT&C1&D3	Sets up modem control (CD and DTR).
ATS2=255	Ignore the **+++** command. The **+++** characters set the modem to command mode. You might need to configure the far-end modem to ignore **+++** because the **+++** command issued to the near-end modem will be transmitted to the far-end modem. The far-end modem might interpret it and cause the connection to hang. This is a bug in the far-end modem. Many modems might operate this way.
ATE0	When **echo off** is set, the modem will not echo keystrokes.
ATM0	Turns off the external audio output from the modem.

1. Warning: Because the Caller ID function activates on the second ring, hackers typically target modems that answer on the first ring. If a modem takes more than one ring to answer, many hackers don't pursue the matter. You are therefore advised to set your modem to at least ATS0=2, thus pretending that your line subscribes to Caller ID.

AT Command Sets

AT commands stands for attention commands that are used to address the modem and force a certain behavior from it. The following is a listing of different command sets that exist and examples of commands used in the modem modules of Cisco 2600 and Cisco 3600 series:

- **Alphabetic** Command Set—Q0 enables output of result codes.
- **Caret** Command Set—**^V** Displays the modem's current flash memory bootstrap revision.
- **Dollar** Command Set—**$B**n sets the serial port rate to n bps, for example **$B 115200**.
- **Percent** Command Set—**%B**n sets the modem port data rate, for example **%B 33600**.
- **Ampersand** Command Set—**&D3** sets the modem on-hook and resets when detecting an on-to-off transition of DTR.
- **Parenthesis** Command Set—**)M1** autoadjusts the power level for cellular modems.
- **Asterisk** Command Set—*** I** displays the modem identifier.
- **Hyphen** Command Set—**-DL** redials the last number dialed.
- **Colon** Command Set—**:Dn** sets manual dial.
- @ Character Command Set—**@E** gives detailed modem call status.
- **Backslash** Command Set—**\F** displays stored phone numbers.
- # Character Command Set—**#E0** enables the escape code sequence in answer mode.

For more info on the AT Commands, consult http://www.cisco.com/univercd/cc/td/doc/product/access/acs_mod/cis3600/analogfw/analogat.htm#12195.

Nonstandard Modem Commands

Many modem commands are not standardized, and they vary from one vendor to another. The following modem configurations and commands are essential for modems that are attached to Cisco access servers:

- Hardware flow control—Use CTS and RTS.
- Lock DTE speed—Sets the serial port of the modem to a fixed data transfer rate. Locking the speed between the modem and DTE device prevents the speed from being negotiated down during the initial call setup.
- Error correction—Sets error control.
- Compression—Uses the best compression algorithm that can be negotiated between the two communicating modems.
- Show configuration—Shows current modem settings.
- Getting help—Shows all of the AT commands for your specific modem.

- Saving the configuration—Saves the configuration that you just entered in the NVRAM of the modem.

Table 4-7 shows some standard modem initialization strings. For nonstandard modem commands, you must refer to the vendor's user manual that comes with each modem you purchase. More information about commands for each modem type can be found at http://www.cisco.com/warp/public/701/21.html.

Table 4-7   *Standard Modem Commands*

Command	Microcom	Hayes	USR
Hardware flow control	**AT\Q3**	**AT&K3**	**AT&H1&R2**
Lock DTE speed	**AT\J0**	**AT&Q6**	**AT&B1**
Error correction	**AT\N6**	**AT&Q5**	**AT&M4**
Compression	**AT%C1**	**AT&Q9**	**AT&K1**
Show configuration	**AT\S1**	**AT&V**	**ATI4**
Getting help[1]	**AT$H**	**AT$H**	**AT$**
Saving the configuration	**AT&W**	**AT&W**	**AT&W**

1. The help feature is not always built in. As an example, I could not get the help on a new PCMCIA 10/100 + 56K Modem card I had, no matter what help command I tried. I called the manufacturer, a major PCMCIA cards provider, to find out that indeed no help had been built for the modem portion of its new combo cards.

Modem Initialization Strings

Initialization strings are used to send commands to modems before they dial out. They are a series of parameter settings that are sent to your modem to configure it to interact with the access server in a specified way. No strings are required when you dial into a modem. The following are some examples of modem initialization strings:

U.S. Robotics (USR) Courier at&fs0=1&c1&d3&h1&r2&b1&m4&k1&w
Hayes Optima/Accura at&fs0=1&c1&d3&k3&q9&w
Microcom QX4232 series at&fs0=1&c1&d3\q3\j0\n6%c1&w

There are numerous other modems from different vendors. Always refer to the user manual from your modem vendor for the proper modem commands to use.

Note that the AppleTalk Remote Access (ARA) 1.0 (or 2.0) client software includes built-in MNP 4 capability. It might have problems if MNP 4 is enabled on the answering modem. Some modems let you disable MNP, but allow LAPM.

For example, you can use the following command strings to disable MNP:

USR Sportster series ats27=16
Practical Peripherals MiniTower series at&q9

Also, for a list of AT commands for various modem types and their specific initializing strings, refer to Appendix D, "AT Commands for Modems and Chat-Scripts."

Automatic Configuration of Modems

Modem autoconfiguration facilitates the configuration of modems on access servers. To set up a modem using modem autoconfiguration, connect the phone line and power cable to the modem, and use the **modem autoconfigure** command on the line with the modem. No other setup function is required for most modems.

To better understand modem autoconfiguration, this section contains the following topics:

- Modem capability database (modemcap file in the Cisco IOS software)—Modemcap is a database of modems and their modem configuration command strings.

- Modem autodiscovery—You can configure a line to automatically attempt to discover the type of modem on the line and to use that modem configuration.

- Modem autoconfiguration—You can configure a line to use a specified modem type.

Modem Capability Database

The modem capability database (modemcap) is a list of modems with a known set of AT configuration commands for setting each modem type's attributes. For example, many modems use the string **AT&F** to reset the modem to its factory default attributes.

Modem attributes have a full name and a two- or three-letter abbreviation.

Factory default, for example, is also referred to as FD. For normal operation, you need not know these abbreviations. If you are familiar with the modem abbreviations, you can add entries to the modemcap database.

The modemcap database contains entries for supported modems. You can do the following tasks to manage a modemcap database entry:

- View modem entries in the modemcap database with the **show modemcap** command.

- View the contents of a modem's modemcap entry.

- Modify a modem's modemcap entry.

- Create a modem database entry.

The **show modemcap** command displays the modems in the modemcap database, as follows:

```
Router#show modemcap
default
codex_3260
usr_courier
usr_sportster
hayes_optima
```

```
global_village
viva
telebit_t3000
microcom_hdms
microcom_server
nec_v34
nec_v11
nec_piafs
cisco_v110
mica
```

In addition, with the modem type specified, it shows a complete list of the specified modem's modemcap entry that includes the following fields:

- Command description
- Command abbreviation (with colon separator)
- Command string

The command **show modemcap codex_3260** shows the AT command string attributes and their values for the Codex 3260 modem, as shown in the following:

```
Router#show modemcap codex_3260
Modemcap values for codex_3260
Factory Defaults (FD): &F
Autoanswer (AA): S0=1
Carrier detect (CD): &C1
Drop with DTR (DTR): &D2
Hardware Flowcontrol (HFL): *FL3
Lock DTE speed (SPD): *SC1
Best Error Control (BER): *SM3
Best Compression (BCP): *DC1
No Error Control (NER): *SM1
No Compression (NCP): *DC0
No Echo (NEC): E0
No Result Codes (NRS): Q1
Software Flowcontrol (SFL): [not set]
Caller ID (CID): &S1
Miscellaneous (MSC): [not set]
Template entry (TPL): default
```

The default modem type has modemcap values for a few of the most common attributes. It does not contain strings for attributes that vary widely by modem type, such as locking speeds, setting hardware flow control, or dealing with compression and error correction.

You can use the **modemcap entry** *modem_name* command or the **show modemcap** *modem_name* command to see the contents of a modem's modemcap entry. The **modemcap entry** *modem_name* command displays modemcap values in a truncated form.

As you will see later in this section, you can also create variant modemcap entries to add new modems or to extend a modem's functionality in the modemcap database.

Modem Autodiscovery

If no modem is specified for a particular line and you have provided the **modem autoconfigure discovery** command, the access server attempts to autodiscover the type of modem to which it is attached. The access server determines the type of modem by sending AT commands to the modem and evaluating the response. The Cisco IOS software initially tries the first of the modemcap strings to see if the modem initializes properly. If not, the Cisco IOS software cycles to the next string and repeats the process until the appropriate string is found. Usually, if none of the strings properly initializes the modem, you must manually configure the modem.

NOTE Sometimes, the router fails to recognize a modem, even though it might be part of the modemcap list. Therefore, if you know that your modem can be configured by using an initialization string from one of these scripts, you can issue the **modem autoconfigure type** *type* command, as explained in the next section.

The following is an example of the **modem autoconfigure discovery** command:

```
Router(config)#line 1 16
Router(config-line)#modem autoconfigure discovery
```

This command instructs the access server to do the following on lines 1 though 16:

- Send the AT string at various baud rates until it receives an OK.
- Send a variety of AT commands that attempt to receive a complete identification of the modem identified in the access server's modem capabilities database.

The specific modemcap entries found on a particular system are determined by the hardware and Cisco IOS software version that are installed.

NOTE Whenever possible, configure the modem to eliminate the overhead of modem autodiscovery. If you list a specific modem type, initialization proceeds more quickly.

If the access server cannot determine the modem type, the default modem entry is used. Any modems that are not currently supported in the list can be manually added to the list to be autodiscovered in future communication, as you will see later in the section, "Fine-tuning Modem Autoconfiguration."

Modem Autoconfiguration

If you know that your modem can be configured by using an initialization string from one of the preconfigured scripts of the modemcap, you can issue the **modem autoconfigure type** *type* command. In this command, *type* is one of the strings in the modemcap list displayed in the "Modem Capability Database" section, earlier in this chapter. If you list a specific modem type, initialization proceeds more quickly than if you let the autodiscovery take place. In the following example, the access server is configured to send an initialization string for a USR Sportster modem on line 1:

```
Router(config)#line 1
Router(config-line)#modem autoconfigure type usr_sportster
```

NOTE   To eliminate the overhead of modem autodiscovery and to avoid modem configuration ambiguity caused by modem autodiscovery, configure the modem type by using the **modem autoconfigure type** command whenever possible.

With automatic modem configuration, each time a modem is reset, a chat-script is executed that sends a string of modem configuration commands (AT commands) to the modem. This modem configuration command string is generated automatically whenever the modem is recycled.

Speed Issues with Modem Autoconfiguration

Here are the results of autoconfiguration tests that were performed on 3640s to determined how long it took a Cisco Router to configured an attached modem:

Test Description	Time
Autodiscovery with no match found (therefore, default settings were applied), unknown discovery	6 seconds
Autodiscovery with a match found (USR Sportster), know discovery	5 seconds
Autoconfigure with modem type specified (type USR)	2 seconds

Fine-tuning Modem Autoconfiguration

If none of the strings from the modemcap properly initializes the modem, you must manually configure the modem or change the modemcap database.

Use the **modemcap edit** *new_modem_name* command to do the following:

- Add a new entry to the modemcap database

- Add new attributes to an existing modem entry in the modemcap database

Figure 4-15 shows the uses of the **modemcap edit usr_new** command. The command line marked with a **1** creates the usr_new entry in the modemcap database and sets the caller-id for the usr_new modem to *U1. The command line marked with a **2** locks the DTE speed on this modem. Finally, the command line marked with a **3** points to another modemcap entry to be used as a template. As a result, any value not found in the current modemcap entry is set by the template modemcap entry. In this example, the **usr_courier** modemcap entry is the template. You can have up to four layers of templates.

Figure 4-15   *Creating and Editing a Variant Modemcap Entry*

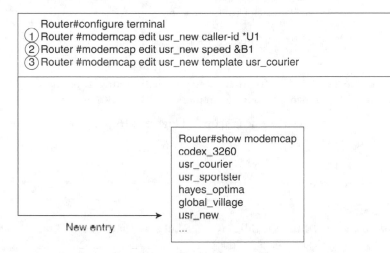

Additional commands that can be used when creating variant modem cap entries are as follows:

- The **modemcap edit** command edits user-created modemcap entries only.

- Use the **no modemcap edit** *modemname* command to remove the specified modem from the modemcap database. With this command, the whole modemcap entry is deleted.

- The **no modemcap edit** *modemname attribute* command removes a modem attribute from a modem's modemcap entry without deleting the entry altogether.

After configuring a modemcap entry with the **modemcap edit** command, use the **show modemcap** *modem_name* command to verify the new modemcap attribute values.

Figure 4-16 shows the output for the new modemcap created in Figure 4-15.

Figure 4-16 *Viewing a Variant Modemcap Entry*

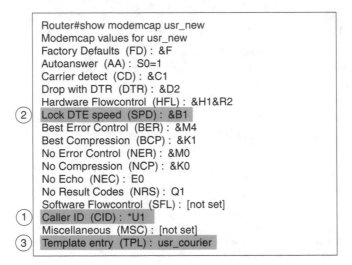

```
Router#show modemcap usr_new
Modemcap values for usr_new
Factory Defaults  (FD) :  &F
Autoanswer  (AA) :  S0=1
Carrier detect  (CD) :  &C1
Drop with DTR  (DTR) :  &D2
Hardware Flowcontrol  (HFL) :  &H1&R2
Lock DTE speed  (SPD) :  &B1
Best Error Control  (BER) :  &M4
Best Compression  (BCP) :  &K1
No Error Control  (NER) :  &M0
No Compression  (NCP) :  &K0
No Echo  (NEC) :  E0
No Result Codes  (NRS) :  Q1
Software Flowcontrol  (SFL) :  [not set]
Caller ID  (CID) :  *U1
Miscellaneous  (MSC) :  [not set]
Template entry  (TPL) :  usr_courier
```

The numbers in the Figure 4-16 output correspond to the numbers in Figure 4-15 that show each **modemcap edit** command from the example.

Specifically, the usr_new modemcap shown in Figure 4-16 is identical to the usr_courier entry, with the following exceptions:

- The DTE speed lock
- The caller ID field
- The template

If you use the **show running-config** command, the usr_new information for the configuration on the previous page appears as follows:

```
usr_new SPD=&B1:CID=*U1:TPL=usr_courier
```

Chat-Scripts for Async Lines

Because asynchronous modems are not standard, you must write custom chat-scripts to perform certain tasks. Chat-scripts are used for the following tasks:

- Modem configuration
- Dialing and remote login commands
- Failure detection

A **chat-script** is a string of text that defines the handshaking that occurs between two DTE devices, or between a DTE and its directly attached. It consists of expect-send pairs that define the string that the local system expects to see from the remote device and which reply the local system should send:

```
(config)#chat-script script-name expect-string send-string
```

For example, you can configure chat-scripts for the following tasks:

- Initializing the directly attached modem
- Instructing the modem to dial out
- Logging in to a remote system

The following is a sample **chat-script** command and a table that describes it:

```
(config)#chat-script Reno ABORT ERROR ABORT BUSY "" "ATZ" OK "ATDT \T" TIMEOUT 30
➥CONNECT \c
```

chat-script Command	Description
Reno	Defines the name of this chat-script as dial.
ABORT ERROR	Stops the chat-script if an error is encountered.
"ATZ"	Without expecting an input string, sends the AT command to the modem to reset it by using the stored profile.
OK "ATDT \T"	When the input string OK is seen, sends the AT command to instruct the modem to dial the telephone number in the dialer string or **start-chat** command.
TIMEOUT 30 CONNECT	Waits up to 30 seconds for the input string CONNECT.
\c	Suppresses a new line at the end of the send string. It is an escape sequence. Indicates the end of the chat-script.

For more information on chat-scripts, please refer to Appendix D, "AT Commands for Modems and Chat-Scripts."

Modem-script versus System-script

Chat-scripts are used as modem-scripts or system-scripts. Modem-scripts are used between DTE to DCE, where system-scripts are sent DTE to DTE.

In the following example, the script called Niagara is used between the router and the modem to successfully handshake with the destination. The Gambling script is used for logging between the router and an end-system at the destination; ! script called Niagara is used for dialing a modem:

```
chat-script Niagara ABORT ERROR "" "AT Z" OK "ATDT \T" TIMEOUT 30 CONNECT \c
!
! Script for logging into a system called Gambling and starting up slip session:
```

```
chat-script Gambling ABORT invalid TIMEOUT 15 name: billw word: wewpass ">" "slip
➥default"
!
Interface async 5
dialer map ip 172.16.12.17 modem-script Niagara system-script Gambling
➥918005551212
```

You can manually start a chat-script on any asynchronous line that is not currently active by using the **start-chat** command. Or, you can configure chat-scripts so they are executed for specific events, such as the following:

- Line activation—Triggered by incoming traffic (Carrier Detect signal going up)
- Connection—Triggered by outgoing traffic (for example, reverse Telnet)
- Line reset—Triggered by async line reset
- Startup—Triggered by access server startup
- Dialer—Triggered by dial-on-demand routing (DDR)

Start-chat: Manual Start of Chat-script

If you wish to manually start a chat-script on a line, you can use the **start-chat** privileged EXEC command.

```
Router#start-chat regexp [line-number [dialer-string]]
```

This command provides modem dialing commands for a chat-script that you want to apply immediately to a line. If you do not specify a line, the script runs on the current line. If the specified line is already in use, the script is not activated, and an error message appears.

The argument *regexp* is used to specify the name of the modem script that is to be executed. The first script that matches the argument in this command and the **dialer map** command will be used.

Verifying and Debugging Modem Autoconfiguration

The **debug confmodem** command displays the modem configuration process, as shown in Example 4-1. Example 4-1 shows an access server modem configuration process on line 97 with a USR Sportster modem attached.

Example 4-1   *Modem Configuration Process—**debug confmodem***

```
Router#debug confmodem
TTY97: detection speed (115200) response ---OK---
TTY97: Modem command: --AT--
TTY97: Modem configuration succeeded
TTY97: Detected modem speed 115200
```

Example 4-1 *Modem Configuration Process*—**debug confmodem** *(Continued)*

```
TTY97: Done with modem configuration
TTY97: detection speed (115200) response ---OK---
TTY97: Modem command: --AT&F&C1&D2&H1&R2&M4&K1&B1S0=1H0--
TTY97: Modem configuration succeeded
TTY97: detection speed (115200) response ---OK---
TTY97: Done with modem configuration
```

You can also use the following commands to verify operations:

- The **show line** command shows the type of modem configured on a line.

- The **clear line** command returns a line to its idle state. Normally, this command returns the line to its conventional function as a terminal line with the interface left in a down state.

Troubleshooting Modem Autoconfiguration

To troubleshoot modem autoconfiguration, consider the following conditions and solutions: the modem is not responding, the modem is not recognized by modem autoconfigure discovery, or there is an original modemcap entry problem.

If the modem is not responding:

- Is the modem plugged in and turned on?

- Is the power-up configuration set to factory default?

- Can you connect the modem through reverse Telnet?

- Do you have a dial tone at the phone jack?

If the modem is not recognized by modem autoconfigure discovery:

- Use the **show line** command to verify the modem configuration that the line is using.

- Does the Cisco access server recognize the modem?

- Use the **modem autoconfigure type** *modem-name* command.

NOTE   Use the **show modemcap** command to verify modemcap support for this modem.

If there is an original modemcap entry problem:

- If you configured your own modemcap entry and reconfiguration appears to function, verify that the DTR attribute is not set to &D3.

And as a last resort, do not forget that you can also check the modem manufacturer's manual.

Summary

You learned in this chapter how to configure an access server for modem connectivity. To do this, you saw how to perform a reverse Telnet session to the modem, how to configure it for basic asynchronous operations, and how to use the modem autoconfiguration.

In Chapter 5, "Configuring Point-to-Point Protocol and Controlling Network Access," you will learn how to establish a PPP session over the lines you have configured for Async connectivity.

Case Study 4-1—Configuring Asynchronous Connections with Modems

In this case study, you have to set up an initial configuration for an access server to provide modem support. You then manually configure the attached modem. Finally, you are required to verify proper operation by dialing the connection from a PC. From the Central site's router, you verify the connected users and list the status of the modem hardware control signals.

Scenario

Complete the tasks of this case study, and then review the case study solution section that follows to see how you did and see where you might need to review the concepts presented in this chapter.

You were asked to configure the external modem on the central site router (Cisco 3640) to receive an asynchronous call placed from the PC, as shown in Figure 4-17.

Figure 4-17 *Telecommuter Calling Back at the Central Site via an Asynchronous Connection*

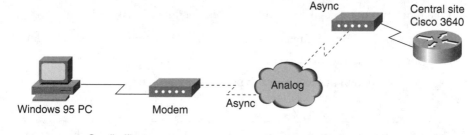

Task 1—Setting Up the Initial Configuration of the Central Site Router

Configure this new router for the first time. Provide it with all parameters necessary during an initial configuration. For example, provide the hostname, ip address, routing protocol, and so on.

Task 2—Configuring the Serial Interface and Line

Step 1   Configure the serial interface to which the external modem is connected, and the corresponding line.

Step 2   From the global configuration mode, configure a hostname to allow reverse.

Task 3—Configuring the Central Site Modem

Step 1   Enter **modem** at the command prompt (Reverse Telnet to line 97 of the Cisco 3640).

Step 2   Enter **AT** and press Return. Observe that you receive an OK from the modem.

Step 3   Enter and describe what each of the following AT commands do (you can use the modem built-in help, the modem manual, or visit the Web site of the modem manufacturer to find the answers):

AT$	AT&$	ATS$
AT&F1	ATS0=1	AT&C1
AT&D2	AT&H1	AT&R2
AT&M4	AT&B1	AT&K1
AT&W0	ATI4	

Task 4—Configuring the PC Modem and Connecting to Central Site

From the remote PC, initiate a reverse Telnet session on the PC modem, and dial in to the central router. Suppose that the phone number to reach CentralC is a four-digit speed-dial number: 1005.

Once the modems have synchronized (trained), you should be prompted with a user access verification in the pcmodem window. Log in, and go into the privileged EXEC mode. Verify users' connectivity to port 97. Also, verify that the Central site router is properly configured.

Task 5—Simplifying Router Modem Configuration with Autoconfigure

Step 1   Turn on a debugging function so you can see the router autoconfiguring the modem.

Step 2   Configure your line 97 so the access server will attempt to autoconfigure the modem as a US Robotics Sportster.

Step 3   Save your configuration.

Solution to Case Study 4-1—Configuring Asynchronous Connections with Modems

The following is a step-by-step discussion of the case study solution.

Task 1 Solution—Setting Up the Initial Configuration of the Central Site Router

Complete the following steps on the Central site router.

NOTE   Some commands that are requested in this case study do not pertain to Async connectivity; they pertain to the initial configuration of any Cisco routers. This is necessary because your central site access server was never configured prior to this case study.

Commands requested during case studies that do not relate to previous chapters are usually commands covered in ICRC and ACRC courses and books.

Configure your Central site router for the following initial configuration:

Command	Description
hostname *hostname*	Provides your router with a name. For this case study, use CentralA.
no ip domain-lookup	Avoids domain lookups of typos.
router igrp *100*	Enables the IGRP routing protocol with the Autonous System *100*.
network *10.0.0.0*	Advertises network 10.0.0.0 with IGRP.
enable secret *cisco*	Specifies an additional layer of security over the **enable password** command by displaying the encrypted *cisco* password.
enable password *san-fran*	Sets the local password to control access to various privilege levels to *san-fran*.
interface e *0/0*	Cisco 3640: most specify the slot, and then the interface.
ip address *address mask*	Let's pick 10.115.0.110 255.255.255.0.
no shut	Enables (activates) the interface.

Task 2 Solution—Configuring the Serial Interface and Line

Step 1 Configure the serial interface to which the external modem is connected and the corresponding line by using the following commands. In this case study, assume that a four-port synchronous/asynchronous network module is located in the fourth slot of a Cisco 3640, and that you are taking the first interface of that card for asynchrounous communications.

NOTE The modem is connected to the first port on this card, thus configuring **interface serial 3/0**. In ICRC and CRLS, you learn that Cisco starts counting at 0. Therefore the fourth slot is called slot 3 and the first port is called port 0—thus 3/0.

Command	Description
interface serial *3/0*	Enters the interface configuration mode of the first interface of the fourth slot of the Cisco 3640.
physical-layer async	Configures the serial interface as an async interface (adds line 97 to the configuration).
line *97*	Configures the line for the following physical layer parameters.
login	Allows login and challenge for a password.
password *cisco*	Sets the login password to *cisco*.
modem inout	Allows incoming and outgoing modem connections.
transport input all	Allows any transport protocol.
speed *115200*	Sets speed between router and modem.
stopbits *1*	One stop bit per byte.
flowcontrol hardware	Uses CTS/RTS flow control.

Step 2 From global configuration mode, configure a hostname to allow reverse Telnet to the attached modem:

Command	Description
ip host *modem 2097 10.115.0.110*	Int E 0/0—IP address picked in Task 1. This command allows a reverse Telnet connection to line 97. The name can be anything you choose (we chose *modem*). As learned previously in this chapter, a reverse Telnet connection is performed by using an IP address of a valid interface—in this case, interface E 0/0.

Task 3 Solution—Configuring the Central Site Modem

Step 1   Enter **modem** at the command prompt. This command (word: **modem**) connects you to the modem on line 97 of the Cisco 3640 via reverse Telnet, as specified in the previous step.

Step 2   You are prompted for a Telnet line password. Enter the password **cisco**, and press Return.

Step 3   Table 4-8 provides a description for each AT command. Results may vary, depending on the manufacturer.

Table 4-8   *AT Commands to Manually Configure the Modem*

AT Command	Description
AT$	HELP, Command Quick Reference (CTRL-S to Stop, CTRL-C to Cancel) <output omitted>
AT&$	HELP, Ampersand Commands (CTRL-S to Stop, CTRL-C to Cancel) <output omitted>
ATS$	HELP, S Register Functions (CTRL-S to Stop, CTRL-C to Cancel) <output omitted>
AT&F1	Hardware Flow Control Configuration
ATS0=1	Auto-Answer on first ring
AT&C1	Modem Controls CD
AT&D2	DTE Controls DTR
AT&H1	CTS
AT&R2	RX to DTE/RTS high
AT&M4	ARQ/Normal Mode
AT&B1	Fixed DTE Speed
AT&K1	Auto Data Compression
AT&W0	Store Configuration to Template 0
ATI4	Displays the modem configuration settings

Task 4 Solution—Configuring the PC Modem

From the PC, initiate a reverse Telnet session on the PC's modem. One way of doing this in Windows 95 is to use Hyperterminal and to establish a connection by selecting Connect using: Direct to COM*X,* where you will choose the COM port number used by your PC's modem.

After reverse Telnet is initiated, type **AT**; you should get an **OK** back from the modem. To call the Central site, type **atdt 1001**, which means "attention, dial tone the number 1001." Your PC modem will initiate a call on the Central site.

NOTE	This case study was developed by using a POTS simulator, which used four-digit phone numbers.

Once the PC modem and the Central site modem are synchronized, log into the Central site by entering the line password you configured in Task 2. In the pcmodem window, you can enter the privileged EXEC mode. You can type **show users** to verify connectivity to the tty port 97. You can also type **show line 97** to verify asynchronous connectivity or type **show run** to display the configuration of the Central site.

```
CentralA#show run

!
version 11.3
no service password-encryption
!
hostname CentralA
!
enable secret 5 $1$kFDB$u7Gnl0ROGlQUxISnDvEP1/
enable password san-fran
!
no ip domain-lookup (no misspelled command lookups)
ip host modem 2097 10.115.0.110 (static route to modem for reverse Telnet
connection)
!
controller T1 1/0
!
interface Ethernet0/0
ip address 10.115.0.110 255.255.255.0
no lat enabled
!
interface Ethernet0/1
no ip address
shutdown
no lat enabled
!
interface Serial3/0
physical-layer async (sets interface to async mode)
no ip address
!
interface Serial3/1
no ip address
shutdown
!
```

Task 5 Solution—Simplifying Router Modem Configuration with Autoconfigure

Step 1 From the privilege mode, enter **debug confmodem** to turn on modem configuration debugging.

Step 2 Enter configuration mode and configure the modem line as follows:

```
line 97
modem autoconfigure type usr_sportster
```

In a few seconds, you should see messages from the command that you entered. Your output should look similar to the following:

```
TTY97: detection speed (115200) response ---OK---
TTY97: Modem command: --AT&F&C1&D2&H1&R2&M4&K1&B1S0=1H0--
TTY97: Modem configuration succeeded
TTY97: detection speed (115200) response ---OK---
TTY97: Done with modem configuration
```

Step 3 To save your configuration, enter the following:

CentralC#copy runn start

Case Study Conclusion

In this case study, you learned how to do the following:

- Configure a line on an access server
- Reverse Telnet to a modem
- Configure a modem
- Initiate a session on a modem
- Autoconfigure an access server's modem

Case Study 4-2—Configuring Remote WAN Routers

This case study presents a remote site that is located in the Northwest Territories that needs to connect to a cross-Canadian WAN.

Scenario

Only analog lines are available for the Yellowknife customer. Therefore, Yellowknife will join the cross-Canadian WAN via Calgary's access server. Because the client has its own long-distance lines between Calgary and Yellowknife, it has decided to nail the line (permanent connection via DDR). Figure 4-18 shows the topology of the WAN. The routers used in this case are Cisco 2509-RJ (2 serial, 1 Ethernet, and 8 Async).

Figure 4-18 *Remote Connection to a Cross-Canadian WAN*

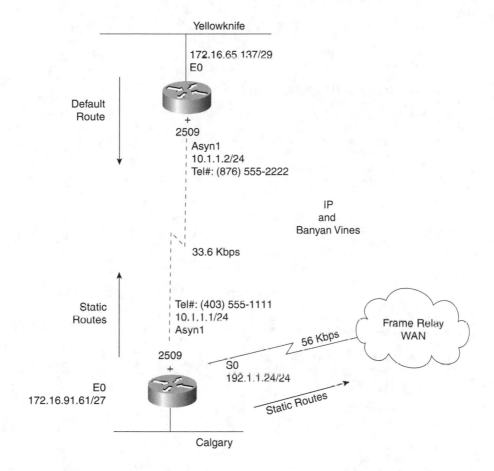

Solution to Case Study 4-2—Configuring Remote WAN Routers

Here is the actual configuration of the Calgary and Yellowknife routers. The bold letters show the lines pertaining to the commands seen in this chapter:

```
Calgary#sh run
Building configuration...

Current configuration:
!
version 11.2
```

```
no service password-encryption
service udp-small-servers
service tcp-small-servers
!
hostname Calgary
!
enable secret 5 $1$yZyJ$AT8R..8Agr2efa652aef6454sde
!
username Yellow password BABA
no ip domain-lookup
ip host Toronto 192.1.1.7
ip host Modem1 2001 172.16.171.161
ip host Halifax 192.1.1.46
ip host Montreal 192.1.1.3
ip host Ottawa 192.1.1.11
ip host Vancouver 192.1.1.26
ip host Edmonton 192.1.1.27
vines routing 4BADBEEF:0001
chat-script Hayes-Optima ABORT ERROR "" "AT Z" OK "ATDT \T" TIMEOUT 30 CONNECT \c
!
interface Ethernet0
 ip address 172.16.171.161 255.255.255.224
 vines metric 2
 vines propagate
 vines update interval 230
!
interface Serial0
 description DLCI-96 Frame Relay Circuit# 0B67851535-274TDON-352
 ip address 192.1.1.24 255.255.255.0
 encapsulation frame-relay
 vines metric 35
 vines propagate
 vines update interval 230
 no fair-queue
 cdp enable
!
interface Async1
 ip address 10.1.1.1 255.255.255.0
 encapsulation ppp
 keepalive 10
 async default routing
 async mode dedicated
 vines metric 50
 no vines propagate
 vines update interval 100
 dialer in-band
 dialer idle-timeout 300
 dialer wait-for-carrier-time 180
 dialer map vines 4BADCAFE:0001 name Yellow modem-script Hayes-Optima broadcast
➥9,18675552222
 dialer map ip 10.1.1.2 name Yellow modem-script Hayes-Optima broadcast
➥9,18675552222
 dialer-group 1
!
no ip classless
```

```
ip route 172.16.94.96 255.255.255.224 192.1.1.23
ip route 172.16.94.128 255.255.255.248 192.1.1.20
ip route 172.16.65.136 255.255.255.248 10.1.1.2
<output omitted>
!
snmp-server community public RO
dialer-list 1 protocol ip permit
dialer-list 1 protocol vines permit
banner incoming ^C


¦ ¦
¦ Out of Bounds ¦
¦ ¦
¦ Authorized Users Only ¦
^C
banner login ^C


¦ ¦
¦ Out of Bounds ¦
¦ ¦
¦ ¦
¦ Authorized Users Only ¦
^C
banner motd ^Cncomm^C
!
line con 0
 exec-timeout 0 0
line 1
 login local
 modem InOut
 modem autoconfigure type hayes_optima
 transport input all
 stopbits 1
 speed 115200
 flowcontrol hardware
line 2 8
line aux 0
 password 7 YYYYYYYYYYYY
 login
 modem Dialin
 modem autoconfigure type usr_sportster
 stopbits 1
line vty 0 4
 password WWWWWWW
 login
!
end


Yellow#sh run
Building configuration...

Current configuration:
```

```
!
version 11.2
no service password-encryption
no service udp-small-servers
no service tcp-small-servers
!
hostname Yellow
!
enable secret 5 $&34%$Bea3..8Agr2efa65wf3f64ewe38$
!
username Calgary password BABA
no ip domain-lookup
ip host Modem1 2001 172.16.65.137
ip host Calgary 10.1.1.1
!
interface Ethernet0
 ip address 172.16.65.137 255.255.255.248
 vines metric 30
 no ip route-cache
 no ip mroute-cache
 no mop enabled
!
interface Serial0
 no ip address
 no ip route-cache
 no ip mroute-cache
 shutdown
!
interface Async1
 ip address 10.1.1.2 255.255.255.0
 encapsulation ppp
 keepalive 10
 async default routing
 async mode dedicated
 vines metric 50
 no vines propagate
 vines update interval 100
 dialer in-band
 dialer idle-timeout 300
 dialer wait-for-carrier-time 180
 dialer map vines 4BADBEEF:0001 name Calgary broadcast
 dialer map ip 10.1.1.1 name Calgary broadcast
 dialer-group 1
!
no ip classless
ip route 0.0.0.0 0.0.0.0 10.1.1.1
!
dialer-list 1 protocol ip permit
dialer-list 1 protocol vines permit
!
line con 0
 exec-timeout 0 0
line 1
 login local
 modem InOut
```

```
    modem autoconfigure type hayes_optima
    transport input all
    stopbits 1
    speed 115200
    flowcontrol hardware
line 2 8
line aux 0
 session-timeout 15
 password cisco
 autobaud
 login
 modem InOut
 transport input all
 stopbits 1
line vty 0 4
 password cisco
 login
!
end
```

Solution Summary

On this router, I configured the interface Async; not Serial. The access server used by Calgary is a Cisco 2509-RJ, which has built-in async interfaces.

Even though the modem attached to the access server was a Hayes Accura 33.6, I had to use the Hayes Optima modemcap to get the connection to work. Also, a chat-script had to be configured for dial-out to take place.

Review Questions

Answer the following questions and then refer to Appendix H, "Answers to Review Questions," for answers and explanations.

1 What does the lock DTE modem attribute do?

2 A user dials into a line and ends up in someone else's session. What is one possible cause?

3 What is reverse Telnet? Describe how it is used with modems.

4 What are the modem autoconfiguration options?

CHAPTER 5

Configuring Point-to-Point Protocol and Controlling Network Access

Remote access is an integral part of the corporate mission. Traveling sales people, executives, remote office staff, and telecommuters all need to communicate by connecting to the main office LAN. The need for electronic information makes remote data access almost as necessary as a telephone.

In Chapter 4, "Configuring Asynchronous Connections with Modems," you learned the technology and tasks necessary to establish an analog dial-up connection. In this chapter, you will learn how to use that dial-up connection to connect to the network and exchange data.

You will learn, more specifically, about the Point-to-Point Protocol (PPP). PPP is often used to link remote nodes and remote LANs together. This chapter focuses especially on the authentication methods used by PPP—Password Authentication Protocol (PAP) and the Challenge Handshake Authentication Protocol (CHAP).

PPP Overview

To make remote connections, remote-node users should have the application software (for example, FTP, Telnet), protocol stacks (for example, TCP/IP), and link-layer drivers (for example, PPP, SLIP) installed on their own remote devices, as shown in Figure 5-1. The higher-layer protocols are encapsulated in the link-layer protocols (such as SLIP and PPP) when they are transmitted across the dial-up line.

Figure 5-1 *Remote Establishes a Connection with the Central Office Access Server*

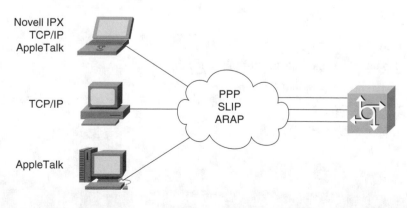

Novell IPX
TCP/IP
AppleTalk

TCP/IP

AppleTalk

PPP
SLIP
ARAP

Point-to-point links between LANs, hosts, terminals, and routers can provide sufficient physical connectivity in many application environments. Many regional and commercial network services provide access to the Internet, and point-to-point links provide an efficient way to access the service provider locally.

The Internet community adopted two schemes for the transmission of IP datagrams over serial point-to-point lines:

- Serial Line Internet Protocol (SLIP)—SLIP is a standard protocol for point-to-point serial connections, using a variation of TCP/IP. SLIP was a predecessor of PPP.

- Point-to-Point Protocol (PPP)—PPP provides router-to-router and host-to-network connections over synchronous and asynchronous circuits.

NOTE   PPP and SLIP are data-link layer protocols (Layer 2 of the OSI model).

Although both SLIP and PPP were designed with IP in mind, SLIP is pretty much limited for use with IP, whereas PPP can be used for other network-layer protocols.

Multilink is especially useful with ISDN when both B channels can be used to achieve 128 Kbps throughput.

NOTE   ARAP and SLIP are not used very frequently in current network configurations, so they are not covered in the course. For additional configuration information, refer to the Cisco IOS documentation CD-ROM or Cisco Connection Online (CCO) at www.cisco.com.

PPP Architecture

PPP is a standard encapsulation protocol for the transport of different network-layer protocols (including, but not limited to, IP) across serial, point-to-point links.

PPP Mechanisms

PPP also describes mechanisms for the following:

- Network-protocol multiplexing
- Link configuration
- Link-quality testing

- Authentication
- Header compression
- Error detection
- Link-option negotiation

PPP Functional Components

PPP has the following three main functional components:

- It has a method for encapsulating datagrams over serial links, based on the ISO HDLC protocol (this is not Cisco HDLC), as shown in Figure 5-2.
- Link Control Protocol (LCP) establishes, configures, authenticates, and tests the data-link connection.
- Network Control Protocols (NCPs) establish and configure different network-layer protocols (such as IP, IPX, and AppleTalk). For example, Internet Protocol Control Protocol (IPCP) is the NCP for IP.

Figure 5-2   *PPP and the OSI Model*

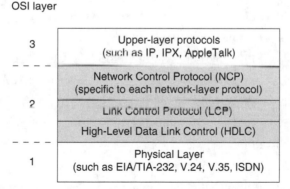

HDLC is the basis of PPP frame format. Figure 5-3 shows the difference between the two frame formats. RFC 1662 describes PPP in HDLC framing in detail.

Figure 5-3 *PPP and HDLC Frame Format*

Flag	Address	Control	Data (Payload)	FCS	Flag
1 byte	1 byte	1 or 2 bytes	1500 bytes	2 (or 4) bytes	1 byte

HDLC ISO frame

Flag	Address	Control	Protocol	LCP	FCS	Flag
1 byte	1 byte	1 byte	1 or 2 bytes	Up to1500 bytes	2 (or 4) bytes	1 byte

PPP frame

Related RFCs

The following is a partial list of RFCs of interest for access products (for a complete listing of RFCs related to material in this book, consult Appendix E, "RFC List"):

- RFC 1055—Nonstandard for transmission of IP datagrams over serial lines: SLIP
- RFC 1144—Compressing TCP/IP headers for low-speed serial links
- RFC 1220—Point-to-Point Protocol extensions for bridging
- RFC 1334—PPP authentication protocols
- RFC 1378—PPP AppleTalk Control Protocol (ATCP)
- RFC 1492—Access control protocol, sometimes called TACACS
- RFC 1549—PPP in HDLC Framing
- RFC 1552—PPP Internetworking Packet Exchange Control Protocol (IPXCP)
- RFC 1570—PPP LCP Extensions
- RFC 1661—Point-to-Point Protocol (PPP)
- RFC 1662—PPP in HDLC-like Framing (obsoletes RFC 1549)
- RFC 1717—PPP Multilink Protocol (MP)
- RFC 1990—PPP Multilink Protocol (MP) (obsoletes RFC 1717)

Configuring Cisco Access Servers

You can configure a Cisco access server to allow a PPP, SLIP, or ARAP session to start automatically or to provide the router's user prompt to your callers, as shown in Figure 5-4.

Figure 5-4 *The Autoselect Process on Cisco Access Servers*

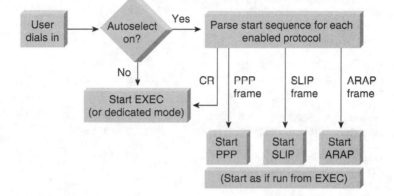

This autosensing feature can be accomplished by using the **autoselect** command issued in the line configuration mode:

```
Router(config)#line  line-number
Router(config-line)#autoselect {arap ¦ ppp ¦ slip ¦ during-login}
```

The **autoselect** command permits the access server to allow an appropriate process to start automatically when a starting character is received. The access server detects either a Return character, which is the start character for an EXEC session, or the start character for one of the three protocols specified (ARAP, PPP, or SLIP). For example, PPP frames always start with a flag character having the value 7E in hexadecimal (or 01111110 in binary) format.

Protocol Flag Values

The following are frame flag hexidecimal values for different protocols:

carriage return	0d
SLIP	c0
ARAP	10
PPP	7E

The **during-login** option of the **autoselect** command causes the username and/or password prompt to display without the need to press the Return key. This option is configured in the remote Windows 95 PC modem configuration by enabling a terminal window to be brought up after dialing. Autoselect starts when the line is active, but the system provides a username and password prompt. Example 5-1 shows a caller's session on an access server configured with the **autoselect during-login** command.

Example 5-1 *A Windows 95 Client Is Dialing to an ISP, which Provides PPP Autoselect Login to its Customers*

```
                Welcome to Communications
              Your Access Ramp to the Internet

User Access Verification
Username: cpaquet
Password:
service>who
    Line     User      Host(s)                 Idle Location
<text omitted>
    8 tty 8    pieriv    Async interface          00:01:03
*   9 tty 9    cpaquet   idle                     00:00:00
   10 tty 10   h20wins   Async interface          00:01:18
    <omitted>
    Se1:19     debris    Sync PPP                 00:00:10
service>
service>ppp
Entering PPP routing mode.
Async interface address is unnumbered (Ethernet0)
Your IP address is 192.1.1.145. MTU is 1500 bytes
Header compression will match your system.
~ }#À!}!Í} }4}"}&} }*} } }%}&£òP◊}'}"}(}"Uä~~ }#À!}!Í} }4}
```

---

no exec Command

If you don't want users to be presented with a user prompt, type **no exec** at the line configuration mode. This command determines whether or not the terminal server starts an EXEC process on the line. By default, the terminal server starts EXECs on all lines. When a user tries to Telnet to a line with the **no exec** command configured, the user gets no response when pressing the Return key at the login screen.

Enabling PPP

To enable PPP on your router, type the following interface command:

```
Router(config-if)#encapsulation ppp
```

For SLIP use:

```
router(config-if)#encapsulation slip
```

Configuring Dedicated or Interactive PPP (and SLIP) Sessions

You can configure one or more asynchronous interfaces on your access server to be in dedicated network interface mode. In dedicated mode, an interface is automatically configured for SLIP or PPP connections. There is no user prompt or EXEC level, and no end-user commands are required to initiate remote-node connections.

To ensure that the dial-in user must run either SLIP or PPP on the specified line, use the **async mode dedicated** command:

```
Router(config-if)# async mode dedicated
```

Dedicated Mode

When the interface is configured for dedicated mode, the end user cannot change the encapsulation method, address, or other parameters.

In interactive mode, a line can be used to make any type of connection, depending on the EXEC command entered by the user. For example, depending on its configuration, the line can be used for Telnet connections, or for SLIP or PPP encapsulation. The user is prompted for an EXEC command before a connection is initiated.

To allow the dial-in user to run SLIP, PPP, or EXEC on the specified line, configure the **async mode interactive** command:

```
Router(config-if)# async mode interactive
```

By default, no async mode is configured. In this state, the line is not available for inbound networking because the SLIP and PPP connections are disabled.

Commands Input Sequence

If you try to configure the line with **autoselect ppp** prior to configuring the **async mode interactive** command, you see the following error message:

```
%Autoselect w/o the interface command 'Async mode interactive' is useless
```

Configuring the Interface Addressing Method for Local Devices

The local address is set by using the **ip address** or **ip unnumbered** command.

- **ip address** command—To assign an IP address to a network interface, configure the following command at the interface configuration mode:

```
Router(config-if)#ip address address mask
```

- **ip unnumbered** command—To conserve network addresses, configure the asynchronous interfaces as "unnumbered." An unnumbered interface does not have an address. When the unnumbered interface generates a packet, it uses the address of the specified interface as the source address of the IP packet, and can be thought of as a referenced IP address. IP unnumbered can be used only in point-to-point connections. The command is as follows:

```
Router(config-if)#ip unnumbered
```

NOTE   A **loopback interface** is a virtual interface that never goes down; therefore, it is an ideal line to use as the reference when using the **ip unnumbered** command.

Configuring the Interface-Addressing Method for Remote Devices

You can control whether addressing is dynamic (the user specifies the address at the EXEC level when making the connection), or whether default addressing is used (the address is forced by the system). If you specify dynamic addressing, the router must be in interactive mode and the user enters the address at the EXEC level.

It is common to configure an asynchronous interface to have a default address and to allow dynamic addressing. With this configuration, the choice between the default address or dynamic addressing is made by the users when they enter the **slip** or **ppp EXEC level** command. If the user enters an address, it is used; if the user enters the default keyword, the default address is used.

You can therefore configure the router to do one of the following:

- Assign a default async address

        or

- Allow an async address to be assigned dynamically by the caller

Assigning a Default Async Address

To assign a predefined default IP address to the remote client node that dials in to the corresponding asynchronous line, use the **peer default ip address** command. Additionally, the **pool** and **dhcp** arguments allow address allocation from a local pool of addresses or a DHCP server. The new command, as of Cisco IOS Release 11.0 and later, is the **async** interface command (for example, **async default ip address** *address*).

```
Router(config-if)#peer default ip address{ip-address ¦ dhcp ¦ pool poolname}
```

Additionally, the **pool** and **dhcp** options to the **peer default ip address** command require a global command to create the pool of addresses. For example, the **ip local pool** *pool-name starting-address end-address*.

DHCP Consideration

If the **peer default ip dhcp** option is chosen, you have to also configure **ip helper address** and **ip dhcp-server**.

Allowing an Async Address to Be Assigned Dynamically

The **async dynamic** address allows the remote dial-in client to enter its own IP address, if it has one:

```
Router(config-ig)#async dynamic address
```

NOTE   When a line is configured for dynamic assignment of asynchronous addresses, the user enters the **slip** or **ppp EXEC** command, and is prompted for an address or logical host name. Assigning asynchronous addresses dynamically is also useful when you want to assign set addresses to users. For example, an application on a personal computer that automatically dials in using SLIP and polls for electronic mail messages can be set up to dial in periodically, and then enter the required IP address and password.

Supplement 5-1 at the end of this chapter provides a summary analysis of the address negotiation between a Windows 95 dial-up workstation and a Cisco IOS router, depending on different configuration scenarios.

PPP Link Control Protocol Options

Earlier in the chapter, you learned about the PPP architecture and how the LCP is used for establishing, configuring, authenticating, and testing the data-link connection. This section presents configuration features that are negotiated through the LCP.

Authentication, using either PAP or CHAP, is used as a security measure with PPP and PPP callback. Authentication allows the dial-up target to identify that any given dial-up client is a valid client with a preassigned username and password.

Callback is a PPP option used to provide call and dial-up billing consolidation. PPP callback was first supported in Cisco IOS Release 11.0(3).

Compression is used to improve throughput across existing lines. PPP compression was first supported in Cisco IOS Release 10.3. As you will see later, Cisco routers support Stacker, Predictor, and MPPC.

Multilink PPP takes advantage of multiple bearer channels to improve throughput. Datagrams are split, sequenced, transmitted across multiple links, and then recombined at the destination. The multiple links together are called a **bundle**. Multilink is especially useful with ISDN, in which both B channels can be used to achieve 128 Kbps throughput. Multilink PPP was first supported in Cisco IOS Release 11.0(3).

The following sections provide you with detailed explanations of LCP options.

PAP and CHAP Authentication

With PPP, callers can be authenticated with PAP or CHAP. You may also elect not to carry any authentication. Figure 5-5 shows the PPP authentication process.

Figure 5-5   *Incoming PPP Session—Authentication Process*

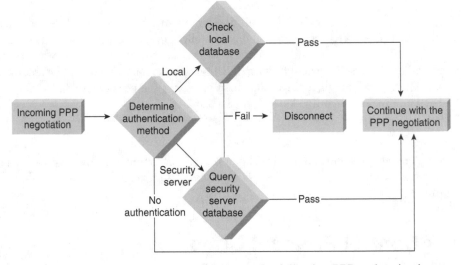

The flowchart presented in Figure 5-5 shows the following PPP authentication process steps:

1 When a user enters the **ppp** command, the system determines the type of authentication configured. If no authentication is configured, the PPP process starts immediately. Otherwise, the system goes to the next step.

2 The system determines the authentication method to be used and does one of the following:

It checks the local database (established with the username password commands) to see whether the given **username/password** pair matches the pair in the local database (CHAP or PAP).

or

It sends an authentication request to the security server (TACACS+ or RADIUS).

3 The system checks the authentication response sent back from the security server or local database. If it is a positive response, the access server starts the PPP process. If the result is negative, the access server rejects the user immediately.

With either PAP or CHAP authentication, you have a two-way process, in which an Id/Password pair is repeatedly sent by the peer to the authenticator until the authentication is acknowledged or the connection is terminated. For PAP, this process provides an insecure authentication method. If you put a protocol analyzer on the line, you can see the password in clear text.

With PAP, there is no protection from playback (if you have a sniffer connected to the line and you capture the packet for later use, you can use the packet to authenticate your way directly into the network by playing back the captured packet).

If you are interested in more secure access control, you should use CHAP rather than PAP as the authentication method. You should use PAP only if it is the only method of authentication that the remote station supports.

NOTE   CHAP passwords are encrypted when they cross the network, whereas PAP passwords are cleartext when they cross the network.

PAP is a one-way authentication when it is between a host and an access server, as shown in Figure 5-6; it is a two-way authentication when it is between routers.

Figure 5-6   *One-Way PAP Authentication between a Host and an Access Server*

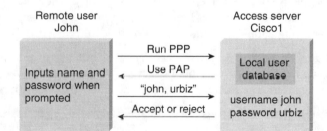

Configuring PAP Authentication

From a configuration perspective, there are two routers in Figure 5-7. Left and Right, connected across an ISDN cloud, are configured for the PAP authentication method.

Figure 5-7 *Example of Access Routers Configured for a Two-Way PAP*

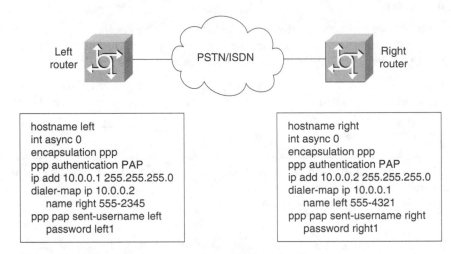

```
hostname left
int async 0
encapsulation ppp
ppp authentication PAP
ip add 10.0.0.1 255.255.255.0
dialer-map ip 10.0.0.2
    name right 555-2345
ppp pap sent-username left
    password left1
```

```
hostname right
int async 0
encapsulation ppp
ppp authentication PAP
ip add 10.0.0.2 255.255.255.0
dialer-map ip 10.0.0.1
    name left 555-4321
ppp pap sent-username right
    password right1
```

Perform the following steps to configure PAP authentication:

1 On the interface, specify **encapsulation ppp**.

2 Enable the use of PAP authentication with the **ppp authentication PAP** command. This entry is made because router Left, during the LCP negotiation, asks router Right to use PAP authentication during the negotiation to identify itself.

3 Configure the addresses, usernames, and passwords. Passwords must be identical at both ends and must be entered on both systems, if PAP is used between routers (two-way authentication). The router name and password are case-sensitive.

4 To ensure that both systems can communicate properly, configure the **dialer-map** command lines for each router. By configuring each router with a **dialer-map** statement, each system knows what to do with authentication issues because the systems have prior knowledge of each other. The **dialer-map** command also contains the telephone number to dial to reach the specified router.

NOTE   The Authentication method specified under the interface is for INCOMING CALLS authentication. It is not the authentication method that the router uses when asked to authenticate. It is the "answering" router prerogative to specify what authentication it entertains from a caller. The caller must comply with the authentication method asked by the answering router. If not, the negotiation fails and the access server disconnects the call.

Configuring CHAP Authentication

When using CHAP authentication, the access server sends a challenge message to the remote node after the PPP link is established, as shown in Figure 5-8. The remote node responds with a value calculated by using a one-way hash function (typically MD5). The access server checks the response against its own calculation of the expected hash value. If the values match, the authentication is acknowledged. Otherwise, the connection is immediately terminated.

Figure 5-8   *One-Way CHAP Authentication between a User and a Cisco Access Server*

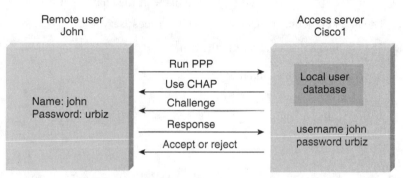

CHAP provides protection against playback attack through the use of a variable challenge value that is unique and unpredictable. The use of repeated challenges every two minutes during any CHAP session is intended to limit the time of exposure to any single attack. The access server (or authentication server, such as TACACS+) controls the frequency and timing of the challenges. A major advantage of the constantly changing challenge string is that the line cannot be sniffed and played back later to gain unauthorized access to the network.

The six following figures show the series of events that occur during a CHAP authentication between two routers.

Placing the Call

Figure 5-9 represents the following three steps:

1   The call comes in to 3640-1. The incoming interface is configured with the **ppp authentication chap** command.

2   LCP negotiates CHAP and MD5.

3   A CHAP challenge from 3640-1 to the calling router is required on this call.

Figure 5-9   *User Placing a Call to a Cisco Access Server*

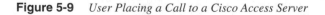

766-1

3640-1

Sending a Challenge

Figure 5-10 illustrates the following steps in the CHAP authentication between the two routers:

1 A CHAP challenge packet is built with the following characteristics:

01	Challenge packet type identifier
id	Sequential number that identifies the challenge
random	A reasonably random number
3640-1	The authentication name of the challenger

2 The id and random values are kept on the access server.

3 The challenge packet is sent to the caller.

Figure 5-10 *The Challenge Is Sent to the Calling Router*

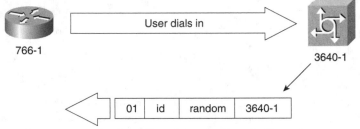

The answering router maintains a list of outstanding challenges.

Processing the Challenge

Figure 5-11 illustrates the receipt and MD5 processing of the challenge packet from the server.

Figure 5-11 *The Challenge Is Received and Processed by the Calling Router*

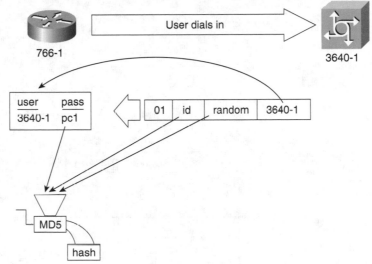

The calling router processes the CHAP challenge packet in the following manner:

1 The id value is fed into the MD5 hash generator.

2 The random value is fed into the MD5 hash generator.

3 The name **3640-1** is used to look up the password.

4 The password is fed into the MD5 hash generator.

The result is the one-way MD5-hashed CHAP challenge that will be sent back in the CHAP response.

NOTE   As mentioned in RFC 1334, no matter what number you process through the MD5 algorithm, the result is always 128 bits long!

Answering the Challenge

Figure 5-12 illustrates the building of the CHAP response packet that will be sent to the access server:

1 The response packet is assembled from the following components:

02	CHAP response packet type identifier
id	Copied from the challenge packet
hash	The output from the MD5 hash generator (the hashed information from the challenge packet)
766-1	The authentication name of this caller

2 The response packet is then sent to the challenger.

Figure 5-12 *Caller Sends the Response to the Answering Cisco Access Server*

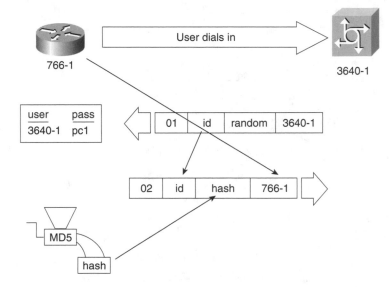

The Verification

Figure 5-13 shows the response-packet processing that occurs on the challenger.

Figure 5-13 *The Answering Access Server Verifies the Answer*

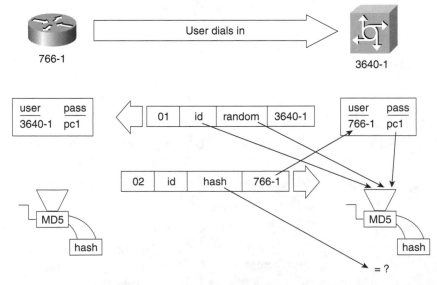

The CHAP response packet is processed in the following manner:

1 The id is used to find the original challenge packet.

2 The id is fed into the MD5 hash generator.

3 The original challenge random value is fed into the MD5 hash generator.

4 The name **766-1** is used to look up the password from one of the following sources:

   - Local database
   - RADIUS server
   - TACACS server

   (Note that with Cisco IOS Release 11.1 and earlier, TACACS is used for the password check only. With Cisco IOS Release 11.2 and later, TACACS is used to verify the hash value.)

5 The password is fed into the MD5 hash generator.

6 The hash value received in the response packet is then compared to the calculated MD5-hashed value.

CHAP authentication succeeds if the calculated and the received hash values are equal.

The Result

Figure 5-14 illustrates the success message being sent to the calling router.

Figure 5-14 *The Answering Router Sends the Pass Result to the Calling Router.*

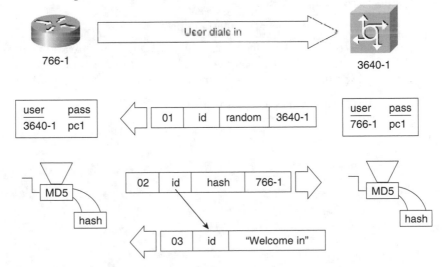

If authentication was successful, a CHAP success packet is built from the following components:

03   CHAP success message type
id   Copied from the response packet
Welcome in is simply a text message of some kind, meant to be a user-readable explanation.

If authentication failed, a CHAP failure packet is built from the following components:

04   CHAP failure message type
id   Copied from the response packet
Authentication failure or a similar text message is meant to be a user-readable explanation.

The success or failure packet is then sent to the caller.

Refer to the section "Verifying and Troubleshooting PPP," later in this chapter, for a look at the complete process with the **debug ppp negotiation** command.

Supplement 5-2, at the end of the chapter, provides a summary of the authentication successes and failures between a Windows 95 workstation and a Cisco IOS router, depending on different scenarios.

Interface Commands for CHAP Authentication

Configuring CHAP is straightforward. As with PAP, you have two routers shown in Figure 5-15: Left and Right, connected across the cloud. Use the following steps as a guide to configuring CHAP authentication:

1 On the interface, specify **encapsulation ppp**.

2 Enable the use of CHAP authentication with the **ppp authentication chap** command. This entry is made because router Left asks router Right to use CHAP authentication to identify itself during the LCP negotiation.

3 Configure the usernames and passwords.

Figure 5-15 *These Routers are Configured for a Two-Way CHAP Authentication*

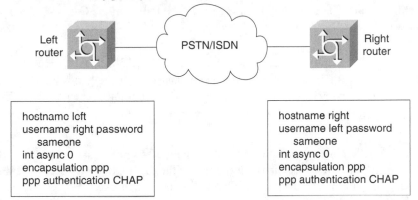

Passwords must be identical at both ends. The router name and password are case-sensitive.

Enabling PAP and CHAP Authentication

You can enable both PAP and CHAP authentication on an interface. The first method specified is requested during link negotiation. If the caller refuses the first method, the second method is tried. The commands are as follows:

```
Router(config-if)#ppp authentication pap chap
```
   or
```
router(config-if)#ppp authentication chap pap
```

PPP Callback

PPP callback provides a client-server relationship between the end points of a point-to-point connection. PPP callback allows a router to request that a dial-up peer router call back. The callback feature can be used to control access and toll costs between the routers.

When PPP callback is configured on the participating routers, the calling router (the callback client) passes authentication information to the remote router (the callback server), which uses the host name and dial string authentication information to determine whether to place a return call. If the authentication is successful, the callback server disconnects, and then places a return call. The remote username of the return call is used to associate it with the initial call, so that the packets can be transmitted.

Both routers on a point-to-point link must be configured for PPP callback; one must function as a callback client, and one must be configured as a callback server. The callback client must be configured to initiate PPP callback requests, and the callback server must be configured to accept PPP callback requests and place return calls.

Return calls are made through the same dialer rotary group, but not necessarily the same line as the initial call. The preceding information can be found on the Cisco Web site at www.cisco.com.

NOTE   If the return call fails (because the line is not answered or the line is busy), no retry occurs. If the callback server has no interface available when attempting the return call, it does not retry.

When the client router dials the initial call, the router's hold-queue timer is started if the command **dialer hold-queue** is configured on the dialing out interface. No calls to the same destination will be made again until the hold-queue timer expires. The timer is stopped if PPP NCP negotiation is successful or if the call fails. The complete command syntax is as follows:

```
dialer hold-queue number of packets timeout seconds
```

NOTE   For rotary groups that include ISDN, the return call never occurs if the enable time is long and another user dials into the last interface before the enable timer expires. For rotary groups that include ISDN, if an interesting packet arrives at the server during the enable time, the dialer may use the last interface for the interesting packet, and the return call is never made.

When planning to implement PPP callback, consider the following:

- Authentication is required for callback to be successful.

- The time between the disconnect of the initial call and dialing the return call is determined by the dialer enable timeout. This interval must be long enough to guarantee that the initial call is completely disconnected.

- The dialer hold-queue timeout determines how long to wait before the client can make another call to the same destination. The server must make the return call before the client hold-queue timer expires, to prevent the client from trying again and possibly preventing the return call from being connected.

- The hold timer on the callback client should be approximately four times larger than the server's hold-queue timer.

Callback: How Does it work?

The asynchronous callback feature supports EXEC, PPP, and ARAP sessions. The main motivation for callback is for telephone bill consolidation and dial-up cost savings. It is not positioned as a security feature; however, if the callback number is assigned in the authentication database, security is enforced because callbacks are made only to assigned telephone numbers. The incoming calls go through the normal login process and must pass authentication before callback can occur, as shown in Figure 5-16.

Figure 5-16 *Flowchart of Callback Operations*

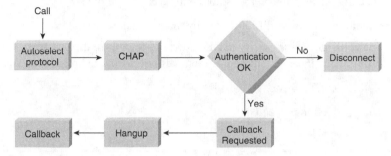

The callback feature employs a two-pass process:

1 On the first pass, the callback engine determines which target line to use for callback to the remote user and hangs up on the incoming line. Then, the callback engine dials back to the remote user through the target line by using the dial string provided.

2 On the second pass, the callback engine proceeds normally, as if there were no callback.

To make callback work properly, you must make sure that callback is configured for each autoselect protocol that is defined for any given remote user. Otherwise, the remote dial-in autoselect process may work, but no callback occurs.

The PPP callback operation consists of the following events:

1 The callback client initiates the call. The client requests callback by using the callback option during the PPP LCP negotiation phase.

2 The callback server acknowledges the callback request and checks its configuration to verify that callback is enabled.

3 The callback client and server authenticate by using either CHAP or PAP authentication. The username is used to identify the dial string for the return call.

4 After successful initial authentication, the callback server router identifies the callback dial string. The callback server compares the username of the authentication to the host name in a dialer map table. The dial string can be identified by a mapping table or by the Callback Option Message field during PPP's LCP negotiations. The Callback Option Message field is defined in RFC 1570.

dialer callback-secure, **ppp callback accept**, and **ppp authentication pap** or **ppp authentication chap** are enabled on an interface, all calls answered on that interface are disconnected after authentication and steps 5–8 occur (as follows):

5   If the dialer callback-secure is not enabled, the callback server maintains the initial call if the authenticated username is not configured for callback.

   The initiating call is disconnected by the callback server.

6   The callback server uses the dial string to initiate the callback. If the return call fails, no additional calls are attempted. Callback is not negotiated on the return call.

7   Authentication occurs.

8   The connection proceeds.

Callback Negotiation

If a caller requests a callback but the server is not set to accept a callback, the answering router maintains the initial call.

Configuring Async Callback

Begin the configuration of PPP callback with the following async callback global configuration mode commands:

```
Router(config-if)#ppp callback accept
Router(config)#username username password password
[callback-dialstring telephone-number]
[callback-line line-number]
[callback-rotary rotary-group-number]
```

Command	Description
username *username* **password** *password*	Creates a local username-based authentication database
[**callback-dialstring** *telephone-number*]	Defines the callback phone number
[**callback-line** *line-number*]	Specifies the line to call back on
[**callback-rotary** rotary-group-number]	Specifies a rotary group to call back on

If you configure callback-dialstring " ", your router accepts the callback phone number from the caller.

Continue the callback configuration by using the async callback commands in the line configuration or async interface mode, as follows:

```
Router(config-if)#ppp callback accept
Router(config-if)#ppp callback initiate
Router(config)#line line-number
Router(config-line)#callback forced-wait seconds
Router(config-line)#script callback script-name
```

Command	Description
ppp callback accept	This interface command allows the specified interface to accept a callback request initiated from a remote node (per RFC 1570).
ppp callback initiate	This interface command allows the router to initiate a callback to a remote node when the remote node is capable of putting itself in an "answer mode" for callback.
callback forced-wait *seconds*	This line option allows an additional wait (in seconds) before the callback chat script is applied to the outgoing target line. This option accommodates modems that require a longer resting period before any input to it can be accepted again.
script callback *script name*	This line command specifies a chat script to issue AT commands to the modem during a callback attempt made to the target async line. This command is used for EXEC and PPP callbacks.

Configuring the Callback Server

A router can call back PPP clients that dial in. As shown in Figure 5-17, configure PPP callback for a server, perform the following steps (the following step numbers correspond to the numbers in Figure 5-17):

1 Configure IP on the dial-in line.

2 Use the **dialer callback-secure** command to disconnect calls that are not properly configured for callback. A callback server with dialer callback-secure configured disconnects any unconfigured dial-in users.

3 Set up dialer map with the **dialer map** and **dialer-group** commands.

4 Use the **ppp callback accept** command to enable callback.

5 Define the ppp authentication method with the **ppp authentication chap** command.

6 Configure dialer callback-server username in a dialer map-class to identify the name in the dialer map as a valid callback client. When callback client router dials in and is authenticated, the call is disconnected. For example, in Figure 5-17, a return call is made to 555-5678, as configured by the **dialer map** command. The **dialer map** command identifies the map-class to be used for this connection.

7 Use the **dialer hold-queue timeout** command to set the server's hold-queue timer, which identifies the number of seconds that a callback client or server holds packets destined for the client while waiting for the return call to be completed.

Figure 5-17 *Example of a PPP Callback Server*

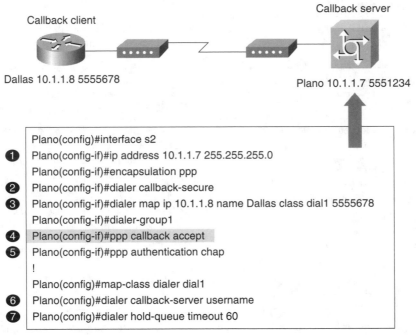

Use the **dialer enable-timeout** command to determine the amount of time that the server waits before making the return call.

PPP Callback—Additional Feature from Cisco

Another command for callback is **dialer callback secure**, which is a Cisco proprietary command. This command ensures that the initial call is always disconnected at the receiving end and that the return call is made only if the username is configured for callback. If the username (hostname in the **dialer map** command) is not configured for callback, the initial call stays up and no return call is made.

Configuring the Callback Client

You can set up a Cisco router to initiate a PPP callback request. As shown in Figure 5-18, configure client PPP callback so that all calls over this interface request callback (the following step numbers correspond to the numbers in Figure 5-18):

1 Configure PPP on the serial or ISDN interface.

2 Set up a dialer map with the **dialer map** and **dialer-group** commands. Be sure that the **dialer map** command has a name field with the correct name of the server; in Figure 5-17, the name is Plano.

3 Configure the router interface as the callback client with the **ppp callback initiate** command.

4 Set the authentication to CHAP with the **ppp authentication** command.

Figure 5-18 *Example of a PPP Callback Client*

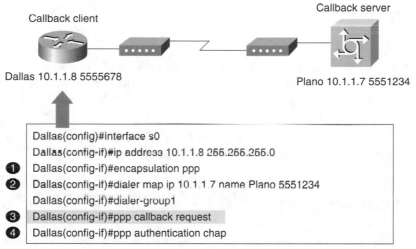

Note that you can use the optional **dialer hold-queue timeout** command to specify the number of seconds that the callback client waits for a return call from the callback server.

PPP Compression

Cisco routers can also maximize performance by using data compression, which enables higher data throughput across the link.

Compression is a negotiated option. So, if you want to use compression but the party you are calling is not configured for compression, no compression will take place.

The Cisco compression schemes are as follows:

- **Predictor**—Determines whether the data is already compressed. If so, the data is just sent—no time is wasted trying to compress already compressed data.

- **Stacker**—A Lempel-Ziv (LZ)-based compression algorithm looks at the data, and only sends each data type once with information about where the type occurs within the data stream. The receiving side uses this information to reassemble the data stream. (Stacker is the only supported algorithm in the Cisco 700 series.)

- **MPPC**—Microsoft Point-to-Point Compression (MPPC) Protocol (RFC 2118) allows Cisco routers to exchange compressed data with Microsoft clients. MPPC uses an LZ-based compression algorithm.

- **TCP header compression**—Used to compress the TCP headers.

The highest compression ratio is usually reached with highly compressible text files. Already compressed files such as JPEG graphics or MPEG files, or files that were compressed with software such as PKZIP or StuffIt, are only compressed 1:1 or even less.

If you frequently transfer already compressed data, such as graphics and video, you need to consider whether you want to globally set up compression. Trying to compress already compressed data can take longer than transferring the data without any compression at all. Ideally, you can attain 2:1 or 3:1 compression for information that was not previously compressed. Expect an average of 1.6:1 compression for mixed compressed and uncompressed source data.

Compressing data can cause performance degradation because it is software, not hardware compression. Compression can be CPU- or memory-intensive.

Configuring Compression

Configuring for compression is simple: from the interface, issue the **compress predictor**, **compress stac**, **compress mppc**, or **ip tcp header-compression** command on both sides of the link.

Compression Algorithm

Predictor is more memory-intensive and less CPU-intensive. Stacker and MPPC are more CPU-intensive and less memory-intensive. **Memory-intensive** means that an extra memory allowance is required.

You need to consider this memory usage when implementing compression on any specific router. If you use a Cisco 2500 series or better, it should be acceptable to use either of these methods if you have sufficient memory in the router. Use caution with smaller systems that have less memory and slower CPUs, and ensure that you are not overloading the router. The interface command to enable compression is:

```
Router(config-if)#compress [predictor¦stac¦mppc]
```

TCP Header Compression

The TCP header compression technique is fully described in RFC 1144. It is supported on serial lines by using HDLC, PPP, and SLIP encapsulation. You must enable the compression on both ends of the connections for TCP header-compression to work. Only TCP headers are compressed—UDP headers are not affected. The following is the interface command used to activate TCP header compression:

```
Router(config-int)#ip tcp header-compression
```

The **ip tcp header-compression passive** command specifies that TCP header compression is not required, but if the router receives compressed headers from a destination, then use header compression for that destination.

PPP Multilink

Multilink over PPP provides load balancing over dialer interfaces—including ISDN, synchronous, and asynchronous interfaces. Multilink PPP (MP) can improve throughput and reduce latency between systems by splitting packets and sending the fragments over parallel circuits, as shown in Figure 5-19. Prior to MP, two or more ISDN B channels could not be used in a standardized way while ensuring sequencing. MP is most effective when used with ISDN.

Figure 5-19 *Multilink PPP Logically Bundles Together Links to Provide a Larger Bandwidth to a Destination*

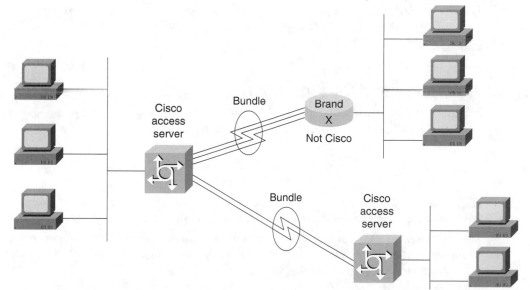

MP solves several problems related to load balancing across multiple WAN links, including the following:

- Multivendor interoperability, as specified by RFC 1990, which replaces RFC 1717
- Packet fragmentation, improving latency of each packet (supports RFC 1990 fragmentation and packet-sequencing specifications)
- Packet sequence and load calculation

Multilink PPP Fragments

Multilink fragments are called **packets** (per RFC 1990, section 3, page 7, which states "individual fragments, which are the 'packets' in the Multilink Protocol.").

This feature negotiates the Maximum Received Reconstructed Unit (MRRU) option during the PPP LCP negotiation to indicate to its peer that it can combine multiple physical links into a bundle.

Prior to the adoption of RFC 1990, there was no standardized way to use both of the B channels and ensure proper sequencing.

MP is interoperable between Cisco routers running Cisco IOS software and Cisco 700 series routers, and with most routers that conform to RFC 1990.

Use Multilink PPP with applications in which bandwidth requirements are dynamic, such as remote LAN access applications for telecommuters or small office, home office (SOHO) environments.

Multilink Operation and Configuration

Multilink PPP is controlled by the addition of a two-, four-, or eight-byte sequencing header in the PPP frame that indicates sequencing for the fragments.

MP Packet Header

RFC 1990 provides for only four-byte headers. The first fragment of a multilink packet in PPP has two headers, one for the fragment and followed by the header for the packet itself.

During PPP negotiation, some hardware platforms could use different header lengths for PPP Multilink, causing potential problems. Please check with the specific platform documentation if you have problems with Multilink PPP.

Transmission channels in the bundle need not be the same types. Asynchronous and synchronous links, for example, can be used to simultaneously transmit fragments of one datagram.

During PPP's LCP option negotiation, a system indicates to its peer that it is willing to multilink by sending the MRRU option as part of the initial LCP option negotiation. Multilink systems must be able to do the following:

- Combine multiple physical links into one logical link (bundle)
- Receive and reassemble upper-layer protocol data units (PDUs)
- Receive PDUs of a negotiated size

After the LCP negotiation is complete, the remote destination must be authenticated and a dialer map with the remote system name must be configured.

The authenticated username, or caller ID, is used to determine to which bundle the link is added.

The **ppp multilink** command activates multilink on an interface. This command and related commands will be explored in greater detail in Chapter 7, "Using ISDN and DDR to Enhance Remote Connectivity."

```
Router(config-if)#ppp multilink
```

The following shows an example of the **show ppp multilink** command. At the bottom of the output, you can see the exact number of channels participating in the bundle:

```
Router#show ppp multilink
Bundle rudder, 3 members, first link is BRI0: B-channel 1
0 lost fragments, 8 reordered, 0 unassigned, sequence 0x1E/0x1E rcvd/sent
```

Verifying and Troubleshooting PPP

This section introduces tools for verifying and troubleshooting a PPP session.

One way to determine whether PAP or CHAP authentication was passed is to use the **show dialer** command. This command must be used to view the progress of asynchronous dial-up connections.

If **show dialer** displays the name of the remote router, it means that you passed PAP or CHAP authentication, as shown in Example 5-2.

Example 5-2 show dialer *Command Example*

```
LA#show dialer int bri0

BRI0 - dialer type = ISDN

Dial String      Successes      Failures      Last called      Last status
2002                    7             0      00:00:05         successful
0 incoming call(s) have been screened.

BRI0:1 - dialer type = ISDN
Idle timer (121 secs), Fast idle timer (20 secs)
Wait for carrier (30 secs), Re-enable (15 secs)
Dialer state is data link layer up
```

continues

Example 5-2 show dialer *Command Example (Continued)*

```
Dial reason: ip (s=10.130.0.1, d=192.168.2.1)
Time until disconnect 117 secs
Connected to 2002 (Boise)

BRI0:2 - dialer type = ISDN
Idle timer (121 secs), Fast idle timer (20 secs)
Wait for carrier (30 secs), Re-enable (15 secs)
Dialer state is idle
```

You can check the **show dialer** command on both routers to verify that the name of the other router is displayed. If it is, then you know that PAP or CHAP authentication is working.

If you do not see the name of the other host, you know that something was misconfigured because the authentication failed in at least one direction.

The **debug ppp negotiation** command is a great tool for troubleshooting the PPP Link Control protocol activities such as authentication, compression, and multilink. Once the LCP is in OPEN state, the NCP negotiation takes place. In the following output, you can observe that for PPP to work, LCP options must be negotiated before any NCP activities take place. You therefore see the following negotiations: CHAP Authentication; CCP (Compression Control Protocol); and finally the NCP protocols IP, IPX, and CDP:

```
Router#debug ppp negotiation
BR0:1 PPP: Treating connection as a callin
BR0:1 PPP: Phase is ESTABLISHING, Passive Open
BR0:1 LCP: State is Listen
BR0:1 LCP: I CONFREQ [Listen] id 116 len 30
BR0:1 LCP:    AuthProto CHAP (0x0305C22305)
BR0:1 LCP:    MagicNumber 0x1109DB3A (0x05061109DB3A)
BR0:1 LCP:    MRRU 1524 (0x110405F4)
BR0:1 LCP:    EndpointDisc 1 Local (0x130B0143656E7472616C42)
BR0:1 LCP: O CONFREQ [Listen] id 68 len 15
BR0:1 LCP:    AuthProto CHAP (0x0305C22305)
BR0:1 LCP:    MagicNumber 0x156A31E0 (0x0506156A31E0)
BR0:1 LCP: O CONFREJ [Listen] id 116 len 19
BR0:1 LCP:    MRRU 1524 (0x110405F4)
BR0:1 LCP:    EndpointDisc 1 Local (0x130B0143656E7472616C42)
BR0:1 LCP: I CONFACK [REQsent] id 68 len 15
BR0:1 LCP:    AuthProto CHAP (0x0305C22305)
BR0:1 LCP:    MagicNumber 0x156A31E0 (0x0506156A31E0)
BR0:1 LCP: I CONFREQ [ACKrcvd] id 117 len 15
BR0:1 LCP:    AuthProto CHAP (0x0305C22305)
BR0:1 LCP:    MagicNumber 0x1109DB3A (0x05061109DB3A)
BR0:1 LCP: O CONFACK [ACKrcvd] id 117 len 15
BR0:1 LCP:    AuthProto CHAP (0x0305C22305)
BR0:1 LCP:    MagicNumber 0x1109DB3A (0x05061109DB3A)
BR0:1 LCP: State is Open
BR0:1 PPP: Phase is AUTHENTICATING, by both
BR0:1 CHAP: O CHALLENGE id 61 len 28 from "BranchB"
BR0:1 CHAP: I CHALLENGE id 56 len 29 from "CentralB"
BR0:1 CHAP: Waiting for peer to authenticate first
```

```
BR0:1 CHAP: I RESPONSE id 61 len 29 from "CentralB"
BR0:1 CHAP: O SUCCESS id 61 len 4
BR0:1 CHAP: Processing saved Challenge, id 56
BR0:1 CHAP: O RESPONSE id 56 len 28 from "BranchB"
BR0:1 CHAP: I SUCCESS id 56 len 4
BR0:1 PPP: Phase is UP
BR0:1 IPCP: O CONFREQ [Closed] id 61 len 10
BR0:1 IPCP:    Address 10.135.0.1 (0x03060A870001)
BR0:1 CCP: O CONFREQ [Closed] id 64 len 10
BR0:1 CCP:    MS-PPC supported bits 0x00000001 (0x120600000001)
BR0:1 CDPCP: O CONFREQ [Closed] id 61 len 4
BR0:1 IPXCP: O CONFREQ [Closed] id 5 len 18
BR0:1 IPXCP:    Network 0x00000BAD (0x010600000BAD)
BR0:1 IPXCP:    Node 0010.7ba6.a3e5 (0x020800107BA6A3E5)
BR0:1 IPCP: I CONFREQ [REQsent] id 56 len 10
BR0:1 IPCP:    Address 10.135.0.2 (0x03060A870002)
BR0:1 IPCP: O CONFACK [REQsent] id 56 len 10
BR0:1 IPCP:    Address 10.135.0.2 (0x03060A870002)
BR0:1 CCP: I CONFREQ [REQsent] id 67 len 10
BR0:1 CCP:    MS-PPC supported bits 0x00000001 (0x120600000001)
BR0:1 CCP: O CONFACK [REQsent] id 67 len 10
BR0:1 CCP:    MS-PPC supported bits 0x00000001 (0x120600000001)
BR0:1 CDPCP: I CONFREQ [REQsent] id 56 len 4
BR0:1 CDPCP: O CONFACK [REQsent] id 56 len 4
BR0:1 IPXCP: I CONFREQ [REQsent] id 15 len 18
BR0:1 IPXCP:    Network 0x00000BAD (0x010600000BAD)
BR0:1 IPXCP:    Node 0010.7be1.4701 (0x020800107BE14701)
BR0:1 IPXCP: O CONFACK [REQsent] id 15 len 18
BR0:1 IPXCP:    Network 0x00000BAD (0x010600000BAD)
BR0:1 IPXCP:    Node 0010.7be1.4701 (0x020800107BE14701)
BR0:1 IPCP: I CONFACK [ACKsent] id 61 len 10
BR0:1 IPCP:    Address 10.135.0.1 (0x03060A870001)
BR0:1 IPCP: State is Open
BR0:1 CCP: I CONFACK [ACKsent] id 64 len 10
BR0:1 CCP:    MS-PPC supported bits 0x00000001 (0x120600000001)
BR0:1 CCP: State is Open
BR0:1 CDPCP: I CONFACK [ACKsent] id 61 len 4
BR0:1 CDPCP: State is Open
BR0:1 IPXCP: I CONFACK [ACKsent] id 5 len 18
BR0:1 IPXCP:    Network 0x00000BAD (0x010600000BAD)
BR0:1 IPXCP:    Node 0010.7ba6.a3e5 (0x020800107BA6A3E5)
BR0:1 IPXCP: State is Open
```

Summary

In this chapter, you learned how to configure PPP between a Central site and a remote site, and how to prepare for PAP or CHAP authentication. You also learned about the operation of PPP multilink and how to troubleshoot a PPP session from the router's point of view.

In Chapter 6, "Accessing the Central Site with Windows 95," you will see the other side of the equation: Windows 95 workstation configuration for dial-up networking.

Case Study—Configuring PPP and Controlling Network Access with CHAP

Complete the tasks of this case study, and then review the case study solution section that follows to see how you did and see where you might need to review the concepts presented in this chapter.

The objective of this case study is to prepare a Cisco access server, so that it can accept incoming calls that request a PPP session. This exercise builds on the case study done in Chapter 4, "Configuring Asynchronous Connections with Modems," in which you learned about the physical line configuration.

In this case study, you learn how to do the following:

- Configure the PPP communications protocol for operation
- Control network access with CHAP authentication
- Configure a local pool address range using the **ip local pool** command

Scenario

Figure 5-20 displays the topology used in this case study.

Figure 5-20 *Preparing the Cisco Router To Accept Incoming PPP Sessions from Remote Users*

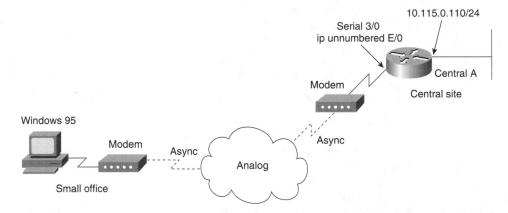

Given a Central site Cisco-IOS router with asynchronous capability, configure the asynchronous serial port so mobile users can call into the site from their PCs.

Task 1—Configuring PPP on Your Central Site Router

Complete the following steps:

Step 1   Enter router configuration mode.

Step 2   In the router configuration mode, configure an IP pool.

Step 3   Enter serial 3/0 configuration mode:

— Configure the serial 3/0 interface to acquire Ethernet 0/0's IP address when processing calls. This serial interface is used by the external modem.

— Obtain an IP address from the lab pool.

— Specify PPP as the encapsulating protocol for data to be transferred between remote users and the router.

— Configure CHAP authentication.

— Return async line to interactive mode.

— Disable Cisco Discovery Protocol.

Step 4   Enter the configuration commands for line 97. Line 97 corresponds to the serial interface 3/0, as explained in Chapter 4's "Router and Modem Configuration" section. You configure the Layer 1 information on the line 97 interface, as follows:

— Enter the configuration mode for line 97.

— Use a local login name.

— Configure autoselect on line 97.

— Configure PPP as the autoselect protocol.

Step 5   In global configuration mode, configure user login and password. This must be entered so the PC user can access the Central site and authenticate using CHAP.

Task 2—Configuring Your Central Site Router to Accept Telnet Connections

You now configure the Central site router to accept incoming Telnet connections. This is necessary if you wish to Telnet to your router from within your LAN/WAN (that is, you are not dialing in the router, but you are accessing this router via your Ethernet connection, for example).

Step 1 Do the following:

— Specify the virtual incoming lines to configure.

— Require a username and password from the local login database (checking users against the local database created with the **username** *name* **password** *password* command).

WARNING Virtual terminals require a password. If you don't set one, it responds to attempted connections by returning an error message and closing the connection.

Step 2 Exit from all configuration modes.

Step 3 Once you are satisfied with your configuration, you should always save it in the router's NVRAM.

Task 3—Verifying Your PPP Configuration

Step 1 Confirm what you have configured, and that the configuration was properly saved.

Step 2 Look at the configuration for line 97.

Solution to Case Study—Configuring PPP and Controlling Network Access with CHAP

The following is a step-by-step discussion of the case study solution.

Task 1 Solution—Configuring PPP on Your Central Site Router

Complete the following steps:

Step 1 Enter router configuration mode by typing **configure terminal** (or **conf t** for the short form).

Step 2 In the router configuration mode, configure an IP pool with the following command:

```
CentralA(config)#ip local pool lab 10.115.0.111 10.115.0.114
```

Lab is the poolname you assigned to the address pool.

Step 3   Execute the following:

— Enter serial interface 3/0 configuration mode:

```
CentralA(config-if)#int s3/0
```

— Configure the serial 3/0 interface to acquire Ethernet 0/0's IP address when processing calls. This serial interface is used by the external modem:

```
CentralA(config-if)#ip unnum ethernet 0/0
```

— Provide the caller with an IP address from the lab pool:

```
CentralA(config-if)#peer default ip address pool lab
```

— Specify PPP as the encapsulating protocol for data to be transferred between remote users and the router:

```
CentralA(config-if)#encapsulation ppp
```

— Configure CHAP authentication:

```
CentralA(config-if)#ppp authentication chap
```

— Place async line to interactive mode:

```
CentralA(config-if)#async mode interactive
```

— Disable Cisco Discovery Protocol:

```
CentralA(config-if)#no cdp enable
```

Step 4   Execute the following:

— Enter the configuration mode for line 97:

```
CentralA(config)#line 97
```

— Use a local login database to authenticate callers:

```
CentralA(config-line)#login local
```

— Configure autoselect on line 97:

```
CentralA(config-line)#autoselect during-login
```

— Configure PPP as the autoselect protocol:

```
CentralA(config-line)#autoselect ppp
```

Step 5   In global configuration mode, configure the local authenticating database for user login and password. In Step 4, you entered the **login local** line command to specify that callers would be authenticated using a local database:

```
Central(config)#username student password cisco
```

Task 2 Solution—Configuring Your Central Site Router to Accept Telnet Connections

You now configure the Central site router to accept incoming Telnet connections. This is necessary if you wish to Telnet to your router from within your LAN/WAN (that is, you are not dialing in the router, but you are accessing this router via your Ethernet connection, for example).

Step 1 Enter the following commands:

— Specify the virtual incoming lines to configure:

```
CentralA(config)#line vty 0 4
```

— Require a username and password from the local login database (checking users against the local database created with the **username** *name* **password** *password* command):

```
CentralA(config-line)#login local
```

Step 2 Exit from all configuration modes:

```
exit
```

Step 3 Once you are satisfied with your configuration, you should always save it in the router's NVRAM:

```
copy running startup
```

Task 3 Solution—Verifying Your PPP Configuration

Step 1 To confirm what you configured and that the configuration was properly saved, you can enter the **show run** command. Your configuration would look like the following:

```
Building configuration...
Current configuration:
!
version 11.3
no service password-encryption
!
hostname CentralA
!
enable secret 5 $1$XvjL$dRrWaKsqFfPqVyrm9cHPK/
enable password san-fran
!
username student password 0 cisco
no ip domain-lookup
ip host modem 2097 10.115.0.110
!
!
!
controller T1 1/0
!
```

```
!
interface Ethernet0/0
ip address 10.115.0.110 255.255.255.0
no lat enabled
!
interface Serial0/0
no ip address
no ip mroute-cache
shutdown
!
interface Serial3/0
physical-layer async
ip unnumbered Ethernet0/0
encapsulation ppp
async mode interactive
peer default ip address pool lab
no cdp enable
ppp authentication chap
!
interface Serial3/1
no ip address
shutdown
!
interface Serial3/2
no ip address
shutdown
!
interface Serial3/3
no ip address
shutdown
!
router igrp 100
network 10.0.0.0
!
ip local pool lab 10.115.0.111 10.115.0.114
ip classless
!
!
line con 0
exec-timeout 0 0
line 65 70
line 97
password cisco
autoselect during-login
autoselect ppp
login local
modem InOut
modem autoconfigure type usr_sportster
transport input all
stopbits 1
speed 115200
flowcontrol hardware
line aux 0
line vty 0 4
login local
!
end
```

Step 2   Look at the configuration for line 97 by entering **show line 97**. The line 97 configuration display would look like the following:

```
CentralA#sh line 97
Tty Typ Tx/Rx A Modem Roty AccO AccI Uses Noise Overruns
I 97 TTY 115200/115200 - inout - - - 1 0 0/0
Line 97, Location: "", Type: ""
Length: 24 lines, Width: 80 columns
Baud rate (TX/RX) is 115200/115200, no parity, 1 stopbits, 8 databits
Status: No Exit Banner, Modem Detected
Capabilities: Hardware Flowcontrol In, Hardware Flowcontrol Out
Modem Callout, Modem RI is CD, Line usable as async interface
Modem Autoconfigure
Modem state: Idle
Group codes: 0
Modem hardware state: CTS noDSR DTR RTS, Modem Configured
    Special Chars: Escape Hold Stop Start Disconnect Activation
    ^^x none - - none
    Timeouts: Idle EXEC Idle Session Modem Answer Session Dispatch
    00:10:00 never none not set
    Idle Session Disconnect Warning
    never
    Login-sequence User Response
    00:00:30
    Modem type is usr_sportster.
    Session limit is not set.
    Time since activation: never
    Editing is enabled.
    History is enabled, history size is 10.
    DNS resolution in show commands is enabled
    Full user help is disabled
    Allowed transports are lat pad v120 mop telnet rlogin nasi. Preferred
    ➥is lat.
    No output characters are padded
    No special data dispatching characters
```

Case Study Conclusion

In this case study, you saw how to prepare a Central site access server so it is now configured to accept asynchronous incoming calls that request a PPP session. In the next case study (at the end of Chapter 6), you will see how to use a Windows 95 workstation to place a call on this Central site router.

Supplement 5-1—IP Address Negotiations

Table 5-1 contains the result of IP address assignments between a Windows 95 caller and the Cisco IOS 11.2. For dial-up networking connections, you can either provide an IP address or have the access server assign one for the duration of the connection. This is adjusted in

Windows 95 from the Dial-Up Networking connection's **Properties** menu by selecting **Server Types, TCP/IP Settings, Specify an IP address**.

Table 5-1   *IPCP Address Negotiation—Test Results*

Router's Settings	Win95 Dial-Up Settings	Router's Reactions
async dynamic address	Specified 10.115.0.13	Accepted for: 10.115.0.13
async dynamic address ip unnumbered e0	Specified 13.13.13.13	Accepted Win95 address of: 13.13.13.13
async dynamic address peer default ip address 10.115.0.177	Specified 13.13.13.13	No router installed Negotiated to 10.115.0.177, which was accepted by Windows 95
async dynamic address peer default ip address pool (pool: 10.115.0.111 through 10.115.0.119)	Specified 10.115.0.116 (which fall in the within the pool range of address)	Accepted for: 10.115.0.116 Because address specified is part of the pool

Supplement 5-2—Authentication Process with Windows 95 and Cisco Routers

Wanting to understand better how Windows 95 and a Cisco router were negotiating the Authentication, I performed the tests shown in Table 5-2, using IOS 11.3(2). When I mention the Win95 encrypted password, I refer to a connection's **Properties** menu, **Server Types**, **Required encrypted password** being activated or deactivated. I also provide the router's configuration request (CONFREQ) and the Windows 95 acknowledgment (CONFACK) or refusal (CONFNAK). Those results were monitored via the **debug ppp negotiation** command.

Table 5-2   *PPP Authentication Negotiation—Test Results*

Router's Settings	Win95 Dial-Up Settings	Results of Authentication
ppp authentication pap CONFREQ: PAP	No encryption required CONFACK: PAP	Passed
ppp authentication pap CONFREQ: PAP	Encryption required CONFNAK: MS-CHAP	Failed

continues

Table 5-2 *PPP Authentication Negotiation—Test Results (Continued)*

Router's Settings	Win95 Dial-Up Settings	Results of Authentication
ppp authentication chap CONFREQ: CHAP	No encryption required CONFACK: CHAP	Passed
ppp authentication chap CONFREQ: CHAP	Encryption required CONFACK: CHAP	Passed
ppp authentication chap pap CONFREQ: CHAP	No encryption required CONFREQ: CHAP	Passed
ppp authentication pap chap CONFREQ: PAP CONFREQ: CHAP	Encryption required CONFNAK: PAP CONFACK: CHAP	Passed

Review Questions

Answer the following questions and then refer to Appendix H, "Answers to Review Questions," for answers and explanations.

1 What are some LCP options for PPP?

2 Describe the usefulness of PPP callback.

3 Describe how CHAP provides security.

Accessing the Central Site with Windows 95

In the last two chapters, you learned how to configure your access server for remote connection. It is now time to examine what has to be done at the user's level to establish a dial-up connection, as shown in Figure 6-1. More precisely, and as shown in Figure 6-1, you will learn how to configure a Windows 95 workstation to place an analog call to a Central site router.

Figure 6-1 *A Windows 95 PC Is Dialing into a Remote Access Server*

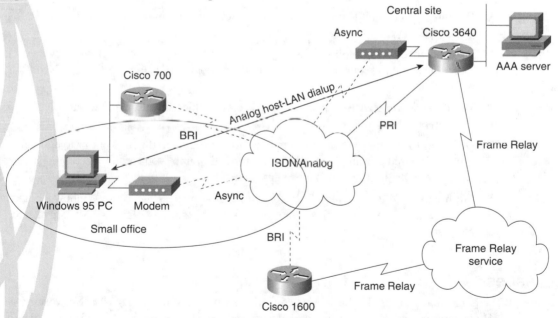

In this chapter, you learn how to configure a PC to dial up and connect to an access server by using Windows 95 Dial-Up Networking.

Windows 95 Dial-Up Networking Overview

Windows 95 provides connectivity to mobile users who wish to exchange data remotely. Out of all the functionalities, the one that interests us the most for the purpose of this chapter is the dial-up networking, which lets you turn your workstation into a dial-up client or server. This section covers some of the connectivity tools that Windows 95 provides to mobile users.

NOTE   Dial-up networking server capabilities are only available if you install Microsoft Plus! for Windows 95. Also, the dial-up server for Windows 95 can accommodate only one modem. Because this book focuses on using Cisco equipment as access servers, you don't have to worry about Microsoft Plus!.

The Basics

Windows 95 provides many tools to help and increase mobile users' productivity:

- **Remote Mail**—Mobile users can remotely exchange e-mail messages with an MS Exchange server by using a client software such as MS Outlook.

- **Direct Cable Connection**—Using a parallel or null modem cable or infrared devices, this tool allows you to set up a two-node, peer-to-peer network using IPX/SPX or NetBEUI protocols.

- **Windows 95 Briefcase**—This tool helps keep your files synchronized when you use two computers.

- **Deferred Printing**—When your laptop is not connected to the network or to a direct printer, deferred printing saves the print information until your printer is reconnected, at which time the printing will happen automatically.

- **Support for Other Vendors' Tolls for Dial-Up**—It is possible to use Windows 95 Dial-Up Networking to dial in other remote access servers such as Windows NT, Shiva, and NetWare.

The Issues

The issues that you should consider when working with Windows 95 Dial-Up Networking include hardware requirements, network design and security requirements, and configuration requirements.

The required hardware for Windows 95 Dial-Up Networking is as follows:

- One or more compatible modems, or an ISDN adapter

- 2 to 3 MB of hard disk space to install Dial-Up Networking

The issues to resolve when working with Windows 95 Dial-Up Networking include the following:

- Considering what type of remote access server that the remote users connect to and which connection protocol to use
- Deciding what type of LAN protocol to install on dial-up client and server: TCP/IP, IPX, or NetBEUI
- Determining what security is required

Finally, a Windows 95 Dial-Up Networking configuration includes the following components:

- Dial-up clients and servers
- Connection protocols
- Network LAN protocols and network servers
- Security

LAN Connection Protocols

Windows 95 makes it easy to configure dial-up clients and servers to access the network. When you install Dial-Up Networking, any protocols that are already installed on the computer are automatically enabled for Dial-Up Networking. Windows 95 includes support for TCP/IP, IPX/SPX, and NetBEUI network protocols. Figure 6-2 shows the different LAN protocols that are supported.

Figure 6-2   *Protocols Supported by Windows 95 Networking*

Connection Protocols	Network Protocols (APIs)
NetWare Connect	IPX/SPX (Windows Sockets/NetBIOS)
PPP	TCP/IP (Windows Sockets/NetBIOS) IPX/SPX (Windows Sockets/NetBIOS) NetBEUI (NetBIOS)
RAS for Windows NT 3.1 or Windows for Workgroups 3.11	NetBEUI (NetBIOS)
SLIP and CSLIP	TCP/IP (Windows Sockets/NetBIOS)

Configuring a Windows 95 Dial-Up Connection

To create a Dial-Up Networking connection using the Make New Connection Wizard, complete the following steps:

1 From the My Computer window, double-click on the Dial-Up Networking folder, as shown in Figure 6-3.

Figure 6-3 *Dial-Up Networking Folder*

2 From the Dial-Up Networking window, double-click Make New Connection, as shown in Figure 6-4.

Figure 6-4 *Creating a New Connection*

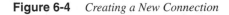

3 Supply information that the Make New Connection Wizard needs to define a connection, including a name for the computer you are dialing and your PC's modem type, as shown in Figure 6-5.

Figure 6-5   *Make New Connection Wizard—Selecting a Name for the Computer You are Dialing and Your PC's Modem Type*

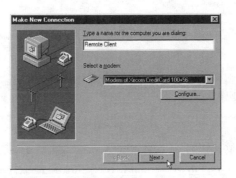

4 Provide the area code, telephone number, and country code of the system that you will call, as shown in Figure 6-6.

Figure 6-6   *Make New Connection Wizard—Defining the System that You Will Call*

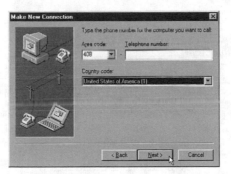

The new icon for your connection appears in the Dial-Up Networking window. You need to provide this information only once for each connection that you define. After the New Connection icon is created, you may want to make it a shortcut and place it on your desktop.

Configuring a Windows 95 Dial-Up Client

To configure the Windows 95 Dial-Up Client, complete the following steps:

1 From the Dial-Up Networking window shown in Figure 6-7, right-click on a connection icon, and then click Properties or click on Properties from the File menu.

Figure 6-7 *The Dial-Up Networking Window*

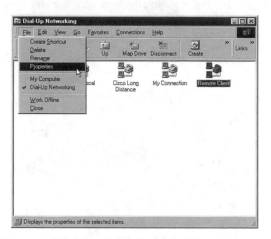

2 From the General tab of the dialog box, click Server Types, as shown in Figure 6-8.

NOTE   Depending on your Windows 95 revision, the Server Types function either appears as a button or a tab.

Figure 6-8 *Figure 6-8 Destination Properties Dialog Box*

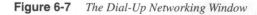

3 From the Server Types dialog box, select the correct remote access server type, as seen in Figure 6-9.

Figure 6-9   *Server Types Dialog Box*

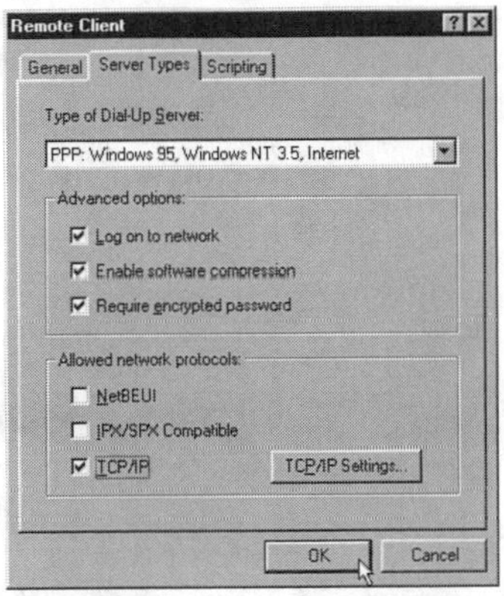

4 From the Server Types dialog box, you can optionally select the following advanced options:

— Log on to network—NT domain only

— Enable software compression—Use Microsoft's compression feature

— Require encrypted password—RAS dial-in

5 From the Server Types dialog box, select from the following allowed network protocols:

— NetBEUI

— IPX/SPX Compatible

— TCP/IP

NOTE   With Windows NT and locally defined usernames on a network access server, you need to configure the username with the *DOMAIN\\username* command string in order for direct network login to work with CHAP authentication.

Verifying a Windows 95 Dial-Up Connection

After you define a remote connection with the Make New Connection Wizard, you can make a connection in two ways:

• Double-click the connection icon in the Dial-Up Networking window, and then click on the Connect button (see Figure 6-10). Figure 6-11 displays the connection dialog box.

Figure 6-10 *Making a Connection*

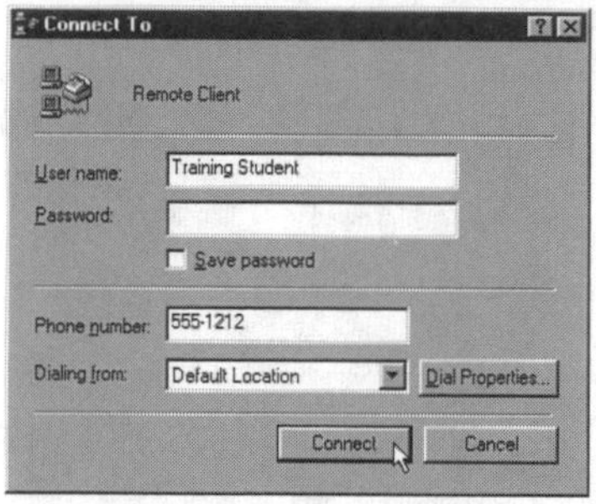

Figure 6-11 *Windows 95 Dialing Out*

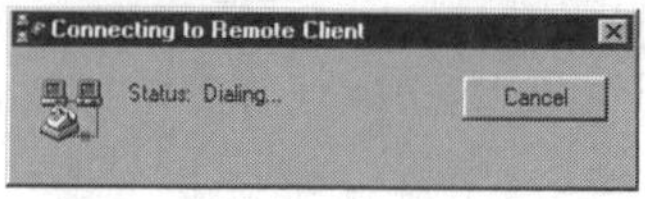

- Connect to a remote network resource when you work in an application other than Windows 95 Dial-Up Networking. If you cannot find the resource on the current network, Windows 95 responds by automatically activating Dial-Up Networking.

After you establish or end a connection, you need not restart the computer or Windows 95.

When you attempt to perform the following tasks, Windows 95 automatically starts Dial-Up Networking:

- When you try to access a network resource and your computer is not connected to a network

- When your application specifies a UNC name (which uses the form *\\servername\sharename*) that cannot be accessed by using the LAN

- When you double-click a link that points to a remote network object (for example, when an application attempts to connect to a file on a network server or when you reconnect to a remote OLE object)

To disable the Dialup Networking prompt in Dial-Up Networking, click the **Connection** menu, and then click **Settings**. Select the **Don't Prompt To Use Dial-Up Networking** option.

Summary

In this chapter, you learned how to configure a PC for Microsoft Windows 95 Dial-Up Networking and how to complete a dial-up networking connection to a Central site router.

Now that you are familiar with ways to connect a single user to an access server, you will learn how to connect a remote access server to the Central site router in Chapter 7, "Using ISDN and DDR to Enhance Remote Connectivity."

Configuring a Windows 95 Dial-Up Connection Using ISDN and DDR to Enhance Remote Connectivity

Complete the tasks of this case study, and then review the case study solution section that follows to see how you did and see where you might need to review the concepts that were presented in this chapter.

In this case study, you will practice how to install a new asynchronous connection device by using Windows 95 Dial-Up Networking. You will also configure Windows 95 Dial-Up Networking and connect to the network. You will see how to initiate connections from the remote client to the access server, how to start the PPP process, and how to launch upper-layer applications to communicate with others.

This case study is the apotheosis of what you learned in Chapters 4 through 6:

- In Chapter 4, "Configuring Asynchronous Connections with Modems," you saw how to prepare your router for an async connection.

- In Chapter 5, "Configuring Point-to-Point Protocol and Controlling Network Access," you saw how to configure your router to support a PPP session.

- In this chapter, you learned how to configure the client portion by using Windows 95 Dial-Up Networking.

Scenario

In this case study, you are a remote user. You wish to use your Windows 95 laptop to connect to the Central office, as shown in Figure 6-12.

Figure 6-12   *A Remote User Calling the Central Office*

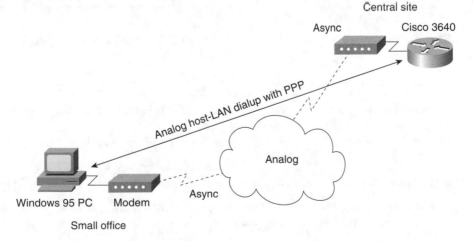

Task 1—Setting Up Windows 95 with Your Network and Dialing

Using Windows 95 Dial-Up networking, create a new dial-up connection to the Central site. When setting up the connection, use the following settings:

- Specify your modem (whether internal or external).
- Use the phone number according to your setup. (In the lab test that we did, the phone number we used was 1001—that's how our POTS simulators were configured.)
- Create a shortcut of the connection on your desktop.

Task 2—Setting Dial-Up Connection Properties

Change the properties of the new connection to provide access only to TCP/IP services. Also, your Windows 95 will receive an IP address upon connecting to the access server.

Task 3—Making the Connection

Step 1   Establish a connection to your Central site. You will be requested to type in a name and a password, which will allow you to start a PPP session with the access server.

NOTE   In the Chapter 5 case study, you were asked during Task 1 to type the following global command:

```
username student password cisco
```
The variables *student* and *cisco* are used to authenticate you when you establish a PPP session.

Step 2   From your Windows 95 station, initiate a Telnet session to your access server.

NOTE   You can reach your access server by Telnetting to the Ethernet address that you configured during Task 1 of the Chapter 5 case study.

Step 3   Once in the access server, verify on which line your current session came in.

Step 4   Once you know on which line your current session came in, look in detail at the parameters concerning your current session.

Step 5   Log off of the session.

Solution to Case Study—Configuring a Windows 95 Dial-Up Connection

The following is a step-by-step discussion of the case study solution.

Task 1 Solution—Setting Up Windows 95 with Your Network and Dialing

Using Windows 95 Dial-Up Networking, create a new dial-up connection to the Central site. To accomplish this task, you should perform the following steps:

NOTE   The following figures represent typical windows found in Windows 95. Variations of these windows may be found in different versions of Windows 95.

Step 1   From the desktop, click Start and select **Programs**, **Accessories**, and then choose **Dial-Up Networking folder**.

The Dial-Up Networking window appears, as shown in Figure 6-13.

Figure 6-13   *Dial-Up Networking Window*

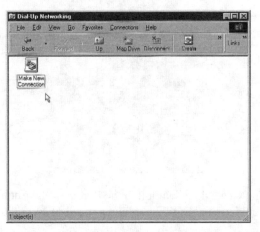

Step 2   Double-click the Make New Connection icon. The window in Figure 6-14 appears.

Figure 6-14 *Make New Connection Wizard*

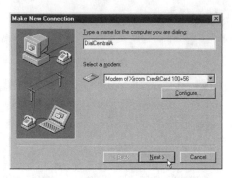

Step 3 Choose a name for the new dial-up connection that you are creating, and type this on the first line. Use a name that is easy to recognize, such as **DialCentralA**.

Step 4 Select the modem that you are using, and then click on the Configure button. The window shown in Figure 6-15 displays.

Figure 6-15 *Modem Properties Window*

Step 5 Click the General tab, and fill in the Port and Maximum speed. For this lab, you should use the COM2 port and a speed of 115200 baud.

Step 6 Click the Connection tab, and verify that the modem settings are 8–N–1. Other options available from this window are Port Settings and Advanced, which you leave at the defaults.

Step 7 Click the Options tab and view the features under this menu. For this lab, just keep the defaults.

Step 8   Click OK, and then click Next in the Make a New Connection window. The dialog box displayed in Figure 6-16 appears.

Figure 6-16   *Configuring the Phone Number to Dial*

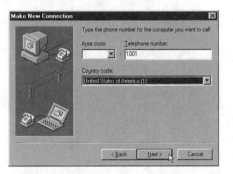

Step 9   Enter the telephone number of the asynchronous line for your Central site router. In this case study, the phone number to reach CentralA is 1001. Click Next. The software notifies you when you have successfully created a new dial-up networking connection with the name you chose during configuration.

Step 10   Click Finish, and you see your newly created icon in the Dial-Up Networking window.

Step 11   If you want to put this icon on your desktop, you can click the right mouse button or select Create Shortcut under the File menu.

Task 2 Solution—Setting Dial-Up Connection Properties

To change the dial-up properties, do the following steps:

Step 1   Select the connection icon that you just created in the Dial-Up Networking folder by clicking on it once.

Step 2   Press the right mouse button, or select File from the Dial-Up Networking window and select Properties. The dialog box displayed in Figure 6-17 should appear.

Figure 6-17 *Connection Window*

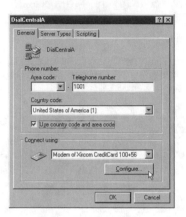

Step 3   In the DialCentralA Connection dialog box, make sure that the telephone number is correct. Deselect the Use country code and area code check box.

Step 4   Select Configure; the Modem Properties window that you already configured appears. You can check all the fields to verify that they are still correct.

Step 5   Close the Modem Properties window and return to the Dial-Up Networking window.

Step 6   Select the Server Types button or tab. The window displayed in Figure 6-18 appears.

Figure 6-18 *Server Types Window*

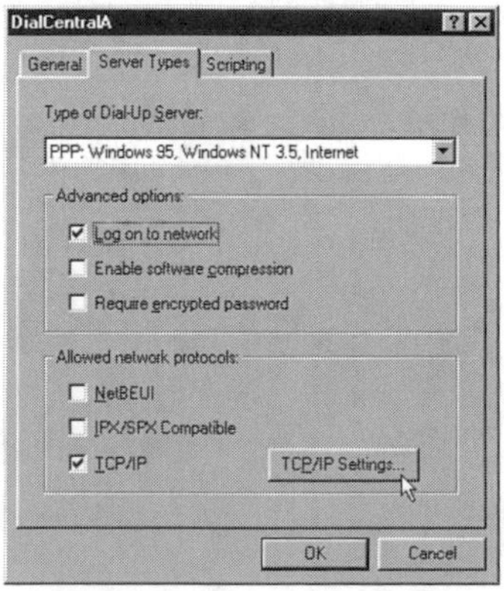

The Server Types window allows you to set the PPP or SLIP protocol. For this lab, you will use the PPP: Windows 95, Windows NT 3.5, Internet choice.

Step 7   Deselect all Advanced options; and under Allowed network protocols, select only TCP/IP.

Step 8   Click on TCP/IP Settings; the window displayed in Figure 6-19 appears.

Figure 6-19   *TCP/IP Settings Window*

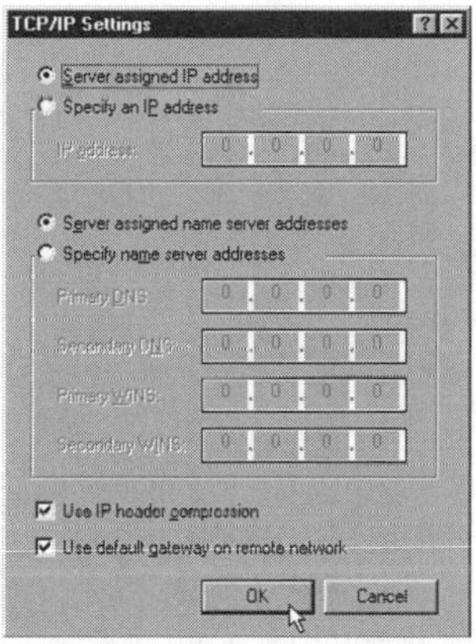

Step 9   In the TCP/IP Settings window, select the Server assigned IP address and Server assigned name server addresses radio buttons. Check the boxes for Use IP header compression and Use default gateway on remote network.

Step 10   Click the OK button and return to the original Dial-Up Networking window.

Task 3 Solution—Making the Connection

Step 1   To make the remote connection, double click the desktop icon that you created. A connection window opens. Enter the username **student** and password **cisco**. Click the Connect button to initiate the dial-up connection. After the connection is made, double-click the icon again to view the protocols used to connect to the host.

Step 2   To Telnet to the router from your Windows 95 station, select Start, Run, Telnet, and type in the Ethernet IP address of your Central site. In this case study, you type **telnet 10.115.0.110**. Log in with the username **student** and the password **cisco**.

Step 3   To verify on which line your current session came in, go to the console of your Cisco access server and enter a **show line** command. Note the A (for active) that precedes line 97. Your display should be similar to that shown in Example 6-1.

Example 6-1   *Output from the* **show line** *Command*

```
CentralA>sh line
 Tty  Typ     Tx/Rx       A  Modem  Roty  AccO  AccI  Uses  Noise  Overruns
*   0  CTY                 -    -     -     -     -     1     0      0/0
   65  TTY                 -  inout   -     -     -     0     0      0/0
   66  TTY                 -  inout   -     -     -     0     0      0/0
   67  TTY                 -  inout   -     -     -     0     0      0/0
   68  TTY                 -  inout   -     -     -     0     0      0/0
   69  TTY                 -  inout   -     -     -     0     0      0/0
   70  TTY                 -  inout   -     -     -     0     0      0/0
A  97  TTY  115200/115200  -  inout   -     -     -     2     0      0/0
  129  AUX     9600/9600   -    -     -     -     -     0     0      0/0
*130  VTY                 -    -     -     -     -     2     0      0/0
  131  VTY                 -    -     -     -     -     0     0      0/0
  132  VTY                 -    -     -     -     -     0     0      0/0
  133  VTY                 -    -     -     -     -     0     0      0/0
  134  VTY                 -    -     -     -     -     0     0      0/0

Line(s) not in async mode -or- with no hardware support:
1-64, 71-96, 98-128
```

Step 4   Once you know on which line your current session came in, look in detail at the parameters concerning your current session. Use the command **show line 97** in this case to see the session in detail. The result of this command is displayed in Example 6-2.

Example 6-2   *Output from the* **show line 97** *Command*

```
CentralA>sh line 97
 Tty  Typ     Tx/Rx       A  Modem  Roty  AccO  AccI  Uses  Noise  Overruns
A  97  TTY  115200/115200  -  inout   -     -     -     2     0      0/0

Line 97, Location: "", Type: ""
Length: 24 lines, Width: 80 columns
Baud rate (TX/RX) is 115200/115200, no parity, 1 stopbits, 8 databits
Status: Ready, Active, No Exit Banner, Async Interface Active
  HW PPP Support Active, Modem Detected
Capabilities: Hardware Flowcontrol In, Hardware Flowcontrol Out
  Modem Callout, Modem RI is CD, Line usable as async interface
  Modem Autoconfigure
Modem state: Ready
Line is running PPP for address 10.115.0.111.
0 output packets queued, 0 input packets.
 Async Escape map is 000000000000000001010000000000000
Group codes:    0
Modem hardware state: CTS DSR  DTR RTS, Modem Configured
```

Step 5   Log off of the session.

Review Questions

Answer the following questions, and then refer to Appendix H, "Answers to Review Questions," for answers and explanations.

1 List the three allowed protocols used for Windows 95 Dial-Up Networking.

2 How do you configure "Lock DTE speed" on a PC modem from Windows 95 Dial-Up Networking?

PART IV

Enhancing On-Demand Connectivity

CHAPTER 7

Using ISDN and DDR Technologies to Enhance Remote Connectivity

ISDN Overview

Prior to the 1960s, the world's communication network was relying mainly on analog facilities. Communication networks have been evolving for the past 40 years toward digital transmission. In 1968, ITU-T convened a meeting to discuss the integration of transmission and switching. Part of the discussions revolved around *Integrated Services Digital Network (ISDN)*.

ISDN developers envisioned that this new technology would provide a digital pipeline, offering integrated access to the broadest range of services. These services were to include voice, networking, packet switching, telemetry, and cable television.

ISDN versus Asynchronous

As its name implies, ISDN uses digital technology. As shown in Figure 7-1, ISDN replaces the traditional analog basic telephone service equipment and wiring scheme with a new higher-speed digital equipment that provides a host of new services.

Figure 7-1 *Local Loops for ISDN and Asynchronous Connections*

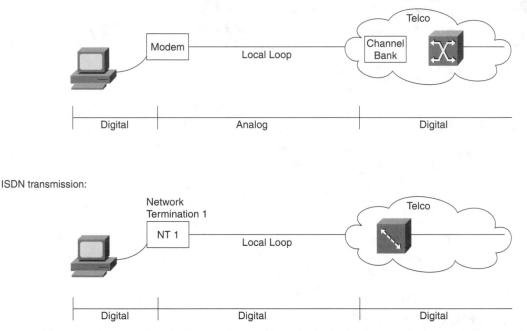

The major impetus for ISDN growth, especially in the United States, is the capability of ISDN to cost-effectively provide reliable service for the World Wide Web and access to other services that require high-speed services.

The ISDN call uses a unique set of protocols to communicate from the local terminal equipment to the ISDN switch in the central office for call setup and teardown. These protocols also allow the service provider to offer many other services besides basic telephone service.

Once the call is set up and the connection made, the process is the same as a traditional call. When the call is to be disconnected, once again the unique ISDN protocols are used to communicate between the local switch and the terminal equipment.

ISDN delivers a faster alternative to the following:

- **Analog dialup modems**—ISDN provides two to four times the bits-per-second transmission rate.
- **Other switched services**—Fast call setup makes a connection in less than one second (compared to 30 to 45 seconds for other switched services).
- **Expensive leased lines**—ISDN provides more than double the bit rate, and for a lower cost.

The primary difference between the basic or analog telephone call process and the ISDN call process is the use of digital signaling and data transmission from end-to-end.

NOTE   ISDN is an access technology that provides a digital local loop. Therefore, ISDN transmissions are digital from end-to-end. With asynchronous connections, the local loop is analog and requires PCM, thus introducing delay in the transmission.

SDN Services and Channelized E1 and T1

The access interface is the physical connection between the user and the provider. Two different access interfaces are currently defined by the ISDN recommendations from the ITU-T. They are called *Basic Rate Interface* (*BRI*) and *Primary Rate Interface* (*PRI*), as shown in Figure 7-2.

Figure 7-2   *Differences between BRI and PRI for Channelized E1 and T1*

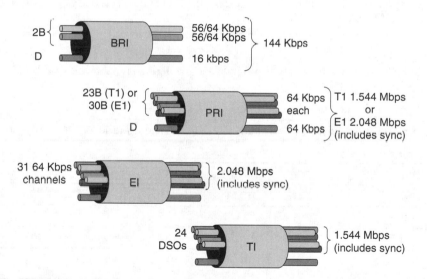

The ISDN bearer service channel—B channel—carries voice or data, usually in frame format. The D channel is the ISDN out-of-band signaling channel, which carries the user-network messages, such as call setup and teardown.

ISDN-BRI specifies the following:

- Two 64 Kbps bearer channels and one 16 Kbps data channel service. BRI connects to an NT1 for four-wire connection.
- Framing and synchronization at 48 Kbps.

- Total speed is two B channels at 64 Kbps each (128), one D channel at 16 Kbps, plus framing and synchronization at 48 Kbps. The total comes to (128+16+48=192)—192 Kbps.

- It is intended to be used at small concentration points.

- It is referred to as a digital signal level zero (DS0) interface.

ISDN-PRI specifies the following:

- 23 or 30 B channels, at 64 Kbps each

- One D channel, at 64 Kbps

- Framing and synchronization use 8 Kbps (North America T1) or 64 Kbps (European E1)

- Total speed 1.544 Mbps (T1) or 2.048 Mbps (E1)

NOTE   In an E1 PRI, there are actually 32 channels: 30 B channels, one D channel, and one synchronization channel. Also, in Europe, the D channel is carried in timeslot 16; in the United States, it is in timeslot 24.

Table 7-1 displays the relationship between the digital signal level, speed, T designation, and number of channels.

Table 7-1   *Digital Signal Levels—Characteristics*

Digital Signal Level	Speed	T Designation	Channels or DS0s
DS0	64 Kbps		1
DS1	1.544 Mbps	T1	24
DS2	6.312 Mbps	T2	96
DS3	44.736 Mbps	T3	672
DS4	274.176 Mbps	T4	4032

NOTE   In some cases, a DS0 can carry only 56 Kbps, usually due to legacy telco equipment or a signaling method called *robbed-bit signaling* (RBS). RBS and other signaling methods will be discussed later in this chapter in the "ISDN Primary Rate Interface" section.

In Europe, the equivalent of a T1 facility is an E1. E1 has 32 64-Kbps channels for a total of 2.048 Mbps.

Other hierarchies of voice and data channels are the Synchronous Optical Network (SONET) and Synchronous Digital Hierarchy (SDH). SONET is a North American telco standard; SDH is used elsewhere. These standards were developed to provide standards for Fiber Optics Transmission Systems (FOTS). Table 7-2 compares SONET and SDH channels.

Table 7-2   *A Comparison between SONET and SDH Levels*

SONET Signal Level	Speed	SDH Equivalent
STS-1/OC-1	51.84 Mbps	STM-0
STS-1/OC-3	155.52 Mbps	STM-1
STS-1/OC-12	622.08 Mbps	STM-4
STS-1/OC-24	1244.16 Mbps	STM-8
STS-1/OC-48	2488.32 Mbps	STM-16
STS-1/OC-192	9953.28 Mbps	STM-64

NOTE   Channelized T1 has 24 B channels at 64 Kbps each and one D channel at 64 Kbps.

Channelized E1 has 30 B channels at 64 Kbps each and one D channel at 64 Kbps.

BRI Call Processing

Figure 7-3 shows the sequence of events that occur during the establishment of a BRI call.

Figure 7-3   *BRI D Channel Performing Call Process*

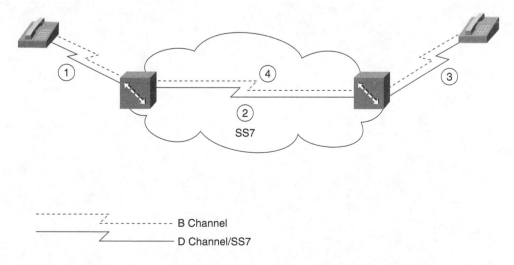

1   When the call is initiated, the D channel comes up. The called number is sent to the local ISDN switch.

2   The local switch uses the SS7 signaling protocols to set up a path and pass the called number to the terminating ISDN switch.

3   The far end switch brings up the D channel to the destination. The D channel is used for call setup, signaling, and call termination, which are the call control functions.

4   When the terminating end answers, the B channel is connected end-to-end. A B channel carries the conversation or data. Both B channels can be used simultaneously to the same or different destinations.

The maximum length of most ISDN local loops in North America is about 18,000 feet (5.5 km), using standard POTS wiring.

NOTE   ISDN is a local-loop technology. Once the ISDN switch processes the call, the communication uses the SS7 infrastructure to reach its destination.

BRI Functional Groups and Reference Points

ISDN technology involves many functional devices, also known as **functional groups**. The ISDN reference points define the communication protocols of these devices.

Each functional group has identical elements, but one group includes the NT2 CPE; the other does not. The following functional groups are illustrated in Figure 7-4:

Figure 7-4   *ISDN Functions and Reference Points*

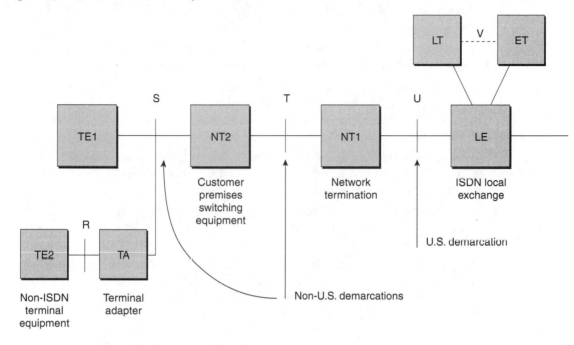

- **Terminal equipment 1 (TE1)** designates a device that is compatible with the ISDN network. A TE1 connects to a Network Termination of either Type 1 or Type 2, such as a digital telephone, a router with ISDN interface, or digital facsimile equipment.

- **Terminal equipment 2 (TE2)** designates a device that is not compatible with ISDN and requires a terminal adapter, such as terminals with X.21, EIA/TIA-232, or X.25 interfaces or a router without ISDN interface (AGS+ and so on).

- **Terminal adapter (TA)** converts standard electrical signals into the form used by ISDN, so that non-ISDN devices can connect to the ISDN network. For example, converting V.35 or EIA/TIA-232 to ISDN or a router without ISDN interface (AGS+ and so on).

- **Network termination type 1 (NT1)** connects four-wire ISDN subscriber wiring to the conventional two-wire local loop facility. The NT1 is part of the CPE in the United States and it is part of the local exchange in Europe.

- **Network termination type 2 (NT2)** directs traffic to and from different subscriber devices and the NT1. The NT2 is an intelligent device that performs switching and concentrating. Often, a PBX is the NT2 device.

- **Line termination (LT)** (located at the exchange side) functions are identical to those of an NT1.

- **Exchange termination (ET).** Subscriber line cards in the ISDN exchange LT and ET are sometimes referred to as the LE (local exchange), which is the ISDN switch for which we must configure.

Reference points are architectural definitions that may or may not have a physical realization as an interface. ISDN reference points are as follows:

- **U reference point** (User reference point)—This reference point is located between NT1 and LT (it corresponds with a subscriber line). There are no ITU-T standards for the U interface. This is the American National Standards Institute (ANSI) standard for the United States.

- **T reference point** (Terminal reference point)—This reference point is located between NT1 and NT2 (or between the NT1 and TE1 or TA, if there is no NT2 device). The T interface uses the same characteristics as the S interface.

- **S reference point** (System reference point)—This reference point is located between NT2 and TE1 or TA. It connects the terminals to the ISDN network. This is the most important interface for the users. The S interface uses the same characteristics as the T interface.

- **R reference point** (Rate reference point)—This reference point is located between TA and TE2 (non-ISDN interface). The TE2 connects to the TA via a standard physical-layer interface. These standards include EIA/TIA-232-C (formerly RS-232-C), V.24, X.21, and V.35.

NOTE   The S/T interface is governed by the ITU I.430 standard. The ANSI T1.601 or ITU I.431 standards govern the U interface, depending on the country.

Some manufacturers define a V reference point in Local Exchanges (LE) between Local Termination (LT) and Exchange Termination (ET). This reference point identifies the network node interface and is transparent to users.

Given all the ISDN abbreviations such as T, S, U, S/T, and so on, what do all of these components and reference points look like in the real world?

As shown in Figure 7-5, a connection is made from the wall jack with a standard two-wire cable to the NT1, and then out of the NT1 with a four-wire connection to your ISDN phone, terminal adapter, Cisco ISDN router, or maybe to an ISDN fax. The S/T interface is implemented using an eight-wire connector to allow for powering the NT and TE capabilities.

Figure 7-5   *Physical Layout of an ISDN Installation*

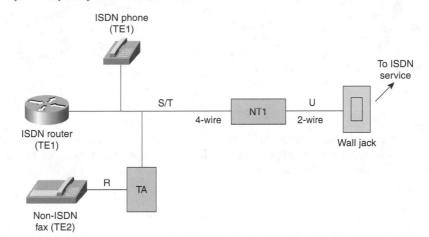

Because all of these connectors look fairly similar (such as RJ-11, RJ-45s and so on), you must be careful about what you plug in and where.

The S/T reference point is a four-wire interface (TX and RX). It is point-to-point and multipoint (passive bus), as shown in Figure 7-5. It uses the ITU I.430 specification. The S/T interface defines the interface between a TE1 or TA, and an NT.

The U interface defines the two-wire interface between the NT and the ISDN cloud.

The R interface defines the interface between the TA and an attached non-ISDN device (TE2).

An NT1 and NT2 combination device is sometimes referred to as an NTU.

ISDN Protocols

The ITU-T groups and organizes the ISDN protocols according to general topics:

E-series—Telephone Network, for example E.164—International ISDN addressing

I-series—Concepts and interfaces, for example I.430—BRI interface

Q-series—Switching and signaling, for example q.921—LAPD (Link Access Procedures for D channel)

PRI—Reference Points

PRI technology is a bit simpler than BRI. The wiring is not multipoint, and there is only the straight connection between the CSU/DSU and the PRI interface (see Figure 7-6).

Figure 7-6 *Standards and Reference Points on ISDN PRI*

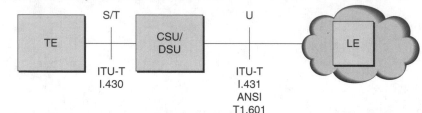

Multipoint refers to the capability to have multiple ISDN devices connected to the network, all connected on the same S-Bus. As a result, there is arbitration at Layer 1 and Layer 2, so multiple devices can access the network without collisions or interruptions between devices that need to share the ISDN network. Because there are not multiple devices, PRI does not require this arbitration.

ISDN Protocol Layers

Similar to other communication standards, ISDN uses many protocols. This section describes the ISDN protocols.

ISDN Layer 1

Layer 1, the physical layer, is responsible for the circuit switching of the connection. It supports the attachments of a TA/NT1, or even the connection of multiple devices. Both the B and the D channel share this physical layer. The standards involved at Layer 1 are as follows:

- I.430 for BRI, which defines the communication across the S/T reference point.
- I.431 for PRI, which is a full-duplex, point-to-point, serial, synchronous connection.
- ANSI T1.601 for BRI, which defines the communication across the U interface for North America.

As shown in Figure 7-7, Layer 2 and Layer 3 operate for the D channel. However, the B channel operates in either an HDLC or PPP encapsulation mode to encapsulate the upper-layer protocols, instead of using Layer 2 and Layer 3 directly.

Figure 7-7   *ISDN Protocols and the OSI Reference Model*

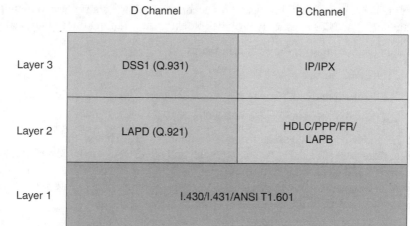

LAPD is the framing protocol used for D channel data. The Digital Subscriber Signaling System No. 1 (DSS1) is the Layer 3 protocol for the D channel. Specifically, only Q.931 is used here, not the entire DSS1 protocol suite.

The D channel is governed by DDR, which is the mechanism for building connections over either an analog or ISDN connection. The B channel is governed by IP or IPX protocols for data transmission.

Figure 7-8 shows what the I.430 BRI frames between the TE and the NT look like.

Figure 7-8   *I.430 Framing (BRI Layer 1)*

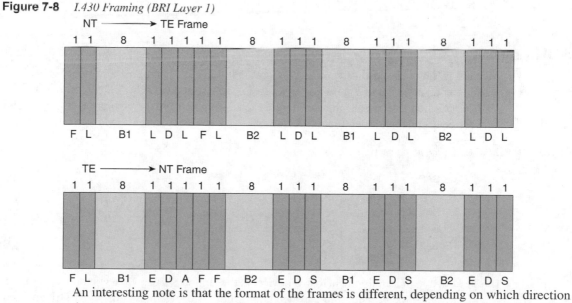

An interesting note is that the format of the frames is different, depending on which direction they are going. Also note that time-division multiplexing is occurring between the D channel and the two B channels. The frame can have 16 bits from each of the B channels and four bits from the D channel. The framing always occurs, even if no data is being transmitted across the B channels. The NT1 constantly provides clocking and framing out to the local exchange.

B channels have the following characteristics:

- ISDN BRI bit rate is 192 Kbps.
- ISDN user bandwidth is 144 Kbps, 2×B channels plus 1 D channel ((2×64) + 16).
- ISDN signaling requirement is 48 Kbps.

The TE and ISDN switch are constantly communicating. That is, there is a constant stream of ones and zeros exchanged between the router and the ISDN switch located at the central office. The stream of data exchanged must follow a specific sequence, such as the one shown in Figure 7-8. Such a sequence, in which each bit has a specific function, is referred to as **framing**. The I.430 standard defines the BRI framing bit field key as follows:

- B1 bit—Bit within the B channel 1
- B2 bit—Bit within the B channel 2
- D bit—D channel bit
- F bit—Framing bit used for synchronization
- L bit—DC balancing bit adjust average bit value
- E bit—Echo of previous D bit
- A bit—Activation bit
- S bit—Spare bit

ISDN Layer 2

With ISDN, all of the hardware addressing occurs in Layer 2, just like a traditional LAN environment. As shown in Figure 7-9, it is possible to have up to eight ISDN terminals on an S/T bus. TEs are therefore differentiated from each through terminal endpoint identifiers (TEIs) and service access point identifiers (SAPIs).

Figure 7-9   *ISDN Can Accommodate Multiple Devices on the S/T Bus*

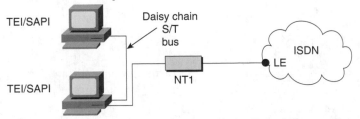

The TEI is a dynamic assignment to that device. In the United States, when you boot up a router, you make some type of request to the switch for a TEI. The switch assigns you a TEI, and you will communicate over the switch using the signaling that uses a SAPI. This is the same concept as is used in the 802.2 frames, in which you need to differentiate between the different processes that are running. You need some special identifiers to provide this discrimination between frames. Some of the messages sent over the ISDN network are for call setup or call teardown, and others are data. The SAPI is a way of prioritizing the calls or giving access to the network first.

Q.920 is the functional specification for ISDN. The actual communication takes place over the network and is specified in Q.921.

WARNING   Cisco 4000 can't share the S-bus.

NOTE   Examples of SAPI values are 0 for Call control procedure and 63 for Layer 2 management function.

TEI groups assignments are 0–63 for non-automatic TEI assignment; 64–126 for automatic TEI assignment; and 127 for group assignment, or broadcast.

ISDN Layer 3—Channel Q.931

ITU Q.931 is specified as the protocol for Layer 3 of the D channel. The protocol messages and its rules for exchange are derived from the DSS1 protocol suite.

The I series specifications define support of the end terminal (end equipment) protocol as it is applied to the Cisco routers. The Q series specifications define the equipment from the network point of view, as supported by the central switch.

These data link layer protocols are not implemented in the NT equipment. They are only implemented in the end equipment, and are used to communicate with the local switch. They are not supported in the NT1 equipment.

ISDN Call Setup

There are a number of ways to place an ISDN call. In an ISDN call, the called party requests a call setup, as shown in Figure 7-10. Before the actual connect and call proceeding, you might see several different messages, such as progress, which indicate how your call is proceeding. This progress message is optional.

The same is true for the alerting message, which is typical of telephone messages, but is not required. Alerting messages are not typical with data transmissions. Most of the time, you see connection messages with data calls. You may not see the Connect acknowledge, but it is valid.

The messages depend on how successful the call and completion acknowledgments are implemented.

Figure 7-10 *Call Setup—Q.931 Activities*

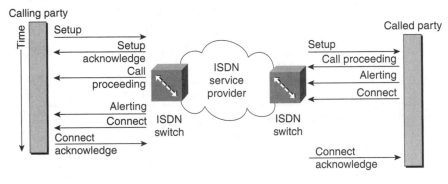

NOTE Different ISDN switches use different call setup and teardown procedures. Depending on the switch type, you may or may not get all the steps shown in Figure 7-10. At a minimum, Call proceeding, Alerting, and Connect should be exchanged.

ISDN Call Teardown

Similar to call setup, the call teardown request is not an end-to-end function, but instead is processed by the switch. The release procedures are based on a three-message approach:

- Release
- Released
- Release complete

The Release message is transmitted through the network as quickly as possible. Figure 7-11 assumes that the called party is generating the release. The process is triggered by a Disconnect message on the D channel, between the calling and called parties. After receipt of this message, the exchange immediately starts the release of the switch path that supports the B channel circuit, and sends a Release message to the succeeding exchange at the same time. The message is passed through the network from all intermediate exchanges to the terminating exchange.

Figure 7-11 *Q.931 Steps During a Call Teardown*

In Figure 7-11, all of the exchanges are characterized as the telco network box. The Release message is intended to inform the exchanges involved in the call as quickly as possible that the call-related circuit connections are to be released. As the involved exchanges release the call, a Released message is eventually transmitted to the terminating exchange, and this transmission causes the following actions:

- It issues a Disconnect message to the calling party.

- It starts a timer T_{12} to ensure receipt of a Released message.

- It connects the switched path.

- When a Released message is received from the preceding exchange, it returns a Release complete message to the preceding exchange.

The T timers are used through the exchanges to ensure that the exchange will repeat the Release message if a Release complete message is not received within the timer period. If not acknowledged, a Reset circuit occurs.

ISDN BRI and DDR Overview

Cisco implements Dial on Demand Routing (DDR) from the perspective of the incoming data to the router.

With DDR, all incoming traffic is classified as either **interesting** or **uninteresting**. As shown in Figure 7-12, if the traffic is interesting, the packet is passed to the router. The router connects to the remote router if it is not currently connected using access-lists and dialer-lists. If the traffic is uninteresting and there is no connection, it does not dial the remote router, thus saving costs.

Figure 7-12 *Dial-On Demand Routing Uses Conditions to Classify the Packets as Either Interesting or Uninteresting*

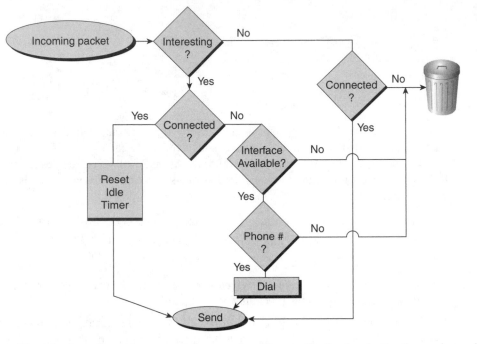

The idle timer is used to reset the connection if no traffic for the destination arrives within the configured timer interval.

WARNING Once a connection is made, all traffic goes through, unless an access-list is applied to the interface. For example, if you configured your DDR link to deny Telnet traffic but allow ping traffic, a user can send a ping to bring up the connection, and then start a Telnet session on the open DDR interface.

Access routers use DDR to connect to remote routers. The access router calls the remote router only when interesting traffic arrives. Dialer-lists specify interesting traffic. The BRI interface is placed in a dial group that is linked to a dialer-list that specifies interesting traffic. You can use multiple dialer-list settings to designate interesting traffic that is mapped for other DDR destination routers.

Access-lists can also be used to produce more granularity in defining interesting packets that initiate DDR calls. For this periodic-use environment, specify static routes so that routing updates will not initiate ISDN calls to remote routers that run up service charges from the ISDN service provider.

DDR commands map a host ID and dialer string to initiate the setup of an ISDN call for interesting traffic. The router then makes an outgoing call from its BRI through the ISDN NT1. If using an external TA, it must support V.25bis_dialing. Calling details for these devices come from dialer commands.

ISDN end stations now use this static route to transmit packet traffic. When no more traffic is transmitted over the ISDN call, an idle timer starts. After the idle timeout occurs, the call disconnects.

There are global and interface tasks that are required to configure ISDN on a router for DDR.

Global tasks do the following:

- Select the switch that matches the ISDN provider's switch at the central office (CO). This requirement is necessary because signaling specifics differ regionally and nationally, despite standards.

- Set destination details. Indicate static routes from the router to other ISDN destinations.

- Establish the criteria for interesting packets in the router that initiate an ISDN call to the appropriate destination.

Interface tasks do the following:

- Select interface specifications. Specify the interface type BRI and the number for this ISDN BRI port. For PRI, the interface task description occurs later in this chapter. The interface uses an IP address and subnet mask.

- Configure ISDN addressing, DDR dialer information, and any ISDN parameters supplied by the ISDN service provider. Indicate that the interface is part of the dialer group using the interesting packets set globally. Additional commands place the ISDN call to the appropriate destination.

Following interface configuration, you can define optional features: the time to wait for the ISDN carrier to respond to the call, and the seconds of idle time before the router times out and drops the call.

Configuring an ISDN BRI

You must specify global and interface parameters to prepare the router for operation in an ISDN environment.

At the global or high level, the administrator must specify the ISDN service provider's CO switch type. There are approximately 10 different switches to choose from, depending on the country where the connection is established.

Although the high-level interface configuration and selection tasks apply to all routers, this section focuses on BRI for access routers. PRI details on the Cisco 3600 and 4000 series, and

7000 family routers and AS5200 series access servers with T1/E1 controllers are covered at the end of this chapter, in the "ISDN Primary Rate Interface" section.

The interface ISDN addressing tasks include assigning the IP address, dialer group, and ISDN service profile statements. The task also includes adding the **dialer map** command that associates a statically mapped destination to a destination IP address, hostname, and ISDN dial number.

Optional features to set for ISDN are covered in more detail in the "Optional Configuration" section at the end of the chapter (these include **isdn caller number**, **isdn rate adaptation**, and **dialer map speed**). Other options are described in the Cisco Documentation CD-ROM.

Step 1—Selecting the ISDN Switch Type

You must specify the type of ISDN switch used by the service providers at the CO.

Selecting the ISDN Switch Type

Some ISDN service providers use one switch, but emulate the software of another switch. Therefore, the switch type that needs to be configured is the one that has been emulated by the switch, and not the actual brand name of the switch installed at the CO.

When you use the **isdn switch-type** command in global mode, all ISDN interfaces on the router are configured for the same switch type. If you use the command in the interface configuration mode, only the interface for which you are configuring assumes that switch type.

Following are the global or interface commands that let you specify the ISDN switch located at the CO to which your router will connect:

```
Router(config)#isdn switch-type switch type
Router(config-if)#isdn switch-type switch type
```

For BRI ISDN service, the switch type can be one of those listed in Table 7-3.

Table 7-3   *ISDN BRI Switch Types*

Switch Type	Description
basic-5ess	AT&T basic rate switches (United States)
basic-dms100	NT DMS-100 (North America)
basic-ni1	National ISDN-1 (North America)
basic-ni2	National ISDN-2 (North America)
basic-1tr6	German 1TR6 ISDN switches
basic-nwnet3	Norwegian Net3 switches

Table 7-3   *ISDN BRI Switch Types (Continued)*

Switch Type	Description
basic-nznet3	New Zealand Net3 switches
basic-ts013	Australian TS013 and TS014 switches
basic-net3	Switch type for NET3 in United Kingdom and Europe
ntt	NTT ISDN switch (Japan)

Depending on the version of Cisco IOS software that you use, you might see different switch types available.

WARNING   If you need to change the specified switch type, you must reboot the router before the different switch-type setting takes effect on the router. To disable the switch on the ISDN interface, specify **isdn switch-type.**

You can apply an ISDN switch type on a per-interface basis, thus extending the existing global **isdn switch-type** command to the interface level. This allows Basic Rate Interfaces (BRIs) and Primary Rate Interfaces (PRIs) to run simultaneously on platforms that support both interface types.

Sequence of Commands for Specifying the ISDN Switch Type

To specify a switch type under your serial interface, you must have configured the E1/T1 controller. But in order to configure the E1/T1 controller, you must have configured the global **isdn switch-type**! Once the E1/T1 controller is configured—following the configuration of the **isdn switch-type**—you can introduce the switch command at the interface level. If you wish to, you can also remove it from the global level. The interface **isdn switch-type** command, if specified, overwrites the **isdn switch-type** specified at the global level.

Step 2—Configuring the Interface

The **interface bri** *interface-number* command designates the interface used for ISDN on a router acting as a TE1.

If the router does not have a native BRI (it is a TE2 device), it must use an external ISDN terminal adapter. On a TE2 router, use the **interface serial** *interface-number* command.

Step 3—Setting the Service Profile Identifiers (SPID), If Necessary

Some service providers use service profile identifiers (SPIDs) to define the services subscribed to by the ISDN device that is accessing the ISDN service provider. The service provider assigns one or more SPIDs to the ISDN device when you first subscribe to the service. If you use a service provider that requires SPIDs, your ISDN device cannot place or receive calls until it sends a valid assigned SPID to the service provider when accessing the switch to initialize the connection.

Purpose of SPIDs

Service providers use SPIDs to define the services you are paying for. Common extra features include call waiting, call holding, multiple subscriber number, caller ID, call transfer, call forwarding, call deflection, and so on.

Currently, only the DMS-100 and NI1 switch types require SPIDs. The AT&T 5ESS-switch type may support a SPID, but it is recommended that you set up that ISDN service without SPIDs. SPIDs have significance at the local access ISDN interface only. Remote routers are never sent SPIDs.

How Are SPID Numbers Chosen?

To keep SPID numbers simple (an oxymoron, it seems), most telcos use part of the ISDN phone number in the SPID nomenclature. Therefore, SPIDs are often the ISDN phone number with some optional numbers. For example, the SPID for the phone number (888)555-1212 could be 888555121200.

A local directory number (LDN) might also be necessary if the router is to answer calls made to the second directory number.

The commands to set SPIDs and LDN on both B channels are as follows:

```
Router(config-if)#isdn spid1 spid-number [ldn]
Router(config-if)#isdn spid2 spid-number [ldn]
```

Commands	Description
isdn spid1 and **isdn spid2**	These commands are used to define, at the router, the SPID number that has been assigned by the ISDN service provider for the respective B channel.

Commands	Description
spid-number	This is the number that identifies the service to which you have subscribed. The ISDN service provider assigns this value.
ldn	This local dial number (optional) must match the called-party information coming in from the ISDN switch in order to use both B channels on most switches. It may be required by the ISDN service provider.

SPIDs Can "Byte"

Using ISDN, I recently configured two Cisco 2520s for DDR for a client wishing to set up a MAN. During the week of the installation, the metropolitan region was split into two different area codes. For the purpose of this story, suppose that the area code 111 was split between 111 and 999. Anything on the central metropolitan area remained 111, and the peripheral area became 999. The telco provided me with the suburban router's ISDN phone numbers—9995551212 and 9995551213—but no SPID numbers. Knowing the telco modus operandi for SPID creation and the switch type, I figured the SPID numbers for the router located in the new area code region to be 999555121200 and 999555121300. Once the router was configured, it indicated, via the **show isdn status**, that the SPIDs were invalid. By contacting the telco, I found out that, although the phone numbers were using the new area code of 999, the SPIDs configured on the switch were not updated to reflect the area code change. So, the phone numbers were **999**5551212 and **999**5551213, but the SPIDs were **111**555121200 and **111**555121300—still using the old area code.

Step 4—Setting the Encapsulation Protocol

The following **encapsulation ppp** command can be used if you want PPP encapsulation for your ISDN interface. This is the case if you want any of the LCP options that PPP offers (for example, CHAP authentication). You must use PPP, PAP, or CHAP if you receive calls from more than one dial-up source. To revert from PPP encapsulation to the default, use the **encapsulation hdlc** command.

```
Router(config-if)#encapsulation [ppp ¦ hdlc]
Router(config-if)#ppp authentication [chap ¦ pap]
```

Configuring Dial-on-Demand Routing (DDR)

Connections initiated by remote offices or telecommuters are brought up on an as-needed basis, which results in substantial cost savings for the company. In dial-on-demand routing scenarios, users are not connected for long periods of time. The number of remote nodes requiring access is relatively low, and the completion time for the dial-in task is short.

Following are the steps involved in configuring a spoke router for DDR. A **spoke router** is the link between a stub network and the WAN. A **stub network** has only a single connection to a router.

1   Define what constitutes interesting traffic by using the **dialer-list** command.

2   Assign this traffic definition to an interface by using the **dialer-group** command.

3   Define the destination address, hostname, telephone number to dial, and optional call parameters by using the **dialer map** command.

4   Define call parameters by using commands such as **dialer idle-timeout**, **dialer fast-idle**, and **dialer load-threshold**.

Step 1—Defining what Constitutes Interesting Traffic

The **dialer-list** command is used to configure dial-on-demand calls that will initiate a connection. The simpler form of the command specifies whether a whole protocol suite, such as IP or IPX, will be permitted or denied to trigger a call. The more complex form references an access-list, which allows finer control of the definition of interesting traffic.

The command syntax to define a DDR dialer-list to control dialing by protocol is as follows:

```
Router(config)#dialer-list dialer-group-number
protocol protocol-name {permit | deny}
```

Command	Description
dialer-list dialer-group-number **protocol** protocol-name {**permit**	**deny**	**list** access-list-number	access-group}	This command defines a DDR dialer-list to control dialing by protocol, or by a combination of protocol and access-list.
dialer-group-number	This is the number of a dialer access group identified in any **dialer-group** interface configuration command.
protocol-name	This is one of the following protocol keywords: **appletalk, bridge, clns, clns_es, clns_is, decnet, decnet_router-L1, decnet_router-L2, decnet_node, ip, ipx, vines,** or **xns**.

You can also specify an access-list for more refined control over the DDR process. Standard or extended access-lists can be used for DDR, and then applied to dialer groups and interfaces. An extended access-list gives you control over the protocol, source address, and destination address in determining interesting packets.

The **access-list** command specifies interesting traffic that initiates a DDR call. The **dialer-list** command is used in conjunction with the access-list. This command associates the access-list with the dialer access group:

```
Router(config)#access-list access-list-number [permit ¦ deny]
{protocol ¦ protocol-keyword}{source source-wildcard ¦ any}
{destination destination-wildcard ¦ any}
[protocol-specific-options] [log]
Router(config)#dialer-list dialer-group list access-list-number
```

Step 2—Assigning the Dialer-List to an Interface

Once the dialer-list is created, it needs to be assigned to the interface responsible for initiating the call. This associating command is as follows:

```
Router(config-if)#dialer-group group-number
```

Command	Description
dialer-group	This command configures an interface to belong to a specific dialing group. The dialer group points to a dialer-list.
group-number	This is the number of the dialer access group to which the specific interface belongs. This access group is defined with the **dialer-list** command, which specifies interesting traffic that initiates a DDR call. Acceptable values are nonzero, positive integers from 1 to 10.

NOTE   For a given protocol and a given dialer group, only one access-list can be specified in the **dialer-list** command.

Step 3—Defining Destination Parameters

Once you define what constitutes interesting traffic, you must provide the interface responsible for initiating the call with all the parameters necessary to reach the destination. The **dialer map** command identifies destination router information, such as the phone number to dial:

```
Router(config-if)#dialer map protocol next-hop-address
[name hostname] [broadcast] dial-string
```

Command	Description
dialer map *protocol next-hop-address* [**name** *hostname*] **broadcast**] *dial-string*	This command configures a serial interface or ISDN interface to call one or multiple sites. The **name** refers to the name of the remote system, and **broadcast** indicates that broadcasts should be forwarded to this address. The *dial-string* is the number to dial to reach the destination.

The **dialer map** command has many other optional parameters available to it. For a complete description of the command and its parameters, refer to the documentation CD-ROM or CCO.

Mapping What?

Cisco commands often contain the word "map," which is used to map statically Layer 2 addresses to Layer 3 addresses. For example, the command **frame-relay map** is used to define a Layer 3 next-hop-address to its Layer 2 address—in this case, a DLCI number. With a **dialer-map** statement, you bundle a Layer 3 address (IP in this chapter) to a dial-up Layer 2 address (which, in this case, is a phone number).

Step 4—Defining Optional Call Parameters

The following additional call parameters can be added to the interface:

```
Router(config-if)#dialer idle-timeout seconds
Router(config-if)#dialer fast-idle seconds
Router(config-if)#dialer load-threshold load [outbound | inbound | either]
```

Command	Description
dialer idle-timeout *seconds*	This command specifies the time that the line can remain idle before it is disconnected. The default time is 120 seconds.
dialer fast-idle *seconds*	This command specifies the time that a line can remain idle before the current call is disconnected to allow another call that is waiting to use the line. The default time is 20 seconds.
dialer load-threshold *load* [**outbound** | **inbound** | **either**]	This command specifies the interface load at which the dialer initiates another call to the destination.
Load	This is a number from 1 to 255 (255 is equal to 100% load and 128 is equal to 50% load).
Outbound	This command calculates the load on outbound data only (the default).
Inbound	This command calculates the load on inbound data only.
Either	This command calculates the load on the maximum of the outbound or inbound data.

Idle-Timeout versus Fast-Idle

Combining the **dialer idle-timeout** and **dialer fast-idle** commands allows you to configure lines to stay up for a longer period of time when there is no contention, but they can also be reused more quickly when there are not enough lines for the current demand.

Also, if you intend to nail the line, set a high timeout value on the receiving router because these commands apply to inbound and outbound calls.

Static and Default Routing

The use of static and default routes eliminates the need to send routing updates over expensive leased lines or to trigger a DDR call.

If you configure as a **leaf node**, sometimes also called a **stub network** (a remote site with no routes behind it), you probably will configure a default or static route for the leaf node to go to just one location, as shown in Figure 7-13. By default, it sends all of its traffic to the cloud or the Central site location.

Figure 7-13 *Static and Default Routes Usage*

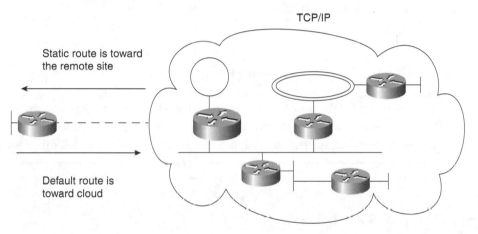

Static Route

At the Central site, you can enter the static route and point it at a specific address, as follows:

```
Router(config)#ip route 172.108.0.0 255.255.0.0 192.254.35.2
```

In order to point to your interface instead of the next hop address, you can also use the following:

```
ip route 172.108.0.0 255.255.0.0 BRI 0
```

Provided that you are using a **dialer-string** command, if you use a **dialer-map** command, DDR does not kick in if the static route is pointing at your interface.

NOTE   A static route is usually necessary to initiate DDR.

Default Route

To configure a default route, use the **ip route** and **ip default-network** commands. Default routes from one host to another are static routes. To set the gateway of last resort, use the 0.0.0.0/0 address as the destination address.

The **ip default-gateway** command is used with a router on which IP routing is disabled. This command provides the router with an address to which it can forward packets whose destination IP addresses are not in its address space. The following is an example of default route configuration:

```
Router(config)#ip route 172.254.50.0 255.255.255.0 172.254.45.1
Router(config)#ip default-network 172.254.50.0
Router(config)#ip route 0.0.0.0 0.0.0.0 172.254.45.1
```

Routing Protocols Intricacies

For RIP, the 0.0.0.0 route is automatically installed as the local gateway of last resort. The **ip default-network 0.0.0.0** command is not necessary. RIP automatically advertises the route to 0.0.0.0, even when redistribute static and a default metric are not configured.

With IGRP, for this redistribution to happen, you must include the **ip default-network** command.

Setting Route Redistribution

Now, we have configured the remote leafs, and they have their static routes established. On the corporate side, it is very important that you be able to distribute those addresses across the network, as desired. To redistribute those routes, you need to configure the routes to be redistributed to a dynamic routing protocol at the core side.

Figure 7-14 shows that we use IGRP as the dynamic routing protocol and redistribute the static routes by entering the **redistribute static** command. In this example, the router advertises that it knows the way to 192.150.42.0.

Figure 7-14 *This Router Advertises Static Routes to Other Routers*

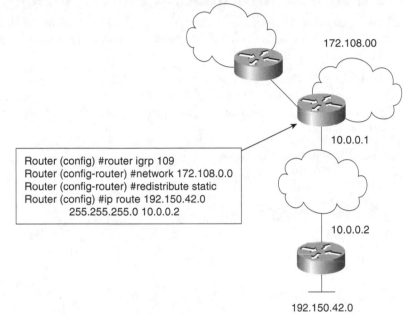

172.108.00

10.0.0.1

Router (config) #router igrp 109
Router (config-router) #network 172.108.0.0
Router (config-router) #redistribute static
Router (config) #ip route 192.150.42.0
          255.255.255.0 10.0.0.2

10.0.0.2

192.150.42.0

Deactivating Routing Updates

Because we use static routes or default routing on our remote networks, we need not pass IGRP routing updates to the rest of the network from the remote sites. As shown in Figure 7-15, to block this traffic, we declare the BRI interface on the corporate side to be passive, which prevents any routing updates from being passed to the remote node.

Figure 7-15 *Blocking Routing Updates by Using the* **passive-interface** *Command*

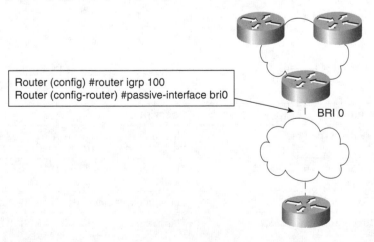

Router (config) #router igrp 100
Router (config-router) #passive-interface bri0

BRI 0

Configuring a Router for Initiating an ISDN Call

Some basic configuration is necessary on a router to provide for dial-on-demand routing. In the following section, you will read about the necessary commands for successful DDR connectivity.

Figure 7-16 shows the topology of router-to-router DDR. Example 7-1 shows how you can combine commands to set up ISDN and DDR. DDR is configured to connect Cisco-a to Cisco-b by using legacy DDR, which uses **dialer map** statements. Cisco-b configuration is shown in Example 7-2.

Figure 7-16   *Topology of a Simple Network Using DDR*

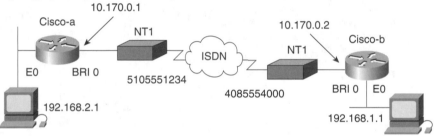

Example 7-1   *Router-A Configuration, Using a Simple **dialer-list** Statement*

```
hostname Cisco-a
isdn switch-type basic-5ess
username Cisco-b password samepass
interface bri 0
 ip address 10.170.0.1 255.255.0.0
 encapsulation ppp
 dialer idle-timeout 300
 dialer map ip 10.170.0.2 name Cisco-b 4085554000
 dialer-group 1
 ppp authentication chap
!
ip route 192.168.1.0 255.255.255.0 10.170.0.2
dialer-list 1 protocol ip permit
```

Table 7-4 describes the commands used in the configuration in Example 7-1.

Table 7-4   *ISDN Basic Configuration*

Command	Description
isdn switch-type	This command selects the AT&T 5ESS switch as the CO ISDN switch type for this interface.
username Cisco-b password samepass	This command sets up a CHAP username and password for the remote router.
interface bri 0	This command enters BRI 0 configuration mode.
ip address 10.170.0.1 255.255.0.0	This command specifies the BRI 0 IP address and net mask.
encapsulation ppp	This command sets up PPP encapsulation for BRI 0.

Table 7-4   *ISDN Basic Configuration (Continued)*

Command	Description
dialer idle-timeout 300	This is the number of seconds of idle time before the router drops the ISDN call.
dialer map	This command establishes how to call the next hop router.
ip	This is the name of the protocol used by this map.
10.170.0.2	This is the IP address for the next-hop router's BRI interface.
Cisco-b	This is the CHAP identification name for the remote router.
4085554000	This is the telephone number used to reach the BRI interface on the remote router for this DDR destination.
dialer-group 1	This command associates the BRI 0 interface with **dialer-list 1**.
ppp authentication chap	This command sets up CHAP PPP authentication for BRI 0.
ip route	This command configures a static route to the subnet on the remote router.
dialer-list 1 protocol ip permit	This command associates permitted IP traffic with dialer-group 1. The router only starts an ISDN call for IP traffic.

In Example 7-1 and Figure 7-16, the network between the serial interfaces of the two routers uses eight bits of subnetting. Static route statements define the IP route to the Cisco-b LAN interfaces over 192.168.1.0. Interesting traffic is defined as any IP traffic that initiates a DDR call to Cisco-b.

The number dialed is for the remote ISDN device. The service provider offering the ISDN service provides this number. Traffic is routed to the LAN shown on the right of Figure 7-16. Before a connection can be made, static routes of how to reach those networks must be in place.

NOTE   When Cisco documentation mentions **legacy DDR**, it refers to configurations that use **dialer-map** statements.

Example 7-2 displays the configuration for Cisco-b from Figure 7-16.

Example 7-2   *Cisco-b Configuration, Using a Simple **dialer-list** Statement*

```
hostname Cisco-b
isdn switch-type basic-5ess
username Cisco-a password samepass
interface bri 0
```

continues

Example 7-2 *Cisco-b Configuration, Using a Simple* **dialer-list** *Statement (Continued)*

```
 ip address 10.170.0.2 255.255.0.0
 encapsulation ppp
 dialer idle-timeout 300
 dialer map ip 10.170.0.1 name Cisco-a 5105551234
 dialer-group 1
 ppp authentication chap
!
ip route 192.168.2.0 255.255.255.0 10.170.0.1
dialer-list 1 protocol ip permit
```

Using an Extended Access-List to Define a Dialer-List

Figure 7-17 shows a more complex topology set up with DDR. This topology is used for the extended configuration shown in Example 7-3, in which you see how you can combine the commands described earlier for DDR to set up an extended access-list to trigger an ISDN call. You may use many of the same commands for configuring a simple ISDN call. Access-lists can be applied to a dialer group to trigger dialing, and then you can apply that dialer-list to the interface.

Figure 7-17 *Using an Access-List to Provide Granularity to a Dialer-List Statement*

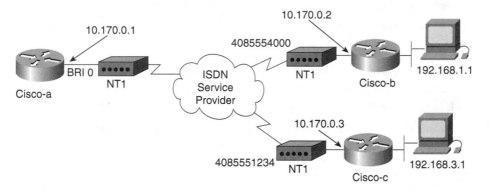

DDR is configured on router Cisco-a, as shown in Example 7-3, to connect with Cisco-b for all IP traffic except Telnet and FTP. The details about what is interesting to DDR are defined in an access-list.

Example 7-3 *Cisco-a Configuration, Using ACL for DDR*

```
hostname Cisco-a
isdn switch-type basic-dms100
username Cisco-b password samepass
username Cisco-c password samepass
interface bri 0
 ip address 10.170.0.1 255.255.0.0
 encapsulation ppp
dialer idle-timeout 300
```

Example 7-3   *Cisco-a Configuration, Using ACL for DDR (Continued)*

```
dialer map ip 10.170.0.2 name cisco-b 4085554000
dialer map ip 10.170.0.3 name cisco-c 4085551234
dialer-group 2
ppp authentication chap
ip route 192.168.1.0 255.255.255.0 10.170.0.2
ip route 192.168.3.0 255.255.255.0 10.170.0.3
access-list 101 deny tcp any any eq ftp
access-list 101 deny tcp any any eq telnet
access-list 101 permit ip any any
dialer-list 2 protocol ip list 101
```

Table 7-5 describes the commands used in the configuration in Example 7-3.

Table 7-5   *ISDN—Legacy DDR Commands*

Command	Description
isdn switch-type	This command selects the ISDN switch type for this interface.
username Cisco-b password samepass	This command sets up the CHAP username and password for the remote router in the local user database.
interface bri 0	This command enters BRI 0 configuration mode, and sets up DDR and ISDN functions.
ip address 10.170.0.1 255.255.0.0	This command specifies the BRI 0 IP address and net mask.
encapsulation ppp	This command sets up PPP encapsulation for BRI 0.
dialer idle-timeout 300	This is the number of seconds of idle time (300 seconds = 5 minutes) before the router drops the ISDN call.
dialer map	This command establishes the IP address and ISDN number to call the next-hop routers.
dialer-group 2	This command associates the BRI 0 interface with **dialer-list 2**.
ppp authentication chap	This command sets up CHAP PPP authentication for BRI 0.

The service provider offering the ISDN service uses a Northern Telecom DMS-100 switch, so the configuration in Example 7-3 uses SPIDs. The service provider provides other details that you must use when you configure your router for ISDN.

Configuring ISDN by using extended access-lists is more common in networks than configuring ISDN by using a dialer-list and dialer map statement is, as shown in the previous configuration example.

Optional Configurations

It is possible to fine-tune a router's configuration to provide for more flexible and efficient connectivity. In this section, you will learn some of those optional configurations for ISDN DDR.

The optional configurations for ISDN include the following:

- B Channel Aggregation
- ISDN Caller Identification
- Called-Party Number Answering
- ISDN Rate Adaptation

B Channel Aggregation

As shown in Figure 7-18, B Channel Aggregation is a mechanism for combining two or more B channels into a single ISDN pipe for the equivalent of 128 Kbps or greater bandwidth. You must use Multilink PPP (MP) to get the full bandwidth—otherwise, you have two separate 64-Kbps channels. Multilink PPP lets you load balance across the two B channels.

Figure 7-18 *Concept of B Channel Aggregation*

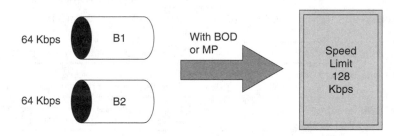

Bandwidth-on-demand (BOD) provides a dynamic method of enabling you to use only the communications bandwidth that is required to do the job. Today's flexible communications facilities allow a subsecond setup of calls, permitting the decision to obtain more bandwidth to be deferred until it's really needed.

Cisco IOS software offers two methods of combining the B channels to obtain BOD:

- Use a generic BOD, a Cisco proprietary implementation of BOD, which is based on a proprietary algorithm available in all systems that are running Cisco IOS Release 10.0 and later.
- Use MP to allocate additional bandwidth when needed.

Cisco Proprietary BOD

The Cisco proprietary BOD is triggered by outgoing traffic levels only. When the traffic level reaches a configured level, the access router assigns the other B channel to share the traffic.

If you have an access server that is connected to an ISDN BRI (2B+D) with BOD configured, only one B channel is usually used for communications. If you transfer a large file, the BOD feature senses the additional traffic and allocates a second B channel. The router load balances the traffic between the two B channels. When you finish transferring the file, the second B channel goes idle, which saves you connect time.

The dialer initiates another call to the destination if a packet is transmitted on a dialer interface and the transmission load on the interface exceeds the specified load threshold. The dialer then makes additional calls, as needed, to expand the bandwidth.

The **dialer load-threshold** command is used to configure (Cisco proprietary) bandwidth-on-demand by setting the maximum load before the dialer places another call to a destination. The following is an example of BOD configuration:

```
Router(config)#int bri 0
Router(config-if)#dialer load-threshold load
```

The *load* value is a number from 1 to 255 that is directly related to the bandwidth of the link, which can be specified by the **bandwidth** command. The lowest value, 1, brings up the second link instantaneously. Any value greater than 1 specifies how much bandwidth on the first B channel must be used before the second B channel is used for BOD. The bandwidth is defined as a ratio of 255, where 128 is 50 percent and 255 is 100 percent of the available bandwidth.

Load Average Calculation

Although the **load-interval** interface configuration command is often used for dial backup purposes to increase or decrease the likelihood of a backup interface being implemented, it can be used on any interface. The **load-interval** command allows you to change the default interval of five minutes to a shorter or longer period of time. If you change it to a shorter period of time, the input and output statistics that display when you use the **show interface** command will be more current and based on more instantaneous data, instead of reflecting a more average load over a longer period of time. The default is 300 seconds (five minutes). The new value has to be a multiple of 30, between 30 and 600 seconds.

Using BOD, the load calculation takes into consideration the outbound traffic exclusively. If you wish both inbound and outbound traffic to be used in the load calculation, use MP.

Multilink PPP

Cisco further enhanced bandwidth-on-demand by basing its implementation on industry-standard Multilink PPP (MP).

NOTE   Some Cisco documentations abbreviate Multilink PPP as MLP. Per RFC 1717 and 1990, the official abbreviation for Multilink PPP is MP.

The MP feature provides load balancing over multiple WAN links, while providing multivendor interoperability, packet fragmentation, proper sequencing, and load calculation on both inbound and outbound traffic. As shown in Figure 7-19, Cisco's implementation of MP supports the fragmentation and packet sequencing specified in RFC 1990, which replaces RFC 1717.

Figure 7-19   *Multilink PPP Fragmenting and Sequencing*

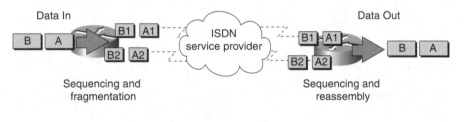

PPP Multilink Terminology

Even though PPP is a Layer 2 protocol and therefore should use the term **frame**, RFC 1990 defines individual fragments as **packets** for a multilink protocol.

MP-based bandwidth-on-demand is available in Cisco IOS Release 11.0 and later, and it is available in Cisco 700 series routers with Release 3.2 and later.

Multilink PPP allows packets to be fragmented and the fragments to be sent at the same time over multiple point-to-point links to the same remote address. The multiple links come up in response to a dialer load threshold that you define. The load can be calculated on inbound traffic, outbound traffic, or either, as needed for the traffic between the specific sites. MP provides bandwidth-on-demand and reduces transmission latency across WAN links.

Use the **dialer load-threshold** *load* command, which has the keywords **inbound**, **outbound**, or **either** for MP-based bandwidth-on-demand. For remote users, configure the load threshold outbound. Then, configure **ppp multilink**, which allows you to turn MP on or off. This command is placed either on the physical interface or in a dialer interface, depending on the interface type, quantity of interfaces configured, and whether dialer rotary groups or dialer profiles are used. The following is an example of multilink activation:

```
Router(config)#int bri 0
Router(config-if)#dialer load-threshold load [inbound ¦ outbound ¦ either ]
Router(config-if)#ppp multilink
```

The **ppp multilink** command can be configured on the following:

- Asynchronous serial interfaces in dialer rotary groups—Multilink PPP is configured in the dialer rotary interface (**int dialer** *number*).

- Individual BRIs—Multilink PPP is configured on the BRI interface (**int bri** *number*).

- Synchronous serial—Multilink PPP is configured on the serial interface (**int serial** *number*)

- Multiple BRIs in dialer rotary groups—Multilink PPP is configured in the dialer rotary interface (**int dialer** *number*), not on the BRI interfaces.

- Multiple BRIs in dialer profiles—For incoming calls, Multilink PPP is configured on the BRI interfaces. For outgoing calls, Multilink PPP is configured in the dialer interface. For both incoming and outgoing calls, Multilink PPP is configured on both the BRI and dialer interfaces.

- PRI B channels in dialer rotary groups—Multilink PPP is configured on the serial interfaces associated with the PRI interface.

NOTE   By default, both B channels of a BRI are in a two-link rotary group. PRIs can have up to 23 links per rotary group for T1 or 30 links for E1.

Example 7-4 illustrates the configuration of BRI 0 for MP.

Example 7-4   *BRI Interface Configured for Multilink PPP*

```
Router(config)#interface bri0
Router(config-if)#no ip address
Router(config-if)#encapsulation ppp
Router(config-if)#ppp multilink
Router(config-if)#dialer idle-timeout 30
Router(config-if)#dialer load-threshold 128 either
```

Configuring Load Threshold Value

You can configure only one end of a link for a load threshold. If you need to configure both the caller and answering routers (they might both have to perform DDR at multipoint), set the threshold at different values. If Router-A is set for an outbound threshold of 50 and the answering router—Router-B—is set for an inbound threshold of 50, they might both attempt to bring up the second link simultaneously. They thus get a busy signal from the other end. This is improbable with ISDN because the call setup is very low. It can, though, be a problem with slower call setup technologies, such as asynchronous links.

In small offices, use the **either** option for load threshold to ensure that the maximum of the inbound and outbound traffic is calculated as the load threshold. As shown in Example 7-5, if multiple rotary groups on a router are configured for multilink, one large bundle is created between the two routers, based on the authentication name (provided that the rotary group dials the same destination).

Example 7-5 *Rotary Group Interface Configured for Multilink PPP*

```
Router(config)#interface dialer1
Router(config-if)#ip address 10.10.10.7 255.255.255.0
Router(config-if)#encapsulation ppp
Router(config-if)#dialer idle-timeout 30
Router(config-if)#dialer map ip 10.10.10.8 name Router 81012345678901
Router(config-if)#dialer load-threshold 128 either
Router(config-if)#dialer-group 1
Router(config-if)#ppp authentication chap
Router(config-if)#ppp multilink
```

PPP authentication plays a part in Multilink PPP. The bundle decision is based on the authentication name of the remote router independently on each side of the link. Each router should use a unique hostname for authentication, with a shared password. If authentication is not configured correctly, Multilink PPP will not work correctly.

When single Multilink BRIs or a rotary group with multiple BRIs are calling a PRI, do not put a **dialer load-threshold** on the PRI or multiple BRI rotary group. Use the **dialer load-threshold** command on the single BRI interface to prevent attempts to bring up a third B channel to a single BRI destination.

ISDN Caller Identification

Calling-line identification screens incoming ISDN calls. The called number supplied in the call message setup request is verified against a table of allowed numbers. This feature prevents charges for calls from unauthorized numbers. In some situations, there are charges for call setup attempts. So, even if the call does not pass caller ID screening, there is a charge for the attempt.

NOTE Caller ID is available only from providers and switches that supply called number values during the call setup phase.

As shown in Figure 7-20, call acceptance does not occur until the router verifies the calling number.

Figure 7-20 *Caller Identification Process*

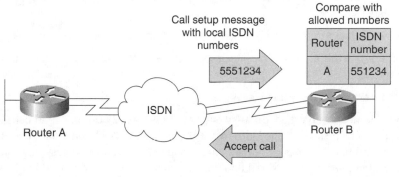

Caller ID screening requires a local switch that is capable of delivering the caller ID to the router or access server. If you enable caller ID screening, but do not have such a switch, no calls are allowed in. In addition, caller ID screening records the number exactly as it was sent, with or without an area code prefix.

The **isdn caller** command can be used to configure ISDN caller ID screening. The number is a telephone number, up to 25 characters in length. As part of this number, enter an *x* or *X* in any position in the number where you can accept any number as a match (a so-called **wildcard** or **don't-care digit**). You can specify up to 64 numbers per interface.

Called-Party Number Answering

Multiple devices can be physically connected at your site, as previously seen in Figure 7-9. You can ensure that only a single device answers an incoming call by verifying the number or subaddress in the incoming call against the device's configured number, subaddress, or both.

ISDN: SAPI and TEI

The SAPI and the TEI taken together create a unique identifier for a specific logical link, which, in turn, represents a specific TE. The TEI is a seven-bit number carried in the address field of the LAPD frame. Although the TEI seven-bit code allows up to 127 devices on an S-bus, there are limits to the number that you can attach: up to eight devices with the 5ess and NI-1 switches, and up to two devices for the DMS-100. Configuring multiple devices on an ISDN line is referred to as **ISDN Multipoint**.

You can specify that the router verify a called-party number or subaddress number in the incoming setup message for ISDN BRI calls, if the number is delivered by the switch. You can do this by configuring the number that is allowed. The following is the interface command that provides a verification of the called-party phone by using the number supplied in the call setup request:

```
Router(config-if)#isdn answer1 [called-party-number][:subaddress]
```

If you wish to allow an additional number for the router, you can configure it with the following command:

```
Router(config-if)#isdn answer2 [called-party-number][:subaddress]
```

If you do not specify the **isdn answer1** or **isdn answer2** command, all calls are processed or accepted. If you specify the **isdn answer1** or **isdn answer2** command, the router must verify the incoming called-party number and the subaddress before processing or accepting the call. The called-party number should not be mistaken for the number used by the router to initiate the call.

ISDN Rate Adaptation

Rate adaptation allows the ISDN channel to adjust to a lower speed, if requested in the call setup by the access router. You must, therefore, use the rate-adaptation feature for cases in which the destination does not use the default DS0 of 64 Kbps, but rather uses 56 Kbps. Figure 7-21 shows a connection with a reduced speed, which is set on the D channel during the call setup process. The manual assignment of calling speed is done on a per-destination basis. If not configured for the lower speed of 56 Kbps, the interface uses the default speed of 64 Kbps. The data rate can be adjusted to 56 Kbps if call setup requests it.

Figure 7-21 *ISDN Rate Adaptation, According to Destination*

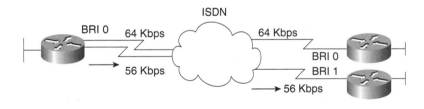

ISDN: 56 Kbps Speed Limit

The 56 Kbps data rate limitation comes from the restricted digital information (RDI) technique. This method stipulates that octets cannot have all zeroes. To meet the RDI requirement of having at least one bit turned on in each octet (called **one-density**), every eighth bit of each octet is set to on. If one bit per octet is borrowed, the data rate drops to 56 Kbps for an original 64 Kbps channel.

For ISDN interfaces only, you can specify an optional speed parameter for **dialer map** commands, as shown following. This option informs the ISDN software whether it should place a call at 56 Kbps or 64 Kbps. If you omit the ISDN speed parameter, the default is 64 Kbps, as follows:

```
Router(config-if)#dialer map protocol next-hop-address[name name]
[speed speed] [broadcast] dial-string
```

Symptoms of ISDN Speed Mismatch

A connection toward a specific destination being dropped following a connect ack might be a symptom that a rate adaptation is needed.

Monitoring the ISDN Interface

In this section, you will learn the commands used in monitoring ISDN interfaces, including their configuration and their performance.

The show interface bri Command

The **show interface bri** command displays information about the BRI D channel or about one or more B channels, provided that your router is a TE1 (has a native BRI), as shown in Example 7-6.

Example 7-6 *The **show interface bri 0** Command Displays D Channel Information*

```
Router#show interface bri 0
BRI0 is up, line protocol is up (spoofing)
  Hardware is BRI
   Description: B1:888-555-1212  B2:888-555-1213
   Internet address is 172.16.1.1/24
   MTU 1500 bytes, BW 64 Kbit, DLY 20000 usec, rely 255/255, load 1/255
   Encapsulation PPP, loopback not set
   Last input 00:00:04, output 00:00:04, output hang never
   Last clearing of "show interface" counters never
   Queueing strategy: fifo
   Output queue 0/40, 0 drops; input queue 0/75, 0 drops
   5 minute input rate 0 bits/sec, 0 packets/sec
   5 minute output rate 0 bits/sec, 0 packets/sec
      729700 packets input, 3621651 bytes, 0 no buffer
      Received 0 broadcasts, 0 runts, 0 giants, 0 throttles
      2 input errors, 0 CRC, 0 frame, 0 overrun, 0 ignored, 2 abort
      809365 packets output, 4050309 bytes, 0 underruns
      0 output errors, 0 collisions, 10 interface resets
      0 output buffer failures, 0 output buffers swapped out
      8 carrier transitions
```

So, if your router acts as a TEI (has a native BRI), use the **show interface bri** command to monitor the interface and the first B channel.

If, on the other hand, the router is a TE2 (has an external terminal adapter), use the **show interface serial** command.

Why Is the Router Spoofing?

The word **spoofing** indicates that the line is not necessarily up, but the dialer is forcing the line to masquerade as up. Spoofing is a state to allow DDR to work (other states are up, down, and so on). The interface dials-on-demand in response to the packets being routed to it. But because no packets are routed to down interfaces, the interface must pretend to be up (spoof), so that packets will be routed to it when it is not connected. By default, a router removes any routes pointing to down interfaces from its routing table. DDR interfaces with BRI remain in spoofing state, even when one or both B channels are up.

The command to display the B1 information is **show interface bri 0 1 2**. Example 7-7 displays information on both B channels.

Example 7-7   *The* show **interface bri 0 1 2** *Command Displays Information On Both B Channels*

```
Router#show interface bri 0 1 2
Router>sh int bri 0 1 2
BRI0:1 is up, line protocol is up
  Hardware is BRI
  MTU 1500 bytes, BW 64 Kbit, DLY 20000 usec, rely 255/255, load 39/255
  Encapsulation PPP, loopback not set, keepalive set (10 sec)
  LCP Open, multilink Open
  Last input 00:00:00, output 00:00:00, output hang never
  Last clearing of "show interface" counters never
  Queueing strategy: fifo
  Output queue 0/40, 0 drops; input queue 4/75, 0 drops
  5 minute input rate 9000 bits/sec, 4 packets/sec
  5 minute output rate 10000 bits/sec, 4 packets/sec
     1116649 packets input, 56234180 bytes, 0 no buffer
     Received 0 broadcasts, 0 runts, 0 giants, 0 throttles
     20 input errors, 7 CRC, 0 frame, 0 overrun, 0 ignored, 13 abort
     1096705 packets output, 39131602 bytes, 0 underruns
     0 output errors, 0 collisions, 7 interface resets
     0 output buffer failures, 0 output buffers swapped out
     24 carrier transitions
BRI0:2 is up, line protocol is down
  Hardware is BRI
  MTU 1500 bytes, BW 64 Kbit, DLY 20000 usec, rely 255/255, load 1/255
  Encapsulation PPP, loopback not set, keepalive set (10 sec)
  LCP Open, multilink Closed
  Closed: VINESCP, XNSCP, IPCP, CCP, CDP, BRIDGECP, LLC2, ATALKCP, IPXCP
          NBFCP
```

Example 7-7 *The* show **interface bri 0 1 2** *Command Displays Information On Both B Channels (Continued)*

```
Last input 00:20:07, output 00:19:19, output hang never
Last clearing of "show interface" counters never
Queueing strategy: fifo
Output queue 40/40, 51 drops; input queue 0/75, 0 drops
5 minute input rate 0 bits/sec, 0 packets/sec
5 minute output rate 0 bits/sec, 0 packets/sec
    1113092 packets input, 55047875 bytes, 0 no buffer
    Received 0 broadcasts, 0 runts, 0 giants, 0 throttles
    61 input errors, 4 CRC, 0 frame, 0 overrun, 0 ignored, 57 abort
    1093367 packets output, 37971979 bytes, 0 underruns
    0 output errors, 0 collisions, 7 interface resets
    0 output buffer failures, 0 output buffers swapped out
    19 carrier transitions
```

The show isdn status Command

The **show isdn status** command displays information about memory, Layer 2 and Layer 3 timers, and the status of PRI channels, as shown in Example 7-8

Author's Note

Example 7-8 is the actual screen output of a MAN router connected to a basic-NI1 switch. The ISDN switch, located at the CO, has allocated an individual TEI number for each B channel.

Example 7-8 *This example Shows the B1 Channel as Established and the B2 Channel in an Initiating Mode*

```
Router#show isdn status
The current ISDN Switchtype = basic-ni1
ISDN BRI0 interface
    Layer 1 Status:
        ACTIVE
    Layer 2 Status:
        TEI = 109, State = MULTIPLE_FRAME_ESTABLISHED
        TEI = 111, State = MULTIPLE_FRAME_ESTABLISHED
    Spid Status:
        TEI 109, ces = 1, state = 8(established)
            spid1 configured, no LDN, spid1 sent, spid1 valid
            Endpoint ID Info: epsf = 0, usid = 70, tid = 0
        TEI 111, ces = 2, state = 5(init)
            spid2 configured, no LDN, spid2 sent, spid2 valid
            Endpoint ID Info: epsf = 0, usid = 71, tid = 0
    Layer 3 Status:
        1 Active Layer 3 Call(s)
    Activated dsl 0 CCBs = 1
        CCB:callid=9800, sapi=0, ces=1, B-chan=1
    Total Allocated ISDN CCBs = 1
```

Some options that you have with the **show isdn status** are as follows:

Command	Description
show isdn status {**memory**	**timers**	**services**}	The **show isdn status** command output displayed provides the output from the logical link Layers 1, 2, and 3.
memory	This command displays memory pool statistics. This keyword is for use by technical development staff only.
timers	This command displays the values of Layer 2 and Layer 3 timers.
services	This command displays the status of PRI channels.

Verifying PPP Multilink

Example 7-9 shows an output of the **show ppp multilink** command. It displays bundle information on a rotary group in the packet multiplexing section, including the number of members in a bundle and the bundle to which a link belongs.

Example 7-9 *An Example of the* **show ppp multilink** *Command Output When Two Active Bundles Are On a System*

```
router#show ppp multilink
Bundle rudder, 3 members, first link is BRI0: B channel 1
  0 lost fragments, 8 reordered, 0 unassigned, sequence 0x1E/0x1E rcvd/sent
Bundle dallas, 4 members, first link is BRI2: B channel 1
  0 lost fragments, 28 reordered, 0 unassigned, sequence 0x12E/0x12E rcvd/sent
```

The **show interface** command also displays information on the status of multilink. As shown by the bolded portion of the screen output in Example 7-10, only the B1 channel has its LCP up. Also, the B1 channel shows the NCP as being open, whereas the B2 channel shows the NCP as being closed because the second link has not come up yet.

Multilink Bundles

The multilink field shows the status as open if multilink is *enabled*, but not necessary when links are bundled.

Example 7-10 *The* **show ppp multilink** *and* **show interface** *Commands*

```
NorthShore>show ppp multilink
Bundle SouthShore, 1 member, Master link is Virtual-Access1
Dialer Interface is BRI0
  0 lost fragments, 0 reordered, 0 unassigned, sequence 0x0/0x0 rcvd/sent
```

Example 7-10 *The* **show ppp multilink** *and* **show interface** *Commands (Continued)*

```
    0 discarded, 0 lost received, 1/255 load
Member Link: 1
BRI0:1
NorthShore>show interface bri 0 1 2
BRI0:1 is up, line protocol is up
  Hardware is BRI
  MTU 1500 bytes, BW 64 Kbit, DLY 20000 usec, rely 255/255, load 1/255
  Encapsulation PPP, loopback not set, keepalive set (10 sec)
  LCP Open, multilink Open
  Last input 00:00:01, output 00:00:01, output hang never
  Last clearing of "show interface" counters never
  Queueing strategy: fifo
  Output queue 0/40, 0 drops; input queue 3/75, 0 drops
  5 minute input rate 0 bits/sec, 0 packets/sec
  5 minute output rate 0 bits/sec, 0 packets/sec
     10814 packets input, 898050 bytes, 0 no buffer
     Received 0 broadcasts, 0 runts, 0 giants, 0 throttles
     0 input errors, 0 CRC, 0 frame, 0 overrun, 0 ignored, 0 abort
     8367 packets output, 779118 bytes, 0 underruns
     0 output errors, 0 collisions, 7 interface resets
     0 output buffer failures, 0 output buffers swapped out
     3 carrier transitions
BRI0:2 is down, line protocol is down
  Hardware is BRI
  MTU 1500 bytes, BW 64 Kbit, DLY 20000 usec, rely 255/255, load 1/255
  Encapsulation PPP, loopback not set, keepalive set (10 sec)
  LCP Closed, multilink Closed
  Closed: VINESCP, IPCP, CDP, NBFCP
  Last input never, output never, output hang never
  Last clearing of "show interface" counters never
  Queueing strategy: fifo
  Output queue 0/40, 0 drops; input queue 0/75, 0 drops
  5 minute input rate 0 bits/sec, 0 packets/sec
  5 minute output rate 0 bits/sec, 0 packets/sec
     0 packets input, 0 bytes, 0 no buffer
     Received 0 broadcasts, 0 runts, 0 giants, 0 throttles
     0 input errors, 0 CRC, 0 frame, 0 overrun, 0 ignored, 0 abort
     0 packets output, 0 bytes, 0 underruns
     0 output errors, 0 collisions, 7 interface resets
     0 output buffer failures, 0 output buffers swapped out
     54 carrier transitions
```

In the previous screen output, you can see that B1 is up, but B2 is still down. Also notice that the LCP list Multilink is opened for B1. The multilink open state appears once the interface is configured for PPP Multilink, regardless of whether other links have joined the bundle.

Troubleshooting Multilink PPP

The **debug dialer** command indicates whether the multilink is up after authentication. As shown in Example 7-11, the **debug dialer** command also shows when the overload occurs.

Example 7-11 *Verifying that the Second B Channel is Coming Up with* **debug dialer**

```
BranchF#debug dialer
BranchF#ping 10.115.0.135
Type escape sequence to abort.
Sending 5, 100-byte ICMP Echos to 10.115.0.135, timeout is 2 seconds:
BRI0: Dialing cause ip (s=10.155.0.1, d=10.115.0.135)
BRI0: Attempting to dial 6000
%LINK-3-UPDOWN: Interface BRI0:2, changed state to up
dialer Protocol up for BR0:2.
%LINEPROTO-5-UPDOWN: Line protocol on Interface BRI0:2, changed state to
up!!!!
Success rate is 80 percent (4/5), round-trip min/avg/max = 32/34/36 ms
BranchF#
BRI0: rotary group to 6000 overloaded (1)
BRI0: Attempting to dial 6000
%ISDN-6-CONNECT: Interface BRI0:2 is now connected to 6000 CentralF
```

If the second link fails to come up, use Table 7-6 to troubleshoot your Multilink PPP configuration.

Table 7-6 *Multilink Troubleshooting*

Problem	Solution
Multilink is open, but no data is passing.	Check **dialer map** statements, and verify that routing is on.
The last link of a bundle dials but never connects.	Check the **debug isdn q931**, **debug modem**, or **debug chat** command output for asynchronous application operation. You might also use the new **debug ppp multilink events** command for help. Multilink may not be enabled.
Data throughput is low.	Verify that fair queuing is not enabled.

Following are different debugging commands that are used to monitor Multilink PPP in an ISDN DDR environment:

- The **debug ppp multilink** command displays packet sequence numbers. It is only useful as a last resort because it does not help troubleshoot when connections are not being bundled.
- The **debug ppp negotiation** command displays the MRRU option negotiation.
- The **debug ppp authentication** command is useful for displaying the steps in the PPP authentication process.

- The **debug isdn events** command also displays information that is useful for monitoring and troubleshooting Multilink PPP.

ISDN debug Commands

The following are debug commands that are helpful when troubleshooting ISDN. Two other ISDN debug commands are **debug isdn q921** and **debug isdn q931**.

ISDN Q921

As shown in Example 7-12, you may use the **debug isdn q921** EXEC command to display data link layer (Layer 2) access procedures that are taking place at the access router on the D channel (LAPD) of its ISDN interface. This command is useful when you want to observe signaling events between the access router and the ISDN switch. The ISDN data link layer interface, provided by the access router, conforms to the user interface specification defined by ITU-T recommendation Q.921.

Example 7-12 *Debugging the ISDN Q921 Message On a Calling Router*

```
SouthShore#debug isdn q921
ISDN BR0: RX <-  SETUP pd = 8  callref = 0x41
        Bearer Capability i = 0x8890
        Channel ID i = 0x8A
        Signal i = 0x40 - Alerting on - pattern 0
        Calling Party Number i = 0x0083, '8885551212'
        Called Party Number i = 0xC1, '5551213'
        Locking Shift to Codeset 5
        Codeset 5 IE 0x2A  i = 0x808D0E, 0x8001068B0A, '8885551212'
➥0x80010A800114800114
ISDN BR0: TX ->  RELEASE_COMP pd = 8  callref = 0xC1
        Cause i = 0x00A2 - No channel available
ISDN BR0: RX <-  SETUP pd = 8  callref = 0x41
        Bearer Capability i = 0x8890
        Channel ID i = 0x8A
        Signal i = 0x40 - Alerting on - pattern 0
        Calling Party Number i = 0x0083, '8885551212'
        Called Party Number i = 0xC1, '5551213'
        Locking Shift to Codeset 5
        Codeset 5 IE 0x2A  i = 0x808D0E, 0x8001068B0A, '8885551212'
0x80010A800114800114
ISDN BR0: TX ->  RELEASE_COMP pd = 8  callref = 0xC1
        Cause i = 0x80A2 - No channel available
SouthShore#
```

The **debug isdn q921** command output is limited to the commands and responses exchanged during peer-to-peer communication carried over the D channel. This debug information does not include data transmitted over the B channels that are also part of the router's ISDN interface.

The peers (data link layer entities and layer management entities on the routers) communicate with each other via an ISDN switch over the D channel.

This command can be used with the **debug isdn event** and the **debug isdn q931** commands at the same time. The displays will be intermingled.

ISDN Q931

You may use the **debug isdn q931** EXEC command to display information about call setup and teardown of ISDN network connections (Layer 3) between the local router (user side) and the network. The ISDN network layer interface provided by the access router conforms to the user interface specification defined by ITU-T recommendation Q.931, which is supplemented by other specifications, such as those for switch types VN2 and VN3. The router tracks only activities that occur on the user side (not the network side) of the network connection.

The display information of the **debug isdn q931** command output is limited to the commands and responses exchanged during peer-to-peer communication carried over the D channel. This debug information does not include data transmitted over the B channels. The peers (network layers) communicate with each other via an ISDN switch over the D channel.

You may also use this command with the **debug isdn event** and the **debug isdn q921** commands at the same time, but the display will be intermingled.

Other ISDN debugging commands available are **debug isdn active** (to show active calls) and **debug isdn history** (to see previous activities).

Table 7-7 presents a graphical representation of the different debug commands and their relation to the OSI model.

Table 7-7   *ISDN and DDR Debugging*

OSI Layer	ISDN	Dialer
3	**debug isdn q931**	**debug dialer** **debug ip packet**
2	**debug isdn events** **debug isdn active** **debug isdn history** **debug isdn q921**	**debug ppp negotiation** **debug ppp authentication**

ISDN Primary Rate Interface

As mentioned at the beginning of this chapter, T1 and E1 provide two-way service over telephone-switching networks. This section describes the tasks that are required to get ISDN PRI up and running.

PRI configuration tasks are as follows:

1 Specify the correct PRI switch type that the router interfaces with at the provider's Central office.

2 Specify the T1/E1 controller, framing type, and line coding for the provider's facility.

3 Set a PRI group timeslot for the T1/E1 facility and indicate the speed used.

4 Identify the interface that you will configure to act with DDR.

Selecting the PRI Switch

You have to use the **isdn switch-type** command to specify the CO PRI switch to which the router connects.

```
Router(config)#isdn switch-type [switch type]
```

With Cisco IOS Release 11.3(3)T, this command is also available as a controller command to allow different switches to be supported on different controllers. If configured as a global command, the specified switch type applies to all controllers. Table 7-8 lists the options for the PRI **isdn switch-type** command.

Table 7-8   *ISDN PRI Switch Types*

isdn switch-type Command	Description
pri-4ess	AT&T 4ESS-Primary switches (U.S.)
pri-5ess	AT&T 5ESS-Primary switches (U.S.)
pri-dms100	NT DMS-100 switches (North America)
pri-ntt	NTT ISDN PRI switches (Japan)
pri-net5	European ISDN PRI switches
None	No switch defined

NOTE   An incompatible switch-selection configuration can result in failure to make ISDN calls. Reloading the router after changing the switch type is required to make the new configuration effective.

Selecting the ISDN PRI Controller for Configuration

The **controller** {**t1** | **e1**} *slot/port* global command identifies a Cisco 7000 family or Cisco 3600 series controller. Use a single *unit number* for the Cisco 4000 series or AS5000 series controllers:

```
Router(config)#controller {t1 ¦ e1} {slot/port  ¦ unit number}
```

controller Command	Description
t1	The controller interface for North American and Japanese facility interfaces.
e1	The controller interface for European facilities and facilities that are used in much of the rest of the world.
slot/port or *unit number*	Specifies the physical slot/port location or unit number of the controller.

Configuring the Framing, Linecoding, and Clocking of the Controller

The **framing** controller configuration command is used to select the frame type used by the PRI service provider:

```
Router(config-controller)#framing {sf ¦ esf ¦ crc4 ¦ no-crc4}
```

framing Command	Description
sf	This is the super frame that is used for some older T1 configurations.
esf	This is the extended super frame that is used for T1 PRI configurations.
crc4 or **no-crc4**	This is the cyclic redundancy check 4 that is used for E1 PRI configurations.

Use the **linecode** command to identify the physical-layer signaling method to satisfy the ones density requirement on the provider's digital facility. Without a sufficient number of ones in the digital bitstream, the switches and multiplexers in a WAN can lose their synchronization for transmitting signals.

```
Router(config-controller)#linecode {ami ¦ b8zs¦ hdb3}
```

linecode Command	Description
ami	This is the alternate mark inversion that is used for T1 configurations.
b8zs	This is the binary 8-zero substitution that is used for T1 PRI configurations.
hdb3	This is the High-Density Bipolar 3 that is used for E1 PRI configurations.

Binary 8-zero substitution (b8zs) accommodates the ones density requirements for T1 carrier facilities, using special bipolar signals encoded over the digital transmission link. It allows 64 Kbps (clear channel) for ISDN channels.

Settings for these two Cisco IOS software controller commands on the router must match the framing and linecode types used at the T1/E1 WAN provider's CO switch.

Use the **clock source** command **line** and **internal** options to configure the T1 clock source for the Cisco 7000 family, and the Cisco 3600 and Cisco 4000 series modules. The AS5000 series uses the **line primary** and **secondary** version of the command to select either the primary or secondary TDM as the clock source. With two controllers in an AS5000 series access server, one will be primary and one will be secondary. With four controllers, one will still be primary with multiple secondaries.

```
Router(config-controller)#clock source {line [primary ¦ secondary] ¦ internal}
```

The following are the usual configurations:

For T1	**framing esf** and **linecode b8zs**
For E1	**framing crc4** and **linecode hdb3**

NOTE   One instance in which you would use **clock source internal** is when two routers are connected back-to-back in a test environment.

Additional ISDN PRI Configuration Parameters

Additional ISDN PRI configuration parameters include the following:

- **pri-group** command
- D channel selection
- Accepting analog calls

The **pri-group** Command

The **pri-group** command configures the specified interface for PRI operation and how many fixed timeslots are allocated on the provider's digital facility.

```
Router(config-controller)#pri-group [timeslots range]
```

Command	Description
pri-group [*timeslots range*]	This is the number of timeslots allocated to this PRI. For T1, use values in the range of 1 to 24; for E1, use values from 1 to 31. The speed of the PRI is the aggregate of the channels assigned

D Channel Selection

The **interface serial** command specifies an interface for PRI D channel operation. The interface is a serial interface to a T1/E1 on the router or access server:

```
Router(config)#interface serial { slot/port: ¦ unit:}{23 ¦ 15}
```

interface serial Command	Description
slot/port	This is the slot/port on the Cisco 7000 family or 3600 series router of the channelized controller, for which this interface represents the D channel.
unit	This is the unit number on the Cisco 4000 or AS5000 series of the channelized controller, for which this interface represents the D channel.
23	This is a T1 interface that designates channelized DS0s 0 to 22 as the B channels and DS0 23 as the D channel.
15	This is an E1 interface that designates 30 B channels and timeslot 16 as the D channel.

WARNING Within an E1 or T1 facility, the channels start numbering at 1 (1 to 31 for E1 and 1 to 24 for T1). Serial interfaces in the Cisco router start numbering at 0. Therefore, channel 16, the E1 signaling channel, is serial port subinterface 15. Channel 24, the T1 signaling channel, becomes serial subinterface 23.

Accepting Analog Calls

The **isdn incoming-voice modem** command allows incoming analog calls to be switched to internal modems that are installed on a digital network module. Software examines the bearer capability fields of the D channel data, and determines whether a call is a normal ISDN call or an analog call being carried on an ISDN B channel. If it is an analog call, it is switched to internal modems. This command is available only for those access servers with the capability for internal modems:

```
Router(config-if)#isdn incoming-voice modem
```

Digital Modems for Analog Calls

Digital modem network modules do not provide network interfaces of their own; they handle analog calls passing through other router interfaces instead. In addition to the digital modem module, the router must contain a PRI network module to connect to the ISDN channel; and must contain another module, such as Ethernet, to provide connectivity to the LAN. The PRI module concurrently handles digital ISDN data connections and remote voice-channel (analog) modem connections, allowing a dynamic mix of digital and modem connections. The digital modem module acts as a pool of available modems that can be used for both incoming and outgoing calls. For more information on digital modems, please visit www.cisco.com.

PRI Configuration Example

PRI includes an extra element that is not present with BRI: the controller, which requires configuration. Figure 7-22 shows a sample network for this PRI configuration example. Example 7-13 presents the controller and interface configuration for ISDN PRI.

Figure 7-22 *Sample Topology for PRI Configuration*

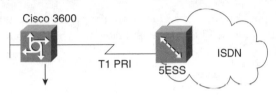

Example 7-13 *Both the Controller and the Interface Require Configuration Parameters for PRI*

```
isdn switch-type primary-5ess
!
controller t1 1/0
pri-group timeslots 1-24
framing esf
linecode b8zs
clock source line primary
!
interface serial 0/0:23
ip address 192.168.11.2 255.255.255.0
isdn incoming-voice modem
```

Table 7-9 describes portions of the configuration presented in Example 7-13.

Table 7-9   *PRI Example Command Descriptions*

Command	Description
isdn switch-type primary-5ess	This command elects a switch type of 5ESS.
controller t1 1/0	This command selects the T1 controller 1/0.
pri-group timeslots 1-24	This command establishes the interface port to function as PRI, with 23 timeslots designated to operate at a speed of 64 Kbps.
framing esf	This command selects esf framing, which is a T1 configuration feature.
linecode b8zs	This command selects **linecode b8zs** for T1.
clock source line	This command specifies the T1 line as the clock source for the 3600.
interface serial 0/0:23	This command uses serial interface 0/0. Subinterface 23 has the D channel (T1).

NOTE   Static mapping and DDR commands are also used for configuring PRI. Although they are also required for ISDN operation, these other commands are omitted from this example because they have been extensively covered in the BRI section of this chapter.

The **controller t1 0** command configures the T1 controller. In the example, the switch type selected is an AT&T model. This example is accurate for some operations in the United States.

Static route statements and DDR commands comparable to BRI are necessary to complete a true PRI configuration.

For an E1 example, the timeslot argument for the **pri-group** command would be **1-31** rather than **1-24,** as shown for a T1 example; and the interface command would be **0/0:15** instead of **0/0:23**.

Summary

In this chapter, you learned the difference between ISDN BRI and PRI, and how to select either one of these services, depending on the applications. The signaling and call sequences of the Q921 and Q931 protocols were examined. A significant portion of the chapter was spent on how to configure and troubleshoot ISDN for dial-on-demand routing and to accept calls.

In the next chapter, you will learn how to optimize the configuration of dial-on-demand routing.

Case Study—Using ISDN and DDR to Enhance Remote Connectivity

Complete the tasks of this case study, review the case study solution section that follows to see how you did, and see where you might need to review the concepts presented in this chapter.

The objective of this case study is to configure a branch office to place a call to the Central office router, as shown in Figure 7-23. You will also see how to configure the Central office equipment to accept an incoming call from the branch office router.

Figure 7-23 *Case Study Sample Network*

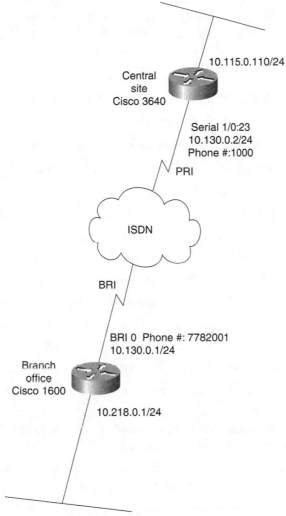

In this case study, you will learn how to do the following:

- Configure ISDN BRI and Legacy DDR on the branch office.
- Configure ISDN PRI and Legacy DDR on the Central site router.
- Place an ISDN BRI to ISDN PRI call from the branch office.

NOTE   Legacy DDR is defined by Cisco as configurations, which uses **dialer map** statements.

Scenario

Given a Central site Cisco-IOS router with ISDN PRI capability and a branch office site Cisco-IOS router with ISDN BRI capability, configure both routers so that you can place an ISDN call between your two company sites.

Task 1—Configuring ISDN BRI On Your Branch Office Router

Complete the following steps on your branch office router:

Step 1 Enter configuration mode for your branch office router.

Step 2 Enter an initial configuration to configure the Central router:

1 Configure the hostname **BranchA** on your branch router.

2 Configure the router to prevent the lookup of misspelled commands.

3 Activate IGRP with the autonomous system number **100**, and ensure that no routing updates will be sent out of interface BRI 0.

4 Configure the enable secret password to be **cisco**.

5 Revive the E 0 interface and provide it with the IP address of **10.218.0.1** with a mask of 24 bits.

6 Configure the line VTY 0 to 4 to request a login with the **cisco** password.

Step 3 In global configuration mode, complete the following steps:

1 Configure the ISDN switch type specified by the telephone company (5ess for this case study).

2 Configure the username of the router to be dialed into, and configure the password to be used. Use **cisco** as the password.

3 Configure the dialer-list to specify the type of interesting traffic that will generate a call to the remote router.

4 Specify the static route to the Central site router's Ethernet 0 interface. Use the Ethernet address of the Central site router.

5 Begin the configuration of the BRI0 interface.

6 Configure the transmission (encapsulation) protocol to be used on this interface to be PPP.

7 Configure PPP data transmission to use CHAP as the authentication protocol for attaching stations.

8 Configure the BRI0 IP address.

9 Assign dialer-list 1 to BRI0.

10   Configure the dialer idle time.

11   Configure a dialer map statement using the PRI address, name of the Central site router, and phone number (this case study uses a four-digit phone number, which simulates subscribing to an ISDN speed dial service).

12   Set the BRI0 interface to active mode.

Step 4   At the end of any configuration, you should monitor your router's performance and behavior. Once you are satisfied with the changes you make, you can save your running configuration with the **copy run start** command.

Step 5   Use the appropriate commands to view the current status of your router's ISDN interface and connections.

Step 6   Turn off ISDN Q.921 debugging.

Task 2—Configuring ISDN PRI on Your Central Site Router

Complete the following steps on your Central site router:

Step 1   Enter configuration mode for your Central site router.

Step 2   Enter the following configuration commands:

1   Configure the ISDN switch type specified by the telephone company (in this case study, you will pretend to be using a primary-5ess).

2   Configure the username of your branch router to be dialed into and the password to be used. Use **cisco** as the password.

3   Configure the dialer-list to specify the type of interesting traffic that will generate a call to the remote router.

4   Specify a static route to the branch office router's Ethernet subnet via its BRI address.

5   Begin the configuration of the T1 interface.

6   Select the linecode type on the T1 line. In this case study, you use **b8zs**.

7   Specify that the interface will clock its transmitted data from a clock recovered from the line's receive data stream.

8   Select the frame type on your T1 line. In this case study, you use the extended super frame format.

9   Enable PRI on your T1 interface to use all 24 channels. Once entered, you will see the 24 channels enabled.

10 Enter the interface configuration mode for the D channel.

11 Configure the transmission (encapsulation) protocol to be used on this interface to be PPP.

12 Configure PPP data transmission to use CHAP as the authentication protocol for attaching stations.

13 Configure the T1 1/0 IP address.

14 Assign dialer-list 1 to T1 1/0.

15 Configure the dialer idle time.

16 Configure a dialer map statement, using the BRI 0 address and name of the branch office router. (Contrary to the branch office router, our Central site does not subscribe to the telco's speed dial service. Therefore, all seven digits of the phone number must be configured to reach the branch office.)

Step 3 Specify that IGRP routing updates will not be sent out of the PRI interface, and that static routes will be redistributed in IGRP.

Step 4 At this point, you usually exit all configurations and save your running configuration.

Step 5 Use the appropriate commands to view the current status of your router's ISDN interface and connections.

Step 6 Turn off ISDN Q.921 debugging.

Task 3—Verifying the ISDN Connection

Step 1 Look at your running configuration on the branch router.

Step 2 Look at your running configuration on the Central site router.

Step 3 From the branch office router, enter the appropriate command to send data to the Ethernet interface of your Central site router. Repeat the test in the other direction. If you turn on Q.931 debugging, you will also see the ISDN call progress.

Solution to Case Study—Using ISDN and DDR to Enhance Remote Connectivity

The following is a step-by-step discussion of the case study solution.

Task 1 Solution—Configuring ISDN BRI on your Branch Office Router

Complete the following steps on your branch office router:

Step 1   Enter configuration mode for your branch office router.

Step 2   Enter an initial configuration using the following commands:

```
hostname BranchA
no ip domain-lookup          Do not look up misspelled commands.
router igrp 100
network 10.0.0.0
passive-interface bri 0      So routing updates do not trigger calls.
enable secret cisco
int e0
ip address 10.218.0.1 255.255.255.0
no shut
line console 0
no exec-timeout
line vty 0 4                 In the previous case study, you saw how to
login                        use a local database for login. Here you
password cisco               see a example of where a line password
                             is used to authenticate users.
```

Step 3   In global configuration mode, enter the following configuration commands:

1   Configure the ISDN switch type specified by the telephone company (5ess for this case study):

```
BranchA(config)#isdn switch-type basic-5ess
```

2   Configure the username of the router to be dialed into and the password to be used. Use **cisco** as the password:

```
BranchA(config)#username CentralA password cisco
```

3   Configure the dialer-list to specify the type of interesting traffic that will generate a call to the remote router:

```
BranchA(config)#dialer-list 1 protocol ip permit
```

4   Specify the static route to the Central site router's Ethernet 0 interface. Use the Ethernet address of the Central site router:

```
BranchA(config)#ip route 10.115.0.0 255.255.255.0 10.130.0.2
```

5   Begin the configuration of the BRI0 interface:

```
BranchA(config)#int bri 0
```

6   Configure the transmission (encapsulation) protocol to be used on this interface to be PPP:

```
BranchA(config-if)#encap ppp
```

7   Configure PPP data transmission to use CHAP as the authentication protocol for attaching stations:

```
BranchA(config-if)#ppp authentication chap
```

8   Configure the BRI0 IP address:

```
BranchA(config-if)#ip address 10.130.0.1 255.255.255.0
```

9   Assign dialer-list 1 to BRI0:

```
BranchA(config-if)#dialer-group 1
```

10   Configure the dialer idle time:

```
BranchA(config-if)#dialer idle-timeout 60
```

11   Configure a dialer map statement using the PRI address, name of the Central site router, and phone number (this case study uses a four-digit phone number, which simulates that you are subscribing to an ISDN speed dial service):

```
BranchA(config-if)#dialer map ip 10.130.0.2 name CentralA 1000
```

12   Set the BRI0 interface to active mode:

```
BranchA(config-if)#no shut
```

Step 4   At the end of any configuration, you should monitor your router's performance and behavior. Once you are satisfied with the changes you make, you can save your running configuration with the **copy run start** command.

Step 5   You can use the following commands to view the current status of your router's ISDN interface and connections:

- **show isdn status**
- **show interface bri 0**
- **debug isdn q921**

Example 7-14 displays the output of these commands.

Example 7-14 *Viewing the Status of the Branch Office Router*

```
BranchA#sh isdn status
Global ISDN Switchtype = basic-5ess
ISDN BRI0 interface
dsl 0, interface ISDN Switchtype = basic-5ess
Layer 1 Status:
ACTIVE
Layer 2 Status:
TEI = 64, Ces = 1, SAPI = 0, State = MULTIPLE_FRAME_ESTABLISHED
Layer 3 Status:
0 Active Layer 3 Call(s)
Activated dsl 0 CCBs = 0
Total Allocated ISDN CCBs = 0

BranchA#sh int bri 0
BRI0 is up, line protocol is up (spoofing)
```

Example 7-14 *Viewing the Status of the Branch Office Router (Continued)*

```
Hardware is BRI
Internet address is 10.130.0.1/24
MTU 1500 bytes, BW 64 Kbit, DLY 20000 usec, rely 255/255, load 1/255
Encapsulation PPP, loopback not set
Last input 00:00:08, output never, output hang never
Last clearing of "show interface" counters never
Input queue: 0/75/0 (size/max/drops); Total output drops: 0
Queueing strategy: weighted fair
Output queue: 0/1000/64/0 (size/max total/threshold/drops)
Conversations 0/1/256 (active/max active/max total)
Reserved Conversations 0/0 (allocated/max allocated)
5 minute input rate 0 bits/sec, 0 packets/sec
5 minute output rate 0 bits/sec, 0 packets/sec
10 packets input, 59 bytes, 0 no buffer
Received 5 broadcasts, 0 runts, 0 giants, 0 throttles
0 input errors, 0 CRC, 0 frame, 0 overrun, 0 ignored, 0 abort
10 packets output, 59 bytes, 0 underruns
0 output errors, 0 collisions, 2 interface resets
0 output buffer failures, 0 output buffers swapped out
1 carrier transitions

BranchA#debug isdn q921
ISDN Q921 packets debugging is on
BranchA#
ISDN BR0: RX <- IDCKRQ ri = 0 ai = 64
ISDN BR0: TX -> IDCKRP ri = 31815 ai = 64
ISDN BR0: RX <- IDCKRQ ri = 0 ai = 64
ISDN BR0: TX -> IDCKRP ri = 16568 ai = 64
ISDN BR0: RX <- RRp sapi = 0 tei = 64 nr = 0
ISDN BR0: TX -> RRf sapi = 0 tei = 64 nr = 0
ISDN BR0: RX <- RRp sapi = 0 tei = 64 nr = 0
ISDN BR0: TX -> RRf sapi = 0 tei = 64 nr = 0
```

Step 6   Turn off ISDN Q.921 debugging. To do so, use the **no debug isdn q921**, **no debug all**, or **undebug all** command.

Task 2 Solution—Configuring ISDN PRI on Your Central Site Router

Complete the following steps on your Central site router:

Step 1   Enter configuration mode for your Central site router.

Step 2   Enter the following configuration commands:

1   Configure the ISDN switch type specified by the telephone company (in this case study, you pretend to be using a primary-5ess):

```
CentralA(config)#isdn switch-type primary-5ess
```

2 Configure the username of your branch router to be dialed into and the password to be used. Use **cisco** as the password:

```
CentralA(config)#username BranchA password cisco
```

3 Configure the dialer-list to specify the type of interesting traffic that will generate a call to the remote router:

```
CentralA(config)#dialer-list 1 protocol ip permit
```

4 Specify a static route to the branch office router's Ethernet subnet via its BRI address:

```
CentralA(config)#ip route 10.218.0.0  255.255.255.0  10.130.0.1
```

5 Begin the configuration of the T1 interface:

```
CentralA(config)#controller t1 1/0
```

6 Select the linecode type on the T1 line. In this case study, you use **b8zs**:

```
CentralA(config-controller)#linecode b8zs
```

7 Specify that the interface will clock its transmitted data from a clock recovered from the line's receive data stream:

```
CentralA(config-controller)#clock source line
```

8 Select the frame type on your T1 line. In this case study, you use the extended super frame format:

```
CentralA(config-controller)#framing esf
```

9 Enable PRI on your T1 interface to use all 24 channels. Once entered, you see the 24 channels enabled:

```
CentralA(config-controller)#pri-group timeslots 1-24
```

10 Enter interface configuration mode for the D channel:

```
CentralA(config)#int serial 1/0:23
```

11 Configure the transmission (encapsulation) protocol to be used on this interface to be PPP:

```
CentralA(config-if)#encap ppp
```

12 Configure PPP data transmission to use CHAP as the authentication protocol for attaching stations:

```
CentralA(config-if)#ppp authentication chap
```

13 Configure the T1 1/0 IP address:

```
CentralA(config-if)#ip address 10.130.0.2  255.255.255.0
```

14 Assign dialer-list 1 to T1 1/0:

```
CentralA(config-if)#dialer-group 1
```

15 Configure the dialer idle time:

```
CentralA(config-if)#dialer idle-timeout 60
```

16 Configure a dialer map statement by using the BRI 0 address and the name of the branch office router. (Unlike the branch office router, your Central site does not subscribe to the telco's speed dial service. Therefore all seven digits of the phone number must be configured to reach the branch office.)

```
CentralA(config-if)#dialer map ip 10.130.0.1 name BranchA  7782001.
```

Step 3 In the global configuration mode, enter the following commands to specify that routing updates will not be sent out of this PRI and that static routes will be redistributed in IGRP:

```
CentralA(config)#router igrp 100
CentralA(config-router)#passive-interface s 1/0:23
CentralA(config-router)#redistribute static
```

Step 4 At this point, you usually exit all configurations and save your running configuration.

Step 5 Use the following commands to view the current status of your router's ISDN interface and connections:

- **show isdn status**
- **show interface s1/0:23**
- **show controller t1 1/0**
- **debug isdn q921**

Example 7-15 displays the output of these commands.

Example 7-15 *Viewing the Status of the Central Office Router*

```
CentralA#sh isdn status
Global ISDN Switchtype = primary-5ess
ISDN Serial1/0:23 interface
dsl 0, interface ISDN Switchtype = primary-5ess
Layer 1 Status:
ACTIVE
Layer 2 Status:
TEI = 0, Ces = 1, SAPI = 0, State = MULTIPLE_FRAME_ESTABLISHED
Layer 3 Status:
0 Active Layer 3 Call(s)
Activated dsl 0 CCBs = 0
Total Allocated ISDN CCBs = 0

CentralA#sh int s1/0:23
Serial1/0:23 is up, line protocol is up (spoofing)
Hardware is DSX1
Internet address is 10.130.0.2/24
MTU 1500 bytes, BW 64 Kbit, DLY 20000 usec, rely 255/255, load 1/255
Encapsulation PPP, loopback not set
```

continues

Example 7-15 *Viewing the Status of the Central Office Router (Continued)*

```
Last input 00:00:06, output 00:00:06, output hang never
Last clearing of "show interface" counters never
Input queue: 0/75/0 (size/max/drops); Total output drops: 0
Queueing strategy: weighted fair
Output queue: 0/1000/64/0 (size/max total/threshold/drops)
Conversations 0/1/256 (active/max active/max total)
Reserved Conversations 0/0 (allocated/max allocated)
5 minute input rate 0 bits/sec, 0 packets/sec
5 minute output rate 0 bits/sec, 0 packets/sec
38 packets input, 151 bytes, 0 no buffer
Received 0 broadcasts, 0 runts, 0 giants, 0 throttles
0 input errors, 0 CRC, 0 frame, 0 overrun, 0 ignored, 0 abort
38 packets output, 151 bytes, 0 underruns
0 output errors, 0 collisions, 6 interface resets
0 output buffer failures, 0 output buffers swapped out
1 carrier transitions
Timeslot(s) Used:24, Transmitter delay is 0 flags

CentralA#sh cont t1 1/0
T1 1/0 is up.
T1 with CSU interface.
Cable Length is LONG, Rcv gain is 36 db and Tx gain is 0 db.
No alarms detected.
Framing is ESF, Line Code is B8ZS, Clock Source is Line.
Data in current interval (203 seconds elapsed):
0 Line Code Violations, 0 Path Code Violations
0 Slip Secs, 0 Fr Loss Secs, 0 Line Err Secs, 0 Degraded Mins
0 Errored Secs, 0 Bursty Err Secs, 0 Severely Err Secs, 0 Unavail Secs
Data in Interval 1:
0 Line Code Violations, 0 Path Code Violations
0 Slip Secs, 756 Fr Loss Secs, 0 Line Err Secs, 0 Degraded Mins
0 Errored Secs, 0 Bursty Err Secs, 0 Severely Err Secs, 756 Unavail Secs
Data in Interval 2:
0 Line Code Violations, 0 Path Code Violations
0 Slip Secs, 900 Fr Loss Secs, 0 Line Err Secs, 0 Degraded Mins
0 Errored Secs, 0 Bursty Err Secs, 0 Severely Err Secs, 900 Unavail Secs
Data in Interval 3:
0 Line Code Violations, 0 Path Code Violations
0 Slip Secs, 900 Fr Loss Secs, 0 Line Err Secs, 0 Degraded Mins
0 Slip Secs, 900 Fr Loss Secs, 0 Line Err Secs, 0 Degraded Mins
<output omitted>

CentralA#deb isdn q921
ISDN Q921 packets debugging is on
CentralA#
ISDN Se1/0:23: RX <- RRp sapi = 0 tei = 0 nr = 16
ISDN Se1/0:23: TX -> RRf sapi = 0 tei = 0 nr = 20
ISDN Se1/0:23: RX <- RRp sapi = 0 tei = 0 nr = 16
ISDN Se1/0:23: TX -> RRf sapi = 0 tei = 0 nr = 20
ISDN Se1/0:23: RX <- RRp sapi = 0 tei = 0 nr = 16
ISDN Se1/0:23: TX -> RRf sapi = 0 tei = 0 nr = 20
```

Step 6   Turn off ISDN Q.921 debugging:

```
CentralA#no deb isdn q921
```

Task 3 Solution—Verifying the ISDN Connection

Step 1   Look at your running configuration on the branch router. It should look like
the configuration in Example 7-16. The bold commands represent the
configuration performed in this case study.

Example 7-16 *The Running Configuration on the Branch Office Router*

```
BranchA#sh run
Building configuration...
Current configuration:
!
version 11.3
no service password-encryption
!
hostname BranchA
!
enable secret 5 $1$NRrJ$daaIONQjK5MsoGX9SmJM70
enable password san-fran
!
username CentralA password 0 cisco
no ip domain-lookup
isdn switch-type basic-5ess
!
!
!
interface Ethernet0
ip address 10.218.0.1 255.255.255.0
!
interface Serial0
no ip address
no ip mroute-cache
shutdown
!
interface BRI0
ip address 10.130.0.1 255.255.255.0
encapsulation ppp
dialer idle-timeout 60
dialer map ip 10.130.0.2 name CentralA 1000
dialer-group 1
isdn switch-type basic-5ess
ppp authentication chap
!
router igrp 100
passive-interface BRI0
network 10.0.0.0
!
ip classless
```

continues

Example 7-16 *The Running Configuration on the Branch Office Router (Continued)*

```
ip route 10.115.0.0 255.255.255.0 10.130.0.2
dialer-list 1 protocol ip permit
!
line con 0
exec-timeout 0 0
line vty 0 4
password cisco
login
!
end
```

Step 2 Look at the running configuration on the Central site router. It should look like the configuration in Example 7-17. The bold commands represent the configuration performed in this case study.

Example 7-17 *The Running Configuration on the Central Site Router*

```
CentralA#sh run
Building configuration...
Current configuration:
!
version 11.3
no service password-encryption
!
hostname CentralA
!
enable secret 5 $1$L.QE$52g1nPy0Tk3AwGd/XdEXK0
enable password san-fran
!
username student password 0 cisco
username BranchA password 0 cisco
no ip domain-lookup
ip host modem 2097 10.115.0.110
isdn switch-type primary-5ess
!
!
!
controller T1 1/0
framing esf
linecode b8zs
pri-group timeslots 1-24
!
!
interface Ethernet0/0
ip address 10.115.0.110 255.255.255.0
no lat enabled
!
interface Serial0/0
no ip address
no ip mroute-cache
shutdown
```

Example 7-17 *The Running Configuration on the Central Site Router (Continued)*

```
no fair-queue
!
interface Serial1/0:23
ip address 10.130.0.2 255.255.255.0
encapsulation ppp
dialer idle-timeout 60
dialer map ip 10.130.0.1 name BranchA 7782001
dialer-group 1
isdn switch-type primary-5ess
ppp authentication chap
!
interface Serial3/0
physical-layer async
ip unnumbered Ethernet0/0
encapsulation ppp
async mode interactive
peer default ip address pool lab
no cdp enable
ppp authentication chap
!
interface Serial3/1
no ip address
shutdown
!
interface Serial3/2
no ip address
shutdown
!
interface Serial3/3
no ip address
shutdown
!
router igrp 100
redistribute static
passive-interface Serial1/0:23
network 10.0.0.0
!
ip local pool lab 10.115.0.111 10.115.0.114
ip classless
ip route 10.218.0.0 255.255.255.0 10.130.0.1
dialer-list 1 protocol ip permit
!
!
line con 0
exec-timeout 0 0
line 65 70
line 97
password cisco
autoselect during-login
autoselect ppp
login local
```

continues

Example 7-17 *The Running Configuration on the Central Site Router (Continued)*

```
modem InOut
modem autoconfigure type usr_sportster
transport input all
stopbits 1
speed 115200
flowcontrol hardware
line aux 0
line vty 0 4
login local
!
end
```

Step 3 From the branch office router, you can enter **ping 10.115.0.110** to send data to the Ethernet interface of your Central site router. Repeat the test in the other direction. If you turn on Q.931 debugging, you also see the ISDN call progress. Output at the branch and Central site should look similar to Examples 7-18 and 7-19.

Example 7-18 *Testing the Branch Office Connectivity with the Central Site*

```
Branch1A#debug isdn q931

Branch1A#ping 10.115.0.110
Type escape sequence to abort.
Sending 5, 100-byte ICMP Echos to 10.115.0.110, timeout is 2 seconds:
ISDN BR0: TX -> SETUP pd = 8 callref = 0x02
Bearer Capability i = 0x8890
Channel ID i = 0x83
Keypad Facility i = '4000'
ISDN BR0: RX <- CALL_PROC pd = 8 callref = 0x82
Channel ID i = 0x8A
ISDN BR0: RX <- CONNECT pd = 8 callref = 0x82
%LINK-3-UPDOWN: Interface BRI0:2, changed state to up.!!!!
Success rate is 80 percent (4/5), round-trip min/avg/max = 32/33/36 ms
Branch1A#
ISDN BR0: TX -> CONNECT_ACK pd = 8 callref = 0x02
%LINEPROTO-5-UPDOWN: Line protocol on Interface BRI0:2, changed state to up
Branch1A#
Branch1A#
%ISDN-6-CONNECT: Interface BRI0:2 is now connected to 4000 CentralA
ISDN BR0: RX <- DISCONNECT pd = 8 callref = 0x81
Cause i = 0x8090 - Normal call clearing
ISDN BR0: TX -> RELEASE pd = 8 callref = 0x01
Cause i = 0x80D1 - Invalid call reference value
ISDN BR0: RX <- RELEASE_COMP pd = 8 callref = 0x81
%ISDN-6-DISCONNECT: Interface BRI0:2 disconnected from 4000 CentralA, call lasted 122
seconds
ISDN BR0: TX -> DISCONNECT pd = 8 callref = 0x02
Cause i = 0x8090 - Normal call clearing
ISDN BR0: RX <- RELEASE pd = 8 callref = 0x82
```

Example 7-18 *Testing the Branch Office Connectivity with the Central Site (Continued)*

```
%LINK-3-UPDOWN: Interface BRI0:2, changed state to down
ISDN BR0: TX -> RELEASE_COMP pd = 8 callref = 0x02
%LINEPROTO-5-UPDOWN: Line protocol on Interface BRI0:2, changed state to down
```

Example 7-19 *Testing the Central Site connectivity to the Branch Office*

```
CentralA#debug isdn q931
ISDN Q931 packets debugging is on....
CentralA#ping 10.218.0.1
Type escape sequence to abort.
Sending 5, 100-byte ICMP Echos to 10.218.0.1, timeout is 2 seconds:
ISDN Se1/0:23: TX -> SETUP pd = 8 callref = 0x0009
Bearer Capability i = 0x8890
Channel ID i = 0xE1808397
Called Party Number i = 0xA1, '7782007'
ISDN Se1/0:23: RX <- CALL_PROC pd = 8 callref = 0x8009
Channel ID i = 0xA98397
ISDN Se1/0:23: RX <- CONNECT pd = 8 callref = 0x8009
%LINK-3-UPDOWN: Interface Serial1/0:22, changed state to up.!
ISDN Se1/0:23: TX -> CONNECT_ACK pd = 8 callref = 0x0009!!!
Success rate is 80 percent (4/5), round-trip min/avg/max = 120/130/140 ms
CentralA#
%LINEPROTO-5-UPDOWN: Line protocol on Interface Serial1/0:22, changed state to up
%ISDN-6-CONNECT: Interface Serial1/0:22 is now connected to 7782001 BranchA
```

Case Study Conclusion

In this case study, you saw how to configure a branch office to communicate via ISDN link to a Central site by using legacy dial-on-demand routing. In the next chapter, you will see how to optimize your dial-on-demand routing configuration.

Review Questions

Answer the following questions and then refer to Appendix H, "Answers to Review Questions," for answers and explanations.

1 What is the difference between ISDN BRI and ISDN PRI?

2 If you are not sure what your ISDN switch type is, where would you obtain this information?

3 What are Q.921 and Q.931?

CHAPTER 8

Optimizing the Use of DDR Interface—Dialer Profiles and Rotary Groups

In the previous chapter, you learned how to configure dial-on-demand routing on an access server. In this chapter, you are introduced to the configuration of dialer profiles and rotary groups, which helps you build more flexibility in your network design by introducing a modular approach.

As seen in Chapter 7, "Using ISDN and DDR to Enhance Remote Connectivity," **dialer-map** statements are convenient when one physical interface is responsible for calling one destination.

The **dialer-map** command can also be used if your router calls multiple destinations that all use the same communication parameters. As an example, if your router performs DDR to three different destinations; and for every call the encapsulation is PPP, the authentication method is CHAP, and the idle-timeout is 300 seconds; you can configure one physical interface with all the parameters and provide it with three separate **dialer-map** statements.

On the other hand, what if your router is responsible for reaching three separate locations that use different communication parameters? Suppose that one location requires PAP authentication when another is doing CHAP authentication. One location might require an ISDN speed of 56 Kbps, whereas the other destinations communicate at 64 Kbps. If this is the case, specific call parameters are defined under three separate physical interfaces, each of them connected to a separate line.

The previous scenario might result in a waste of resources and money. You would have to procure a router with three WAN interfaces, and you would have to pay for three lines that might be used for only a few minutes daily.

You need a mechanism in which physical interfaces are not locked with permanent configurations, but assumes call parameters on an as-needed basis. Once the call is finished, the same interface is freed of the previous configuration and is ready to service another calling destination.

This mechanism is called **dialer interface**. The dialer interface is not a physical interface; it is an entity that allows you to propagate an interface configuration to multiple interfaces. When a physical interface is being used for dialing, it inherits the parameters configured for the dialer interface.

After an interface configuration is propagated to a set of physical interfaces, those interfaces can be used to place calls by using standard DDR criteria. Using the dialer interface allows you to specify one set of dialer maps that can apply to multiple physical lines.

Dialer interfaces provide flexibility through rotary groups and dialer profiles. The following sections explain the differences between these two configurations.

Dialer Rotary Overview

Dialer rotary groups simplify the configuration of physical interfaces by allowing you to apply a single logical interface configuration to a set of physical interfaces. The single logical interface is a dialer rotary group, which is defined by specifying a dialer interface. Physical interfaces are assigned to the dialer rotary group and inherit all of the dialer interface configuration parameters. When many destinations are configured, any of the physical interfaces in a rotary group can be used for outgoing calls.

Creating and Configuring a Rotary Group

To configure a rotary group, you place each BRI interface in a rotary group. In Figure 8-1, all of the BRIs are assigned to dialer rotary-group 1. All of these BRI lines are also set in a hunt group. A **hunt group** is a series of telephone lines that are programmed so that as incoming calls arrive, if the first line is busy, the second line is tried, and then the third line is tried, and so on until a free line is found. This way, an incoming call should not end up with a busy signal.

Figure 8-1   *Creating a Hunt Group with Multiple BRIs*

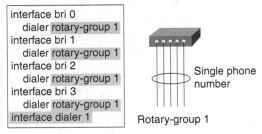

NOTE   You may still have to perform some of the configuration on the physical interface rather than at the dialer rotary interface. For example, if you connect to a switch that requires SPIDs, you have to enter each of the SPIDs separately at each of the physical BRI interfaces.

The rest of the interface configuration is done on the interface dialer 1, the new rotary you created.

NOTE	If you install multiple BRIs or PRIs to service remote users, request one phone number from the service provider. You then assign all of the interfaces to one rotary group, or hunt group, so that you only need to dial one number for either configuration. Using one number requires only one set of dialer map statements on the remote routers instead of multiple statements, which also makes debugging much easier and less complicated.

The **interface dialer** command in global configuration mode creates a dialer rotary group:

```
Router(config)#interface dialer group-number
```

Then, you use the **dialer rotary-group** command in interface (BRI, Async, and so on) configuration mode to include that interface in the specified rotary group, as shown in the syntax that follows. You have to use this command on each interface that you wish to include in the rotary group.

```
Router(config-if)#dialer rotary-group rotary-number
```

The syntaxes for the **interface dialer** and **dialer rotary-group** commands are explained in the following table.

Command	*Description*
interface dialer *group-number*	Defines a dialer rotary group. The group number ranges from 0 through 255.
dialer rotary-group *group-number*	Includes an interface in a dialer rotary group.

Configuring the Interface Dialer

In the previous chapter, you saw how to configure call parameters under a physical interface. The following are some commands required for setting up rotary groups.

The command **dialer string** is used to specify the phone number to dial when placing a call from an interface to a specific destination. A modem chat-script must be defined and used to implement dialing on asynchronous interfaces. The syntax is as follows:

```
Router(config-if)#dialer string dial-string
```

---

dialer string and dialer group Commands

If a **dialer string** command is specified without a **dialer group** command with access lists defined, dialing is never initiated. If the **debug dialer** command is enabled, an error message displays and indicates that dialing never will occur.

By default, packets are dropped during the time required to establish a connection. To prevent this, use the **dialer hold-queue** command, which allows interesting outgoing packets to be held in a queue while dialing takes place. The number of packets allowed in a queue ranges from 0 to 100. The syntax is as follows:

```
Router(config-if)#dialer hold-queue number
```

Dealing with Dialer Timers

Because DDR links are considered temporary, some timers are necessary to regulate the connection for operations, such as the length of time a connection stays up if there is contention for using the same line.

After placing a call, the router must be told how long to keep the connection up, once it has not seen an interesting packet for a certain amount of time. The **dialer idle-timeout** command specifies the idle time (in seconds) before the line is disconnected. Every time the router processes an interesting packet, it resets this timer. The default is 120 seconds. This command, which is used on lines for which there is no contention, applies to inbound and outbound calls. This is an inactivity timer. The syntax for the **dialer idle-timeout** command follows:

```
Router(config-if)#dialer idle-timeout seconds
```

Intricacies of Idle Timers

The answering router also starts an idle-timeout timer as soon as it answers a call, and can break your connection after 120 seconds (default timer is for 120 seconds). You can fix this by configuring a very high idle-timeout value on the answering router, defining interesting traffic with a **dialer-list** statement, and configuring the corresponding dialer-group on the answering interface (so the answering router knows what is interesting traffic and can reset its timer).

The **dialer fast-idle** command specifies the amount of time that a connected line remains idle before it is disconnected to allow a second call, which is destined for a second location over this same line, to be placed. This command, which is used on lines for which there is contention, applies to inbound and outbound calls. The line is considered idle when no interesting packets are being sent across it. If the line becomes idle for the configured length of time, the current call is disconnected immediately and the line is available for new calls. The default fast-idle time is 20 seconds. This is an inactivity timer for contended interfaces. The syntax for the **dialer fast-idle** command is as follows:

```
Router(config-if)#dialer fast-idle seconds
```

On local calls, analog modems can take 20 to 30 seconds to synchronize to each other, including the time to dial and answer. International calls take longer than local calls to connect. The **dialer wait-for-carrier-time** command (as follows) specifies how long (in seconds) to wait for carrier tone. On asynchronous interfaces, this command sets the total time allowed for the chat-script to run. The default time is 30 seconds. For asynchronous lines, it is better to increase the value of this parameter to 60 seconds to compensate for the possible delay in the telephone network.

```
Router(config-if)#dialer wait-for-carrier-time seconds
```

As you saw in the previous chapter, some configurations are required on only some category of interfaces. An example of this is the SPID configuration, required only for ISDN BRI interfaces. Similarly, specific configuration is required when performing DDR with async interfaces.

The **dialer in-band** command enables DDR and V.25bis dialing on the dialer or async interface. V.25bis is an ITU-T standard for in-band signaling to bit synchronous DCE devices. A variety of devices support V.25bis, ranging from analog V.32 modems to ISDN terminal adapters to inverse multiplexers.

The syntax for the **dialer in-band** command is as follows:

```
Router(config-if)#dialer in-band
```

Other examples of peculiar commands are **isdn incoming-voice modem** and **interface group-async**.

The **isdn incoming-voice modem** command is used to configure the D channel to switch incoming analog calls to the internal modems. The syntax for the **isdn incoming-voice modem** command is as follows:

```
Router(config)#interface serial 1/0:23
Router(config-if)#isdn incoming-voice modem
```

The **interface group-async** command is used to create an asynchronous group interface, which can be associated with other asynchronous interfaces. This association allows you to configure the group interface and all of its members' interfaces with a single command entered at the asynchronous group interface command line. Although you can have more than one group interface on a router, a member interface can be associated with only one group. The syntaxes of commands for creating a group-async, **interface group-async**; and to associate members, **group-range,** are as follows:

```
Router(config)#interface group-async 1
Router(config-if)#group-range 65 70
```

In-Band Signaling

DDR over serial lines requires the use of dialing devices that support V.25bis. V.25bis is an International Telecommunication Union Telecommunication (ITU-T) Standardization Sector standard for in-band signaling to bit synchronous data communications equipment (DCE) devices. A variety of devices support V.25bis, including analog V.32 modems, ISDN terminal adapters, and inverse multiplexers. This is according to the Cisco Web site at www.cisco.com/univercd/cc/td/doc/cisintwk/ics/cs002.htm.

If you are using a TE2 (non-native ISDN router), your TA will require the **dialer in-band** command.

Dialer Profile Overview

Dialer profiles separate the logical configuration from the interface that receives or makes calls. Profiles can define encapsulation, access control lists and minimum or maximum calls, and turn features on or off.

With dialer profiles, the logical and physical configurations are dynamically bound to each other on a per-call basis, which allows physical interfaces to dynamically take on different characteristics based on incoming or outgoing calls, as shown in Figure 8-2.

Figure 8-2　*A Logical Interface, Called a Dialer Profile, Borrows a Physical Interface to Make a Connection to a Specific Destination*

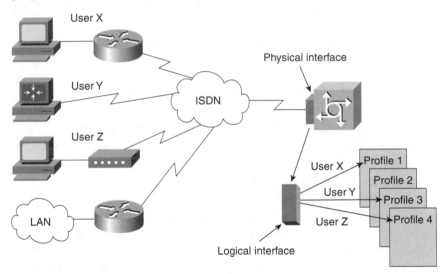

Dialer profiles help users design and deploy complex and scalable circuit-switched internetworks by implementing a new DDR model in Cisco routers and access servers. Dialer profiles separate the logical portion of DDR—such as the network layer, encapsulation, and dialer parameters—from the physical interface that places or receives calls.

Dialer profiles address several dialup issues:

- **One configured interface per ISDN interface**—Before dialer profiles, all ISDN B channels inherited the physical interface's configuration.

- **Dialer map complexity**—Before dialer profiles, one dialer map was required per dialer per protocol, making multiprotocol configurations very complex.

- **Limited dial backup**—When a Basic Rate Interface (BRI) or Primary Rate Interface (PRI) is used to back up an interface, all the B channels are down and the whole interface is idle. In addition, the one-to-one relationship between interfaces and backup interfaces does not scale well to a packet-switching environment, in which many virtual circuits might need to be backed up individually and floating static routes are not desirable.

Dialer profiles let you create different configurations for B channels on an ISDN PRI interface. Using dialer profiles, you can do the following:

- Configure B channels of an ISDN interface with different IP subnets or IPX networks.
- Use different encapsulations of B channels of an ISDN interface. However, only Point-to-Point Protocol (PPP) and High-Level Data Link Control (HDLC) encapsulation are now supported.
- Set different DDR parameters for B channels of an ISDN interface.
- Eliminate the waste of ISDN B channels by letting ISDN BRI interfaces belong to multiple dialer pools.

NOTE	The main difference between a **rotary group** and a **dialer profile** is that a physical interface participates in only one rotary group. With a dialer profile, a physical interface can belong to many different pools.

Components of Dialer Profile

As illustrated in Figure 8-3, a dialer profile consists of the following elements:

- Dialer interface
- Dialer map-class (optional)
- Dialer pool
- Physical interfaces

Figure 8-3 *Elements of a Dialer Profile*

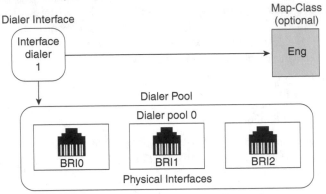

Dialer Interface

A **dialer interface** is a logical entity that uses a per-destination dialer profile.

All configuration settings specific to the destination go into the dialer interface configuration. Multiple dialer maps can be specified for the same dialer interface. A dialer map can be associated with different per-call parameters, defined with each dialer map-class.

The dialer interface is configured with the following characteristics:

- IP address of destination network
- Encapsulation type
- PPP authentication type
- Dialer remote name (for PPP CHAP)
- Dialer string or dialer map
- Dialer pool number
- Dialer group number
- Dialer list number
- Multilink PPP
- The optional dialer idle timeout and dialer in-band

The configuration commands that create the relationships between the elements of a dialer profile are shown in Figure 8-4. The commands and the configuration mode in which they are used are described in the table that follows the figure.

Figure 8-4   *Representation of Dialer Profile Configuration Concepts and Commands*

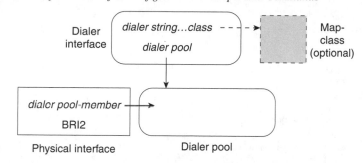

Command	Description
dialer string *number* **class** *map-class-name*	A dialer interface command that specifies the phone number of the destination. The use of the optional keyword **class** followed by the *map-class-name* is to point to a specific map-class and use the configuration commands of that map-class in the call.
dialer pool *number*	A dialer interface command that specifies the pool of physical interfaces available to reach the destination subnetwork. A number between 1 and 255 identifies the pool.
dialer pool-member *number*	An interface configuration command that associates and places a physical interface in a specifically numbered pool.

To configure a dialer profile like any other DDR interface, perform the following tasks:

1 Configure one or more dialer interfaces.

2 Configure a dialer string and (optionally) a dialer map-class to specify different characteristics on a per-call basis.

3 Configure the physical interfaces and attach them to a dialer pool. You can configure any number of dialer interfaces for a router. Each dialer interface is the complete configuration for a destination. The **interface dialer global** command creates a dialer interface and enters interface configuration mode.

A dialer profile has the command listed in Example 8-1. The command is explained in the table that follows the example.

Example 8-1   *Command Used with Dialer Profiles*

```
interface dialer1
ip address 10.1.1.1
255.255.255.0
encapsulation ppp
dialer remote-name Smalluser
dialer string 5554540
dialer pool 3
```

continues

Example 8-1 *Command Used with Dialer Profiles (Continued)*

```
dialer-group 1
ppp authentication chap
ppp multilink
!
interface dialer2
ip address 10.2.2.2
255.255.255.0
encapsulation ppp
dialer remote-name Mediumuser
dialer string 5551234 class Eng
dialer load-threshold 50 either
dialer pool 1
dialer-group 2
ppp multilink
interface dialer3
ip address 10.3.3.3 255.255.255.0
encapsulation ppp
dialer remote-name Poweruser
dialer string 4155551234 class Eng
dialer hold-queue 10
dialer idle-timer 9999
dialer pool 2
dialer-group 2
ppp multilink
!
map-class dialer Eng
dialer isdn speed 56
dialer fast-idle 30
dialer hold-queue 75
```

Command	Description
ip address *address mask*	Specifies the IP address and mask of the destination network.
dialer remote-name *name*	Specifies the remote router name, which is passed for CHAP authentication.
dialer string *string* **class** *map-class-name*	Defines the destination router's phone number and supports optional map classes. See the following paragraphs for more information on dialer map classes.

Command	Description
dialer load-threshold *load*	Specifies at what traffic load additional links will **[outbound|inbound|either]**be brought up for Multilink PPP. Valid values are 1 to 255. Optionally, you may specify which direction of traffic is used to calculate the actual load. If you want the links to remain in a Multilink PPP bundle indefinitely, use a very high dialer idle-timeout value (9999, for example) instead of a dialer load-threshold.
dialer hold-queue *number–of-packets*	Specifies the length of the queue for packets waiting for the line to come up. Valid values are from 0 to 100.
dialer pool *number*	Binds a dialer interface to a dialer pool configured with the **dialer remote-name** command, which gives the CHAP username for a remote user. Valid values are from 1 to 255.
dialer-group *group-number*	Specifies a dialer list that defines interesting packets to trigger a call for DDR. The **dialer-list** command can reference access lists to more specifically define interesting packets. Valid values are from 1 to 10.
ppp multilink	Specifies that this dialer interface uses Multilink PPP. This command is placed on the physical interface for incoming calls, in the dialer profile for outgoing calls, and on both the interface and dialer profile when incoming and outgoing calls are expected.

Dialer Map Class

The **dialer map class** is an optional element that defines specific characteristics for a call to a specified dial string.

For example, the map class for one destination might specify an ISDN speed of 56 Kbps, whereas a map class for a different destination might specify an ISDN semipermanent connection. The dialer map class can also contain optional dialer-timing parameters, including dialer fast-idle, dialer idle-timeout, and dialer wait-for-carrier-time. A map class is an optional element of a dialer profile and can be used by (or referenced from) multiple dialer interfaces.

Map classes are optional. They are used to specify different characteristics for different types of calls on a per-destination basis.

Figure 8-5 shows the usefulness of map class. Calls to three different destinations require many parameters that are the same from one destination to another. Instead of re-entering these commands under each of the concerned dialer interfaces, it is being told to refer itself to the map class for further configuration parameters. As you can see, the same map class can be used for multiple dialer interfaces. The configuration parameters of a map class are specific to one or more destinations.

After the interface is configured, an optional dialer map class can be defined. In Figure 8-5, the dialer interface dialer3 is associated with map-class Eng. Any dialer associated with this map-class sets the ISDN line speed to 56 Kbps.

Figure 8-5 *One Map Class Has Configuration Parameters that Are Applicable to Three Different Dialer Profiles*

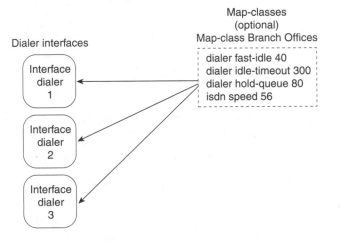

You can use the **map-class dialer** *class-name* command to specify a map class and enter the map-class configuration mode.

In this example, the **dialer isdn speed 56** command specifies an ISDN bit rate of 56 Kbps for use in the map class. You can set the speed to 56; 64 is the default value.

Additionally, the other map class commands listed in the following table are available in map-class configuration mode.

Command	Description
dialer isdn [speed 56|spc]	Specifies the ISDN line speed of 56 kbps (64 kbps is the default; this parameter is only used with 56 kbps line speed). Note that 64 is not a valid option. [**spc**] is used for ISDN only, specifying that an ISDN semipermanent connection is to be used for calls associated with this map.
dialer idle-timeout *seconds*	Specifies the idle timer values to use for the call. This timer disconnects the call if there has been no interesting data for the specified time. Defaults to 120 seconds.
dialer fast-idle *seconds*	Specifies the fast idle timer value to use for a call. This timer specifies a quick disconnect time if there is another call waiting for the same interface, and the interface is idle. The waiting call does not have to wait for the idle timer to expire. Defaults to 20 seconds.

Command	Description
dialer wait-for-carrier-time *seconds*	Specifies the wait for carrier (CD) time value to use for the call. If no carrier is detected within the time value specified, the call is abandoned.

Dialer Pool

Each dialer interface references a **dialer pool**, which is a group of one or more physical interfaces associated with a dialer profile.

A physical interface can belong to multiple dialer pools. Contention for a specific physical interface is resolved with a configured priority, which is optional.

Physical Interfaces

A virtual interface must be associated with a dialer pool. The dialer is a group of one or many physical interfaces in charge of placing the call.

Dialer profiles support PPP or HDLC encapsulation, PPP authentication (PAP or CHAP), and Multilink PPP, if used. All other settings are part of the dialer interface configuration that is applied to the physical interface on a per-call basis.

Use the **dialer pool-member** command to assign a physical interface to a dialer pool. You can assign an interface to multiple dialer pools by using this command to specify several dialer pool numbers.

Use the priority option of this command to set the interface's priority within a dialer pool, which is only used when dialing out. You can use a combination of synchronous, serial, BRI, or PRI interfaces with dialer pools. The following table lists the commands used to set the pool membership priority.

Command	Description
dialer pool-member *number*	The dialer pooling number. This is a decimal value from 1 to 255.
priority *priority*	Sets the priority of the physical interface within the dialer pool. This is a decimal value from 1 to 255. Interfaces with the highest-priority number are selected first when dialing out. Use this to determine which interfaces are used the most, or which ones are reserved for special pool uses.

Command	Description
min-link *minimum*	Sets the minimum number of ISDN B channels on an interface reserved for this dialer pool. This is a number from 1 to 255 (used for dialer backup).
max-link *maximum*	Sets the maximum number of ISDN B channels on an interface reserved for this dialer pool. This is a number from 1 to 255.

Encapsulation type, PPP authentication, and Multilink PPP are all configured on the physical interface. This association to the physical interface is important because before an incoming call is bound to a dialer interface, the router negotiates the Link Control Protocol (LCP) layer of PPP (which includes the authentication type and whether PPP multilink will be used). Then, the router authenticates the remote router with the method specified (PAP or CHAP). Based on the response to this challenge, the router will try to bind the call to the correct dialer profile. At this point, the dialer profile is applied and takes over, and the call is completed and the routers are connected.

Example of Dialer Profile Configuration

The dialer interfaces are visible only to the upper-layer protocols, not to the physical interfaces making up the dialing pool. Because one dialer interface maps to one destination, addressing, access lists, and static routes can be specified on a per-destination basis, regardless of which interface actually carries out the call. Example 8-2 contains a sample dialer profile configuration.

Example 8-2 *Example of Dialer Profiles Using Map Classes*

```
interface Dialer1
 ip address 10.1.1.1 255.255.255.0
 encapsulation ppp
 dialer remote-name Smalluser
 dialer string 4540
 dialer pool 3
 dialer-group 1
interface Dialer2
 ip address 10.2.2.2 255.255.255.0
 encapsulation ppp
 dialer remote-name Mediumuser
 dialer string 5264540 class Eng
 dialer load-threshold 50 either
 dialer pool 1
 dialer-group 2
interface Dialer3
 ip address 10.3.3.3 255.255.255.0
 encapsulation ppp
 dialer remote-name Poweruser
 dialer string 4156884540 class Eng
 dialer load-threshold 80
```

Example 8-2 *Example of Dialer Profiles Using Map Classes (Continued)*

```
 dialer pool 2
 dialer-group 2
interface BRI0
 encapsulation PPP
 dialer pool-member 1 priority 100
 ppp authentication chap
interface BRI1
 encapsulation ppp
 dialer pool-member 1 priority 50
 dialer pool-member 2 priority 50
 dialer pool-member 3 min-link 1
 ppp authentication chap
interface BRI2
 encapsulation ppp
 dialer pool-member 2 priority 100
 ppp authentication chap
interface BRI3
 encapsulation ppp
 dialer pool-member 2 priority 150
 ppp authentication chap
map-class dialer Eng
 isdn speed 56
 dialer hold-queue 10
 dialer idle-timeout 180
```

Dialer commands can be configured under the dialer interface directly. The same command may appear more than once, possibly with different parameters. The order of precedence is as follows (from highest to lowest):

```
Map-class parameters
Interface parameters
```

Refer to Example 8-2 for examples of the use and syntax for the **map-class** command.

Verifying a Dialer Profile Configuration

The **show dialer interface bri** *number* command displays information in the same format as the legacy DDR statistics on incoming and outgoing calls.

In Example 8-3, the message that says **Dialer state is data link layer up** suggests that the dialer came up properly. If you see a message saying **physical layer up**, the line protocol came up, but the Network Control Protocol (NCP) did not.

Example 8-3 *Verifying Dialer Profile Operations*

```
NASX#show dialer interface bri0
BRI0 - dialer type = ISDN
Dial String      Successes       Failures      Last called      Last status
5553872                 6              0          19 secs       successful
```

continues

Example 8-3 *Verifying Dialer Profile Operations (Continued)*

```
0 incoming call(s) have been screened.
BRI0: B-Channel 1
Idle timer (120 secs), Fast idle timer (20 secs)
Wait for carrier (30 secs), Re-enable (15 secs)
Dialer state is data link layer up
Dial reason: ip (s=10.1.1.8, d=10.1.1.1)
Interface bound to profile Dialer0
Time until disconnect 102 secs
Current call connected 00:00:19
Connected to 5553872 (system1)

BRI0: B-Channel 2
Idle timer (120 secs), Fast idle timer (20 secs)
Wait for carrier (30 secs), Re-enable (15 secs)
Dialer state is idle
```

The source and destination address of the packet that initiated the dialing is shown in the **Dial reason** line.

Summary

In this chapter, you learned how to select the appropriate dial-up features for a given situation (branch office, central site, and so on), how to configure rotary groups and dialer profiles, and how to verify and troubleshoot these rotaries.

You also learned that some equipment and commands can be configured to allow analog calls on PRI interfaces.

In the next chapter, you will learn how a Cisco 700 router, typically used in small offices, can call a Central site using ISDN BRI interfaces.

Case Study—Using Dialer Profiles to Enhance DDR

Complete the tasks of this case study, and then review the case study solution section that follows to see how you did and where you might need to review the concepts presented in this chapter.

In this case study, you will learn how to configure the Central site router to receive async calls through the PRI interface to terminate on the internal MICA. Then, you learn how to configure a dialer interface on the Central site router, so the Branch Office can reach it by using its BRI interface. Through this case study, you will demonstrate that PRI connections can receive both ISDN and analog calls.

Scenario

Figure 8-6 shows the topology for this case study.

Figure 8-6 *The Central Site Is Called by a Remote User Using Win 95 and a Branch Office*

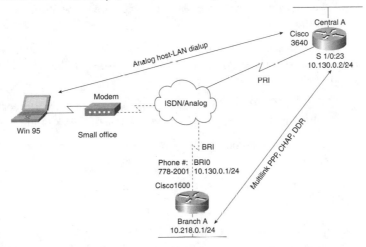

Given a Central site with an ISDN PRI interface and internal modems, you will be asked to configure the router to receive both async calls and BRI calls. Incoming async (analog) calls will be directed to the internal modems. Then, you will have to configure a dialer interface to receive ISDN BRI calls from the Branch office.

Task

Execute the following steps to configure the Central site PRI to receive incoming async calls and create a dialer interface.

Step 1   Under the PRI D channel, provide the command that will have analog calls sent to the internal modem. Also, link this serial interface to the dialer pool.

Step 2   Configure an asynchronous group. Create an asynchronous group interface and provide commands for the following requirements:

— Async lines 65 to 70 will service this interface.

— This interface will not have its own IP address; instead, it will borrow the interface E0 address.

— The encapsulation will be PPP with CHAP authentication.

— This interface will be using DDR on its async lines.

— Incoming calls can start either a PPP or an EXEC session.

— This interface is associated with the dialer list 1.

— The incoming PPP session will be issued an IP address from the ASYNCLAB pool of addresses.

— The disconnect will take place after 60 seconds without interesting traffic.

Step 3 Configure physical characteristics of the lines that are associated with the async-group interface. Provide the commands for the following configuration requirements:

— The EXEC, IP, or SLIP session will be automatically decided by the router upon receiving the first byte of data of the incoming connection.

— The router will consult the local username database to authenticate callers.

— The modem can receive and place calls.

— The router will autoconfigure the MICA modem.

— The lines are authorized to transport for input and output any traffic (Telnet, rlogin, lat, and so on).

— The flowcontrol will be done by the modem signaling with one stopbit.

Step 4 Configure the dialer interface to be used for receiving calls from the branch office. Provide all the necessary commands for an authenticated PPP session, for identifying interesting traffic, and any other commands you should configure on a dialer interface.

Step 5 Assign a static route to reach the branch office using the dialer interface. Also, prevent IGRP routing updates from going out of your interface dialer.

Solution to Case Study—Using Dialer Profiles to Enhance DDR

The following is a step-by-step discussion of the case study solution.

Step 1 Under the PRI D channel, the following command will have analog calls sent to the internal modem:

```
CentralA(config-if)#isdn incoming-voice modem
```

The following links this serial interface to the dialer pool:

```
CentralA(config-if)#dialer pool-member 1
```

Step 2 To configure an asynchronous group:

```
CentralA(config)#interface group-async 1
```

The following list shows the commands for the Step Two configuration requirements:

— To have async lines 65 to 70 service this interface:

```
CentralA(config-if)#group-range 65 70
```

— To make the interface not have its own IP address, and instead borrow the interface E0 address:

```
CentralA(config-if)#ip unnumbered e 0/0
```

— To have the encapsulation be PPP with CHAP authentication:

```
CentralA(config-if)#encapsulation ppp
CentralA(config-if)#ppp authentication chap
```

— To ensure that this interface will be using DDR on its async lines:

```
CentralA(config-if)#dialer in-band
```

— To make incoming calls, start either a PPP or an EXEC session:

```
CentralA(config-if)#async mode interactive
```

— To associate this interface with the dialer list 1:

```
CentralA(config-if)#dialer-group 1
```

— To have the incoming PPP session be issued an IP address from the ASYNCLAB pool of addresses:

```
CentralA(config-if)#peer default ip address pool lab
```

— To make the disconnect take place after 120 seconds without interesting traffic:

```
CentralA(config-if)#dialer idle-timeout 120
```

Step 3 Configure the physical characteristics of the lines that are associated with the async-group interface. The following list shows the commands for the Step 3 configuration requirements:

— To have the EXEC, IP, or SLIP session be automatically decided by the router upon receiving the first byte of data of the incoming connection:

```
CentralA(config)#line 65 70
CentralA(config-line)#autoselect during-login
CentralA(config-line)#autoselect ppp
```

— To have the router consult the local username database to authenticate callers:

```
CentralA(config-line)#login local
```

— To ensure that the modem can receive and place calls:

```
CentralA(config-line)#modem inout
```

— To have the router autoconfigure the MICA modem:

```
CentralA(config-line)#modem autoconfigure type mica
```

— To make the lines authorized to transport for input and output any traffic (Telnet, rlogin, lat, and so on):

```
CentralA(config-line)#transport input all
```

— To have the flowcontrol be done by the modem signaling with one stopbit:

```
CentralA(config-line)#stopbits 1
CentralA(config-line)#flowcontrol hardware
```

Step 4 The following shows how to configure the dialer interface to be used for receiving calls from the branch office. It also shows how to provide all the necessary commands for an authenticated PPP session, for identifying interesting traffic, and any other commands you should configure on a dialer interface:

```
CentralA(config)#interface dialer 1
CentralA(config-if)#ip address 10.130.0.2 255.255.255.0
CentralA(config-if)#dialer in-band
CentralA(config-if)#dialer idle-timeout 60
CentralA(config-if)#dialer-group 1
CentralA(config-if)#no fair-queue
CentralA(config-if)#encapsulation ppp
CentralA(config-if)#ppp authentication chap
CentralA(config-if)#no peer default ip address
CentralA(config-if)#ppp multilink
CentralA(config-if)#dialer remote-name BranchA
CentralA(config-if)#dialer string 7782001
CentralA(config-if)#dialer pool 1
```

Step 5 To assign a static route to reach the branch office by using the dialer interface and to prevent IGRP routing updates from going out of your interface dialer:

```
CentralA(config)#ip route  10.218.0.0  255.255.255.0  dialer 1
CentralA(config)#router igrp 100
CentralA(config-router)#passive-interface dialer 1
```

The new configuration can be seen in bold letters in Example 8-4.

Example 8-4 *Central Router Configured with Group-Async and Dialer Interfaces*

```
!
version 11.3
no service password-encryption
!
hostname CentralA
!
enable secret 5 $1$XvjL$dRrWaKsqFfPqVyrm9cHPK/
enable password san-fran
!
```

Example 8-4 *Central Router Configured with Group-Async and Dialer Interfaces (Continued)*

```
username student password 0 cisco
username BranchA password 0 cisco
no ip domain-lookup
ip host modem 2097 10.115.0.110
isdn switch-type primary-5ess
!
!
!
controller T1 1/0
framing esf
linecode b8zs
pri-group timeslots 1-24
!
!
interface Ethernet0/0
ip address 10.115.0.110 255.255.255.0
no lat enabled
!
interface Serial0/0
no ip address
no ip mroute-cache
shutdown
!
interface Serial1/0:23
no ip address
encapsulation ppp
dialer pool-member 1
isdn switch-type primary-5ess
isdn incoming-voice modem
hold-queue 75 in
!
interface Serial3/0
physical-layer async
ip unnumbered Ethernet0/0
encapsulation ppp
async mode interactive
peer default ip address pool lab
no cdp enable
ppp authentication chap
!
interface Serial3/1
no ip address
shutdown
!
interface Serial3/2
no ip address
shutdown
!
interface Serial3/3
no ip address
shutdown
```

continues

Example 8-4   *Central Router Configured with Group-Async and Dialer Interfaces (Continued)*

```
!
interface Group-Async1
ip unnumbered Ethernet0/0
encapsulation ppp
dialer in-band
dialer idle-timeout 60
dialer-group 1
async mode interactive
peer default ip address pool asynclab
no cdp enable
ppp authentication chap
group-range 65 70
!
interface Dialer1
ip address 10.130.0.2 255.255.255.0
encapsulation ppp
dialer remote-name BranchA
dialer idle-timeout 60
dialer string 7782001
dialer pool 1
dialer-group 1
no peer default ip address
no fair-queue
ppp authentication chap
ppp multilink
!
router igrp 100
passive-interface Dialer1
network 10.0.0.0
!
ip local pool lab 10.115.0.111 10.115.0.114
ip classless
ip route 10.218.0.0 255.255.255.0 Dialer1
dialer-list 1 protocol ip permit
!
!
line con 0
exec-timeout 0 0
line 65 70
autoselect during-login
autoselect ppp
login local
modem InOut
modem autoconfigure type mica
transport input all
stopbits 1
flowcontrol hardware
line 97
password cisco
autoselect during-login
autoselect ppp
```

Example 8-4 *Central Router Configured with Group-Async and Dialer Interfaces (Continued)*

```
login local
modem InOut
modem autoconfigure type usr_sportster
transport input all
stopbits 1
speed 115200
flowcontrol hardware
line aux 0
line vty 0 4
login local
!
end
```

NOTE   The Central site router is thus capable of receiving analog calls over the PRI and of switching them to the internal modems.

Case Study Conclusion

With the proper configuration and interfaces, an access server can receive both ISDN and analog calls using PRI interfaces.

Review Questions

Answer the following questions, and then refer to Appendix H, "Answers to Review Questions," for answers and explanations.

1 How do dialer profiles simplify configurations?

2 What features do map classes provide to dialer interfaces?

3 Describe a network that might not benefit from dialer profiles.

CHAPTER 9

Configuring a Cisco 700 Series Router

In the previous chapter, you learned how to configure Cisco access servers for ISDN and how to optimize the connections. In this chapter, you will learn how to provide connectivity to the Central site for a small office/home office (SOHO) that is equipped with a Cisco 700 Series Router, as shown in Figure 9-1.

Figure 9-1   *SOHO Connecting to a Central Site*

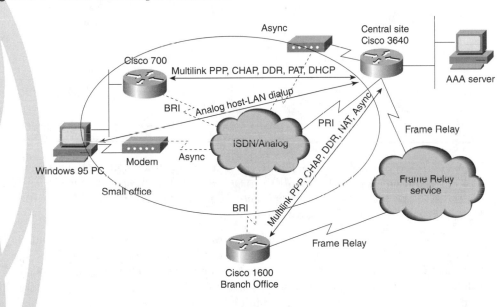

Cisco 700 Series Overview

All the routers in the Cisco 700 series product family offer maximum flexibility for remote access. The product family now includes the Cisco 761M, 762M, 765M, 766M, 771M, 772M, 775M, and 776M routers. These products offer two optional analog telephone interfaces to allow devices such as standard telephones, facsimile machines, and modems to share an ISDN BRI line, eliminating the need for multiple telephone lines or expensive ISDN telephones, as shown in Figure 9-2. Four of the Cisco 700 models offer support for two basic telephone service lines, as well as support for supplemental telephone services over ISDN. These telephone services include call waiting, cancel call waiting, call hold, call retrieve, three-way call conferencing, and call transfer.

Figure 9-2 *Cisco 700 Used by Telecommuters, Home Offices, and Small Offices*

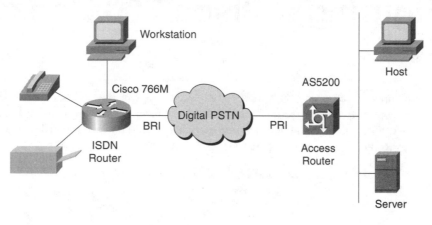

NOTE   Earlier models of the 700 series had model numbers without the M suffix. The M suffix indicates that the routers have 1.5 MB of system RAM.

The Cisco 700 series routers all support IP and IPX routing, transparent bridging, Simple Network Management Protocol (SNMP) management, and multilevel authentication. All Cisco 700 series routers support the Multilink Point-to-Point Protocol (MP), providing up to 128 Kbps (precompressed) of ISDN bandwidth.

All models in this family also feature ClickStart software, which allows users to configure Cisco 700 series routers by using a standard World Wide Web browser, such as Netscape Navigator. ClickStart is a graphical, user-friendly configuration interface that breaks the installation process into simple steps by prompting the user for the required information, thus enabling the user to set up a new router in just a few minutes.

The integrated packaging, documentation, user-friendly software, and match-the-colors cabling design of Cisco Fast Step allows users with no technical experience to have a Cisco 700 series router set up, tested, and connected to the Internet/intranet in less than 30 minutes. Cisco Fast Step software is a free, easy-to-use Microsoft Windows 95 or NT version 4-based tool that simplifies the setup and monitoring of Cisco routers for small offices and home offices. Once setup is completed, the monitor facility of Fast Step provides instant router status and ISDN connection information.

Cisco 800 Series Routers

Cisco has another SOHO router. It is the Cisco 800. The new Cisco 800 Series of Integrated Services Digital Network (ISDN) access routers provides big-business networking benefits to small offices and corporate telecommuters. With Cisco IOS software technology, the Cisco 800 Series offers secure, manageable, high-performance solutions for Internet and corporate LAN access. You can find more information on the Cisco 800 series router at www.cisco.com.

Cisco 700 Series Features

The Cisco 700 series is fully interoperable with Cisco IOS-based routers such as the Cisco 1600, Cisco 1700, Cisco 2500, Cisco 3600, Cisco 4000, and Cisco 7000 series using Multilink PPP for IP or IPX routing.

The Cisco 700 series is designed to minimize the complexity of configuring and operating multiprotocol routers. All Cisco 700 series routers come with the Cisco Fast Step software.

ClickStart, a Web-based application, simplifies initial configuration. Flash memory and TFTP downloading eliminate the expense of recalling units or sending a person to the remote site to perform software upgrades.

Personal network profiles make the process of connecting and disconnecting multiple sites transparent to the user. They enable Cisco 700 users to create customized sets of configuration parameters, such as filters, demand thresholds, network addresses, calling phone numbers, and passwords for each remote site that is dialed. Personal network profiles allow on-demand calls to be made to different telephone numbers, based on demand filters that are tailored for each remote site.

Because the Cisco 700 series supports remote management using SNMP and Telnet, a network management team at the Central site can perform all common monitoring functions.

NOTE With version 4.1 of the Cisco IOS-700, Combinet Proprietary Protocol (CPP) is no longer available, and PPP is the default.

Networking Features

The Cisco 700 series has industry-standard networking features designed to enhance interoperability, starting with PPP protocol support. Multilevel authentication using Challenge Handshake Authentication Protocol (CHAP) and Password Authentication Protocol (PAP) is supported. PPP dial-back security is available to control router access.

B-channel aggregation is supported with industry-standard Multilink PPP. All Cisco 700 series routers support Multilink PPP, which aggregates both B channels, providing up to 128 Kbps of ISDN bandwidth.

Cisco 700 series routers also support data compression that is compatible with the Cisco IOS, with a compression ratio of up to 4:1. When Multilink PPP is combined with a 4:1 compression ratio, an aggregate throughput of up to 512 Kbps is possible. The Cisco 700 series does not include data compression; this capability can be added via software at a very low cost by ordering the Standard Feature Set.

Access-lists provide packet filtering for bridging and routing.

Cisco 700 series routers can function as a Dynamic Host Configuration Protocol (DHCP) relay agent or DHCP server. When configured, Cisco 700 series routers will relay DHCP requests and responses between DHCP clients and a specified DHCP server. In addition, port and address translation (PAT) enables local hosts on a private IP network to communicate over a public network such as the Internet.

Routing and WAN Features

The Cisco 700 series offers the benefits of IP and IPX routing in a modem-sized package. When connecting to other Cisco routers, concurrent bridging is also supported.

The Cisco 700 series supports Routing Information Protocol (RIPv1 and RIPv2) for IP routing updates, with extensions to support demand circuits. IPX routing support includes Novell IPX Router Specification, Revision A, 9/2/92, with support for IPX spoofing. Cisco's snapshot routing is also supported.

DDR ensures that connections will not be inadvertently kept up when they are not in use, which keeps ISDN charges to a minimum. DDR allows ISDN connections to occur only when the router senses traffic that has been defined as "interesting" by the user or network administrator. Access-lists prevent broadcast traffic on the LAN from bringing up the ISDN connection unnecessarily.

With two ISDN BRI B channels, the Cisco 700 series can support simultaneous sessions with two sites or share network traffic between the channels. For example, as bandwidth needs increase, such as when a large file transfer is initiated, the second B channel is brought up automatically to carry the additional traffic.

This bandwidth-on-demand is supported with industry-standard Multilink PPP, which is also used for standards-based B-channel aggregation. Support for bandwidth-on-demand using Multilink PPP and 4:1 data compression enable cost-efficient WAN connections.

ISDN and Telephony Features

The Cisco 760 series routers are designed for both North American and international applications. They support all major ISDN central office switches in use worldwide. The 765 router is especially designed for international use because it has been homologated (certified) for use in more than 25 countries. It generates local tone (425 Hz) for international basic (analog) telephone service support. Cisco 760 series routers have met U.S. and international regulatory approvals, such as UL 1459, FCC part 15 class B, and FCC part 68 certification.

The Cisco 765 and 766 models also provide support for supplemental telephone services over ISDN, the first such products to offer this feature. Supplemental telephone services supported include call waiting, cancel call waiting, call hold, and call retrieve. These supplemental services for ISDN may not be available from certain central office switches; carriers; and Post, Telephone, and Telegraphs (PTTs).

The Cisco 762, 764, and 766 routers include a built-in NT1 device to provide an all-in-one solution for ISDN users in North America. In addition to the integrated NT1, the routers also provide an external S/T port to support additional ISDN devices such as ISDN telephones.

The Cisco 765 and Cisco 766 routers are similar to the Cisco 761 and 762 routers. However, they support two RJ-11 interfaces for sharing the ISDN BRI line with up to two analog devices (such as standard telephones, fax machines, and modems), which eliminate the need for multiple telephone lines or expensive ISDN telephones. Using Cisco's call-priority feature, the Cisco 765 and 766 can drop one or both ISDN BRI B channels that are being used for data to accept or initiate analog calls.

The personal network profiles enable Cisco 760 users to assign multiple ISDN phone numbers to each profile for flexibility in reaching the destination router.

Initial configuration options for the Cisco 765 and 766 routers can be entered by using a standard touch-tone telephone.

The Cisco 700 series supports ISDN BRI via a built-in RJ-45 connector.

The Cisco 700 series is compatible with international central office switch-types, which include I-CTR3 (also known as NET3 or Euro-ISDN for most of Europe), INS HSD64 and 128 (Japan), VN3 (France), 1TR6 (Germany), and TPH (Australia).

North American switch support includes AT&T 5ESS, Northern Telecom DMS 100, and NI-1 ISDN standards.

Cisco IOS-700 Release 4.x—Summary of Features

Cisco IOS-700 Release 4.0 includes many new features to ease configuration and administration:

- SAP helper address for NetWare networks
- Stacker compression with IOS routers

- IPX ping and IPX default route
- Automated callback initiated by the D channel
- Second number fail-over
- RIP snapshot routing
- DHCP relay agent and server
- Port and address translation

In addition to the preceding features, the Cisco IOS-700 offers the following key benefits:

- **DHCP relay agent**   Forwards DHCP requests and responses between DHCP clients and a specified DHCP server. DHCP automates TCP/IP addressing, which saves administration time and reduces the number of IP addresses that a site may require.

- **DHCP server**   The Cisco 700 series can assign and manage IP addresses from a specified address pool to DHCP clients.

- **Port and address translation (PAT)**   Allows the remote LAN to be configured by using private network addresses that are invisible to the outside world. All data from the remote LAN appears to be coming from the Cisco 700 series router itself. A Cisco 700 series user needs only a single IP node address, regardless of the number of remote workstations, which provides significant potential savings when connecting to an Internet service provider (ISP), and greatly relieves the network management burden for both ISPs and corporate network managers.

DHCP is a client/server protocol that allows local hosts (called DHCP clients) to request and receive IP configuration parameters from a DHCP server. These parameters include the IP address, subnet mask, default gateway, and WINS and DNS server. DHCP is specified in RFC 2132 (obsoletes RFC 1541).

Cisco 700 series routers with Release 4.0 software support PAT. PAT enables local hosts on a private IP network to communicate over a public network such as the Internet. All traffic designated to an external address has its source IP address translated before the packet is forwarded over the public network. IP packets returning to the private network will have their IP addresses translated back to a private IP address.

Profile Overview

There are two modes in which you can set parameters: the **system mode** and the **profile mode**, as explained in *Annex A* of the Cisco 700 documentation. System-mode parameters affect the configuration on a global level. Profiles are individual parameters that are maintained in configuration sets. Profile-mode parameters affect the way the router handles the connection to a device.

You do not have to reconfigure the router every time that you connect to a different device. Instead of using one set of configuration parameters for all devices, you can use different profiles to communicate with a variety of devices.

For example, you can create a user-defined profile, called 2500, which contains the parameters to be used when communicating with a Cisco 2500 series router over the WAN. You can customize your Cisco 700 series router to maintain up to 17 user-defined profiles. Profiles are saved in the Cisco 700 series router nonvolatile RAM (NVRAM).

NOTE

A **profile** is a set of configurations, customized for and associated with a specific remote device. After being defined by the user, profiles are saved and stored in a Cisco 700 series router's nonvolatile random access memory (NVRAM), which is the memory used to store the router's configurations. When the router is turned on, the profiles are loaded.

In addition to user-defined profiles, there are three permanent profiles on the Cisco 700, as shown in Figure 9-3. The following profiles can be modified, but not deleted:

- **LAN**   Determines how data is passed from the router to the LAN. It is used for routing and with the Ethernet connection.

- **Internal**   Determines how data is passed between the bridge engine and the IP/IPX router engine. Used when routing is enabled on LAN or USER profiles. It stores the parameters used to communicate between the LAN and WAN ports on the Cisco 700 series router.

- **Standard**   Used for incoming ISDN connections that do not have a profile. If authentication is not required and the destination device that you are connecting to does not have a user-defined profile, the router uses the Standard profile.

Figure 9-3 *Cisco 700 Series—Profiles*

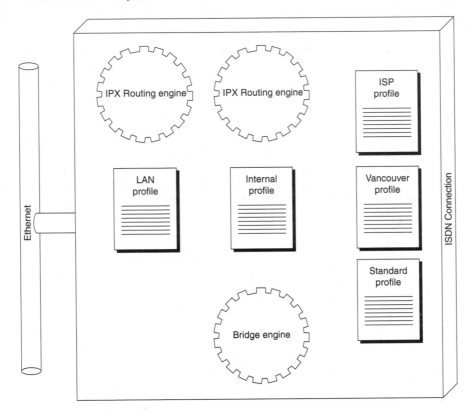

| NOTE | The Standard profile does not support routing, as shown in Figure 9-4. This profile should be used to provide the appropriate configuration and security measures for unknown callers. |

Figure 9-4   *Profiles—Manufacturer Defaults*

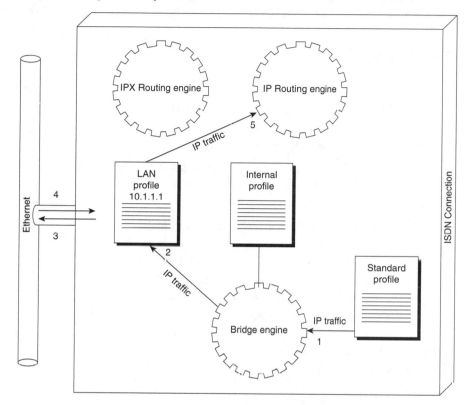

NOTE   Traffic flows from profile to profile through engines—a routing engine or a bridging engine.

Profiles enable users to create customized sets of configuration parameters, such as filters, demand thresholds, and passwords for each remote site that is dialed. Profiles allow on-demand calls to be made to different telephone numbers, based on demand filters that are tailored for each remote site.

Up to 20 profiles (16 user, LAN, standard, system, and internal) can be configured on Cisco 700 series routers.

System parameters are independent of profiles and affect the router as a system. System parameters can be changed only at the system-level prompt, shown as follows:

```
Router_name>
```

As an example of profiles, Figure 9-3 shows three possible connections for the WAN side of the router: two connections are to and from a known caller, and one connection is from an unknown caller.

Profile template characteristics are as follows:

- The profile template consists of all the profile parameters, as seen at the system level. All profiles are based on the profile template by inheriting these values. The profile template is modified by configuring the profile parameters at the system level.

- Any profile that has a specific profile parameter redefined within the profile is not affected by a change to the profile template configuration.

- After you configure the profile template, you can customize individual profiles by entering profile mode for that specific profile and redefining the profile's parameters.

- Profiles are either active or inactive:

  — An active profile immediately creates a virtual connection to that profile's associated remote device. After a virtual connection is created, a demand call can be made to that profile's associated remote device.

  — Inactive profiles have no connection associated with them. No demand calls can be made with a profile that is configured as inactive.

  — Activity status is configured with the **set profile** command. To display these settings for an individual profile, use the **show profile** command while in profile mode for the profile.

Profile guidelines are as follows:

- LAN and Internal profiles provide the same basic function.

- Any protocol routed in the LAN profile must be routed in the User profile in order to allow that protocol to be forwarded.

- Any protocol routed in the Internal profile may be routed or bridged in the User profile.

- If IP routing is for the Internal profile, the router is a pingable device.

- For IP to be bridged, the Internal profile must be enabled instead of IP routing.

Profile parameters are parameters that can be configured on a per-profile basis, and therefore apply only to the connection with the remote router. After creating a new profile, these parameters can be reconfigured within that profile. Any configuration changes to profile parameters while in profile mode apply only to that profile. The following are some common user profile parameters set on a Cisco 700:

- Demand Parameters
- Called Number
- Subnet Mask
- PPP Authentication

- Default Gateway
- Passwords
- CHAP Host Secret
- PAP Host Password
- IP Parameters

Cisco 700 User Interface

The user interface has a UNIX-like directory structure, as shown in Figure 9-5. Commands are set by entering **set** commands on the command-line interface. Also, to navigate from one profile to another, the **cd** (change directory) command is used.

Figure 9-5   *Cisco 700 Uses a UNIX-like Directory Structure for USER Profiles*

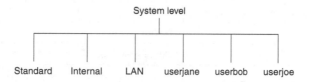

The **set** commands are automatically saved in NVRAM, and **reset** commands remove commands from NVRAM. To initialize the system, enter **set default**. The **set default** command is the same as the **erase start** command, followed by the **reload** command in the Cisco IOS software.

The **show** command displays information and parameters.

You can save **set** commands in a text file off-line, and copy and paste them at the command-line prompt to configure the router.

Configuring the Cisco 700 Series

You must specify system level, LAN profile, and user profile parameters to prepare the Cisco 700 router for operation in an ISDN environment.

- **System level configuration**   Select the switch that matches the ISDN provider's switch at the CO. This requirement is necessary because, despite standards, signaling specifics differ regionally and nationally. Set destination details, such as the directory numbers, and enter Service Profile Identifiers (SPIDs), if required. System-level configuration also includes assigning a system name and setting Multilink PPP off if you are connecting to a Cisco IOS router running Release 11.0(3) or earlier.

- **LAN profile configuration**   Specify an IP address and subnet mask for the Ethernet interface. Specify the types of packets to be routed. In this case, turn IP routing on and set IP RIP update to periodic.

- **User profile configurations**   Specify the characteristics of each user that you plan to dial. In our application, there is only one user—the ISP on the other end of the ISDN connection. Assign the user a name, set IP routing on, set the framing type, set the ISDN phone number you will dial, set the encapsulation type, and set the static route.

Once these profiles are created, you can define optional features, including caller ID, authentication type, and timeout value for the ISDN connection.

System Level Configuration

Use the **set switch** global command to specify the CO switch to which the router connects. For BRI ISDN service, the switch type can be one of those listed in Table 9-1.

Table 9-1   *Cisco 700 ISDN Switch Commands*

Command	Description
set switch switch-type	Defines the type of switch you are using
5ess	AT&T basic rate switches (U.S.)
dms	NT DMS-100 (North America)
ni-1	National ISDN-1 (North America)
1tr6	German 1TR6 ISDN switches
net3	Switch type for NET3 in United Kingdom and Europe
perm64	Dedicated line service--B channel 1 runs at 64 Kbps; channel 2 not used
perm128	Dedicated line service--both B channels combined to give 128 Kbps

NOTE   Auto-detect of ISDN switch type is available in later versions of the IOS-700. Separate IOS-700 images may require country-specific switches. The default if no switch is specified is basic-5ess.

Several ISDN providers use ISDN switches that operate on dial-in numbers called **SPIDs**. The SPIDs are used to authenticate that call requests are within contract specifications. These switches include National ISDN-1 and DMS-100 ISDN switches, as well as the AT&T 5ESS switch. The **set 1 spid** and **set 2 spid** commands are used on some switches and are replacements for subaddresses. The local SPID number is supplied by the service provider.

The following command line shows the syntax for the first BRI 64 Kbps channel, followed by a table list of ISDN-related commands:

```
IOS-700>set 1 spid spid-number [ldn]
```

Command	Description
set 1 spid *spid-number* **set 2 spid** *spid-number*	Number identifying the service to which you have subscribed. This value is assigned by the ISDN service provider.
ldn *number*	Local dial number (optional). This number must match the called-party information coming in from the ISDN switch in order to use both B channels on most switches.
set 1 dir *number* **set 2 dir** *number*	Directory number to which you have subscribed. This value is assigned by the ISDN service provider.

The system profile sets parameters that apply to all profiles on the selected router, unless overridden in the user profile. This is also called the *global configuration*. Example 9-1 shows a sample system-level configuration.

Example 9-1 *System-Level Configuration*

```
>set system R700
R700>set switch dms
R700>set 1 spid 0805555111101
R700>set 2 spid 0805555999902
R700>set 1 dir 5551111
R700>set 2 dir 5559999
```

LAN Profile Configuration

If you want to activate the IP routing on the LAN profile, you have to provide the address and subnet mask command to the Cisco 700. Also, you have to activate the routing with the **set ip routing on** command. Example 9-2 shows a sample LAN profile configuration.

Example 9-2 *LAN Profile Configuration*

```
IOS-700>cd lan
IOS-700:LAN>set ip address 192.168.1.1
IOS-700:LAN>set ip netmask 255.255.255.0
IOS-700:LAN>set ip routing on
IOS-700:LAN>set bridging off
```

Potential Profile Pitfalls

Let's discuss issues of bridging and routing with the different Cisco 700 profiles.

There are different strategies available for bridging and routing with a Cisco 700 series router. Depending on the strategy, sometimes problems happen. Here is an example: If IP routing is activated on the LAN profile and IP routing is not turned on the standard profile, as shown in Figure 9-6, the IP traffic will pass from the standard profile to the bridge engine (1), pass to the LAN profile (2), and come out on the Ethernet interface/LAN profile (3). The difficulty arises with the return-trip packets (4). The return traffic is routed from the LAN profile to the IP Routing Engine (5). Having no access to the standard profile, the return traffic gets caught and stops in the routing engine. The following is a typical misconfiguration:

```
cd lan
set bridging on
set ip routing on
set ip address 10.1.1.1
cd internal
set bridging on
cd standard
set bridging on
```

Figure 9-6 *Problem with LAN Profile Routing and Internal Profile Bridging*

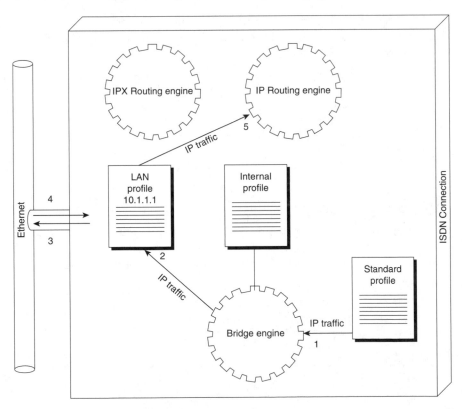

The solution is to turn off routing on the LAN interface and apply Layer 3 configuration to the internal profile.

If the IP routing is activated on the internal profile, as shown in Figure 9-7, the IP traffic will pass from standard profile to the bridge engine (1), pass to the LAN profile (2), and pass to the Ethernet interface LAN profile (3). The return traffic will then go from the Ethernet segment to the LAN profile (4), go to the bridging engine (5), go to the Internal profile (6), go to the IP Routing engine (7), go back out to the Internal profile (8), go toward the Bridge engine (9), and go to the Bridge engine that sends the packet out to the standard profile (10). The following is a typical proper configuration when standard profile is involved:

```
cd lan
set bridging on
cd internal
set bridging on
set ip routing on
set ip address 10.1.1.1
cd standard
set bridging on
```

Figure 9-7 *The Solution—LAN profile bridging and INTERNAL profile routing*

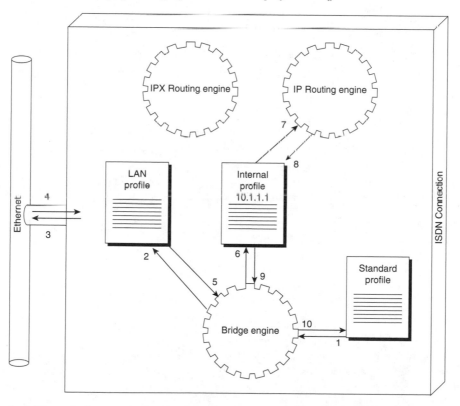

A similar solution can be implemented when using a user profile, as shown in Figure 9-8. If both IP routing and bridging are turned on for the Chicago profile, all IP traffic flows to the IP Routing engine (1). Not shown in Figure 9-8 is that all other traffic (AppleTalk, NetBEUI, and

IPX/SPX) would flow to the Bridge engine. The IP traffic flows from the IP routing engine to the Internal profile (2) and then flows to the Bridge engine (3). All traffic, whether it is IP or non-routed traffic like NetBEUI, flows to the LAN profile (4), and flows on to the Ethernet segment (5).

The return trip traffic flows from the Ethernet segment into the LAN profile (6), and then flows to the Bridge engine (7). The IP traffic flows to the internal profile (8), and then flows to the Routing engine (9), followed by the Chicago profile (10). Traffic other than IP flows from the Bridge engine to the Chicago profile (not shown on Figure 9-8).

The following is a typical correct configuration when a user profile is involved:

```
cd lan
set bridging on
cd internal
set bridging on
set ip routing on
set ip address 10.1.1.1
cd standard
set bridging off
set user Chicago
set bridging off
set ip routing on
set ip address 192.168.1.1
```

Figure 9-8 *The Solution with User Profile—LAN Profile Bridging And Internal Profile Routing*

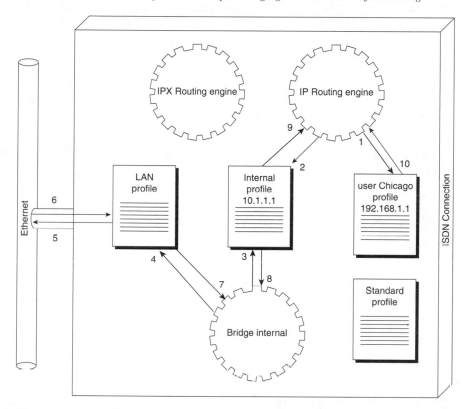

If you change an IP address of a profile, the IP routing is suspended, even if it still appears under the same profile when performing the **upload** command. To reactivate the IP routing process, you have to either **reload** the Cisco 700 or type under the profile **set ip routing on**.

User Profile Configuration

Use the **set encapsulation ppp** command if you want PPP encapsulation for your ISDN interface and if you want any of the LCP options that PPP offers (for example, CHAP authentication). You must use PPP PAP or CHAP if you will receive calls from more than one dial-up source. This command must be entered if you are connecting to a Cisco IOS router.

In addition to these commands, each user profile must include the username (**set user** *username*), ip address (**set ip address** *ip address*), and subnet mask (**set ip netmask** *netmask*) of the user. You must also turn on IP routing using the **set ip routing on** command.

NOTE	If you do not include the subnet mask, the default mask for that class of address is assumed. As an example, if you are using the address 172.16.2.53 without configuring a network mask, the Cisco 700 assumes the mask to be 255.255.0.0, which is the default mask for a class B address.

If you want to route IP with PPP, you must turn off CPP by using the **set encapsulation ppp** command.

Routing IP using CPP is only recommended for connections between 700 products, not between a Cisco 700 and a Cisco IOS router. To route between non-CPP products, you should configure IP routing with PPP.

NOTE	With version 4.1 of the Cisco IOS-700, encapsulation with PPP is the default.

The **set number** *number* command configures the phone number that is used to dial the ISP or remote router. This command is used in a user profile. The following is an example of this command:

```
IOS-700:User3>set number 14085551234
```

Enabling Profiles

A **connection** is a dynamically created link to a remote site. Connections are closely related to profiles because all connections are associated with a profile that defines the configuration of the connection.

A **virtual connection** is a connection without any existing physical channels. An **active connection** is a connection with one or more existing physical channels. Profiles can be set to be either active or inactive. When a profile has been created, setting it to active creates a virtual connection to the associated remote device. After a call is made to the associated remote device, the connection becomes an active connection.

Virtual and active connections behave similarly. The only difference is that active connections are forwarding packets. Virtual connections exist in order to monitor packet traffic until a demand filter causes a call to be initiated. When this happens, the virtual connection becomes an active connection.

When the call is finished, the physical link between the two devices is disconnected. However, the virtual connection to the remote router might be configured to remain active.

If the profile is configured to remain active after a link disconnects, a virtual connection remains. The virtual connection monitors the LAN traffic. If packets destined for the WAN are detected, the router opens up the physical connection and forwards the packets.

If the remote user makes a call to you, the remote device is identified and associated with the virtual connection created by the user's profile. This causes the connection to become active.

When creating a profile, it can be set active or inactive by using the **set active profile-name** or the **set inactive profile-name** commands.

Setting IP Default Routes

For the user profile specified, usually the Central site router, you can enter the default route and point it at a specific address, as follows:

```
700:user>set ip route destination 0.0.0.0/0 gateway 0.0.0.0 propagate on cost 1
```

The address used is the IP address of the BRI interface Central site router. All traffic for this user goes to the same IP address. To enable static routes, you must also set bridging off and make the Central site user profile active by using the following commands:

Command	Description
propagate on	Propagates routes and RIP updates.
cost *number*	Specifies the RIP hop count.

NOTE   Normally the **propagate on** command is not used because it will cause the BRI link to come up whenever there is a routing update.

Configuring IP Routing

In Example 9-3, the 700 router (R700) has a static route to the (Cisco IOS) router Central, as shown in Figure 9-9. Only the LAN and USER profiles are shown. You must also configure the system profile for the 700 router. The router-configuration information must be supplied by the ISP, and depends on the configuration of the ISP and the switch type.

Figure 9-9 *A Cisco 700 router Communicating with a Cisco IOS-Based Router*

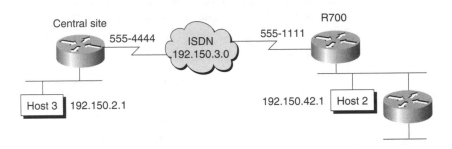

Example 9-3 *Cisco 700 Configuration for Connecting to a Central Site IOS-Based Router*

```
R700> cd LAN
R700:LAN> set ip address 192.150.42.16
R700:LAN> set ip netmask 255.255.255.0
R700:LAN> set ip routing on
R700:LAN> set ip rip update periodic
R700:LAN> cd
R700> set user Central
R700:Central> set number 5554444
R700:Central > set ip routing on
R700:Central > set rip update off
R700:Central > set ip route destination 0.0.0.0/0 gateway 0.0.0.0 prop on
R700:Central > set bridging off
R700:Central > cd
R700> set active Central
```

PPP's IP Control Protocol (IPCP) allows for the negotiation of certain parameters, such as an IP address and a specific compression protocol. Some points to remember when using IPCP negotiation on a Cisco 700 follow:

- A user profile is required to run PPP. IP routing must be turned on in order to receive an IPCP negotiated address.

- If a manually configured IP address exists on the Internal profile, the IPCP address will be assigned to the WAN (user) profile.

- If a manually configured IP address exists on the LAN profile, the IPCP address will be assigned to the Internal profile.

- If the LAN IP address is manually configured, the WAN interface must be unnumbered because the IPCP address will be assigned to the Internal profile.

- The remote site router needs to be configured to hand off IPCP addresses. A sample configuration for the remote router (Central) to hand off an IPCP address follows:

```
Central(config)#ip local pool test 700 192.150.3.10 192.150.3.19
Central(config)#interface bri0
Central(config-if)#peer default ip address pool test
```

This configuration specifies the IP address to be used when the 700 dials into the Central site.

Cisco 700—Configuration Example

Example 9-4 shows a comprehensive configuration of a Cisco 700 for dial-on demand routing to a Central site, as displayed in Figure 9-10. The capital letters in Example 9-4 represent the characters that allow a unique abbreviation of the command. For the purpose of this book, you will find a separator line between the different configuration levels. The first part of the configuration encompasses system-level commands. The second part of Example 9-4 shows the configuration of the Ethernet interface. The third part shows the configuration of the Internal profile used for routing. Finally, the last part of the example is the configuration for the USER profile called Central. Remember that user profiles inherit the system-level configuration by default.

Figure 9-10 *Cisco 700 Configuration—System, LAN, and USER Profiles*

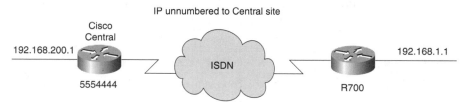

Example 9-4 *IP Routing Example*

```
>SEt SYStem R700
R700>SEt SWitch 5ESS
R700>SEt ENCapsulation PPp
R700>SEt PPp AUthentication INcoming CHap
R700>SEt PPp AUthentication OUtgoing CHap
R700>SEt PPp SEcret Client
------------------------------------------------------------
R700>cd LAN
R700:LAN>SEt BRidging ON
------------------------------------------------------------
R700>cd Internal
R700:INTERNAL>SEt BRidging ON
R700:INTERNAL>SEt IP ROuting ON
R700:INTERNAL>SEt IP 192.168.1.1
R700:INTERNAL>SEt IP BRidging OFf
R700:INTERNAL>SEt USer Central
------------------------------------------------------------
R700:Central>SEt BRidging OFf
R700:Central>SEt IP ROUTING ON
R700:Central>SEt IP ROUTE DEstination 0.0.0.0/0 GAteway 0.0.0.0
R700:Central>SEt NUmber 5554444
R700:Central>SEt ACtive
R700:Central>SEt PPp SEcret Host
```

Table 9-2 contains descriptions for the commands used in Example 9-4.

Table 9-2   *Command Description of IP Routing Example*

Command	Description
SEt SYStem R700	Defines the system name as R700.
SEt SWitch 5ESS	Configures for the AT&T 5ESS switch.
SEt ENCapsulation PPp	Configures PPP encapsulation over a WAN interface.
SEt PPp AUthentication INcoming CHap	Applies CHAP authentication to incoming WAN calls. The argument could also be chap pap.
SEt PPp AUthentication OUtgoing CHap	Applies CHAP authentication to outgoing WAN calls. This is the challenge I will send out. The default is none. The Cisco 700 is often used to call an ISP or your Central Office, in which case you will not send out an authentication challenge.
SEt PPp SEcret Client password	Specifies the CHAP password used by 700 to authenticate; must match on remote.
cd LAN	Switches to LAN profile.
SEt BRidging OFf	Packets that are not routed are dropped.
SEt IP 192.168.1.1	Sets the IP address on the Ethernet interface.
SEt IP ROUTING ON	Enables IP routing over the LAN interface.
SEt USer Central	Creates a user profile named "Central."
SEt BRidging OFf	Turns off bridging on this profile.
SEt IP ROUTING ON	Turns on IP routing for this profile.
SEt IP ROUTE DEstination 0.0.0.0/0 GAteway 0.0.0.0.	Configures an unnumbered route to the Central site.
SEt NUmber 5264444	Sets the number to call to reach this user.
SEt ACtive	Enables a virtual connection to Central. Incoming packets from the LAN cause the R700 router to dial the Central site.
SEt PPp SEcret HOst password	Sets password expected by 700 in response from remote.

Additional Interface Configuration

You can add the interface functions desired or required by the particular ISDN situation, as follows:

- Filter inbound call setups with caller ID screening.
- Use callback with or without authorization.

- Implement Multilink PPP for better bandwidth use.
- Cisco 700 routers implement Multilink PPP by default.

NOTE   You must manually turn off the multilink capability if your router is connecting to a Cisco IOS router running Release 11.0(3) or earlier.

Caller ID

Different commands are used on the Cisco 700 series router and the Cisco IOS router to configure caller ID. The commands for the Cisco 700 series router are issued at the system prompt level. The commands for the Cisco IOS router are issued at the BRI 0 interface level. Figure 9-11 and the command descriptions in Tables 9-3 and 9-4 provide examples of caller ID.

Figure 9-11 *Caller ID Scenario*

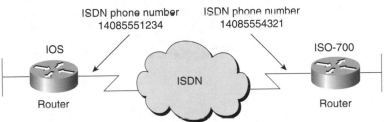

Table 9-3   *Cisco 700 Caller ID Commands*

Cisco IOS-700 Commands	Description
set caller id on	Enables caller ID on the ISDN interface.
set callidreceive 14085551234	Allows calls to be authorized, if received from the 14085551234 telephone number.

Table 9-4   *Cisco IOS Caller ID commands*

Cisco IOS Commands	Description
interface bri0	Specifies the ISDN interface on which you want caller ID authentication.
isdn caller 14085554321	Allows ISDN calls to be authorized on this interface if they are received from the 14085554321 telephone number.

The Prefix Issue

You may not see the 1 of the long-distance phone call during the caller ID because the switch is only passing the actual phone number including the area code. If the CO ISDN switch does not pass the control character, such as the 1, the command should be **set callidreceive 4085554321**.

PPP Callback—No Authorization

With this feature, you use the **set ringback** number command on the side initiating the call, and **set callback on** on the other end. The caller is Left700 and the callee is Right700, as shown in Figure 9-12. Example 9-5 shows the command to implement this callback.

Figure 9-12 *PPP Callback Scenario*

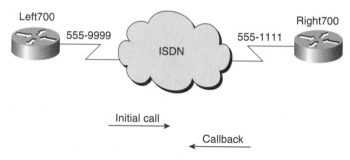

Example 9-5 *PPP Callback—No Authentication*

```
Left700>cd Right700
Left700:Right700>set ringback 5559999

Right700>cd Left700
Right700:Left700>set callback on
```

PPP Callback—Receive Number Authorization

With PPP callback authorization, the calling number of the router initiating the call is used to authorize on the callback router. The configuration in Example 9-6 refers to Figure 9-12.

Example 9-6 *PPP Callback with Caller ID Screening*

```
Left700>cd Right700
Left700:Right700>set ringback 5559999
Left700:Right700>set ppp callback request always

Right700>cd Left700
```

Example 9-6 *PPP Callback with Caller ID Screening (Continued)*

```
Right700:Left700>set ppp callback reply on
Right700:Left700>set callback id on
Right700:Left700>set callback receive 5559999
```

Cisco 700 and Cisco IOS Configuration Examples

The following pages will provide you with different configurations for IP or IPX, and for PAP or CHAP authentication for both the Cisco 700 and the IOS-based routers.

IP Traffic with CHAP Authentication between a Cisco 700 and an IOS-Based Router

In this example, you will see how to configure a Cisco 700 for remote connectivity to a Central site IOS router, as shown in Figure 9-13.

Figure 9-13 *Cisco 700 Calling Central Site, IOS Router*

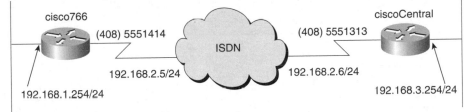

Cisco 700 Configuration

Example 9-7 shows the Cisco 700 configuration. It has been separated to provide you with a distinction between the different profile's configurations. The first part represents the system-level configuration. The second part is the LAN profile. The last part contains the user profile commands.

Example 9-7 *Additional Configuration on a Cisco 700 Series Router*

```
set system cisco766
set ppp multilink on
set switch 5ess
set ppp authentication incoming chap
set ppp authentication outgoing chap
set ppp secret client
pass1
pass1
------------------------------------------------------------
cd lan
set ip address 192.168.1.254
set netmask 255.255.255.0
```

continues

Example 9-7 *Additional Configuration on a Cisco 700 Series Router (Continued)*

```
set ip routing on
set ip rip update periodic
set bridging off
- - - - - - - - - - - - - - - - - - - - - - - - - - - - - - - - - - - - - - - - - - - - - - - - - - - - - - -
set user ciscoCentral
set number 4085551313
set compression stac
set ppp secret host
pass1
pass1
set ip routing on
set ip framing none
set ip address 192.168.2.5
set ip netmask 255.255.255.0
set ip rip version 1
set bridging off
cd
set active ciscoCentral
```

Table 9-5 contains the command descriptions for the configuration in Example 9-7.

Table 9-5   *Cisco 700 Series Router—Additional Commands*

Command	Description
set system cisco766	Defines the name of the router.
set ppp multilink on	Turns MP on for connection to the Cisco IOS router.
set switch 5ess	Identifies the ISDN switch type.
set ppp authentication incoming chap	Sets incoming authentication to CHAP.
set ppp authentication outgoing chap	Sets outgoing authentication to CHAP.
set ppp secret client	Sets the client CHAP secret password.
pass1	Password entered twice.
cd lan	Changes to the LAN profile.
set ip address 192.168.1.254	Sets the IP address of the Ethernet interface.
set netmask 255.255.255.0	Sets the subnet mask.
set ip routing on	Turns on IP routing.
set ip rip update periodic	Sets RIP updating to periodic--every 30 seconds.
set bridging off	Sets bridging to off.
set user ciscoCentral	Defines a new user called ciscoCentral.
set number 4085551313	Sets the number to be called to reach this user.
set compression stac	Sets the compression type to STAC for this user.

Table 9-5   *Cisco 700 Series Router—Additional Commands (Continued)*

Command	Description
set ppp secret host	Sets the host chap secret password.
pass1	Password entered twice.
set ip routing on	Sets IP routing to on for this user.
set ip framing none	Sets IP framing to IPCP for this user.
set ip address 192.168.2.5	Sets the IP address for user ciscoCentral.
set ip netmask 255.255.255.0	Sets the netmask for this user.
set ip rip version 1	Sets the version of RIP for this user.
set ip rip update snapshot	Sets the RIP updates to snapshot for this user.
set bridging off	Sets bridging to off.
set active ciscoCentral	Makes this user profile active.

Cisco IOS Configuration

Example 9-8 shows the configuration for the Central site to connect on the Cisco 700, as shown in Figure 9-13.

Example 9-8   *IOS-Based Central Site Router's Additional Configuration*

```
hostname ciscoCentral
username cisco766 password pass1
isdn switch-type basic-5ess
ip routing
interface ethernet 0
ip address 192.168.3.254 255.255.255.0
interface bri 0
encapsulation ppp
dialer rotary-group 0
<output omitted>
interface dialer 0
encapsulation ppp
ppp authentication chap
ppp multilink
dialer load-threshold 1
compress stac
dialer in-band
ip address 192.168.2.6 255.255.255.0
dialer map ip 192.168.2.5 name cisco766 speed 56 broadcast 4085551414
dialer-group 1
router rip
network 192.168.3.0
network 192.168.2.0
dialer-list 1 protocol ip permit
```

Table 9-6 contains the command description for the configuration of the IOS router shown in Example 9-8.

Table 9-6 *Additional Configuration Commands of Central Site IOS-Based Router*

Command	Description
hostname ciscoCentral	Sets the host name of the router.
username cisco766 password pass1	Defines a user called **cisco766** with a password of **pass1**.
isdn switch-type basic-5ess	Sets the ISDN switch type.
ip routing	Turns on IP routing.
interface ethernet 0	Enters interface E 0 configuration mode.
ip address 192.168.3.254 255.255.255.0	Defines the IP address and subnet mask of the interface.
interface bri 0	Enters interface BRI 0 configuration mode.
encapsulation ppp	Sets the encapsulation to PPP for each bri interface.
dialer rotary-group 0	Sets the dialer group to 0 for each BRI interface.
interface dialer 0	Sets the parameters for dialer group 0.
encapsulation ppp	Sets encapsulation to PPP for dialer group 0.
ppp authentication chap	Sets authentication to CHAP for dialer group 0.
ppp multilink	Sets Multilink PPP for dialer group 0.
dialer load-threshold 1	Sets the volume to bring up another line.
compress stac	Sets the compression type to STAC for dialer group 0.
dialer in-band	Sets all activity for this dialer group to in-band.
ip address 192.168.2.6 255.255.255.0	Sets the IP address and mask for this dialer group.
dialer map ip 192.168.2.5 name cisco766 speed 56 broadcast 4085551414	Sets the dialer-map parameters.
dialer-group 1	Associates this dialer interface to dialer group 1 router rip. Sets RIP to active on this router.
network 192.168.3.0	Assigns network numbers for this router.
network 192.168.2.0	Assigns network numbers for this router.
dialer-list 1 protocol ip permit	Allows IP packets to be routed using dialer-list 1.

TIP   When configuring PPP CHAP with IOS and 700 routers, remember that the password of **set ppp secret client** has to be the same as the **set ppp secret host** and the same as the **username password** statement. Also, the username statement and the dialer map name statement are case-sensitive. The passwords are case-sensitive as well.

IP Traffic with PAP Authentication between Two Cisco 700s

This is an example of the way two Cisco 700 routers could be configured to exchange IP packets with PAP Authentication. Figure 9-14 represents this scenario.

Figure 9-14 *IP Segments Using PAP Authentication*

Remote Office Configuration

The small office/home office router's configuration is displayed in Example 9-9.

Example 9-9 *Cisco 700 Series SOHO Router's Configuration Using PAP*

```
>set systemname SOHO
SOHO>set ppp password client
Enter Password: Knight
ReEnter Password:  Knight
SOHO>set encapsulation ppp
SOHO>set ppp authentication incoming pap
SOHO>cd LAN
SOHO:LAN>set bridging off
SOHO:LAN>set ip routing on
SOHO:LAN>set ip rip update periodic
SOHO:LAN>set ip 192.168.3.1
SOHO>set user Central
SOHO:Central>set bridging off
SOHO:Central>set ip routing on
SOHO:Central>set ip rip update demand
SOHO:Central>set ip 192.168.2.2
SOHO:Central>set ip framing none
SOHO:Central>set timeout 120
SOHO:Central>set 1 number 14165551234
SOHO:Central>set 1 number 14165551234
SOHO:Central>set ppp password host
Enter Password:  merry
ReEnter Password: merry
SOHO:Central>set ppp authentication outgoing pap
```

NOTE   The **systemname** is used as the userid during PPP authentication. The **systemname** is case-sensitive and must match the user profile name on the far end unit.

Central Site Configuration

The Central office is also equipped with a Cisco 700 and has the configuration displayed in Example 9-10.

Example 9-10 *Configuration of a Central Site Equipped with a Cisco 700*

```
>set systemname Central
Central> set ppp password client
Enter password:  merry
ReEnter password:  merry
Central>set encapsulation ppp
Central>set ppp authentication incoming pap
Central>cd LAN
Central:LAN>set bridging off
Central:LAN>set ip routing on
Central:LAN>set ip rip update periodic
Central:LAN>set ip 192.168.1.1
Central:LAN>cd
Central:LAN>set user SOHO
Central:SOHO>set bridging off
Central:SOHO>set ip routing on
Central:SOHO>set ip rip update demand
Central:SOHO>set ip 192.168.2.1
Central:SOHO>set ip framing none
Central:SOHO>Set timeout 120
Central:SOHO>Set 1 number 14165551222
Central:SOHO>Set 2 number 14165551222
Central:SOHO>set ppp password host
Enter password: Knight
ReEnter password:  Knight
Central:SOHO>set ppp authentication outgoing pap
```

IPX Traffic with CHAP Authentication between a Cisco 700 and an IOS-based Router

This is an example of the way a Cisco 700 could be configured to exchange IPX traffic with a Central site equipped with an IOS-based router. Figure 9-15 represents this scenario.

Figure 9-15 *IPX Segments Using CHAP Authentication*

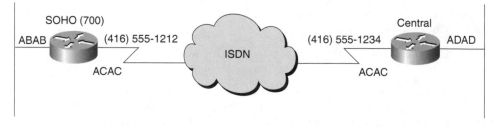

NOTE   In the example in Figure 9-15, the ISDN link will stay up all the time due to the RIP and SAP update.

Remote Office Configuration

The small office/home office will have the configuration displayed in Example 9-11.

Example 9-11 *Cisco 700 Series SOHO Router Configuration for IPX Routing*

```
>set systemname SOHO
SOHO>set ppp secret client
Enter password: merry
ReEnter password: merry
SOHO>set encapsulation ppp
SOHO>set ppp authentication incoming chap
SOHO>cd LAN
SOHO:LAN>set bridging off
SOHO:LAN>set ipx routing on
SOHO:LAN>set ipx network ABAB
SOHO:LAN>set ipx framing 802.3
SOHO:LAN>set ipx rip update periodic
SOHO> set user Central
SOHO:Central>set bridging off
SOHO:Central >set 1 number 14165551234
SOHO:Central >set 2 number 14165551234
SOHO:Central >set ipx routing on
SOHO:Central >set ipx framing none
SOHO:Central >set ipx rip update periodic
SOHO:Central >set ipx network ACAC
SOHO:remote>set ppp secret host
Enter password: merry
ReEnter password: merry
SOHO:remote>set ppp authentication outgoing chap
```

Central Site Configuration

The Cisco IOS configuration could be as shown in Example 9-12.

Example 9-12 *IOS-based Central Site Router IPX Routing Configuration*

```
hostname Central
Username SOHO password merry
ipx routing
interface ethernet 0
  ipx network ADAD
Interface BRI 0
  ipx network ACAC
  encapsulation ppp
  dialer map ipx ACAC.0234.a234.0012 name SOHO broadcast 14165551222
  dialer-group 1
```

continues

Example 9-12 *IOS-based Central Site Router IPX Routing Configuration (Continued)*

```
 ppp authentication chap
 ppp multilink
dialer-list 1 protocol ipx permit
```

Authentication Quick Reference Guide

Multiple configuration permutations are possible for CHAP and PAP authentication of Cisco 700 series routers. Tables 9-7 through 9-10 provide the settings for PAP or CHAP authentication on several combinations of two Cisco 700 and/or IOS-based routers.

Table 9-7   *Cisco 700 Series Routers with CHAP Authentication*

Central, CHAP, Cisco 700	Remote, CHAP, Cisco 700
Set ppp authentication outgoing chap	Set ppp authentication outgoing chap
Set ppp authentication incoming chap	Set ppp authentication incoming chap
Set ppp secret client Enter password: merry ReEnter password: merry	Set ppp secret host Enter password: merry ReEnter password: merry
Set systemname Central	Set user Central
Set user Remote	Set systemname Remote
Set ppp secret host Enter password: Knight ReEnter password: Knight	Set ppp secret client Enter password: Knight ReEnter password: Knight

NOTE   The remote site will have the configuration, as shown in Table 9-7.

```
Remote:Central>set ppp secret client Knight
```
The command to specify the secret password to use when the remote site is logging into Central is *Knight*. Thus, the following command on *Central*:
```
Central:Remote>set ppp secret host Knight
```
In Table 9-7, the routers are doing a two-way authentication, using a different password in both directions. This can be done if both routers are Cisco 700 series because you can specify which password to use, depending on whether the routing is acting as a host or a client.

Table 9-8   *Cisco 700 Series Routers with PAP Authentication*

Central, PAP, Cisco 700	Remote, PAP, Cisco 700
Set ppp authentication outgoing pap	Set ppp authentication outgoing pap

Table 9-8   *Cisco 700 Series Routers with PAP Authentication (Continued)*

Central, PAP, Cisco 700	Remote, PAP, Cisco 700
Set ppp authentication incoming pap	Set ppp authentication incoming pap
Set ppp secret client Enter password: merry ReEnter password: merry	Set ppp secret host Enter password: merry ReEnter password: merry
Set systemname Central	Set user Central
Set user Remote	Set systemname Remote
Set ppp password host Enter password: Knight ReEnter password: Knight	Set ppp password client Enter password: Knight ReEnter password: Knight

Table 9-9

Central, CHAP, Cisco IOS-Based	Remote, CHAP, Cisco 700
ppp authentication chap	Set ppp authentication outgoing chap
	Set ppp authentication incoming chap
hostname Central	Set user Central
Username Remote password merry	Set systemname Remote
Username Remote password merry	Set ppp secret host Enter password: merry ReEnter password: merry
Username Remote password merry	Set ppp secret client Enter password: merry ReEnter password: merry

NOTE   As recommended on the Cisco Web site, the same password (**merry**) is entered in three places for successful authentication: at the **set ppp secret client** command on the Cisco 700, at the **set ppp secret host** command on the Cisco 700, and at the **username password** global-configuration command on the Cisco IOS-based access server. This password is case-sensitive on each device.

Table 9-10   *PAP with an IOS-Based Central Router and Cisco 700 Series Remote Router*

Central, PAP, Cisco IOS-Based	Remote, PAP, Cisco 700
ppp authentication pap	Set ppp authentication outgoing pap
	Set ppp authentication incoming pap

continues

Table 9-10 *PAP with an IOS-Based Central Router and Cisco 700 Series Remote Router (Continued)*

Central, PAP, Cisco IOS-Based	Remote, PAP, Cisco 700
hostname Central	Set user Central
Username Remote password merry	Set systemname Remote
Username Remote password merry	Set ppp password host Enter password: merry ReEnter password: merry
Username Remote password merry	Set ppp password client Enter password: merry ReEnter password: merry

Monitoring IP Routing

Example 9-13 shows a partial output from the **show ip configuration all** and **show ip route all** commands. The **show ip configuration** command displays the name of the profile (if you are in profile mode), whether IP routing is enabled for the profiles, the IP address and netmask for the connection, the RIP version used for the profile (not shown), and so on. The **show ip route all** command shows the destination network address for a given profile, the type of interface used to reach that destination (either WAN for ISDN or NET for Ethernet), and the local gateway for the route.

Example 9-13 *Display of a* **show ip configuration all** *Command*

```
R700:Central>show ip configuration all
Profile      Routing      Frame       IP Address      Netmask
Internal     ON           ETH2        192.168.1.1     255.255.255.0
Central      ON           IPCP        192.168.99.1    255.255.255.0
Profile PAT Multicast Summarization
Internal     OFF          OFF         OFF
Central      OFF          OFF         OFF


R700:Central>show ip route all
Profile      Type         Destination      Bits     Gateway
Central      WAN          192.168.99.1     24       192.168.1.1
Internal     NET          192.168.1.1      24       DIRECT
```

Table 9-11 explains some other commands that are useful when you monitor and/or troubleshoot Cisco 700 connections.

Table 9-11 *Addition Monitoring and Troubleshooting Commands*

Command	Description
call 1 <phone number>	The Cisco 700 can initiate a manual call via its ISDN port.
disconnect <connection number or channel number or **all**>	Manually disconnects a manual or DDR call.

Table 9-11   *Addition Monitoring and Troubleshooting Commands (Continued)*

Command	Description
diag ppp on/off	Monitors the status of the ppp negotiation.
log calls	Monitors and keeps track of call status.
log messages ver time	Monitors Q931 traffic.
show status	Displays the status line for ISDN connection.
show negotiation	Displays negotiated parameters.

Cisco 700 Series and DHCP

DHCP automates IP address network assignment and administration, and may reduce the number of IP addresses that a site may require. A DHCP client can automatically discover and incorporate local configuration parameters without user intervention. In turn, the network manager need not enter per-client configuration parameters. DHCP is especially useful for mobile users who need part-time network access.

A DHCP server also services existing Bootstrap Protocol (BOOTP) clients with no client modifications. There are two primary differences between DHCP and BOOTP:

- DHCP provides a mechanism whereby clients can request and receive an IP address for a certain period of time, called a **finite lease** in the RFC. This allows for addresses to be reused once their lease has expired, thereby conserving IP addresses that are in scarce supply.

- DHCP provides a mechanism for a client to acquire all of the IP-configuration parameters that it needs in order to operate.

Cisco 700—DHCP Functionality

The Cisco 700 series router with 4.x software can function as a DHCP server or a DHCP relay agent.

As a DHCP server, the Cisco 700 series router will allocate an IP address from a specified IP address pool to a DHCP client, as shown in Figure 9-16.

Figure 9-16 *Cisco 700 Configured as a DHCP Server*

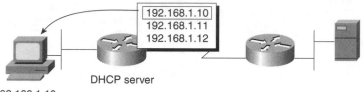

As a DHCP relay agent, the Cisco 700 series router will relay DHCP requests and responses between DHCP clients on the local Ethernet segment and a remote DHCP server across the WAN segment, as shown in Figure 9-17.

Figure 9-17 *Cisco 700 Configured as a DHCP Relay Agent*

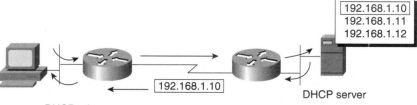

Using the Cisco 700 as a relay agent eliminates the need to have a DHCP server on every segment.

The relay agent fills in the IP address in the gateway field of the DHCP request, so the server can set the scope (what range of addresses) from which the client will be assigned an address. In an IOS router, DHCP relay is enabled by the use of the **ip helper interface** command.

DHCP Server Configuration

Example 9-14 shows the required commands to configure a Cisco 700 as a DHCP server, as shown in Figure 9-18.

Example 9-14 *Cisco 700 Series Router DHCP Server Configuration*

```
>SEt SYStem LA766
LA766>SEt DHcp SERver
LA766>SEt DHcp ADdress 192.168.200.2 252
LA766>SEt DHcp NETmask 255.255.255.0
LA766>SEt DHcp GAteway PRImary 192.168.200.1
LA766>SEt DHcp DNS PRImary 192.168.1.1
LA766>SEt DHcp WINS PRImary 192.168.1.1
LA766>SEt DHcp Domain WayNet
```

Figure 9-18 *DHCP Server Configuration*

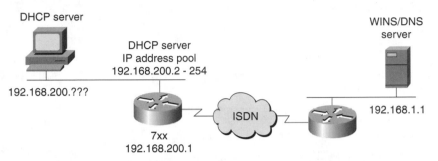

Table 9-12 contains command descriptions for the configuration in Example 9-14.

Table 9-12   *Cisco 700 Series Router DHCP Commands*

Command	Description
SEt DHcp SERver	Enables DHCP server functionality on the Cisco 700.
SEt DHcp ADdress 192.168.200.2 252	Specifies the starting address of the pool and the number of addresses in the pool. In this case, the assigned addresses can range from 192.168.200.2 to 192.168.200.254.
SEt DHcp NETmask 255.255.255.0	Specifies the subnet mask that DHCP clients will use.
SEt DHcp GAteway PRImary 192.168.200.1	Specifies the 700 as the default gateway. Note that this address should match the IP address configured on the LAN profile.
SEt DHcp DNS PRImary 192.168.1.1	Specifies the DNS address for DHCP clients.
SEt DHcp WINS PRImary 192.168.1.1	Specifies the WINS server for DHCP clients.
Set DHcp Domain WayNet	Specifies the NT domain of the DHCP server.

Some points to remember when configuring the DHCP server are as follows:

- When the DHCP server is initialized, default addresses are used if no existing LAN or Internal addresses exist. If a manually configured LAN or Internal address exists, the router defines the default gateway, netmask, and DHCP address pool based on this address. If neither exists, it uses the default settings of 10.0.0.1 as the LAN IP address, 255.0.0.0 as the subnet mask, 10.0.0.2 as the starting DHCP client address, and 10.0.0.1 (the LAN interface address) as the primary gateway address.

- Unlike DHCP relay, DHCP server and IPCP will not automatically initiate a call, even if AUTO is OFF.

- In order for the DHCP server parameters to be automatically generated and used based on the LAN or Internal IP address, each DHCP parameter must be set to 0 or to none.

- To reset the DHCP server configuration, each value must be reset by using the **reset** command.

DHCP Relay Agent Configuration

Configuring a DHCP relay agent on a Cisco 700 series router is easy. At the system level, you only need to add one command:

```
SEt DHcp RElay ip address of DHCP server
```

To view DHCP configuration, enter the following:

```
SHow DHcp Config
```

Example 9-15 is a configuration example of a Cisco 700 relay agent, as seen in Figure 9-19.

Example 9-15 *Cisco 700 Series DHCP Relay Agent*

```
>SEt SYStem LA766
LA766>SEt SWitch 5ESS
LA766>SEt ENCapsulation PPp
LA766>SEt PPp Authentication INcoming CHap
LA766>SEt PPp Authentication OUtgoing CHap
LA766>SEt PPp SEcret Client
LA766>SEt DHcp RElay 192.168.1.1
```

Figure 9-19 *Cisco 700 DHCP Relay Agent Example*

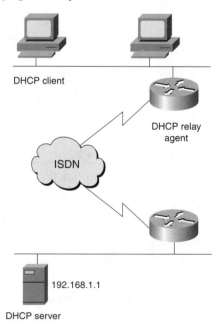

No change is made to the user profiles, to the LAN profile on the Cisco 700, or to the Central site router.

Some points to remember when configuring the DHCP relay agent are as follows:

- The IP address on the Internal or the LAN profile must be in the same network as that of the DHCP clients.

- A configuration in which both the Internal and LAN IP addresses exist will not work with DHCP relay. A LAN profile IP address or an Internal profile IP address can be used, but not both. If the Internet Protocol Control Protocol (IPCP) is to be used in conjunction with DHCP relay, a manually configured LAN IP address must not already exist because the IPCP address will be placed on the Internal profile.

- DHCP relay and IPCP initiate a call automatically, even if autodetection is set to off.

- DHCP relay and DHCP server are mutually exclusive. The router can function as one or the other, but not both.

- Upon rebooting, the 700 waits 90 seconds before it attempts to get an IPCP address. This allows for ISDN line initialization.

- Make sure that the gateway address set in the remote DHCP server is that of the 700 LAN profile.

Monitoring DHCP

Use the **show dhcp config** command, as shown in Example 9 16, to see useful information about the DHCP environment: the IP address range in the IP address pool (the starting IP address plus the count equals the range), the default gateway, and the WINS and DNS server addresses. All of these configuration parameters will be returned to a DHCP client that requests an IP configuration from the Cisco 700.

Example 9-16 *Display of the* **show dhcp config** *Command*

```
LA766>show dhcp config
Environment
  DHCP Server      ON
  DHCP Relay       OFF
IP Address Pool
  Start IP Address      192.168.200.2
  Count      252
  Subnet Mask      255.255.255.0
DNS Configuration
  Primary DNS Server      192.168.1.1
  Secondary DNS Server      192.168.1.1
  Domain      ""
Gateways
  Primary Gateway      192.168.200.1
  Secondary Gateway      NONE
WINS Configuration
  Primary WINS Server      192.168.1.1
  Secondary WINS Server      NONE
Address In Use
  IP Address      Mac Address
2 IP addresses allocated, 250 free
```

Summary

In this chapter, you learned the characteristics of the Cisco 700. You also learned how to configure the Cisco 700 series to connect with an IOS-based router via ISDN links. This chapter concludes with the standard configuration of routers for dial-on-demand routing.

With the next chapter, you will begin Part V, "Enabling Permanent Connections to the Central Site," and embark on the study of building a WAN with permanent connections—mainly via X.25 and Frame Relay.

Case Study—Configuring a Cisco 700 Series Router

Complete the tasks of this case study, and then review the case study solution section that follows to see how you did and see where you might need to review the concepts presented in this chapter.

In this case study, you are asked to configure a Cisco 700 series router to communicate with an access server using PPP and CHAP. You will also be required to add commands to an IOS-based access server to enable it to communicate with a Cisco 700 series router.

Scenario

You are asked to configure routers for both a remote office and a Central site with IP routing and addresses to communicate over the ISDN network. Figure 9-20 presents the network topology.

Figure 9-20 *SOHO Router Connecting to IOS-based Central Router*

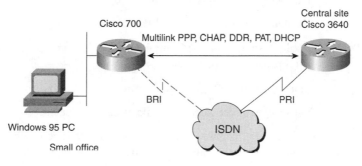

Task 1—Resetting the Cisco 700 to Default Settings

Before you attempt to configure your Cisco 700, you should check the current configuration. To ensure that you start with a clean Cisco 700 router, you can reset it to its original settings.

Step 1   After you hook the Cisco 700 console port to your terminal, reset the Cisco 700 to its original settings.

Step 2   After the 766 reboots, display the current default settings.

Task 2—Configuring the Cisco 700 to Communicate with the Central Site Router

Complete the following steps to configure your Cisco 700 series router to communicate with the Central site router.

Step 1   Provide a name to your Cisco 700. You could call it HomeA.

Step 2   Prepare your Cisco 700 to present the password **cisco** when it receives a CHAP request from the Central site router.

Step 3   Configure your Cisco 700 LAN profile to use an IP address, such as 10.118.0.1 with a mask of 24 bits. Also, enable routing on the LAN profile.

Step 4   You are now required to configure your Cisco 700 series router with a profile for the Central site that it wishes to connect to:

— Create a user profile, which identifies the router to which you will connect. You could call that profile CentralA.

— Provide the BRI interface of the Cisco 700 with an IP address (for the Cisco 700, use 10.30.1.2; for the Central site IOS-based router, use 10.30.1.1). These addresses will use a 24-bit mask.

— Configure the phone number to dial to reach the Central site ISDN connection. Pretend that you are subscribing to a speed-dial service and that your router simply has to dial 1000 to reach the Central site.

— Configure a timeout value of 90 seconds for calls.

— Enable IP routing on the CentralA profile. You could also turn off bridging on the same profile.

— Set a default route to point to CentralA.

— Don't forget to activate the profile after it is created.

Step 5   Initiate a call from the Cisco 700 to the Central site router. What would you expect to see? Would the call go through?

Task 3—Configuring the Cisco 3640 to Communicate with the Cisco 700

You will now configure the Central site router so you can establish a connection between the Cisco 700 and the Central site router.

Step 1   Configure the Central site router so it will accept calls from the remote site.

Step 2   Configure the PRI interface so it will perform CHAP authentication and multilink PPP.

Step 3   On the Central site router, configure a dialer interface, which you will call dialer 2, to be used as a connection to the Cisco 700. Provide this dialer interface with an IP address of the same subnet as the ISDN interface of the Cisco 700—that is, 10.30.1.1 with a mask of 24 bits. Remember all of the other commands that are necessary for a dialer interface to work for DDR.

Step 4   Configure a static map to the home office LAN segment.

Step 5   Ensure that your Central site will not be sending routing updates out of interface dialer 2.

Step 6   On the Central router, configure an access-list to specify IP as the only interesting DDR traffic except for IGRP updates.

Task 4—Placing a Manual ISDN Call from the Cisco 700

To test the capability of the two routers to communicate, have the Cisco 700 place a call to the Central site router.

Task 5—Configuring the Cisco 700 to Receive Incoming Calls from the Central Site

Finish the configuration on the home office router so it can receive incoming calls from the Central site and authenticate with CHAP.

NOTE   One of the default commands with a Cisco 700 series is **set ppp authentication incoming chap pap**. This command configures your Cisco 700 series router to accept and respond to incoming authentication requests, whether the request is for CHAP or PAP authentication.

That is the reason you were not asked in this case study to provide a command that would specify what kind of authentication request your router would entertain.

Step 1   Provide the configuration for your Cisco 700 series router that will ensure a two-way authentication using CHAP.

Step 2   Provide a command to specify that the password used by the Central site when authenticating will be **cisco.**

Step 3   Look at your Cisco 700 series router's configuration to confirm that all the required commands are configured.

Step 4   Look at the Central site router to confirm proper configuration.

Solution to Case Study—Configuring a Cisco 700 Series Router

The following is a step-by-step discussion of the case study solution.

Task 1 Solution—Resetting the Cisco 700 to Default Settings

Step 1   To reset a Cisco 700 to its default, enter the command **set default**.

Step 2   To display the configuration of a Cisco 700, enter the command **upload**.

Task 2 Solution—Configuring the Cisco 700 to Communicate with the Central Site Router

Step 1 Provide a name to your Cisco 700. You could call it HomeA:

```
set system HomeA
```

Step 2 Prepare your Cisco 700 to present the password cisco when it receives a CHAP request from the Central site router:

```
set ppp secret client cisco
```

Step 3 Configure your Cisco 700 LAN profile to use an IP address, such as 10.118.0.1 with a mask of 24 bits. Also, enable routing on the LAN profile:

```
cd lan
set ip address 10.118.0.1
set ip netmask 255.255.255.0
set ip routing on
```

Step 4 You will now be required to configure your Cisco 700 series router with a profile for the Central site it wishes to connect to:

— Create a user profile, which identifies the router to which you will connect. You could call that profile CentralA:

```
cd
set user CentralA
```

— Provide the BRI interface of the Cisco 700 with an IP address; let's say for Cisco 700, 10.30.1.2 (you could give to the Central site IOS-based router the address of 10.30.1.1). These addresses will use a 24-bit mask:

```
set ip address 10.30.1.2
set ip netmask 255.255.255.0
```

— Configure the phone number to dial to reach the Central site ISDN connection. Pretend you are subscribing to a speed-dial service and to reach the Central site, your router simply has to dial 1000:

```
set number 1000
```

— Configure a timeout value of 90 seconds for calls:

```
set timeout 90
```

— Enable IP routing on the CentralA profile. You could also turn off bridging on the same profile:

```
set ip routing on
set bridging off
```

— Set a default route to point to CentralA:

```
set ip route destination 0.0.0.0/0 gateway 10.30.1.1
```

> — Don't forget to activate the profile after it is created:
>
> ```
> set active
> ```

Step 5 Initiate a call from the Cisco 700 to the Central site router. What would you expect to see? Would the call go through?

The call should not go through because the Central site access has not yet been configured.

Task 3 Solution—Configuring the Cisco 3640 to Communicate with the Cisco 700

Step 1 Configure the Central site router to accept calls from the remote:

```
username HomeA password cisco
```

Step 2 Configure the PRI interface to perform CHAP authentication and multilink PPP:

```
interface s 1/0:23
ppp authentication chap
ppp multilink
no fair-queue
```

Step 3 On the Central site router, configure a dialer interface (which you will call dialer 2) to be used as a connection to the Cisco 700. Provide this dialer interface with an IP address of the same subnet as the ISDN interface of the Cisco 700—that is, 10.30.1.1 with a mask of 24 bits. Remember all the other commands that are necessary for a dialer interface to work for DDR:

```
interface dialer 2
ip address 10.30.1.1
encapsulation ppp
dialer remote-name HomeA
dialer string 2002
dialer pool 1
dialer-group 2
no fair-queue
ppp authentication chap
ppp multilink
```

Step 4 Configure a static map to the home office LAN segment:

```
ip route 10.118.0.0 255.255.255.0 Dialer2
```

Step 5 Ensure that your Central site will not be sending routing updates out of interface dialer 2:

```
router igrp 100
```

```
              passive-interface Dialer2
```

Step 6   On the Central Router, configure an access-list to specify IP as the only
interesting DDR traffic, except for IGRP updates:

```
dialer-list 2 protocol ip list 102
access-list 102 deny igrp any any
access-list 102 permit ip any any
```

Task 4 Solution—Placing a Manual ISDN Call from the Cisco 700

To test the capability of the two routers to communicate, you will have the Cisco 700 place a
call to the Central site router:

```
cd CentralA
call 1000
```

Task 5 Solution—Configuring the Cisco 700 to Receive Incoming Calls from the Central Site

Now, finish the configuration on the home office router so it can receive incoming calls from
the Central site and authenticate with CHAP.

Step 1   Provide the configuration for your Cisco 700 series router that will ensure a
two-way authentication using CHAP:

```
set ppp authentication outgoing chap
```

Step 2   Provide a command to specify that the password used by the Central site
when authenticating will be **cisco:**

```
set ppp secret host
Enter password: cisco
Re-Enter password: cisco
```

Step 3   Look at your Cisco 700 series router's configuration to confirm that all the
required commands are configured. The configuration is displayed in
Example 9-17.

Example 9-17 *Default Settings*

```
HomeA> upload
CD
SET SCREENLENGTH 20
SET COUNTRYGROUP 1
SET LAN MODE ANY
SET WAN MODE ONLY
SET AGE OFF
SET MULTIDESTINATION OFF
SET SWITCH 5ESS
```

Example 9-17 *Default Settings (Continued)*

```
SET AUTODETECTION OFF
SET 1 DELAY 30
SET 2 DELAY 30
SET BRIDGING ON
SET LEARN ON
SET PASSTHRU OFF
SET SPEED AUTO
SET PLAN NORMAL
SET 1 AUTO ON
SET 2 AUTO ON
SET 1 NUMBER
SET 2 NUMBER
SET 1 BACKUPNUMBER
SET 2 BACKUPNUMBER
SET 1 RINGBACK
SET 2 RINGBACK
SET 1 CLIVALIDATENUMBER
SET 2 CLIVALIDATENUMBER
SET CLICALLBACK OFF
SET CLIAUTHENTICATION OFF
SET SYSTEMNAME HomeA
LOG CALLS TIME VERBOSE
SET UNICASTFILTER OFF
DEMAND 1 THRESHOLD 0
DEMAND 2 THRESHOLD 48
DEMAND 1 DURATION 1
DEMAND 2 DURATION 1
DEMAND 1 SOURCE LAN
DEMAND 2 SOURCE BOTH
TIMEOUT 1 THRESHOLD 0
TIMEOUT 2 THRESHOLD 48
TIMEOUT 1 DURATION 0
TIMEOUT 2 DURATION 0
TIMEOUT 1 SOURCE LAN
TIMEOUT 2 SOURCE BOTH
SET REMOTEACCESS PROTECTED
SET LOCALACCESS ON
SET CLICKSTART ON
SET LOGOUT 5
SET CALLERID OFF
SET PPP AUTHENTICATION IN CHAP PAP
SET PPP CHAPREFUSE NONE
SET PPP AUTHENTICATION OUT CHAP
SET PPP AUTHENTICATION ACCEPT EITHER
SET PPP TAS CLIENT 0.0.0.0
SET PPP TAS CHAPSECRET LOCAL ON
SET PPP SECRET CLIENT ENCRYPTED 02050d480809
SET PPP CALLBACK REQUEST OFF
SET PPP CALLBACK REPLY OFF
SET PPP NEGOTIATION INTEGRITY 10
SET PPP NEGOTIATION COUNT 10
```

continues

Example 9-17 *Default Settings (Continued)*

```
SET PPP NEGOTIATION RETRY 3000
SET PPP TERMREQ COUNT 2
SET PPP MULTILINK ON
SET COMPRESSION OFF
SET PPP BACP ON
SET PPP ADDRESS NEGOTIATION LOCAL OFF
SET PPP IP NETMASK LOCAL OFF
SET IP PAT UDPTIMEOUT 5
SET IP PAT TCPTIMEOUT 30
SET IP RIP TIME 30
SET CALLDURATION 0
SET SNMP CONTACT ""
SET SNMP LOCATION ""
SET SNMP TRAP COLDSTART OFF
SET SNMP TRAP WARMSTART OFF
SET SNMP TRAP LINKDOWN OFF
 TRAP LINKUP OFF
SET SNMP TRAP AUTHENTICATIONFAIL OFF
SET DHCP OFF
SET DHCP DOMAIN
SET DHCP NETBIOS_SCOPE
SET VOICEPRIORITY INCOMING INTERFACE PHONE1 ALWAYS
SET VOICEPRIORITY OUTGOING INTERFACE PHONE1 ALWAYS
SET CALLWAITING INTERFACE PHONE1 ON
SET VOICEPRIORITY INCOMING INTERFACE PHONE2 ALWAYS
SET VOICEPRIORITY OUTGOING INTERFACE PHONE2 ALWAYS
SET CALLWAITING INTERFACE PHONE2 ON
SET CALLTIME VOICE INCOMING OFF
SET CALLTIME VOICE OUTGOING OFF
SET CALLTIME DATA INCOMING OFF
SET CALLTIME DATA OUTGOING OFF
SET USER LAN
SET IP ROUTING ON
SET IP ADDRESS 10.118.0.1
SET IP NETMASK 255.255.255.0
SET IP FRAMING ETHERNET_II
SET IP PROPAGATE ON
SET IP COST 1
SET IP RIP RECEIVE V1
SET IP RIP UPDATE OFF
SET IP RIP VERSION 1
SET USER Internal
SET IP FRAMING ETHERNET_II
SET USER Standard
SET PROFILE ID 000000000000
SET PROFILE POWERUP ACTIVATE
SET PROFILE DISCONNECT KEEP
SET IP ROUTING ON
SET IP ADDRESS 0.0.0.0
SET IP NETMASK 0.0.0.0
SET IP FRAMING NONE
```

Example 9-17 *Default Settings (Continued)*

```
SET IP RIP RECEIVE V1
SET IP RIP UPDATE OFF
SET IP RIP VERSION 1
SET USER CentralA
SET PROFILE ID 000000000000
SET PROFILE POWERUP ACTIVATE
SET PROFILE DISCONNECT KEEP
SET BRIDGING OFF
SET 1 NUMBER 1000
SET 2 NUMBER 1000
TIMEOUT 1 DURATION 90
TIMEOUT 2 DURATION 90
SET PPP SECRET HOST ENCRYPTED 1511021f0725
SET IP ROUTING ON
SET IP ADDRESS 10.30.1.2
SET IP NETMASK 255.255.255.0
SET IP FRAMING NONE
SET IP PROPAGATE ON
SET IP COST 1
SET IP RIP RECEIVE V1
SET IP RIP UPDATE OFF
SET IP RIP VERSION 1
SET IP ROUTE DEST 0.0.0.0/0 GATEWAY 10.30.1.1 PROPAGATE OFF COST 1
CD
LOGOUT
SET
```

Step 4 Look at the Central site router to confirm the proper configuration. The configuration is displayed in Example 9-18.

Example 9-10 *Central Site Configuration*

```
Central
A#show running-config
Building configuration...
Current configuration:
!
version 11.3
no service password-encryption
!
hostname CentralA
!
enable secret 5 $1$XvjL$dRrWaKsqFfPqVyrm9cHPK/
enable password san-fran
!
username student password 0 cisco
username BranchA password 0 cisco
username HomeA password 0 cisco
no ip domain-lookup
ip host modem 2097 10.115.0.110
isdn switch-type primary-5ess
```

continues

Example 9-18 *Central Site Configuration (Continued)*

```
!
!
!
controller T1 1/0
framing esf
linecode b8zs
pri-group timeslots 1-24
!
!
interface Ethernet0/0
ip address 10.115.0.110 255.255.255.0
no lat enabled
!
interface Serial0/0
no ip address
no ip mroute-cache
shutdown
!
interface Serial1/0:23
no ip address
encapsulation ppp
dialer pool-member 1
isdn switch-type primary-5ess
isdn incoming-voice modem
no fair-queue
ppp authentication chap
ppp multilink
hold-queue 75 in
!
interface Serial3/0
physical-layer async
ip unnumbered Ethernet0/0
encapsulation ppp
async mode interactive
peer default ip address pool lab
no cdp enable
ppp authentication chap
!
interface Serial3/1
no ip address
shutdown
!
interface Serial3/2
no ip address
shutdown
!
interface Serial3/3
no ip address
shutdown
!
interface Group-Async1
```

Example 9-18 *Central Site Configuration (Continued)*

```
ip unnumbered Ethernet0/0
encapsulation ppp
dialer in-band
dialer idle-timeout 90
dialer-group 1
async mode interactive
peer default ip address pool lab
no cdp enable
ppp authentication chap
group-range 65 70
!
interface Dialer1
ip address 10.130.0.2 255.255.255.0
encapsulation ppp
dialer remote-name BranchA
dialer idle-timeout 60
dialer string 7782001
dialer pool 1
dialer-group 1
ppp authentication chap
!
interface Dialer2
ip address 10.30.1.1 255.255.255.0
encapsulation ppp
dialer remote-name HomeA
dialer string 2002
dialer pool 1
dialer-group 2
no fair-queue
ppp authentication chap
ppp multilink
!
router igrp 100
passive-interface Dialer1
passive-interface Dialer2
network 10.0.0.0
!
ip local pool lab 10.115.0.111 10.115.0.114
ip classless
ip route 10.118.0.0 255.255.255.0 Dialer2
ip route 10.218.0.0 255.255.255.0 Dialer1
dialer-list 1 protocol ip permit
dialer-list 2 protocol ip list 102
access-list 102 deny igrp any any
access-list 102 permit ip any any
!
!
line con 0
exec-timeout 0 0
line 65 70
autoselect during-login
```

continues

Example 9-18 *Central Site Configuration (Continued)*

```
autoselect ppp
login local
modem InOut
modem autoconfigure type mica
transport input all
stopbits 1
flowcontrol hardware
line 97
password cisco
autoselect during-login
autoselect ppp
login local
modem InOut
modem autoconfigure type usr_sportster
transport input all
stopbits 1
speed 115200
flowcontrol hardware
line aux 0
line vty 0 4
login local
!
end
CentralA#
```

Case Study Conclusion

In this case study, you reviewed the different commands required on the Cisco 700 and on the IOS-based router to establish an ISDN DDR connection between a SOHO and a Central site.

Review Questions

Answer the following questions and then refer to Appendix H, "Answers to Review Questions," for answers and explanations.

1 Discuss profiles and how they are used in a Cisco 700 series router.

2 Describe DHCP server and client operation.

PART V

Enabling Permanent Connections to the Central Site

CHAPTER 10

Using X.25 for Remote Access

With Part V of this book, we embark on the study of permanent wide area network connections. This chapter focuses on X.25 technology. It covers how X.25 works, how to implement it, and how it can provide permanent connectivity between two offices, as shown in Figure 10-1.

Figure 10-1 *Branch Office and Central Office, Permanently Connected Using X.25*

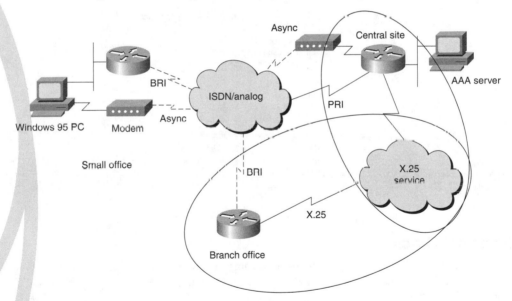

X.25 Overview

X.25 is a standard that defines the connection between a terminal and a packet-switching network. X.25 offers the closest approach to worldwide data communication available, and virtually every nation uses some X.25-addressable network.

X.25 originated in the early 1970s. The networking industry commonly uses the term **X.25** to refer to the entire suite of X.25 protocols.

Engineers designed X.25 to transmit and receive data between alphanumeric "dumb" terminals through analog telephone lines. X.25 enabled dumb terminals to remotely access applications on mainframes or minicomputers.

Because modern desktop applications need LAN-to-WAN-to-LAN data communication, engineers designed newer forms of wide-area technology: Integrated Services Digital Network (ISDN) and Frame Relay. In many situations, these newer WANs complement or extend X.25, rather than replace it.

Many different network-layer protocols can be transmitted across X.25 virtual circuits (VCs), which results in tunneling that has datagrams or other Layer 3 packets within the X.25 Layer 3 packets. This setup is shown in Figure 10-2. Each Layer 3 packet keeps addressing legal for its respective protocol, whereas the X.25 VC transports the packet across the WAN.

Figure 10-2 *X.25 Uses Virtual Circuits to Carry Datagrams*

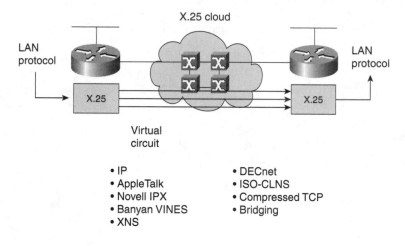

X.25 Protocol Stack

The X.25 packet-switching protocol suite compares to the lower three layers of the Open System Interconnection (OSI) model, as shown in Figure 10-3.

Figure 10-3 *X.25 and the OSI Model*

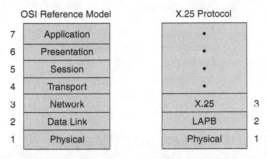

In general, X.25 is used as an overengineered data link in the internetworking world. Both X.25 at Layer 3 and Link Access Procedure, Balanced (LAPB) at Layer 2 provide reliability and sliding windows. Layers 3 and 2 were designed with strong flowcontrol and error checking to reduce the requirement for these functions external to X.25.

X.25 evolved in the days of analog circuits, when error rates were much higher than today. For analog circuit technology at Layer 1, it is more efficient to build more reliability into the network at the hardware level. With digital or fiber-optic technologies, the error rates have dropped dramatically. Newer technologies, such as Frame Relay, have taken advantage of drops in error rates by providing a stripped-down, "unreliable" data link.

X.25 was designed in the days of alphanumeric terminals and computing on central time-sharing computers. Demands on the packet switch were lower than today. Today's complex applications on desktop workstations demand more bandwidth and speed. Newer technologies such as ISDN and X.25 over Frame Relay add packet-switching capability.

X.25 DTE and DCE

Data terminal equipment (DTE) and data circuit-terminating equipment (DCE) for X.25 identify the responsibilities of the two stations on an X.25 attachment. The X.25 protocol implements virtual circuits between the X.25 DTE and X.25 DCE.

Although the terms **DTE** and **DCE** occur at all three layers associated with the X.25 stack, the use shown in the figure identifies responsibilities that are independent of the Physical layer DTE/DCE. The terms DTE/DCE are independent of the typical plug-gender and clock-source definitions used at the Physical layer.

The X.25 DTE is typically a router or a packet assembler/disassembler (PAD).

The X.25 packet-level DCE typically acts as a boundary function to the public data network (PDN) within a switch or concentrator. The X.25 switch at the carrier site may also be called data switching equipment (DSE). X.25's use of DTE/DCE terminology differs from the usual Physical layer interpretation.

The way X.25 traffic is carried within the carrier cloud depends on the implementation. In some cases, X.25 is also used within the cloud.

NOTE   X.25 DTE is usually a subscriber's router or PAD.

X.25 DCE is usually a PDN's switch or concentrator.

The Packet Assembler/Deassembler (PAD)

The PAD is a device that collects data from a group of asynchronous terminals and periodically outputs the data in X.25 packets, as represented in Figure 10-4. A PAD also takes data packets from a host and turns them into a character stream that can be transmitted to the terminals. The operation of the terminal-PAD interface, the services offered by a PAD, and the PAD-host control interaction are defined by the International Telecommunication Union Telecommunication Standardization Sector (ITU-T) recommendations.

Figure 10-4 *The PAD Collects Data and Outputs It into X.25 Packets*

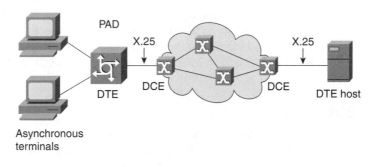

Public data network (PDN)

ITU-T Recommendations for PAD Services

Some ITU-T recommendations defining the PAD are as follows:

- X.3—Specifies the parameters for terminal-handling functions (such as baud rate, flowcontrol, character echoing, and other functions) for a connection to an X.25 host. The X.3 parameters are similar in function to Telnet options or the AT command set for modems.

- X.28—Specifies the user interface for locally controlling a PAD. X.28 identifies the keystrokes that you would enter at a terminal to set up the PAD, similar to the AT command set for modems.

- X.29—Specifies a protocol for setting the X.3 parameters via a network connection. When a connection is established, the destination host can request that the PAD or terminal change its parameters by using the X.29 protocol. A PAD cannot tell the destination host to change its X.3 parameters, but it can communicate that its own parameters were changed.

- X.75—Specifies the gateway between the clouds. It defines the signaling system between two PDNs. X.75 is essentially an NNI.

X.121—The X.25 Addressing Standard

The format of X.25 addresses is defined by the ITU-T X.121 standard:

- The first four digits specify the Data Network Identification Code (DNIC). The first three digits specify the country code. The fourth digit is the provider number assigned by the ITU-T. Countries that require more than ten provider numbers are assigned multiple country codes. The U.S., for example, is assigned country codes 310 through 316 to represent the country code, and the fourth digit is assigned by the ITU-T.

- The remaining 8 to 10 or 11 digits specify the network terminal number (NTN) that is assigned by the packet-switched network (PSN) provider.

NOTE	For your specific DNIC code, consult your service provider. For a listing of ITU-T country code assignments, refer to the ITU-T Recommendation X.121. The ITU-T Web site is www.itu.org.

A sample of the DNIC country codes is listed in Table 10-1.

Table 10-1   *X.121 DNIC Country codes*

Region X.121	Country Code Range
Zone 1 Oceans for ImmarSAT	100s
Zone 2 (predominantly Europe)	200s
United Kingdom	234–237
Germany	262–265
France	208–209
Austria	232
Belgium	206
Zone 3 (predominantly North America)	300s
United States	310–316

continues

Table 10-1   *X.121 DNIC Country codes (Continued)*

Region X.121	Country Code Range
Canada	302–303
Jamaica	338
Zone 4 (predominantly Asia)	400s
Japan	440–443
Zone 5 (predominantly Australia, New Zealand, and Pacific islands)	500s
Australia	505
New Zealand	530
Zone 6 (predominantly Africa)	600s
South Africa	655
Morocco	604
Zone 7 (predominantly South America)	700s
Brazil	724
Argentina	722

For different network protocols to connect across X.25, statements are entered on the router to map the next-hop Network layer address to an X.121 address. For example, an IP Network layer address is mapped to an X.121 address to identify the next-hop host on the other side of the X.25 network.

These statements are logically equivalent to the LAN Address Resolution Protocol (ARP) that dynamically maps a Network layer address to a data-link media access control (MAC) address. Maps are required for each protocol because ARP is not supported in an X.25 network. Mapping statements are a manual configuration step required when setting up X.25 on the router.

Unlike the ARP that dynamically maps a Network layer address, static X.25 map statements must be configured manually.

X.25 Encapsulation

Movement of Network layer data through the internetwork usually involves encapsulation of datagrams inside media-specific frames. As each media frame arrives at the router and is discarded, the router analyzes the datagram and places it inside a new frame as it is forwarded.

The X.25 specification maps to Layers 1 through 3 of the OSI reference model. Layer 3 X.25 describes packet formats and packet-exchange procedures between peer Layer 3 entities. Layer 2 X.25 is implemented by Link Access Procedure, Balanced (LAPB).

The same layer of the OSI reference model occurs twice. As shown in Figure 10-5, Layer 3 occurs twice: once for the IP datagram and once for X.25. When the system forwards a datagram to an X.25 interface, the maps are consulted to determine the X.25 destination.

Figure 10-5 *Protocol Datagrams Are Reliably Carried Inside LAPB Frames and X.25 Packets*

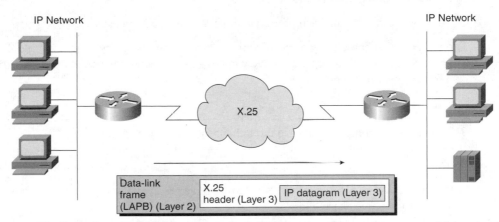

Similarly, in an X.25 environment, the LAPB frame arrives at the router, which extracts the datagram from the packet or packets. The router discards the encapsulating frame and analyzes the datagram to identify the format and next-hop. Based on the route determination, the router re-encapsulates the datagram in framing suitable for the outgoing media as it forwards the traffic.

X.25 Virtual Circuits

VCs are used interchangeably with the terms **virtual circuit number (VCN)**, **logical channel number (LCN)**, and **virtual channel identifier (VCI)**.

A VC can be a permanent virtual circuit (PVC) or, more commonly, a switched virtual circuit (SVC). An SVC exists only for the duration of the session.

Three phases are associated with SVCs:

* Call setup
* Information transfer
* Call clear

A PVC is similar to a leased line. Both the network provider and the attached X.25 subscriber must provision the virtual circuit. PVCs use no call setup or call clear that is apparent to the subscriber. Any provisioned PVCs are always present, even when no data traffic is being transferred.

The X.25 protocol offers simultaneous service to many hosts (for example, a multiplex connection service). An X.25 network can support any legal configuration of SVCs and PVCs over the same physical circuit attached to the X.25 interface. However, configuring a large number of VCs over a serial interface may result in poor performance. X.25's original design aim assumed service for time-sharing and terminal-to-host applications, not contemporary computer-to-computer applications.

Cisco routers provide numbering for up to 4095 VCs per X.25 interface.

Throughput for encapsulating a specific protocol can be improved by using multiple SVCs. Multiple SVCs provide a larger effective window size, especially for protocols that offer their own higher-layer resequencing.

NOTE   SVCs may be combined to improve throughput for a particular protocol.

This combination of SVCs does not benefit traditional X.25 applications, such as those available from a time-sharing host.

Single Protocol Virtual Circuits

The Cisco router's traditional encapsulation method enables different protocols to transport their datagrams through an X.25 cloud because the router uses separate virtual circuits. Each protocol is specified in an individual **x25 map** command that references the X.121 address used to reach the destination.

Multiprotocol Virtual Circuits

In Cisco IOS Release 10.2 and later releases, a single virtual circuit to a host can carry traffic from multiple protocols. One X.25 map statement contains several protocol addresses, mapped to a single X.121 address associated with the destination host.

This capability uses the method described in RFC 1356. Each of the supported protocols can map to a destination host. Because routing multiple protocols over a VC generates higher traffic loads, combining SVCs, as described earlier in this chapter, may improve throughput.

X.25 Encapsulation

Two methods are available to encapsulate traffic in X.25: Cisco's long-available encapsulation method and the IETF's standard method (defined in RFC 1356). The latter allows hosts to exchange several protocols over a single virtual circuit. Cisco's encapsulation method is the default (for backward compatibility), unless the interface configuration command specifies IETF.

Configuring X.25

When you select X.25 as a WAN protocol, you must set appropriate interface parameters. Interface tasks are as follows:

- Define the X.25 encapsulation (DTE is the default).
- Assign the X.121 address (usually supplied by the PDN service provider).
- Define map statements to associate X.121 addresses with higher-level protocol addresses.

Other configuration tasks can be performed to control data throughput and to ensure compatibility with the X.25 network service provider. Commonly used parameters include the number of VCs allowed and packet size negotiation.

X.25 is a flow controlled protocol. The default flow control parameters must match on both sides of a link. Mismatches because of inconsistent configurations can cause severe internetworking problems.

NOTE   Before configuring X.25 parameters, you must enter interface configuration mode and assign a higher layer address, such as an IP address to the interface.

Configuring the X.121 address

The **x25 address** command defines the local router's X.121 address (one address per interface). The value specified must match the address designated by the X.25 PDN:

```
Router(config-if)#x25 address x.121-address
```

The **x25 map** command provides a static conversion of higher-level addresses to X.25 addresses. The command correlates the network-layer addresses of the peer host to the peer host's X.121 address:

```
Router(config-if)#x25 map protocol address x.121-address [options]
```

The following table describes the **x25 map** command.

Table 10-2   *Description of the* **x25 map** *Command*

x25 map Command	Description
protocol	Selects the protocol type. Supported protocols are ip, xns, decnet, ipx, appletalk, vines, apollo, bridge, clns, and compressed tcp.
address	Specifies the protocol address (not specified for bridged or CLNS connections).
x.121-address	Specifies the X.121 address. Both the protocol address and the X.121 addresses are required to specify the complete network protocol-to-X.121 mapping.
options	Used to customize the connection (optional). One commonly used option is **broadcast**. The broadcast option causes the Cisco IOS software to direct any broadcasts sent through this interface to the specified X.121 address.

If you try to communicate with a host that understands multiple protocols over a single VC, use the following **x25 map** command:

```
Router(config-if)#x25 map protocol address
    [protocol2 address2]* x.121-address [options]
```

This communication requires the multiprotocol encapsulations defined by RFC 1356. In the preceding **x25 map** command, the * means that a maximum of nine network protocol addresses may be associated with one host destination in a single configuration command.

NOTE   Bridging is not supported with the **x25 map** command. To bridge a protocol over X.25, use the **x25 map bridge** command.

Configuring X.25 SVCs

To activate X.25 on an interface, you must enter the **encapsulation x25** command to specify the encapsulation style to be used on the serial interface:

```
Router(config-if)#encapsulation x25 [dte | dce]
```

The router can be an X.25 DTE device, which is typically used when the X.25 PDN is used to transport various protocols. The router can also be configured as an X.25 DCE device, which is typically used when the router acts as an X.25 switch.

NOTE   If you change the interface configuration from an X.25 DCE to X.25 DTE or vice versa, the interface configuration will change to the default interface settings.

Configuring X.25 SVC Examples

Figure 10-6 shows a sample network to be configured for X.25.

Figure 10-6 *Typical X.25 Network to Be Configured*

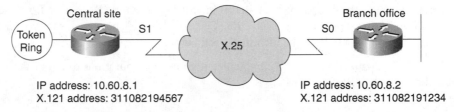

IP address: 10.60.8.1
X.121 address: 311082194567

IP address: 10.60.8.2
X.121 address: 311082191234

Example 10-1 shows the Central site SVC configuration for the network in Figure 10-6.

Example 10-1 *Central Site X.25 Configuration*

```
Central(config)#interface serial 1
Central(config-if)#encapsulation x25
Central(config-if)#x25 address 311082194567
Central(config-if)#ip address 10.60.8.1 255.255.248.0
Central(config-if)#x25 map ip 10.60.8.2 311082191234 broadcast
```

Example 10-2 shows the branch office SVC configuration for the network in Figure 10-6.

Example 10-2 *Branch Office X.25 Configuration*

```
Branch(config)#interface serial 0
Branch(config-if)#encapsulation x25
Branch(config-if)#x25 address 311082191234
Branch(config-if)#ip address 10.60.8.2 255.255.248.0
Branch(config-if)#x25 map ip 10.60.8.1 311082194567 broadcast
```

Table 10-3 describes the commands that are used in this example.

Table 10-3   *Basic X.25 Configuration Commands*

Command	Description
encapsulation x25	Sets the encapsulation style on interface serial 1 to X.25 type.
x25 address 311082194567	Establishes the X.121 address of serial 1.
x25 map	To set up the LAN protocols-to-remote host mapping for X.25 WAN protocol.
ip	A Layer 3 protocol specified for address association.
10.60.8.2	IP address of serial 0 that is mapped.
311082191234	The X.121 address of the host that defines the IP address.

IP routing on Cisco A forwards datagrams destined for subnet 10.60.8.0 to interface serial 1. The interface map identifies the destination to the X.25 cloud. In this typical configuration, Cisco A tries to establish an SVC to Cisco B using its X.121 source address and a destination X.121 address of 311082191234 when it sends packets to 10.60.8.2.

Upon receipt of the setup request, Cisco B identifies the remote IP address from the source X.121 address and accepts the connection. Once the SVC is connected, each router uses it as a point-to-point data link for the identified destination.

The two X.25 attachments need complementary map configurations to establish the VC that will encapsulate IP datagrams.

<table>
<tr><td>NOTE</td><td>This example illustrates the use of the **broadcast** option on the **x25 map** command. It is not typically used in cases when you do not want the link to continually come up to send broadcasts.</td></tr>
</table>

The sample network in Figure 10-7 illustrates an X.25 network if multiple circuits are established from the Central site router. In Example 10-3, the separate **x25 map** statements are configured to create separate links to each branch office. In this case, the same network layer protocol, IP, is used.

Figure 10-7 *Multiple SVC Mapped at the Central Site*

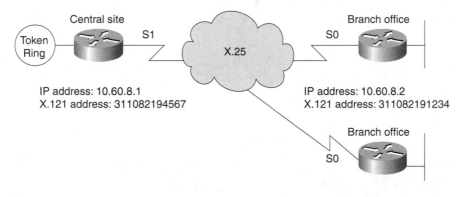

IP address: 10.60.8.1
X.121 address: 311082194567

IP address: 10.60.8.2
X.121 address: 311082191234

IP address: 10.60.8.3
X.121 address: 311082198901

Example 10-3 *Central Site X.25 Configuration to Multiple Destinations*

```
Central(config)#interface serial 1
Central(config-if)#encapsulation x25
Central(config-if)#x25 address 311082194567
Central(config-if)#ip address 10.60.8.1 255.255.248.0
Central(config-if)#x25 map ip 10.60.8.2 311082191234 broadcast
Central(config-if)#x25 map ip 10.60.8.3 311082198901 broadcast
```

Configuring X.25 PVCs

As you did when configuring X.25 SVCs, use the **encapsulation x25** command to specify the encapsulation style to be used on the serial interface:

```
Router(config-if)#encapsulation x25 [dte | dce]
```

As you did when configuring X.25 SVCs, use the **x25 address** command to define the local router's X.121 address (one address per interface). The value specified must match the address designated by the X.25 PDN:

```
Router(config-if)#x25 address x.121-address
```

Instead of establishing an1414 SVC with the **x25 map** command, you can establish a permanent virtual circuit (PVC). PVCs are the X.25 equivalent of leased lines; they are never disconnected. You do not need to configure an address map before defining a PVC; an encapsulation PVC implicitly defines a map. To establish an encapsulation PVC, enter the **x25 pvc** command in interface configuration mode. Command syntax follows:

```
Router(config-if)#x25 pvc circuit protocol address
    [protocol2 address2]* x.121-address [options]
```

The following table describes the **x25 pvc** command.

Table 10-4   *Description of the* **x25 pvc** *Command*

x25 pvc Command	Description
circuit	Virtual circuit channel number, which must be less than the virtual circuits assigned to the SVCs.
protocol	Protocol type entered by keyword. Supported protocols are appletalk, bridge, clns, compressedtcp, decnet, ip, ipx, qllc, vines, and xns. As many as nine protocol and address pairs can be specified in one command line.
address	Protocol address of the host at the other end of the PVC.
x121-address	X.121 address.
options	Used to customize the connection (optional). One commonly used option is **broadcast**. The broadcast option causes the Cisco IOS software to direct any broadcasts sent through this interface to the specified X.121 address.

Multiple protocols can be routed on the same PVC. Multiple circuits can also be established on an interface by creating another PVC.

NOTE   Before configuring X.25 parameters, you must enter interface configuration mode and assign a higher layer address, such as an IP address to the interface.

Configuring X.25 PVC Examples

The example in Figure 10-8 demonstrates how to use the PVC to exchange IP traffic between the Central site and branch office router.

Figure 10-8 *X.25 PVCs Link the Branch Office with the Central Site*

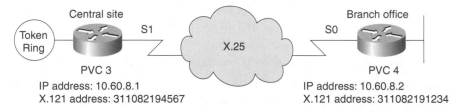

In this example, the public network has established a PVC through its network, connecting PVC number three to PVC number four. On the Central site router, a connection is established between the Central site router and the branch office IP address, 10.60.8.2. On the branch office router, a connection is established between the branch office and Central site IP address, 10.60.8.1.

Example 10-4 shows the Central site PVC configuration for the network shown in Figure 10-8.

Example 10-4 *Central Site X.25 PVC Configuration*

```
Central(config)#interface serial 1
Central(config-if)#encapsulation x25
Central(config-if)#x25 address 311082194567
Central(config-if)#ip address 10.60.8.1 255.255.248.0
Central(config-if)#x25 pvc 4 ip 10.60.8.2 311082191234 broadcast
```

Example 10-5 shows the branch office PVC configuration for the network shown in Figure 10-8.

Example 10-5 *Branch Office X.25 PVC configuration*

```
Branch(config)#interface serial 0
Branch(config-if)#encapsulation x25
Branch(config-if)#x25 address 311082191234
Branch(config-if)#ip address 10.60.8.2 255.255.248.0
Branch(config-if)#x25 pvc 3 ip 10.60.8.1 311082194567 broadcast
```

Additional X.25 Configuration Tasks

It may be necessary to perform additional configuration steps so that the router will work correctly with the service provider network. Crucial X.25 parameters are as follows:

- Virtual circuit (VC) range—Incoming, two-way, and outgoing
- Default packet sizes—Input and output
- Default window sizes
- Window modulus

Configuring X.25 VC Ranges

Table 10-5 summarizes additional configuration tasks for VC assignment. The complete range of VCs is allocated to PVCs or SVCs, depending on your requirements. SVCs are commonly used.

Table 10-5   *X.25 VC Ranges*

VC Use	Range	Default	Command
PVC	1–4095	No default, but the number must be greater than zero.	**x25 pvc circuit**
SVC	1–4095	0	**x25 lic circuit**
Incoming only	1–4095	0	**x25 hic circuit**
SVC	1–4095	1	**x25 ltc circuit**
Two-Ways	1–4095	1024	**x25 htc circuit**
SVC	1–4095	0	**x25 loc circuit**
Outgoing Only	1–4095	0	**x25 hoc circuit**

NOTE   Decode the abbreviations used in the command column of Table 10-5, as follows:

i   incoming

t   two-way

o   outgoing

l   low

h   high

c   circuit

The circuit numbers must be assigned so that an incoming range comes before a two-way range, both of which come before an outgoing range. Any PVCs must take a circuit number that comes before any SVC range. The following numbering scheme lists the proper order for these VC assignment commands:

```
1 ≤ PVCs < (lic ≤ hic) < (ltc ≤ htc) < (loc ≤ hoc) ≤ 4095
```

(Where lic is a low incoming circuit number, hic is a high incoming circuit number, ltc is a low two-way circuit number, htc is a high two-way circuit number, loc is a low outgoing circuit number, and hoc is a high outgoing circuit number.)

If both limits of a range are zero, the range is unused.

X.25 ignores any events on a VC number that are not in an assigned VC range; it considers the out-of-range VC as a protocol error. The network administrator specifies the VC ranges for an X.25 attachment. For correct operation, the X.25 DTE and DCE devices must have identically configured ranges. Numbers configured for any PVCs must also agree on both sides of an attachment (not necessarily end-to-end).

The following example may help you understand why you would configure VC ranges. If you acquire 10 circuits from your SVC provider and use all 10 on a given situation, incoming calls cannot get through. You can partition the 10 circuits to be dedicated to different calling situations—incoming, outgoing, or either:

1	Incoming
2	Incoming
3	Incoming
4	Either
5	Either
6	Either
7	Either
8	Outgoing
9	Outgoing
10	Outgoing

If many incoming calls are coming in, some circuits are still available for outgoing calls.

Configuring X.25 Packet Sizes

The **x25 ips** and **x25 ops** commands set the default maximum input/output packet size:

To set the incoming packet size, use the **x25 ips** command:

```
Router(config-if)#x25 ips bytes
```

To set the outgoing packet size, use the **x25 ops** command:

```
Router(config-if)#x25 ops bytes
```

Table 10-6 describes the **x25 ips** and **x25 op**s command.

Table 10-6   *Description of* **x25 ips** *and* **x25 ops** *Commands*

x25 ips and x25 ops Commands	Description
bytes	Maximum packet size assumed for VCs that do not negotiate a size. Supported values are 16, 32, 64, 128, 256, 512, 1024, 2048, and 4096. Default is 128 bytes.

The input and output values should match unless the network supports asymmetric transmissions. If the stations of an X.25 attachment conflict on the VC's maximum packet size, the VC is unlikely to work.

Fragmentation is a feature of X.25. The PAD will reassemble the IP packet at the destination.

NOTE   Before configuring the maximum packet size on your X.25 WAN connection, ask your service provider what is the maximum packet size your provider supports.

Configuring Window Parameters

Use the **x25 win** and **x25 wout** commands to set the default window size. The window size specifies the number of packets that can be received or sent without receiving or sending an acknowledgment. Both ends of an X.25 link must use the same default window size.

Therefore, to specify default unacknowledged packet limits, use the following commands:

```
Router(config-if)#x25 win packets
Router(config-if)#x25 wout packets
```

Table 10-7 describes the **x25 win** and **x25 wout** commands.

Table 10-7   *Description of the* **x25 win** *and* **x25 wout** *Commands*

x25 win and x25 wout Commands	Description
packets	Packet window size, assumed for VCs that do not negotiate a size. Range is one to one less than the modulus. The default is two packets.

The **x25 modulo** command specifies the packet-numbering modulus. It affects the maximum number of window sizes. Modulo 8 is widely used and allows VC sizes up to seven packets. Modulo 128 is rare, but it allows VC window sizes up to 127 packets.

The command to define packet-level window counter limits is as follows:

```
Router(config-if)#x25 modulo modulus
```

Table 10-8 describes the **x25 modulo** command.

Table 10-8   *Description of the* **x25 modulo** *Command*

x25 modulo Command	Description
modulus	Either 8 or 128.

Both ends of an X.25 link must use the same modulo.

Additional X.25 Configuration Options Example

Example 10-6 shows additional commands that you can configure for X.25 connections.

Example 10-6 *Specifying X.25 Windows and Packets Sizes*

```
Router(config)#interface serial 0
Router(config-if)#encapsulation x25
Router(config-if)#x25 address 311082198756
Router(config-if)#x25 ips 1024
Router(config-if)#x25 ops 1024
Router(config-if)#x25 win 7
Router(config-if)#x25 wout 7
```

An X.121 address is assigned to interface serial 0. The input and output packet and window sizes, and the maximum number of VCs for any protocol are also defined. See Table 10-9 for descriptions of the preceding example.

Table 10-9   *X.25 Windows and Packets Sizes Commands*

Command	Description
x25 address 311082198756	Specifies the address of the interface.
x25 ips 1024 **x25 ops 1024**	Sets both the input and output default packet sizes to 1024 to match the values defined for the network attachment. Maximum value is 4096.
x25 win 7 **x25 wout 7**	Sets both the input and output window sizes to 7 to match the values defined for the network attachment.
x25 default	Identifies X.25 as the default protocol to use on an interface.

The typical default packet size provided worldwide by PDNs is 128 bytes. In the United States and Europe, default packet sizes of 1024 are common. Other countries can also provide higher packet sizes. The Layer 3 default maximum packet size is subject to the limit that lower layers are able to support.

Verifying X.25 Configuration

Use the **show interfaces** command to display status and counter information about an interface. This serial interface has its encapsulation type configured for X.25 operation. The output from this command, displayed in Example 10-7, also displays LAPB information:

Example 10-7 *Display of a* **show** *Command for an Interface Configured for X.25*

```
CentralA#sh int s 3/1
Serial3/1 is up, line protocol is up
Hardware is CD2430 in sync mode
Internet address is 10.140.1.1/24
MTU 1500 bytes, BW 128 Kbit, DLY 20000 usec, rely 255/255, load 1/255
```

Example 10-7 *Display of a* **show** *Command for an Interface Configured for X.25 (Continued)*

```
Encapsulation X25, loopback not set
X.25 DTE, address 311010100101, state R1, modulo 8, timer 0
Defaults: idle VC timeout 0
cisco encapsulation
input/output window sizes 2/2, packet sizes 128/128
Timers: T20 180, T21 200, T22 180, T23 180
Channels: Incoming-only none, Two-way 1-1024, Outgoing-only none
RESTARTs 1/0 CALLs 0+0/0+0/0+0 DIAGs 0/0
LAPB DTE, state CONNECT, modulo 8, k 7, N1 12056, N2 20
T1 3000, T2 0, interface outage (partial T3) 0, T4 0
VS 5, VR 3, tx NR 3, Remote VR 5, Retransmissions 0
Queues: U/S frames 0, I frames 0, unack. 0, reTx 0
IFRAMEs 5/3 RNRs 0/0 REJs 0/0 SABM/Es 0/1 FRMRs 0/0 DISCs 0/0
Last input 00:00:29, output 00:00:29, output hang never
Last clearing of "show interface" counters never
Queueing strategy: fifo
Output queue 0/40, 0 drops; input queue 0/75, 0 drops
5 minute input rate 0 bits/sec, 0 packets/sec
5 minute output rate 0 bits/sec, 0 packets/sec
<Output Omitted>
```

Summary

In this chapter, you learned how to configure an X.25 WAN connection and assign X.121 addresses to the router's interfaces. You also learned how to map higher-level addresses to X.25 addresses and how to verify the X.25 configuration of your router.

In the next chapter, you will learn about the successor of X.25, Frame Relay.

Case Study—Using X.25 for Remote Access

Complete the tasks of this case study, and then review the case study solution section that follows to see how you did and see where you might need to review concepts presented in this chapter.

In this case study, you will specify the command to provide X.25 encapsulation on serial lines and assign an X.121 address to a router interface. You will issue the appropriate router commands to convert higher-level protocol addresses to X.121 addresses and verify X.25 configuration in the router.

Scenario

Configure both the branch office and the Central site routers so they can communicate in X.25 by using their synchronous interfaces, as shown in Figure 10-9.

Figure 10-9 *The Branch Office and the Central Site are Interconnected via a X.25 Network*

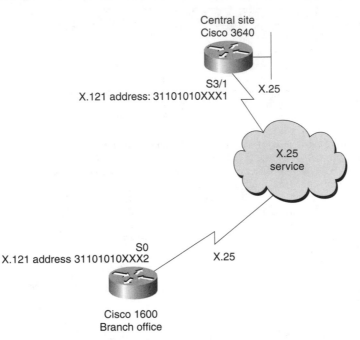

The two sites will use the following IP and X.121 addresses.

Central Site Serial:

    ip address10.140.1.1 255.255.255.0
    X.121 address311010100101

Branch Office Serial 0:

    ip address10.140.1.2 255.255.255.0
    X.121 address311010100102

Task 1—Configuring X.25 at the Central Site

Step 1   At the Central site router console, provide all the configuration on the serial interface that will do the following:

    — Ensure that the encapsulation is X.25.

    — Provide the X.25 address.

    — Ensure that your Central site router is aware of the relation between the branch office IP address and its X.121 address. Also, ensure that the broadcast will be passed to the branch office.

    — Provide your Central site serial interface with an IP address.

Step 2 Ensure that your Central site serial interface is properly configured.

Task 2—Configuring X.25 at the Branch Office

Step 1 At the branch office router console, provide all the configuration that will do the following:

— Ensure that the encapsulation is X.25.

— Provide the X.25 address.

— Ensure that your branch office router is aware of the relation between the Central site IP address and its X.121 address. Also, ensure that broadcasts will be passed to the central office.

— Provide your branch office serial interface with an IP address.

Step 2 Ensure that your branch office serial interface is properly configured.

Solution to Case Study—Using X.25 for Remote Access

The following is a step-by-step discussion of the case study solution.

Task 1 Solution—Configuring X.25 at the Central Site

Step 1 At the Central site router console, provide all the configuration on the serial interface that will do the following:

— Ensure that the encapsulation is X.25:

```
CentralA(config)#interface s3/1
CentralA(config-if)#encapsulation x25
```

— Provide the X.25 address:

```
CentralA(config-if)#x25 address 311010100101
```

— Ensure that your Central site router is aware of the relation between the branch office IP address and its X.121 address. Also, ensure that the broadcast will be passed to the branch office:

```
CentralA(config-if)#x25 map ip 10.140.1.2 311010100102 broadcast
```

— Provide your Central site serial interface with an IP address:

```
CentralA(config-if)#ip address 10.140.1.1 255.255.255.0
```

Step 2 Ensure that your Central site serial interface is properly configured. Example 10-8 shows the verification of this.

Example 10-8 *Verification of the Central Site Configuration with the* **show interface** *Command*

```
CentralA#sh int s 3/1
Serial3/1 is up, line protocol is up
Hardware is CD2430 in sync mode
Internet address is 10.140.1.1/24
MTU 1500 bytes, BW 128 Kbit, DLY 20000 usec, rely 255/255, load 1/255
Encapsulation X25, loopback not set
X.25 DTE, address 311010100101, state R1, modulo 8, timer 0
Defaults: idle VC timeout 0
cisco encapsulation
input/output window sizes 2/2, packet sizes 128/128
Timers: T20 180, T21 200, T22 180, T23 180
Channels: Incoming-only none, Two-way 1-1024, Outgoing-only none
RESTARTs 1/0 CALLs 0+0/0+0/0+0 DIAGs 0/0
LAPB DTE, state CONNECT, modulo 8, k 7, N1 12056, N2 20
T1 3000, T2 0, interface outage (partial T3) 0, T4 0
VS 5, VR 3, tx NR 3, Remote VR 5, Retransmissions 0
Queues: U/S frames 0, I frames 0, unack. 0, reTx 0
IFRAMEs 5/3 RNRs 0/0 REJs 0/0 SABM/Es 0/1 FRMRs 0/0 DISCs 0/0
Last input 00:00:29, output 00:00:29, output hang never
Last clearing of "show interface" counters never
Queueing strategy: fifo
Output queue 0/40, 0 drops; input queue 0/75, 0 drops
5 minute input rate 0 bits/sec, 0 packets/sec
5 minute output rate 0 bits/sec, 0 packets/sec
8 packets input, 31 bytes, 0 no buffer
Received 0 broadcasts, 0 runts, 0 giants, 0 throttles
0 input errors, 0 CRC, 0 frame, 0 overrun, 0 ignored, 0 abort
9 packets output, 71 bytes, 0 underruns
0 output errors, 0 collisions, 3 interface resets
0 output buffer failures, 0 output buffers swapped out
0 carrier transitions
DCD=up DSR=up DTR=up RTS=up CTS=up


CentralA#sh run
Building configuration...
Current configuration:
!
version 11.3
no service password-encryption
!
hostname CentralA
!
enable secret 5 $1$L.QE$52g1nPy0Tk3AwGd/XdEXK0
enable password san-fran
!
username student password 0 cisco
username BranchA password 0 cisco
username HomeA password 0 HomeA
```

Example 10-8 *Verification of the Central Site Configuration with the* **show interface** *Command (Continued)*

```
<output omitted>
!
interface Serial3/1
ip address 10.140.1.1 255.255.255.0
encapsulation x25
no ip mroute-cache
x25 address 311010100101
x25 map ip 10.140.1.2 311010100102 broadcast
!
<output omitted>
```

Task 2 Solution—Configuring X.25 at the Branch Office

Step 1 At the branch office router console, provide all the configuration that will do the following:

— Ensure that the encapsulation is X.25:

```
BranchA(config-if)#interface s0
BranchA(config-if)#encapsulation x25
```

— Provide the X.25 address:

```
BranchA(config-if)#x25 address 311010100102
```

— Ensure that your branch office router is aware of the relation between the Central site IP address and its X.121 address. Also, ensure that broadcast will be passed to the central office:

```
BranchA(config-if)#x25 map ip 10.140.1.1 311010100101 broadcast
```

— Provide your branch office serial interface with an IP address:

```
BranchA(config-if)# ip address 10.140.1.2 255.255.255.0
```

Step 2 Ensure that your branch office serial interface is properly configured. Example 10-9 shows the verification of this.

Example 10-9 *Verification of the Branch Office Configuration with the* **show interface** *Command*

```
BranchA#sh int s0
Serial0 is up, line protocol is up
Hardware is QUICC Serial
Internet address is 10.140.1.2/24
MTU 1500 bytes, BW 1544 Kbit, DLY 20000 usec, rely 255/255, load 1/255
Encapsulation X25, loopback not set
X.25 DTE, address 311010100102, state R1, modulo 8, timer 0
Defaults: idle VC timeout 0
cisco encapsulation
input/output window sizes 2/2, packet sizes 128/128
Timers: T20 180, T21 200, T22 180, T23 180
Channels: Incoming-only none, Two-way 1-1024, Outgoing-only none
```

continues

Example 10-9 *Verification of the Branch Office Configuration with the* **show interface** *Command (Continued)*

```
RESTARTs 0/0 CALLs 0+0/0+0/0+0 DIAGs 0/0
LAPB DTE, state CONNECT, modulo 8, k 7, N1 12056, N2 20
T1 3000, T2 0, interface outage (partial T3) 0, T4 0
VS 3, VR 2, tx NR 2, Remote VR 3, Retransmissions 0
Queues: U/S frames 0, I frames 0, unack. 0, reTx 0
IFRAMEs 3/2 RNRs 0/0 REJs 0/0 SABM/Es 0/1 FRMRs 0/0 DISCs 0/0
Last input never, output 00:00:40, output hang never
Last clearing of "show interface" counters never
Queueing strategy: fifo
Output queue 0/40, 0 drops; input queue 0/75, 0 drops
5 minute input rate 0 bits/sec, 0 packets/sec
5 minute output rate 0 bits/sec, 0 packets/sec
6 packets input, 22 bytes, 0 no buffer
Received 0 broadcasts, 0 runts, 0 giants, 0 throttles
0 input errors, 0 CRC, 0 frame, 0 overrun, 0 ignored, 0 abort
5 packets output, 97 bytes, 0 underruns
0 output errors, 0 collisions, 19 interface resets
0 output buffer failures, 0 output buffers swapped out
1 carrier transitions
DCD=up DSR=up DTR=up RTS=up CTS=up

BranchA#sh run
Building configuration...
Current configuration:
!
version 11.3
no service password-encryption
!
hostname BranchA
!
enable secret 5 $1$NRrJ$daaIONQjK5MsoGX9SmJM70
enable password san-fran
!
username CentralA password 0 cisco
<output omitted>
!
interface Serial0
ip address 10.140.1.2 255.255.255.0
encapsulation x25
no ip mroute-cache
x25 address 311010100102
x25 map ip 10.140.1.1 311010100101 broadcast
!
<output omitted>
```

Review Questions

Answer the following questions and then refer to Appendix H, "Answers to Review Questions," for answers and explanations.

1 Explain the difference between an X.25 DTE and DCE.

2 Assume you want an IP connection over an X.25 link. What must you do to map the network layer address to the X.121 address?

3 How can you limit traffic by lowering the amount of acknowledgements sent across the X.25 link?

CHAPTER 11

Frame Relay Connection and Traffic Flow Control

In the previous chapter, you were introduced to X.25. Frame Relay, presented in this chapter, is a next-generation protocol to X.25.

This chapter presents the Frame Relay technology, including its benefits and its requirements. You will see how Frame Relay can be used to connect a Central site with its branch offices, as shown in Figure 11-1. You will be introduced to the reachability issue caused by split horizon and how to configure subinterfaces to solve this problem.

Figure 11-1 *Frame Relay Connections between the Central Site and a Branch Office*

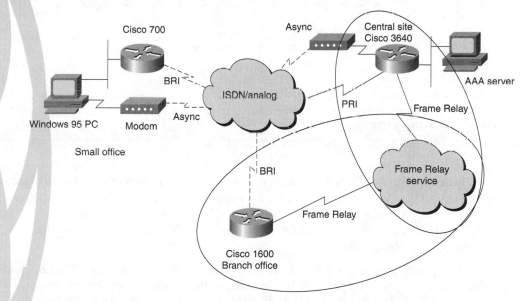

You will learn about Frame Relay traffic shaping, used for Quality of Service, and how to configure it. You will also see how to verify and troubleshoot Frame Relay configurations.

Frame Relay Overview

Frame Relay is an International Telecommunication Union Telecommunication Standardization Sector (ITU-T; formerly the Consultative Committee for International Telegraph and Telephone [CCITT]) and American National Standards Institute (ANSI) standard that defines the process for sending data over a public data network (PDN). It is a connection-oriented, data-link technology that is streamlined to provide high performance and efficiency, as shown in Figure 11-2. It relies on upper-layer protocols for error correction, and today's more dependable fiber and digital networks. It uses the services of many different Physical layer facilities at speeds that typically range from 56 Kbps up to 2 Mbps.

Figure 11-2 *Frame Relay Uses Connection-Oriented Virtual Circuits*

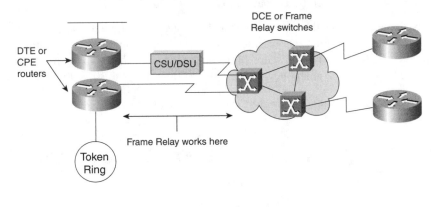

NOTE   The Frame Relay forum can be found at www.frforum.com.

Note that Frame Relay defines the interconnection process between your customer premises equipment (CPE—also known as data terminal equipment [DTE]) such as a router, and the service provider's local access-switching equipment (known as data communications equipment [DCE]). It does not define the way the data is transmitted within the service provider's Frame Relay cloud.

Frame Relay differs significantly from X.25 in its functionality and format. In particular, Frame Relay is a more streamlined protocol. It does not have the windowing and retransmission strategies of X.25. This simplicity facilitates higher performance and greater efficiency that is appropriate for use over faster, less error-prone networks. As a result, Frame Relay is appropriate for uses that require high throughput, such as LAN interconnection. Frame Relay is a purely Layer 2 protocol.

The network providing the Frame Relay service can be either a carrier-provided public network or a network of privately owned equipment serving a single enterprise.

Frame Relay over switched virtual circuits (SVCs) is not discussed in this chapter or this course because it is not widely supported by service providers at this time. The service provider must also support SVCs in order for Frame Relay to operate over SVCs.

Frame Relay Operation

Frame Relay provides a means for statistically multiplexing many logical data conversations (referred to as **virtual circuits**) over a single physical transmission link by assigning connection identifiers to each pair of DTE devices. The service provider's switching equipment constructs a table that maps connection identifiers to outbound ports. When a frame is received, the switching device analyzes the connection identifier and delivers the frame to the pre-established associated outbound port.

The virtual circuits can be either permanent virtual circuits (PVCs) or switched virtual circuits (SVCs). PVCs are permanently established connections that are used when there is frequent and consistent data transfer between DTE devices across a Frame Relay network.

With ANSI T1.617, ITU-T Q.933 (Layer 3), and Q.922 (Layer 2), Frame Relay now supports SVCs. SVCs are temporary connections, used when there is only sporadic data transfer between DTE devices across the Frame Relay network. Because they are temporary, SVC connections require call setup and termination for each connection. Cisco IOS Release 11.2 or later supports Frame Relay SVCs. You will need to determine whether your carrier supports SVCs before implementing them.

A data-link connection identifier (DLCI) identifies the logical virtual circuit between the CPE and the Frame Relay (FR) switch. The Frame Relay switch maps the DLCIs between each pair of routers to create a PVC. DLCIs have local significance in that the identifier references the point between the local router and the Frame Relay switch to which it is connected. Your Frame Relay provider sets up the DLCI numbers to be used by the routers for establishing PVCs.

Local Significance

DLCIs have local significance; that is, the end devices at two different ends of a connection may use a different DLCI to refer to that same connection. Figure 11-5 provides an example of one VC identified at each end by two different DLCI numbers.

Because the DLCIs have only local significance, the only real restriction on the use of DLCIs is that they are not used for more than one destination from the same port.

You configure an available DLCI number to map this provided Frame Relay number to a network address. For example, an administrator might map to an IP address of the interface on

Router A in Figure 11-3. This mapping in the router points to a static route, which is the PVC to that remote router. For example, the administrator can configure a Frame Relay map for 172.16.11.3 by using the PVC identified as DLCI 500.

Figure 11-3   *In Frame Relay, a Locally Significant DLCI Is Mapped to Your WAN Network Address*

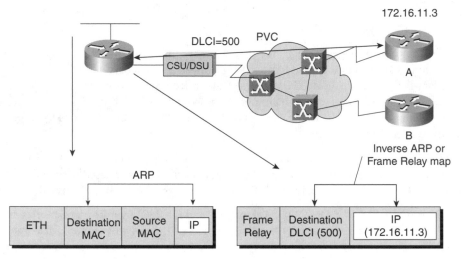

On Cisco routers, the address mapping can be either configured manually, or dynamic address mapping can be used. With dynamic address mapping, Frame Relay Address Resolution Protocol (ARP) provides a given DLCI and requests next-hop protocol addresses for a specific connection. The router then updates its mapping table and uses the information in the table to forward packets on the correct route. Frame Relay ARP is also known as Inverse ARP.

When packets are sent across the network, the intermediate switches will look up the DLCI in the map table and do the following:

- If the DLCI is defined on the link, the switch will forward packets toward their destination.
- If the DLCI is not defined on the link, the switch will discard the frame.

DLCI Numbering Scheme

The Frame Relay service provider will assign the DLCI numbers for your WAN. Usually, DLCIs 0 to 15 and 1008 to 1023 are reserved for special purposes. Therefore, service providers are typically assigned DLCIs in the range of 16 to 1007.

Multicasts can use DLCI 1019 through 1020. Cisco LMI uses DLCI 1023 and ANSI/ITU-T uses DLCI 0 (there is a discussion on LMI in the following section).

Frame Relay Signaling

Local Management Interface (LMI) is a signaling standard between the CPE device and the FR switch that is responsible for managing the connection and maintaining status between the devices. As shown in Figure 11-4, LMIs include support for the following:

- A keepalive mechanism, which verifies that data is flowing
- A multicast mechanism, which provides the network server with its local DLCI
- The multicast addressing, which gives DLCIs global rather than local significance in Frame Relay networks
- A status mechanism, which provides an ongoing status on the DLCIs known to the switch

Figure 11-4 *The Connection Between the Router and the Frame Relay Switch Is Managed by the LMI Signaling Standard*

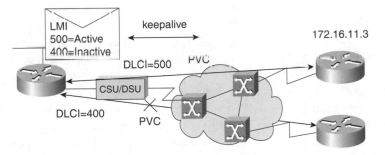

Although the LMI is configurable, beginning in Release 11.2, the Cisco router tries to autosense which LMI type the Frame Relay switch is using by sending one or more full status requests to the Frame Relay switch. The Frame Relay switch responds with one or more LMI types. The router configures itself with the last LMI type received. Three types of LMIs are supported:

- **cisco**   LMI type, defined jointly by Cisco, StrataCom, Northern Telecom, and Digital Equipment Corporation, nicknamed "the gang of four"
- **ansi**   Annex D of the ANSI standard T1.617
- **q933a**   ITU-T Q.933 Annex A

Additional Frame Relay Standards

Other key ANSI standards are T1.606, which defines the Frame Relay architecture; and T1.618, which describes data transfer. The International Telecommunication Union Telecommunication Standardization sector specifications include I.122, which defines ITU-T Frame Relay architecture; and Q.922, which standardizes data transfer. Use of these LMI standards is especially widespread in Europe.

Regarding the Cisco LMI, Compaq acquired Digital and Cisco acquired StrataCom. We could call it "the gang of three": Cisco, Compaq, and Nortel. Resistance being futile, most Frame Relay switching equipment supports the Cisco LMI.

An administrator setting up a connection to a Frame Relay network must choose the appropriate LMI from the three supported types to ensure proper Frame Relay operation.

Frame Relay Extensions

In addition to the basic Frame Relay protocol functions for transferring data, the "gang of four" promoted the following extensions:

Virtual circuit status messages (common)   These messages provide communication and synchronization between the network and the user device. They periodically report the existence of new PVCs and the deletion of already existing PVCs, and generally provide information about PVC integrity. Virtual circuit status messages prevent the sending of data into black holes, that is, over PVCs that no longer exist.

Multicasting (optional)   Multicasting allows a sender to transmit a single frame, but have it delivered by the network to multiple recipients. Thus, multicasting supports the efficient conveyance of routing protocol messages and address-resolution procedures that typically must be sent to many destinations simultaneously.

Global addressing (optional)   Global addressing gives connection identifiers global rather than local significance, which allows them to be used to identify a specific interface to the Frame Relay network. Global addressing makes the Frame Relay network resemble a local area network (LAN) in terms of addressing; address resolution protocols therefore perform over Frame Relay exactly as they do over a LAN.

Simple flow control (optional)   This provides for an XON/XOFF flow-control mechanism that applies to the entire Frame Relay interface. It is intended for those devices whose higher layers cannot use the congestion notification bits and that need some level of flow control.

The source for this information is www.cisco.com.

When an inverse ARP request is made, the router updates its map table with three possible LMI connection states, as follows:

- **Active state**   Indicates that the connection is active and that routers can exchange data.

- **Inactive state**   Indicates that the local connection to the Frame Relay switch is working, but the remote router's connection to the Frame Relay switch is not working.

- **Deleted state**   Indicates that no LMI is being received from the Frame Relay switch, or that there is no service between the CPE router and Frame Relay switch.

Configuring Frame Relay

A basic Frame Relay configuration assumes that you want to configure Frame Relay on one or more physical interfaces. Perform the following steps to enable Frame Relay:

1 Select the interface and enter interface configuration mode.

2 Configure a network layer address, for example, an IP address.

3 Select the encapsulation type used to encapsulate data traffic end-to-end:

```
router(config-if)#encapsulation frame-relay [cisco ¦ ietf]
```
cisco is the default. Use it if connecting to another Cisco router. Select **ietf** if connecting to a non-Cisco router.

4 If using Cisco IOS Release 11.1 or earlier, specify the LMI-type used by the FR switch:

```
router(config-if)#frame-relay lmi-type {ansi ¦ cisco ¦ q933i}
```

cisco is the default.

With IOS Release 11.2 or later, the LMI type is autosensed, so no configuration is needed.

Frame Relay Keepalives

If you configure under the serial interface no keepalive, the LMI will stop. (You can find more information on Frame Relay on Cisco Connection Online.) For example, according to CCO, "Keepalives (messages sent through a connection to ensure that both sides will continue to regard the connection as active) and PVC status messages are examples of these messages, and are the common LMI features that are expected to be a part of every implementation that conforms to the consortium specification."

---

5 Configure addressing mapping. Figure 11-3 provides a visual representation of address mapping.

Use the **frame-relay map** command to configure static address mapping. In Figure 11-5, the headquarters router is configured with a static map to the branch router. The syntax for the command is as follows:

```
Router(config-ig)#frame-relay map protocol protocol-address dlci [broadcast]
↪[ietf ¦ cisco]
```

frame-relay map Command	Description
protocol	Selects the protocol type. Supported protocols are appletalk, clns, decnet, ip, xns, and vines.
protocol-address	Specifies the protocol address (not specified for bridged or CLNS connections).
dlci	DLCI number used to connect to the specified protocol address on the interface.
broadcast	(Optional) Broadcasts should be forwarded when multicast is not enabled.
ietf	(Optional) Enables the Internet Engineering Task Force (IETF) encapsulation.
cisco	(Optional) Enables the Cisco encapsulation. This is the default.

Figure 11-5 *Basic Frame Relay Configuration with a Map Command*

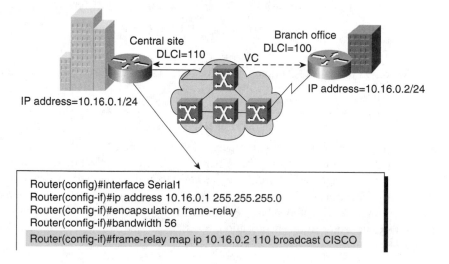

```
Router(config)#interface Serial1
Router(config-if)#ip address 10.16.0.1 255.255.255.0
Router(config-if)#encapsulation frame-relay
Router(config-if)#bandwidth 56
Router(config-if)#frame-relay map ip 10.16.0.2 110 broadcast CISCO
```

Frame Relay Encapsulation and Mapping

There are two possible encapsulations of frame in Frame Relay. Cisco's own frame encapsulation has a four-byte header, with two bytes for the DLCI and two bytes to identify the packet type. The IETF standard is in accordance with RFCs 1294 and 1490, and it uses a two-byte header, as shown in Figure 11-6. Configure IETF based on map entries and protocol for more flexibility. Use this method of configuration for backward compatibility and interoperability. [source: www.cisco.com]

On the subject of Frame Relay Inverse and mapping, some administrators let Inverse ARP discover the DLCIs, and then do the hard-coding entry of mapping Layer 3 addresses to DLCI numbers with the **frame-relay map** command. This strategy makes it easier for your support staff to gain information on the Frame Relay network.

Earlier, you had to configure the encapsulation on the serial interface with the **frame-relay encapsulation** command.

In this example, the default encapsulation, which is Cisco, is applied to all the VCs available on that serial interface. This is fine if the destinations' routers are all Cisco. If the equipment at the destinations were non-Cisco, you would have to configure with **frame-relay encapsulation ietf**. So, every frame leaving your router would be encapsulated in an IETF format.

What if most destinations use the Cisco encapsulation, but one destination requires the IETF? In such a case, you would specify, under the interface, the general encapsulation to be used by most destinations. Because the default encapsulation is Cisco, you would not have to mention it in part of the **encapsulation frame-relay**, as shown in the following example. You would specify the exception using the **frame-relay map** command:

```
router(config-if)#encapsulation frame-relay
router(config-if)#frame-relay map ip 192.1.1.7 73 IETF
```

Figure 11-6 *Frame Relay Format*

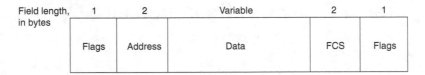

On Cisco routers, address mapping can be either configured manually with static address mapping, or dynamic address mapping can be used.

If you use dynamic address mapping, Frame Relay Inverse ARP provides a given DLCI and requests next-hop protocol addresses for a specific connection. The router then updates its mapping table and uses the information in the table to route outgoing traffic. Dynamic address mapping is enabled by default for all protocols enabled on a physical interface. No additional commands are necessary.

If you use static address mapping, you must use the **frame-relay map** command to statistically map destination network protocol addresses to a designated DLCI.

TIP	If your Frame Relay environment supports LMI and Reverse ARP, dynamic address mapping will take place. Therefore, no static address mapping will be required from you.

NOTE	There are two standards for Frame Relay encapsulations: Cisco or EITF. The encapsulation method can be configured either on an interface or per-destination basis.

The following example represents a Frame Relay interface using EITF frames to communicate to the two destinations shown:

```
Router(config-if)#encapsulation frame-relay IETF
Router(config-if)#frame-relay map ip 131.108.123.2 48 broadcast
Router(config-if)#frame-relay map ip 131.108.123.3 49 broadcast
```

On the other hand, it is possible to configure encapsulation strictly per destination. In the following example, IETF encapsulation is configured on a per-DLCI basis. This configuration has the same result as the configuration in the first example.

```
Router(config-if)#encapsulation frame-relay
Router(config-if)#frame-relay map ip 131.108.123.2 48 broadcast ietf
Router(config-if)#frame-relay map ip 131.108.123.3 49 broadcast ietf
```

The following example shows a case in which most destinations use Cisco's encapsulation, but one site requires EITF frames:

```
Router(config-if)#encapsulation frame-relay
Router(config-if)#frame-relay map ip 131.108.123.2 48 broadcast
Router(config-if)#frame-relay map ip 131.108.123.3 49 broadcast ietf
Router(config-if)#frame-relay map ip 131.108.123.4 50 broadcast
```

Verifying Frame Relay Configuration and Operations

After you configure Frame Relay, you can verify that the connections are active by using different show commands.

show interface serial Command

The **show interface serial** command displays information regarding the encapsulation, Layer 1, and Layer 2 status. It also displays information about the multicast DLCI, the DLCIs used on the Frame Relay-configured serial interface, and the LMI DLCI used for the local management interface, as displayed in Example 11-1.

Example 11-1 *The* **show interface serial** *Command Provides Information on Frame Relay Configuration*

```
Router#show interface serial 0
Serial0 is up, line protocol is up
Hardware is CD2430 in sync mode
MTU 1500 bytes, BW 128 Kbit, DLY 20000 usec, rely 255/255, load 1/255
Encapsulation FRAME-RELAY, loopback not set, keepalive set (10 sec)
LMI enq sent 112971, LMI stat recvd 112971, LMI upd recvd 0, DTE LMI up
LMI enq recvd 0, LMI stat sent 0, LMI upd sent 0
LMI DLCI 1023 LMI type is CISCO frame relay DTE
FR SVC disabled, LAPF state down
Broadcast queue 0/64, broadcasts sent/dropped 32776/0, interface broadcasts 14
Last input 00:00:00, output 00:00:03, output hang never
Last clearing of "show interface" counters never
Input queue: 0/75/0 (size/max/drops); Total output drops: 0
Queueing strategy: weighted fair
<Output Omitted>
```

Local Loop Identifier—Circuit Number

A typical Frame Relay WAN is composed of numerous sites that are connected to the central office via a local loop. The Telco identifies these individual local loops with a circuit number, such as: 05QHDQ101545–080TCOM-002. Telco technicians typically leave a label on the CSU/DSU with the circuit number. When you call the telco for help with troubleshooting your Frame Relay WAN, you will be required to provide the circuit number.

To simplify the management of your WAN, use the description command at the interface level to record the circuit number:

```
Halifax(config)#interface serial 0
Halifax(config-if)#description Cicuit-05QHDQ101545-080TCOM-002
Halifax(config-if)#^z
Halifax#show interface serial 0
Serial 0 is up, line protocol is up Hardware is MCI Serial
Description Cicuit-05QHDQ101545-080TCOM-002
Internet address is 150.136.190.203, subnet mask  255.255.255.0
MTU 1500 bytes, BW 1544 Kbit, DLY 20000 usec, rely 255/255, load 1/255
```

show frame-relay pvc Command

The **show frame-relay pvc** command displays the status of each configured connection, as well as traffic statistics. This command is also useful for viewing the number of BECN and FECN packets received by the router, as shown in Example 11-2.

Example 11-2 *The* **show frame-relay pvc** *Command Provides Information on PVCs*

```
Router#show frame-relay pvc 110

PVC Statistics for interface Serial0 (Frame Relay DTE)

DLCI = 110, DLCI USAGE = LOCAL, PVC STATUS = ACTIVE, INTERFACE = Serial0
```

continues

Example 11-2 *The* **show frame-relay pvc** *Command Provides Information on PVCs (Continued)*

```
input pkts 14055        output pkts 32795       in bytes 1096228
out bytes 6216155       dropped pkts 0          in FECN pkts 0
in BECN pkts 0          out FECN pkts 0         out BECN pkts 0
in DE pkts 0            out DE pkts 0
out bcast pkts 32795    out bcast bytes 6216155
```

show frame-relay map Command

The **show frame-relay map** command displays the current map entries and information about the connections, as shown in Example 11-3.

Example 11-3 *The* **show frame-relay map** *Command Provides Information on Layer 2 and Layer 3 Addresses*

```
Router#show frame-relay map
Serial2 (up): IP 131.108.122.2 dlci 20(0x14,0x0440), dynamic
        CISCO, BW= 56000, status defined, active
```

show frame-relay lmi Command

The **show frame-relay lmi** command displays LMI traffic statistics, as seen in Example 11-4. For example, it shows the number of status messages exchanged between the local router and the Frame Relay switch.

Example 11-4 *The* **show frame-relay lmi** *Command Provides Statistics on the Frame Relay Connection*

```
Router#show frame-relay lmi

LMI Statistics for interface Serial0 (Frame Relay DTE) LMI TYPE = CISCO
Invalid Unnumbered info         0 Invalid Prot Disc 0
Invalid dummy Call Ref          0 Invalid Msg Type 0
Invalid Status Message          0 Invalid Lock Shift 0
Invalid Information ID          0 Invalid Report IE Len 0
Invalid Report Request          0 Invalid Keep IE Len 0
Num Status Enq. Sent 113100     Num Status msgs Rcvd 113100
Num Update Status Rcvd 0        Num Status Timeouts 0
```

Frame Relay Topologies

Frame Relay allows you to interconnect your remote sites in a variety of ways; by default, interfaces that support Frame Relay are multipoint connection types. Example topologies, as shown in Figure 11-7, include the following:

- A **star topology**, also known as a hub-and-spoke configuration, is the most popular Frame Relay network topology. In this topology, remote sites are connected to a Central site that generally provides a service or application.

- This is the least expensive topology because it requires the fewest PVCs. In this scenario, the Central router provides a multipoint connection because it is typically using a single interface to interconnect multiple PVCs.

- In a **full-mesh topology**, all routers have virtual circuits to all other destinations. This method, although costly, provides direct connections from each site to all other sites, and allows for redundancy. When one link goes down, a router at site A can reroute traffic through site C, for example. As the number of nodes in the full-mesh topology increases, the topology becomes increasingly more expensive.

- In a **partial-mesh topology**, not all sites have direct access to a Central site.

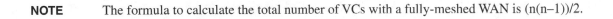

NOTE   The formula to calculate the total number of VCs with a fully-meshed WAN is (n(n−1))/2.

Figure 11-7 *Frame Relay Topologies*

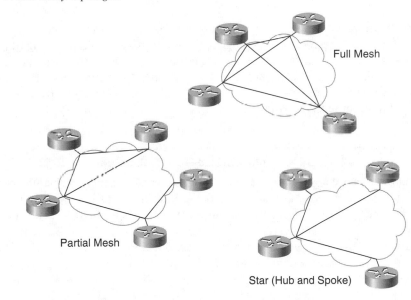

By default, interfaces that support Frame Relay are multipoint connection types. This type of connection is not a problem when only one PVC is supported by a single interface. However, it is a problem when multiple PVCs are supported by a single interface. In this situation, routing updates received by the Central router cannot be broadcast to the other remote sites.

Depending on the traffic patterns in your network, you may want to have additional PVCs connect to remote sites that require heavy data traffic. In any of these cases, when a single interface must be used to interconnect multiple sites, you may have reachability issues because of the nonbroadcast multiaccess (NBMA) nature of Frame Relay. With Frame Relay running multiple PVCs over a single interface, the primary issue is with split horizon.

Reachability Issues with Routing Updates

By default, a Frame Relay network provides NBMA connectivity between remote sites. NBMA connectivity means that although all locations can reach each other, depending on the topology, routing update broadcasts received by one router cannot be forwarded to all locations because Frame Relay networks use split horizon to reduce the number of routing loops.

Non-Broadcast Multiaccess (NBMA)

NBMA networks are those networks that support many (more than two) routers, but have no broadcast capability, such as Frame Relay.

Split horizon reduces the number of routing loops by not allowing a routing update received on one interface to be forwarded through the same interface. As shown in Figure 11-8, Central router's interface S0 receives a routing update from router BranchA. Central router is connecting three PVCs over a single interface. Split horizon forbids the Central router to send out updates via the same interface that it used to receive them. Therefore, BranchB and BranchC routers will never receive the update.

Split Horizon—an Explanation

Split horizon says that you cannot advertise a route out of the same interface through which you learned the route. This means that BranchB and BranchC will still receive an update from A. However, the update will not contain any information that is learned through that interface. The information from another interface on A will go to both BranchB and BranchC. Split horizon is actually not an issue if you do not want BranchB and BranchC to know about each other's local networks. [source: Karen Bagwell, CCIE and CCSI]

Figure 11-8 *Split Horizon at Work In a Partially Meshed Network without Subinterfaces*

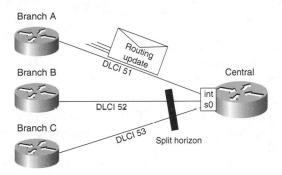

There are two inherent problems with multiple PVCs terminating in one interface: split horizon and the support for broadcast traffic.

Broadcasts are not a problem if there is only a single PVC on a physical interface because this would be more of a point-to-point connection type.

Another issue with routers that support multipoint connections over a single interface is that when many DLCIs terminate in a single router, that router must replicate routing updates and service advertising updates on each DLCI to the remote routers. The updates can consume access-link bandwidth and cause significant latency variations in user traffic. The updates can also consume interface buffers and lead to higher packet-rate loss for both user data and routing updates.

The amount of broadcast traffic and the number of virtual circuits terminating at each router should be evaluated during the design phase of a Frame Relay network. Overhead traffic, such as routing updates, can affect the delivery of critical user data, especially when the delivery path contains low-bandwidth (56 Kbps) links.

One common solution to split horizon is subinterfaces, which are covered in the upcoming section.

Solution for Split Horizon Issues—Subinterfaces

The simplest answer to resolving the reachability issues brought on by split horizon might seem to be to simply turn off split horizon. However, two problems exist with this solution. First, only IP allows you to disable split horizon; IPX and AppleTalk do not. Second, disabling split horizon increases the chances of routing loops in your network.

To enable the forwarding of broadcast routing updates in a Frame Relay network, you can configure the router with logically assigned interfaces called subinterfaces. **Subinterfaces** are logical subdivisions of a physical interface. In split-horizon routing environments, routing updates received on one subinterface can be sent out another subinterface. In subinterface configuration, each virtual circuit can be configured as a point-to-point connection, which allows the subinterface to act similar to a leased line.

NOTE
A key reason for using subinterfaces is to allow distance-vector routing protocols to perform properly in an environment in which split horizon is activated.

Subinterfaces themselves do not enable the forwarding of broadcasts. Instead, each destination is perceived to be on its own interface. Therefore, the router receiving a broadcast on subinterface S0.1, for example, is capable of reforwarding the same routing information out of its interfaces S0.2 and S0.3.

In Figure 11-9, reconsider the situation in which BranchA sends a routing update to Central. With subinterfaces, Central receives the update on its interface S 0.1 and is therefore able to pass to BranchB and BranchC the same update, sending it out through interfaces S0.2 and S0.3.

Figure 11-9   *Partially Meshed Frame Relay Network Using Subinterfaces*

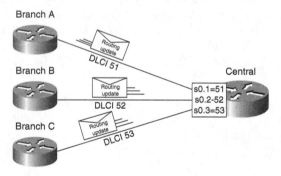

Configuring Frame Relay Subinterfaces

You can configure subinterfaces to support the following connection types:

- **Point-to-point**   A single subinterface is used to establish one PVC connection to another physical or subinterface on a remote router. In this case, the interfaces would be in the same subnet, and each interface would have a single DLCI. Each point-to-point connection is its own subnet. In this environment, broadcasts are not a problem because the routers are point-to-point and act like a leased line.

- **Multipoint**   A single subinterface is used to establish multiple PVC connections to multiple physical interfaces or subinterfaces on remote routers. In this case, all the participating interfaces would be in the same subnet, and each interface would have its own local DLCI. In this environment, because the subinterface is acting like a regular NBMA Frame Relay network, broadcast traffic is subject to the split horizon rule.

Figure 11-10 provides the visual representation for this example of subinterface configuration:

```
Router(config)#<Output Omitted>
Router(config-if)#interface Serial0
Router(config-if)#no ip address
Router(config-if)#encapsulation frame-relay

Router(config)#interface Serial0.2 point-to-point
Router(config-if)#ip address 10.17.0.1 255.255.255.0
Router(config-if)#frame-relay interface-dlci 110
!
Router(config)#interface Serial0.3 point-to-point
Router(config-if)#ip address 10.18.0.1 255.255.255.0
Router(config-if)#frame-relay interface-dlci 120
!
<output omitted>
```

Figure 11-10 *Configuring Subinterfaces*

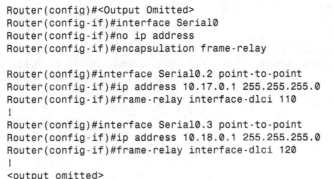
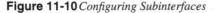
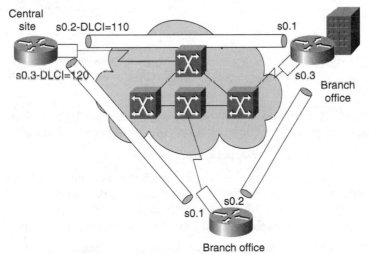

To configure subinterfaces on a physical interface, perform the following steps:

1 Select the interface that you want to create subinterfaces on, and enter the interface configuration mode.

2 Remove any network layer address that is assigned to the physical interface. If the physical interface has an address, frames will not be received by the local subinterfaces.

3 Configure Frame Relay encapsulation, as discussed in the "Configuring Basic Frame Relay" section.

4 Select the subinterface you want to configure:

```
Router(config-if)#interface serial number subinterface-number
     {multipoint | point-to-point}
```

interface serial Command	Description
number	The physical interface number, such as **interface serial 0**.
subinterface-number	Subinterface number in the range 1 to 4294967293. The interface number that precedes the period (.) must match the interface number to which this subinterface belongs. The number of subinterfaces that is possible on one interface is dependent on the interface descriptor block (IDB). The IDB is a set of data structures that provide a hardware and software view of network interfaces.
multipoint	Select this if you want the router to forward broadcasts and routing updates that it receives. Select this if you're routing IP and you want all routers to be in the same subnet.
point-to-point	Select this if you do not want the router to forward broadcasts or routing updates, and if you want each pair of point-to-point routers to have its own subnet.

5 Configure a network layer address on the subinterface. If the subinterface is point-to-point and you are using IP, you can use the **ip unnumbered** command:

```
Router(config-if)#ip unnumbered interface
```

If you use this command, it is recommended that the interface be the loopback interface. This is because the Frame Relay link will not work if this command is pointing to an interface that is not fully operational, and a loopback interface is less likely to fail. When using **ip unnumbered**, it should have two ends on the same major network.

6 If you configured the subinterface as multipoint or point-to-point, you must configure the local DLCI for the subinterface to distinguish it from the physical interface:

```
Router(config-if)#frame-relay interface-dlci dlci-number
```

frame-relay interface-dlci Command	Description
dlci-number	Defines the local DLCI number being linked to the subinterface. This is the only way to link an LMI-derived PVC to a subinterface because LMI does not know about subinterfaces.

This command is required for all point-to-point subinterfaces. It is also required for multipoint subinterfaces for which Inverse ARP is enabled. It is not required for multipoint subinterfaces that are configured with static route maps. Do not use this command on physical interfaces.

NOTE   If you defined a subinterface for point-to-point communication, you cannot reassign the same subinterface number to be used for multipoint communication without first rebooting the router. Instead, you must avoid using that subinterface number and use a different subinterface number.

Frame Relay Traffic-Shaping Overview

Frame Relay service providers use a parameter called **committed information rate (CIR)** to provision network resources to a Frame Relay user and regulate usage according to the assigned parameters. A mechanism written for the Frame Relay protocol exists for letting Frame Relay users know that congestion has been encountered within the Frame Relay network. This mechanism relies on the forward explicit congestion notification/backward explicit congestion notification (FECN/BECN) bits in the Q.922 header of the frame. The network or the user can selectively set the discard eligible (DE) bit in frames, and then drop these frames when congestion is encountered.

The traffic shaping over Frame Relay feature provides the following capabilities:

- **Rate enforcement on a per-virtual circuit basis**   You can configure a peak rate to limit outbound traffic to either the CIR or some other defined value, such as the Excess Information Rate (EIR).

- **Generalized BECN support on a per-virtual circuit (VC) basis**   The router can monitor BECNs and throttle traffic based on BECN-marked packet feedback from the Frame Relay network.

- **Priority/custom/weighted fair queuing (PQ/CQ/WFQ) support at the VC level**   This allows for finer granularity in the prioritization and queuing of traffic, thus giving you more control over the traffic flow on an individual VC.

Traffic Shaping and Flow Terminology

The traffic shaping over Frame Relay feature applies to Frame Relay PVCs and SVCs.

You should be familiar with some terminology related to Frame Relay traffic flow. Common Frame Relay terms related to traffic flow follow:

- **Local access rate**   The clock speed (port speed) of the connection (local loop) to the Frame Relay cloud. It is the rate at which data travels into or out of the network, regardless of other settings.

- **Committed Information Rate (CIR)**   The rate, in bits per second, that the Frame Relay switch agrees to transfer data. The rate is usually averaged over a period of time, referred to as the **committed rate measurement interval (Tc)**. In general, the duration of Tc is proportional to the "burstiness" of the traffic.

- **Oversubscribe and oversubscription**   Oversubscription is when the sum of the CIRs on all the VCs coming in to a device exceeds the access line speed. Oversubscription can occur when the access line can support the sum of CIRs purchased, but not of the CIRs plus the bursting capacities of the VCs. If oversubscription occurs, packets are dropped.

- **Committed Burst (Bc)**   The maximum number of bits that the switch agrees to transfer during any committed rate measurement interval (Tc). The higher the Bc-to-CIR ratio is, the longer the switch can handle a sustained burst. For example, if the Tc is two seconds and the CIR is 32 Kbps, the Bc is 64 Kbps. The Tc calculation is Tc = Bc/CIR.

NOTE   Tc is not a recurrent time interval. It is used strictly to measure inbound data, during which it acts like a sliding window. Inbound data triggers the Tc interval.

- **Excess Burst (Be)**   The maximum number of uncommitted bits that the Frame Relay switch attempts to transfer beyond the CIR. Excess Burst is dependent on the service offerings available from your vendor, but it is typically limited to the port speed of the local access loop.

- **Forward Explicit Congestion Notification (FECN)**   When a Frame Relay switch recognizes congestion in the network, it sends an FECN packet to the destination device, indicating that congestion has occurred, as shown in Figure 11-11.

- **Backward Explicit Congestion Notification (BECN)**   When a Frame Relay switch recognizes congestion in the network, it sends a BECN packet to the source router, instructing the router to reduce the rate at which it is sending packets, as shown in Figure 11-11. With Cisco IOS Release 11.2 or later, Cisco routers can respond to BECN notifications. This topic is discussed later in this chapter.

- **Discard Eligibility (DE) indicator**   When the router detects network congestion, the FR switch will drop packets with the DE bit set first. The DE bit is set on the oversubscribed traffic—that is, the traffic that was received after the CIR was met.

Figure 11-11 *Forward and Backward Congestion Notification*

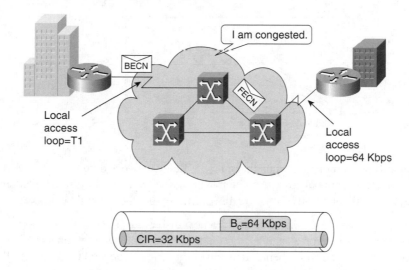

The CIR, by itself, does not provide much flexibility when dealing with varying traffic rates. In practice, the Frame Relay switch measures traffic over a time interval that is specific to each logical connection, as you will see in Figure 11-12.

Figure 11-12 *The Frame Relay Switch Measures Traffic over a Time Interval Specific to Each Logical Connection*

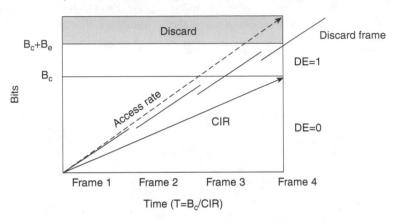

B_C and B_E are amounts of data that a Frame Relay network agrees to transfer over a time interval, T. B_C is the maximum amount in excess of the B_C that the network attempts to transfer under normal conditions. However, the traffic beyond the B_C will be marked DE.

Notice in Figure 11-12 that the actual frame transfer rate parallels the access rate; when a frame is being transmitted on a channel, that channel is dedicated to that transmission. The horizontal lines represent no frames being transmitted. In general, the sum of CIRs for all logical connections must be less than or equal to the physical line rate.

Using Traffic Shaping over Frame Relay

The traffic shaping over Frame Relay feature can be used in the following typical situations:

- When you have a Frame Relay network topology that consists of a high-speed (T1 line speed) connection at the Central site and low-speed (less than 56 Kbps) connections at the branch sites.

- When you have a Frame Relay network that is constructed with many VCs to different locations on a single physical line into the network.

- If you notice that your Frame Relay connections occasionally get congested.

- When you have several different types of traffic (such as IP, SNA, or Internetwork Packet Exchange (IPX) to transmit on the same Frame Relay VC, and want to ensure that the different traffic types receive a certain amount of bandwidth.

When you have a Frame Relay network topology that consists of a high-speed (T1 line speed) connection at the Central site and low-speed (<56 Kbps) connections at the branch sites, as shown in Figure 11-13, you can use the traffic shaping over Frame Relay feature. Because of the speed mismatch, a bottleneck often exists for traffic on a VC when the Central site tries to communicate with the branch site. This bottleneck results in poor response times for traffic, such as Systems Network Architecture (SNA) or interactive Telnet when it is stuck behind a large File Transfer Protocol (FTP) packet on the low-speed line. Packets get dropped at the bottleneck, resulting in lost SNA sessions and possibly causing the Central site to retransmit unacknowledged packets, making the congestion problem worse. The rate-enforcement capability of the traffic-shaping feature can be used to limit the rate at which data is sent on the VC at the Central site. Rate enforcement can also be used in conjunction with the existing DLCI prioritization feature to further improve performance in this situation.

Figure 11-13 *As an Example, Use Traffic Shaping When a Disproportionately Large Bandwidth Site Communicates with a Significantly Smaller Bandwidth Site*

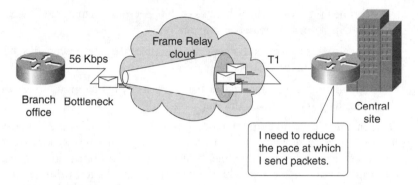

When you have a Frame Relay network that is constructed with many VCs to different locations on a single physical line into the network, these VCs send traffic as fast as the physical line speed allows. The rate-enforcement capability enables you to control the transmission speed used by the router by other criteria, such as the CIR or EIR. The rate-enforcement feature can preallocate the bandwidth that each VC receives on the physical line into the network, effectively creating a virtual time-division-multiplexing network.

If you notice that your Frame Relay connections occasionally get congested, you may want the router to throttle traffic instead of sending it in to the network. Throttling the traffic may help prevent packet loss in the network. The BECN-based throttling capability that is provided with the traffic shaping feature allows you to have the router dynamically throttle traffic, based on receiving BECN-tagged packets from the network. This throttling holds packets in the router's buffers to reduce the data flow from the router into the Frame Relay network. The throttling is done on a per-VC basis, and the rate is dynamically increased as fewer BECNs are received.

Quite often, you may have several different types of traffic—such as IP, SNA, or Internetwork Packet Exchange (IPX)—to transmit on the same Frame Relay VC, and want to ensure that the different traffic types receive a certain amount of bandwidth. Using custom queuing, with the per-VC queuing and rate-enforcement capabilities, enables you to configure VCs to perform this task. Prior to the Cisco IOS Release 11.2, custom queuing was only defined at the interface level. Now it can be defined at the VC level.

Configuring Frame Relay Traffic Shaping

To enable Frame Relay traffic shaping, perform the following steps.

1 **Specify a map class.** Specify a map class to be defined with the **map-class frame-relay** command:

```
Router(config)#map-class frame-relay map-class-name
```

2 **Define the map class.** When you define a map class for Frame Relay, you can do the following:

— Define the average and peak rates (in bits per second) that are allowed on virtual circuits associated with the map class.

— Specify that the router dynamically fluctuates the rate at which it sends packets, depending on the BECNs it receives.

— Specify either a custom queue-list or a priority queue-group to use on virtual circuits associated with the map class.

Once in map class configuration mode, you can define the average and peak rates, specify that the router dynamically fluctuate the rate at which it sends packets—depending on the BECNs it receives, or specify either a custom queue-list or a priority queue-group to use on virtual circuits associated with the map class. See the following section, "Ways to Define a Map Class," for different ways to define a map class for traffic shaping.

3 **Enable Frame Relay on an interface.** Once you have defined a map class with queuing and traffic-shaping parameters, enter interface configuration mode and enable Frame Relay encapsulation on an interface with the **encapsulation frame-relay** command, discussed earlier in this chapter in the "Configuring Frame Relay" section.

```
Router(config-if)#encapsulation frame-relay
```

4 **Enable Frame Relay traffic shaping on an interface with the frame-relay traffic-shaping command**. Enabling Frame Relay traffic shaping on an interface enables both traffic shaping and per-virtual circuit queuing on all the PVCs and SVCs on the interface. Traffic shaping enables the router to control the circuit's output rate and react to congestion notification information if also configured:

```
Router(config-if)#frame-relay traffic-shaping
```

5 **Map the map class to virtual circuits on the interface.** ap a map class to all virtual circuits on the interface with the **frame-relay class** *map-class-name command*. The *map-class-name* argument must match the *map-class-name* of the map class you configured:

```
Router(config-if)#frame-relay class map-class-name
```

NOTE   The map class can be mapped to the interface or to a specific subinterface on the interface.

Ways to Define a Map Class

This section shows the different ways to define a map class for traffic shaping.

Traffic Shaping through Rate Enforcement

Define the average and peak rates if the data is being sent faster than the speed at which the destination is receiving. If you define the average and peak rates (in bits per second) that are allowed on virtual circuits associated with the map class, use the **frame-relay traffic-rate** *average [peak]* command.

```
Router(config-map-class)#frame-relay traffic-rate average [ peak]
```

frame-relay traffic-rate Command	Description
average	Average rate in bits per second; it is equivalent to specifying the contracted CIR.
peak (Optional)	Peak rate, in bits per second. Peak = CIR + Be/Tc = CIR(1 + Bc/Bc) = CIR + EIR.

Traffic Shaping through Dynamic Enforcement

Specify that the router dynamically fluctuate the rate at which it sends packets, depending on the BECNs that it receives if you want the sending router to adjust its transmission rate based on the BECNs received. To select BECN as the mechanism to which traffic shaping will adapt, use the **frame-relay adaptive-shaping becn** command.

NOTE   The **frame-relay adaptive-shaping** command replaces the **frame-relay becn-response-enable** command.

Traffic Shaping through Queuing

Specify either a custom queue-list or a priority queue-group to use on virtual circuits associated with the map class if you want to use Cisco queuing mechanisms to control traffic flow.

NOTE   Queuing is covered in Chapter 13, "Managing Network Performance with Queuing and Compression."

To specify a custom queue-list, use the **frame-relay custom-queue-list** *number* command.

To specify a priority queue-list, use the **frame-relay priority-group** *number* command. The number is a required number assigned to the custom or priority queue list. The command syntax for both of these commands is described in Table 11-1.

Table 11-1 *Frame Relay Custom Queuing Commands*

Command	Description
frame-relay custom-queue-list *number*	Assigns a custom queue to virtual circuits associated with the map class. Use this command when you want to guarantee a particular protocol or service. Use this command after you have defined a custom queue by using the queue-list commands. Only one form of queuing may be associated with a particular map class, so subsequent definitions overwrite previous ones.
frame-relay priority-group *number*	Assigns a priority queue to virtual circuits associated with the map class. Use this command when you want to guarantee an absolute priority for a protocol or service. Use this command after defining the priority queue using priority-list commands. Only one form of queuing may be associated with a particular map class, so subsequent definitions overwrite previous ones.

Traffic Shaping Examples

Figure 11-14 illustrates a typical Frame Relay environment. The Central site has a T1-speed local loop connection and the branch offices have slower (in this case, 9.6 Kbps) local loop connections. In addition, the CIR for each PVC going from the Central site to each branch office is 9.6 Kbps.

Figure 11-14 *Typical Frame Relay Topology, in which a Central Site has a Larger Bandwidth Available than Branch Office Site—this Topology Makes It an Ideal Candidate for Traffic Shaping*

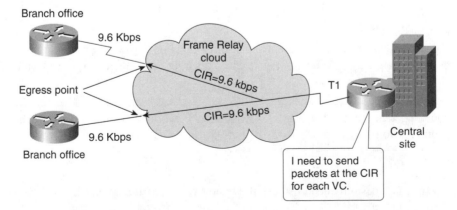

In this environment, the following process occurs:

1 The Central site may send data across the T1-speed line. Even though the CIR is 9.6 Kbps, the router continues to send the data based on the T1 rate.

2 The data goes through the cloud.

3 When the data reaches the local loop that is connected to the branch office, a bottleneck occurs because the data is being sent faster than the speed of the branch office local loop. At this point, packets are buffered at the egress point of the network, which increases line response time and can cause problems, particularly for latency-sensitive protocols such as SNA.

With the problem that occurs in the given process, the solution is to slow the speed at which the Central site router is sending data. With the traffic shaping over Frame Relay feature, you can define and enforce a rate on the VC at which the router will send data. The pace you set can be the CIR, EIR, or some other value.

Rate Enforcement Example

Perform the following steps to configure traffic shaping over Frame Relay rate enforcement:

1 Define a map class and enter map class configuration mode:

```
Router(config)#map-class frame-relay map-class-name
```

2 Define the rate enforcement parameters to use:

```
Router(config-map-class)#[no] frame-relay traffic-rate average [peak]
```

average is the average rate (equivalent to CIR).

peak is the "peak rate" (equivalent to CIR + Bc/t = CIR(1 + Be/Bc)). The default peak value is the line rate (derived from the bandwidth command). For SVCs, the configured peak and average rates are converted to the equivalent CIR, Be, and Bc values for use by SVC signaling. Only one command format ("traffic rate" or CIR, Be, and Bc) will be accepted in one map class. The user is warned when entering a second command type that the previous one is being overwritten.

3 Enable both traffic shaping and per-VC queuing for all VCs (PVCs and SVCs) on a Frame Relay interface:

```
Router(config-if)#frame-relay traffic-shaping
```

For VCs where no specific traffic shaping or queuing parameters are specified, a set of default values is used.

4 Associate a map class with an interface or subinterface:

```
Router(config)#frame-relay class name
```

Each VC created on the interface/subinterface inherits all of the relevant parameters defined in the **frame-relay-class** *name*. For each VC, the precedence rules are as follows:

— Use a map class associated with VC if it exists.

— If not, use a map class associated with subinterface, if it exists.

— If not, use a map class associated with interface, if it exists.

— If not, use the default parameters.

5 (Optional) Apply a map class to a specific DLCI for which a Frame Relay map statement exists:

```
Router(config-map-class)#frame-relay interface-dlci
         dlci [broadcast] [ietf | cisco]
```

Example 11-5 shows a traffic-shaping configuration example.

Example 11-5 *Traffic-Shaping Configuration Example*

```
Central(config)#interface Serial2
Central(config-if)#no ip address
Central(config-if)#encapsulation frame-relay
Central(config-if)#frame-relay traffic-shaping
Central(config-if)#frame-relay class branch
!
<output omitted>
!
Central(config)#map-class frame-relay branch
Central(config-map-class)#frame-relay traffic-rate 9600 18000
```

Dynamic Enforcement Example

Figure 11-15 illustrates a Frame Relay environment in which different sites might have different speeds for local loop connections to the Frame Relay cloud.

Figure 11-15 *Switches Notify Outgoing Router of Congestion Using BECN*

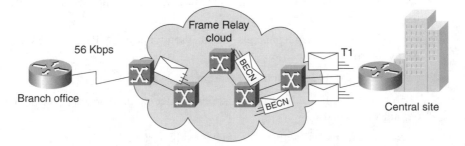

In this environment, the following process can occur:

1 Central site sends data to router branch site.

2 One of the switches within the cloud determines that it is getting congested with traffic. In this case, the congested switch will send a BECN packet to the Central router.

NOTE   Prior to the traffic shaping over Frame Relay feature, the Central router would note that the BECN was received, but would not slow its transmission rate.

---

3 At this point, packets begin dropping within the switch that is encountering the congestion. As previously discussed, this environment can cause problems, particularly for latency-sensitive protocols such as SNA.

With the problem in this given process, the solution is to enable the Central router to dynamically fluctuate the rate at which it sends packets, depending on the BECNs that it receives. For example, if the Central router begins receiving many BECNs, it will reduce the packet transmit rate. As the BECNs become intermittent, the router will increase the packet transmit rate.

Perform the following steps to configure traffic shaping over Frame Relay BECN support:

1 Define a map class and enter map class configuration mode, as previously discussed.

2 Make sure that BECN support is enabled:

```
Router(config-map-class)#frame-relay adaptive-shaping becn
```

BECN support is enabled by default. When enabled, BECNs received from the network on this VC are used to further regulate the output rate on the VC. As the frequency of BECNs increases, the output rate is steadily reduced from *peak to average* (equivalent of CIR). As congestion eases in the network and the frequency of BECNs decreases, the output rate is allowed to increase gradually to its configured *peak*.

3 Enable both traffic shaping and per-VC queuing for all VCs (PVCs and SVCs) on a Frame Relay interface:

```
Router(config-if)#frame-relay traffic-shaping
```

For VCs, where no specific traffic shaping or queuing parameters are specified, a set of default values is used.

4 Associate a map class with an interface or subinterface, as previously discussed:

```
Router(config-if)#frame-relay class name
```

5 (Optional) Apply the map class to a specific DLCI for which a **frame-relay map** statement exists, as previously discussed:

```
Router(config-map-class)#frame-relay interface-dlci
    dlci [broadcast] [ietf ¦ cisco]
```

Example 11-6 shows traffic-shaping through a BECN example.

Example 11-6 *Traffic-Shaping BECN Support*

```
Router(config)#interface serial 0
Router(config-if)#encapsulation frame-relay
Router(config-if)#frame-relay traffic-shaping
Router(config-if)#frame-relay class becnnotify
!
…
!
Router(config)#map-class frame-relay becnnotify
Router(config-map-class)#frame-relay adaptive-shaping becn
```

Queuing Example

In Example 11-7, the virtual circuits on subinterfaces Serial0.1 and Serial0.2 inherit class parameters from the main interface, namely those defined in **slow_vcs**. However, the virtual circuit defined on subinterface Serial0.2 (DLCI 102) is specifically configured to use map class **fast_vcs**.

Map class **slow_vcs** uses a peak rate of 9600 and an average rate of 4800 bits per second. Because BECN feedback is enabled by default, the output rate will be cut back as low as 4800 Bps in response to received BECNs. This map class is configured to use custom queuing by using **queue-list 1**. In Example 11-7, **queue-list 1** has three queues, with the first two being controlled by access list 100 and 115.

Map class **fast_vcs** uses a peak rate of 64,000 and average of 16,000 Bps. Because BECN feedback is enabled by default, the output rate will be cut back as low as 4800 Bps in response to received BECNs. This map class is configured to use priority queuing using **priority-group 2**.

Example 11-7 *The* **show running-config** *Command on a Router with Traffic-Shaping Queuing*

```
interface Serial 0
no ip address
encapsulation frame-relay
frame-relay lmi-type ansi
frame-relay traffic-shaping
frame-relay class slow_vcs
!
interface Serial0.1 point-to-point
ip address 10.128.30.1 255.255.255.248
ip ospf cost 200
bandwidth 10
frame-relay interface-dlci 101
!
interface Serial0.2 point-to-point
ip address 10.128.30.9 255.255.255.248
ip ospf cost 400
bandwidth 10
frame-relay interface-dlci 102
class fast_vcs
```

Example 11-7 *The* **show running-config** *Command on a Router with Traffic-Shaping Queuing (Continued)*

```
!
interface Serial0.3 point-to-point
ip address 10.128.30.17 255.255.255.248
ip ospf cost 200
bandwidth 10
frame-relay interface-dlci 103
map-class frame-relay slow_vcs
frame-relay traffic-rate 4800 9600
frame-relay custom-queue-list 1
!
map-class frame-relay fast_vcs
frame-relay traffic-rate 16000 64000
frame-relay priority-group 2
!
access-list 100 permit tcp any any eq 2065
access-list 115 permit tcp any any eq 256
!
priority-list 2 protocol decnet high
priority-list 2 ip normal
priority-list 2 default medium
!
queue-list 1 protocol ip 1 list 100
queue-list 1 protocol ip 2 list 115
queue-list 1 default 3
queue-list 1 queue 1 byte-count 1600 limit 2
queue-list 1 queue 2 byte-count 600 limit 20
queue-list 1 queue 3 byte-count 500 limit 20
```

Map class **slow_vcs** uses a peak rate of 9600 and average rate of 4800 Bps. Because BECN feedback is enabled by default, the output rate will be cut back as low as 4800 Bps in response to received BECNs. This map class is configured to use custom queuing using **queue-list 1**. In this example, **queue-list 1** has three queues, with the first two being controlled by access lists 100 and 115.

Map class **fast_vcs** uses a peak rate of 64,000 and average rate of 16,000 Bps. Because BECN feedback is enabled by default, the output rate will be cut back as low as 4800 Bps in response to received BECNs. This map class is configured to use priority-queuing using **priority-group 2**.

Verifying Frame Relay Traffic Shaping

As shown in Example 11-8, the **show frame-relay pvc** command, previously discussed, includes the parameters used in traffic shaping, if enabled, and the queuing algorithm in use.

Example 11-8 *Verifying Frame Relay Traffic Shaping with the* **show frame-relay pvc** *Command*

```
Router#show frame-relay pvc 110

PVC Statistics for interface Serial0 (Frame Relay DTE)

DLCI = 110, DLCI USAGE = LOCAL, PVC STATUS = ACTIVE, INTERFACE = Serial0.1
input pkts 14186        output pkts 33081        in bytes 1106836
out bytes 6268930       dropped pkts 0           in FECN pkts 0
in BECN pkts 0          out FECN pkts 0          out BECN pkts 0
in DE pkts 0            out DE pkts 0
out bcast pkts 33066                             out bcast bytes
6267370
Shaping adapts to BECN
pvc create time 1w6d, last time pvc status changed 1w6d
cir 56000          bc 7000              be 0          limit 875
interval 125
mincir 0           byte increment 875                BECN response
no
pkts 33082         bytes 6268960      pkts delayed 0          bytes
delayed 0
shaping inactive
Serial0.1 dlci 110 is first come first serve default queueing
Output queue 0/40, 0 drop, 0 dequeued
```

Case Study—Establishing a Dedicated Frame Relay Connection and Controlling Traffic Flow

Complete the tasks of this case study and then review the case study solution section that follows to see how you did and see where you might need to review concepts presented in this chapter.

In this case study, you will configure a Frame Relay interface and subinterface, apply traffic-shaping techniques, and verify the proper operation of Frame Relay.

Scenario

You are the WAN manager of a Frame Relay network set in a star topology. You have to configure Frame Relay on the Central site and branch office routers, as shown in Figure 11-16. Also, you have to configure subinterfaces on the Central site router so there is one VC connection to each branch using the Frame Relay network.

The bandwidth available at the Central site is larger than the bandwidth found at branch offices. Therefore, enable Frame Relay traffic shaping to control traffic flow from the Central site.

Figure 11-16 *Frame Relay WAN: Central Site Exchanges with One of the Branch Offices*

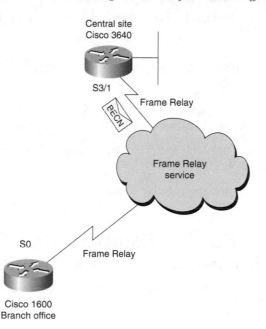

Task 1—Configuring Frame Relay Subinterfaces on the Central Site Router

Because your WAN is in a star topology, your Central site has only one Frame Relay PVC. So, you must configure subinterfaces to make VC connections to multiple branch offices:

Step 1   Prepare the interface 3/1 for Frame Relay connection.

Step 2   Configure a point-to-point subinterface on your Central site router to connect to one of the branch office routers. The connection will be made by using the Cisco LMI.

Step 3   Confirm the status of your serial interface 3/1 and of the **frame-relay pvc**.

Task 2—Configuring Frame Relay on the Branch Office Router

Step 1   Configure the Serial Interface 0 (int S 0) to communicate with the Central site. The branch office uses the Cisco LMI.

Step 2   Verify that the serial interface is properly configured and that a PVC is available.

Task 3—Verifying Frame Relay Operation

Ensure that your router has Frame Relay connectivity and that it is learning routes.

Task 4—Enabling Frame Relay Traffic-Shaping BECN Support from the Central Site

There is congestion on your Frame Relay WAN. You identify that the congestion is the result of dissimilar bandwidth between the Central site and the branch offices.

Configure your Central site's router to adapt to congestion notices that it receives from the Frame Relay network.

Confirm that traffic shaping is active on PVC.

Solution to Case Study—Establishing a Dedicated Frame Relay Connection and Controlling Traffic Flow

The following is a step-by-step discussion of the case study solution.

Task 1 Solution: Configuring Frame Relay Subinterfaces on the Central Site Router

Step 1   Configure your Central site router's serial interface for Frame Relay as follows:

— Enter serial interface 3/1 configuration mode:

```
CentralA(config)#interface serial 3/1
```

— Enable Frame Relay encapsulation on the interface:

```
CentralA(config-if)#encapsulation frame-relay
```

— Specify cisco as the LMI type. The following command is not necessary because Cisco LMI is the default:

```
CentralA(config-if)#frame-relay lmi-type cisco
```

— Activate the interface:

```
CentralA(config-if)# no shutdown
```

NOTE   IP addresses are configured on the subinterfaces; no IP address is specified on the interface.

Step 2   Configure your Central site router's serial subinterface for Frame Relay as follows:

— Enter serial subinterface 3/1.1 configuration mode. Specify the connection as a point-to-point connection:

```
CentralA(config)#interface serial 3/1.1 point-to-point
```

— Assign an IP address to the subinterface. Any IP address would do, providing that it is part of the same subnet used by every Frame Relay interface on your WAN:

```
CentralA(config-subif)#ip address 10.140.1.1 255.255.255.0
```

— Set the bandwidth to 64 Kbps. This command is said to be passive. The routing algorithm to calculate the best route uses the bandwidth value— in this case, 64:

```
CentralA(config-subif)#bandwidth 64
```

— Identify the connection with the local DLCI. In this case study, we pretend that the VC configure by the service provider to link the Central site and the branch office is DLCI 110:

```
CentralA(config-subif)#frame-relay interface-dlci 110
```

Step 3   Verify the status of the interface, as displayed in Example 11-9.

Example 11-9 *Monitoring a Frame Relay Interface*

```
CentralA#sh interface s3/1
Serial3/1 is up, line protocol is up
Hardware is CD2430 in sync mode
MTU 1500 bytes, BW 128 Kbit, DLY 20000 usec, rely 255/255, load 1/255
Encapsulation FRAME-RELAY, loopback not set, keepalive set (10 sec)
LMI enq sent 411, LMI stat recvd 411, LMI upd recvd 0, DTE LMI up
LMI enq recvd 0, LMI stat sent 0, LMI upd sent 0
LMI DLCI 1023 LMI type is CISCO frame relay DTE
FR SVC disabled, LAPF state down
Broadcast queue 0/64, broadcasts sent/dropped 108/0, interface broadcasts 52
Last input 00:00:01, output 00:00:01, output hang never
Last clearing of "show interface" counters never
Input queue: 0/75/0 (size/max/drops); Total output drops: 0
Queueing strategy: weighted fair
Output queue: 0/1000/64/0 (size/max total/threshold/drops)
Conversations 0/1/256 (active/max active/max total)
Reserved Conversations 0/0 (allocated/max allocated)
5 minute input rate 0 bits/sec, 0 packets/sec
5 minute output rate 0 bits/sec, 0 packets/sec
727 packets input, 25126 bytes, 0 no buffer
Received 411 broadcasts, 0 runts, 0 giants, 0 throttles
0 input errors, 0 CRC, 0 frame, 0 overrun, 0 ignored, 0 abort
798 packets output, 42594 bytes, 0 underruns
0 output errors, 0 collisions, 9 interface resets
0 output buffer failures, 0 output buffers swapped out
```

continues

Example 11-9 *Monitoring a Frame Relay Interface (Continued)*

```
2 carrier transitions
DCD=up DSR=up DTR=up RTS=up CTS=up


CentralA#sh frame-relay pvc

PVC Statistics for interface Serial3/1 (Frame Relay DTE)

DLCI = 110, DLCI USAGE = LOCAL, PVC STATUS = ACTIVE, INTERFACE = Serial3/1.1

input pkts 23 output pkts 28 in bytes 2632
out bytes 4254 dropped pkts 0 in FECN pkts 0
in BECN pkts 0 out FECN pkts 0 out BECN pkts 0
in DE pkts 0 out DE pkts 0
out bcast pkts 13 out bcast bytes 2694
pvc create time 00:06:37, last time pvc status changed 00:06:38
```

NOTE   The point-to-point subinterface will not come up until the branch is configured.

Task 2 Solution—Configuring Frame Relay on the Branch Office Router

Step 1   Configure Frame Relay on the branch office router:

— Enter serial interface 0 configuration mode:

```
BranchA(config)#interface serial 0
```

— Enable Frame Relay encapsulation on the interface:

```
BranchA(config-if)#encapsulation frame-relay
```

— Assign an IP address to the interface. We use an IP address reserved for the Frame Relay connection. As you can see, it is part of the same subnet as the address we assigned on CentralA's Frame Relay interface:

```
BranchA(config-if)#ip address 10.140.1.2 255.255.255.0
```

— Set the bandwidth to 64 Kbps:

```
BranchA(config-if)#bandwidth 64
```

— Specify cisco as the LMI type:

```
BranchA(config-if)#frame-relay lmi-type cisco
```

— Activate the interface:

```
BranchA(config-if)#no shutdown
```

Step 2   Verify that the serial interface is properly configured and that a PVC is available, as shown in Example 11-10.

Example 11-10   *Monitoring a Frame Relay Interface with the* **show interface** *Command*

```
BranchA#sh interface s0
Serial0 is up, line protocol is up
Hardware is QUICC Serial
Internet address is 10.140.1.2/24
MTU 1500 bytes, BW 64 Kbit, DLY 20000 usec, rely 255/255, load 1/255
Encapsulation FRAME-RELAY, loopback not set, keepalive set (10 sec)
LMI enq sent 399, LMI stat recvd 399, LMI upd recvd 0, DTE LMI up
LMI enq recvd 0, LMI stat sent 0, LMI upd sent 0
LMI DLCI 1023 LMI type is CISCO frame relay DTE
FR SVC disabled, LAPF state down
Broadcast queue 0/64, broadcasts sent/dropped 69/0, interface broadcasts 57
Last input 00:00:05, output 00:00:05, output hang never
Last clearing of "show interface" counters never
Input queue: 0/75/0 (size/max/drops); Total output drops: 0
Queueing strategy: weighted fair
Output queue: 0/1000/64/0 (size/max total/threshold/drops)
Conversations 0/1/256 (active/max active/max total)
Reserved Conversations 0/0 (allocated/max allocated)
5 minute input rate 0 bits/sec, 0 packets/sec
5 minute output rate 0 bits/sec, 0 packets/sec
774 packets input, 42693 bytes, 0 no buffer
Received 399 broadcasts, 0 runts, 0 giants, 0 throttles
2 input errors, 0 CRC, 2 frame, 0 overrun, 0 ignored, 0 abort
701 packets output, 25047 bytes, 0 underruns
0 output errors, 0 collisions, 25 interface resets
0 output buffer failures, 0 output buffers swapped out
6 carrier transitions
DCD=up DSR=up DTR=up RTS=up CTS=up


BranchA#sh frame-relay pvc

PVC Statistics for interface Serial0 (Frame Relay DTE)

DLCI = 100, DLCI USAGE = LOCAL, PVC STATUS = ACTIVE, INTERFACE = Serial0
input pkts 166      output pkts 95      in bytes 27898
out bytes 11736      dropped pkts 0      in FECN pkts 0
in BECN pkts 0      out FECN pkts 0      out BECN pkts 0
in DE pkts 0      out DE pkts 0
out bcast pkts 70      out bcast bytes 9136
pvc create time 01:06:58, last time pvc status changed 00:16:17
```

Task 3 Solution—Verifying Frame Relay Operation

From the Central site router, you could view the state of your Frame Relay WAN with the **show ip route** and the **show frame-relay map** commands.

Task 4 Solution—Enabling Frame Relay Traffic-Shaping BECN Support from the Central Site

To correct the congestion problem and provide traffic shaping, you could do the following steps:

Step 1 Enter global configuration mode for the Central site router:

```
CentralA#conf terminal
```

Step 2 Enter map class configuration mode and specify a map class name. You could use **TSLAB** as the map class name, as in "Traffic Shaping Lab":

```
CentralA(config)#map-class frame-relay TSLAB
```

Step 3 Define the BECN support as the map class parameter:

```
CentralA(config-map-class)#frame-relay adaptive-shaping becn
```

Step 4 Configure Frame Relay traffic shaping on the interface, as follows:

— Enter interface configuration mode for serial interface 3/1:

```
CentralA(config-map-class)#interface serial 3/1
```

— Enable Frame Relay traffic shaping on the interface:

```
CentralA(config-if)#frame-relay traffic-shaping
```

— Enter serial subinterface 3/1 configuration mode:

```
CentralA(config-if)#interface serial 3/1.1
```

— Associate the map class that you defined with the subinterface:

```
CentalA(config-subif)#frame-relay class TSLAB
```

NOTE If you are using a Cisco router configured for Frame Relay switching in your Frame Relay cloud, the router does not deliver BECN notifications like an IGX would. So you cannot verify the throttling back of traffic based on the BECNs in this laboratory exercise.

Step 5 You could use the **show frame-relay pvc** command to verify that traffic shaping is enabled. Your output would look like that shown in Example 11-11.

Example 11-11 *The* **show frame-relay pvc** *Command Display*

```
CentralA#sh frame-relay pvc

PVC Statistics for interface Serial3/1 (Frame Relay DTE)

DLCI = 110, DLCI USAGE = LOCAL, PVC STATUS = ACTIVE, INTERFACE = Serial3/1.1

input pkts 35      output pkts 40      in bytes 4324
out bytes 6684      dropped pkts 0 in      FECN pkts 0
```

Example 11-11 *The* **show frame-relay pvc** *Command Display (Continued)*

```
in BECN pkts 0      out FECN pkts 0 out      BECN pkts 0
in DE pkts 0      out DE pkts 0
out bcast pkts 25      out bcast bytes 5124
Shaping adapts to BECN
pvc create time 00:12:55, last time pvc status changed 00:12:55
```

Case Study Conclusion

In this case study, you configured interfaces and subinterfaces for Frame Relay. You also had to develop a traffic-shaping plan for the WAN.

Review Questions

Answer the following questions and then refer to Appendix H, "Answers to Review Questions," for answers and explanations.

1 What is a DLCI and how is it used to route Frame Relay traffic?

2 Why would you use Frame Relay subinterfaces?

3 List and describe three Frame Relay traffic-shaping features.

CHAPTER 12

Enabling Backup to a Permanent Connection

In the two previous chapters, you learned how to enable permanent connections between a Central site and a branch office by using X.25 or Frame Relay. How can you provide connectivity between the two sites if the permanent connection goes down?

This chapter describes the need and circumstances for using the Cisco dial-backup functionality.

You will learn how to configure a backup connection for a primary link, such as a Frame Relay serial connection, if the link goes down or is overutilized.

Dial Backup Overview

A **backup interface** is an interface that stays idle until certain circumstances occur, and then it is activated. The backup interface can be a physical interface or an assigned backup interface to be used in a dialer pool. Backup interface examples for a primary line can be an Integrated Services Digital Network (ISDN), an asynchronous interface, a dialer pool, or another serial interface.

NOTE
The backup interface is referred to often in Cisco documentation as the **secondary link**.

A backup interface can be configured to activate when the following situations occur:

- The primary line goes down
- The primary line reaches a certain load threshold

Configuring Dial Backup

Backup interfaces are beneficial for redundancy, in case primary lines fail. The example in Figure 12-1 illustrates an ISDN backup for a Frame Relay network.

Figure 12-1 *When the Primary Link Fails, the Backup (Secondary) Link Takes Over by Establishing a Connection to the Destination*

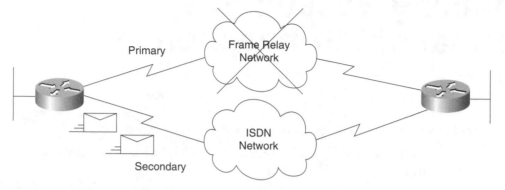

To configure backup if a primary line goes down, perform the following steps:

1 Select the primary interface, and configure it as needed (for dial-on-demand routing, Frame Relay interfaces and subinterfaces, X.25, and so on):

   ```
   Router(config)#interface serial 0
   ```

2 Use the following command on the primary interface to specify the interface or dialer interface to use for backup. (Interface number specifications vary from router to router. For example, some routers require you to just specify the port number; others require you to specify the slot and port.)

   ```
   Router(config-if)#backup interface interface-type number
   ```

3 Define the period of time to wait before enabling the backup link after the primary link goes down with the following command syntax, which is explained in the table that follows:

   ```
   Router(config-if)#backup delay {enable-delay | never} {disable-delay | never}
   ```

backup delay Command	Description
enable-delay	Number of seconds that elapse after the primary line goes down before the Cisco IOS software activates the secondary line.
disable-delay	Number of seconds that elapse after the primary line comes up, before the Cisco IOS software deactivates the secondary line.
never	Prevents the secondary line from being activated or deactivated.

Example of Dial Backup for Link Failure

In Figure 12-2, interface serial 0 (S0) is the primary interface. You can see from the configuration displayed in the figure that if the primary interface is down for 40 seconds, the backup interface (BRI0) will be activated. The secondary line will deactivate 20 seconds after the primary line is re-enabled.

NOTE   The example in Figure 12-2 illustrates only the commands to enable a backup. The interface must also be configured as needed (for DDR, Frame Relay, X.25, and so on).

Figure 12-2   *Dial Backup Configuration for a Link Failure*

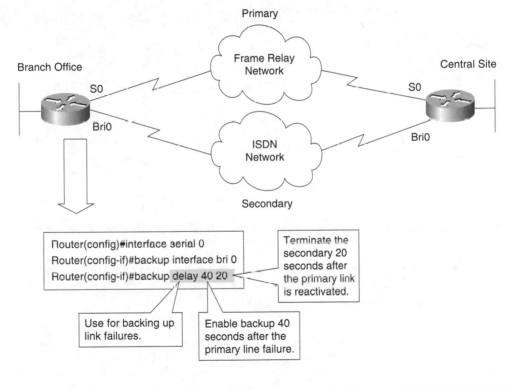

Floating Static Route

An alternative to dial backup for link failure is a floating static route. **Floating static routes** are static routes that have an administrative distance greater than the administrative distance of dynamic routes. Administrative distances can be configured on a static route, so that the static route is less desirable than a dynamic route. In this manner, the static route is not used when the dynamic route is available. If the dynamic route is lost, however, the static route can take over, and traffic can be sent through this alternative route. When this alternative route is provided by a DDR interface, DDR is used as a backup mechanism.

Activating a Dial Backup to Support Primary Line Traffic

You can configure a backup to activate the secondary line, based on the traffic load on the primary line. The software monitors the traffic load and computes a five-minute moving average. If this average exceeds the value you set for the line (as shown in Figure 12-3), the secondary line is activated. Depending on how the line is configured, some or all of the traffic will flow onto the secondary dial-up line.

Figure 12-3 *When the Primary Link Load Exceeds a Threshold, the Backup Link Comes to the Rescue by Establishing a Second Connection to the Destination*

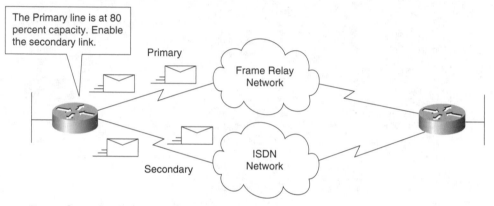

To configure backup if a primary line reaches or exceeds a certain threshold, perform the following steps:

1 Select the primary interface and configure it as needed (for dial-on-demand routing, Frame Relay interfaces, X.25, and so on):

```
Router(config)#interface serial 0
```

NOTE   The **backup load** command can't be configured for Frame Relay subinterfaces.

---

2 Use the following command on the primary interface to specify the backup to be used if a dial backup is needed:

```
Router(config-if)#backup interface interface-type number
```

3 To set the traffic load threshold for dial backup service, use the following command syntax, which is explained in the table that follows:

```
Router(config-if)#backup load {enable-threshold | never}
{disable-threshold | never}
```

backup load Command	Description
enable-threshold	Percentage of the primary line's available bandwidth that the traffic load must exceed to enable dial backup.
disable-load	Percentage of the primary line's available bandwidth that the traffic load must be less than to disable dial backup.
never	Prevents the secondary line from being activated or deactivated.

Example of Dial Backup for Excessive Traffic Load

In Figure 12-4, interface serial 0 is the primary interface. From the configuration in the figure, you can tell that if the primary interface is down for 40 seconds, the backup interface (BRI 0) will be activated. The secondary line will deactivate 20 seconds after the primary line is re-enabled.

NOTE	The example in Figure 12-4 illustrates only the commands to enable a backup. The interface must also be configured as needed (for DDR, Frame Relay, X.25, and so on).

Figure 12-4   *Dial Backup Configuration for an Excess Load on the Primary Link*

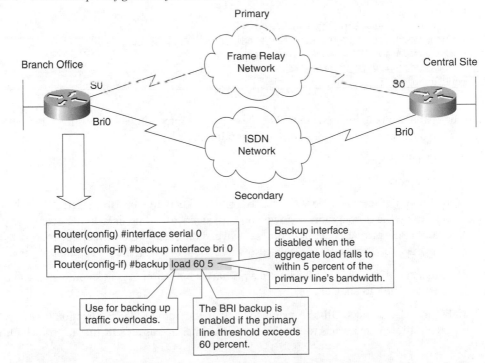

Backup Interface Operations

When a backup interface is specified on a primary line, the backup interface is placed in standby mode. Once in standby mode, the backup interface is effectively shut down until enabled. The backup route between the two company sites is not resolvable and it does not appear in the routing table. Example 12-1 displays the output of the **show interface dialer 1** command when it is run on the backup interface of the network displayed in Figure 12-5.

Figure 12-5   *The Backup Interface Is in Standby Mode*

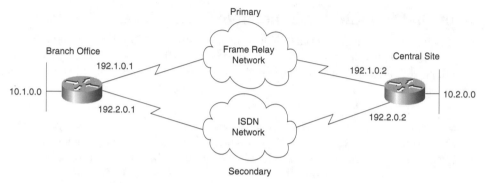

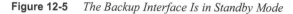

Example 12-1 *The Backup Interface is in Standby Mode*

```
Branch#show interface dialer 1
Dialer1 is standby mode, line protocol is down
  Hardware is Unknown
  Internet address is 192.2.0.1/24
  MTU 1500 bytes, BW 56 Kbit, DLY 20000 usec, rely 255/255, load 1/255
  Encapsulation PPP, loopback not set
  DTR is pulsed for 1 seconds on reset
<Output Omitted>
```

The primary link in Figure 12-5 will be the only route appearing in the routing table. The branch office router continues to monitor the two following events:

- Carrier detect
- Keepalives

If the branch office router does not receive either a keepalive or carrier detect response, it assumes that the primary line is down and activates the backup link. In the event of a primary line failure, the primary interface comes down and the backup is enabled. The routing table now reflects the backup route as the only resolvable route between the two company sites.

If a physical link is used as a backup to a primary connection, it is in standby mode and cannot be used as a link to another site.

In Figure 12-6, Branch Office A wants to back up its Frame Relay connection with ISDN BRI. Branch Office A also wants to use the same BRI interface as a DDR link to Branch Office B, however. If Branch Office A places the physical BRI link in standby mode, it is deactivated and does not activate until the primary line fails or reaches a specified threshold. Thus, the BRI link cannot be used to connect to Branch Office B.

Figure 12-6   *A Physical Interface Cannot Be Active and a Backup at the Same Time*

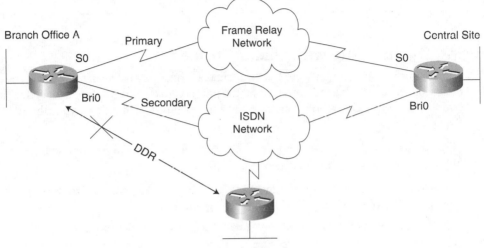

Branch Office B

Dialer Profiles as Backup Interfaces

With dialer profiles, the BRI connection in Figure 12-6 can be used to back up the primary Frame Relay link between the Central site and branch office. At the same time, it can be configured for DDR between Branch Office A and Branch Office B (as shown in Figure 12-7). Configure one dialer profile to act as the backup line. This profile is in standby mode until engaged. Configure another dialer profile for Legacy DDR between the Branch Office A and Branch Office B sites. Make the physical BRI interface a member of both dialer pools.

Figure 12-7   *Dialer Interface Can Be Used as the Backup without Deactivating the Physical Interface*

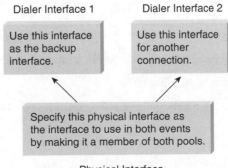

Dialer Interface 1   Dialer Interface 2

Use this interface as the backup interface.

Use this interface for another connection.

Specify this physical interface as the interface to use in both events by making it a member of both pools.

Physical Interface

NOTE	When you use a BRI for a dial backup, neither of the B channels can be used while the interface is in standby mode. In addition, when a BRI is used as a backup interface and the BRI is configured for Legacy DDR, only one B channel is usable. Once the backup is initiated over one B channel, the second B channel is unavailable. When the backup interface is configured for dialer profiles, both B channels can be used.

Configuring Dial Backup with Dialer Profiles

Dialer interfaces can be configured as the logical intermediary between physical interfaces. The dialer interface is the backup interface for the primary link. If the primary connection fails or is overutilized, the dialer interface kicks in and enlists a physical interface, typically BRI, to place the call.

To configure a dialer interface and a specific physical interface to function as backup to other physical interfaces, perform the following steps:

1 Create and configure a dialer interface, as you did in Chapter 8, "Optimizing the Use of DDR Interface—Dialer Profiles and Rotary Groups."

2 The following table reviews ways to configure a dialer interface.

Command	Description
interface *type number*	Specify the interface to be used as backup.
encapsulation ppp	Specify PPP encapsulation on the interface.
ppp authentication chap	Specify CHAP authentication.

3 Make the interface to be used as backup a member of the dialer pool by using the **dialer pool member** *number* command.

Command	Description
dialer pool member *number*	Make the interface a member of the dialer pool. The number must match the appropriate dialer pool number.

4 You must then configure the primary interface to use a backup.

5 Enter interface configuration mode for the primary interface.

6 Assign an address to your interface.

7 Specify the backup interface dialer to be used with the **backup interface dialer** *number* command.

Command	Description
backup interface *interface-type number*	Specify the interface or dialer interface to use for backup. Interface number specifications vary from router to router. For example, some routers require you to specify just the port number, whereas others require you to specify the slot and port.

Example 12-2 shows the configuration of a site that backs up a leased line by using a BRI interface. One dialer interface, dialer 0, is defined. The leased line (serial 0) is configured to use the dialer interface (dialer 0) as a backup. The dialer interface uses dialer pool 1, which has physical interface bri 0 as a member. Thus, physical interface bri 0 can back up the serial interface.

Example 12-2 *A Dialer Profile Provides Backup to Two Serial Interfaces*

```
interface dialer 0
ip unnumbered loopback0
encapsulation ppp
dialer remote-name Remote0
dialer pool 1
dialer string 5551212
dialer-group 1
interface bri 0
encapsulation ppp
dialer pool-member 1
ppp authentication chap
interface serial 0
ip unnumbered loopback0
backup interface dialer 0
backupdelay 5 10
```

Routing with the Load Backup Feature

This section discusses the way load sharing and load balancing work with different routing protocols when the load backup feature is on.

Load Backup with OSPF

If the routing protocol used is OSPF, the load backup feature will load share between the primary and backup links after the backup link is activated.

The cost assigned to the primary link and the backup link must be equal if both links are to be utilized, however. If one link has a lower cost than the other, all routing occurs over the link with the lower cost even if both lines are up.

NOTE	The cost mentioned in the preceding paragraph refers to the value assigned to a link in OSPF. This metric is based on the speed of the media.

OSPF does not support load balancing between the primary link and the backup connection. If load balancing is to occur in this environment, each connection must be able to support comparable bandwidth environments (a 56 Kbps serial backs up a 56 Kbps serial connection).

Load Backup with IGRP and EIGRP

If the routing protocol used is IGRP or EIGRP, or if you have a static route configured, the load backup feature will load share between the primary and backup links after the backup link is activated. The metric assigned to the primary link and the backup link must be the same if both links are to be utilized, however. If one link has a lower metric than the other, all routing occurs over the link with the lower metric, even if both lines are up. If load balancing is to occur in this environment, each connection must be able to support comparable bandwidth environments (a 56 Kbps serial backs up a 56 Kbps serial connection).

Instead of relying on equal metrics to load share and load balance, the variance router configuration command can also be used to control load balancing in an IGRP/EIGRP environment. Use the **variance** *multiplier* command to configure unequal-cost load balancing by defining the difference between the best metric and the worst acceptable metric.

Figure 12-8 shows a sample network and the configuration to create load balancing between primary and backup lines. The table that follows covers the **variance** command.

Figure 12-8   *Load Balancing Command for IGRP/EIGRP*

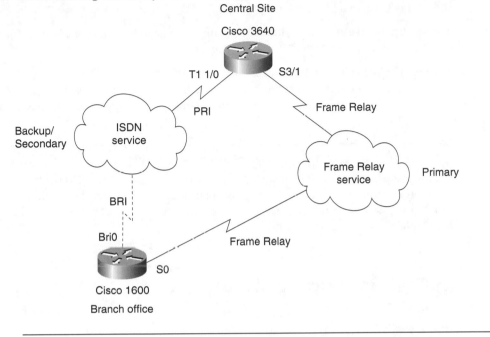

Command	Description
variance *multiplier*	The range of metric values that is accepted for load balancing. Acceptable values are nonzero, positive integers. The default value is 1, which means equal-cost load balancing. In the example in Figure 12-8, the multiplier is set to 4.

Setting this value lets the communication server determine the feasibility of a potential route. A route is feasible if the next communication server in the path is closer to the destination than the current communication server, and if the metric for the entire path is within the variance. Only paths that are feasible can be used for load balancing and included in the routing table.

If the following two conditions are met, the route is deemed feasible and can be added to the routing table:

- The local best metric must be greater than the metric learned from the next communication server.

- The multiplier times the local best metric for the destination must be greater than or equal to the metric through the next communication server.

In Figure 12-8, the **variance 4** command says to use both paths, even if the backup path's metric is four times worse than the primary path.

You can use the **traffic-share** {**balanced** | **min**} command to control the way traffic is distributed among IGRP/EIGRP load sharing routes.

The **traffic-share balanced** command distributes traffic proportionally to the ratios of the metrics. As a result of the **variance 4** command, the best route transports four times the traffic of the worst route. The **traffic-share min command** specifies routes that have minimum costs.

Load Sharing Functioning

Load sharing is done per conversation basis. A **conversation** is defined as the traffic of a single transport layer session or network layer flow that crosses a given interface. The conversation is called from the source and destination address, protocol type, port number, or other attributes in the relevant communications layer.

Verifying Dial Backup Configuration

To verify a backup line link for a primary line connection, enter the **show interface** *type number* command.

The primary interface output in Example 12-3 illustrates that Dialer1 is specified as a backup if the serial subinterface 3/1.1 fails. If the serial link fails, the backup will be enabled 20 seconds later. The backup will deactivate 40 seconds after the serial subinterface reactivates.

Example 12-3 *Primary Interface* **show interface** *Output*

```
CentralA#show interface s 3/1.1
Serial3/1.1 is up, line protocol is up
  Hardware is CD2430 in sync mode
  Internet address is 10.140.1.1/24
  Backup interface Dialer1, failure delay 20 sec, restore delay 40 sec
  MTU 1500 bytes, BW 56 Kbit, DLY 20000 usec, rely 255/255, load 1/255
  Encapsulation FRAME-RELAY
<Output Omitted>
```

The backup interface output in Example 12-4 shows the backup link in standby mode until the primary line fails.

Example 12-4 *Backup Interface* **show interface** *Output*

```
Router#show interface dialer 1
Dialer1 is standby mode, line protocol is down
  Hardware is Unknown
```

Example 12-4 *Backup Interface* **show interface** *Output (Continued)*

```
 Internet address is 192.2.0.1/24
  MTU 1500 bytes, BW 56 Kbit, DLY 20000 usec, rely 255/255, load 1/255
<Output Omitted>
```

Summary

This chapter explained how to configure a backup connection that activates upon primary line failures or when the primary line reaches a specified threshold. You have also seen how to configure a dialer interface to act as a backup to physical interfaces. The next chapter focuses on managing your network performance by using queuing and compression methods.

Case Study—Enabling a Backup to a Permanent Connection

Complete the tasks of this case study, and then review the case study solution section that follows to see how you did and where you might need to review the concepts presented in this chapter.

In this case study, you are required to configure a dial backup connection to a primary link.

Scenario

Given critical timely information traveling across the Frame Relay connection between the Central site and remoter office, configure the remote's BRI line to back up the primary Frame Relay connection, in case the primary connection fails. Figure 12-9 displays the network you could use to complete this case study.

Figure 12-9 *Network for Case Study*

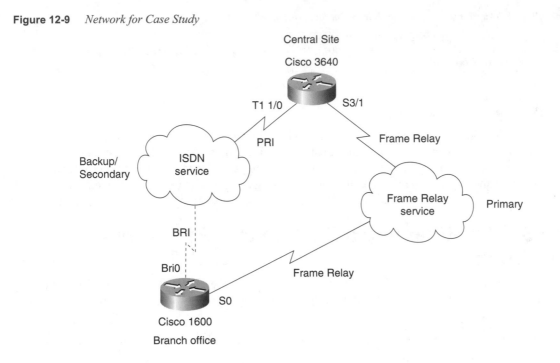

Task 1—Prepare the Branch Office Router's BRI Interface to Be a Dial Backup

Complete the following steps on the branch office router:

Step 1 Enter global configuration mode, and configure the following on the branch office router to specify interesting traffic:

— Remove any existing dialer list.

— Create a dialer list 1, which is associated with access list 101.

— For access list 101, specify that you wish to deny IGRP updates over the link, but that all other IP traffic is allowed.

Step 2 Specify that the BRI 0 interface can now pass routing updates. While in standby mode, it will not pass updates.

Step 3 From the BRI 0 interface, ensure that no other dialer map statement points to the Central site. Then, create a new dialer map statement pointing to the Central site, and ensure that this dialer map specifies that broadcasts can be sent over.

Task 2—Establish a Backup Connection for the Central Site's Frame Relay Link

Complete the following steps on the Central site router:

Step 1   Specify that the dialer 1 interface can now pass routing updates. While in standby mode, it will not pass updates.

Step 2   Enter primary line interface configuration mode and specify the backup interface:

— Enter serial 3/1.1 configuration mode. This central site primary link is connected to a Frame Relay network.

— Specify dialer 1 as the backup interface.

— Specify dialer 1 to engage 20 seconds after the primary link fails and to disengage 40 seconds after the primary link comes back up.

Task 3—Verify and Enable the Dial Backup

Complete the following steps on the Central site router:

Step 1   Look at the **show interface dialer 1** output to verify that dialer 1 is in standby mode. Look at the **show interface serial 3/1.1** output to verify that dialer 1 is its dial backup. Also review the **show ip route** command output.

What would be the route to the branch office Ethernet?

Step 2   Switch to the branch office router and shut branch office's serial 0 interface.

Step 3   Switch back to the Central site router and wait until the dialer 1 interface activates and the Frame Relay routes are eliminated from the routing table. Ping the branch Ethernet.

Step 4   Enter the **show ip route** command again. What is the route to the branch Ethernet now?

Solution to Case Study—Enabling a Backup to a Permanent Connection

The following is a step-by-step discussion of the case study solution.

Task 1 Solution—Prepare the Branch Office Router's BRI Interface to Be a Dial Backup

Complete the following steps on the branch office router:

Step 1   Enter global configuration mode and configure the following on the branch office router to specify interesting traffic:

— Remove any existing dialer list.

```
BranchA(config)#no dialer-list 1
```

— Associate the dialer list 1 to access list 101.

```
BranchA(config)#dialer-list 1 protocol ip list 101
```

— For access list 101, specify that you wish to deny IGRP updates over the link, but that all other IP traffic is allowed.

```
BranchA(config)#access-list 101 deny igrp any any
BranchA(config)#access-list 101 permit ip any any
```

Step 2   Specify that the BRI 0 interface can now pass routing updates. While in standby mode, it will not pass updates:

```
BranchA(config-router)#router igrp 100
BranchA(config-router)#no passive-interface bri 0
```

With the preceding configuration, the BRI 0 interface can now pass routing updates when it is activated.

Step 3   From the BRI 0 interface, ensure that no other dialer map statement points to the central site. Then, create a new dialer map statement pointing to the central site, and ensure that this dialer map specifies that broadcasts can be sent over:

— Remove the existing dialer map:

```
BranchA(config-if)#no dialer map ip 10.130.0.2 name CentralA 1000
```

— Re-create the dialer map and allow broadcasts:

```
BranchA(config-if)#dialer map ip 10.130.0.2 name CentralA
broadcast 1000
```

Task 2 Solution—Establish a Backup Connection for the Central Site's Frame Relay Link

Complete the following steps on the Central site router:

Step 1   Specify that the dialer 1 interface can now pass routing updates. While in standby mode, it will not pass updates:

```
CentralA(config-router)#router igrp 100
CentralA(config-router)#no passive-interface dialer 1
```

As shown in the preceding, the dialer 1 interface can now pass routing updates when it is activated.

Step 2   Enter primary line interface configuration mode and specify the backup interface:

— Enter serial 3/1.1 configuration mode. This Central site primary link is connected to a Frame Relay network:

```
CentralA(config)#int serial 3/1.1
```

— Specify dialer 1 as the backup interface:

```
CentralA(config-if)#backup interface dialer 1
```

— Specify dialer 1 to engage 20 seconds after the primary link fails and to disengage 40 seconds after the primary link comes back up:

```
CentralA(config-if)#backup delay 20 40
```

Task 3 Solution—Verify and Enable the Dial Backup

Complete the following steps on the Central site router:

Step 1   Example 12-5 has the output of the **show interface dialer 1** command to verify that dialer 1 is in standby mode. Example 12-6 has the output of the **show interface serial 3/1.1** command to verify that dialer 1 is its dial backup. Finally, Example 12-7 displays the output of the **show ip route** command.

Example 12-5   *The Output of the* **show interface dialer 1** *Command on the Central Site Router*

```
CentralA#sh int d 1
Dialer1 is standby mode, line protocol is down
Hardware is Unknown
Internet address is 10.130.0.2/24
MTU 1500 bytes, BW 56 Kbit, DLY 20000 usec, rely 255/255, load 1/255
Encapsulation PPP, loopback not set
DTR is pulsed for 1 seconds on reset
Last input never, output never, output hang never
Last clearing of "show interface" counters never
Queueing strategy: fifo
Output queue 0/40, 0 drops; input queue 0/75, 0 drops
5 minute input rate 0 bits/sec, 0 packets/sec
5 minute output rate 0 bits/sec, 0 packets/sec
0 packets input, 0 bytes, 0 no buffer
Received 0 broadcasts, 0 runts, 0 giants, 0 throttles
0 input errors, 0 CRC, 0 frame, 0 overrun, 0 ignored, 0 abort
0 packets output, 0 bytes, 0 underruns
0 output errors, 0 collisions, 0 interface resets
0 output buffer failures, 0 output buffers swapped out
0 carrier transitions
CentralA#
```

Example 12-6 *The Output of the* **show interface serial 3/1.1** *Command on the Central Site Router*

```
CentralA#sh int s 3/1.1
Serial3/1.1 is up, line protocol is up
Hardware is CD2430 in sync mode
Internet address is 10.130.1.1/24
Backup interface Dialer1, failure delay 20 sec, restore delay 40 sec
MTU 1500 bytes, BW 64 Kbit, DLY 20000 usec, rely 255/255, load 1/255
Encapsulation FRAME-RELAY
```

Example 12-7 *The Output of the* **show ip route** *Command*

```
CentralA#sh ip route
Codes: C - connected, S - static, I - IGRP, R - RIP, M - mobile, B - BGP
D - EIGRP, EX - EIGRP external, O - OSPF, IA - OSPF inter area
N1 - OSPF NSSA external type 1, N2 - OSPF NSSA external type 2
E1 - OSPF external type 1, E2 - OSPF external type 2, E - EGP
i - IS-IS, L1 - IS-IS level-1, L2 - IS-IS level-2, * - candidate default
U - per-user static route, o - ODR
Gateway of last resort is not set
10.0.0.0/24 is subnetted, 15 subnets
I  10.30.2.0 [100/180671] via 10.115.0.115, 00:00:37, Ethernet0/0
S  10.118.0.0 is directly connected, Dialer2
C  10.115.0.0 is directly connected, Ethernet0/0
I  10.122.0.0 [100/180671] via 10.115.0.130, 00:00:21, Ethernet0/0
I  10.119.0.0 [100/180671] via 10.115.0.115, 00:00:37, Ethernet0/0
C  10.140.1.0 is directly connected, Serial3/1.1
I  10.140.2.0 [100/158350] via 10.115.0.115, 00:00:37, Ethernet0/0
I  10.140.5.0 [100/158350] via 10.115.0.130, 00:00:22, Ethernet0/0
I  10.150.0.0 [100/160350] via 10.115.0.130, 00:00:22, Ethernet0/0
I  10.135.0.0 [100/160350] via 10.115.0.115, 00:00:38, Ethernet0/0
I  10.222.0.0 [100/160250] via 10.150.0.1, 00:00:02, Serial3/1.1
I  10.150.0.0 [100/158450] via 10.115.0.110, 00:00:22, Ethernet0/0
I  10.219.0.0 [100/158450] via 10.115.0.115, 00:00:39, Ethernet0/0
I  10.218.0.0 [100/158350] via 10.140.1.2, 00:00:04, Serial3/1.1
CentralA#
```

The route to the branch office Ethernet is via the Central site Serial 3/1.1 interface.

Step 2   Switch to the branch office router and shut branch office's serial 0 interface. You are now simulating a lost connection of the primary interface.

Step 3   Switch back to the Central site router and wait until the dialer 1 interface activates and the Frame Relay routes are eliminated from the routing table. Ping the branch Ethernet. You should be able to reach the Branch Office Ethernet interface going out via the Central router Dialer 1 interface.

Step 4   Example 12-8 displays the new output of the **show ip route** command.

Example 12-8 *The New Output of the* **show ip route** *Command*

```
CentralA#sh ip route
Codes: C - connected, S - static, I - IGRP, R - RIP, M - mobile, B - BGP
Codes: C - connected, S - static, I - IGRP, R - RIP, M - mobile, B - BGP
D - EIGRP, EX - EIGRP external, O - OSPF, IA - OSPF inter area
N1 - OSPF NSSA external type 1, N2 - OSPF NSSA external type 2
E1 - OSPF external type 1, E2 - OSPF external type 2, E - EGP
i - IS-IS, L1 - IS-IS level-1, L2 - IS-IS level-2, * - candidate default
U - per-user static route, o - ODR
Gateway of last resort is not set
10.0.0.0/8 is variably subnetted, 14 subnets, 2 masks
I 10.30.2.0/24 [100/180671] via 10.115.0.115, 00:01:07, Ethernet0/0
S 10.118.0.0/24 is directly connected, Dialer2
C 10.115.0.0/24 is directly connected, Ethernet0/0
I 10.122.0.0/24 [100/180671] via 10.115.0.130, 00:00:24, Ethernet0/0
I 10.119.0.0/24 [100/180671] via 10.115.0.115, 00:01:07, Ethernet0/0
I 10.140.2.0/24 [100/158350] via 10.115.0.115, 00:01:07, Ethernet0/0
I 10.140.1.0/24 [100/158350] via 10.115.0.110, 00:00:24, Ethernet0/0
I 10.130.0.0/24 [100/160350] via 10.115.0.110, 00:00:25, Ethernet0/0
I 10.135.0.0/24 [100/160350] via 10.115.0.115, 00:01:07, Ethernet0/0
C 10.130.0.0/24 is directly connected, Dialer1
C 10.130.0.1/32 is directly connected, Dialer1
I 10.222.0.0/24 [100/158450] via 10.115.0.130, 00:00:25, Ethernet0/0
I 10.219.0.0/24 [100/158450] via 10.115.0.115, 00:01:07, Ethernet0/0
I 10.218.0.0/24 [100/180671] via 10.130.0.1, 00:00:06, Dialer1
```

The new route to the branch Ethernet is via the Dialer 1 interface.

Case Study Conclusion

Now, if you were to bring down the primary link, you would see the backup link kick in to supplement.

Review Question

Answer the following question and then refer to Appendix H, "Answers to Review Questions," for an answer and explanation.

   1 What are two circumstances or scenarios in which a backup interface will be enabled?

CHAPTER 13

Managing Network Performance with Queuing and Compression

This chapter covers why you may need to implement queuing technologies on your WAN connection. It also describes how to implement the queuing technologies available from Cisco IOS software so that you can prioritize traffic over your WAN connection. It then explains how you can use compression to optimize WAN utilization.

Queuing Overview

A protocol-dependent switching process handles traffic that arrives at a router interface. The switching process includes the delivery of traffic to an outgoing interface buffer. First-in, first-out (FIFO) queuing is the classic algorithm for packet transmission. With FIFO, transmission occurs in the same order as messages are received. Until recently, FIFO queuing was the default for all router interfaces. If user needs require traffic to be reordered, the department or company must establish a queuing policy, other than FIFO queuing, which ensures that sensitive traffic goes out first (see Figure 13-1).

Figure 13-1 *Reordering the Packets So Time-Sensitive Traffic is Processed First*

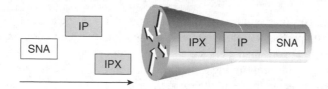

Cisco IOS software offers three queuing options as alternatives to FIFO queuing:

- **Weighted fair queuing (WFQ)** prioritizes interactive traffic over file transfers to ensure satisfactory response time for common user applications.

- **Priority queuing** ensures the timely delivery of a specific protocol or type of traffic because that traffic is transmitted before all others.

- **Custom queuing** establishes bandwidth allocations for each different type of traffic.

Table 13-2 in the "Queuing Comparison" section, later in this chapter, offers a helpful comparison of all of the queuing methods.

The Need for Traffic Prioritization

The need to prioritize packets arises from the diverse mixture of protocols and their associated behaviors found in today's data networks. Different types of traffic that share a data path through the network can affect each other.

Depending on the application and overall bandwidth, users may or may not perceive any real performance degradation. For instance, delay-sensitive, interactive, transaction-based applications may require a higher priority than, say, a file transfer to satisfy users. Desktop video conferencing requires a specified amount of bandwidth to perform acceptably. If your network is designed so that multiple protocols share a single data path between routers, prioritization may be a requirement.

Prioritization is most effective on WAN links in which the combination of bursty traffic and relatively lower data rates can cause temporary congestion. Depending on the average packet size, prioritization is most effective when applied to links at T1/E1 bandwidth speeds or lower. If there is no congestion on the WAN link, there is no reason to implement traffic prioritization.

NOTE   Prioritization is most effective on bursty WAN links (T1/E1 or below) that experience temporary congestion.

If a WAN link is constantly congested, traffic prioritization may not resolve the problem. Adding bandwidth might be the appropriate solution.

Establishing a Queuing Policy

A queuing policy helps network managers to meet two challenges: to provide an appropriate level of service for all users and to control expensive WAN costs.

Typically, the corporate goal is to deploy and maintain a single enterprise network, even though the network supports disparate applications, organizations, technologies, and user expectations. Consequently, network managers are concerned about providing all users with an appropriate level of service, while continuing to support mission-critical applications and having the ability to integrate new technologies at the same time.

Because the major cost of running a network is also related to WAN circuit charges, network managers must strike the appropriate balance between the capacity and cost of these WAN circuits, and the level of service provided to their users.

To meet these challenges, queuing allows network managers to prioritize, reserve, and manage network resources—and to ensure the seamless integration and migration of disparate technologies without unnecessary costs.

Choosing a Cisco IOS Queuing Option

Determining the best Cisco IOS queuing option for your traffic needs involves the following general guidelines (as represented in Figure 13-2):

1 Determine whether the WAN is congested.

   If traffic does not back up, there is no need to sort the traffic—it is serviced as it arrives. However, if the offered load exceeds the transmission capacity for periods of time, then there is an opportunity to sort the traffic with one of the Cisco IOS-queuing options.

2 Decide whether strict control over traffic prioritization is necessary and whether automatic configuration is acceptable.

   Proper queuing configuration is a nontrivial task. To effectively perform this task, the network manager must study the types of traffic using the interface, determine how to distinguish them, and decide their relative priority. This done, the manager must install the filters and test their effect on the traffic. Traffic patterns change over time, so the analysis must be repeated periodically.

3 Establish a queuing policy.

   A queuing policy results from the analysis of traffic patterns and the determination of the relative traffic priorities discussed in Step 2.

4 Determine whether any of the traffic types you identified in your traffic pattern analysis can tolerate a delay.

Figure 13-2 *Flow Chart of Queuing Options*

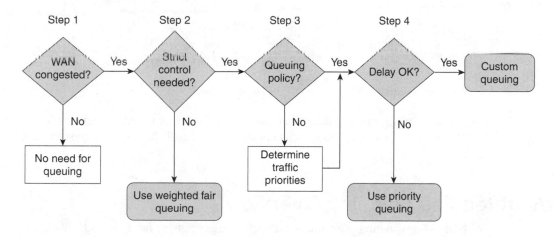

Queuing: Return Policy

For queuing to be pertinent, you should have a matching return policy; the answering router should handle packets comparably.

First In, First Out Queuing Overview

When FIFO queuing is in effect, traffic is transmitted in the order received, without regard for the bandwidth consumption or the associated delays (as shown in Figure 13-3). As a result, file transfers and other high-volume network applications often generate series of packets of associated data. These related packets are known as **packet trains**.

Figure 13-3 *FIFO Queuing*

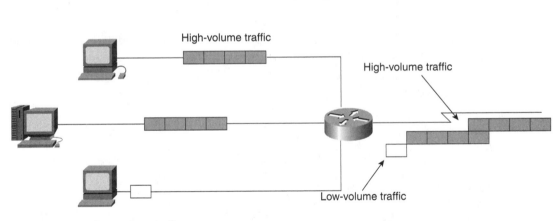

Packet trains are groups of packets that tend to move together through the network, as shown in Figure 13-3. These packet trains can consume all available bandwidth and starve out other traffic.

Weighted Fair Queuing Overview

Weighted fair queuing is an automated method that provides fair bandwidth allocation to all network traffic. Weighted fair queuing provides traffic-priority management that dynamically sorts traffic into messages that make up a conversation. Weighted fair queuing then breaks up the "train" of packets within each conversation to ensure that the bandwidth is shared fairly between individual conversations.

Weighted fair queuing overcomes an important limitation of FIFO queuing. Weighted fair queuing breaks up packet trains to ensure that low-volume traffic is transferred in a timely fashion. Weighted fair queuing gives low-volume traffic, such as Telnet sessions, priority over high-volume traffic, such as File Transfer Protocol (FTP) sessions. Weighted fair queuing gives concurrent file transfers balanced use of link capacity.

Fair queuing is enabled by default for physical interfaces whose bandwidth is less than or equal to 2.048 Mbps; and that do not use Link Access Procedure, Balanced (LAPB), X.25, compressed Point-to-Point Protocol (PPP), or Synchronous DataLink Control (SDLC) encapsulations. Fair queuing is not an option for these protocols.

The weighted fair queuing algorithm arranges traffic into conversations. The discrimination of traffic into conversations is based on packet header addressing.

Common conversation discriminators are the following:

- Source/destination network address
- Source/destination MAC address
- Source/destination port or socket numbers
- Frame Relay data-link connection identifier (DLCI) value
- Quality of service/type of service (QoS/ToS) value

In Figure 13-4, the weighted fair queuing algorithm has identified three conversations.

Figure 13-4 *Messages Are Sorted in Conversations*

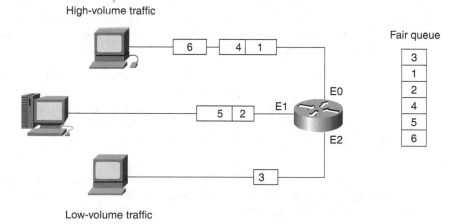

The weighted fair queuing algorithm places packets of the various conversations in the fair queue before transmission. The order of removal from the fair queue is determined by the virtual delivery time of the last bit of each arriving packet. Small, low-volume packets are given priority over large, high-volume conversation packets.

After low-volume conversations are serviced, high-volume conversations share the remaining link capacity fairly, and interleave or alternate transmission Timeslots. In this figure, high-volume conversation packets are queued in order of arrival after the low-volume packet.

The queuing algorithm ensures the proper amount of bandwidth for each message. With weighted fair queuing, two equal-size file transfers get equal bandwidth, rather than the first file transfer using most of the link's capacity.

In Figure 13-4, packet 3 is queued before packets 1 or 2 because packet 3 is a small packet in a low-volume conversation.

The result of the queuing order and the transmission order is that short messages, which do not require much bandwidth, are given priority and the short messages arrive at the other end of the link first.

As a result, packet 3 is transmitted before packets 1 or 2.

Configuring Weighted Fair Queuing

The **fair-queue** command enables fair queuing on an interface

```
Router(config-if)#fair-queue {congestive-discard-threshold}
```

where the *congestive-discard-threshold* number is the number of messages creating a congestion threshold, after which messages for high-volume traffic will no longer be queued; the maximum packets in a conversation held in a queue before they are discarded. Valid values are 1 to 512, inclusive. The default is 64 messages. The **fair-queue 128** command sets the congestive discard threshold number to 128.

The congestive discard policy applies only to high-volume conversations that have more than one message in the queue. The discard policy tries to control conversations that would monopolize the link. If an individual conversation queue contains more messages than the congestive discard threshold, that conversation will not have any new messages queued until that queue's content drops below one-fourth of the congestive-discard value.

NOTE   Weighted fair queuing is used by default on serial interfaces at E1 speeds (2.048 Mbps) and below. Weighted fair queuing is disabled on serial interfaces that use X.25 or compressed PPP. LAN interfaces and serial lines, operating at E3 or T3 speeds, are not available for weighted fair queuing.

The **fair-queue** command enables fair queuing on an interface. In Figure 13-5, interface serial 1 is attached to a Frame Relay network and is configured to operate at a 56 Kbps link speed. The **fair-queue 128** command sets the congestive discard threshold number to 128.

Figure 13-5 *Weighted Fair Queuing Example*

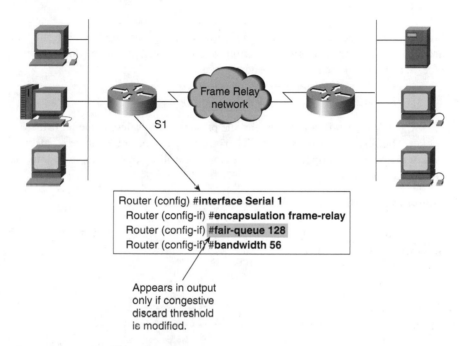

```
Router (config) #interface Serial 1
  Router (config-if) #encapsulation frame-relay
  Router (config-if) #fair-queue 128
  Router (config-if) #bandwidth 56
```

Appears in output
only if congestive
discard threshold
is modified.

Because conversations may not have any new messages queued until that queue's content drops below one-fourth of the congestive-discard value, a queue must contain fewer than 32 entries (1/4 of 128).

Priority Queuing Overview

Priority output queuing provides a mechanism to use strict priority in selecting which packets to send first on an interface. This technique is useful in environments in which traffic has a hierarchy of importance, and more important traffic should not be delayed by less important traffic.

Priority queuing categorizes and prioritizes datagrams that travel on an interface. Traffic can be assigned to the various queues, according to protocol or Transmission Control Protocol (TCP) port number. Priority queuing controls time-sensitive traffic (such as Digital Equipment Corporation local-area transport) or mission-critical traffic (such as transaction processing) on low-bandwidth serial links.

With priority queuing, the high-priority queue is always emptied before the medium-priority queue, and so on (as shown in Figure 13-6). As a result, traffic in lower-priority queues might not get forwarded in a timely manner or get forwarded at all. For this reason, priority queuing provides the network administrator the most control over deciding which traffic gets forwarded.

NOTE   Weighted fair queuing automatically prioritizes traffic to ensure that all traffic is given fair access to bandwidth. Use priority queuing when you must guarantee that certain types of traffic receive as much of the available bandwidth as needed.

An incoming packet is compared with the priority list to select a queue. If there is room, the packet is buffered in memory and waits to be dispatched after the queue is selected. If the queue is full, the packet is dropped. For this reason, controlling queue size is an important configuration task.

Figure 13-6 *Priority Queuing Operation*

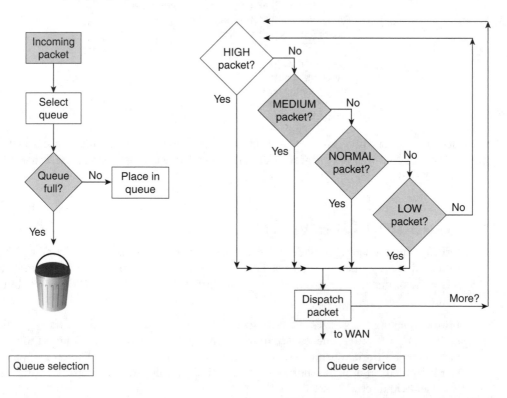

Compare Priority Queuing to class levels on the Titanic. The first-class passengers had a much greater chance of escaping than the passengers in steerage did. Similarly, packets in the high queue escape the router, and the low-priority packets drown.

The queuing process empties the high-priority queue before the queuing software services the medium-priority queue. The dispatching algorithm controls the queuing process. The dispatching algorithm checks a queue for a packet and then dispatches it. Therefore, the high queue must be empty before the medium queue will get any service. As a result, mission-critical traffic in the high queue is always transmitted before traffic in other queues.

NOTE

You must configure a default queue for traffic that is not identified by the priority list.

Be careful when you define the packets that belong in the high queue because these packets are always processed first. If the high queue is always filled, packets in other queues do not have a chance to be transmitted.

Configuring Priority Queuing

To configure priority queuing, perform the following tasks:

1 Create an output priority queuing list.

A **priority list** is a set of rules that describe the way packets should be assigned to priority queues. You can establish queuing priorities based on the protocol type or on packets entering from a specific interface. All Cisco supported protocols are allowed.

2 Assign a default queue.

You must explicitly assign a queue for packets that were not specified in the priority list.

3 Specify the queue sizes (optional).

You can specify the maximum number of allowable packets in each queue. In general, it is not recommended that the default queue sizes be changed.

4 Assign the priority list number to an interface.

Only one list can be assigned per interface. Once assigned, the priority list rules are applied to all traffic that passes through the interface.

Step 1—Create an Output Priority Queuing List

You can set a priority queue, either by protocol type or by incoming interface type.

Create an output priority queuing list with the **priority-list protocol** command:

```
Router(config)#priority-list list-number protocol protocol-name
    {high | medium | normal | low} queue-keyword keyword-value
```

priority-list protocol Command	Description
list-number	User-specified number from 1 to 16 that identifies the priority list. In Cisco IOS releases prior to 11.2, only 10 priority lists were supported.
protocol-name	Can be aarp, arp, apollo, appletalk, bridge (transparent), clns, clns_es, clns_is, compressedtcp, cmns, decnet, decnet_node, decnet_router-l1, decnet_router-l2, ip, ipx, pad, rsrb, stun, vines, xns, or x25.

queue-keyword and *keyword-values* represent some of the following arguments:

byte-count	Can be: gt (greater than), lt (less than).
list	Specifies an access-list for IP, AppleTalk, IPX, VINES, XNS, or bridging.
tcp/udp port	For IP only; can be the port number or port name.
fragments	IP packets whose fragment offset field is nonzero are matched by this command. Note that packets with a nonzero fragment offset do not contain TCP or UDP headers, so other instances of this command that use the tcp or udp keyword will always fail to match such packets.

You can also create an output priority queuing list with the **priority-list interface** command. Use this command to set queuing priorities for all traffic arriving on an incoming interface:

```
Router(config)#priority-list list-number interface interface-type
    interface-number {high | medium | normal | low}
```

priority-list interface Command	Description
list-number	User-specified number from 1 to 16 that identifies the priority list.
interface-type	Specifies the name of the interface with incoming packets.
interface-number	Number of the specified interface.

WARNING   Queuing is a process. Be aware that any new line is added at the bottom of the queue list.

Step 2—Assign a Default Queue

The default queue is normal. Use the **priority-list default** command to assign packets to a queue if no other priority list conditions are met:

```
Router(config)#priority-list list-number default
   {high | medium | normal | low}
```

Step 3—Specify the Queue Sizes (optional)

Use the optional **priority-list queue-limit** command to change the default maximum number of packets in each queue:

```
Router(config)#priority-list list-number queue-limit
   high-limit medium-limit normal-limit low-limit
```

priority-list queue-limit Command	Description
list-number	User-specified number from 1 to 16 that identifies the priority list.
queue-limit	Default number of datagrams.
high-limit	Default of 20 datagrams.
medium-limit	Default of 40 datagrams.
normal-limit	Default of 60 datagrams.
low-limit	Default of 80 datagrams.

Step 4—Assign the Priority List Number to an Interface

Once you define the priority list, enter interface configuration mode, and enter the **priority-group** command to link a priority list to an interface:

```
Router(config-if)#priority-group list
```

Priority-group Command	Description
list	Arbitrary number from 1 to 16 that identifies the priority list selected by the user.

In the configuration shown in Figure 13-7, **priority-list 2** specifies the following:

- Telnet (TCP port 23) traffic is assigned to the high-priority queue.

- Traffic from source network 131.108.0.0 is assigned to the high-priority queue, as specified by access-list 1. The list 1 argument in the second line of the configuration specifies that access-list 1 be used to sort packets for placement in the high-priority queue.

- All traffic arriving from Ethernet interface 0 is assigned to the medium-priority queue.

- All other IP traffic is assigned to the normal-priority queue.

- All other traffic not specified in priority-list 2 is assigned to the low-priority queue.

- Queue-size limits have been changed from the default values to the following:

    — 15 datagrams for the high queue

    — 20 datagrams for the medium queue

    — 20 datagrams for the normal queue

    — 30 datagrams for the low queue

WARNING   Figure 13-7 shows an example of priority queuing. It might not be the best policy for your environment.

Figure 13-7 *Priority Queuing Example*

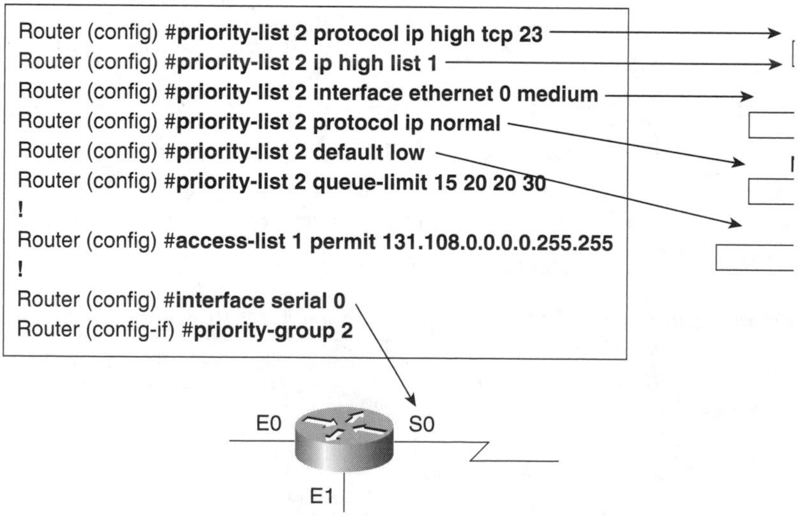

NOTE   Priority list 2 is linked to interface serial 0 by the **priority-group 2** command.

Custom Queuing Overview

Custom queuing lets you guarantee bandwidth for traffic by assigning queue space to each protocol. Custom queuing eliminates a potential priority-queuing problem. When priority queuing is used, it is possible that packets from higher-priority queues could consume all the available interface bandwidth. As a result, packets in the lower-priority queues might not get forwarded in a timely manner, or at all.

Custom queuing eliminates this problem. With custom queuing, you reserve a certain percentage of bandwidth for each specified class of traffic. You can use custom queuing to allocate bandwidth, based on a protocol or source interface.

Using custom queuing, you can use filters to assign types of traffic to one of 16 possible queues. The router services each queue sequentially, transmitting a configurable quantity of traffic from each queue before servicing the next queue.

As a result, one type of traffic never monopolizes the entire bandwidth. You can control the percentage of the interface's bandwidth that a queue consumes by configuring the number of bytes transmitted from a queue at one time.

Custom queuing is particularly important for time-sensitive protocols, such as Systems Network Architecture (SNA), which require predictable response time.

NOTE   Queue 0 is a system queue that handles system packets such as keepalives.

Queue 0 is emptied before the other custom queues.

Custom Queuing Operation

As shown in Figure 13-8, custom queuing has two components:

- **Traffic filtering**—The forwarding application—such as IP, IPX, or AppleTalk—applies a set of filters or access-list entries to each message that it forwards. The messages are placed in queues, based on the filtering.

- **Queued message forwarding**—Custom queuing uses a round-robin dispatching algorithm to forward traffic. Each queue continues to transmit packets until the configured byte limit is reached. When this queue's threshold is reached or the queue is empty, the queuing software services the next queue in sequence.

Figure 13-8 *Custom Queuing Operation*

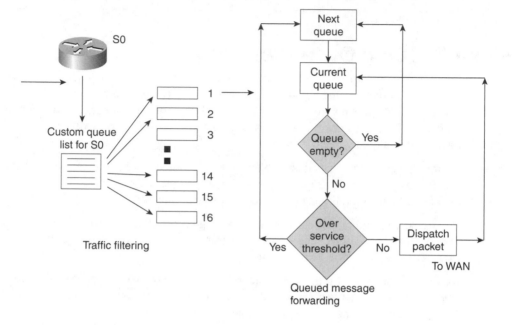

NOTE When priority queuing, custom queuing, or weighted fair queuing is enabled, IP traffic is classified by fast-switching logic. All other traffic is processed as switched.

Configuring Custom Queuing

To configure custom queuing, perform the following tasks:

1 Set custom queue filtering for a protocol or for an interface.

You can configure custom queuing to filter for an interface or a protocol. For example, you can do the following:

— Send all traffic from Token Ring interface 0 to custom queue 1.

— Send all IP traffic to custom queue 2.

— Send all IPX traffic to custom queue 3.

— Send all AppleTalk traffic to custom queue 4.

2 Assign a default custom queue. You can assign a queue for those packets that do not match the custom queue filtering.

3 (Optional) Change the queue capacity. You can designate the maximum number of packets that a queue can contain.

4 Configure the service threshold per queue. To allocate more bandwidth to a protocol's traffic or traffic from an interface, you increase the size of a queue.

5 Assign the custom queue list to an interface. The filters of the queue list are applied to all traffic that passes through the interface.

Step 1—Set Queue Priority

You can create an output custom queuing list by using the protocol or the interface as discriminating criteria.

Use the **queue-list protocol** command to specify inclusion of a protocol in a particular queue. To create an output custom queuing list with the **queue-list protocol** command, use the following syntax:

```
Router(config)#queue-list list-number protocol
    protocol-name queue-number queue-keyword keyword-value
```

queue-list protocol Command	Description
list-number	Number of the queue list from 1 to 16.
protocol-name	Required argument that specifies the protocol type. Can be: aarp, arp, apollo, appletalk, bridge (transparent), clns, clns_es, clns_is, compressed tcp, cmns, decnet, decnet_node, decnet_router-11, decnet_router-12, ip, ipx, pad, rsrb, stun, vines, xns, or x25.
queue-number	Number of the queue, from 1 to 16.
queue-keyword	Keyword value: gt, lt, list, tcp, or udp.

You can also create an output custom queuing list with the **queue-list interface** command. Use the **queue-list interface** command to establish queuing priorities on incoming interfaces:

```
Router(config)#queue-list list-number interface
    interface-type interface-number queue-number
```

queue-list interface Command	Description
list-number	Number of the queue list, from 1 to 16.
interface-type	Required argument that specifies the name of the interface.
interface-number	Number of the specified interface.
queue-number	Number of the queue, from 1 to 16.

In Cisco IOS Release 11.0, the maximum number of queues that can be used for custom queuing increased from 10 to 16. 16 queues are assigned by default.

Step 2—Assign a Default Custom Queue

Use the **queue-list default** command to assign packets to a queue if no other queue list conditions are met:

```
Router(config)#queue-list list-number default queue-number
```

queue-list default Command	Description
list-number	Number of the queue list, from 1 to 16.
queue-number	Number of the queue, from 1 to 16.

WARNING   If no default queue is specified, default traffic is queued to queue 1.

Step 3—Use the optional queue-list queue limit Command

To limit the length of a particular queue, use the optional **queue-list queue limit** command:

```
Router(config)# queue-list list-number queue queue-number
    limit limit-number
```

queue-list queue limit Command	Description
list-number	Number of the queue list, from 1 to 16.
queue-number	Number of the queue, from 1 to 16.
limit-number	Maximum number of packets in a queue at any time. Range is 0 to 32,767 entries; default is 20.

Step 4—Configure the Service Threshold Per Queue

Use the **queue-list queue byte-count** command to set the minimum byte count transferred from a given queue at a time. This value is specified on a per-queue basis:

```
Router(config)#queue-list list-number queue queue-number
    byte-count byte-count-number
```

queue-list queue byte-count Command	Description
list-number	Number of the queue list, from 1 to 16.
queue-number	Number of the queue, from 1 to 16.
byte-count-number	Specifies the minimum number of bytes that the system allows to be delivered from a given queue during a particular cycle. The default is 1500 bytes.

NOTE	Because the router will not split a packet for the purpose of queuing, if a queue threshold (the maximum byte count) is reached during the transmission of a packet, the whole packet is still allowed to go through.

For example, the default threshold of 1500 bytes is used on a given queue. The first packet assigned to that queue is 1100 bytes, and the second packet is 300 bytes. The threshold has not been reached yet because the byte count is currently at 1400 bytes. The next packet assigned to the same queue is therefore processed, regardless of its size. If the third packet is 1000 bytes, the whole packet is processed for a total byte count of 2400 bytes. The fourth packet will be put on hold while the router services the subsequent queues.

Step 5—Assign the Custom Queue List to an Interface

Use the **custom-queue-list** command to link a queue list to an interface:

```
Router(config)#custom-queue-list list
```

custom-queue-list Command	Description
list	Number of the queue list (from 1 to 16) made available to control the interface's available bandwidth.

Custom Queuing Example

Figure 13-9 illustrates the following important custom-queuing features:

- FTP traffic (TCP port 20) is assigned to queue 1. The **queue-list 1 protocol ip 1 tcp 20** command designates FTP data traffic by identifying TCP port 20.
- Non-FTP IP traffic is assigned to queue 2.
- IPX traffic is assigned to queue 3.
- AppleTalk traffic is assigned to queue 4.
- All other traffic is assigned to queue 5.
- FTP traffic receives more bandwidth.

The **queue-list 1 queue 1 byte-count 4500** command allocates 4500 bytes to queue 1. This command increases the transfer capacity of queue 1 from the default of 1500 bytes to 4500 bytes. As a result, FTP traffic is allocated more bandwidth than any other type of traffic.

Figure 13-9 *Custom Queuing Example*

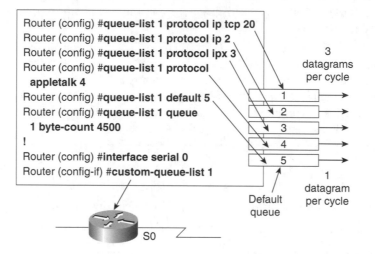

```
Router (config) #queue-list 1 protocol ip tcp 20
Router (config) #queue-list 1 protocol ip 2
Router (config) #queue-list 1 protocol ipx 3
Router (config) #queue-list 1 protocol
  appletalk 4
Router (config) #queue-list 1 default 5
Router (config) #queue-list 1 queue
  1 byte-count 4500
!
Router (config) #interface serial 0
Router (config-if) #custom-queue-list 1
```

Verifying Queuing Operation

Use the **show queuing** command, displayed in Example 13-1, to display detailed queuing information about all interfaces where fair queuing is enabled.

Example 13-1 *Verifying Queuing with the* **show queueing** *Command*

```
Router#show queueing S0
Current fair queue configuration:
Interface Serial 0
Input queue: 0/75/0 (size/max/drops); Total output drops: 0
Output queue: 18/64/30 (size/threshold/drops)
Conversations 2/8 (active/max active)
Reserved Conversations 0/0 (allocated/max allocated)
(depth/weight/discards) 3/4096/30
Conversation 117, linktype: ip, length: 556, flags: 0x280
source: 172.16.128.115, destination: 172.16.58.89, id: 0x1069, ttl: 59,
TOS: 0 prot: 6, source port 514, destination port 1022
(depth/weight/discards) 14/4096/0
Conversation 155, linktype: ip, length: 1504, flags: 0x280
source: 172.16.128.115, destination: 172.16.58.89, id: 0x104D, ttl: 59,
TOS: 0 prot: 6, source port 20, destination port 1554
```

NOTE The word *queuing* is spelled *queueing* for the **show queueing** command.

In Example 13-1, there are two active conversations (117 and 155) on interface Serial 0.

You can also use the **show interfaces** command, displayed in Example 13-2, to display queuing information for the router's interfaces.

Use the **show queuing custom** command to display custom queue information, as shown in Example 13-2.

Example 13-2 *The* **show queueing custom** *Command Displays Information on the Queue*

```
Router#show queueing custom
Current custom queue configuration:
List Queue Args
3 5 default
3 1 interface Serial 3
3 3 protocol ip
3 3 byte-count 1518
```

In Example 13-2, custom queue list 3 information is displayed. Table 13-1 explains this output.

Table 13-1   **show queueing custom** *Command Output*

Queue Arguments	Description
5 default	Defines the default queue. 1 interface Serial 3. All traffic for interface Serial 3 is sent to queue 1.
3 protocol ip	IP traffic is sent to queue 3.
3 byte-count 1518	Specifies the minimum number of bytes delivered from queue 3 during a single cycle.

You can use the **show queueing priority** command to display priority queuing information. You can use the **show queueing fair** command to display weighted fair queuing information.

Queuing Comparison

Table 13-2 provides a summary of the differences between WFQ, priority queuing, and custom queuing.

Table 13-2   *Comparison Between Different Queuing Methods*

Weighted Fair Queuing	Priority Queuing	Custom Queuing
No queue lists	4 queues	16 queues
Low volume given priority	High priority queue serviced first	Round-robin service
Conversation dispatching	Packet dispatching	Threshold dispatching

continues

Table 13-2 *Comparison Between Different Queuing Methods (Continued)*

Weighted Fair Queuing	Priority Queuing	Custom Queuing
Interactive traffic gets priority	Critical traffic gets through	Allocation of available bandwidth
File transfer gets balanced access	Designed for low-bandwidth links	Designed for higher-speed, low-bandwidth links
Enabled by default	Must configure	Must configure

The primary distinction between custom queuing and priority queuing is that custom queuing guarantees some level of service to all traffic, whereas priority queuing guarantees that one type of traffic will get through, possibly at the expense of all others. As a result, a low queue can be starved out and never allowed to transmit if there is a limited amount of available bandwidth or if the transmission frequency of the critical traffic is high.

Weighted fair queuing differs from priority and custom queuing in several ways. Priority and custom queuing must be explicitly enabled on an interface, whereas weighted fair queuing is enabled by default. Weighted fair queuing does not use queue lists to determine the preferred traffic on a serial interface. Instead, the fair queue algorithm dynamically sorts traffic into messages that are part of a conversation. The messages are queued for low-volume conversations, usually interactive traffic; and are given priority over high-volume, bandwidth-intensive conversations, such as file transfers. When multiple file transfers are occurring, the transfers are given comparable bandwidth.

Optimizing Traffic Flow with Data Compression

Many strategies and techniques exist for optimizing traffic over WAN links, including queuing and access-lists. One of the more effective methods, however, is compression.

This section discusses how to optimize the WAN traffic over the WAN link by compressing data on the WAN link.

Compression Overview

Data-compression technology maximizes bandwidth and increases WAN link throughput by reducing frame size and thereby allowing more data to be transmitted over a link.

Figure 13-10 graphically displays the following various types of data compression that Cisco equipment supports:

- Link compression (also known as per interface compression)
- Payload compression (also known as per-virtual circuit compression)
- TCP header compression

- Microsoft Point-to-Point Compression (MPPC)
- Other compression considerations mentioned in the following note.

Figure 13-10 *Compression Allows More Efficient Use of Bandwidth*

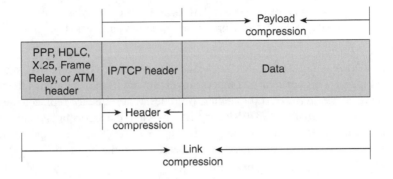

The default method of transmitting data across a serial link is the uncompressed format. This allows headers to be used in the normal switching operation, but can consume more bandwidth than desired.

NOTE   Cisco 3600 series routers now support a compression port module that provides high-performance, hardware-based data compression using simultaneous Stacker compression algorithms. Independent, full-duplex compression and decompression capabilities are used on Point-to-Point (PPP) encapsulated packets.

The data compression AIM provides hardware-based compression and decompression of packet data transmitted and received on the serial network interfaces of the Cisco 2600 series router without occupying the Port Module Slot, which might otherwise be used for additional customer network ports. Supported are the industry standard Limpel Zif Stac (LZS) and Microsoft point-to-point compression (MPPC) algorithms over Point-to-Point Protocol (PPP) or Frame Relay. High-level Data Link Control (HDLC) is not supported. The Data Compression AIM requires Cisco IOS Release 12.0(1)T or later.

The data compression AIM provides a cost-effective, hardware-based compression that yields a higher level of performance than that available from the main chassis CPU running the Cisco IOS compression feature. The data compression AIM series cards provide enhanced versatility, network peripheral integration, and performance for the Cisco 2600 series routers. The data compression AIM delivers higher levels of WAN bandwidth optimization by supporting compression ratios of up to 4:1 with 8 Mbps throughput.

Link Compression Over a Point-to-Point Connection

Link compression (also known as **per-interface compression**) involves compressing both the header and payload section of a data stream. Unlike header compression, link compression is protocol-independent.

The link compression algorithm uses STAC or Predictor to compress the traffic in another link layer, such as PPP or LAPB, to ensure error correction and packet sequencing (Cisco HDLC uses STAC compression only):

- **Predictor**—Predicts the next sequence of characters in the data stream by using an index to look up a sequence in a compression dictionary. It then examines the next sequence in the data stream to see if it matches. If it does, that sequence replaces the looked-up sequence in a maintained dictionary. If it does not, the algorithm locates the next character sequence in the index, and the process begins again. The index updates itself by hashing a few of the most recent character sequences from the input stream.

- **STAC**—Developed by STAC Electronics, STAC is a Lempel-Ziv (LZ)-based, compression-based algorithm. It searches the input data stream for redundant strings and replaces them with what is called a **token**, which turns out to be shorter than the original redundant data string.

If the data flow transverses across a point-to-point connection, use link compression. In a link-compression environment, the complete packet is compressed and the switching information in the header is not available for WAN-switching networks. Thus, the best applications for link compression are point-to-point environments with a limited hop path. Typical examples are leased lines or ISDN.

NOTE   Predictor is memory-intensive, and Stacker is CPU-intensive.

Payload Compression

Payload compression (also known as **per-virtual circuit compression**) only compresses the data portion of the data stream. The header is left intact.

When designing an internetwork, the customer cannot assume that an application will go over point-to-point lines. If link compression were used, the header may not be readable at a particular hop.

When using payload compression, the header is left unchanged and packets can be switched through a WAN packet network. Payload compression is appropriate for virtual network services such as X.25, SMDS, Frame Relay, and ATM. It uses the STAC compression method that was discussed previously.

TCP IP Header Compression

The TCP header compression subscribes to the Van Jacobson Algorithm, which is defined in RFC 1144. TCP/IP header compression lowers the overhead generated by the disproportionately large TCP/IP headers as they are transmitted across the WAN.

TCP/IP header compression is protocol-specific and only compresses the TCP/IP header. So, the Layer 2 header is still intact and a packet with a compressed TCP/IP header can still travel across a WAN link.

It is beneficial on small packets with few bytes of data, such as Telnet. Cisco's header compression supports X.25, Frame Relay, and dial-on-demand WAN link protocols. Because of processing overhead, header compression is generally used at lower speeds, such as 64 Kbps links.

Microsoft Point-to-Point Compression

Microsoft Point-to-Point Compression (MPPC) Protocol (RFC 2118) allows Cisco routers to exchange compressed data with Microsoft clients. MPPC uses an LZ-based compression mechanism. Use MPPC when exchanging data with a host using MPPC across a WAN link.

Windows 95 Compression

This section contains two examples for the personal benefit of the reader—they are not covered in the standard BCRAN course.

The Windows 95 client software supports both MPPC and LZS, whereas the Microsoft's NT server only supports MPPC, which is negotiated during the Compression Control Protocol (CCP) process.

As you learned in Chapter 5, "Configuring Point-to-Point Protocol and Controlling Network Access," the MPPC algorithm is also optimized to work efficiently in typical PPP scenarios (1500 byte MTU, for example). Note that MPPC is a layer-compression mechanism, and it should not be used with modem compression enabled on the client PC.

In Chapter 5, you learned that PPP options are negotiated. Once the authentication is successful, the compression method is negotiated between both parties. In Example 13-3, you see the result of the **debug ppp negotiation** command.

Example 13-3 *Output of* **debug ppp negotiation** *Command*

```
Router#debug ppp negotiation
R0:1 PPP: Treating connection as a callin
BR0:1 PPP: Phase is ESTABLISHING, Passive Open
BR0:1 LCP: State is Listen
BR0:1 LCP: I CONFREQ [Listen] id 116 len 30
BR0:1 LCP:    AuthProto CHAP (0x0305C22305)
<output omited>
```

continues

Example 13-3 *Output of* **debug ppp negotiation** *Command (Continued)*

```
BR0:1 PPP: Phase is AUTHENTICATING, by both
BR0:1 CHAP: O CHALLENGE id 61 len 28 from "BranchB"
BR0:1 CHAP: I CHALLENGE id 56 len 29 from "CentralB"
BR0:1 CHAP: Waiting for peer to authenticate first
BR0:1 CHAP: I RESPONSE id 61 len 29 from "CentralB"
BR0:1 CHAP: O SUCCESS id 61 len 4
BR0:1 CHAP: Processing saved Challenge, id 56
BR0:1 CHAP: O RESPONSE id 56 len 28 from "BranchB"
BR0:1 CHAP: I SUCCESS id 56 len 4
BR0:1 PPP: Phase is UP
<output omited>
BR0:1 CCP: I CONFREQ [REQsent] id 67 len 10
BR0:1 CCP:    MS-PPC supported bits 0x00000001 (0x120600000001)
BR0:1 CCP: O CONFACK [REQsent] id 67 len 10
BR0:1 CCP:    MS-PPC supported bits 0x00000001 (0x120600000001)
<output omited>
BR0:1 CCP: I CONFACK [ACKsent] id 64 len 10
BR0:1 CCP:    MS-PPC supported bits 0x00000001 (0x120600000001)
BR0:1 CCP: State is Open
BR0:1 CDPCP: I CONFACK [ACKsent] id 61 len 4
BR0:1 CDPCP: State is Open
BR0:1 IPXCP: I CONFACK [ACKsent] id 5 len 18
BR0:1 IPXCP:    Network 0x00000BAD (0x010600000BAD)
BR0:1 IPXCP:    Node 0010.7ba6.a3e5 (0x020800107BA6A3E5)
BR0:1 IPXCP: State is Open
```

In Chapter 5, you saw that in order for Layer 3 packets to be exchanged during a PPP session, the LCP had to be opened first. Also, before any MPPC packets may be communicated, PPP must reach the NCP phase, and the CCP Control Protocol must reach the Opened state, as shown in Example 13-4.

Example 13-4 *Output of* **show interface** *Command*

```
BranchB#sh int bri 0 1
BRI0:1 is up, line protocol is up
  Hardware is BRI
  MTU 1500 bytes, BW 64 Kbit, DLY 20000 usec, rely 255/255, load 1/255
  Encapsulation PPP, loopback not set, keepalive set (10 sec)
  LCP Open
  Open: IPCP, CCP, CDPCP, IPXCP
  Last input 00:00:00, output 00:00:00, output hang never
  Last clearing of "show interface" counters never
  Input queue: 0/75/0 (size/max/drops); Total output drops: 0
  Queueing strategy: weighted fair
  Output queue: 0/1000/64/0 (size/max total/threshold/drops)
     Conversations  0/1/256 (active/max active/max total)
     Reserved Conversations 0/0 (allocated/max allocated)
  5 minute input rate 0 bits/sec, 0 packets/sec
  5 minute output rate 0 bits/sec, 0 packets/sec
     2253 packets input, 81870 bytes, 0 no buffer
     Received 2253 broadcasts, 0 runts, 0 giants, 0 throttles
```

Example 13-4 *Output of* **show interface** *Command (Continued)*

```
0 input errors, 0 CRC, 0 frame, 0 overrun, 0 ignored, 0 abort
2199 packets output, 77282 bytes, 0 underruns
0 output errors, 0 collisions, 0 interface resets
0 output buffer failures, 0 output buffers swapped out
181 carrier transitionsCompression Considerations
```

Compression Considerations

Other considerations that you may wish to consider when selecting a compression algorithm to optimize your WAN utilization follow:

- **Modem compression**—In dial environments, compression can occur in the modem. Two common modem-compression standards are Microcom Networking Protocol 5 (MNP5) and the ITU V.42bis. MNP5 and V.42bis offer up to two times and four times compression, respectively. The two specifications are not compatible. The modems at both ends of the connection negotiate the standard to use. If compression is being done at the modem, do not configure the router to run compression.

- **Encrypted data**—Compression is a Layer 2 function and encryption occurs at Layer 3. When a data stream is encrypted by the client application, it is then passed onto the router for routing and/or compression services. When the compression engine receives the encrypted data stream, which by definition has no repetitive patterns, the data expands and does not compress. LZS then compares the before and after images to determine which is the smallest. and then sends the uncompressed data as it was originally received if expansion occurred. So, if data is encrypted, do not compress the encrypted data using a Layer 2 compression algorithm.

  The solution to this problem is to compress at Layer 3 and then encrypt at the same layer. Cisco is very active in providing a solution to this problem with its' work on the IP Security (IPSec) Protocol and the IP Compression Protocol (IPComp). IPSec is a standards-based method of providing privacy, integrity, and authenticity to information transferred across IP networks. IPSec provides IP network-layer encryption. IPComp is a mechanism to reduce the size of IP datagrams and is especially useful when encryption is applied to IP datagrams, in which Layer 2 (PPP) compression is not effective. [Source: www.cisco.com.]

- **CPU cycles versus memory**—The amount of memory that a router must have and that the network manager must plan on varies, according to the protocol being compressed, the compression algorithm, and the number of concurrent circuits on the router. Memory requirements will be higher for Predictor than for STAC, and payload will use more memory than link compression. Likewise, link compression utilizes more CPU cycles.

NOTE   For more information on compression, consult
http://www.cisco.com/warp/public/732/net_foundation/compr_wp.htm.

Configuring Data Compression

Use the **compress [predictor|stac|mppc]** command to configure point-to-point software compression for a LAPB, PPP, or HDLC link. Data-compression schemes used in internetworking devices are referred to as **lossless compression algorithms**. These schemes reproduce the original bit streams exactly, with no degradation or loss, which is a feature required by routers and other devices to transport data across the network:

```
Router(config-if)#compress [predictor¦stac¦mppc]
```

Use the **frame-relay payload-compress** command to enable STAC compression on a specified Frame Relay point-to-point interface or subinterface:

```
Router(config-if)#frame-relay payload-compress
```

Use the **x25 map compressdtcp** command to map compressed TCP headers to an X.121 address for a given link.

Use the **ip tcp header-compression** command to enable TCP header compression. The passive keyword compresses outgoing TCP packets, only if incoming TCP packets on the same interface are compressed. If passive is not specified, the router will compress all traffic:

```
Router(config-if)#ip tcp header-compression [passive]
```

WARNING Never recompress data. Remember that compressed data does not compress; it expands.

Summary

In this chapter, you learned why queuing is necessary, how to identify alternative queuing protocols, and how to determine the best queuing method that should be implemented.

You also learned how to configure weighted fair, priority, and custom queuing on your network interfaces; and how to verify proper queuing configuration, troubleshoot incorrect configurations, and enable data compression.

In the next chapter, you will embark in a new section of this book, which covers scaling and troubleshooting your remote access network.

Case Study—Managing Network Performance with Queuing and Compression

Complete the tasks of this case study, and then review the case study solution section that follows to see how you did and where you might need to review the concepts presented in this chapter.

In this case study, you have to solve a congestion problem by implementing queuing.

Scenario

Your WAN is experiencing congestion. Devise a queuing strategy for the WAN link between the Central site and branch office, as shown in Figure 3-11, so that each kind of traffic is guaranteed some bandwidth. Once the strategy is developed, you are responsible for configuring the Central router.

Figure 13-11 *Manage the Traffic Flow Between the Central Site and the Branch Office*

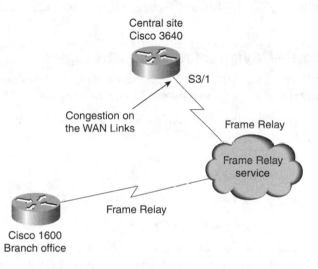

Task 1—Devise a Queuing Strategy

Complete the following steps.

Step 1   Plan the queuing so that the following requirements are meant:

— FTP traffic should be allowed to use up to 43% of the bandwidth.

— Telnet traffic should be allowed to use up to 29% of the bandwidth.

— IP traffic should be allowed to use up to 14% of the bandwidth.

— All other traffic should share, at the most, 14% of the bandwidth.

Step 2   Configure the Central router to implement the strategy developed in Step 1.

Task 2—Verify Your Queuing Configuration

Complete the following steps on the Central site router:

Step 1   Determine which command you would use to verify the queuing activity on the Central router.

Step 2   Determine which command you would use to debug the queuing activity on the Central router.

Solution to Case Study—Managing Network Performance with Queuing and Compression

The following is a step-by-step discussion of the case study solution.

Task 1 Solution—Devise a Queuing Strategy

In the scenario, all traffic must have a certain guaranteed bandwidth. Therefore, a **custom queuing** strategy is more appropriate for this case study.

Step 1   Assuming that other traffic will use the default custom queue size of 1500 bytes, develop the following plan. If 14% of the traffic has a queue size of 1500 bytes:

FTP traffic—43% is equal to 4500 bytes.

Telnet traffic—29% is equal to 3000 bytes.

IP traffic—14% is equal to 1500 bytes.

Step 2   The following commands have to be configured on the Central router to implement the strategy outlined in Step 1:

```
CentralA(config)#queue-list 1 protocol ip 1 tcp ftp
CentralA(config)#queue-list 1 protocol ip 2 tcp telnet
CentralA(config)#queue-list 1 protocol ip 3
CentralA(config)#queue-list 1 queue 1 byte-count 4500
CentralA(config)#queue-list 1 queue 2 byte-count 3000
CentralA(config)#queue-list 1 default 4
```

Because queues 3 and 4 are using the default queue size of 1500 bytes, no adjustment is necessary. Queue-list 1 now needs to be assigned to an interface.

Eliminate the Frame Relay traffic-shaping feature, as seen in Chapter 11, so you can enable custom queuing:

```
CentralA(config)#interface s3/1
CentralA(config-if)#no frame-relay traffic-shaping
```

Assign queue list 1 to traffic traveling over the serial interface:

```
CentralA(config-if)#custom-queue-list 1
```

Task 2 Solution—Verify Your Queuing Configuration

Step 1   Which command would you use to verify the queuing activity on the Central router? You would use the **show queueing custom** command. The output would look like that displayed in Example 13-5.

Example 13-5 *Display of the* **show queueing custom** *Command*

```
CentralA#sh queueing custom
Current custom queue configuration:
List Queue      Args
1    4          default
1    1          protocol ip tcp port ftp
1    2          protocol ip tcp port telnet
1    3          protocol ip
1    1          byte-count 4500
1    2          byte-count 3000
```

Step 2   Which command would you use to debug the queuing activity on the Central router? You would use the **debug custom-queue** command. Your traffic would look like that displayed in Example 13-6.

Example 13-6 *Display of the* **debug custom-queue** *Command*

```
CentralA#debug custom-queue
Custom output queueing debugging is on
CentralA#
CQ: Serial3/1 output (Pk size/Q: 292/1) Q # was 3 now 1
CQ: Serial3/1 output (Pk size/Q: 148/3) Q # was 1 now 3
CQ: Serial3/1 output (Pk size/Q: 292/1) Q # was 3 now 1
```

If you were to initiate a ping to BranchA E 0 while the debug is active, you would see the output in Example 13-7.

Example 13-7 *Display of the* **debug custom-queue** *Command Output Following a* **ping**

```
CentralA#ping 10.218.0.1
Type escape sequence to abort.
Sending 5, 100-byte ICMP Echos to 10.218.0.1, timeout is 2 seconds:
!!!!!
Success rate is 100 percent (5/5), round-trip min/avg/max = 60/60/60 ms
CentralA#
CQ: Serial3/1 output (Pk size/Q: 104/3) Q # was 1 now 3
CQ: Serial3/1 output (Pk size/Q: 104/3) Q # was 3 now 3
CQ: Serial3/1 output (Pk size/Q: 104/3) Q # was 3 now 3
CQ: Serial3/1 output (Pk size/Q: 104/3) Q # was 3 now 3
CQ: Serial3/1 output (Pk size/Q: 104/3) Q # was 3 now 3
CQ: Serial3/1 output (Pk size/Q: 292/1) Q # was 3 now 1
CQ: Serial3/1 output (Pk size/Q: 148/3) Q # was 1 now 3
```

If you were to start a telnet session, you would see the output in Example 13-8.

Example 13-8 *Display of the* **debug custom-queue** *Command Output for a Telnet Session*

```
CentralA#telnet 10.218.0.1
Trying 10.218.0.1 ... Open
User Access Verification
Password:
CQ: Serial3/1 output (Pk size/Q: 48/2) Q # was 1 now 2
CQ: Serial3/1 output (Pk size/Q: 44/2) Q # was 2 now 2
CQ: Serial3/1 output (Pk size/Q: 56/2) Q # was 2 now 2
CQ: Serial3/1 output (Pk size/Q: 44/2) Q # was 2 now 2
CQ: Serial3/1 output (Pk size/Q: 47/2) Q # was 2 now 2
CQ: Serial3/1 output (Pk size/Q: 47/2) Q # was 2 now 2
CQ: Serial3/1 output (Pk size/Q: 53/2) Q # was 2 now 2
CQ: Serial3/1 output (Pk size/Q: 47/2) Q # was 2 now 2
CQ: Serial3/1 output (Pk size/Q: 44/2) Q # was 2 now 2
```

If you clear the router's routing table, the router would request updates from its neighbors. You would see the debug screen output in Example 13-9.

Example 13-9 *Display of the* **debug custom-queue** *Output Following Routing Updates Requests*

```
CentralA#clear ip route *
CentralA#
CQ: Serial3/1 output (Pk size/Q: 36/3) Q # was 1 now 3
CQ: Serial3/1 output (Pk size/Q: 134/3) Q # was 3 now 3
CQ: Serial3/1 output (Pk size/Q: 134/3) Q # was 3 now 3
```

Example of Custom Queue Configuration

Example 13-10 shows a sample configuration output of a router configured with the step listed in this case study.

Example 13-10 *Running Configuration Following Custom Queuing Configuration*

```
CentralA#sh running config
Building configuration...
Current configuration:
!
<output omitted>
!
interface Serial3/1
no ip address
encapsulation frame-relay
custom-queue-list 1
frame-relay lmi-type cisco
<output omitted>
!
queue-list 1 protocol ip 1 tcp ftp
queue-list 1 protocol ip 2 tcp telnet
queue-list 1 protocol ip 3
queue-list 1 default 4
```

Example 13-10 *Running Configuration Following Custom Queuing Configuration (Continued)*

```
queue-list 1 queue 1 byte-count 4500
queue-list 1 queue 2 byte-count 3000
!
<output omitted>
!
end
```

NOTE   Because **no frame-relay traffic shaping** is the default, it does not appear in the **show run** screen output.

Case Study Conclusion

In this case study, you had to come up with a queuing strategy that would ensure that every traffic had some bandwidth available. You configured a custom queue and verified its proper operations.

Review Questions

Answer the following questions and then refer to Appendix H, "Answers to Review Questions," for answers and explanations.

1   When would you use weighted fair queuing, custom queuing, and priority queuing?

2   When is it best to use payload compression instead of link compression?

PART VI

Scaling Remote Access Networks

CHAPTER 14

Scaling IP Addresses with Network Address Translation

This chapter introduces students to the IP address-depletion problem. Cisco provides a way to implement the same IP addresses in multiple subnetworks, reducing the need for registered IP addresses. Figure 14-1 provides a graphical representation of where NAT could be applied.

Figure 14-1 *Chapter Activities—NAT and PAT*

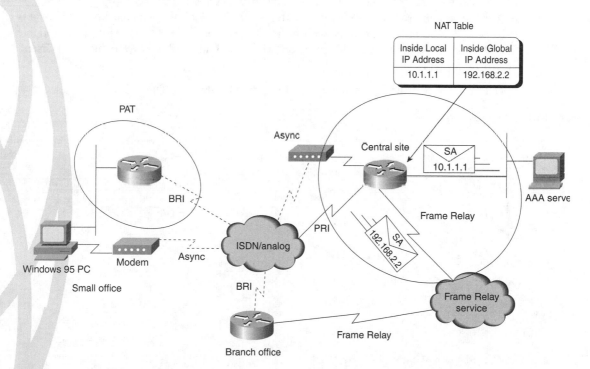

You will learn about Network Address Translation (NAT), and how to configure and troubleshoot a Cisco router for NAT operation. You will also read about how to configure and troubleshoot a Cisco 700 series router for Port Address Translation (PAT).

NOTE	The inside local and inside global IP address schemes that are used in this chapter are reserved and not to be used in the public network. The figures and examples in this chapter use a 10.0.0.0 network to illustrate inside local addresses and the 192.168.0.0 network to represent inside global addresses.

NAT Overview and Terminology

IP address depletion is a key problem facing the public network. To maximize the use of your registered IP addresses, Cisco IOS Release 11.2 software and subsequent releases implement NAT. This feature, which is Cisco's implementation of RFC 1631 (the IP Network Address Translator), is a solution that provides a way to use the same IP addresses in multiple internal subnetworks, thereby reducing the need for registered IP addresses.

The NAT functionality allows privately addressed networks to connect to public networks such as the Internet. The privately addressed "inside" network sends a packet through the NAT router; the addresses are converted to legal, registered IP addresses, which enables the packets to be passed to the public networks, such as the Internet. These features were formerly available only through pass-through firewall gateways. This functionality is now available in all Cisco enterprise routers.

NAT terminology is defined in Table 14-1 and is represented in Figure 14-2.

Figure 14-2 *NAT Terminology*

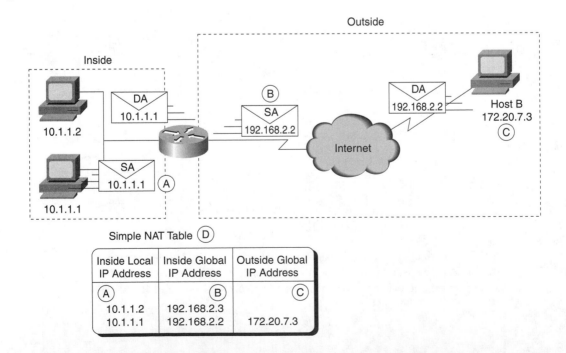

Inside Local IP Address	Inside Global IP Address	Outside Global IP Address
Ⓐ	Ⓑ	Ⓒ
10.1.1.2	192.168.2.3	
10.1.1.1	192.168.2.2	172.20.7.3

Table 14-1 *Cisco's implementation of NAT uses the following terms related to NAT.*

Term	Definition
Inside local IP address	The IP address assigned to a host on the inside network. The address was globally unique but obsolete, allocated from RFC 1918, Address Allocation for Private Internet Space, or randomly picked.
Inside global IP address	A legitimate IP address (assigned by the NIC or service provider) that represents one or more inside local IP addresses to the outside world. The address was allocated from a globally unique address space, typically provided by the Internet Service Provider (ISP).
Outside global IP address	The IP address that was assigned to a host on the outside network by its owner. The address was allocated from a globally routable address space.
Outside local IP address	The IP address of an outside host, as it appears to the inside network. The address was allocated from address space routable on the inside, or possibly allocated from RFC 1918, for example.
Simple translation entry	A translation entry that maps one IP address to another.
Extended translation entry	A translation entry that maps one IP address and port pair to another address port pair.

NAT technology enables private IP internetworks that use nonregistered IP addresses to connect to the public network, as shown in Figure 14-3. A NAT router is placed on the border of a stub domain (inside network) and a public network (outside network), and translates the internal local addresses into globally unique IP addresses before sending packets to the outside network. NAT takes advantage of the fact that relatively few hosts in a stub domain communicate outside of the domain at any given time. Therefore, only a subset of the IP addresses in a stub domain must be translated into globally unique IP addresses for outside communication.

Figure 14-3 *Network Using NAT to Connect to the Internet*

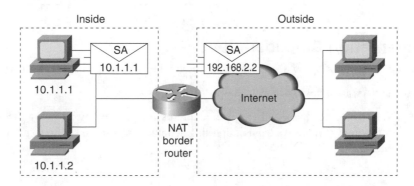

If your internal addresses must change because you changed service providers or because two intranets merged (two companies merged, for example), NAT can be used to translate the appropriate addresses. NAT enables you to change the addresses incrementally, without changing to hosts or routers except for those bordering stub domains. This eliminates duplicate address ranges without readdressing host computers.

The translation performed by using NAT can be either static or dynamic. **Static translation** occurs when you specifically configure addresses in a lookup table. A specific inside address maps into a prespecified outside address. The inside and outside addresses are statically mapped one-for-one. **Dynamic translation** occurs when the NAT border router is configured to understand which inside addresses must be translated, and which pool of addresses may be used for the outside addresses. There can be multiple pools of outside addresses. Multiple internal hosts can also share a single outside IP address, which conserves address space. Address sharing is accomplished by port multiplexing, or changing the source port on the outbound packet so that replies can be directed back to the appropriate router.

For load sharing, you can map outside IP addresses to inside IP addresses by using the Transmission Control Protocol (TCP) load distribution feature. Load distribution can also be accomplished by using NAT where one external address maps to this address. Then, the round-robin between inside machines occurs. In this case, incoming new connections are distributed across several machines. Each connection may state information that a given connection must remain on one server.

NOTE   Use NAT if the following is true:

- You need to connect to the Internet and your hosts do not have globally unique IP addresses.

- You change over to a new ISP that requires you to renumber your network.

- Two intranets with duplicate addresses merge.

- You want to support basic load sharing.

NAT Implementation Considerations

Before implementing NAT, you should evaluate the following considerations.

Typical NAT advantages are as follow:

- NAT conserves the legally registered addressing scheme by allowing the privatization of intranets, yet it allows legal addressing scheme pools to be set up to gain access to the Internet.

- NAT also reduces the instances in which addressing schemes overlap. If a scheme was originally set up within a private network, the network was connected to the public network (which may use the same addressing scheme). Without address translation, the potential for overlap exists globally.

- NAT increases the flexibility of connection to the public network. Multiple pools, backup pools, and load sharing/balancing pools can be implemented to help ensure reliable public network connections. Network design is also simplified because planners have more flexibility when creating an address plan.

- Deprivatization of a network requires the renumbering of the existing network; the costs can be associated with the number of hosts that require conversion to the new addressing scheme. NAT allows the existing scheme to remain, and it still supports the new assigned addressing scheme outside the private network.

Typical NAT disadvantages are as follows:

- NAT increases delay. Switching path delays, of course, are introduced because of the translation of each IP address within the packet headers. Performance may be a consideration because NAT is currently done by using process switching. The CPU must look at every packet to decide whether it has to translate it, and then alter the IP header—and possibly the TCP header. It is not likely that this process will be easily cacheable.

- One significant disadvantage, when implementing and using NAT, is the loss of end-to-end IP traceability. It becomes much harder to trace packets that undergo numerous packet address changes over multiple NAT hops. This scenario does, however, lead to more secure links because hackers who want to determine a packet's source will find it difficult, if not impossible, to trace or obtain the origination source or destination address.

- NAT also forces some applications that use IP addressing to stop functioning because it hides end-to-end IP addresses. Applications that use physical addresses instead of a qualified domain name will not reach destinations that are translated across the NAT router. Sometimes, this problem can be avoided by implementing static NAT mappings.

NAT Operation

NAT can be used to perform several functions. This section describes in detail the operation of the following NAT functions:

- **Translating inside local addresses**—Establishes a mapping between inside local and global addresses.

- **Overloading inside global addresses**—You can conserve addresses in the inside global address pool by allowing source ports in TCP connections or User Datagram Protocol (UDP) conversations to be translated. When different inside local addresses map to the same inside global address, each inside host's TCP or UDP port numbers are used to distinguish between them.

- **TCP load distribution**—A dynamic form of destination translation can be configured for some outside-to-inside traffic. When a mapping scheme is established, destination addresses that match an access-list are replaced with an address from a rotary pool. Allocation is done on a round-robin basis, and is done only when a new connection is opened from the outside to the inside. All non-TCP traffic is passed untranslated (unless other translations are in effect).

- **Handling overlapping networks**—NAT can be used to resolve addressing issues that arise when inside addresses overlap with addresses in the outside network. This can occur when two companies merge, both with duplicate addresses in the networks. It can also occur if you switch ISPs and the address you were assigned by your old ISP is reassigned to another client.

NOTE   NAT functions:

- Translation Inside Local addresses

- Overloading Inside Global Addresses

- TCP Load Distribution

- Handling Overlapping Networks

Traffic Types Supported in Cisco IOS NAT

The following traffic types are supported by Cisco IOS NAT:

- Any TCP/UDP traffic that does not carry source and/or destination IP addresses in the application data stream
- HTTP
- TFTP
- Telnet
- Archie
- finger
- NTP
- NFS
- rlogin, rsh, rcp

Although the following traffic types carry IP addresses in the application data stream, they are supported by Cisco IOS NAT:

- IMCP
- FTP (including PORT and PASV commands)
- NetBIOS over TCP/IP (datagram, name, and session services)
- Progressive Networks' RealAudio
- White Pines' CuSeeMe
- Xing Technologies' Streamworks
- DNS "A" and "PTR" queries
- H.323/NetMeeting [12.0(1)/12.0(1)T and later]
- VDOLive [11.3(4)11.3(4)T and later]
- Vxtreme [11.3(4)11.3(4)T and later]
- IP Multicast [12.0(1)T] (source address translation only)

The following traffic types are not supported by Cisco IOS NAT:

- Routing table updates
- DNS zone transfers
- BOOTP
- talk, ntalk
- SNMP
- NetShow

The source for the Cisco NAT support information is the Cisco IOS Network Address Translation (NAT) Packaging Update, found at www.cisco.com.

Translating Inside Local Addresses

Figure 14-4 illustrates NAT operation when it is used to translate addresses from inside your network to destinations outside of your network.

Figure 14-4 *Translating Addresses*

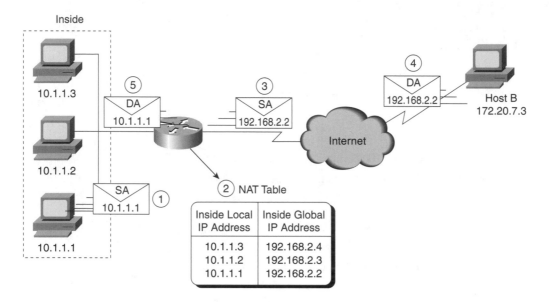

The steps in the following list correspond to the numbered NAT operation steps in Figure 14-4:

1 User at host 10.1.1.1 opens a connection to outside Host B.

2 The first packet that the border router receives from Host 10.1.1.1 causes the router to check its NAT table.

   If a translation is found because it has been statically configured, the router continues to Step 3. If no translation is found, the router determines that address 10.1.1.1 must be translated. The router allocates a new address and sets up a translation of the inside local address 10.1.1.1 to a legal inside global address from the dynamic address pool. This type of translation entry is referred to as a **simple entry**.

3 The border router replaces 10.1.1.1's inside local IP address with the selected inside global address, 192.168.2.2, and forwards the packet.

4 Host B receives the packet and responds to that node by using the inside global IP address 192.168.2.2.

5 When the border router receives the packet with the inside global IP address, the router performs a NAT table lookup by using the inside global address as the reference. The router then translates the address to 10.1.1.1's inside local address and forwards the packet to 10.1.1.1. Host 10.1.1.1 receives the packet and continues the conversation. For each packet, the router performs Step 2 through Step 5.

Overloading Inside Global Addresses

Figure 14-5 illustrates NAT operation when a single inside global address can be used to represent multiple inside local addresses simultaneously. In this example, an extended translation entry table is used. In the table, the combination of address and port makes each global IP address unique. The use of ports to make an address unique is actually Port Address Translation (PAT), which is a subset of NAT.

Figure 14-5 *Overloading Addresses*

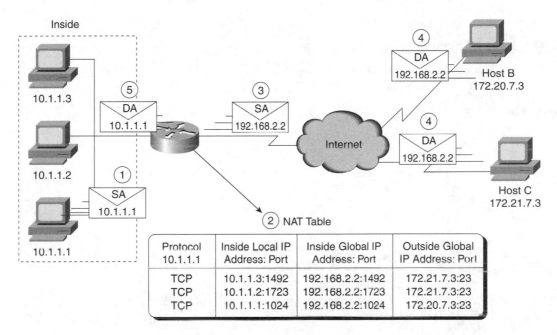

The steps in the following list correspond to the numbered NAT operation steps in Figure 14-5:

1 User at Host 10.1.1.1 opens a connection to Host B.

2 The first packet that the router receives from 10.1.1.1 causes the router to check its NAT table.

   If no translation is found, the router determines that address 10.1.1.1 must be translated. The router allocates a new address and sets up a translation of the inside local address 10.1.1.1 to a legal global address. If overloading is enabled and another translation is active, the router will reuse the global address from that translation and save enough information to be able to distinguish it from the other translation entry. This type of entry is called an **extended entry**.

3 The router replaces 10.1.1.1's inside local IP address with the selected inside global address, 192.168.2.2, and forwards the packet.

4   Outside Host B receives the packet and responds to that node using the inside global IP address 192.168.2.2.

5   When the router receives the packet with the inside global IP address, the router performs a NAT table lookup using the inside global address and port number, and the outside address and port number as the references. The router then translates the address to 10.1.1.1's inside local address and forwards the packet to 10.1.1.1. Host 10.1.1.1 receives the packet and continues the conversation. For each packet, the router performs Step 2 through Step 5.

TCP Load Distribution

Figure 14-6 illustrates NAT operation when NAT is used to map one virtual host to several real hosts.

Figure 14-6 *TCP Load Distribution*

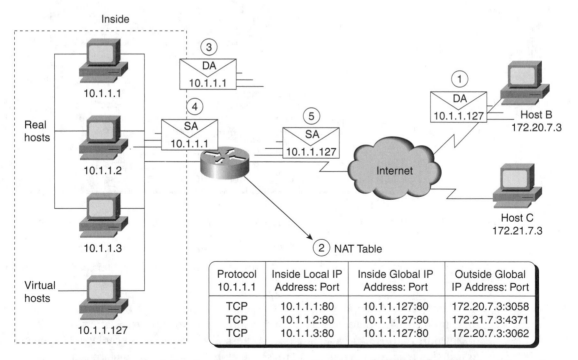

The steps in the following list correspond to the numbered NAT operation steps shown in Figure 14-6:

1   User on Host B (172.20.7.3) opens a TCP connection to the virtual host at 10.1.1.127.

2   The router receives the connection request and creates a new translation allocating the next real host (10.1.1.1) for the inside local IP address.

3 The router replaces the destination address with the selected real host address, and then forwards the packet.

4 Host 10.1.1.1 receives the packet and responds.

5 The router receives the packet and performs a NAT table lookup using the inside local address and port number, and using the outside address and port number as the key. The router then translates the source address to the address of the virtual host and forwards the packet.

The next connection request causes the router to allocate 10.1.1.2 for the inside local address.

Handling Overlapping Networks

Figure 14-7 illustrates NAT operation when addresses in the inside network overlap with addresses that are in the outside network.

Figure 14-7 *Overlapping Addresses*

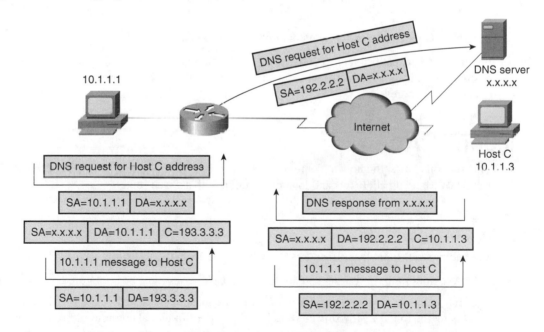

The steps in the following list correspond to the numbered addresses NAT operation steps shown in Figure 14-7:

1   User at 10.1.1.1 opens a connection to Host C (10.1.1.3), and 10.1.1.1 does a name-to-address lookup to a Domain Name System (DNS) server.

2   The router intercepts the DNS reply and translates the returned address if there is an overlap. In this case, 10.1.1.3 overlaps with an inside address. To translate the return address of Host C, the router creates a simple translation entry that maps the overlapping address 10.1.1.3 to an address from a separately configured outside local address pool. In this example, the address is 193.3.3.3.

3   The router then forwards the DNS reply to 10.1.1.1. The reply has Host C's address as 193.3.3.3. At this point, 10.1.1.1 opens a connection to 193.3.3.3.

4   When the router receives the packet for Host C, the router sets up a translation that maps the inside local address; and the global, outside global, and local addresses. The router replaces the source address of 10.1.1.1 with the inside global address of 192.2.2.2, and replaces the destination address of 193.3.3.3 with Host C's outside global address 10.1.1.3.

5   Host C receives a packet and continues the conversation.

For each packet sent between 10.1.1.1 and Host C, the router does a lookup, replaces the destination address with the inside local address, and replaces the source address with the outside local address.

Configuring NAT

This section shows you how to configure static and dynamic NAT, and how to use NAT to handle overlapping addresses and load distribution with a Cisco router.

Static NAT Configuration

To enable basic, static local IP address translation, perform the following steps:

1   At a minimum, IP routing and appropriate IP addresses must be configured on the router.

2   If you use static address translations for inside local addresses, define the addresses by using the **ip nat inside source static** *local-ip global-ip* global configuration command, as shown in Table 14-2. To remove the static translation, use the no form of this command.

Table 14-2   *Static NAT Command Variables*

ip nat inside source static Command	Description
local-ip	Sets up a single static translation. This argument establishes the local IP address assigned to a host on the inside network. The address could be randomly chosen, allocated from RFC 1918, or obsolete.
global-ip	Sets up a single static translation. This argument establishes the globally unique IP address of an inside host as it appears to the outside world.

3 Enable NAT on at least one inside and one outside interface by entering interface configuration mode and entering the **ip nat** {**inside** | **outside**} command.

Only packets moving between inside and outside interfaces can be translated. For example, if a packet is received on an inside interface but is not destined for an outside interface, it will not be translated.

Example 14-1 shows a sample static NAT configuration. The corresponding topology is shown in Figure 14-8.

Figure 14-8   *Static NAT*

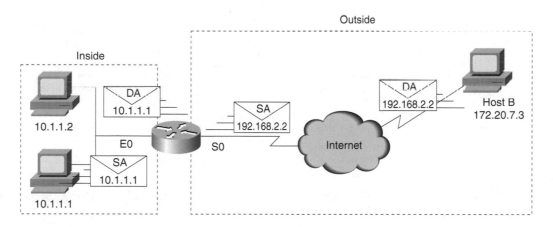

Example 14-1   *Static NAT Configuration*

```
ip nat inside source static 10.1.1.1 192.168.2.2
!
interface Ethernet0
ip address 10.1.1.10 255.255.255.0
ip nat inside
!
interface Serial0
ip address 172.16.2.1 255.255.255.0
ip nat outside
```

Dynamic NAT Configuration

To enable dynamic local IP address translation, perform the following steps:

1   At a minimum, IP routing and appropriate IP addresses must be configured on the router.

2   Define a standard IP access-list for the inside network by using the **access-list** *access-list-number* {**permit** | **deny**} *local-ip-address* command.

3   Define an IP NAT pool for the inside network by using the **ip nat pool** *pool-name start-ip end-ip* {**netmask** *netmask* | **prefix-length** *prefix-length*} [**type rotary**] command, which is explained in Table 14-3.

Table 14-3   **ip nat pool** *Command*

ip nat pool Command	Description
pool-name	Name of the pool.
start-ip	Starting IP address that defines the range of addresses in the address pool.
end-ip	Ending IP address that defines the range of addresses in the address pool.
netmask *netmask*	Network mask that indicates which address bits belong to the network and subnetwork fields, and which bits belong to the host field. Specify the netmask of the network to which the pool address belongs.
prefix-length *prefix-length*	Number that indicates how many bits of the netmask are ones (how many bits of the address indicate the network). Specify the netmask of the network to which the pool addresses belong.
type rotary	(Optional) Indicates that the range of addresses in the address pool identifies real inside hosts, among which TCP load distribution will occur.

1   Map the access-list to the IP NAT pool by using the **ip nat inside source list** *access-list-number* **pool** *name* command.

2   Enable NAT on at least one inside and one outside interface with the **ip nat** {**inside** | **outside**} command.

Only packets moving between inside and outside interfaces can be translated. For example, if a packet is received on an inside interface but is not destined for an outside interface, it will not be translated.

Example 14-2 shows a sample dynamic NAT configuration.

Example 14-2   *Dynamic NAT Configuration*

```
ip nat pool dyn-nat 192.168.2.1 192.168.2.254 netmask 255.255.255.0
ip nat inside source list 1 pool dyn-nat
!
interface Ethernet0
ip address 10.1.1.10 255.255.255.0
ip nat inside
!
interface Serial0
ip address 172.16.2.1 255.255.255.0
ip nat outside
!
access-list 1 permit 10.1.1.0 0.0.0.255
```

Inside Global Address Overloading Configuration

To configure inside global address overloading, perform the following steps:

1   At a minimum, IP routing and appropriate IP addresses must be configured on the router.

2   Configure dynamic address translation.

3   When you define the mapping between the access-list and the IP NAT pool by using the **ip nat inside source list** *access-list-number* **pool** *name* **overload** command, add the **overload** keyword to the command.

4   Enable NAT on the appropriate interfaces by using the **ip nat** {**inside** | **outside**} command.

Example 14-3 shows a sample address-overloading configuration. The corresponding topology is shown in Figure 14-9.

Figure 14-9   *Address Overloading*

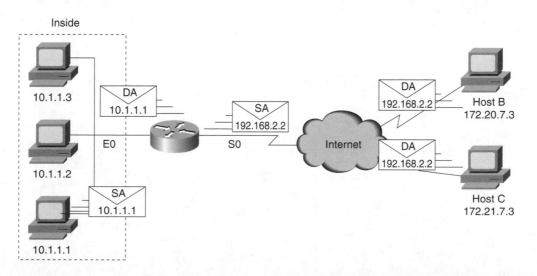

Example 14-3 *NAT Configuration with Address Overloading*

```
ip nat pool ovrld-nat 192.168.2.2 192.168.2.2 netmask 255.255.255.0
ip nat inside source list 1 pool ovrld-nat overload
!
interface Ethernet0/0
ip address 10.1.1.10 255.255.255.0
ip nat inside
!
interface Serial0/0
ip address 172.16.2.1 255.255.255.0
ip nat outside
!
access-list 1 permit 10.1.1.0 0.0.0.255
```

TCP Load Distribution Configuration

To configure TCP load distribution, perform the following steps:

1 At a minimum, configure IP routing and appropriate IP addresses on the router.

2 Define a standard IP access-list with a permit statement for the virtual host.

3 Define an IP NAT pool for the real hosts, making sure that it is a rotary type pool using the **ip nat pool** *name start-ip end-ip* {**netmask** *netmask* | **prefix-length** *prefix-length*} **type rotary** command.

4 Define a mapping between the access-list and the real host pool by using the **ip nat inside destination list** *access-list-number* **pool** *name* command.

5 Enable NAT on the appropriate interface, as previously discussed, by using the **ip nat** {**inside** | **outside**} command.

Example 14-4 shows an example of TCP load distribution configuration. The corresponding topology is shown in Figure 14-10.

Figure 14-10 *TCP Load Distribution Configuration*

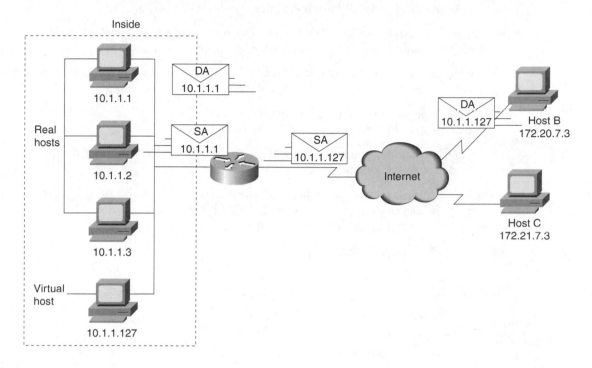

Example 14-4 *NAT Configuration with Load Distribution*

```
ip nat pool real-hosts 10.1.1.1 10.1.1.3 prefix-length 24 type rotary
ip nat inside destination list 2 pool real-hosts
!
interface serial0
ip address 192.168.1.129 255.255.255.224
ip nat outside
!
interface ethernet0
ip address 10.1.1.254 255.255.255.0
ip nat inside
!
access-list 2 permit 10.1.1.127
```

NAT to Translate Overlapping Addresses Configuration

To configure overlapping address translation, perform the following steps:

  1 At a minimum, IP routing and appropriate IP addresses must be configured on the router.

  2 Define the standard IP access-list for the inside network, as discussed in the "Dynamic NAT Configuration" section.

3   Define an IP NAT pool for the inside network by using the **ip nat pool** *name start-ip end-ip* {**netmask** *netmask* | **prefix-length** *prefix-length*} command.

4   Define an IP NAT pool for the outside network by using the **ip nat pool** *name start-ip end-ip* {**netmask** netmask | **prefix-length** *prefix-length*} command.

5   Define mapping between the access-list and the inside global pool by using the **ip nat inside source list** *access-list-number* **pool** *name* [**overload**] command.

6   Define mapping between the access-list and the outside local pool by using the **ip nat outside source list** *access-list-numbe*r **pool** *name* command.

7   Enable NAT on the appropriate interface, as previously discussed, by using the **ip nat** {**inside** | **outside**} command.

Example 14-5 shows a sample configuration of NAT used for translating overlapping addresses. In this example, one single router is responsible for performing the translation for inside and outside traffic. The corresponding topology is shown in Figure 14-11.

Figure 14-11 *NAT Used for Translating Overlapping Addresses*

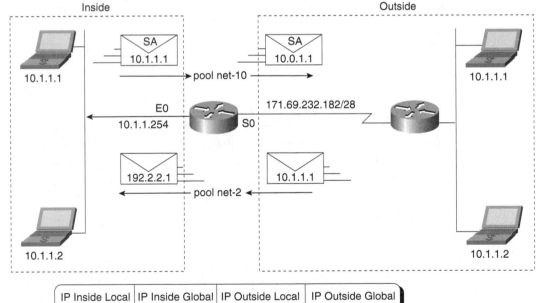

IP Inside Local	IP Inside Global	IP Outside Local	IP Outside Global
10.1.1.1	10.0.1.1	192.2.2.1	10.1.1.1

Example 14-5 *NAT Configuration with Overlapping Addresses*

```
ip nat pool net-2 192.2.2.1 192.2.2.254 prefix-length 24
ip nat pool net-10 10.0.1.1 10.0.1.254 prefix-length 24
ip nat outside source list 1 pool net-2
ip nat inside source list 1 pool net-10
!
interface Serial0
ip address 171.69.232.182 255.255.255.240
ip nat outside
!
interface Ethernet0
ip address 10.1.1.254 255.255.255.0
ip nat inside
!
access-list 1 permit 10.1.1.0 0.0.0.255
```

Verifying and Troubleshooting NAT

This section discusses NAT verification commands on a Cisco IOS router. You can display translation information and clear address translation entries from the NAT translation with the commands covered in this section.

Verifying NAT

The **show ip nat translations** command can be used to verify the active translations. The screen output in Example 14-6 shows a basic translation.

Example 14-6 **show ip nat translation** *Display*

```
Router#show ip nat translation
Pro    Inside global     Inside local     Outside local    Outside global
---    192.2.2.1         10.1.1.1         ---              ---
---    192.2.2.2         10.1.1.2         ---              ---
Router#
```

Example 14-7 is a sample of NAT with overloading. Two different inside hosts appear on the outside with a single IP address, both for a telnet session—destination TCP port 23. Unique source TCP port numbers are used to distinguish between hosts.

Example 14-7 **show ip nat translation** *Display with Address Overloading*

```
Router#sh ip nat trans
Pro  Inside global       Inside local      Outside local     Outside global
tcp  192.168.2.1:11003   10.1.1.1:11003    172.16.2.2:23     172.16.2.2:23
tcp  192.168.2.1:1067    10.1.1.1:1067     172.16.2.3:23     172.16.2.3:23
```

You can use the **show ip nat statistics** command to see NAT statistics.

Dynamic NAT Timeouts

By default, dynamic address translations time out after some period of non-use. You can change the default values on timeouts, if necessary. When overloading is not configured, simple translation entries time out after 24 hours.

If you have configured overloading, you have finer control over the translation entry timeout because each entry contains more context about the traffic that is using it. The following are the timeout values with NAT overloading:

UDP timeout value:	5 minutes
DNS timeout value:	1 minute
TCP timeout value:	24 hours
Finish and Reset value:	1 minute

Troubleshooting NAT

If you need to use a trace on NAT operation, use can use the **debug ip nat** command to display a line of output for each packet that gets translated. Example 14-8 is an example of a debug of address translation inside-to-outside.

Example 14-8 **debug ip nat** *Display*

```
Router#debug ip nat
NAT: s=10.1.1.1->192.168.2.1, d=172.16.2.2 [0]
NAT: s=172.16.2.2, d=192.168.2.1->10.1.1.1 [0]
NAT: s=10.1.1.1->192.168.2.1, d=172.16.2.2 [1]
NAT: s=10.1.1.1->192.168.2.1, d=172.16.2.2 [2]
NAT: s=10.1.1.1->192.168.2.1, d=172.16.2.2 [3]
NAT*: s=172.16.2.2, d=192.168.2.1->10.1.1.1 [1]
NAT: s=172.16.2.2, d=192.168.2.1->10.1.1.1 [1]
NAT: s=10.1.1.1->192.168.2.1, d=172.16.2.2 [4]
NAT: s=10.1.1.1->192.168.2.1, d=172.16.2.2 [5]
NAT: s=10.1.1.1->192.168.2.1, d=172.16.2.2 [6]
NAT*: s=172.16.2.2, d=192.168.2.1->10.1.1.1 [2]
```

You can decode the above debug output by using the following key points:

* The asterisk next to NAT indicates that the translation is occurring in the fast path. The first packet in a conversation will always go through the slow path (be process-switched). The remaining packets will go through the fast path if a cache entry exists.

* s=10.1.1.1 is the source address.

* d=172.16.2.2 is the destination address.

- 10.1.1.1->192.168.2.1 indicates that the address was translated.

- The value in brackets is the IP identification number. This information may be useful for debugging because it enables you to correlate with other packet traces from sniffers, for example.

Clearing NAT Translation Entries

To clear all translated entries, use the **clear ip nat translation** * command, as displayed in Example 14-9. The star symbol is a wildcard, meaning all. In the output, the **show ip nat translations** command shows us the active translation. Then the **clear ip nat translation** * command is typed to clear any active translation. No entries appear following another **show ip nat translations** command.

Example 14-9 *Effect of* **clear ip nat translation** * *Command*

```
router#show ip nat trans
Pro Inside global       Inside local      Outside local     Outside global
tcp 192.168.2.1:11003   10.1.1.1:11003    172.16.2.2:23     172.16.2.2:23
tcp 192.168.2.1:1067    10.1.1.1:1067     172.16.2.3:23     172.16.2.3:23
router#
router#clear ip nat trans *
router#show ip nat trans
router#<nothing>
```

Specific Spelling of the Word "Translation"

The word *translation* is singular with the **clear ip nat translation** command and is plural with the **show ip nat translations** command.

It is possible to clear a simple translation entry containing an inside translation, or both an inside and outside translation, by using the **clear ip nat translation inside** *global-ip local-ip* [**outside** *local-ip global-ip*] command.

You can clear a simple translation entry that contains an outside translation by using **clear ip nat translation outside** *local-ip global-ip* command.

If you wish to clear an extended entry (in its various forms), use the **clear ip nat translation** *protocol* **inside** *global-ip global-port local-ip local-port* [*outside local-ip local-port global-ip global-port*]. The following is a sample of how this command would appear:

```
router#clear ip nat trans udp
    inside 192.168.2.2 10.1.1.2 1220 171.69.2.132 53 171.69.2.132 53
```

NOTE   If NAT is properly configured but translations are not occurring, clear the NAT translations and check if the translations occur.

Configuring and Troubleshooting PAT On the 700 Router

PAT, a subset of NAT, is the only address-translation feature in the Cisco 700 series routers. If you wish to enable address translation on a 700 series router, use PAT.

Cisco 700 series routers with Release 4.0 software support PAT. PAT enables local hosts on a private IP network to communicate over a public network such as the Internet. All traffic that is designated to an external address will have its source IP address and source port number translated before the packet is forwarded over the public network. IP packets returning to the private network will have their IP addresses translated back to private IP addresses.

PAT conserves network address space by enabling a single IP address to be assigned to an entire LAN. All WAN traffic is mapped to a single node—the Integrated Services Digital Network (ISDN)-side IP address of the Cisco 700 series router, as shown in Figure 14-12.

Figure 14-12 *PAT performed On a Cisco 700 series*

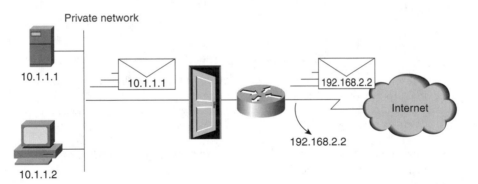

All traffic on the public network appears to come from the Cisco 700, making the remote LAN invisible to the outside world.

NOTE   The advantage of using PAT on a Cisco 700 series router is that it enables hosts on private networks to communicate over public networks and it conserves IP addresses.

PAT Porthandler Operation

If users need to access a specific remote server on the private network, PAT allows packets with a specific well-known port number to get through (for example, File Transfer Protocol (FTP) or Telnet), as shown in Figure 14-13. Only one server of each type (FTP, Telnet, and so on) can be on the remote LAN. Use a static address for the remote servers so they can be found. You can set a static host route at the Central site to get to the remote server. On a Cisco 700 running PAT, either a static or dynamic address can be used.

Figure 14-13 *Only Packets Destined for the Server (By Type) Are Allowed Through*

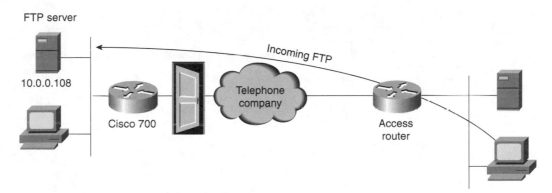

Configuring PAT

Use this complete configuration on the remote Cisco 700 series router to enable IP unnumbered across the WAN, Dynamic Host Configuration Protocol (DHCP) server functionality, and PAT to a Cisco router. The **Set IP PAT ON** and **SEt IP PAT POrt FTP 10.0.0.108** commands (bold in Example 14-10) enable PAT and set up the porthandler functionality for the remote site shown in Figure 14-14. This configuration works for Cisco 700 Release 4.1 or later.

Figure 14-14 *PAT configured on the remote LAN*

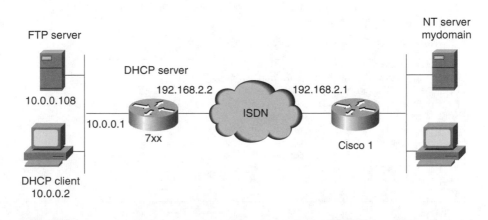

Example 14-10 *Cisco 700 PAT Porthandler Configuration*

```
>cd Internal
Internal>SEt IP 10.0.0.1
>SEt SYStem 7xx
>7xx>SEt User Cisco1
>7xx:Cisco1>Set IP PAT ON (must be configured before the set ip pat port command)
7xx:Cisco1>cd
7xx>SEt PPp AUthentication CHAp
7xx>SEt PPp SEcret CLient
7xx>SEt DHcp SERver
7xx>SEt DHcp DNS PRImary 192.168.2.2
7xx>SEt DHcp WINS PRImary 198.168.2.2
7xx>SEt DHcp DOmain mydomain
7xx> SEt IP PAT POrt FTP 10.0.0.108 (set ip pat port default, allows all services)
7xx>SEt USer Cisco1
7xx:Cisco1> SEt BRidging OFf
7xx:Cisco1> SEt IP ROUTING ON
7xx:Cisco1> SEt IP ROUTE DEstination 0.0.0.0 GAteway 0.0.0.0
7xx:Cisco1>SEt Number 5558899
7xx:Cisco1>SEt PPp Secret Host
7xx:Cisco1>SEt Active
```

Cisco 700—PAT and DHCP Relay Agent

A configuration in which PAT is on and DHCP relay is enabled is not valid. DHCP relay attempts to cross from a public to a private domain. PAT prevents access to the private domain. DHCP relay fails because it must reference the router's private address. Cisco 700 DHCP relay is covered in Chapter 9, "Configuring a Cisco 700 Series Router."

Monitoring PAT

Use the **show ip pat** command to display PAT statistics and the currently active translated sessions. Notice, in the Example 14-11 screen output, that TCP port 21 for the FTP service is being handled by the FTP server 10.0.0.108.

Example 14-11 *The* **show ip nat** *Command on a Cisco 700*

```
7xx:Cisco1>show ip pat
Dropped - icmp 0, udp 0, tcp 0, map 0, frag 0
Timeout - udp 5 minutes, tcp 30 minutes
Port handlers [no default]:
Port      Handler        Service
-------------------------------------
21        10.0.0.108     FTP
23        Router         TELNET
67        Router         DHCP Server
68        Router         DHCP Client
69        Router         TFTP
```

Example 14-11 *The* **show ip nat** *Command on a Cisco 700 (Continued)*

```
80         Router         HTTP
161        Router         SNMP
162        Router         SNMP-TRAP
520        Router         RIP
```

Summary

In this chapter, you learned how NAT and PAT solve the limited IP address problem. Also, you learned to configure PAT and NAT operations.

Case Study—Scaling IP Addresses with Network Address Translation

Complete the tasks of this case study, and then review the case study solution section that follows to see how you did and see where you might need to review the concepts presented in this chapter.

In this case study, you will specify the command to configure dynamic and static NAT, and how to verify that NAT is operating properly using the debug commands.

Scenario

Configure both dynamic and static NAT translation so that the inside local address on your interface is translated to a global IP address that can be communicated on the Internet, as shown in Figure 14-15. The Cisco 3640 acts like an Internet router.

Figure 14-15 *NAT Performed from the Private LAN to the Internet*

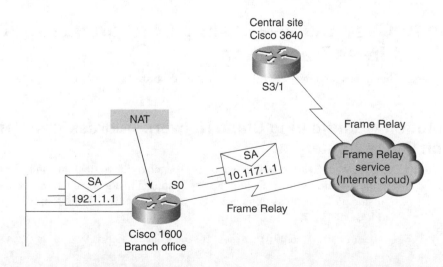

Task 1—Configuring Static Network Address Translation on the Branch Office Router

Step 1   Enter global configuration mode on the branch office router and configure the router. Create a static translation entry, mapping inside local addresses to the outside global address to be used. For this case study, let's use the loopback address of 192.1.1.1 to be translated to 10.117.1.1.

Step 2   Enter interface configuration mode, and configure the interfaces as inside and outside interfaces after you create a loopback interface and you provide it with the previously mentioned IP address.

Step 3   On the Central site router (acting as an Internet router), configure a static route to the new inside global network. Remember that the inside global address used by the Cisco 1600 router is 10.117.1.1. Also (as seen in Chapter 11, "Frame Relay Connection and Traffic Flow Control"), the Cisco 1600 Serial 0 interface address is 10.140.1.2.

Step 4   On the branch router, activate the **debug** command to monitor active NAT translation.

Step 5   From the branch router, initiate an extended ping to the Central site router. With an extended ping, you may specify the source ip address of the ping. You specify 192.1.1.1. What do you expect to see?

Task 2—Configuring Dynamic Network Address Translation on the Branch Office Router

Now that you have practiced the Static NAT commands, think of what the command would be if you were to use dynamic NAT. Redo the same steps as in Task 1, but use dynamic NAT.

Solution to Case Study—Scaling IP Addresses with Network Address Translation

The following is a step-by-step discussion of the case study solution.

Task 1 Solution—Configuring Static Network Address Translation on the Branch Office Router

Step 1   Enter global configuration mode on the branch office router and configure the router. Create a static translation entry, mapping inside local addresses to the outside global address to be used. For this case study, use the loopback address of 192.1.1.1 to be translated to 10.117.1.1:

```
BranchA(config)#ip nat inside source 192.1.1.1 10.117.1.1
```

Step 2 Enter interface configuration mode and configure the interfaces as inside and outside interfaces, once you have created a loopback interface and you have provided it with the previously mentioned IP address:

```
BranchA(config)#interface loopback 1
BranchA(config-if)# ip address 192.1.1.1 255.255.255.0
BranchA(config-if)#ip nat inside
BranchA(config)#interface serial 0
BranchA(config-if)#ip nat outside
```

Step 3 On the Central site router (acting as an Internet router), configure a static route to the new inside global network:

```
CentralA(config)# ip route 10.117.1.0 255.255.255.0 10.140.1.2
```

Step 4 On the branch router, activate the debug command to monitor active NAT translation:

```
BranchA#debug ip nat on
```

Step 5 From the branch router, initiate an extended ping to the Central site router. With an extended ping, you may specify the source ip address of the ping. You specify 192.1.1.1. What do you expect to see?

In the Example 14-12 output, 10.115.0.110 is the Ethernet 0 interface of CentralA.

Example 14-12 *Debugging an IP NAT Transaction*

```
BranchA#debug ip nat
IP NAT debugging is on
BranchA#ping
Protocol [ip]:
Target IP address: 10.115.0.110
Repeat count [5]:
Datagram size [100]:
Timeout in seconds [2]:
Extended commands [n]: y
Source address or interface: 192.1.1.1
Type of service [0]:
Set DF bit in IP header? [no]:
Validate reply data? [no]:
Data pattern [0xABCD]:
Loose, Strict, Record, Timestamp, Verbose[none]:
Sweep range of sizes [n]:
Type escape sequence to abort.
Sending 5, 100-byte ICMP Echos to 10.115.0.110, timeout is 2 seconds:
!!!!!
Success rate is 100 percent (5/5), round-trip min/avg/max = 64/67/68 ms
BranchA#
NAT: s=192.1.1.1->10.117.1.1, d=10.115.0.110 [50]
NAT*: s=10.115.0.110, d=10.117.1.1->192.1.1.1 [50]
NAT: s=10.115.0.110, d=10.117.1.1->192.1.1.1 [50]
NAT: s=192.1.1.1->10.117.1.1, d=10.115.0.110 [51]
NAT*: s=10.115.0.110, d=10.117.1.1->192.1.1.1 [51]
NAT: s=10.115.0.110, d=10.117.1.1->192.1.1.1 [51]
```

continues

Example 14-12 *Debugging an IP NAT Transaction (Continued)*

```
NAT:  s=192.1.1.1->10.117.1.1, d=10.115.0.110 [52]
NAT*: s=10.115.0.110, d=10.117.1.1->192.1.1.1 [52]
NAT:  s=10.115.0.110, d=10.117.1.1->192.1.1.1 [52]
NAT:  s=192.1.1.1->10.117.1.1, d=10.115.0.110 [53]
NAT*: s=10.115.0.110, d=10.117.1.1->192.1.1.1 [53]
NAT:  s=10.115.0.110, d=10.117.1.1->192.1.1.1 [53]
NAT:  s=192.1.1.1->10.117.1.1, d=10.115.0.110 [54]
NAT*: s=10.115.0.110, d=10.117.1.1->192.1.1.1 [54]
NAT:  s=10.115.0.110, d=10.117.1.1->192.1.1.1 [54]
```

Task 2 Solution—Configuring Dynamic Network Address Translation on the Branch Office Router

Here are the steps you had to follow to remove the static translation and introduce dynamic NAT:

Step 1 Enter global configuration mode on the branch office router and prepare to configure the router. Remove the **ip nat inside source static 192.1.1.1 10.140.1.2** command.

Step 2 In global configuration mode, create an access-list that permits traffic that originates from the inside network:

```
BranchA(config)#access-list 10 permit 192.1.1.1
```

Step 3 Configure a dynamic NAT pool for private-to-public address space translation:

```
BranchA(config)#ip nat pool NATLAB 10.117.1.1  10.117.1.254 netmask
    255.255.255.0
```

Step 4 Associate the defined NAT pool to an inside NAT boundary; associate the NATLAB to access-list 10:

```
BranchA(config)#ip nat inside source list 10 pool NATLAB        .
```

NOTE Your inside and outside NAT interfaces were already defined in Task 1.

Case Study Conclusion

In this case study, you prepared a router for static and dynamic NAT to translate local addresses to global addresses.

Review Questions

Answer the following questions, and then refer to Appendix H, "Answers to Review Questions," for answers and explanations.

1   What is the difference between a simple translation entry and an extended translation entry? State how each one is used.

2   Give one or more examples when NAT could be used.

3   Your networks are addressed by using 10.1.1.1/24 subnets. Your ISP provides you a globally unique address of 192.1.1.0/24. What commands do you use to translate from 10.1.1.0/24 to 192.1.1.0/24?

4   When viewing the output of the **show ip nat translations** command, how can you determine when an inside global address is being used for overloading inside global addresses?

CHAPTER 15

Using AAA to Scale Access Control in an Expanding Network

In the previous chapters, you learned how to configure your Cisco routers to provide remote access to users. Controlling access is a major concern of remote access networks.

This chapter describes the access-control features of Cisco Secure and the operation of a Cisco Secure server. It also describes how to configure a router to access a preconfigured Cisco Secure server; and how to use authentication, authorization, and accounting (AAA), as shown in Figure 15-1.

Figure 15-1 *The AAA Server Authenticates Users*

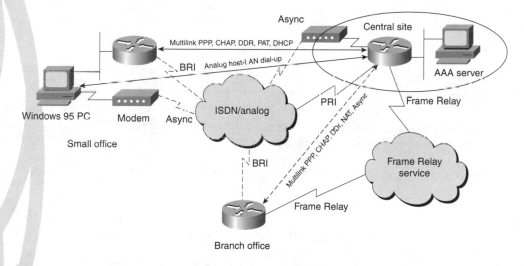

Overview of Cisco Access Control Solutions

As shown in Figure 15-2, Cisco provides the following security solutions:

- **Clients**   The dial clients can utilize CiscoRemote or token cards as a secure means for dial-up. Token cards such as SDI, Enigma, and CryptoCards are supported.

- **Client protocols**   Cisco IOS software supports Point-to-Point Protocol (PPP), Challenge Handshake Authentication Protocol (CHAP), Password Authentication Protocol (PAP), and MS-CHAP protocols for dial-up security. We recommend using PPP with CHAP authentication. If Remote Access Dial-In User Service (RADIUS) or token cards were implemented, the requirement would be PAP.

- **Access servers**   Cisco IOS software supports the following protocols to provide a secure means for dial-up: dialer profiles, access control list, per-user access control lists, lock and key, Layer 2 Forwarding Protocol (L2F), and Kerberos V.

- **Central site protocols**   For security verification between the network access server and the network security server, the network access server supports Terminal Access Controller Access System plus (TACACS+), RADIUS, and Kerberos V protocols.

- **Security servers**   Cisco Secure is the umbrella under which Cisco has a variety of security server solutions. Cisco Secure UNIX and Cisco Secure NT provide your network with AAA capabilities. Cisco offers both the PIX Firewall and the Centuri Firewall for the Cisco Secure NT platform.

Figure 15-2 *Overview of Cisco Security Solutions*

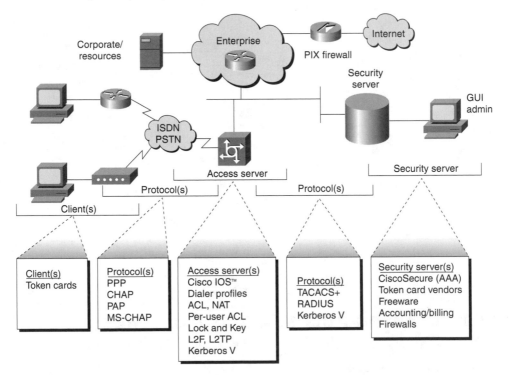

NOTE   For more comprehensive training on Cisco security options, attend the Managing Cisco
Network Security (MCNS) course.

One of the security solutions shown in Figure 15-2 is a Cisco Secure server. It incorporates a
multiuser, Web-based Java configuration and management tool that simplifies server
administration, and enables multiple system administrators to simultaneously manage security
services from multiple locations. The graphical user interface (GUI) of the Cisco Secure Access
Control Server (ACS) supports Microsoft and Netscape Web browsers, providing multiplatform
compatibility. Token cards from CRYPTOCard, Enigma Logics, and Security Dynamics
Technologies are now fully supported. Token cards are the strongest method used to
authenticate users who are dialing in and to prevent unauthorized users from accessing
proprietary information. Cisco Secure ACS 2.0 now supports industry-leading relational
database technologies from Sybase, Inc., and Oracle Corporation. Traditional scalability,
redundancy, and nondistributed architecture limitations are removed with the integration of
relational database technologies such as Sybase's SQLAnywhere. Storage and management of
user and group profile information is greatly simplified.

Additional features included in Cisco Secure are an automatic account disable for the
prevention of brute force attacks and a server attribute called Maxsessions, which limits the
number of login sessions or Integrated Services Digital Network (ISDN) B channels required
for a user or a Virtual Private Dial Network (VPDN) profile.

Overview of Cisco Secure

Cisco Secure has three major components, as shown in Figure 15-3:

- **The AAA server**   Shown at the bottom of the figure, it interacts with TACACS+ and
  RADIUS.

- **The Netscape Fastrack server**   This is shown on the left side as a Web browser.

- **The relational database management system (RDBMS)**   This is shown on the right
  side of Figure 15-3.

Figure 15-3 *Cisco Secure Components*

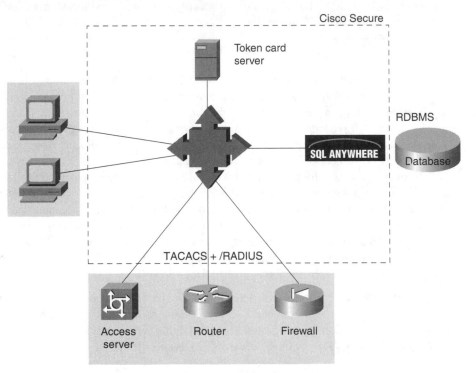

The UNIX version of Cisco Secure comes bundled with Netscape's Fastrack Web Server. The Web Server is the portion of the product that interfaces with the GUI Admin Client.

The Cisco Secure server can operate with an external RDBMS. The open database connectivity (ODBC) interface allows Cisco Secure to operate with several database applications. The server has support for Oracle and Sybase Enterprise database applications. The RDBMS that comes bundled with Cisco Secure is SQLAnywhere and is a nonscalable RDBMS.

Cryptocard Authentication Server is bundled with the product, but it is not necessary for implementation. This server is complete and natively supports the use of a Cryptocard as a token card security measure.

NOTE   Cisco Secure ACS operates successfully with Oracle Version 7.3, Sybase SQL Server Version 11, and Sybase SQLAnywhere by means of ODBC.

The Web-based interface lets you easily manage your Cisco Secure ACS database through the same type of Web browser that you use to view the Internet. Using the Web-based interface, you can log in to the Cisco Secure ACS database, change your password for the Cisco Secure ACS database, and perform Cisco Secure ACS system administrator tasks, such as adding or deleting user and group profiles, and assigning attributes and permissions.

The Cisco Secure ACS stores these profiles for each network user in its RDBMS, which contains AAA information.

The GUI client for Cisco Secure must have Java and JavaScript enabled.

Understanding AAA

Configuring the Cisco Secure server is the first part of a two-part process to develop an operational access-control system. The second involves configuring the network access server so that it functions properly with the Cisco Secure server. These steps are critical and must be completed with extreme precision. Failure to configure the network access server properly may result in being locked out of the router.

The three parts of AAA are defined as follows:

- **Authentication**   Authentication determines the identity of users and whether they should be allowed access to the network. Authentication allows network managers to bar intruders from their networks.

- **Authorization**   Authorization allows network managers to limit the network services available to each user. Authorization also helps to restrict the exposure of the internal network to outside callers. Authorization allows mobile users to connect to the closest local connection and still have the same access privileges, if they were directly connected to their local networks. You can also use authorization to specify which commands a new system administrator can issue on specific network devices.

- **Accounting**   System administrators might need to bill departments or customers for connection time or resources used on the network (for example, bytes transferred). Accounting tracks this kind of information. You can also use the accounting syslog to track suspicious connection attempts into the network and trace malicious activity.

Router Access Modes

Understanding router access modes is the key to understanding the AAA commands and how they work to secure your network access server.

With the exception of the **aaa accounting system** command, all of the AAA commands apply to either character mode or packet mode. Table 15-1 can help you decode the meaning of an

AAA command by associating the AAA command element with the connection mode to the router.

Table 15-1   *Router Access Modes*

Modes	Router ports	AAA command element
Character mode (line mode or interactive login)	tty, vty, aux, con	login, exec, nasi connection, arap, enable, command
Packet mode (interface mode or link protocol session)	async, group-async BRI, PRI, serial, dialer profiles, dialer rotaries	ppp, network, arap

Primary applications for the Cisco Secure ACS include securing dial-up access to a network and securing the management of routers within a network. Both applications have unique authentication, authorization, and accounting requirements. With the Cisco Secure ACS, system administrators can select a variety of authentication methods to provide a set of authorization privileges. These router ports need to be secured by using the Cisco IOS software and a Cisco Secure server.

NOTE   The AppleTalk Remote Access Protocol (ARAP) is an exception. ARAP behaves as both a character mode and packet mode connection. For example, ARAP authentication takes place in character mode, whereas ARAP access-lists apply to packet mode.

Configuring AAA

The first steps in configuring the network access server are to globally enable AAA, specify the Cisco Secure server that will provide AAA services for the network access server, and configure the encryption key that is used to encrypt the data transfer between the network access server and the Cisco Secure server.

Enabling AAA and Identifying the Server

To activate TACACS+, use the **tacacs-server key** command:

```
Router(config)#aaa new-model
Router(config)#tacacs-server host 192.168.229.76 single-connection
Router(config)#tacacs-server key shared1
```

To activate RADIUS, use the **radius-server key** command:

```
Router(config)#aaa new-model
Router(config)#radius-server host 192.168.229.76
Router(config)#radius-server key shared1
```

Table 15-2 explains the elements of the preceding configurations.

Table 15-2   *AAA Activation Commands*

Command	Description
aaa new-model	Enables AAA on the router.
tacacs-server host *ip address* **single-connection**	Indicates both the address of the Cisco Secure server and the desire to use the TCP single-connection feature of Cisco Secure. This feature improves performance by maintaining a single TCP connection for the life of the session between the network access server and the Cisco Secure server, rather than opening and closing TCP connections for each session (the default).
tacacs-server key *key*	Establishes the shared secret encryption key between the network access server and the Cisco Secure server.
radius-server host *ip address*	Specifies a RADIUS AAA server.
radius-server key *key*	Specifies an encryption key to be used with the RADIUS AAA server.

AAA Authentication Commands

The **aaa authentication** command, in global configuration mode, is the basic command to enable the AAA authentication process. Many precise authentication commands derive from **aaa authentication**, such as the following:

- **aaa authentication arap**
- **aaa authentication enable default**
- **aaa authentication local-override**
- **aaa authentication login**
- **aaa authentication nasi**
- **aaa authentication password-prompt**
- **aaa authentication ppp**
- **aaa authentication username-prompt**

The following are some frequent command combinations used for authentication.

aaa authentication login Command

You can configure AAA authentication for users wishing to access the EXEC prompt. The **aaa authentication login** global configuration command is used for AAA authentication in this case (Table 15-3 covers this command):

```
Router(config)#aaa authentication login {default ¦ list-name} method1
➥[...[method4]]
```

Table 15-3   aaa authentication login *Command*

Command	Description
default	Uses the listed authentication methods that follow this argument as the default list of methods when a user logs in.
list-name	Character string used to name the following list of authentication methods that are activated when a user logs in.
method	At least one (and up to four) of the keywords.

NOTE   On the console, login will succeed without any authentication checks if **default** is not set.

To create a default list that is used if no list is assigned to a line, use the **authentication login** command with the **default** argument, followed by the methods you want to use in default situations.

The additional methods of authentication are used only if the previous method returns an error, not if it fails. To ensure that the authentication succeeds, even if all methods return an error, specify **none** as the final method in the command line.

If authentication is not specifically set for a line, the default is to deny access and no authentication is performed. The keywords for the **aaa authentication login** methods are covered in Table 15-4.

Table 15-4   aaa authentication login *Methods*

Keyword	Description
enable	Uses the enable password for authentication.
krb5	Uses Kerberos 5 for authentication.
line	Uses the line password for authentication.
local	Uses the local username database for authentication.
none	Uses no authentication.
radius	Uses RADIUS authentication.
tacacs+	Uses TACACS+ authentication.
krb5-telnet	Uses Kerberos 5 Telnet authentication protocol when using Telnet to connect to the router.

For example, the following creates an AAA authentication list called **MIS-access**. This authentication first tries to contact a TACACS+ server. If no server is found, TACACS+ returns an error and AAA tries to use the enable password. If this attempt also returns an error (because no enable password is configured on the server), the user is allowed access with no authentication:

```
Router(config)#aaa authentication login MIS-access tacacs+ enable none
```

aaa authentication enable default Command

You can configure AAA authentication to determine whether a user can access the privileged command level. The **aaa authentication enable default** global configuration command is used for AAA authentication in this case:

```
Router(config)#aaa authentication enable default method1 [...[method4]]
```

If a default authentication routine is not set for a function, the default is **none** and no authentication is performed.

On the console, the enable password is used if it exists. If no password is set, the process will succeed anyway. The keywords for the **aaa authentication enable default** methods are covered in Table 15-5.

Table 15-5   **aaa authentication enable default** *Methods*

Keyword	Description
if-needed	Does not authenticate if user has already been authenticated on a TTY line.
line	Uses the line password for authentication.
none	Uses no authentication.
radius	Uses RADIUS authentication.
tacacs+	Uses TACACS+ authentication.

NOTE   This command is used with TACACS+, but it cannot be used with TACACS or extended TACACS.

For example, the following creates an authentication list that first tries to contact a TACACS+ server. If no server can be found, AAA tries to use the enable password. If this attempt also returns an error (because no enable password is configured on the server), the user is allowed access with no authentication.

```
Router(config)#aaa authentication enable default tacacs+ enable none
```

aaa authentication ppp Command

You can configure AAA authentication to specify one or more AAA authentication methods for use on serial interfaces running Point-to-Point Protocol (PPP) and TACACS+:

```
Router(config)#aaa authentication ppp {default | list-name} method1
➥[...[method4]]
```

The additional methods of authentication are used only if the previous method returns an error; not if it fails. Specify **none** as the final method in the command line to have authentication succeed, even if all methods return an error. Table 15-6 covers the keywords for the **aaa authentication ppp** methods.

Table 15-6 **aaa authentication ppp** *Methods*

Keyword	Description
enable	Uses the enable password for authentication.
line	Uses the line password for authentication.
none	Uses no authentication.
radius	Uses RADIUS authentication.
tacacs+	Uses TACACS+ authentication.

The following example creates an AAA authentication list called **MIS-access** for serial lines that use PPP. This authentication first tries to contact a TACACS+ server. If this action returns an error, the user is allowed access with no authentication:

```
Router(config)#aaa authentication MIS-access ppp tacacs+ none
```

The aaa authentication local-override Command

You can configure the router with the **aaa authentication local-override** global configuration command, so the user is always prompted for the username. The system then checks to see whether the entered username corresponds to a local account. If the username does not correspond to one in the local database, login proceeds with the methods configured with other AAA commands (such as **aaa authentication login**).

Character Mode (Per-Line) Authentication Example

Example 15-1 shows sample authentication commands. The **aaa authentication login** was previously covered in this section. The **default** and **optional** list names that you create with the **aaa authentication login** command are used with the **authentication login command**.

The **authentication login** command is a per-line command that is used with AAA to specify the name of a list of AAA authentication methods to try at login. If no list is specified, the default list is used (whether or not it is specified in the command line).

Example 15-1 *Comprehensive Authentication Configuration Example*

```
Router(config)#aaa authentication login default tacacs+ local
Router(config)#aaa authentication login Callers tacacs+ local
Router(config)#line con 0
Router(config-line)#login authentication Callers
Router(config-line)#line 1 48
Router(config-line)#login authentication Callers
Router(config-line)#line vty 0 4
Router(config-line)#
```

Note that because **line vty 0 4** does not specify any **login authentication** command, the default method is used.

Table 15-7 explains the preceding commands.

Table 15-7 *Comprehensive Authentication Example—Command Descriptions*

Command	Description
aaa authentication login default tacacs+ local	Default login is TACACS+ server. If no response from the server, use the local username/password database.
aaa authentication login *Callers* **tacacs+ local**	Used for character mode username/password challenge. The list name is *Callers* and the method is TACACS+.
line con 0	Enters console configuration mode.
login authentication *Callers*	Specifies that the AAA list name assigned is *Callers*; the console login requires TACACS+ for authentication.
line 1 48 **login authentication** *Callers*	On lines 1 through 48, the AAA list name assigned is *Callers*; these lines require TACACS+ for authentication.
line vty 0 4	On lines vty 0 through 4, the default list is used. In this case, it specifies the enable password with the **aaa authentication login default tacacs+ local** command.

AAA Authorization Commands

You can configure the access server to restrict the user to perform only certain functions after successful authentication. Use the **aaa authorization** command in global configuration mode to select the function authorized and the method of authorization, as follows:

```
Router(config)#aaa authorization
    {network ¦ exec ¦ commands level ¦ config-commands ¦ reverse-access}
    {if-authenticated ¦ local ¦ none ¦ radius ¦ tacacs+ ¦ krb5-instance}
```

Command	Description
network	All network services, including SLIP, PPP, and ARAP.
exec	EXEC process.
commands *level*	All EXEC commands at the specified level (0-15).
config-commands	For configuration mode commands.
reverse-access	For reverse Telnet connections.
if-authenticated	Allows the user to use the requested function if the user is authenticated.
local	Uses the local database for authorization (with the username password commands).
none	Performs no authorization.
radius	Uses RADIUS for authorization.
tacacs+	Uses TACACS+ for authorization.
krb5-instance	Uses the instance defined by the **kerberos instance map** command.

Character Mode Authorization Example

Example 15-2 shows an example of a character mode authorization.

Example 15-2 *AAA Authentication and Authorization Configuration Example*

```
Router(config)#aaa new-model
Router(config)#aaa authentication login default local
Router(config)#aaa authentication enable default tacacs+ enable
Router(config)#aaa authorization exec tacacs+ local
Router(config)#aaa authorization command 1 tacacs+ local
Router(config)#aaa authorization command 15 tacacs+ local
```

Character mode authorization commands are as described in Table 15-8.

Table 15-8 *AAA Authentication and Authorization Commands*

Command	Description
aaa authentication enable default tacacs+ enable	Determines whether the user can access the enabled command level.
aaa authorization exec tacacs+ local	Determines whether the user is allowed access to an EXEC shell and, if so, what shell attributes are permitted or denied. The method is TACACS+. If there is no response from the TACACS+ server, then the method is local—using the local username and password database.

Table 15-8   *AAA Authentication and Authorization Commands (Continued)*

Command	Description
aaa authorization command *n* **tacacs+ local**	Runs authorization for all commands at the specified privilege level (*n*). You can have every line entered by a user authorized by TACACS+.

Packet Mode Authentication and Authorization Example

Example 15-3 shows an example of packet mode authentication and authorization with AAA.

Example 15-3   *AAA Authentication and Authorization Configuration for PPP Traffic*

```
Router(config)#username admin password password
Router(config)#aaa new-model
Router(config)#aaa authentication ppp default if-needed tacacs+
Router(config)#aaa authentication ppp Callers if-needed tacacs+
Router(config)#aaa authorization network tacacs+ if-authenticated
Router(config)#interface groupasync1
Router(config-if)#ppp authentication chap (default list implied)
Router(config-if)#interface async16
Router(config-if)#ppp authentication chap Callers
Router(config-if)#line 1 16
```

Table 15-9 contains descriptions of the commands used in the preceding configuration.

Table 15-9   *AAA Authentication and Authorization Commands for PPP*

Command	Description
username admin password *password*	Creates or adds to the local database with a username of **admin** and the specified password.
aaa authentication ppp *Callers* **if-needed tacacs+**	Used for packet mode username/password challenge. Uses the list *Callers* only if needed (if not authenticated during login). If not, uses TACACS+.
aaa authorization network tacacs+ if-authenticated	Determines whether the user is permitted to make packet mode connections. If so, specifies what packet mode attributes are permitted or denied. Method is TACACS+. If no response from TACACS+, checks to see whether user has been authenticated.
interface async16 ppp authentication chap *Callers*	On line async16, uses list *Callers* for CHAP authentication.
line 1 16	On lines 1 to 16, uses default list.

AAA Accounting Commands

Use the **aaa accounting** command in global configuration mode for auditing and billing purposes, as follows:

```
Router(config)#aaa accounting
    {command level | connection | exec | network | system}
    {start-stop | stop-only | wait-start} {tacacs+ | radius}
```

Command	Description
command *level*	Audits all commands at the specified privilege level (0–15).
connection	Audits all outbound connections, such as Telnet and rlogin.
exec	Audits the EXEC process.
network	Audits all network service requests, such as SLIP, PPP, and ARAP.
system	Audits all system-level events, such as reload.
start-stop	Sends a start accounting notice at the beginning of a process and a stop accounting notice at the end of a process. The start accounting record is sent in the background. The requested user process begins, regardless of whether the start accounting notice was received by the accounting server.
stop-only	Sends a stop accounting notice at the end of the requested user process.
wait-start	As in start-stop, sends both a start and a stop accounting notice to the accounting server. However, if you use the **wait-start** keyword, the requested user service does not begin until the start accounting notice is acknowledged. A stop accounting notice is also sent.
{**tacacs+** | **radius**}	Uses TACACS+ for accounting or enables RADIUS-style accounting.

AAA Accounting Example

Completing the access control functionality, the Cisco Secure ACS serves as a central repository for accounting information. Each session that is established can be fully accounted for and stored on the server. This accounting information can be used for security audits, capacity planning, or bill-back network usage.

Example 15-4 is an example of an AAA configuration for accounting.

Example 15-4   aaa accounting *Configuration*

```
Router(config)#aaa accounting network start-stop tacacs+
Router(config)#aaa accounting exec start-stop tacacs+
Router(config)#aaa accounting command 15 start-stop tacacs+
Router(config)#aaa accounting connection start-stop tacacs+
Router(config)#aaa accounting system wait-start tacacs+
```

Table 15-10 contains descriptions of the commands used in the preceding configuration.

Table 15-10   **aaa accounting** *Commands*

Command	Description
aaa accounting network start-stop tacacs+	Runs start-stop accounting for all packet mode service requests and uses the TACACS+ server.
aaa accounting exec start-stop tacacs+	Runs start-stop accounting for all character mode service requests and uses the TACACS+ server.
aaa accounting command 15 start-stop tacacs+	Runs start-stop accounting for all commands at privilege level 15.
aaa accounting connection start-stop tacacs+	Runs start-stop accounting for all outbound Telnet and rlogin sessions.
aaa accounting system start-stop tacacs+	Runs start-stop accounting for all system-level events that are not associated with users, such as configuration changes and reloads.

AAA and Virtual Profiles

Virtual profiles provide the next step in dialer profile evolution. As dialer profiles kept the profile specific to a particular user on a single network access server, the AAA server contains multiple virtual profiles for many users.

Dialer profiles can be further scaled through the use of AAA architecture:

* Per-user configurations from a centralized AAA server
* Support for RADIUS/TACACS+ servers
* Use standards-based vendor-specific Attribute/Value pairs
* No proprietary lock-in

Virtual profiles allow profiles to be applied to non-dial-on-demand routing (DDR) enabled interfaces, and allow for centralized configuration management and smaller configurations on routers.

NOTE   With virtual profiles, caller profiles are stored on a centralized AAA server, not on individual access routers.

The steps in virtual profile operation, which are shown in Figure 15-4, are as follows:

1 Check authentication.

2 Authentication is OK.

3 Clone the virtual access interface from the virtual template interface.

4 Request user configuration information.

5 User configuration information is sent and applied to the virtual access interface.

Figure 15-4 *Virtual Profiles Operation*

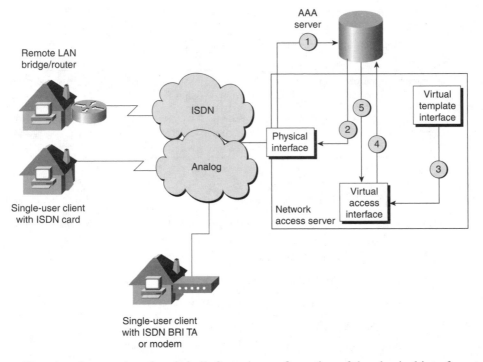

The virtual access interface is built from the configuration of the physical interface, to which are added the virtual template interface configuration and the user-specific configuration of the virtual profile from the AAA server, as shown in Figure 15-5. At this point, the complete virtual access interface is available to handle data to and from the user accessing the network.

Figure 15-5 *Building a Virtual Profile*

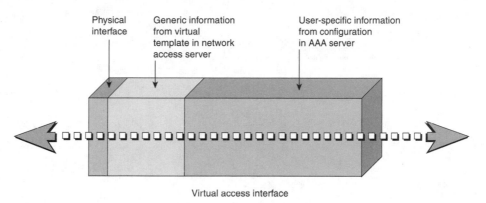

Physical
interface

Generic information
from virtual
template in network
access server

User-specific information
from configuration
in AAA server

Virtual access interface

Summary

In this chapter, you learned the Cisco Secure features and operations, and how to configure a router with AAA commands. You also saw how to configure an AAA server to control access in a remote access network.

Case Study—Using AAA to Scale Access Control in an Expanding Network

Complete the tasks of this case study, and then review the case study solution section that follows to see how you did and see where you might need to review concepts presented in this chapter.

In this case study, you have to configure a Central site access server to locate a TACACS+ server. The Central site access server has to allow PPP connections to authenticate incoming calls using the TACACS+ server. Also, you are asked to create a back door on the console port of the Central site access server to prevent being locked out.

Scenario

You are required to configure the Central site access server. The preconfigured AAA server is located on the same Ethernet segment as the Ethernet interface of your central router, as shown in Figure 15-6.

Figure 15-6 *Case Study Topology*

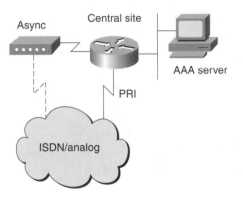

Task 1—Configure the Central Site Access Server for AAA

Log in to the console of your Central site router, and enter global configuration mode.

Enter the appropriate commands to configure the following:

— Enable AAA access control.

— Specify that the router will use the local user database before attempting another form of authentication.

— Specify that the default authentication method for login is TACACS+.

— Specify that a login authentication list called BackDoor is used for authenticating using the enable password.

— Specify that the default authentication method for PPP incoming connections is TACACS+.

— Specify that authorization for exec processes will be from TACACS+.

— Specify that authorization for network processes will be from TACACS+.

— Specify that start-stop accounting will be used on all exec processes.

— Specify that start-stop accounting will be used on all network processes.

Create a local database with the following information on the access server:

— A caller (user) named **student** will offer the password **cisco**.

— An administrator named **admin** will offer the password **TheGreatWhiteNorth**.

WARNING	Do not exit or end the configuration session at this point. If you do, you will be unable to access your Central site router. Complete the remaining configuration steps.

Create a back door on the console to allow you to access the router without using TACACS+.

Configure the address and key of the TACACS+ server to be used for AAA, as follows. The key is Cisco Secure and the ip address of the server is 10.115.0.200.

Task 2—Verify the Console Back Door

Verify that you can log on to the router via its console port and that you can access the privileged mode by using the login name **admin** and **GreatWhiteNorth** as a password.

Task 3—Verify that a Valid Network Login Attempt Will Succeed

From your PC, use Windows Dial-up Networking to place a call to the Central site router. When prompted to provide a username, type `student`. When asked to provide a password, type `cisco`.

Task 4—Verify that an Invalid Network Login Attempt Fails

From the console of the small office site router (home office), ping the Ethernet address of the Central site router. Are you successful at pinging the Central site router's Ethernet interface?

Case Study Solution—Using AAA to Scale Access Control in an Expanding Network

The following is a step-by-step discussion of the case study solution.

Task 1—Configure the Central Site Access Server for AAA

Log in to the console of your Central site router and enter global configuration mode.

Enter the appropriate commands to configure the following:

— Enable AAA access control:

```
Router(config)#aaa new-model
```

— Specify that the router will use the local user database before attempting another form of authentication:

```
Router(config)#aaa authentication local-override
```

— Specify that the default authentication method for login is TACACS+:

```
Router(config)#aaa authentication login default tacacs+
```

— Specify that a login authentication list called BackDoor is used for authenticating by using the **enable** password:

```
Router(config)#aaa authentication login BackDoor enable
```

— Specify that the default authentication method for PPP incoming connections is TACACS+:

```
Router(config)#aaa authentication ppp default tacacs+
```

— Specify that authorization for exec processes will be from TACACS+:

```
Router(config)#aaa authorization exec tacacs+
```

— Specify that authorization for network processes will be from TACACS+:

```
Router(config)#aaa authorization network tacacs+
```

— Specify that start-stop accounting will be used on all exec processes:

```
Router(config)#aaa accounting exec start-stop tacacs+
```

— Specify that start-stop accounting will be used on all network processes:

```
Router(config)#aaa accounting network start-stop tacacs+
```

Create a local database with the following information on the access server:

— A caller (user) named student who will offer the password **cisco**:

```
CentralA(config)#username student password cisco
```

— An administrator named admin who will offer the password **TheGreatWhiteNorth**:

```
CentralA(config)#username admin password TheGreatWhiteNorth
```

WARNING   Do not exit or end the configuration session at this point. If you do, you will be unable to access your Central site router. Complete the remaining configuration steps.

Create a back door on the console to allow you to access the router without using TACACS+:

```
Router(config)#line console 0
Router(config-line)#login authentication BackDoor
```

Configure the address and key of the TACACS+ server to be used for AAA, as follows. The key is Cisco Secure and the ip address of the server is 10.115.0.200:

```
Router(config)#tacacs-server host 10.115.0.200
Router(config)#tacacs-server key ciscosecure
```

Task 2—Verify the Console Back Door

Verify that you can log on the router via its console port and that you can access the privileged mode by using the login name **admin** and **TheGreatWhiteNorth** as a password:

Step 1   Connect to the console of the Central site router.

Step 2   Press Return. You should be prompted for a password.

Step 3   Enter the enable secret password. If your backdoor is configured properly, you will be granted access.

Step 4   If you were able to gain access to the console of your Central site router, proceed to Task 3. If you were not successful, troubleshoot your configuration.

Task 3—Verify that a Valid Network Login Attempt will Succeed

From your PC, use Windows Dial-up Networking to place a call to the Central Cisco site router. In this case, you are using PPP to communicate and you will be prompted for authentication. When prompted to provide a username, type student. When asked to provide a password, type cisco:

Step 1   From your PC, use Windows Dial-up Networking to place a call to the Central site router.

Step 2   Use the username student and the password cisco for access.

Step 3   If you were able to log in, proceed to Task 4. If not, troubleshoot your configuration.

Task 4— Verify that an Invalid Network Login Attempt Fails

From the console of the small office site router (home office), ping the Ethernet address of the Central site router. Are you successful at pinging the Central site router's Ethernet interface?

This network login attempt should fail.

When the SOHO router, named HomeA, connects to CentralA, it is requested to authenticate itself. Cisco 766 routers pass their hostname as a username during the PPP authentication negotiation; in this case, it will pass HomeA.

CentralA has been configured to pass on to the AAA incoming PPP session for authentication. The Cisco Secure server is configured for username **student** and **admin**, not for **HomeA**.

Case Study Conclusion

In this case study, you were able to create and use a back door for the Central site console, use a valid network login for access to the Central site router, and have an invalid network login attempt fail.

Review Questions

Answer the following questions and then refer to Appendix H, "Answers to Review Questions," for answers and explanations.

1 What is authentication?

2 What is authorization?

3 What is accounting in regard to a dial-up networking environment?

Appendixes

Summary of BCRAN Commands

The following is a list of some of the commands that you may find in the BCRAN textbook, organized into various categories. Note that only the command is listed here; parameters are not included. For details on the parameters and the way that the command works, please see the Command Reference on the Cisco Documentation CD or the Cisco Web site.

General Commands

Command	Description
disconnect	Disconnects the specified session or all sessions.
Ctrl-Shift-6	Suspends a session.
modemcap entry	Displays modemcap values in a truncated manner.
show modemcap	Displays the modems in the modemcap database.
debug confmodem	Displays the modem-configuration process.
debug ppp negotiation	Displays PPP option negotiation.
debug ppp authentication	Displays PPP authentication negotiation.
debug dialer	Indicates whether the multilink is up after authentication.
debug chat	Checks to see if there is a chat-script running.
debug modem	Displays modem line activity on an access server.
debug isdn q931	Displays information about call setup and teardown of ISDN network connections (Layer 3) between the local router (user side) and the network.
debug isdn q921	Displays data link layer (Layer 2) access procedures that are taking place at the access router on the D channel (LAPD) of its ISDN interface.
debug ppp multilink	Displays packet sequence numbers.

continues

Command	Description
debug isdn events	Displays ISDN events occurring on the user side (on the router) of the ISDN interface.
debug ip nat	Displays a line of output for each packet that gets translated.
show ppp multilink	Displays bundle information on a rotary group in the packet multiplexing section, including the number of members in a bundle and the bundle to which a link belongs.
show dialer	Displays general diagnostic information for interfaces configured for DDR.
show interface	Displays statistics for an interface.
show isdn	Displays information about memory, Layer 2 and Layer 3 timers, and the status of bearer channels.
show queueing custom	Displays custom queuing information.
show queueing priority	Displays priority queuing information.
show queueing fair	Displays weighted fair queuing information.
show ip nat translations	Displays active NAT translations.
show ip nat statistics	Displays NAT statistics.
clear ip nat translation *	Clears all translated entries—use the * as a wildcard to clear all entries.

General Configuration Commands

Command	Description
line	Configures a console port line, auxiliary port line, or virtual terminal lines.
modemcap edit	Configures an attribute of a modem.
modemcap entry	To store and compress information about the capability of a specified modem, use the **modemcap entry** command. Use the no form of this command to disable the feature.
chat-script	Creates a script to place a call over a modem.
username *username* **password** *password*	Specifies the password for the caller.

Command	Description
map-class dialer	Defines a class of shared configuration parameters associated with the **dialer map** command.
interface *type port*	Configures an interface type and enters interface configuration mode.
access-list	Configures an access-list mechanism for filtering packets.
isdn switch-type	Specifies the central office switch type at the global level.
controller	Enters the T1/E1 configuration mode.
priority-list	Creates an output priority queuing list.
queue-list	Creates an output custom queuing list.
custom-queue-list	Assigns a custom queue list to an interface.
ip nat inside source static	Defines the addresses to use for static address translations for inside local addresses.
ip nat pool	Defines an IP NAT pool.

General Interface Configuration Commands

Command	Description
async dynamic address	Allows the remote dial-in client to enter its own IP address, if it has one.
async mode dedicated	Ensures that the dial-in user must run either SLIP or PPP.
async mode interactive	Allows the dial-in user to run SLIP, PPP, or EXEC on the specified line.
backup delay	Defines the period of time to wait before enabling the backup link when the primary link goes down.
backup interface	On the primary interface, specifies the interface or dialer interface to use for backup.
backup load	Sets the traffic load threshold for dial backup service.
compress	Configures compression on an interface.
dialer callback-secure	Configures an interface to make return calls when callback is successfully negotiated.

continues

Command	Description
dialer fast-idle	Specifies the time that a line can remain idle before the current call is disconnected, to allow another call that is waiting to use the line.
dialer hold-queue	Specifies the time that the line can remain idle before it is disconnected.
dialer idle-timeout	Specifies the idle time (in seconds) before the line is disconnected.
dialer isdn	Specifies the bit rate used on the B channel associated with a specified map class, and specifies whether to set up semipermanent connections for this map class.
dialer load-threshold	Specifies the interface load at which the dialer initiates another call to the destination.
dialer map	Configures a serial or ISDN interface to call one or multiple sites, or to receive calls from multiple sites.
dialer pool	A dialer interface command that specifies the pool of physical interfaces available to reach the destination subnetwork.
dialer pool-member	An interface configuration command that associates and places a physical interface in a specifically numbered pool.
dialer remote-name	Specifies the remote router name, which is passed during authentication.
dialer rotary-group	Specifies the phone number to dial when placing a call from an interface to a specific destination.
dialer string	Specifies the string (telephone number) to be called for interfaces calling a single site.
dialer wait-for-carrier-time	Specifies how long (in seconds) to wait for a carrier tone.
dialer-group	Controls access by configuring an interface to belong to a specific dialing group.
dialer-list	Defines a DDR dialer list to control dialing by protocol, or by a combination of protocol and access-list.
encapsulation	Specifies the encapsulation type to be used.
fair-queue	Enables fair queuing on an interface.
ip address	Assigns an IP address to a network interface.
ip nat	Enables NAT on interface.

Command	Description
ip unnumbered	Conserves network addresses. Unnumbered interfaces do not have an address. Network resources are conserved because fewer network numbers are used and routing tables are smaller. That interface must be up and running for IP to be working on an unnumbered interface.
isdn answer1, isdn answer2	Ensures that the router verifies a called-party number or subaddress number in the incoming setup messages for ISDN BRI calls, if the number is delivered by the switch.
isdn caller	Configures ISDN caller ID screening.
isdn spid1, isdn spid2	Defines at the router the SPID number that has been assigned by the service profile for bearer channel.
isdn switch-type	Specifies the Central office switch type on the ISDN interface.
peer default ip	Assigns a predefined default IP address to the remote client node that dials in to the corresponding asynchronous line.
ppp authentication	Enables CHAP, PPP, or both authentication methods on an interface.
ppp callback	Enables a PPP client to dial into an asynchronous interface and request a callback.
ppp multilink	Enables PPP multilink on an interface.
priority-group	Links a priority list to an interface.
isdn incoming-voice modem	Allows incoming analog calls to be switched to internal modems installed on a digital network module.

General IP Commands

Command	Description
ip route	Establishes static routes.
ip default-network	Selects a network as a candidate route for computing the gateway of last resort.

IP Interface Configuration Command

Command	Description
ip tcp header-compression passive	Specifies that tcp header compression is not required, but if the router receives compressed headers from a destination, use header compression for that destination.

General AAA Commands

Command	Description
aaa new-model	Enables AAA on the router.
radius-server host	Specifies a RADIUS AAA server.
radius-server key	Specifies an encryption key to be used with the RADIUS AAA server.
tacacs-server host	Indicates the address of the CiscoSecure server.
tacacs-server key	Establishes the shared secret encryption key between the network access server and the CiscoSecure server.
aaa authentication enable default	Enables AAA authentication to determine whether a user can access the privileged command level.
aaa authentication local-override	Configures the Cisco IOS software to check the local user database for authentication before attempting another form of authentication.
aaa authentication login	Sets AAA authentication at login.
aaa authentication ppp	Specifies one or more AAA authentication methods for use on serial interfaces running PPP.
aaa authorization	Sets parameters that restrict a user's network access.
aaa authorization config-commands	Disables AAA configuration command authorization in the EXEC model.
aaa new-model	Enables the AAA access control model.
login authentication	Enables AAA authentication for logins.

General Line Configuration Commands

Command	Description
login	Sets a login password on this line. Without the password, no connection is allowed.
password	Sets the password to be used when logging in to this line.
flowcontrol hardware	Uses RTS/CTS for flow control.
speed	Sets the maximum speed (in bits per second) between the modem and the access server. The **speed** command sets both the transmit and receive speeds.
transport input all	Allows all protocols to be passed to the access server through this line.
stopbits	Sets the number of stop bits transmitted per byte.
modem inout	Uses the modem for both incoming and outgoing calls, or modem dial-in for incoming calls only (modem dial-in is the default).
modem dialin	Enables a modem attached to the router to accept incoming calls only.
exec	Allows the EXEC process on this line.
modem autoconfigure discovery	Configures a line to discover what kind of modem is connected to the router, and to configure that modem automatically.
modem autoconfigure type	Directs a line to attempt to configure the attached modem using the entry for **modem-name**.
autoselect	Permits the access server to allow an appropriate process to start automatically when a starting character is received on the line.
callback forced-wait	Allows an additional wait (in seconds) before the callback chat-script is applied to the outgoing target line.
script callback	Specifies a chat-script to issue AT commands to the modem during a callback attempt made to the target async line.

Map-Class Command

Command	Description
dialer callback-server username	To enable an interface to make return calls when callback is successfully negotiated, use the **dialer callback-server** interface configuration command. This command is typed at the map-class command mode.

T1/E1 Controller Commands

Command	Description
framing	Configures the frame type used by the PRI service provider.
lincode	Identifies the physical-layer signaling method to satisfy the density requirement on the provider's digital facility.
clock source	Configures the T1 clock source for the Cisco 7000 family, Cisco 3600, and Cisco 4000 series modules.
pri-group timeslots	Configures the specified interface for PRI operation and the number of fixed timeslots that are allocated on the provider's digital facility.

General WAN Commands

Command	Description
debug frame-relay lmi	Starts the console display of LMI-related events on the router.
debug ppp authentication	Starts the console display of the PPP authentication–related events on the router.
show frame-relay lmi	Displays the LMI traffic statistics.
show frame-relay map	Displays the route maps (between network layer addresses and DLCIs), both static and dynamic.
show frame-relay pvc	Displays the status of each configured PVC, as well as traffic statistics.

Command	Description
show x25 map	Displays the route maps (between network layer addresses and X.121 addresses), both static and dynamic.
show x25 vc	Displays the status of active SVCs and PVCs.

WAN Configuration Commands

Command	Description
map-class frame-relay	Specifies a map class to be defined.
frame-relay traffic-rate	Defines the average and peak rates if the data is being sent faster than the speed at which the destination is receiving.
frame-relay adaptive-shaping becn	Specifies that the router dynamically fluctuates at the rate at which it sends packets, depending on the BECNs it receives.
frame-relay custom-queue-list	Assigns a custom queue to virtual circuits associated with the map class.
frame-relay priority-group	Assigns a priority queue to virtual circuits associated with the map class.
frame-relay traffic-shaping	Enables Frame Relay traffic shaping on an interface.
frame-relay class	Maps a map class to all virtual circuits on the interface.
frame-relay payload-compress	Enables STAC compression on a specified Frame Relay point-to-point interface or subinterface.
encapsulation	Defines the data-link encapsulation for an interface (PPP, HLDC, X25, DTE default—can use DCE and Frame Relay).
frame-relay interface-dlci	Assigns a DLCI to the subinterface (only used on subinterfaces, which are defined by the **interface** *type.subinterface number* {**point-to-point|multipoint**} command).
frame-relay lmi-type	Defines the LMI (Local Management Interface) format (to match the Frame Relay switch).
frame-relay map	Defines how an interface reaches a destination; maps protocol addresses to DLCI to the destination; and defines options, including broadcast.
x25 address	Defines the X.25 (X.121) address of the interface.

continues

Command	Description
x25 hic	Defines the highest incoming SVC circuit number.
x25 hoc	Defines the highest outgoing SVC circuit number.
x25 htc	Defines the highest two-way SVC circuit number.
x25 ips	Defines the default maximum incoming packet size.
x25 lic	Defines the lowest incoming SVC circuit number.
x25 loc	Defines the lowest outgoing SVC circuit number.
x25 ltc	Defines the lowest two-way SVC circuit number.
x25 map	Defines how an interface reaches a destination; maps protocol addresses to X.25 addresses of the destination; and defines options, including broadcast.
x25 modulo	Defines the packet-level window counter limit.
x25 ops	Defines the default maximum outgoing packet size.
x25 pvc	Defines the PVC circuit numbers.
x25 route	Defines a static route in the X.25 routing table for X.25 switching.
x25 win	Defines the default incoming window size.
x25 wout	Defines the default outgoing window size.

Cisco 700 IOS System Commands

Command	Description
cd	Changes to another profile.
set 1 dir	This is the directory number to which you have subscribed.
set 1 spid	This is the number identifying the service to which you have subscribed for channel B1.
set 2 dir	This is the directory number to which you have subscribed.
set 2 spid	This is the number identifying the service to which you have subscribed for channel B2.
set authentication incoming	Sets the authentication that the Cisco 700 will agree to receive.

Command	Description
set authentication outgoing	Sets the authentication that the Cisco 700 series will send.
set dhcp address	Specifies the starting address of the pool and the number of addresses in the pool.
set dhcp dns	Specifies the DNS address for DHCP clients.
set dhcp domain	Specifies the NT domain of the DHCP server.
set dhcp gateway	Specifies the 700 as the default gateway.
set dhcp netmask	Specifies the subnet mask that the DHCP clients will use.
set dhcp relay	Configures a DHCP relay agent.
set dhcp server	Enables DHCP server functionality on the Cisco 700.
set dhcp wins	Specifies the WINS server for DHCP clients.
set encapsulation	Sets the encapsulation for the user profile default template to PPP.
set ppp multilink	Turns MP on for connection to the Cisco IOS router.
set ppp secret client	Sets the client CHAP secret password.
set switch switch-type	Defines the service provider switch-type.
set system	Defines the name of the router.
set user	Defines a new user.
show dhcp config	Displays the DHCP configuration.
show ip configuration all	Displays the IP configuration for all profiles.
show ip route all	Shows the destination network address for a given profile.
show negotiation	Displays negotiated parameters.
show status	Displays the status line for an ISDN connection.

Cisco 700 IOS Profile Commands

Command	Description
set active	Makes a profile active.
set bridging	Sets the bridging state.
set compression	Sets the compression type.

continues

Command	Description
set ip address	Sets the IP address of the profile.
set ip framing none	Sets IP frames to IPCP for this profile (PPP).
set ip netmask	Sets the subnet mask.
set ip rip update	Specifies when IP RIP packets will be sent.
set ip rip update	Sets the RIP updates for this profile.
set ip rip version	Sets the version of RIP for this user.
set ip route	Sets a static router.
set ip routing	Turns on IP routing.
set ipx framing none	Sets IPX frames to IPXCP for this profile (PPP).
set ipx network	Sets the IPX network number for this profile.
set ipx rip update	Specifies when IPX RIP packets will be sent.
set ipx routing	Enables IPX routing on the profile.
set number	Sets the phone number to be called with this profile.
set number	Sets the phone number dialed.
set ppp secret host	Sets the password expected by 700 in response from the remote.

Summary of ICRC Commands

The following is a list of some of the commands you may find in the ICRC course material, organized in various categories. Note that only the command is listed here; parameters are not included. For details on the parameters and how the command works, please see the Command Reference on the Cisco Documentation CD or on the Cisco Web site. The source for this information is "ICRC Annexes" from the GeoTrain Corporation (Cisco Systems Certified Training Partner—Distinguished).

General Commands

Command	Meaning
?	Provides help.
\<Ctrl> \<A>	Moves to the beginning of the command line.
\<Ctrl> \<B>	Moves backward one character.
\<Ctrl> \<C>	Aborts from setup mode.
\<Ctrl> \<E>	Moves to the end of the command line.
\<Ctrl> \<F>	Moves forward one character.
\<Ctrl> \<N> or \<down arrow>	Recalls last (previous) command.
\<Ctrl> \<P> or \<up arrow>	Recalls more recent command.
\<Ctrl> \<Shift> \<6> \<X>	This is the escape sequence used to suspend a session.
\<Ctrl> \<Z>	Exits from configuration mode back to privileged EXEC mode.
\<Esc> \<B>	Moves to the beginning of the previous word.
\<Esc> \<F>	Moves forward one word.
\<Tab>	Completes a keyword.
clear counters	Resets the show interface counters to zero.
clock set	Sets the router's clock.
configure terminal	Enters configuration mode.
copy flash tftp	Copies a file from Flash memory to a TFTP server.
copy running-config startup-config	Copies configuration from RAM to NVRAM (overwrites).
copy running-config tftp	Copies configuration from RAM to TFTP server (overwrites).

continues

Command	Meaning
copy startup-config running-config	Executes configuration from NVRAM into RAM (executes line-by-line; does not overwrite).
copy tftp flash	Copies a file from a TFTP server to Flash memory.
copy tftp running-config	Copies configuration from TFTP server to NVRAM (overwrites).
debug	Starts the console display of the events on the router.
disable	Exits privileged EXEC mode.
disconnect	Disconnects a Telnet session.
enable	Enters privileged mode.
erase startup-config	Erases the configuration in NVRAM.
exit	Exits from the router.
logging on	Sends debug output to Syslog server.
logout	Exits from the router.
ping	Sends an echo and expects an echo reply (**extend ping** also allows ping for protocols other than IP).
setup	Enters prompted dialog to establish an initial configuration.
show access-lists	Displays the contents of all access-lists configured.
show cdp entry	Displays a single-cached CDP entry.
show cdp interface	Displays values of CDP timers and CDP interface status.
show cdp neighbors	Displays a summary of CDP information received from neighbors.
show cdp neighbors detail	Displays detailed CDP information received from neighbors.
show controller	Displays the Layer 1 information about an interface (including cable type and DCE/DTE status for serial interfaces).
show flash	Displays information about flash memory.
show history	Displays the list of recorded command lines during the current terminal session.
show interface	Displays information about interfaces or an interface, including the state of the interface.
show logging	Displays what logging is configured.
show memory	Displays statistics about a router's memory.
show processes	Displays information about the active processes.
show protocols	Displays the status of any Layer 3 protocols.

Command	Meaning
show running-config	Displays the active configuration (in RAM).
show startup-config	Displays the backup configuration (in NVRAM).
show version	Displays the configuration of the system hardware, software version, and configuration register value.
telnet	Connects to a host.
terminal history size	Changes the number of command lines that the system will record during the current terminal session.
terminal monitor	Forwards debug and error output to your Telnet session (use **terminal no monitor** to turn this off).
trace	Traces the route that packets are taking through the network.
undebug	Turns off debugging (also use **no debug**).

General Configuration Commands

Command	Meaning
banner	Specifies a banner for the router (can be motd, idle, or exec banner).
boot system	Specifies the source of IOS images.
cdp holdtime	Sets the amount of time that a receiving device should hold the CDP packets being sent from the router before being discarded.
cdp run	Enables CDP on the router (CDP is enabled by default; use **no cdp run** to disable it).
cdp timer	Sets the time interval at which the router sends CDP updates.
config-register	Sets the 16-bit configuration register.
enable password	Specifies the enable password for the router.
enable secret	Specifies the enable secret password for the router.
exec-timeout	Sets the time that the EXEC command interpreter will wait for input from the terminal before exiting the session (use **exec-timeout 0 0** to extend the timeout indefinitely).
hostname	Specifies the router's name.
interface	Enters interface configuration mode (ethernet, serial, loopback, and so on). Also used to enter subinterface configuration mode. For virtual interfaces (loopback, tunnel, and so on) for a specific interface, it creates that interface the first time that this command is used.

continues

Command	Meaning
line	Enters line configuration mode (console, aux, and vty).
login	Enables password-checking on a line.
password	Specifies the password for a line.
service password-encryption	Specifies that any passwords that are set subsequent to this command will be encrypted. Use **no service password-encryption** after all such passwords are set.

General Interface Configuration Commands

Command	Meaning
bandwidth	Sets bandwidth of the interface (used by some routing protocols).
cdp enable	Enables CDP on an interface (CDP is enabled by default; use **no cdp enable** to disable it).
clock rate	Sets clockrate in bps (used if interface is DCE); note that the **clockrate** command also works.
description	Adds a text description to the interface.
early-token release	For Token Ring, allows more than one token on the ring at one time.
interface	Enters interface configuration mode (or subinterface mode, if it is already in interface mode).
media-type 10baset	On Cisco routers with more than one connector for an Ethernet interface, selects the media-type connector for the Ethernet interface.
ring-speed	For Token Ring, sets the ring speed (4 or 16 Mbps).
shutdown	Administratively shuts down an interface (use **no shutdown** to bring the interface up).

General IP Commands

Command	Meaning
debug ip igrp	Starts the console display of the IP IGRP-related transactions or events on the router.
debug ip rip	Starts the console display of the IP RIP-related events on the router.

Command	Meaning
show hosts	Displays the cached list of host names and addresses (both static and obtained from a DNS server).
show ip access-list	Displays the IP access-lists configured.
show ip interface	Displays IP-specific information about an interface, including whether access-lists are applied.
show ip protocol	Displays the IP routing protocols that are running.
show ip route	Displays the IP routing table.
show ip traffic	Displays statistics on IP traffic.
term ip netmask-format	Specifies the format of network masks for the current session (bit count, decimal, or hexadecimal).

IP Configuration Commands

Command	Meaning
access-list	Defines access-lists: IP standard = numbers 1–99; IP extended = numbers 100–199.
ip access-group	Activates an access-list on an interface.
ip access-list	Defines a named access-list in IOS 11.2 or later.
ip address	Assigns an ip address and subnet mask to an interface.
ip default-network	Defines a default route.
ip domain-lookup	Turns on name service (DNS) lookups (use **no ip domain-lookup** to turn off DNS lookups).
ip helper-address	Defines an address to which the router will forward certain broadcasts (this is usually a server address).
ip host	Defines a static host name to IP address mapping.
ip name-server	Defines one or more hosts that supply host name information (DNS).
ip netmask-format	Specifies the format of IP network masks for the current line (bit count, decimal, or hexadecimal).
ip route	Defines a static route to an IP destination.
ip routing	Enables IP routing on the router.
ip unnumbered	Enables IP processing on a serial interface without assigning an explicit IP address to the interface.

continues

Command	Meaning
network	Defines the networks that the routing protocol runs on. Starts up the routing protocol on all interfaces that are in that network and allows the router to advertise that network.
router igrp	Defines IGRP as an IP routing protocol and enters configuration mode for that protocol.
router rip	Defines RIP as an IP routing protocol and enters configuration mode for that protocol.

General IPX Commands

Command	Meaning
debug ipx routing	Starts the console display of the IPX routing-related events on the router.
debug ipx sap	Starts the console display of the IPX SAP-related events on the router.
show ipx access-list	Displays the IPX access-lists configured.
show ipx interface	Displays IPX-specific information about an interface, including whether access-lists are applied.
show ipx route	Displays the IPX routing table.
show ipx servers	Displays the IPX server list.
show ipx traffic	Displays statistics on IPX traffic.

IPX Configuration Commands

Command	Meaning
access-list	Defines access-lists: IPX standard = numbers 800–899; IPX extended = numbers 900–999; IPX SAP = numbers 1000–1099.
ipx access-group	Activates an IPX standard or extended access-list on an interface.
ipx delay	Defines the delay tick metric to associate with an interface.
ipx encapsulation	Assigns an IPX encapsulation type to an interface or subinterface.
ipx input-sap-filter	Activates an IPX SAP access-list input on an interface.
ipx maximum-paths	Enables round-robin load sharing over multiple equal metric paths.

Command	Meaning
ipx network	Assigns IPX network number (primary or secondary) to an interface.
ipx output-sap-filter	Activates an IPX SAP access-list output on an interface.
ipx route	Defines a static route to an IPX destination.
ipx router rip	Defines RIP as the IPX routing protocol and enters the configuration mode for that protocol.
ipx router-sap-filter	Activates an input IPX SAP filter, identifying from which router SAP advertisements can be received.
ipx routing	Enables IPX routing on the router.
network	Defines the networks that the routing protocol will run on. Starts up the routing protocol on all interfaces that are in that network and allows the router to advertise that network.

General AppleTalk Commands

Command	Meaning
debug appletalk routing	Starts the console display of the AppleTalk routing-related events on the router.
show appletalk access-list	Displays the AppleTalk access-lists configured.
show appletalk globals	Displays information and settings about the router's global AppleTalk configuration parameters.
show appletalk interface	Displays AppleTalk-specific information about an interface, including whether access-lists are applied.
show appletalk route	Displays the AppleTalk routing table.
show appletalk traffic	Displays statistics on AppleTalk traffic.
show appletalk zone	Displays the AppleTalk zone information table.

AppleTalk Configuration Commands

Command	Meaning
access-list	Defines access-lists: AppleTalk = numbers 600–699.
appletalk access-group	Activates an AppleTalk access-list on an interface.
appletalk cable-range	Assigns AppleTalk cable-range to an interface (for phase 2 or extended addressing).

continues

Command	Meaning
appletalk discovery	Enables an interface to learn cable range and zone name (or use **appletalk cable-range 0-0**).
appletalk maximum-paths	Enables round-robin load sharing over multiple equal metric paths.
appletalk network	Assigns AppleTalk network number to an interface (for phase 1, or non-extended addressing).
appletalk protocol	Selects an AppleTalk routing protocol (RTMP, EIGRP, AURP).
appletalk route	Defines a static route to an AppleTalk destination.
appletalk routing	Enables AppleTalk routing on the router.
appletalk zip-reply-filter	Activates an AppleTalk access-list for zone-filtering input on an interface.
appletalk zone	Assigns an AppleTalk zone name to an interface.

General WAN Commands

Command	Meaning
debug frame-relay lmi	Starts the console display of LMI-related events on the router.
debug ppp authentication	Starts the console display of the PPP authentication–related events on the router.
show frame-relay lmi	Displays the LMI traffic statistics.
show frame-relay map	Displays the route maps (between network layer addresses and DLCIs), both static and dynamic.
show frame-relay pvc	Displays the status of each configured PVC, as well as traffic statistics.
show x25 map	Displays the route maps (between network layer addresses and X.121 addresses), both static and dynamic.
show x25 vc	Displays the status of active SVCs and PVCs.

WAN Configuration Commands

Command	Meaning
bandwidth	Defines the bandwidth (in kilobits per second) of the interface (used in routing protocol calculations).

Command	Meaning
encapsulation	Defines the data-link encapsulation for an interface (PPP, HLDC, X25, DTE—default—can use DCE, Frame Relay).
frame-relay interface-dlci	Assigns a DLCI to the subinterface (only used on subinterfaces, which are defined by the **interface** *type subinterface number* {**point-to-point**|**multipoint**} command).
frame-relay inverse-arp	Enables inverse arp on an interface (only needed if it was disabled at some point; the default is enabled).
frame-relay intf-type	Defines the network function performed by the router when it is functioning as a Frame Relay switch (dte, dce, or nni).
frame-relay lmi-type	Defines the LMI (Local Management Interface) format (to match the Frame Relay switch).
frame-relay local-dlci	Defines the local DLCI number for an interface; only needed if an LMI-type is not used in your network or you are doing back-to-back testing between routers.
frame-relay map	Defines the way an interface will reach a destination; maps protocol addresses to DLCI to the destination; defines options, including broadcast.
frame-relay route	Defines a static route in the Frame Relay routing table for Frame Relay switching.
frame-relay switching	Enables the router to perform Frame Relay switching.
ip bandwidth-percent eigrp	Defines the percentage of bandwidth that EIGRP can use for routing traffic.
keepalive	Defines the interval (in seconds) at which keepalives are sent on this interface to the Frame Relay switch.
ppp authentication chap	Sets password authentication using CHAP on an interface.
ppp authentication pap	Sets password authentication using PAP on an interface.
ppp chap hostname	Defines the hostname to be used for CHAP authentication; used so that multiple routers that are in a pool can appear as one hostname.
ppp chap password	Defines a password to be used to authenticate a peer whose name is not found in this router's username list.
ppp multilink	Enables multilink PPP.
ppp pap sent-username	Enables an interface to send PAP information when calling.
username	Defines host name and password for verification (used in PAP or CHAP).
x25 address	Defines the X.25 (X.121) address of the interface.

continues

Command	Meaning
x25 hic	Defines highest incoming SVC circuit number.
x25 hoc	Defines highest outgoing SVC circuit number.
x25 htc	Defines highest two-way SVC circuit number.
x25 ips	Defines default maximum incoming packet size.
x25 lic	Defines lowest incoming SVC circuit number.
x25 loc	Defines lowest outgoing SVC circuit number.
x25 ltc	Defines lowest two-way SVC circuit number.
x25 map	Defines how an interface will reach a destination; maps protocol addresses to X.25 address of the destination; defines options, including broadcast.
x25 modulo	Defines packet-level window counter limit.
x25 ops	Defines default maximum outgoing packet size.
x25 pvc	Defines PVC circuit numbers.
x25 route	Defines a static route in the X.25 routing table for X.25 switching.
x25 win	Defines default incoming window size.
x25 wout	Defines default outgoing window size.

General DECnet Commands

Command	Meaning
debug decnet routing	Starts the console display of the DECnet routing-related events on the router.
show decnet interface	Displays DECnet-specific information about an interface, including whether access-lists are applied.
show decnet route	Displays the DECnet routing table.
show decnet traffic	Displays statistics on DECnet traffic.

DECnet Configuration Commands

Command	Meaning
access-list	Defines access-lists: DECnet = numbers 300–399.
decnet access-group	Activates an access-list on an interface.
decnet cost	Enables DECnet on the interface and defines the outgoing cost of the interface.
decnet node-type	Establishes the routing characteristics of this router, such as Level 1 or Level 2 responsibility.
decnet routing	Enables DECnet rouging on the router.

General Vines Commands

Command	Meaning
debug vines routing	Starts the console display of the Vines routing-related events on the router.
show vines interface	Display Vines-specific information about an interface, including whether access-lists are applied.
show vines neighbor	Displays the contents of the neighbor table, including host names, MAC addresses, encapsulation types, and interface port information.
show vines route	Displays the Vines routing table.

Vines Configuration Commands

Command	Meaning
vines access-group	Activates an access-list on an interface.
vines access-list	Defines access-lists: numbers 1–300.
vines arp-enable	Allows the router to assign client addresses.
vines metric	Enables Vines routing on the interface and defines the metric to be used for the interface.
vines routing	Enables Vines routing on the router.
vines serverless	Allows the propagation of certain broadcast packets by the router to the nearest server.

Open Systems Interconnection (OSI) Reference Model

The source for this appendix is www.cisco.com.

The Open Systems Interconnection (OSI) reference model describes how information from a software application in one computer moves through a network medium to a software application in another computer. The OSI reference model is a conceptual model that is composed of seven layers, each specifying particular network functions. The model was developed by the International Organization for Standardization (ISO) in 1984, and it is now considered to be the primary architectural model for intercomputer communications. The OSI model divides the tasks involved with moving information between networked computers into seven smaller, more manageable task groups. A task or group of tasks is then assigned to each of the seven OSI layers. Each layer is reasonably self-contained, so that the tasks assigned to each layer can be implemented independently. This enables the solutions offered by one layer to be updated without adversely affecting the other layers. The following list details the seven layers of the Open System Interconnection (OSI) reference model:

- **Layer 7**—Application layer
- **Layer 6**—Presentation layer
- **Layer 5**—Session layer
- **Layer 4**—Transport layer
- **Layer 3**—Network layer
- **Layer 2**—Data Link layer
- **Layer 1**—Physical layer

Figure C-1 illustrates the seven-layer OSI reference model.

Figure C-1   *The OSI Reference Model Contains Seven Independent Layers*

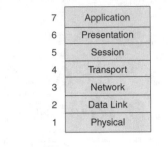

Characteristics of the OSI Layers

The seven layers of the OSI reference model can be divided into two categories: **upper layers** and **lower layers**.

The **upper layers** of the OSI model deal with application issues and generally are implemented only in software. The highest layer, Application, is closest to the end user. Both users and application-layer processes interact with software applications that contain a communications component. The term **upper layer** is sometimes used to refer to any layer above another layer in the OSI model.

The **lower layers** of the OSI model handle data transport issues. The Physical layer and Data Link layer are implemented in hardware and software. The other lower layers generally are implemented only in software. The lowest layer, the Physical layer, is closest to the physical network medium (the network cabling, for example), and it is responsible for actually placing information on the medium.

Figure C-2 illustrates the division between the upper and lower OSI layers.

Figure C-2   *Two Sets of Layers Make Up the OSI Layers—Application and Data Transport*

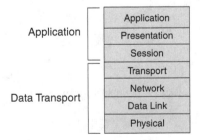

Protocols

The OSI model provides a conceptual framework for communication between computers, but the model itself is not a method of communication. Actual communication is made possible by using communication protocols. In the context of data networking, a **protocol** is a formal set of rules and conventions that governs how computers exchange information over a network medium. A protocol implements the functions of one or more of the OSI layers. Many communication protocols exist, but all tend to fall into one of the following groups: **LAN protocols**, **WAN protocols**, **network protocols**, and **routing protocols**. **LAN protocols** operate at the Physical and Data-Link layers of the OSI model and define communication over the various LAN media. **WAN protocols** operate at the lowest three layers of the OSI model and define communication over the various wide-area media. **Routing protocols** are network-layer protocols that are responsible for path determination and traffic switching. Finally, **network protocols** are the various upper-layer protocols that exist in a given protocol suite.

OSI Model and Communication Between Systems

Information being transferred from a software application in one computer system to a software application in another must pass through each of the OSI layers. If, for example, a software application in System A has information to transmit to a software application in System B, the application program in System A will pass its information to the Application layer (Layer 7) of System A. The Application layer then passes the information to the Presentation layer (Layer 6), which relays the data to the Session layer (Layer 5), and so on down to the Physical layer (Layer 1). At the Physical layer, the information is placed on the physical network medium and is sent across the medium to System B. The Physical layer of System B removes the information from the physical medium, and then its Physical layer passes the information up to the Data Link layer (Layer 2), which passes it to the Network layer (Layer 3), and so on until it reaches the Application layer (Layer 7) of System B. Finally, the Application layer of System B passes the information to the recipient application program to complete the communication process.

Interaction between OSI Model Layers

A given layer in the OSI layers generally communicates with three other OSI layers: the layer directly above it, the layer directly below it, and its peer layer in other networked computer systems. The Data Link layer in System A, for example, communicates with the Network layer of System A, the Physical layer of System A, and the Data Link layer in System B. Figure C-3 illustrates this example.

Figure C-3   *OSI Model Layers Communicate with Other Layers*

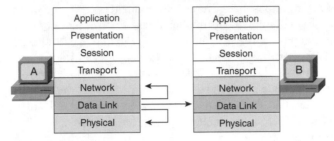

OSI Layer Services

One OSI layer communicates with another layer to make use of the services provided by the second layer. The services provided by adjacent layers help a given OSI layer communicate with its peer layer in other computer systems. Three basic elements are involved in layer services: the service user, the service provider, and the service access point (SAP).

In this context, the service **user** is the OSI layer that requests services from an adjacent OSI layer. The service **provider** is the OSI layer that provides services to service users. OSI layers can provide services to multiple service users. The **SAP** is a conceptual location at which one OSI layer can request the services of another OSI layer.

Figure C-4 illustrates how these three elements interact at the Network and Data Link layers.

Figure C-4   *Service Users, Providers, and SAPs Interact at the Network and Data Link Layers*

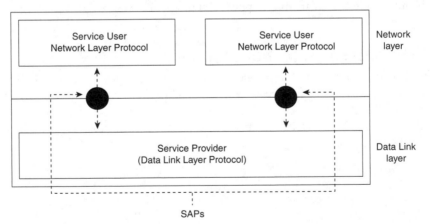

OSI Model Layers and Information Exchange

The seven OSI layers use various forms of control information to communicate with their peer layers in other computer systems. This **control information** consists of specific requests and instructions that are exchanged between peer OSI layers.

Control information typically takes one of two forms: headers and trailers. **Headers** are prepended to data that has been passed down from upper layers. **Trailers** are appended to data that has been passed down from upper layers. An OSI layer is not required to attach a header or trailer to data from upper layers.

Headers, trailers, and data are relative concepts, depending on the layer that analyzes the information unit. At the Network layer, an information unit, for example, consists of a Layer 3 header and data. At the Data Link layer, however, all the information passed down by the Network layer (the Layer 3 header and the data) is treated as data.

In other words, the data portion of an information unit at a given OSI layer potentially can contain headers, trailers, and data from all the higher layers. This is known as **encapsulation**. Figure C-5 shows how the header and data from one layer are encapsulated into the header of the next lowest layer.

Figure C-5   *Headers and Data Can Be Encapsulated During Information Exchange*

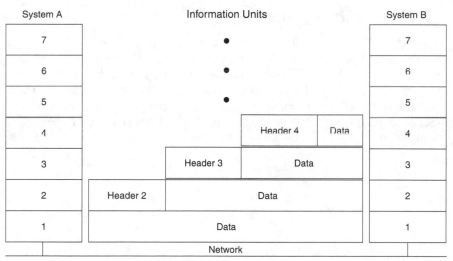

Information Exchange Process

The information exchange process occurs between peer OSI layers. Each layer in the source system adds control information to data, and each layer in the destination system analyzes and removes the control information from that data.

If System A has data from a software application to send to System B, the data is passed to the Application layer. The Application layer in System A then communicates any control information required by the Application layer in System B by prepending a header to the data. The resulting information unit (a header and the data) is passed to the Presentation layer, which prepends its own header containing control information intended for the Presentation layer in System B.

The information unit grows in size as each layer prepends its own header (and, in some cases, a trailer) that contains control information to be used by its peer layer in System B. At the Physical layer, the entire information unit is placed onto the network medium.

The Physical layer in System B receives the information unit and passes it to the Data Link layer. The Data Link layer in System B then reads the control information contained in the header prepended by the Data Link layer in System A. The header is then removed, and the remainder of the information unit is passed to the Network layer. Each layer performs the same actions: The layer reads the header from its peer layer, strips it off, and passes the remaining information unit to the next highest layer. After the Application layer performs these actions, the data is passed to the recipient software application in System B, in exactly the form in which it was transmitted by the application in System A.

OSI Model Physical Layer

The Physical layer defines the electrical, mechanical, procedural, and functional specifications for activating, maintaining, and deactivating the physical link between communicating network systems. Physical layer specifications define characteristics such as voltage levels, timing of voltage changes, physical data rates, maximum transmission distances, and physical connectors. Physical layer implementations can be categorized as either LAN or WAN specifications. Figure C-6 illustrates some common LAN and WAN Physical layer implementations.

Figure C-6 *Physical Layer Implementations Can Be LAN Or WAN Specifications*

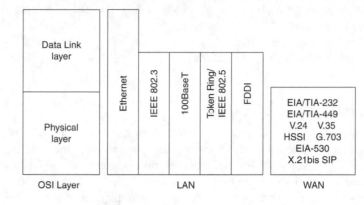

Physical Layer Implementations

OSI Model Data Link Layer

The Data Link layer provides the reliable transit of data across a physical network link. Different Data Link layer specifications define different network and protocol characteristics, including physical addressing, network topology, error notification, sequencing of frames, and flowcontrol. Physical addressing (as opposed to network addressing) defines the way devices are addressed at the Data Link layer. Network topology consists of the Data Link layer specifications that often define how devices are to be physically connected, such as in a bus or a ring topology. Error notification alerts upper-layer protocols that a transmission error has occurred, and the sequencing of data frames reorders frames that are transmitted out of sequence. Finally, flowcontrol moderates the transmission of data so that the receiving device is not overwhelmed with more traffic than it can handle at one time.

The Institute of Electrical and Electronics Engineers (IEEE) has subdivided the Data Link layer into two sublayers: Logical Link Control (LLC) and Media Access Control (MAC). Figure C-7 illustrates the IEEE sublayers of the Data Link layer.

Figure C-7 *The Data Link Layer Contains Two Sublayers*

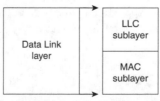

The Logical Link Control (LLC) sublayer of the Data Link layer manages communications between devices over a single link of a network. LLC is defined in the IEEE 802.2 specification, and supports both connectionless and connection-oriented services used by higher-layer protocols. IEEE 802.2 defines a number of fields in Data Link layer frames that enable multiple higher-layer protocols to share a single physical data link. The Media Access Control (MAC) sublayer of the Data Link layer manages protocol access to the physical network medium. The IEEE MAC specification defines MAC addresses, which enable multiple devices to uniquely identify one another at the Data Link layer.

OSI Model Network Layer

The Network layer provides routing and related functions that enable multiple data links to be combined into an internetwork. This is accomplished by the logical addressing (as opposed to the physical addressing) of devices. The Network layer supports both connection-oriented and connectionless service from higher-layer protocols. Network layer protocols typically are routing protocols, but other types of protocols are implemented at the Network layer as well. Some common routing protocols include Border Gateway Protocol (BGP), an Internet interdomain routing protocol; Open Shortest Path First (OSPF), a link-state, interior gateway protocol developed for use in TCP/IP networks; and Routing Information Protocol (RIP), an Internet routing protocol that uses hop count as its metric.

OSI Model Transport Layer

The Transport layer implements reliable internetwork data transport services that are transparent to upper layers. Transport layer functions typically include flowcontrol, multiplexing, virtual circuit management, and error checking and recovery.

Flowcontrol manages data transmission between devices so that the transmitting device does not send more data than the receiving device can process. Multiplexing enables data from several applications to be transmitted onto a single physical link. Virtual circuits are established, maintained, and terminated by the Transport layer. Error checking involves creating various mechanisms for detecting transmission errors; whereas error recovery involves taking an action, such as requesting that data be retransmitted, to resolve any errors that occur.

Some Transport layer implementations include Transmission Control Protocol, Name Binding Protocol, and OSI transport protocols. Transmission Control Protocol (TCP) is the protocol in the TCP/IP suite that provides reliable transmission of data. Name Binding Protocol (NBP) is the protocol that associates AppleTalk names with addresses. OSI transport protocols are a series of transport protocols in the OSI protocol suite.

OSI Model Session Layer

The Session layer establishes, manages, and terminates communication sessions between Presentation layer entities. Communication sessions consist of service requests and service responses that occur between applications located in different network devices. These requests and responses are coordinated by protocols implemented at the Session layer. Some examples of Session layer implementations include Zone Information Protocol (ZIP), the AppleTalk protocol that coordinates the name binding process; and Session Control Protocol (SCP), the DECnet Phase IV session-layer protocol.

OSI Model Presentation Layer

The Presentation layer provides a variety of coding and conversion functions that are applied to Application layer data. These functions ensure that information sent from the Application layer of one system will be readable by the Application layer of another system. Some examples of Presentation layer coding and conversion schemes include common data representation formats, conversion of character representation formats, common data-compression schemes, and common data-encryption schemes.

Common data representation formats—or the use of standard image, sound, and video formats—enable the interchange of application data between different types of computer systems. Conversion schemes are used to exchange information with systems by using different text and data representations, such as EBCDIC and ASCII. Standard data-compression schemes enable data that is compressed at the source device to be properly decompressed at the destination. Standard data-encryption schemes enable data encrypted at the source device to be properly deciphered at the destination.

Presentation layer implementations are not typically associated with a particular protocol stack. Some well-known standards for video include QuickTime and Motion (MPEG). QuickTime is an Apple Computer specification for video and audio, and MPEG is a standard for video compression and coding.

Among the well-known graphic image formats are Graphics Interchange Format (GIF), Joint Photographic Experts Group (JPEG), and Tagged Image File Format (TIFF). GIF is a standard for compressing and coding graphic images. JPEG is another compression and coding standard for graphic images, and TIFF is a standard coding format for graphic images.

OSI Model Application Layer

The Application layer is the OSI layer closest to the end user, which means that both the OSI Application layer and the user interact directly with the software application.

This layer interacts with software applications that implement a communicating component. Such application programs fall outside the scope of the OSI model. Application layer functions typically include identifying communication partners, determining resource availability, and synchronizing communication.

When identifying communication partners, the Application layer determines the identity and availability of communication partners for an application with data to transmit. When determining resource availability, the Application layer must decide whether sufficient network resources for the requested communication exist. In synchronizing communication, all communication between applications requires cooperation that is managed by the Application layer.

Two key types of application-layer implementations are TCP/IP applications and OSI applications. TCP/IP applications are protocols such as Telnet, File Transfer Protocol (FTP), and Simple Mail Transfer Protocol (SMTP), which exist in the Internet Protocol suite. OSI applications are protocols that exist in the OSI suite—such as File Transfer, Access, and Management (FTAM); F Virtual Terminal Protocol (VTP); and Common Management Information Protocol (CMIP).

Information Formats

The data and control information that is transmitted through internetworks takes a wide variety of forms. The terms used to refer to these information formats are not used consistently in the internetworking industry, but sometimes are used interchangeably. Common information formats include frame, packet, datagram, segment, message, cell, and data unit.

A **frame** is an information unit whose source and destination are Data Link layer entities. A frame is composed of the Data Link layer header (and possibly a trailer), and upper-layer data. The header and trailer contain control information intended for the Data Link layer entity in the destination system. Data from upper-layer entities is encapsulated in the Data Link layer header and trailer. Figure C-8 illustrates the basic components of a Data Link layer frame.

Figure C-8   *Data from Upper-Layer Entities Makes Up the Data Link Layer Frame*

Frame

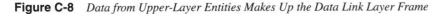
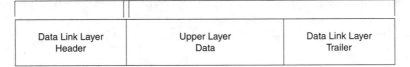

| Data Link Layer Header | Upper Layer Data | Data Link Layer Trailer |

A **packet** is an information unit whose source and destination are Network layer entities. A packet is composed of the Network layer header (and possibly a trailer), and upper-layer data. The header and trailer contain control information intended for the Network layer entity in the destination system. Data from upper-layer entities is encapsulated in the Network layer header and trailer. Figure C-9 illustrates the basic components of a Network layer packet.

Figure C-9   *Three Basic Components Make Up a Network Layer Packet*

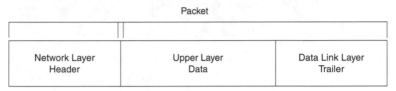

The term **datagram** usually refers to an information unit whose source and destination are Network layer entities that use connectionless network service.

The term **segment** usually refers to an information unit whose source and destination are Transport layer entities.

A **message** is an information unit, whose source and destination entities exist above the Network layer (often the Application layer).

A **cell** is an information unit of a fixed size, whose source and destination are Data Link layer entities. Cells are used in switched environments, such as Asynchronous Transfer Mode (ATM) and Switched Multimegabit Data Service (SMDS) networks. A cell is composed of the header and payload. The header contains control information intended for the destination Data Link-layer entity and is typically five bytes long. The payload contains upper-layer data that is encapsulated in the cell header and is typically 48 bytes long.

The length of the header and the payload fields always are exactly the same for each cell. Figure C-10 depicts the components of a typical cell.

Figure C-10   *Two Components Make Up a Typical Cell*

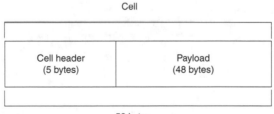

Data unit is a generic term that refers to a variety of information units. Some common data units are service data units (SDUs), protocol data units, and bridge protocol data units (BPDUs). SDUs are information units from upper-layer protocols that define a service request to a lower-layer protocol. PDU is OSI terminology for a packet. BPDUs are used by the spanning-tree algorithm as hello messages.

AT Commands for Modems and Chat-Scripts

The source for this appendix is Cisco Connection Online (www.cisco.com).

Entering AT Commands

The following is a list of items to keep in mind when you issue AT commands to a modem:

- To use the AT command set, the modem requires communications software to put the computer in terminal mode, so that the keyboard entry bypasses the processor and goes directly to the modem.

- Enter commands in either uppercase or lowercase, not mixed case.

- All commands except **A/**, **A>**, and **+++** are preceded by the AT prefix, and are executed when you press **Return** or **Enter**.

- Command length limit is 64 characters. The modem does not count the AT prefix, **Return**, or spaces.

- A missing numeric argument is assumed to be zero. For example, the hang-up command **ATH** is the equivalent of **ATH0**.

- The modem usually operates in one of two modes: command mode (no connection is established with another modem) or online mode.

When in online mode, the only command that the modem recognizes is the escape code (+++), which forces the modem back to command mode in two different ways. If DIP switch 9 is off, the modem disconnects before returning to command mode. If DIP switch 9 is on (factory setting), the modem maintains the connection and enters online-command mode, a state in which it maintains the connection and can also accept commands.

The command mode local echo default is no echo: the modem does not display commands sent from the keyboard. To enable local echo, install the modems with DIP switch 4 off, or send the following command to the modem: **ATE1**.

AT Command Sets

This section contains the following information:

- Basic command set (see Table D-1)
- Ampersand command set (see Table D-2)

- Percent command set (see Table D-3)
- Result code options for the **X**n command (see Table D-4)

Table D-1   *Basic Modem Command Set*

Command	Function
&	See the ampersand command set in Table D-2.
%	See the percent command set in Table D-3.
$	Help basic command summary request.
>	Repeat the last command continuously until canceled by pressing any key. If used in a dial string, automated redialing terminates after ten attempts.
/	Pause for 125 milliseconds.
+++	Escape code that is preceded and followed by a guard time of at least one second of no data transmission. The modem responds to +++ by returning to command mode and (depending on the setting of DIP switch 9) it hangs up and sends a NO CARRIER result code (switch 9 off), or it retains the phone line connection and sends an OK result code (switch 9 on).
A	Force answer mode when the modem has not received an incoming call.
A/	Re-execute the last issued command one time. **A/** does not require the AT prefix or a **Return**.
A>	Re-execute the last issued command continuously until canceled by pressing any key. Dial strings are re-executed ten times, after which the execution terminates. This command does not take the AT prefix or a **Return**.
AT	Attention: lets the modem know commands are being issued to it. Must precede all other commands except **A/**, **A>**, and **+++**.
Bn	Handshake options. **B0** ITU-T V.25 answer sequence. This is the default setting that is also required to answer overseas calls at 1,200 Bps and above. **B1** Bell answer tone. **B2** Force Bell 208B mode (synchronous, 4,800 Bps).
Cn	Transmitter enabled/disabled. **C0** Transmitter disabled; receive-only condition. **C1** Transmitter enabled.

Table D-1   *Basic Modem Command Set (Continued)*

Command	Function
D	Dial the number that follows and enter Originate mode. Optional parameters:
	P
	Pulse dial. This is the default setting.
	T
	Tone dial.
	,
	Pause for 2 seconds.
	;
	Return to command mode after dialing.
	"
	Dial the letters that follow.
	!
	Transfer call (flash switch-hook).
	W
	Wait for second dial tone (with X3 or higher).
	@
	Wait for an answer (with X3 or higher).
	R
	Reverse frequencies.
D$	Help dial command summary request.
DL	Dial the last-dialed number.
DL?	Display the number stored in the last-dialed number buffer.
DSn	Dial the phone number stored in NVRAM at position n (n = 0-3).
En	Command mode local echo (display) of keyboard commands ON/OFF. Default = setting of DIP switch 4.
	E0
	Local echo off.
	E1
	Local echo on.

continues

Table D-1   *Basic Modem Command Set (Continued)*

Command	Function
Fn	Online local echo of transmitted data on or off. Sometimes referred to as the duplex setting.
	F0
	Local echo on. Sometimes called half duplex. Modem copies to the screen data it sends to the remote system.
	F1
	Local echo off. This is the default setting. Sometimes called full duplex. Receiving system may send a remote echo of data.
Hn	On/off hook control.
	H0
	Hang up (go on hook).
	H1
	Go off hook. Busy out phone line.
In	Inquiry.
	I0
	Display product code.
	I1
	Display results of ROM checksum.
	I2
	Display results of RAM test.
	I3
	Display call duration or real time (see K*n*).
	I4
	Display current modem settings.
	I5
	Display NVRAM settings.
	I6
	Display link diagnostics.
	I7
	Display product configuration.
	I8
	Reserved.

Table D-1   *Basic Modem Command Set (Continued)*

Command	Function
	I9
	Display standard feature group B settings.
	I10
	View link security account status.
K*n*	Modem clock operation: Call-duration or real-time mode.
	K0
	Return call duration at ATI3 and ATI6. When modem is offline, it returns the duration of the last call. This is the default setting.
	K1
	Return actual time at ATI3 and ATI6. Clock is set using ATI3=HH:MM:SS K1.
O*n*	Return online after command execution.
	O0
	Return online (normal).
	O1
	Return online and retrain. Use if there were errors in a non-ARQ data transfer.
O0	Return online (normal).
O1	Return online and retrain. Use if there were errors in a non-ARQ data transfer.
P	Pulse dial (default).
Q*n*	Quiet mode: result codes displayed/suppressed. Default = setting of DIP switch 3.
	Q0
	Result codes displayed.
	Q1
	Result codes suppressed (quiet).
	Q2
	Result codes suppressed in answer mode.
S$	Help S-register summary request.
S*r***?**	Query contents of register *r*.
S*r***=***n*	Set S-register value: *r* is any S-register; *n* must be a decimal number between 0 and 255.
S*r.b***=***n*	Alternative command for setting bit-mapped registers: *r* is the bit-mapped register; *.b* is the bit; *n* is 0 (off) or 1 (on).
T	Tone dial.

continues

Table D-1   *Basic Modem Command Set (Continued)*

Command	Function
V*n*	Return result codes in words or numbers (written/numeric mode). Default = setting of DIP switch 2. **V0** Numeric mode. **V1** Written mode.
X*n*	Result code set options. Default = X1, extended set, codes 0-5, 10, and the remaining connect codes in Table D-4.
Z	Software reset. If DIP switch 10 is off, the modem loads the settings in NVRAM. If DIP switch 10 is on, the modem loads the &F0 template, clearing all flow control and high performance settings.

Table D-2   *Ampersand Command Set*

Command	Function
&$	Help extended command summary request.
&A*n*	Enable/disable additional result code subsets. See the **X***n* command in Table D-1. **&A0** ARQ result codes disabled. **&A1** ARQ result codes enabled. **&A2** V32 modulation codes enabled. **&A3** Additional error control indicator (LAPM, MNP, or NONE) and data compression type (V42 *bis* or MNP Level 5). This is the default setting.
&B*n*	Serial port rate. **&B0** Serial port rate switches to follow connection. **&B1** Serial port rate remains fixed at the computer setting. Allowable rates are 115.2, 57.6, 38.4, 19.2, 9.6 Kbps; and 4,800, 2,400, 1,200, and 300 Bps. This is the default setting. **&B2** In answer mode, shift to the fixed serial port rate for ARQ calls; follow the connection rate for non-ARQ calls.

Table D-2   *Ampersand Command Set (Continued)*

Command	Function
&Cn	Carrier Detect (CD) signal, modem to computer. The setting of DIP switch 6 determines CD operations at power-on and reset.
	&C0
	CD override (CD always on).
	&C1
	Modem sends CD signal when it connects with another modem, drops CD on disconnect.
&Dn	Data Terminal Ready (DTR) signal, computer to modem. DIP switch 1 sets DTR operations at power-on and reset.
	&D0
	DTR override (DTR always on).
	&D1
	If issued before connecting, the modem enters online command mode during a call when DTR is toggled. &D1 functions similarly to the escape code (+++). Return online with ATO, or hang up with ATH.
	&D2
	Normal DTR. Terminal must send DTR for modem to accept commands.
&Fn	Load one of four (ROM) templates into RAM (n = 0, 1, 2, or 3).
&Gn	Guard tone for 2,400/1,200 Bps calls from overseas.
	&G0
	No guard tone (U.S., Canada). This is the default setting.
	&G1
	550 Hz guard tone (some European countries).
	&G2
	1800 Hz guard tone. Requires B0 setting.

continues

Table D-2   *Ampersand Command Set (Continued)*

Command	Function
&H*n*	Transmit data flow control.
	&H0
	Flow control disabled.
	&H1
	Hardware (Clear to Send) flow control. This is the default setting.
	&H2
	Software (XON/XOFF) flow control.
	&H3
	Hardware and software flow control.
&I*n*	Received data software flow control.
	&I0
	Flow control disabled. This is the default setting.
	&I1
	XON/XOFF to local modem and remote computer.
	&I2
	XON/XOFF to local modem only.
	&I3
	Host mode, Hewlett-Packard protocol.
	&I4
	Terminal mode, Hewlett-Packard protocol.
	&I5
	Same as &I2 in ARQ mode. In non-ARQ mode, XON/XOFF to remote modem for link flow control.
&K*n*	Data compression.
	&K0
	Disabled.
	&K1
	Auto enable/disable. This is the default setting. Disabled if modem is set to &B0 and serial port rate switches to match link rate.
	&K2
	Enabled, regardless of &B*n* setting.
	&K3
	Selective data compression—MNP Level 5 disabled.

Table D-2 *Ampersand Command Set (Continued)*

Command	Function
&L*n*	Normal/leased phone line.
	&L0
	Normal phone line. This is the default setting.
	&L1
	Leased line; enables the modem to reconnect.
&M*n*	Error Control (ARQ).
	&M0
	Normal mode, error control disabled.
	&M1
	Online synchronous mode without V.25 *bis*.
	&M2
	Reserved.
	&M3
	Reserved.
	&M4
	Normal/ARQ mode. This is the default setting. Normal connection if ARQ connection cannot be made.
	&M5
	ARQ mode. Modem hangs up if ARQ connection cannot be made.
	&M6
	V.25 *bis* mode, using a character-oriented Binary Synchronous communications protocol.
	&M7
	V.25 *bis* synchronous mode, using HDLC Protocol.

continues

Table D-2   *Ampersand Command Set (Continued)*

Command	Function
&N*n*	Link rate variable or fixed. With fixed link rate, modem hangs up if called or if calling modem is operating at a different rate.
	&N0
	Variable link operations. Negotiates highest possible link rate with remote modem. This is the default and the recommended setting.
	&N1 300 Bps
	&N2 1200 Bps
	&N3 2400 Bps
	&N4 800 Bps
	&N5 7200 Bps
	&N6 9600 Bps
	&N7 12 Kbps
	&N8 14.4 Kbps
	&N9 16.8 Kbps
	&N10 19.2 Kbps
	&N11 21.6 Kbps
	&N12 24 Kbps
	&N13 26.4 Kbps
	&N14 28.8 Kbps
&P*n*	Pulse dialing make/break ratio.
	&P0
	U.S./Canada make/break ratio. This is the default setting.
	&P1
	U.K. make/break ratio.

Table D-2   *Ampersand Command Set (Continued)*

Command	Function
&R*n*	Received data hardware (RTS) flow control.
	&R0
	Delay between DTE's RTS signal and the modem's CTS response; duration set by S26.
	&R1
	Ignore RTS.
	&R2
	Received data sent to computer only when RTS is high; used only if computer supports RTS. This is the default setting.
&S*n*	Data Set Ready (DSR) operations.
	&S0
	DSR override, always on. This is the default setting.
	&S1
	Modem sends computer a DSR signal when it detects a modem tone on the phone line.
	&S2
	On loss of carrier, modem sends computer a pulsed DSR signal; Clear to Send (CTS) follows Carrier Detect (CD).
	&S3
	This is the same as &S2, but without CTS following CD.
	&S4
	DSR follows CD.
	&S5
	CTS follows CD, with DSR normal.

continues

Table D-2   *Ampersand Command Set (Continued)*

Command	Function
&T*n*	Modem testing. The following analog tests (&T1 and &T8) are only valid for the quad analog modem and the quad analog/digital configured for analog mode.
	&T0
	End test.
	&T1
	Initiate analog loopback testing.
	&T2
	Reserved.
	&T3
	Initiate local digital loopback testing.
	&T4
	Grant remote digital loopback. This is the default setting.
	&T5
	Prohibit remote digital loopback.
	&T6
	Initiate remote digital loopback testing.
	&T7
	Initiate RDL with self-test and error correction.
	&T8
	Initiate analog loopback with self-test and error correction.
	&T9
	Generates a tone to verify the digital signal processor's capability to generate analog tones and T1 line diagnostics. Command syntax is **AT&T8=***Freq,Amp*, where the Frequency can be from 300 to 4,000 Hz and the amplitude can range from -40 to 0 dBm. Press any key to cancel the tone testing.
	&T10
	Sets the modem to receive analog test tones. This test reports the received tones in frequency and amplitude to the DTE interface on a five-second basis (either to a connected terminal interface or through an SNMP manager). Press any key to cancel the tone testing.
&W	Write current settings to NVRAM.

Table D-2   *Ampersand Command Set (Continued)*

Command	Function
&Xn	Synchronous clock source. The **&X1** and **&X2** commands are only valid for analog modems; they are not supported for digital T1 applications.
	&X0
	Modem's transmit clock. This is the default setting.
	&X1
	DTE's transmit clock.
	&X2
	Modem's receiver clock.
&Yn	Break handling. Destructive breaks clear the buffer; expedited breaks are sent immediately to the remote system. Under data compression, destructive breaks cause both modems to reset their compression tables.
	&Y0
	Destructive, don't send break.
	&Y1
	Destructive, expedited. This is the default setting.
	&Y2
	Nondestructive, expedited.
	&Y3
	Nondestructive, unexpedited; modem sends break in sequence with data received from computer.
&Zn=L	Write the last dialed number to NVRAM at position n (n = 0, 1, 2, or 3).
&Zn=s	Write the following dial string (s) to NVRAM at position n (n = 0, 1, 2, or 3).
&Zn?	Display the phone number stored in NVRAM at position n (n = 0, 1, 2, or 3).

Table D-3   *Percent Command Set*

Command	Function
%$	Help percent command summary request.

continues

Table D-3 *Percent Command Set (Continued)*

Command	Function
%A=	Set up the host security account. The **%A=** command is automatically written to NVRAM and does not require an **&W** command.
	You must specify two fields:
	The account password.
	This identifies the host security account. It can be up to eight characters (ASCII characters 32–127) and is case-sensitive.
	Prompt for phone number (Y/N).
	Y indicates that the host modem will prompt the remote user to enter a phone number; the host modem disconnects and then dials back. **N** indicates that no prompt will be made.
	The fields are entered after the equal sign, separated by a comma, as in the following example for an account with the password BILL and dialback prompting enabled:
	AT%A=BILL,Y<Enter>
%B*n*	Configure the serial port rate during a remote access session.
	%B0 110 Bps
	%B1 300 Bps
	%B2 600 Bps
	%B3 1200 Bps
	%B4 2400 Bps
	%B5 4800 Bps
	%B6 9600 Bps
	%B7 19,200 Bps
	%B8 38,400 Bps
	%B9 57,600 Bps
	%B10 115,200 Bps

Table D-3   *Percent Command Set (Continued)*

Command	Function
%C*n*	Configuration control during remote access session.

%C0

Defer configuration. This is the default setting. Configuration changes are deferred until the call is ended, and take effect for subsequent connections. This command does not have to be entered; it is the default unless one of the following %C values is entered.

%C1

Restore configuration. Use this command to cancel any configuration changes made during remote access and restore the original configuration. However, commands that have been written to NVRAM (with &W) will not be restored to their previous settings. Additionally, if immediate configuration changes are forced (with %C2), those changes cannot be reversed with %C1.

%C2

Execute configuration. Forces configuration changes to take effect immediately, during the current connection. Do not force immediate configuration changes unless absolutely necessary because this may result in an unreliable connection or even a loss of connection.

Command	Function
%CN*n*=*s*	Sets the Carrier Access Code number, where *n* is a position in NVRAM (from 1-3) and *s* is a numeric string containing from 1 to 10 digits. This code allows programming of Dialed Number Indicate Service or Automatic Number Indicate, a service offered by the telephone company.

continues

Table D-3 *Percent Command Set (Continued)*

Command	Function
%CI*n*=*s*	Sets the carrier access code-associated initialization string, where *n* is a position in NVRAM (1, 2, 3, or 4) and *s* is a configuration string of up to 30 characters. Do not include the AT attention prefix in the initialization string.
	%CN*n*=*s* and %CI*n*=*s* allow you to configure a stored initialization string feature in the quad modems. First, define up to three full or partial telephone numbers that may be dialed to access the modem, using the AT%CN*n*=*s* command. An initialization string (without the AT command prefix) can then be associated with the carrier access code number by using the AT%CI*n*=*s* command. Four initialization strings may be stored: three of them to match the carrier access code of a specified carrier access code number, and the fourth to be executed if the modem receives an unknown carrier access code (no full or partial match).
	When a call comes in, the quad modem compares the number dialed against the defined carrier access code numbers. An initialization string is then used to configure the modem to answer the call.
	The carrier access code numbers defined, with their associated initialization strings, can be viewed by entering the **ATI9** command.
	The quad modem identifies the carrier access code on incoming calls by returning special RING result codes, as follows.
	No DNIS or ANI information received: RING (normal).
	Only DNIS information received: RING/5 (where 5 is the DNIS number).
	ANI and DNIS information received: RING/5/5551212 (where 5 is the DNIS and 5551212 is the ANI).
	Only ANI information received: RING//5551212 (where two slashes indicate no DNIS, and 5551212 is the ANI).
	The CAC associated with the last call received is displayed on the current settings screen (obtained by issuing the command **ATI4**), as follows:
	LAST DNIS #: nn. .nn
	or
	LAST ANI #: nn. .nn

Table D-3   *Percent Command Set (Continued)*

Command	Function
%D*n*	Toggle between analog and digital modes (quad analog/digital modems only).
	%D0
	Analog mode. A digital-only modem returns an error if sent this command.
	%D1
	Digital mode. An analog only modem returns an error if sent this command. When set to %D1, the modem displays the message **DCE=Digital (DS0)** on the I4 command screen to indicate that the modem has been configured for digital and is linked with the T1 NAC. If no T1 link is established, the modem displays the message **DCE=Digital (DS)?** It may take up to 30 seconds to establish a T1 link. If this message persists, there is either no T1 module present or there is a hardware problem.
%E=*n*	Use the **%E=*n*** command to edit the link security configuration, where n = 1, 2, 3, or 4.
	%E=1
	Erase local access password.
	%E=2
	Erase autopass password.
	%E=3
	Erase password account.
	%E=4
	Erase account status information.
%F*n*	Configure the data format during a remote access session.
	%F0
	No parity, eight data bits.
	%F1
	Mark parity, seven data bits.
	%F2
	Odd parity, seven data bits.
	%F3
	Even parity, seven data bits.
%L=	Set the local access password for link security.
%P*n*	Assign remote access password.
	%P0
	Create password that allows viewing privileges only.
	%P1
	Create password that allows viewing and configuration privileges.

continues

Table D-3   *Percent Command Set (Continued)*

Command	Function
%P*n=s*	Set the following password string (*s*) at position *n* (*n* = 0 or 1).
%P*n*?	Display the password stored at position *n* (*n* = 0 or 1).
%S=	Access link security settings by entering the local access password.
%T	Tone recognition. Enables modem, when off-hook, to detect the tone frequencies of dialing modems.
%V=	Set link security autopass password for both the host and remote modem.

Table D-4   *Result Code Options for the X*n *Command*

Result Codes	Setting							
	X0	X1	X2	X3	X4	X5	X6	X7
0/OK	x	x	x	x	x	x	x	x
1/CONNECT	x	x	x	x	x	x	x	x
2/RING	x	x	x	x	x	x	x	x
3/NO CARRIER	x	x	x	x	x	x	x	x
4/ERROR	x	x	x	x	x	x	x	x
5/CONNECT 1200		x	x	x	x	x	x	x
6/NO DIAL TONE			x		x		x	x
7/BUSY				x	x	x	x	x
8/NO ANSWER				x	x	x	x	x
9/RESERVED								
10/CONNECT 2400		x	x	x	x	x	x	x
11/RINGING						x	x	x
12/VOICE						x	x	
13/CONNECT 9600		x	x	x	x	x	x	x
18/CONNECT 4800		x	x	x	x	x	x	x
20/CONNECT 7200		x	x	x	x	x	x	x
21/CONNECT 12000		x	x	x	x	x	x	x
25/CONNECT 14400		x	x	x	x	x	x	x
43/CONNECT 16800		x	x	x	x	x	x	x
85/CONNECT 19200		x	x	x	x	x	x	x
91/CONNECT 21600		x	x	x	x	x	x	x

Table D-4   *Result Code Options for the **X**n Command (Continued)*

Result Codes	Setting							
	X0	X1	X2	X3	X4	X5	X6	X7
99/CONNECT 24000		x	x	x	x	x	x	x
103/CONNECT 26400		x	x	x	x	x	x	x
107/CONNECT 28800		x	x	x	x	x	x	x
Functions	X0	X1	X2	X3	X4	X5	X6	X7
Adaptive dialing			x	x	x	x	x	x
Wait for second dial tone (W)				x	x	x	x	x
Wait for answer (@)				x	x	x	x	x
Fast dial			x		x		x	x

Modem Troubleshooting Tips

Table D-5 contains troubleshooting tips on modem access and control.

Table D-5   *Modem Troubleshooting Tips*

Problem	Likely Cause
Connection refused.	Someone already has a connection to that port or an EXEC is running on that port or the modem failed to lower CD after a call disconnected, resulting in an EXEC that remained active after disconnect. To force the line back into an idle state, clear the line from the console and try again. If it still fails, ensure that you have set **modem inout** command for that line. If you don't have modem control, either turn off EXEC on the line (by using the **exec-timeout** line-configuration command) before making a reverse connection or configure the modem by using an external terminal. As a last resort, disconnect the modem, clear the line, make the Telnet connection, and then attach the modem. This prevents a misconfigured modem from denying you line access.
Connection appears to hang.	Try entering **^U** (clear line), **^Q** (XON), and press **Return** a few times to try to establish terminal control.
EXEC does not come up; autoselect is on.	Press **Return** to enter EXEC.

continues

Table D-5   *Modem Troubleshooting Tips (Continued)*

Problem	Likely Cause
Modem does not hang up after entering **quit**.	The modem is either not receiving DTR information, or you have not set up modem control on the router.
Interrupt another user's session when you dial in.	The modem is either not dropping CD on disconnect, or you have not set up modem control on the Cisco router.
Connection hangs after entering **+++** on the dialing modem, followed by an ATO.	The answering modem saw and interpreted the **+++** when it was echoed to you. This is a bug in the answering modem, which is common to many modems. There may be a switch to work around this problem; check the modem's documentation.
Losing data.	You may have Hardware Flow Control only on for either the router's line (DTE) or the modem (DCE). Hardware Flow Control should be on for both or off for both, but not for only one.
Using MDCE.	Turn MDCE into an MMOD by moving pin 6 to pin 8 because most modems use CD and not DSR to indicate the presence of a carrier. You can also program some modems to provide a carrier info via DSR.

Sample Modem Scripts

Listed as follows are several modem command strings that are appropriate for use with your access server. For use with the access server, **Speed=***xxxxx* is a suggested value only. Set the DTE speed of the modem to its maximum capability. This can be done by making a reverse telnet connection in the EXEC mode to the port on the access server where the modem is connected, and then sending an **at** command, which is followed by a carriage return.

In the following example, the modem is attached to asynchronous interface 2 on the access server. The IP address indicated as the server-ip-address is the IP address of the Ethernet 0 interface. The administrator connects from the EXEC to asynchronous interface 2, which has its IP address assigned from Ethernet 0:

```
2511> telnet server-ip-address port-number
2002
```

This appendix closes with a list of AT commands for typical configuration of common modems used with Cisco remote access servers.

AST Premium Exec Internal Data/Fax (MNP 5)
Init=AT&F&C1&D3\G0\J0\N3\Q2S7=60S0=1&W
Speed=9600

ATi 9600etc/e (V.42bis)
Init=AT&FW2&B1&C1&D3&K3&Q6&U1S7=60S0=1&W
Speed=38400

AT&T Paradyne KeepInTouch Card Modem (V.42bis)
Init=AT&FX6&C1&D3\N7\Q2%C1S7=60S0=1&w
Speed=57600

AT&T ComSphere 3800 Series (V.42bis)
Init=AT&FX6&C1&D2\N5\Q2%C1"H3S7=60S0=1&W
Speed=57600

AT&T DataPort Fax Modem (V.42bis)
Init=AT&FX6&C1&D2\N7\Q2%C1S7=60S0=1&W
Speed=38400

Boca Modem 14.4K/V.32bis (V.42bis)
Init=AT&FW2&C1&D3&K3&Q5%C1\N3S7=60S36=7S46=138S95=47S0=1&W
Speed=57600

CALPAK MXE-9600
Init=AT&F&C1&D3S7=60S0=1&W
Speed=9600

Cardinal 2450MNP (MNP 5)
Init=AT&F&C1&D3\J0\N3\Q2\V1%C1S7=60S0=1&w
Speed=9600

Cardinal 9650V32 (MNP)
Init=AT&F&B1&C1&D3&H1&I1&M6S7=60S0=1&W

Cardinal 9600V42 (V.42bis)
Init=AT&FW2&C1&D3&K3&Q5\N3%C1%M3S7=60S46=138S48=7S95=3S0=1&W
Speed=38400

Cardinal 14400 (V.42bis)
Init=AT&F&C1&D3&K3&Q5\N3%C1%M3S7=60S46=138S48=7S95=47S0=1&W
Speed=57600

COMPAQ SpeedPAQ 144 (V.42bis)
Init=AT&F&C1&D3&K3&Q5\J0\N3%C1S7=60S36=7S46=2S48=7S95=47S0=1&W
Speed=57600

Data Race RediMODEM V.32/V.32bis
Init=AT&F&C1&D3&K3&Q6\J0\N7\Q3\V2%C1S7=60S0=1&W
Speed=38400

Dell NX20 Modem/Fax (MNP)
Init=AT&F&C1&D3%C1\J0\N3\Q3\V1W2S7=60S0=1&W
Speed=9600

Digicom Systems (DSI) 9624LE/9624PC (MNP 5)
Init=AT&F&C1&D3*E1*F3*S1S7=60S0=1&W

Digicom Systems (DSI) 9624LE+ (V.42bis)
Init=AT&F&C1&D3*E9*F3*N6*S1S7=60S0=1&W
Speed=38400

Everex Evercom 24+ and 24E+ (MNP 5)
Init=AT&F&C1&D3\J0\N3\Q2\V1%C1S7=60S0=1&W

Everex EverFax 24/96 and 24/96E (MNP 5)
Init=AT&F&C1&D3\J0\N3\Q2\V1%C1S7=60S0=1&W
Speed=9600

Everex Evercom 96+ and 96E+ (V.42bis)
Init=AT&FW2&C1&D3\J0\N3\Q2\V2%C1S7=60S0=1&W
Speed=38400

Freedom Series V.32bis Data/FAX Modem
Init=AT&F&C1&D3&K3&Q6\J0\N7\Q3\V2%C1S7=60S0=1&W
Speed=38400

Gateway 2000 TelePath
Init=AT&FW2&C1&D3&K3&Q5\N3%C1S7=60S36=7S46=138S48=7S95=47S0=1&W
Speed=38400

Gateway 2000 Nomad 9600 BPS Internal Modem
Init=AT&F&C1&D3%C1\J0\N3\Q2S7=60S0=1&W
Speed=38400

GVC SM-96V (V.42bis)
Init=AT&F&C1&D3%C1\J0\N6\Q2\V1S7=60S0=1&W
Speed=38400

GVC SM-144V (V.42bis)
Init=AT&F&C1&D3%C1\J0\N6\Q2\V1S7=60S0=1&W
Speed=57600

Hayes Smartmodem Optima 9600 (V.42bis)
Init=AT&FW2&C1&D3&K3&Q5S7=60S46=138S48=7S95=47S0=1&W
Speed=38400

Hayes Smartmodem Optima 14400 (V.42bis)
Init=AT&FW2&C1&D3&K3&Q5S7=60S46=138S48=7S95=47S0=1&W
Speed=57600

Hayes Optima 28800 (V.34)
Init=AT&FS0=1&C1&D3&K3&Q6&Q5&Q9&W
Speed=115200

Hayes V-series Smartmodem 9600/9600B (V.42)
Init=AT&F&C1&D3&K3&Q5S7=60S0=1&W
Speed=9600

Hayes V-series ULTRA Smartmodem 9600 (V.42bis)
Init=AT&F&C1&D3&K3&Q5S7=60S46=2S48=7S95=63S0=1&W
Speed=38400

Hayes V-series ULTRA Smartmodem 14400 (V.42bis)
Init=AT&FW2&C1&D3&K3&Q5S7=60S38=10S46=2S48=7S95=63S0=1&W
Speed=38400

Hayes ACCURA 24 EC (V.42bis)
Init=AT&FW2&C1&D3&K3&Q5S7=60S36=7S46=138S48=7S95=47S0=1&W

Hayes ACCURA 96 EC (V.42bis)
Init=AT&FW2&C1&D3&K3&Q5S7=60S36=7S46=138S48=7S95=47S0=1&W
Speed=38400

Hayes ACCURA 144 EC (V.42bis)
Init=AT&FW2&C1&D3&K3&Q5S7=60S36=7S46=138S48=7S95=47S0=1&W
Speed=57600

Hayes ISDN System Adapter
Init=AT&FW1&C1&D3&K3&Q0S7=60S0=1&W
Speed=57600

IBM 7855 Modem Model 10 (MNP)
Init=AT&F&C1&D3\N3\Q2\V1%C1S7=60S0=1&W

IBM Data/Fax Modem PCMCIA (V.42bis)
Init=AT&F&C1&D3&K3&Q5%C3\N3S7=60S38=7S46=138S48=7S95=47S0=1&W
Speed=57600

Identity ID9632E
Init=AT&F&C1&D3S7=60S0=1&W
Speed=9600

Infotel V.42X (V.42bis)
Init=AT&F&C1&D3S7=30S36=7S0=1&W
Speed=9600

Infotel V.32 turbo (V.42bis)
Init=AT&FW1&C1&D3&K3&Q5S7=60S0=1&w
Speed=38400

Infotel 144I (V.42bis)
Init=AT&F&C1&D3&K3&Q5\N3%C1S7=60S36=7S46=138S48=7S95=47S0=1&W
Speed=38400

Intel 9600 EX (V.42bis)
Init=AT&F&C1&D3\J0\N3\Q2\V2%C1"H3S7=60S0=1&W
Speed=38400

Intel 14400 EX (V.42bis)
Init=AT&F&C1&D3\J0\N3\Q2\V2%C1"H3S7=60S0=1&W
Speed=38400

Macronix MaxFax 9624LT-S
Init=AT&F&C1&D3&K3&Q9\J0\N3\Q3%C1S7=60S36=7S46=138S48=7S95=47S0=1&W
Speed=9600

Megahertz T3144 internal (V.42bis)
Init=AT&F&C1&D3%C1\J0\N3\Q2\V2S7=60S0=1&W
Speed=57600

Megahertz T324FM internal (V.42bis)
Init=AT&F&C1&D3%C1\J0\N3\Q2\V1S7=60S46=138S48=7S0=1&W
Speed=9600

Megahertz P2144 FAX/Modem (V.42bis)
Init=AT&F&C1&D3%C1\J0\N7\Q2\V2S7=60S0=1&W
Speed=38400

Megahertz T396FM internal (V.42bis)
Init=AT&FW2&C1&D3%C1\J0\N7\Q2\V2S7=60S0=1&W
Speed=38400

Megahertz CC3144 PCMCIA card modem (V.42bis)
Init=AT&F&C1&D3&K3&Q5%C3\N3S7=60S38=7S46=138S48=7S95=47S0=1&W
Speed=57600

Microcom AX/9624c (MNP 5)
Init=AT&F&C1&D3\G0\J0\N3\Q2%C1S7=60S0=1&W
Speed=9600

Microcom AX/9600 Plus (MNP 5)
Init=AT&F&C1&D3\J0\N3\Q2S7=60S0=1&W
Speed=9600

Microcom QX/V.32c (MNP 5)
Init=AT&F&C1&D3\J0%C3\N3\Q2S7=60S0=1&W
Speed=38400

Microcom QX/4232hs (V.42bis)
Init=AT&F&C1&D3\J0%C3\N3\Q2-K0\V2S7=60S0=1&W
Speed=38400

Microcom QX/4232bis (V.42bis)
Init=AT&F&C1&D3\J0%C3\N3\Q2-K0\V2W2S7=60S0=1&W
Speed=38400

Microcom Deskporte 28800 (V.34)
Init=AT&F&c1&q1E0S0=1&W
Speed=115200

Microcom MicroPorte 542 (V.42bis)
Init=AT&F&C1&D3&Q5S7=60S46=138S48=7S95=47S0=1&W
Speed=9600

Microcom MicroPorte 1042 (V.42bis)
Init=AT&F&C1&D3%C3\J0-M0\N6\Q2\V2S7=60S0=1&W
Speed=9600

Microcom MicroPorte 4232bis (V.42bis)
Init=AT&F&C1&D3%C3%G0\J0-M0\N6\Q2\V2S7=60S0=1&W
Speed=38400

Microcom DeskPorte FAST
Init=ATX4S7=60-M1\V4\N2L1S0=1&W
Speed=57600

Motorola/Codex 3220 (MNP)
Init=AT&F&C1&D3*DC1*FL3*MF0*SM3*XC2S7=60S0=1&W

Motorola/Codex 3220 Plus (V.42bis)
Init=AT&F&C1&D3*DC1*EC0*MF0*SM3*XC2S7=60S0=1&W
Speed=38400

Motorola/Codex 326X Series (V.42bis)
Init=AT&F&C1&D3*FL3*MF0*SM3*TT2*XC2S7=60S0=1&W
Speed=38400

MultiTech MultiModem V32EC (V.42bis)
Init=AT&FX4&C1&D3$BA0&E1&E4&E15#L0S7=60S0=1&W
Speed=38400

MultiTech MultiModem V32 (no MNP or V.42)
Init=AT&F&C1&D3S7=60S0=1&W
Speed=9600

MultiTech MultiModem 696E (MNP)
Init=AT&F&C1&D3$BA0&E1&E4&E15S7=60S0=1&W

MultiTech MultiModem II MT932 (V.42bis)
Init=AT&FX4&C1&D3$BA0&E1&E4&E15#L0S7=60S0=1&W
Speed=38400

MultiTech MultiModem II MT1432 (V.42bis)
Init=AT&FX4&C1&D3#A0$BA0&E1&E4&E15#L0S7=60S0=1&W
Speed=57600

NEC UltraLite 14.4 Data/Fax Modem (V.42bis)
Init=AT&F&C1&D3&K3&Q4\J0\N7\Q2W2%C1S7=60S0=1&W
Speed=38400

Practical Peripherals PC28800SA (V.42bis)
Init=AT&F&C1&D3&K3&Q5S7=60S36=7S46=2S48=7S95=47S0=1&W
Speed=115200

Practical Peripherals PM9600SA (V.42bis)
Init=AT&F&C1&D3&K3&Q5S46=138S48=7S7=60S0=1&W
Speed=38400

Practical Peripherals PM14400FX (V.42bis)
Init=AT&F&C1&D3&K3&Q5S7=60S36=7S46=2S48=7S95=47S0=1&W
Speed=57600

Practical Peripherals PM14400SA (V.42bis)
Init=AT&F&C1&D3&K3&Q5S7=60S36=7S46=2S48=7S95=47S0=1&W
Speed=57600

Prometheus ProModem 9600 Plus (V.42)
Init=AT&F&C1&D3*E7*F3S7=60S0=1&W

Prometheus ProModem Ultima (V.42bis)
Init=AT&F&C1&D3*E9*F3*N6*S1S7=60S0=1&W
Speed=38400

Racal Datacomm ALM 3223 (V.42bis)
Init=AT&F&C1&D3\M0\N3\P2\Q1\V1S7=60S0=1&W
Speed=38400

Supra FAXModem V.32bis (V.42bis)
Init=AT&FN1W2&C1&D1&K3&Q5\N3%C1S7=60S36=7S48=7S95=45S0=1&W
Speed=57600

Telebit T1600 (V.42bis)
Init=AT&FX2&C1&D3&R3S7=60S51=6S58=0S59=15S68=2S180=2S190=1S0=1&W
Speed=38400

Telebit T2500 (V.42bis)
Init=AT~&FX2S7=60S51=5S52=2S66=1S68=2S97=1S98=3S106=1S131=1S0=1&W

Telebit T3000 (V.42bis)
Init=AT&FX2&C1&D3S51=6S59=7S68=2S7=60S0=1&W
Speed=38400

Telebit QBlazer (V.42bis)
Init=AT&FX2&C1&D3S59=7S68=2S7=60S0=1&W
Speed=38400

Texas Instruments V.32bis Internal Modem
Init=AT&F&C1&D3%C1\J0\N7\Q2\V2S7=60S0=1&W
Speed=38400

Toshiba T24/DF Internal
Init=AT&F&C1&D3\J0\N3\Q2%C1S7=60S36=7S46=138S48−7S0=1&W
Speed=9600

Universal Data Systems FasTalk V.32/42b (V.42bis)
Init=AT&F&C1&D3\J0\M0\N7\V1\Q2%C1S7=60S0=1&W
Speed=38400

Universal Data Systems V.32 (no MNP or V.42)
Init=AT&F&C1&D2S7=60S0=1&W
Speed=9600

Universal Data Systems V.3224 (MNP 4)
Init=AT&F&C1&D2\J0\N3\Q2S7=60S0=1&W

Universal Data Systems V.3225 (MNP 5)
Init=AT&F&C1&D2\J0\N3\Q2%C1S7=60S0=1&W

Universal Data Systems V.3227 (V.42bis)
Init=AT&F&C1&D2\J0\M0\N7\Q2%C1S7=60S0=1&W
Speed=38400

Universal Data Systems V.3229 (V.42bis)
Init=AT&F&C1&D3\J0\M0\N7\Q2%C1S7=60S0=1&W
Speed=38400

US Robotics Sportster 9600 (V.42bis)
Init=AT&FX4&A3&B1&D3&H1&I0&K1&M4S7=60S0=1&W
Speed=38400

US Robotics Sportster 14400 (V.42bis)
Init=AT&FX4&A3&B1&D3&H1&I0&K1&M4S7=60S0=1&W
Speed=57600

US Robotics Sportster 14400 (V.42bis)
Init=AT&FX4&B1&C1&D2&H1&K1&M4E0X7Q0V1S0=1&W
Speed=57600

US Robotics Sportster 28800 (V.34)
Init=AT&FS0=1&C1&D2&H1&R2&N14&B1&W
Speed=115200

US Robotics Courier V.32bis (V.42bis)
Init=AT&FX4&A3&C1&D2&M4&H1&K1&B1S0=1&W
Speed=38400

US Robotics Courier HST Dual Standard (V.42bis)
Init=AT&FB0X4&A3&C1&D2&M4&H1&K1&B1&R2&S1S0=1&W
Speed=115200

US Robotics Courier HST (V.42bis)
Init=AT&FB0X4&A3&C1&D2&M1&H1&K1&B1S0=1&W
Speed=115200

US Robotics WorldPort 2496 FAX/Data (V.42bis)
Init=AT&FX4&C1&D3%C1"H3\J0-J1\N3\Q2\V2S7=60S0=1&W
Speed=57600

US Robotics WorldPort 9696 FAX/Data (MNP 5)
Init=AT&FX4&C1&D3%C1\J0\N3\Q2\V2S7=60S0=1&W

US Robotics WorldPort 9600 (MNP 5)
Init=AT&FX4&C1&D3%C1\J0\N3\Q2\V2S7=60S0=1&W

US Robotics WorldPort 14400 (V.42bis)
Init=AT&FX4&A3&B1&C1&D3&H1&K1&M4S7=60S0=1&W
Speed=57600

Ven-Tel PCM 9600 Plus (MNP)
Init=AT&FB0&C1&D3\N3\Q3%B0%C1%F1S7=60S0=1&W

ViVa 9642e (V.42bis)
Init=AT&F&C1&D3&K3&Q5\N3%C3S7=60S36=7S46=138S48=7S95=47S0=1&W
Speed=38400

ViVa 14.4/FAX (V.42bis)
Init=AT&F&C1&D3&K3&Q5\N3%C3S7=60S36=7S46=138S48=7S95=47S0=1&W
Speed=38400

ZOOM V.32 turbo (V.42bis)
Init=AT&FW1&C1&D3&K3&Q5%C1\N3S7=60S36=7S46=138S48=7S95=47S0=1&W
Speed=38400

ZOOM V.32bis (V.42bis)
Init=AT&FW1&C1&D3&K3&Q9%C1\N3S7=60S36=7S95=47S0=1&W
Speed=38400

Zyxel U-1496 (V.42bis)
Init=AT&FX6&B1&C1&D2&N0&K4&H3S7=60S0=1&W
Speed=57600

For the latest information on modem configuration, visit www.cisco.com.

RFC List

The following is a list of RFCs referenced in this book:

RFC Number	RFC Title	Chapter Referenced
1055	Nonstandard for Transmission of IP Datagrams Over Serial Lines: SLIP	5
1144	Compressing TCP/IP Headers for Low-Speed Serial Links	5, 13
1220	Point-to-Point Protocol Extensions for Bridging	5
1294	Multiprotocol Interconnect over Frame Relay	11
1331	The Point-to-Point Protocol (PPP) for the Transmission of Multiprotocol Datagrams over Point-to-Point Links	5
1334	PPP Authentication Protocols	5
1356	Multiprotocol Interconnect on X.25 and ISDN in the Packet Mode	10
1378	The PPP AppleTalk Control Protocol (ATCP)	5
1490	Multiprotocol Interconnect Over Frame Relay	11
1492	Access Control Protocol, Sometimes Called TACACS	5
1541	Dynamic Host Configuration Protocol	9
1549	PPP in HDLC Framing	5
1552	The PPP Internetworking Packet Exchange Control Protocol (IPXCP)	5
1570	PPP LCP Extension	5
1631	The IP Network Address Translator (NAT)	14
1661	The Point-to-Point Protocol (PPP)	5
1662	PPP in HDLC-like Framing	5
1717	The PPP Multilink Protocol (MP)	5, 7, 8
1918	Address Allocation for Private Internets	14
1990	The PPP Multilink Protocol (MP)	5, 7
2002	IP Mobility support	Appendix F
2006	The Definitions of Managed Objects for IP Mobility Support using SMIv2.	Appendix F
2118	Microsoft Point-To-Point Compression (MPPC) Protocol	5, 13
2132	DHCP Options and BOOTP Vendor Extensions	9

Emerging and Complementary Technologies

This appendix introduces you to topics related to remote access networks. These topics are presented in this appendix because they are in addition to the topics covered with the BCRAN course framework. Of course, the topics related to remote access networks are not limited to those presented here.

The following information was extracted from Cisco Connection Online at www.cisco.com. You are encouraged to consult Cisco's Web site to expand your knowledge of these subjects.

Cable Modems

Cable modems send two-way, high-speed data transmissions using the same coaxial lines that transmit cable television. Some cable service providers are promising data speeds up to 6.5 times faster than T1 leased lines. This speed makes cable an attractive medium for transferring large amounts of digital information quickly, including complex files such as video clips, audio files, and large chunks of data. Information that would take two minutes to download using ISDN can be downloaded in two seconds through a cable modem connection.

Cable modem access provides speeds superior to leased lines, with lower costs and simpler installation. When the cable infrastructure is in place, a firm can connect through the installation of a modem or router. And because cable modems do not use the telephone system infrastructure, there are no local loop charges. Products such as Cisco's uBR904 cable modem make cable access an even more attractive investment by integrating a fully functional Cisco IOS router, four-port hub, and cable modem into one unit. This combination allows businesses to replace combinations of routers, bridges, hubs, and single-port cable modems with one product. In addition, the uBR cable modem is designed to grow as a company grows, accommodating additional users without creating a need for new equipment.

Cable modems provide a full-time connection. As soon as users turn on their computers, they are connected to the Internet. This setup removes the time and effort of dialing in to establish a connection. Cable's always-on connection also means that a company's information pipe is open at all times. This setup increases the vulnerability of data to hackers, and is a good reason to install firewalls and configure cable routers to maximize security. Fortunately, the industry is moving toward the standardization of cable modems, and the move is likely to address encryption needs. For instance, new models of Cisco's uBR904 cable modem will provide IP security and firewall capabilities. These features protect company LANs and provide VPN tunneling support for authenticated and encrypted connectivity.

Because the connection is permanently established, cable modems cannot dial in to different networks or locations. Any network connection must take place through the Internet. For example, employees using a cable modem at home to surf the Web can connect to a company LAN only if the business connects its LAN to the Internet. Moving through the Internet in this way can restrict the speedy connection of cable modems. To battle this problem, cable access service providers such as Cox Communications are in the process of developing services that combine cable and T1 connections to provide fast and reliable remote-office-to-corporate-network connections.

Availability may be the biggest barrier to cable modem adoption by businesses. This is because only a few office buildings have been outfitted for cable reception, compared to the almost 85 percent of households in North America that are wired for cable.

Some cable operators are in the process of replacing traditional one-way cable systems with the more interactive two-way architecture known as **hybrid fiber coaxial (HFC)**. Because of this upgrade and the need to expand networks to include businesses, the market penetration of cable modems is expected to lag behind DSLs.

XDSL

Digital scriber line (DSL) technology provides dedicated, high-speed Internet access by using existing copper telephone lines. In simple terms, DSL "carves off" a portion of the telephone line to use exclusively for data transmission, and provides high-speed Internet access without interfering with regular phone services. Routers and modems assist at either end of the communication.

Businesses that find their current access speed stifling or want to reduce the cost of data communications may be interested in DSL service. DSL can support high-speed Internet access, remote collaboration, virtual private networking, full-motion video, and other high-bandwidth applications.

DSL is often referred to as **xDSL**, with the "x" referring to the numerous flavors of DSL that are being implemented across the country, including ADSL and SDSL. **ADSL (asymmetrical DSL)** provides faster downloading speed because traffic to the user (downstream) is given more bandwidth than traffic from the user (upstream). **SDSL (symmetrical DSL)** assigns equal amounts of bandwidth to each direction.

Like a leased line such as a T1, DSL is a dedicated connection, providing around-the-clock Internet connection and instantaneous e-mail delivery. Unlike a leased line, DSL does not require the installation of a special cable, nor does it carry with it the expensive local-loop charges that phone companies tack on to T1 use. Some consider DSL to be a more secure solution than cable modem access because it uses a private communications channel—a phone line. Cable lines are shared by many.

DSL gives companies the capability to increase their bandwidth on the fly as their needs change—it is often simply a matter of asking your service provider to increase the amount of bandwidth available to your firm. A business might start with a 256 K access, and then boost it to as high as 1.5 Mbps as the company grows. By choosing networking products that accommodate these upgrades, companies can establish faster connections without purchasing new equipment. Expanding small and medium-sized businesses might also want to look for DSL routers that accommodate more than one DSL line. This scenario reduces the expense associated with expanding to a second DSL line if or when it is needed.

Because of the high number of existing telephone lines, DSL service is expected to reach a large portion of the market. Many of the existing lines need to be upgraded, however, before they can support DSL service.

VPN and Layer 2 Tunneling Protocol

Cisco is a leader in delivering technologies that transform access **Virtual Private Networks (VPNs)** from a promising idea into a practical reality. With the availability of Layer 2 Tunneling Protocol (L2TP) to Cisco IOS software, Cisco offers a standard way to provide Access VPN connectivity. Cisco's end-to-end hardware and Cisco IOS software networking products provide sophisticated security for sensitive private transmissions over the public infrastructure, quality of service through traffic differentiation, reliability for mission-critical applications, scalability for supporting large bandwidths of data, and comprehensive network management to enable a complete Access VPN solution.

VPNs enable today's increasingly mobile workforce to connect to their corporate intranets or extranets whenever, wherever, or however they require; improving productivity and flexibility while reducing access costs.

To provide a low-cost, easily accessible pathway to a corporate intranet or extranet, Access VPNs simulate a private network—but over a shared infrastructure, such as the Internet. They offer access for mobile users, telecommuters, and small offices through a range of technologies—including dial, ISDN, xDSL, mobile IP, and cable.

A key building block for Access VPNs is L2TP (Layer 2 Tunneling Protocol), an extension to the Point-to-Point (PPP) protocol and a fundamental building block for VPNs. L2TP merges the best features of two other tunneling protocols: Layer 2 Forwarding (L2F) from Cisco Systems and Point-to-Point Tunneling (PPTP) from Microsoft. L2TP is an Internet Engineering Task Force (IETF) emerging standard, which is currently under co-development and endorsed by Cisco Systems, Microsoft, Ascend, 3Com, and other networking industry leaders.

Mobile IP

Mobile IP, request for comment 2002 (RFC 2002), enables a host to be identified by a single IP address, even while the device physically moves its point of attachment from one network to another. This allows for the transparent forwarding of data packets to a single address. This IETF proposed standard functionality provides the unique capability to maintain sessions, regardless of movement between locations on different networks, because there are no address changes to be dealt with. Mobility becomes an issue that the mobile IP protocol can transparently negotiate to allow users new freedoms. Movement from one point of attachment to another is seamlessly achieved without the intervention or the knowledge of the user. Mobile IP is the first protocol to offer such mobility transparently to applications. Roaming from a wired network to a wireless or wide area network can also be achieved with ease. Therefore, mobile IP provides ubiquitous connectivity for users, whether they are within their enterprise networks or away from home. Access to the resources within the network remains the same from the perspective of the user. This allows for truly transparent mobility, with respect to all devices that communicate with the mobile node and all intermediate devices within networks.

An added benefit of mobile IP is that it allows users to gain access to their enterprise networks and the Internet in the same way, no matter where they are physically. They can access resources in the same way while they are within the bounds of their enterprise network and also when they dial in from hotel rooms or customer sites. Mobile IP provides a solution that can work in all connectivity situations. It enables users to connect to media of any kind, automatically locate a mobility agent, and register their current location with a home gateway. The home gateway then forwards any traffic received for this mobile user to his current location. If the user moves, it will notify the home gateway of the move because the mobile IP software is automatically monitoring for this condition. In this way, sessions can be seamlessly maintained, despite movement. When the user returns home, the mobile IP protocol automatically discovers this, and informs its home gateway that it has arrived home. The host will behave as any other IP device normally would.

Cisco IOS software increases the overall offering of this mobility solution because many value-added features can be used in conjunction with mobile IP. All IOS features for differentiation of services, accounting, traffic engineering, and queuing can be used in conjunction with mobile IP. By always being able to identify a user by an IP address, it is also possible to simplify certain configurations within the network. Access-lists, and queuing or traffic-shaping configurations could remain static, for example. Netflow statistics and accounting data would be obtained in a straightforward manner. And it is possible to manage the mobile IP functionality in the network the same way that the rest of the IOS platform elements are monitored. Cisco has implemented full MIB support for mobile IP, as specified in RFC 2006.

Easy IP

With Cisco IOS Easy IP, router-configuration tasks are minimized: simply plug in the router, configure the dial-up number for a central access server, and connect the LAN devices to the router. With Cisco IOS Easy IP, a Cisco router automatically assigns private IP addresses (RFC 1918) to SOHO hosts via the Dynamic Host Configuration Protocol (DHCP), automatically negotiates its own registered IP address from a central server via the Point-to-Point Protocol/Internet Control Protocol (PPP/IPCP), and enables all SOHO hosts to access the global Internet by using a single registered IP address. Because Cisco IOS Easy IP utilizes existing port-level multiplexed Network Address Translation (NAT) functionality within Cisco IOS software, IP addresses on the remote LAN are invisible to the Internet, and the remote LAN is more secure.

Cisco IOS Easy IP does the following:

- Dramatically lowers Internet access costs for remote networks
- Eases IP address management
- Simplifies remote access to the Internet
- Improves remote network security

Cisco IOS Easy IP enables true mobility; client IP addresses are transparently configured via DHCP each time they power up on the network.

Cisco IOS Easy IP enables ISPs to allocate a single registered IP address to each remote LAN so that any host on the LAN can access the Internet. It allows ISPs to maximize their customer bases while minimizing the required number of registered IP addresses. This feature simplifies and reduces costs associated with global IP address management tasks for ISPs and their customers. Because only a single registered IP address is required to support all users on an entire remote LAN, customers and ISPs can use their registered IP addresses more efficiently. Cisco IOS Easy IP also reduces management tasks and costs associated with VLSM-based addressing for each remote LAN.

Cisco DialOut Utility

Cisco DialOut Utility, Release 1.5, is a software utility that allows you to send faxes or use communication software from any workstation connected to a network access server (NAS). The Cisco DialOut Utility adds one or more virtual communication (com) ports to your Microsoft Windows workstation. These com ports are used to represent com ports on the NAS. Individual workstations do not require modems, offering substantial savings in a large network and increased savings as the network grows.

The Cisco DialOut Utility is designed to run on Windows 95, Windows 98, and Windows NT.

Multichassis Multilink PPP

Multilink PPP provides the capability of splitting and recombining packets to a single end-system across a logical pipe (also called a **bundle**), which is formed by multiple links. Multilink PPP provides bandwidth on demand, and reduces transmission latency across WAN links.

Multichassis Multilink PPP, on the other hand, provides the additional capability for links to terminate at multiple routers with different remote addresses. MMP can also handle both analog and digital traffic.

This feature is intended for situations with large pools of dial-in users, in which a single chassis cannot provide enough dial-in ports. This feature allows companies to provide a single dial-up number to its users, and to apply the same solution to analog and digital calls. This feature allows Internet service providers, for example, to allocate a single ISDN rotary number to several ISDN PRIs across several routers.

X.25 Over D Channel

ISDN uses the D channel to carry signal information. ISDN can also use the D channel in a BRI to carry X.25 packets. The D channel has a capacity of 16 Kbps, and the X.25 over D channel can utilize up to 9.6 Kbps.

X.25 traffic over the D channel can be used as a primary interface, where low-volume, sporadic interactive traffic is the normal mode of operation. (This feature is not available on the ISDN Primary Rate Interface—PRI).

X.25 and Frame Relay Switching

This appendix discusses how to configure the router to act as an X.25 and Frame Relay switch. It is sometimes useful to simulate a WAN cloud and its components. It is therefore possible to take a router and configure it as a switch. This functionality was used in preparing for the case studies of Chapters 10 and 11.

Setting Up the Router as an X.25 Switch

The router can be configured to switch X.25 traffic over a Transmission Control Protocol (TCP) connection, as shown in Figure G-1.

Figure G-1 *Setting Up the Router as a Switch*

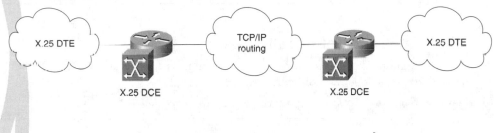

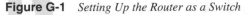

In this mode, the backbone is comprised of routers switching IP datagrams. A few X.25 devices, such as Packet Assembler/Disassembler (PADs), connect to each other across the routed IP backbone network.

The switching performance of IP is higher than native X.25 switching equipment. This use of a TCP/IP cloud provides customers with high-performance, concurrent switching of X.25, IP, and other protocols.

NOTE A router can act as a local or a remote switch. A router can switch X.25 traffic over TCP. This is referred to as XOT.

To enable X.25 switching, enter the **x25 routing** command in global configuration mode.

X.25 traffic can be routed locally between serial ports. In this case, static routing statements map X.121 addresses to serial ports. The router allows X.25 interfaces that are attached to different ports to make switched virtual circuit (SVC) connections, which is called local X.25 switching.

Remote X.25 switching allows X.25 interfaces that are attached to different routers to establish SVCs and permanent virtual circuits (PVCs). Remote X.25 switching is accomplished by tunneling all the X.25 call setup and data traffic between routers in a TCP connection. To enable remote switching, use the **x.25 route** command:

```
Router(config)#x25 route [# position] x.121-address [cud pattern] interface type-
➥ number
```

x25 route Command	Description
# position	(Optional) A positional value that specifies the line number in the table where the entry will be placed.
x.121-address	Destination X.121 address pattern.
cud *pattern*	(Optional) Call User Data (CUD) pattern, which is a printable ASCII string. Caution: This must be the value provided by the X.25 service provider.
type-number	The destination interface number, such as serial 0.

Complete X.25 Switch Configuration

shows configuration output from a router that is acting as an X.25 switch that switches SVCs. In this example, a 3600 was configured as an X.25 Switch.

Example G-1   **show run** *Output from a Router that is Acting as an X.25 Switch that Switches SVCs*

```
x25-switch#sh run
Building configuration...

Current configuration:
!
version 11.3
no service password-encryption
!
hostname x25-switch
!
!
x25 routing
!
!
interface Ethernet0/0
 no ip address
 shutdown
 no lat enabled
```

Example G-1 **show run** *Output from a Router that is Acting as an X.25 Switch that Switches SVCs (Continued)*

```
!
interface Serial1/0
 no ip address
 encapsulation x25 dce
 no ip mroute-cache
 clockrate 64000
!
interface Serial1/1
 no ip address
 encapsulation x25 dce
 no ip mroute-cache
 clockrate 64000
!
!
ip classless
!
x25 route 311082194567 interface Serial1/0
x25 route 311082191234 interface Serial1/1
!
line con 0
line aux 0
line vty 0 4
 login
!
end
```

Setting up the Router as a Frame Relay Switch

Local Frame Relay switching enables the Cisco router to switch Frame Relay frames between interfaces, based on the data link connection identifier (DLCI) number in the frame header. A router interface performing PVC switching is usually configured as a Frame Relay switch, as shown in Figure G-2.

Figure G-2 *Router Switches PVCs between Serial Interfaces*

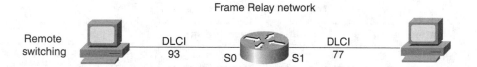

Remote Frame Relay switching enables the router to encapsulate Frame Relay frames in IP datagrams and tunnel them across an IP backbone, as shown in Figure G-3. The Cisco generic routing encapsulation (GRE) tunnel protocol is used for remote Frame Relay switching. The router is usually configured as a Frame Relay data communications equipment (DCE).

Figure G-3 *Tunneling between Routers in an IP Network Forms a Frame Relay Backbone*

Configuring Switching

Use the **frame-relay switching** command to configure the router to function within a Frame Relay network.

```
Router(config)#frame-relay switching
```

Use the **frame-relay route** command to link traffic inside the router between two serial ports when the router is functioning as a Frame Relay switch. The router is performing PVC switching between the serial ports.

```
Router(config-if)#frame-relay route in-dlci out-interface out-dlci
```

frame-relay route Command	Description
in-dlci	DLCI on which the packet is received on the interface.
out-interface	Interface that the router uses to transmit the packet.
out-dlci	DLCI that the router uses to transmit the packet over the specified out-interface.

Use the **frame-relay intf-type** command to configure the interface to function as a Frame Relay switch. The type of Frame Relay switch is determined by the router's function within the Frame Relay network.

```
Router(config-if)#frame-relay intf-type [dte ¦ dce ¦ nni]
```

frame-relay intf-type Command	Description
dte	(Optional) Router is connected to a Frame Relay network.
dce	(Optional) Router is connected to another router and is acting as a switch.
nni	(Optional) Router functions as a switch and is connected to another switch performing Network-to-Network Interface (NNI) support.

Frame Relay Switching Example

Figure G-4 shows an example of a network with Frame Relay switching. Table G-1 explains the configurations in the figure.

Figure G-4   *Frame Relay Switching Example*

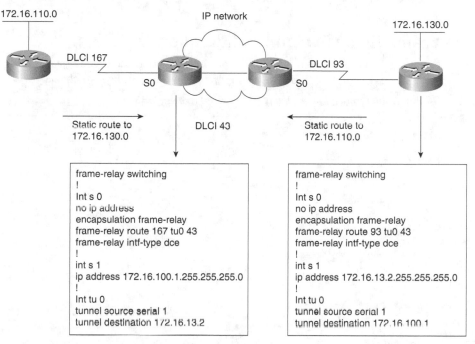

Table G-1   *Explanation of the Frame Relay Switching Example Network Configuration*

Command	Description
167	Specifies the DLCI of the arriving (source) traffic to be switched.
tu0	Specifies the outgoing interface to use.
43	Specifies the outgoing DLCI to use when forwarding the traffic.
frame-relay intf-type dce	Establishes interface S0 as the DCE. In this back-to-back Frame Relay connection, one interface must act as the DCE.
tunnel source serial 1	Defines that software-only tunnel interface 0 will use physical interface serial 1 as the entry into the tunnel.
tunnel destination 172.16.13.2	Defines that the tunnel will deliver traffic to IP address 172.16.13.2 as the tunnel destination.

The router is configured as a remote Frame Relay switch. Traffic arriving on S0 using DLCI 167 will be switched to output interface S1, and DLCI 43 will be used in the source identifier. The traffic will be carried through the IP network by using a GRE tunnel having a next-hop destination of 172.16.100.1.

The tunnel uses the same DLCI number.

Complete Frame Relay Switch Configuration

Example G-1 shows the configuration output from a router that is acting as a Frame Relay switch. In this example, a 3600 was configured as a Frame Relay switch.end

Example G-2 **show run** *Output from a Router that is Acting as a Frame Relay Switch*

```
3640-switch#sh run
Building configuration...

Current configuration:
!
version 11.3
no service password-encryption
!
hostname 3640-switch
!
enable password cisco
!
frame-relay switching
!
! <output omitted>
!
interface Serial1/0
 no ip address
 encapsulation frame-relay
 clockrate 64000
 frame-relay intf-type dce
 frame-relay route 110 interface Serial1/1 100
!
interface Serial1/1
 encapsulation frame-relay
 clockrate 64000
 frame-relay intf-type dce
 frame-relay route 100 interface Serial1/0 110
!
! <Output Omitted>
!
!
ip classless
!
!
line con 0
line aux 0
line vty 0 4
 login
!
end
```

Answers to Review Questions

This appendix provides answers to the review questions at the end of each chapter.

Chapter 2—Selecting Cisco Products for Remote Connections

1 Identify the types of WAN connections discussed in this chapter and the appropriate protocols used on each connection.

- Dedicated (uses synchronous serial)—Typical encapsulation protocols are PPP, SLIP, and HDLC.
- Circuit-switched (uses asynchronous serial or ISDN)—Typical encapsulation protocols are PPP or SLIP.
- Packet-switched (uses synchronous serial)—Typical encapsulation protocols are X.25, Frame Relay, and ATM.

2 Describe the considerations when implementing a WAN connection at a Central site, branch office, and telecommuter site. Some of the considerations appropriate for each site follow:

- **Central site** Multiple access connections, cost, access control, quality of service, redundancy, and scalability.
- **Branch office** Multiple access connections, cost, access control, redundancy, authentication, and service availability.
- **Telecommuter site** Cost, authentication, and service availability.

3 Identify available Cisco equipment designed for a telecommuter site, a branch office, and a Central site. Some of the Cisco equipment appropriate for each site follows:

- **Telecommuter site** 700 series, 800 series, and 1000 series
- **Branch office** 1600 series, 1700 series, 2500 series, and 2600 series
- **Central site** 3600 series, AS5X00 series, 4000 series, and 7000 series

Chapter 3—Assembling and Cabling the WAN Components

1 Which cables are necessary to make the proper physical asynchronous serial, ISDN, and synchronous serial connections?

> To make serial connections, Cisco supports the following standards: EIA/TIA-232, EIA/TIA-449, V.35, X.21, and EIA-530. ISDN BRI requires straight cables with RJ-45 connections. ISDN PRI requires cross cables with RJ-48 connections for T1 and DB-15 connections for E1.

2 How can you verify that you properly installed a network module in a modular router?

> All network modules have an enable LED, which indicates that the module has passed its self-tests and is available to the router. If the LED light is off, you probably did not install the module correctly.

Chapter 4—Configuring Asynchronous Connections with Modems

1 What does the lock DTE modem attribute do?

> The lock DTE attribute locks the data speed between the modem and the DTE device. This prevents the speed from being lowered during modem-to-modem negotiation or "training." Locking the speed maintains the highest possible data rate to take advantage of modem compression.

2 A user dials into a line and ends up in someone else's session. What is one possible cause?

> The last session was not terminated. The access server did not drop or disconnect the session properly.

3 What is reverse Telnet? Describe how it is used with modems.

> Reverse Telnet allows connections through an access server to an attached device or service; Telnet usually allows login to a host. The outgoing port from the access server is specified in some manner. With modems, reverse Telnet allows you to "log in" to a modem that is connected to a router in order to reach the command-line interface for the modem for testing and configuration.

4 What are the modem autoconfiguration options?

> You can use the autodiscovery feature if you do not know what type of modem is being configured. The command is **modem autoconfigure** *discovery*. Or, you can specify a specific type of modem to be autoconfigured, as long as the initialization parameters are set in the modemcap database. The command is **modem autoconfigure** *type*.

Chapter 5—Configuring Point-to-Point Protocol and Controlling Network Access

1 What are some LCP options for PPP?

- **Authentication**—Allows the dial-up target to identify that any given dial-up client is a valid client with a preassigned username and password. Two authentication options are PAP and CHAP.
- **Callback**—A PPP option used to provide call and dial-up billing consolidation.
- **Compression**—Used to improve throughput across existing links.
- **Multilink**—Makes use of the multiple bearer channels to improve throughput.

2 Describe the usefulness of PPP callback.

PPP callback provides billing consolidation, not security.

3 Describe how CHAP provides security.

CHAP provides protection against playback attack through the use of a randomly generated challenge value that is unique and unpredictable. The use of repeated challenges every two minutes during any CHAP session is intended to limit the time of exposure to any single attack.

Chapter 6—Accessing the Central Site with Windows 95

1 List the three allowed protocols used for Windows 95 Dial-Up Networking.

The three allowed protocols used for Windows 95 are NetBEUI, IPX/SPX Compatible, and TCP/IP.

2 How do you configure "Lock DTE speed" on a PC modem from Windows 95 Dial-Up Networking?

You lock the DTE speed from the PC by setting the Maximum speed option in the modem properties window.

Chapter 7—Using ISDN and DDR Technologies to Enhance Remote Connectivity

1 What is the difference between ISDN BRI and ISDN PRI?

ISDN BRI includes two 64-Kbps bearer channels and one 16-Kbps data channel. An ISDN PRI connection includes 23 or 30 64-Kbps B channels and one data channel.

2 If you are not sure what your ISDN switch type is, where can you obtain this information?

You can get this information from your ISDN service provider or from your ISP.

3 What are Q.921 and Q.931?

Q.921 is the Layer 2 framing protocol used for the D channel data. It is responsible for the communication between the terminal equipment and the ISDN switch of the local central office. LAPD frames are used in the D channel. Q.931 is the Layer 3 protocol used for the D channel. It is responsible for the call setup, connect, and call teardown.

Chapter 8—Optimizing the Use of DDR Interface—Dialer Profiles and Rotary Groups

1 How do dialer profiles simplify configurations?

By creating one logical configuration in a dialer profile, you can link physical interfaces to the profile's configuration, rather than configure each physical interface separately.

2 What features do map classes provide to dialer interfaces?

Map classes allow a network administrator to configure specific calling requirements for specific destinations. By using map classes, these calling requirements can be referenced as needed. Each map class contains a set of characteristics, such as timer values and speed. A destination that requires those specific characteristics references the map class, and those characteristics are applied to the configuration.

3 Describe a network that might not benefit from dialer profiles.

A network in which all call parameters are the same might not benefit from dialer profiles as much as a network in which there are many destinations with different calling requirements.

Chapter 9—Configuring a Cisco 700 Series Router

1 Discuss profiles and how they are used in a Cisco 700 series router.

The Cisco 700 series uses profiles to represent an interface or destination to be called. Additionally, there is a system profile that is the global configuration for the router. The LAN profile contains the configuration for the Ethernet interface. A user profile is created for each destination that needs to be called and contains the configuration for that destination. User profiles may be thought of as the configurations for the WAN interface.

2 Describe DHCP server and client operation.

DHCP servers contain a pool of addresses that are used to assign an address to a DHCP client when the client boots and requests an address in a broadcast message.

Chapter 10—Using X.25 for Remote Access

1 Explain the difference between an X.25 DTE and DCE.

> Data terminal equipment (DTE) and data circuit-terminating equipment (DCE) for X.25 identify the responsibilities of the two stations on an X.25 attachment. The DTE is an end system, typically a router or a PAD. The DCE is typically a boundary function between the DTE and the public network.

2 Assume that you want an IP connection over an X.25 link. What must you do to map the network layer address to the X.121 address?

> To map a network layer address to an X.121 address you must create a static map with the **x25 map** *protocol address x.121-address* command for an SVC. On PVCs, use the **x25 pvc** *circuit protocol address x.121-address* command.

3 How can you limit traffic by lowering the amount of acknowledgements sent across the X.25 link?

> You can adjust the incoming or outgoing packet window size before an acknowledgment is sent. The window size specifies the number of packets that can be received or sent without receiving or sending an acknowledgment. If you raise the window size, you lower the number of acknowledgment packets and total packets sent. The commands to do this are **x25 win** *packets* and **x25 wout** *packets*.

Chapter 11—Frame Relay Connection and Traffic Flow Control

1 What is a DLCI and how is it used to route Frame Relay traffic?

> A data-link connection identifier (DLCI) identifies the logical virtual circuit between the CPE and the Frame Relay switch. The Frame Relay switch maps the DLCIs between each pair of routers to create a PVC. DLCIs have local significance in that the identifier references the point between the local router and the Frame Relay switch to which it is connected.

2 Why would you use Frame Relay subinterfaces?

> If you want to avoid reachability issues brought on by split horizon, you can create a subinterface, which is a logical subdivision of a physical interface. You can also create subinterfaces if you want granularity in the way the physical interface is configured. With some exceptions, you can set different parameters on the different subinterfaces, as opposed to the entire interface.

3 List and describe three Frame Relay traffic-shaping features.

> - **Rate enforcement**   Used to define and enforce a rate at which packets are being sent.
> - **BECN support**   Used to throttle back the rate at which packets are sent, based on BECN notifications from the switch.

- **Queuing**   You may have different types of traffic, such as IP, SNA, or IPX transmitted over the same Frame Relay VC, and you can use queues to ensure that different types of traffic receive a certain amount of bandwidth.

Chapter 12—Enabling Backup to a Permanent Connection

1   What are two circumstances or scenarios in which a backup interface will be enabled?

A backup interface is enabled if a primary line fails or reaches a specified level of high link utilization.

Chapter 13—Managing Network Performance with Queuing and Compression

1   When would you use weighted fair queuing, custom queuing, and priority queuing?

- Use weighted fair queuing when no strict control is required on a link. Weighted fair queuing is used to interleave low- and high-volume traffic over the same link so that low-volume traffic can be transmitted in a timely manner instead of waiting behind a large file transfer.

- Use priority queuing when you need absolute strict priority in selecting which packets to send first. This technique is useful in environments in which traffic has a hierarchy of importance. The drawback is that some traffic theoretically may never get through with priority queuing. The solution to this problem is to consider custom queuing.

- Use custom queuing if you need to guarantee a certain amount of bandwidth for specific kinds of traffic.

2   When is it best to use payload compression versus link compression?

If the connection is anything other than a point-to-point connection, use payload compression. Payload compression does not compress the payload header like link compression does. The packet header is readable when switched through a WAN packet network.

Chapter 14—Scaling IP Addresses with Network Address Translation

1   What is the difference between a simple translation entry and an extended translation entry? State how each one is used.

A simple entry is used for inside local address translation. An extended entry is used to overload inside global addresses by allowing a single inside address to represent multiple inside local addresses simultaneously.

2 Give one or more examples when NAT could be used.

NAT can be used to connect to the Internet, but not all hosts have unique IP addresses. NAT allows nonregistered IP use. It can also be used to modify your internal addresses, enabling you to change the address incrementally. NAT can also be used for basic load sharing.

3 Your networks are addressed by using 10.1.1.1/24 subnets. Your ISP provides you a globally unique address of 192.1.1.0/24. What commands do you use to translate from 10.1.1.0/24 to 192.1.1.0/24?

```
access-list 1 permit 10.1.1.1 0.0.0.254
ip nat pool reviewtest 192.1.1.1 192.1.1.254 netmask 255.255.255.0
ip nat inside source list 1 pool reviewtest
! configured on the inside interface
 int e 0
ip nat inside
! configured on the outside interface
 int s 0
ip nat outside
```

4 When viewing the output of the **show ip nat translations** command, how can you determine when an inside global address is being used for overloading inside global addresses?

An inside address is listed for each inside local address that it represents. If it represents three inside local addresses, it will appear three times with a different port number.

Chapter 15—Using AAA to Scale Access Control in an Expanding Network

1 What is authentication?

Who are you? Authentication verifies the identity of a user or system.

2 What is authorization?

Authorization is what you can have and what network resources are available to you. Authorization grants authority to use specific network resources or allows specific privileges.

3 What is accounting in regard to a dial-up networking environment?

Accounting is what resources you used and for how long you used them. Accounting tracks the usage (time used) of network resources and which ones were used.

BCRAN Case Study Addresses and Dial-Up Phone Numbers

Overview

This appendix provides the addresses and phone numbers used in the case studies found in this book.

While I prepared the case studies for this book, six pods were internetworked together using the Ethernet interface of the central routers to create a multi-pod WAN. Most case studies were performed using Pod A. During configuration verification output, such as with the **show ip route** command, you might see addresses from other pods. The following addresses will help you to identify routes and routers.

BCRAN Case Study Addresses and Dial-Up Phone Number Matrix, Part I

Pod	Station Name	Ethernet/IP Address	Lab - IP Address Pool Range	BRI / Address	PRI Address / Dialer 1	Dialer 2 to Home
A	CentralA	10.115.0.110	10.115.0.111–114		10.130.0.2	10.30.1.1
	BranchA	10.218.0.1		10.130.0.1		
	HomeA	10.118.0.1		10.30.1.2		10.30.1.2
	PCA	10.118.0.2				
B	CentralB	10.115.0.115	10.115.0.116–119		10.135.0.2	10.30.2.1
	BranchB	10.219.0.1		10.135.0.1		
	HomeB	10.119.0.1		10.30.2.2		10.30.2.2
	PCB	10.119.0.2				
C	CentralC	10.115.0.120	10.115.0.121–124		10.140.0.2	10.30.3.1
	BranchC	10.220.0.1		10.140.0.1		
	HomeC	10.120.0.1		10.30.3.2		10.30.3.2
	PCC	10.120.0.2				

Pod	Station Name	Ethernet/IP Address	Lab - IP Address Pool Range	BRI / Address	PRI Address / Dialer 1	Dialer 2 to Home
D	CentralD	10.115.0.125	10.115.0.126–129		10.145.0.2	10.30.4.1
	BranchD	10.221.0.1		10.145.0.1		
	HomeD	10.121.0.1		10.30.4.2		10.30.4.2
	PCD	10.121.0.2				
E	CentralE	10.115.0.130	10.115.0.131–134		10.150.0.2	10.30.5.1
	BranchE	10.222.0.1		10.150.0.1		
	HomeE	10.122.0.1		10.30.5.2		10.30.5.2
	PCE	10.122.0.2				
F	CentralF	10.115.0.135	10.115.0.136–139		10.155.0.2	10.30.6.1
	BranchF	10.223.0.1		10.155.0.1		
	HomeF	10.123.0.1		10.30.6.2		10.30.6.2
	PCF	10.123.0.2				

(Use 24 Bit Subnetting)

BCRAN Case Study Addresses and Dial-Up Phone Number Matrix, Part II

Pod	Station Name	Asynchronous Telephone #	ISDN-BRI Phone #	ISDN-PRI Phone #	Serial Address /Frame Relay	DLCI to get to...	NAT Addresses
A	CentralA	1001		1000	10.140.1.1	100	10.117.1.1–254
	BranchA		2001		10.140.1.2	110	
	HomeA		2002				
	PCA	1002					
B	CentralB	1003		2000	10.140.2.1	120	10.117.2.1–254
	BranchB		2003		10.140.2.2	130	
	HomeB		2004				
	PCB	1004					

Pod	Station Name	Asynchro-nous Telephone #	ISDN-BRI Phone #	ISDN-PRI Phone #	Serial Address /Frame Relay	DLCI to get to...	NAT Addresses
C	CentralC	1005		3000	10.140.3.1	140	10.117.3.1–254
	BranchC		2005		10.140.3.2	150	
	HomeC		2006				
	PCC	1006					
D	CentralD	1007		4000	10.140.4.1	160	10.117.4.1–254
	BranchD		2007		10.140.4.2	170	
	HomeD		2008				
	PCD	1008					
E	CentralE	1009		5000	10.140.5.1	200	10.117.5.1–254
	BranchE		2009		10.140.5.2	210	
	HomeE		2010				
	PCE	1010					
F	CentralF	1011		6000	10.140.6.1	220	10.117.6.1–254
	BranchF		2011		10.140.6.2	230	
	HomeF		2012				
	PCF	1012					

(Use 24 Bit Subnetting)

Pod Topology

Figures I-1 through I-6 show locations of IP addresses.

Figure I-1   *Pod A Topology*

Pod A Network

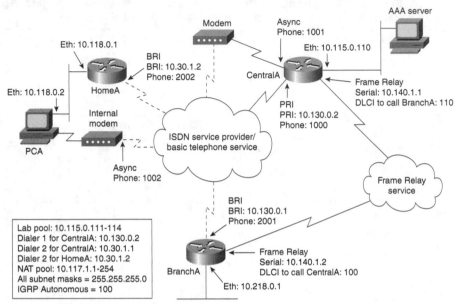

Figure I-2   *Pod B Topology*

Pod B Network

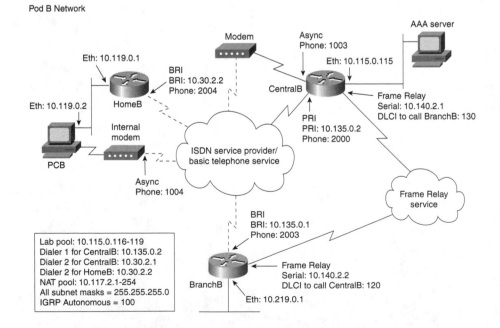

Figure I-3   *Pod C Topology*

Pod C Network

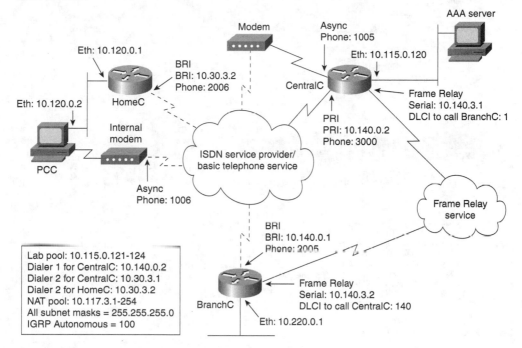

Lab pool: 10.115.0.121-124
Dialer 1 for CentralC: 10.140.0.2
Dialer 2 for CentralC: 10.30.3.1
Dialer 2 for HomeC: 10.30.3.2
NAT pool: 10.117.3.1-254
All subnet masks = 255.255.255.0
IGRP Autonomous = 100

Figure I-4   *Pod D Topology*

Pod D Network

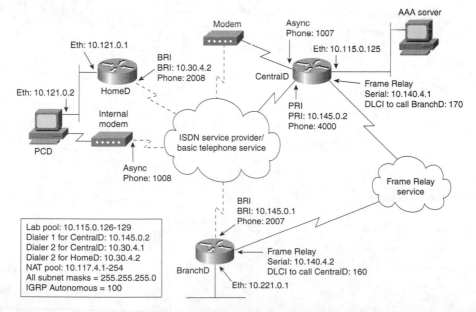

Lab pool: 10.115.0.126-129
Dialer 1 for CentralD: 10.145.0.2
Dialer 2 for CentralD: 10.30.4.1
Dialer 2 for HomeD: 10.30.4.2
NAT pool: 10.117.4.1-254
All subnet masks = 255.255.255.0
IGRP Autonomous = 100

Figure I-5   *Pod E Topology*

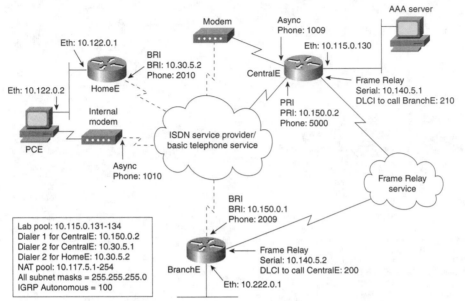

Pod E Network

Figure I-6   *Pod F Topology*

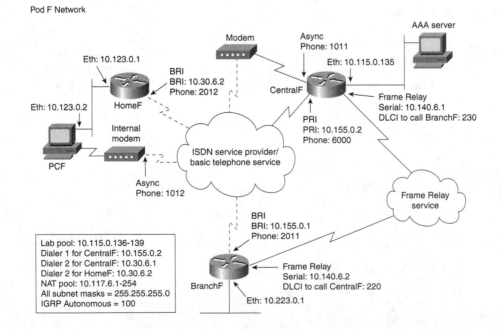

Pod F Network

This glossary assembles and defines the terms and acronyms used in this book. Most of the terms are related to remote access. Many of the definitions have yet to be standardized, and many terms have several meanings. Multiple definitions and acronym expressions are included where they apply.

For current information, visit the Internetworking Terms and Acronyms page on the Cisco Press Publications site:

> http://www.cisco.com/cpress/cc/td/doc/cisintwk/ita/index.htm

NUMERIC

10BaseT. 10-Mbps baseband Ethernet specification, using two pairs of twisted-pair cabling (Category 3, 4, or 5): one pair for transmitting data and the other for receiving data. 10BaseT, which is part of the IEEE 802.3 specification, has a distance limit of approximately 328 feet (100 meters) per segment.

802.x. Set of IEEE standards for the definition of LAN protocols.

A

AAA. Authentication, authorization, and accounting (pronounced "triple a").

access server. Communications processor that connects asynchronous devices to a LAN or WAN through network and terminal emulation software. Performs both synchronous and asynchronous routing of supported protocols. Sometimes called a **network access server (NAS)**.

access-list. List kept by routers to control access to or from the router for a number of services (for example, to prevent packets with a certain IP address from leaving a particular interface on the router).

accounting management. One of five categories of network management defined by ISO for management of OSI networks. Accounting management subsystems are responsible for collecting network data relating to resource usage.

ACK. See *acknowledgment*.

acknowledgment. Notification sent from one network device to another to acknowledge that some event occurred (for example, receipt of a message). Sometimes abbreviated as **ACK**. Compare to *NAK*.

ACL. See *access-list.*

ACRC. Acronym for Advanced Cisco Routers Configuration course.

ACS. Acronym for Access Control Server.

ADSL. Acronym for Asymmetric Digital Subscriber Line. One of four DSL technologies. ADSL is designed to deliver more bandwidth downstream (from the central office to the customer site) than upstream. Downstream rates range from 1.5 to 9 Mbps, whereas upstream bandwidth ranges from 16 to 640 Kbps. ADSL transmissions work at distances up to 18,000 feet (5,488 meters) over a single copper twisted-pair. Compare to *ADSL, HDSL,* and *VDSL.*

algorithm. Well-defined rule or process for arriving at a solution to a problem. In networking, algorithms are commonly used to determine the best route for traffic from a particular source to a particular destination.

AMI. Acronym for Alternate Mark Inversion. Line-code type used on T1 and E1 circuits. In AMI, a zero is represented by 01 during each bit cell; and a one is represented by 11 or 00, alternately, during each bit cell. AMI requires that the sending device maintain ones density. Ones density is not maintained independently of the data stream. Sometimes called **binary coded alternate mark inversion**. Compare to *B8ZS.*

analog. Electrical circuit that is represented by means of continuous variable physical quantities (such as voltages and frequencies), as opposed to discrete representations (such as the 0/1, off/on representation of digital circuits).

analog transmission. Signal transmission over wires or through the air, in which information is conveyed through variations of combinations of signal amplitude, frequency, and phase.

ANSI. Acronym for American National Standards Institute. Voluntary organization—composed of corporate, government, and other members—that coordinates standards-related activities, approves U.S. national standards, and develops positions for the United States in international standards organizations. ANSI helps develop international and U.S. standards relating to communications and networking (among other things). ANSI is a member of the IEC and the ISO.

ARA. Acronym for AppleTalk Remote Access. Protocol that provides Macintosh users direct access to information and resources at a remote AppleTalk site. Also known as **ARAP.**

ARP. Acronym for Address Resolution Protocol. Internet protocol used to map an IP address to a MAC address. Defined in RFC 826.

ARPA. Acronym for Advanced Research Projects Agency. Research and development organization that is part of DoD. ARPA is responsible for numerous technological advances in communications and networking. ARPA evolved into DARPA, and then became ARPA again (in 1994).

ARPANET. Acronym for Advanced Research Projects Agency Network. Landmark packet-switching network established in 1969. ARPANET was developed in the 1970s by BBN and funded by ARPA (and later DARPA). It eventually evolved into the Internet. The term ARPANET was officially retired in 1990.

ARQ. Acronym for Automatic Repeat Request. Communication technique in which the receiving device detects errors and requests retransmissions.

ASCII. Acronym for American Standard Code for Information Interchange. Eight-bit code for character representation (seven bits plus parity).

assigned numbers. RFC [STD2] documents the currently assigned values from several series of numbers used in network protocol implementations. This RFC is updated periodically, and current information can be obtained from the IANA. If you develop a protocol or application that requires the use of a link, socket, port, protocol, and so forth, contact the IANA to receive a number assignment.

async. Subset of tty.

asynchronous transmission. Term describing digital signals that are transmitted without precise clocking. Such signals generally have different frequencies and phase relationships. Asynchronous transmissions usually encapsulate individual characters in control bits (called start and stop bits) that designate the beginning and end of each character. Compare to *synchronous transmission.*

attenuation. Loss of communication signal energy.

AUI. Acronym for Attachment Unit Interface. IEEE 802.3 interface between a Media Attachment Unit (MAU) and a Network Interface Card (NIC). The term AUI can also refer to the rear panel port to which an AUI cable might attach.

authentication. In security, the verification of the identity of a person or process.

average rate. Average rate, in kilobits per second (Kbps), that a given virtual circuit transmits.

B

B8ZS. Acronym for binary 8-zero substitution. Line-code type used on T1 and E1 circuits, in which a special code is substituted whenever eight consecutive zeros are sent over the link. This code is then interpreted at the remote end of the connection. This technique guarantees ones density independently of the data stream. Sometimes called **bipolar 8-zero substitution**. Compare to *AMI*.

backbone. Part of a network that acts as the primary path for traffic that is most often sourced from and destined for other networks.

Backward Explicit Congestion Notification. See *BECN*.

bandwidth. Difference between the highest and lowest frequencies available for network signals. The term is also used to describe the rated throughput capacity of a given network medium or protocol.

bandwidth reservation. Process of assigning bandwidth to users and applications served by a network. Involves assigning priority to different flows of traffic, based on how critical and delay-sensitive they are. This makes the best use of available bandwidth, and if the network becomes congested, lower-priority traffic can be dropped. Sometimes called **bandwidth allocation**.

baseband. Characteristic of a network technology in which only one carrier frequency is used. Ethernet is an example of a baseband network. Also called **narrowband**. Compare to *broadband*.

Basic Rate Interface. See *BRI*.

baud. Unit of signaling speed that is equal to the number of discrete signal elements transmitted per second. Baud is synonymous with bits per second (Bps) if each signal element represents exactly one bit.

Bc. Committed Burst. Negotiated tariff metric in Frame Relay internetworks. The maximum amount of data (in bits) that a Frame Relay internetwork is committed to accept and transmit at the CIR.

B channel. Bearer channel. This is an ISDN communication channel that bears or carries voice, circuit, or packet conversations. The B channel is the fundamental component of ISDN interfaces, and it carries 64,000 bits per second in either direction. Compare to *D channel*.

BCRAN. Acronym for *Building Cisco Remote Access Networks*.

BDR. Acronym for Backup Designated Router.

Be. Excess Burst. Negotiated tariff metric in Frame Relay internetworks. The number of bits that a Frame Relay internetwork attempts to transmit after Bc is accommodated. Be data is generally delivered with a lower probability than Bc data because Be data can be marked as DE by the network. See also *Bc* and *DE*.

bearer channel. See *B channel*.

BECN. Acronym for Backward Explicit Congestion Notification. Bit set by a Frame Relay network in frames traveling in the opposite direction of frames encountering a congested path. DTE receiving frames with the BECN bit set can request that higher-level protocols take flow control action, as appropriate. Compare to *FECN*.

best-effort delivery. Network system that does not use a sophisticated acknowledgment system to guarantee the reliable delivery of information.

binary. Numbering system characterized by ones and zeros (1 = on; 0 = off).

binary 8-zero substitution. See *B8ZS*.

bit. Binary digit used in the binary numbering system. Can be 0 or 1.

bit-oriented protocol. Class of data-link layer communication protocols that can transmit frames, regardless of frame content. Compared to byte-oriented protocols, bit-oriented protocols provide full-duplex operation and are more efficient and reliable. Compare to *byte-oriented protocol*.

BOD. Acronym for Bandwidth on Demand.

BRI. Acronym for Basic Rate Interface. The most common kind of ISDN interface available in the U.S. BRI contains two B channels, each with 64-Kbps capacity; and a single D channel (16 Kbps), which is used for signaling and call progress messages. Compare to *PRI*.

broadband. Transmission system that multiplexes multiple independent signals onto one cable. In telecommunications terminology, any channel having a bandwidth greater than a voice-grade channel (4 kHz). In LAN terminology, a coaxial cable on which analog signaling is used. Also called **wideband**. Contrast with *baseband*.

broadcast. Data packet that will be sent to all nodes on a network. Broadcasts are identified by a broadcast address. Compare to *multicast* and *unicast*.

BRS. Acronym for Bit-Robbing Signaling.

buffer. Storage area used for handling data in transit. Buffers are used in internetworking to compensate for differences in processing speed between network devices. Bursts of data can be stored in buffers until they can be handled by slower processing devices. Sometimes referred to as a *packet buffer.*

byte. Term used to refer to a series of consecutive binary digits that are operated upon as a unit (for example, an eight-bit byte).

byte-oriented protocol. Class of data-link communications protocols that uses a specific character from the user character set to delimit frames. These protocols have largely been replaced by bit-oriented protocols. Compare to *bit-oriented protocol.*

C

cable. Transmission medium of copper wire or optical fiber that is wrapped in a protective cover.

call setup time. Time required to establish a switched call between DTE devices.

carrier. Electromagnetic wave or alternating current of a single frequency, suitable for modulation by another data-bearing signal.

Carrier Detect. See *CD.*

CCITT. Acronym for Consultative Committee for International Telegraph and Telephone. International organization responsible for the development of communications standards. Now called the **ITU-T**. See also *ITU-T.*

CCO. Acronym for Cisco Connection Online. Cisco's Web site.

CCP. Acronym for Compression Control Protocol.

CD. Acronym for Carrier Detect. Signal that indicates whether an interface is active. Also, a signal generated by a modem indicating that a call has been connected.

Central Office. See *CO.*

Centrex. LEC service that provides local switching applications similar to those provided by an on-site PBX. With Centrex, there is no onsite switching; all customer connections go back to the CO.

channel. Communication path. Multiple channels can be multiplexed over a single cable in certain environments.

channelized E1. Access link, operating at 2.048 Mbps, which is subdivided into 30 B channels and one D channel. Supports DDR, Frame Relay, and X.25.

channelized T1. Access-link, operating at 1.544 Mbps, which is subdivided into 24 channels (23 B channels and one D channel) of 64 Kbps each. The individual channels or groups of channels connect to different destinations. Supports DDR, Frame Relay, and X.25. Also referred to as **fractional T1**.

CHAP. Acronym for Challenge Handshake Authentication Protocol. Security feature that is supported on lines using PPP encapsulation, which prevents unauthorized access. CHAP does not prevent unauthorized access; it merely identifies the remote end. The router or access server then determines whether that user is allowed access. Compare to *PAP.*

chat-script. String of text that defines the login "conversation" that occurs between two systems. Consists of expect-send pairs that define the string that the local system expects to receive from the remote system and what the local system should send as a reply.

checksum. Method for checking the integrity of transmitted data. A checksum is an integer value that is computed from a sequence of octets taken through a series of arithmetic operations. The value is recomputed at the receiving end and compared for verification.

CIR. Acronym for Committed Information Rate. Rate at which a Frame Relay network agrees to transfer information under normal conditions, averaged over a minimum increment of time. CIR, measured in bits per second, is one of the key negotiated tariff metrics. See also *Bc.*

circuit. Communications path between two or more points.

CiscoSecure. A complete line of access control software products that complement any dial network solution, enabling the centralization of security policies.

clear channel. Channel that uses out-of-band signaling (as opposed to in-band signaling), so that the channel's entire bit rate is available.

Clear To Send. See *CTS.*

client. Node or software program (front-end device) that requests services from a server.

CO. Acronym for Central Office, a facility that serves local telephone subscribers. In the CO, subscribers' lines are joined to switching equipment that allows them to connect to each other for both local and long distance calls.

CODEC. Acronym for coder-decoder. Device that typically uses pulse code modulation to transform analog signals into a digital bit stream and digital signals back into analog.

Committed Burst. See *Bc*.

Committed Information Rate. See *CIR*.

common carrier. Licensed, private utility company that supplies communication services to the public at regulated prices.

Common Transport Semantic. See *CTS*.

conversation. This is the traffic for a single transport layer session or network layer flow that crosses a given interface. This conversation is called from the source and destination address, protocol type, port number, or other attributes in the relevant communications layer.

cost. In OSPF, the value assigned to a link. This metric is based on the speed of the media.

CPE. Acronym for Customer Premises Equipment. Terminating equipment (such as terminals, telephones, and modems), which are supplied by the telephone company, installed at customer sites, and connected to the telephone company network.

CPP. Acronym for Combined Proprietary Protocol.

CR. Acronym for carriage return.

CRC. Acronym for Cyclic Redundancy Check. Error-checking technique, in which the frame recipient calculates a remainder by dividing frame contents by a prime binary divisor, and compares the calculated remainder to a value stored in the frame by the sending node.

CSU. Acronym for Channel Service Unit. Digital interface device that connects end-user equipment to the local digital telephone loop. Often referred to, together with DSU, as **CSU/DSU**. See also *DSU*.

CTS. Acronym for Clear To Send. Circuit in the EIA/TIA-232 specification that is activated when DCE is ready to accept data from DTE.

Customer Premises Equipment. See *CPE*.

Cyclic Redundancy Check. See *CRC*.

D

DARPA. Acronym for Defense Advanced Research Projects Agency. U.S. government agency that funded research for and experimentation with the Internet. Evolved from ARPA, and then, in 1994, changed back to ARPA.

DASA. Acronym for Dial Access Stacking Architecture.

Data Encryption Standard. See *DES*.

Data Network Identification Code. See *DNIC*.

Data Set Ready. See *DSR*.

Data Terminal Equipment. See *DTE*.

Data Terminal Ready. See *DTR*.

datagram. Logical grouping of information sent as a network layer unit over a transmission medium without prior establishment of a virtual circuit. IP datagrams are the primary information units in the Internet. The terms **cell**, **frame**, **message**, **packet**, and **segment** are also used to describe logical information groupings at various layers of the OSI reference model and in various technology circles.

Data-Link Connection Identifier. See *DLCI*.

DB connector. Data bus connector. Type of connector used to connect serial and parallel cables to a data bus. DB connector names are in the format DB-x, where *x* represents the number of wires within the connector. Although each line is connected to a pin on the connector, not all pins are always assigned a function. DB connectors are defined by various EIA/TIA standards.

DCE. Acronym for Data Circuit-Terminating Equipment (ITU-T expansion). Devices and connections of a communications network that comprise the network end of the user-to-network interface. The DCE provides a physical connection to the network, forwards traffic, and provides a clocking signal used to synchronize data transmission between DCE and DTE devices. Modems and interface cards are examples of DCE. Compare to *DTE*.

D channel. Data channel. This is an ISDN communication channel used for sending information between the ISDN equipment and the ISDN Central office switch. The D channel can also carry "user" packet data at rates up to 9.6 Kbps. It operates as a full-duplex channel, at speeds of 16 Kbps (BRI) or 64 Kbps (PRI) ISDN channel. Compare to *B channel*.

DDR. Acronym for Dial-On Demand Routing. Technique whereby a router can automatically initiate and close a circuit-switched session as transmitting stations demand. The router spoofs keepalives so that end stations treat the session as active. DDR permits routing over ISDN or telephone lines using an external ISDN terminal adapter or modem.

DE. Discard Eligible indicator. When the router detects network congestion, the FR switch drops packets with the DE bit set first. The DE bit is set on the oversubscribed traffic; that is, the traffic that was received after the CIR was sent.

decryption. Reverse application of an encryption algorithm to encrypted data, thereby restoring that data to its original, unencrypted state. See also *encryption*.

dedicated line. Communications line that is indefinitely reserved for transmissions, rather than being switched as transmission is required. See also *leased line*.

default route. Routing table entry that is used to direct frames for which a next-hop is not explicitly listed in the routing table.

delay. Time between the initiation of a transaction by a sender and the first response received by the sender. Also, the time required to move a packet from source to destination over a given path.

demarc. Demarcation point between carrier equipment and CPE.

demodulation. Process of returning a modulated signal to its original form. Modems perform demodulation by taking an analog signal and returning it to its original (digital) form. See also *modulation*.

demultiplexing. Separating multiple input streams that were multiplexed into a common physical signal back into multiple output streams. See also *multiplexing*.

DES. Acronym for Data Encryption Standard. Standard cryptographic algorithm developed by the U.S. National Bureau of Standards.

destination address. Address of a network device that is receiving data. See also *source address*.

DHCP. Acronym for Dynamic Host Configuration Protocol. Provides a mechanism for allocating IP addresses dynamically so that addresses can be reused when hosts no longer need them.

dial backup. Feature that provides protection against WAN downtime by allowing the network administrator to configure a backup serial line through a circuit-switched connection.

Dial-On Demand Routing. See *DDR*.

dial-up line. Communications circuit that is established by a switched-circuit connection using the telephone company network.

digital. The use of a binary code to represent information, such as 0/1, or on/off.

Digital Signal level 0. See *DS-0*.

DLCI. Acronym for Data-Link Connection Identifier. Value that specifies a PVC or SVC in a Frame Relay network. In the basic Frame Relay specification, DLCIs are locally significant (connected devices might use different values to specify the same connection). In the LMI extended specification, DLCIs are globally significant (DLCIs specify individual end devices). See also *LMI*.

DMS. The name of digital Central office switches from Northern Telecom. Model numbers start with BCS.

DNIC. Acronym for Data Network Identification Code. Part of an X.121 address. DNICs are divided into two parts: the first specifies the country in which the addressed PSN is located; the second specifies the PSN itself.

DNS. Acronym for Domain Name System. System used in the Internet for translating names of network nodes into addresses.

DoD. Department of Defense. U.S. government organization that is responsible for national defense. The DoD frequently funds communication protocol development.

Domain. In the Internet, a portion of the naming hierarchy tree that refers to general groupings of networks based on organization-type or geography.

Domain Name System. See *DNS*.

dot address. Refers to the common notation for IP addresses in the form *n.n.n.n*, where each number *n* represents, in decimal, one byte of the four-byte IP address. Also called **dotted notation** or **four-part dotted notation**.

dotted decimal notation. Syntactic representation for a 32-bit integer that consists of four eight-bit numbers written in base 10 with periods (dots) separating them. Used to represent IP addresses in the Internet, as in 192.67.67.20. Also called **dotted quad notation**.

DR. Acronym for Designated Router.

DS. Acronym for Digital Signal.

DS-0. Acronym for Digital Signal level 0. Framing specification used in transmitting digital signals over a single channel at 64 Kbps on a T1 facility. Compare to *DS-1* and *DS-3*.

DS-1. Acronym for Digital Signal level 1. Framing specification used in transmitting digital signals at 1.544 Mbps on a T1 facility (in the United States) or at 2.108-Mbps on an E1 facility (in Europe). Compare to *DS-0* and *DS-3*.

DS-3. Acronym for Digital Signal level 3. Framing specification used for transmitting digital signals at 44.736 Mbps on a T3 facility. Compare to *DS-0* and *DS-1*.

DSL. Acronym for Digital Subscriber Line. Public network technology that delivers high bandwidth over conventional copper wiring at limited distances. There are four types of DSL: ADSL, HDSL, SDSL, and VDSL. All are provisioned via modem pairs, with one modem located at a central office and the other at the customer site. Because most DSL technologies do not use the whole bandwidth of the twisted-pair, there is room remaining for a voice channel. See also *ADSL, HDSL, SDSL,* and *VDSL*.

DSR. Acronym for Data Set Ready. EIA/TIA-232 interface circuit that is activated when DCE is powered-up and ready for use.

DSU. Acronym for Data Service Unit. Device used in digital transmission that adapts the physical interface on a DTE device to a transmission facility, such as T1 or E1. The DSU is also responsible for such functions as signal timing. Often referred to together with CSU, as **CSU/DSU**. See also *CSU*.

DTE. Acronym for Data Terminal Equipment. Device at the user end of a user-network interface that serves as a data source, destination, or both. DTE connects to a data network through a DCE device (for example, a modem) and typically uses clocking signals generated by the DCE. DTE includes such devices as computers, protocol translators, and multiplexers. Compare to *DCE*.

DTMF. Acronym for Dual Tone Multifrequency. Use of two simultaneous voice-band tones for dialing (such as touch-tone).

DTR. Acronym for Data Terminal Ready. EIA/TIA-232 circuit that is activated to let the DCE know when the DTE is ready to send and receive data.

dynamic address resolution. Use of an address resolution protocol to determine and store address information on demand.

E

E1. Wide-area digital transmission scheme used predominantly in Europe that carries data at a rate of 2.048 Mbps. E1 lines can be leased for private use from common carriers. Compare to *T1*. See also *DS-1*.

EIA/TIA. Acronym for Electronic Industries Association/Telecommunications Industry Association.

EIA/TIA-232. Common physical layer interface standard, developed by EIA and TIA, which supports unbalanced circuits at signal speeds of up to 64 Kbps. Closely resembles the V.24 specification. Formerly called RS-232.

EIA/TIA-449. Popular physical layer interface developed by EIA and TIA. Essentially, a faster (up to 2 Mbps) version of EIA/TIA-232, capable of longer cable runs. Formerly called RS-449.

EIA-530. Refers to two electrical implementations of EIA/TIA-449: RS-422 (for balanced transmission) and RS-423 (for unbalanced transmission).

e-mail. Electronic mail. Widely used network application, in which text messages are transmitted electronically between end users over various types of networks using various network protocols.

encapsulation. Wrapping of data in a particular protocol header. For example, Ethernet data is wrapped in a specific Ethernet header before network transit. Also, when bridging dissimilar networks, the entire frame from one network is simply placed in the header used by the data-link layer protocol of the other network.

encryption. Application of a specific algorithm to data to alter its appearance, thus making it incomprehensible to those who are not authorized to see the information. See also *decryption*.

ESF. Acronym for Extended Superframe. Framing type used on T1 circuits that consists of 24 frames of 192 bits each, with the 193rd bit providing timing and other functions. ESF is an enhanced version of SF. See also *SF*.

Excess Burst. See *Be*.

Extended Superframe Format. See *ESF*.

F

FCC. Acronym for Federal Communications Commission. U.S. government agency that supervises, licenses, and controls electronic and electromagnetic transmission standards.

FCS. Acronym for Frame Check Sequence. Extra characters added to a frame for error-control purposes. Used in HDLC, Frame Relay, and other data-link layer protocols.

FECN. Acronym for Forward Explicit Congestion Notification. Bit set by a Frame Relay network to inform DTE receiving the frame that congestion was experienced in the path from source to destination. DTE receiving frames with the FECN bit set can request that higher-level protocols take flow-control action, as appropriate. Compare to *BECN*.

FIFO. Acronym for First In, First Out. With FIFO, transmission occurs in the same order as messages are received.

filter. Generally, a process or device that screens network traffic for certain characteristics, such as source address, destination address, or protocol; and determines whether to forward or discard that traffic based on the established criteria.

firewall. Router or access server, or several routers or access servers, designated as a buffer between any connected public networks and a private network. A firewall router uses access lists and other methods to ensure the security of the private network.

flapping. Intermittent interface failures.

flow. Stream of data traveling between two endpoints across a network (for example, from one LAN station to another). Multiple flows can be transmitted on a single circuit.

flow control. Technique for ensuring that a transmitting entity, such as a modem, does not overwhelm a receiving entity with data. When the buffers on the receiving device are full, a message is sent to the sending device to suspend the transmission until the data in the buffers has been processed.

foreign exchange. If your local Central office is not scheduled to have ISDN for a while, it may be possible to obtain ISDN service from a nearby Central office. This is called foreign exchange. There are additional charges associated with this type of service.

FR. See *Frame Relay*.

fragmentation. Process of breaking a packet into smaller units when transmitting over a network medium that cannot support the original size of the packet.

frame. Logical grouping of information sent as a data-link layer unit over a transmission medium. Often refers to the header and trailer, used for synchronization and error control, which surround the user data contained in the unit. The terms **cell**, **datagram**, **message**, **packet**, and **segment** are also used to describe logical information groupings at various layers of the OSI reference model and in various technology circles.

Frame Relay. Industry-standard, switched data-link layer protocol that handles multiple virtual circuits, using HDLC encapsulation between connected devices. Frame Relay is more efficient than X.25, the protocol for which it is generally considered to be a replacement. See also *X.25*.

frequency. Number of cycles, measured in hertz, of an alternating current signal per unit time.

FTP. Acronym for File Transfer Protocol. Application protocol, part of the TCP/IP protocol stack, used for transferring files between network nodes. FTP is defined in RFC 959.

full duplex. Capability for simultaneous data transmission between a sending station and a receiving station.

full mesh. Term describing a network in which devices are organized in a mesh topology, with each network node having either a physical circuit or a virtual circuit connecting it to every other network node. A full mesh provides a great deal of redundancy, but because it can be prohibitively expensive to implement, it is usually reserved for network backbones. See also *mesh* and *partial mesh*.

G

gateway. In the IP community, this older term refers to a routing device. Today, the term **router** is used to describe nodes that perform this function, and **gateway** refers to a special-purpose device that performs an application-layer conversion of information from one protocol stack to another.

GRD. Ground. Provides the ground reference for voltage measurements.

H

half duplex. Capability for data transmission, in only one direction at a time, between a sending station and a receiving station.

HAN. Acronym for Home Area Network. See also *LAN, MAN,* and *WAN.*

handshake. Sequence of messages exchanged between two or more network devices to ensure transmission synchronization.

HBD3. Line code type used on E1 circuits.

HDLC. Acronym for High-Level Data Link Control. Bit-oriented synchronous data-link layer protocol, developed by ISO. Derived from SDLC, HDLC specifies a data-encapsulation method on synchronous serial links by using frame characters and checksums.

HDSL. Acronym for High-Data-Rate Digital Subscriber Line. One of four DSL technologies. HDSL delivers 1.544 Mbps of bandwidth each way over two copper twisted-pairs. Because HDSL provides T1 speed, telephone companies use HDSL to provision local access to T1 services whenever possible. The operating range of HDSL is limited to 12,000 feet (3658.5 meters), so signal repeaters are installed to extend the service. HDSL requires two twisted-pairs, so it is deployed primarily for PBX-network connections, digital loop carrier systems, interexchange POPs, Internet servers, and private data networks. Compare to *ADSL, SDSL,* and *VDSL.*

High-Speed Serial Interface. See *HSSI.*

HSSI. Acronym for High-Speed Serial Interface. Network standard for high-speed (up to 52 Mbps) serial connections over WAN links.

hub. Hardware or software device that contains multiple independent (but connected) modules of network and internetwork equipment. Hubs can be active (where they repeat signals sent through them) or passive (where they do not repeat, but merely split signals sent through them).

hunt group. A series of telephone lines programmed so that as incoming calls arrive, if the first line is busy, the second line is tried, and then the third is tried, and so on until a free line is found. This way, an incoming call should not end up with a busy signal.

I

ICMP. Acronym for Internet Control Message Protocol. Network layer Internet protocol that reports errors and provides other information relevant to IP packet processing. Documented in RFC 792.

ICRC. Acronym for Introduction to Cisco Router Configuration.

IDN. Acronym for International Data Number. ITU-T standard describing an addressing scheme used in X.25 networks. X.121 addresses are sometimes called IDNs.

IEEE. Acronym for Institute of Electrical and Electronics Engineers. Professional organization whose activities include the development of communications and network standards. IEEE LAN standards are today's predominant LAN standards.

IETF. Acronym for Internet Engineering Task Force. Task force, consisting of over 80 working groups, which is responsible for developing Internet standards. The IETF operates under the auspices of ISOC.

in-band signaling. Transmission within a frequency range that is normally used for information transmission. Compare to *out-of-band signaling*.

Integrated Services Digital Network. See *ISDN*.

IOS. Acronym for Internetwork Operating System.

IP sec. Standards-based method of providing privacy, integrity, and authenticity to information transferred across IP networks. Provides IP network-layer encryption.

ISDN. Acronym for Integrated Services Digital Network. Communication protocol, offered by telephone companies, which permits telephone networks to carry data, voice, and other source traffic.

ISO. Acronym for International Organization for Standardization. International organization that is responsible for a wide range of standards, including those relevant to networking. ISO developed the OSI reference model, a popular networking reference model.

ISOC. Acronym for Internet Society. International nonprofit organization, founded in 1992, which coordinates the evolution and use of the Internet. In addition, ISOC delegates authority to other groups related to the Internet, such as the IAB. ISOC is headquartered in Reston, Virginia (United States).

ISP. Acronym for Internet Service Provider. A company that provides Internet access to other companies and individuals.

ITU-T. Acronym for International Telecommunication Union Telecommunication Standardization Sector. International body that develops worldwide standards for telecommunications technologies. The ITU-T carries out the functions of the former CCITT.

J

jitter. Analog communication-line distortion caused by the variation of a signal from its reference timing positions. Jitter can cause data loss, particularly at high speeds.

K

Kb. Kilobit. Approximately 1,000 bits.

Kbps. Kilobits per second.

keepalive. Message sent by one network device to inform another network device that the virtual circuit between the two is still active.

Kerberos. Developing standard for authenticating network users. Kerberos offers two key benefits: it functions in a multivendor network, and it does not transmit passwords over the network.

L

L2F Protocol. Layer 2 Forwarding Protocol. Protocol that supports the creation of secure, virtual private dial-up networks over the Internet.

L2TP. Layer 2 Tunneling Protocol. Emerging IETF standard that combines Layer 2 Forwarding Protocol (L2F) and Point-to-Point Tunneling protocol (PPTP).

LAN. Acronym for Local Area Network. High-speed, low-error data network that covers a relatively small geographic area (up to a few thousand meters). LANs connect workstations, peripherals, terminals, and other devices in a single building or other geographically limited area. LAN standards specify cabling and signaling at the physical and data-link layers of the OSI model. Ethernet, FDDI, and Token Ring are widely used LAN technologies. See also *HAN, MAN* and *WAN*.

LAPB. Acronym for Link Access Procedure, Balanced. Data-link layer protocol in the X.25 protocol stack. LAPB is a bit-oriented protocol derived from HDLC.

LAPD. Acronym for Link Access Procedure on the D channel. ISDN data-link layer protocol for the D channel. LAPD was derived from the LAPB protocol and was designed primarily to satisfy the signaling requirements of ISDN basic access. Defined by ITU-T Recommendations Q.920 and Q.921.

LCP. Acronym for Link Control Protocol. Protocol that establishes, configures, and tests data-link connections for use by PPP. See also *PPP*.

LDN. Acronym for Local Directory Number.

leased line. Transmission line reserved by a communications carrier for the private use of a customer. A leased line is a type of dedicated line. See also *dedicated line*.

LED. Acronym for Light Emitting Diode. Semiconductor device that emits light produced by converting electrical energy. Status lights on hardware devices are typically LEDs.

line of sight. Characteristic of certain transmission systems (such as laser, microwave, and infrared systems), in which no obstructions in a direct path between transmitter and receiver can exist.

link. Network communications channel, consisting of a circuit or transmission path and all related equipment between a sender and a receiver. Most often used to refer to a WAN connection. Sometimes referred to as a **line** or a **transmission link**.

LMI. Acronym for Local Management Interface. Set of enhancements to the basic Frame Relay specification. LMI includes support for a keepalive mechanism, which verifies that data is flowing; a multicast mechanism, which provides the network server with its local DLCI and the multicast DLCI; global addressing, which gives DLCIs global rather than local significance in Frame Relay networks; and a status mechanism, which provides an ongoing status report on the DLCIs known to the switch. Known as **LMT** in ANSI terminology.

load balancing. In routing, the capability of a router to distribute traffic over all its network ports that are the same distance from the destination address. Good load-balancing algorithms use both line speed and reliability information. Load balancing increases the use of network segments, thus increasing effective network bandwidth.

local loop. Also known as the last mile. Line from the premises of a telephone subscriber to the telephone company CO.

M

MAN. Acronym for Metropolitan Area Network. Network that spans a metropolitan area. Generally, a MAN spans a larger geographic area than a LAN, but a smaller geographic area than a WAN. Compare to *LAN* and *WAN*.

MAU. Acronym for Media Attachment Unit. Known as a transceiver.

Maximum Transmission Unit. See *MTU*.

MD5. Acronym for Message Digest 5. Algorithm used for message authentication. MD5 verifies the integrity of the communication, authenticates the origin, and checks for timeliness.

mesh. Network topology, in which devices are organized in a manageable, segmented manner with many, often redundant, interconnections strategically placed between network nodes. See also *full mesh* and *partial mesh*.

MLP. Sometimes used in Cisco documentation to refer to Multilink PPP.

MNP5. Modem-compression standards from Microcom Networking Protocol.

modem. Modulator-demodulator. Device that converts digital and analog signals. At the source, a modem converts digital signals to a form suitable for transmission over analog communication facilities. At the destination, the analog signals are returned to their digital form. Modems allow data to be transmitted over voice-grade telephone lines.

modulation. Process by which the characteristics of electrical signals are transformed to represent information. Types of modulation include AM, FM, and PAM.

MP. Acronym for Multilink PPP.

MPPC. Acronym for Microsoft Point-to-Point Compression.

MS-CHAP. Authentication method developed by Microsoft and used with PPP connections.

MTU. Acronym for Maximum Transmission Unit. Maximum packet size, in bytes, which a particular interface can handle.

multiaccess network. Network that allows multiple devices to connect and communicate simultaneously.

multicast. Single packets, copied by the network and sent to a specific subset of network addresses. These addresses are specified in the Destination Address Field. Compare to *broadcast* and *unicast*.

multiplexing. Scheme that allows multiple logical signals to be transmitted simultaneously across a single physical channel. Compare to *demultiplexing*.

N

NAK. Negative acknowledgment. Response sent from a receiving device to a sending device, indicating that the information received contains errors. Compare to *acknowledgment*.

NAS. Acronym for Network Access Server.

NASI. Acronym for NetWare Asynchronous Support Interface.

NAT. Acronym for Network Address Translation. Mechanism for reducing the need for globally unique IP addresses. NAT allows an organization with addresses that are not globally unique to connect to the Internet by translating those addresses into globally routable address space. Also known as **Network Address Translator**.

NBMA. Acronym for Nonbroadcast Multiaccess. Term describing a multiaccess network that either does not support broadcasting or in which broadcasting is not feasible.

NCP. Acronym for Network Control Protocol. Series of protocols for establishing and configuring different network-layer protocols, such as for AppleTalk, over PPP. See also *PPP*.

NetBEUI. Acronym for NetBIOS Extended User Interface. Enhanced version of the NetBIOS protocol used by network operating systems such as LAN Manager, LAN Server, Windows for Workgroups, and Windows NT. NetBEUI formalizes the transport frame and adds additional functions. NetBEUI implements the OSI LLC2 protocol.

network. Collection of computers, printers, routers, switches, and other devices that can communicate with each other over some transmission medium.

NI1. National ISDN 1. A specification for a "standard" ISDN phone line. The goal is for National ISDN 1 to become a set of standards to which every manufacturer can conform. For example, ISDN phones that conform to the National ISDN 1 standard will work, regardless of the Central office that the customer is connected to. Note: Future standards, denoted as NI2 and NI3, are currently being developed.

NIUF. Acronym for North American ISDN Forum.

NNI. The standard interface between two Frame Relay switches that meet the same criteria.

NRZ. Acronym for Nonreturn To Zero. Signals that maintain constant voltage levels with no signal transitions (no return to a zero-voltage level) during a bit interval. Compare to *NRZI*.

NRZI. Acronym for Nonreturn To Zero Inverted. Signals that maintain constant voltage levels with no signal transitions (no return to a zero-voltage level), but interpret the presence of data at the beginning of a bit interval as a signal transition and the absence of data as no transition. Compare to *NRZ*.

NT-1. Network termination 1. In ISDN, a device that provides the interface between customer premises equipment and Central office switching equipment.

null modem. Small box or cable used to join computing devices directly, rather than over a network.

NVRAM. Acronym for Nonvolatile Random Access Memory.

O

OC. Acronym for Optical Carrier. Series of physical protocols (OC-1, OC-2, OC-3, and so forth), defined for SONET optical-signal transmissions. OC signal levels put STS frames onto multimode fiber-optic lines at a variety of speeds. The base rate is 51.84 Mbps (OC-1); each signal level thereafter operates at a speed divisible by that number (thus, OC-3 runs at 155.52 Mbps).

octet. Eight bits. In networking, the term octet is often used (rather than byte) because some machine architectures employ bytes that are not eight bits long.

ODBC. Acronym for Open DataBase Connectivity.

OLE. Acronym for Object Linking and Embedding. A compound document standard developed by Microsoft Corporation. It enables creating objects with one application, and then linking or embedding them in a second application. These objects keep their original format and links to the application that created them.

ones density. Scheme that allows a CSU/DSU to recover the data clock reliably. The CSU/DSU derives the data clock from the data that passes through it. To recover the clock, the CSU/DSU hardware must receive at least one one-bit value for every eight bits of data that pass through it. Also called **pulse density**.

OSI. Acronym for Open System Interconnection. International standardization program created by ISO and ITU-T to develop standards for data networking that facilitate multivendor equipment interoperability.

OSI reference model. Open System Interconnection reference model. Network architectural model developed by ISO and ITU-T. The model consists of seven layers, each of which specifies particular network functions such as addressing, flowcontrol, error control, encapsulation, and reliable message transfer. The lowest layer (the physical layer) is closest to the media technology. The lower two layers are implemented in hardware and software, whereas the upper five layers are implemented only in software. The highest layer (the application layer) is closest to the user. The OSI reference model is used universally as a method for teaching and understanding network functionality.

OUI. Acronym for Organizational Unique Identifier. Three octets assigned by the IEEE in a block of 48-bit LAN addresses.

out-of-band signaling. Transmission that uses frequencies or channels outside the frequencies or channels that are normally used for information transfer. Out-of-band signaling is often used for error reporting in situations in which in-band signaling can be affected by whatever problems the network might be experiencing. Compare to *in-band signaling*.

P

packet. Logical grouping of information that includes a header containing control information and (usually) user data. Packets are most often used to refer to network layer units of data. The terms **datagram**, **frame**, **message**, and **segment** are also used to describe logical information groupings at various layers of the OSI reference model and in various technology circles. See also *PDU*.

packet switching. Networking method, in which nodes share bandwidth with each other by sending packets.

PAD. Acronym for Packet Assembler/Disassembler. Device used to connect simple devices (such as character-mode terminals) that do not support the full functionality of a particular protocol to a network. PADs buffer data, and assemble and disassemble packets sent to such end devices.

PAP. Acronym for Password Authentication Protocol. Authentication protocol that allows PPP peers to authenticate one another. The remote router that attempts to connect to the local router is required to send an authentication request. Unlike CHAP, PAP passes the password and host name or username in the clear (unencrypted). PAP does not prevent unauthorized access, but merely identifies the remote end. The router or access server then determines whether that user is allowed access. PAP is supported only on PPP lines. Compare to *CHAP*.

partial mesh. Network in which devices are organized in a mesh topology, with some network nodes organized in a full mesh, but with others that are only connected to one or two other nodes in the network. A partial mesh does not provide the level of redundancy of a full mesh topology, but is less expensive to implement. Partial mesh topologies are generally used in the peripheral networks that connect to a fully meshed backbone. See also *full mesh* and *mesh*.

PAT. Acronym for Port Address Translation. A subset of NAT.

payload. Portion of a cell, frame, or packet that contains upper-layer information (data).

PBX. Acronym for Private Branch Exchange. A small version of the phone company's larger central switching office. A PBX is a private telephone switch. It is connected to groups of lines from one or more central offices, and to all of the telephones at the location served by the PBX.

PCM. Acronym for Pulse Code Modulation. Transmission of analog information in digital form through sampling and encoding the samples with a fixed number of bits.

PDN. Acronym for Public Data Network. Network operated either by a government (as in Europe) or by a private concern to provide computer communications to the public, usually for a fee. PDNs enable small organizations to create a WAN without all the equipment costs of long-distance circuits.

PDU. Acronym for Protocol Data Unit. OSI term for packet.

peak rate. Maximum rate, in kilobits per second, at which a virtual circuit can transmit.

Permanent Virtual Circuit. PVC. Virtual circuit that is permanently established. PVCs save bandwidth associated with circuit establishment and tear down in situations where certain virtual circuits must exist all the time. In ATM terminology, called a **permanent virtual connection**.

ping. Packet internet groper. ICMP echo message and its reply. Often used in IP networks to test the reachability of a network device.

playback. With playback, you capture the packet for later use if you have an analyzer connected to the line.

point of demarcation. The physical point where the phone company ends its responsibility with the wiring of the phone line.

POP. Acronym for Point Of Presence. A long distance carrier's office in your local community. A POP is the place where your long distance carrier, or IXC, terminates your long distance lines just before those lines are connected to your local phone company's lines or to your own direct hookup. Each IXC can have multiple POPs within one LATA. All long-distance phone connections go through the POPs.

POTS. Acronym for Plain Old Telephone System. See *PSTN*.

PPP. Acronym for Point-to-Point Protocol. Successor to SLIP that provides router-to-router and host-to-network connections over synchronous and asynchronous circuits. Whereas SLIP was designed to work with IP, PPP was designed to work with several network layer protocols, such as IP, IPX, and ARA. PPP also has built-in security mechanisms, such as CHAP and PAP. PPP relies on two protocols: LCP and NCP. See also *CHAP, LCP, NCP, PAP,* and *SLIP.*

PPTP. Acronym for Point-to-Point Tunneling Protocol. See *L2TP.*

PRI. Acronym for Primary Rate Interface. ISDN interface to primary rate access. Primary rate access consists of a single 64-Kbps D channel, plus 23 (T1) or 30 (E1) B channels for voice or data. Compare to *BRI.*

PSTN. Acronym for Public Switched Telephone Network. General term referring to the variety of telephone networks and services in place worldwide. Sometimes called POTS.

PTT. Acronym for Post, Telephone, Telegraph.

PVC. Acronym for Permanent Virtual Circuit (virtual circuit that is permanently established). PVCs save bandwidth associated with circuit establishment, and tear down in situations in which certain virtual circuits must exist all the time. In ATM terminology, it is called a permanent virtual connection. See also *SVC.*

Q

Q.920/Q.921. ITU-T specifications for the ISDN UNI data-link layer.

Q.922A. ITU-T specification for Frame Relay encapsulation.

Q.931. ITU-T specification for signaling to establish, maintain, and clear ISDN network connections.

queue. A backlog of packets waiting to be forwarded over a router interface.

R

RADIUS. Database for authenticating modem and ISDN connections and for tracking connection time.

rate enforcement. See *traffic policing.*

RDI. Acronym for Restricted Digital Information.

RJ-45. Registered jack connector. Standard connector used for 10BaseT and other types of network connections.

ROBO. Acronym for Remote Office, Branch Office.

RS-232. Popular physical layer interface. Now known as EIA/TIA-232. See also *EIA/TIA-232.*

RTS. Acronym for Request To Send. EIA/TIA-232 control signal that requests a data transmission on a communications line.

RxD. Receive Data. The DTE receives data from the DCE.

S

S/T-interface. A four-wire ISDN circuit. The S/T interface is the part of an ISDN line that connects to the terminal equipment.

SAPI. Acronym for Service Access Point Identifier.

SDLC. Acronym for Synchronous Data Link Control. SNA data-link layer communications protocol. SDLC is a bit-oriented, full-duplex serial protocol that has spawned numerous similar protocols, including HDLC and LAPB.

SDSL. Acronym for Single-Line Digital Subscriber Line. One of four DSL technologies. SDSL delivers 1.544 Mbps, both downstream and upstream, over a single copper twisted-pair. The use of a single twisted-pair limits the operating range of SDSL to 10,000 feet (3048.8 meters). Compare to *ADSL, IIDSL,* and *VDSL.*

SF. Acronym for Super Frame. Common framing type used on T1 circuits. SF consists of 12 frames of 192 bits each, with the 193rd bit providing error checking and other functions. SF is superseded by ESF, but is still widely used. Also called D4 framing. See also *ESF.*

SLIP. Acronym for Serial Line Internet Protocol. Standard protocol for point-to-point serial connections using a variation of TCP/IP. Predecessor of PPP.

SMTP. Acronym for Simple Mail Transfer Protocol. Internet protocol providing e-mail services.

SOHO. Acronym for Small Office, Home Office. Networking solutions and access technologies for offices that are not directly connected to large corporate networks.

SONET. Acronym for Synchronous Optical Network. High-speed (up to 2.5 Gbps) synchronous network specification, developed by Bellcore and designed to run on optical fiber. STS-1 is the basic building block of SONET. Approved as an international standard in 1988.

source address. Address of a network device that is sending data. See also *destination address.*

speed matching. Feature that provides sufficient buffering capability in a destination device to allow a high-speed source to transmit data at its maximum rate, even if the destination device is a lower-speed device.

SPID. Acronym for Service Profile Identifier. Number that some service providers use to define the services to which an ISDN device subscribes. The ISDN device uses the SPID when accessing the switch that initializes the connection to a service provider. The ISDN switch needs to have a unique identification number for each ISDN set to which it sends calls and signals.

split-horizon. Routing technique, in which information about routes is prevented from exiting the router interface through which that information was received. Split-horizon updates are useful for preventing routing loops.

spoofing. Scheme used by routers to cause a host to treat an interface as if it were up and supporting a session. The router spoofs replies to keepalive messages from the host, in order to convince that host that the session still exists. Spoofing is useful in routing environments such as DDR, in which a circuit-switched link is taken down when there is no traffic to be sent across it to save toll charges.

SS7. Acronym for Signaling System 7. Standard CCS system used with BISDN and ISDN. Developed by Bellcore.

subinterface. One of a number of virtual interfaces on a single physical interface.

subnet mask. 32-bit address mask used in IP to indicate the bits of an IP address that are being used for the subnet address. Sometimes referred to simply as **mask**.

subnetwork. In IP networks, a network that shares a particular subnet address. Subnetworks are networks segmented by a network administrator, in order to provide a multilevel, hierarchical routing structure while shielding the subnetwork from the addressing complexity of attached networks. Sometimes called a **subnet**.

Super Frame. See *SF.*

SVC. Acronym for Switched Virtual Circuit. Virtual circuit that is dynamically established on demand and is torn down when transmission is complete. SVCs are used when data transmission is sporadic. Called a **switched virtual connection** in ATM terminology. Compare to *PVC*.

switch. Network device that filters, forwards, and floods frames, based on the destination address of each frame. The switch operates at the data-link layer of the OSI model.

synchronization. Establishment of common timing between sender and receiver.

synchronous transmission. Term describing digital signals that are transmitted with precise clocking. Such signals have the same frequency, with individual characters encapsulated in control bits (called start bits and stop bits) that designate the beginning and end of each character. Compare to *asynchronous transmission.*

T

T1. Digital WAN carrier facility. T1 transmits DS-1 formatted data at 1.544 Mbps through the telephone-switching network by using AMI or B8ZS coding.

TACACS. Acronym for Terminal Access Controller Access Control System. Authentication protocol, developed by the DDN community, which provides remote access authentication and related services, such as event logging. User passwords are administered in a central database rather than in individual routers, providing an easily scalable network security solution.

TCP. Acronym for Transmission Control Protocol. Connection-oriented transport layer protocol that provides reliable full-duplex data transmission. TCP is part of the TCP/IP protocol stack. See also *TCP/IP.*

TCP/IP. Acronym for Transmission Control Protocol/Internet Protocol. Common name for the suite of protocols developed by the U.S. DoD in the 1970s to support the construction of worldwide internetworks. TCP and IP are the two best-known protocols in the suite. See also *IP, TCP,* and *UDP.*

TEI. Acronym for Terminal Endpoint Identifier. Field in the LAPD address that identifies a device on an ISDN interface.

telco. Telephone company.

traffic policing. Process used to measure the actual traffic flow across a given connection and compare it to the total admissible traffic flow for that connection. Traffic outside of the agreed-upon flow can be tagged (where the CLP bit is set to 1) and discarded en route if congestion develops. Traffic policing is used in ATM, Frame Relay, and other types of networks.

traffic shaping. Use of queues to limit surges that can congest a network. Data is buffered and then sent into the network in regulated amounts to ensure that the traffic will fit within the promised traffic envelope for the particular connection. Traffic shaping is used in ATM, Frame Relay, and other types of networks. Also known as **metering**, **shaping**, and **smoothing**.

Transmission Control Protocol. See *TCP*.

twisted-pair. Two insulated wires, usually made of copper, which are twisted together and often bound into a common sheath to form multi-pair cables. In ISDN, the cables are the basic path between a subscriber's terminal or telephone, and the PBX or the Central office.

TxD. Transmit Data. The DTE transmits data to the DCE.

U

UART. Acronym for Universal Asynchronous Receiver/Transmitter. Integrated circuit, attached to the parallel bus of a computer, which is used for serial communications. The UART translates between serial and parallel signals, provides transmission clocking, and buffers data sent to or from the computer.

UDP. Acronym for User Datagram Protocol. Connectionless transport layer protocol in the TCP/IP protocol stack. UDP is a simple protocol that exchanges datagrams without acknowledgments or guaranteed delivery, requiring that error processing and retransmission be handled by other protocols.

U-interface. A two-wire ISDN circuit that is essentially today's standard one-pair telephone company local loop made of twisted wire. The U-interface is the most common ISDN interface and extends from the central office.

UNC. Acronym for Universal Naming Convention or Uniform Naming Convention. A PC format for specifying the location of resources on a local-area network (LAN). UNC uses the following format: \\server-name\shared-resource-pathname.

unicast. Message sent to a single network destination. Compare to *broadcast* and *multicast*.

V

V.32. ITU-T standard serial line protocol for bidirectional data transmissions at speeds of 4.8 or 9.6 Kbps.

v.32bis. ITU-T standard that extends V.32 to speeds up to 14.4 Kbps.

v.34. ITU-T standard that specifies a serial line protocol. V.34 offers improvements to the V.32 standard, including higher transmission rates (28.8 Kbps) and enhanced data compression.

v.35. ITU-T standard that describes a synchronous, physical layer protocol used for communications between a network access device and a packet network. V.35 is most commonly used in North America and in Europe, and is recommended for speeds up to 48 Kbps.

v.42bis. Modem compression standard from ITU-T.

VC. See *virtual circuit.*

VDSL. Acronym for Very-High-Data-Rate Digital Subscriber Line. One of four DSL technologies. VDSL delivers 13 to 52 Mbps downstream and 1.5 to 2.3 Mbps upstream over a single copper twisted-pair. The operating range of VDSL is limited to 1,000 to 4,500 feet (304.8 to 1,372 meters). Compare to *ADSL, HDSL,* and *SDSL.*

virtual circuit. Logical circuit, created to ensure reliable communication between two network devices. A virtual circuit is defined by a VPI/VCI pair, and can be either permanent (PVC) or switched (SVC). Virtual circuits are used in Frame Relay and X.25. In ATM, a virtual circuit is called a **virtual channel**. Sometimes abbreviated as VC.

VPDN. Acronym for Virtual Private Dial-Up Network. See also *VPN.*

VPN. Acronym for Virtual Private Network. Enables IP traffic to travel securely over a public TCP/IP network by encrypting all traffic from one network to another. A VPN uses "tunneling" to encrypt all information at the IP level.

W - X - Y - Z

WAIS. Acronym for Wide Area Information Server. Distributed database protocol, developed to search for information over a network. WAIS supports full-text databases, which allow an entire document to be searched for a match (as opposed to other technologies that allow only an index of keywords to be searched).

WAN. Acronym for Wide Area Network. Data communications network that serves users across a broad geographic area and often uses transmission devices provided by common carriers. Frame Relay, SMDS, and X.25 are examples of WANs. Compare to *LAN, MAN,* and *HAN.*

WFQ. Acronym for Weighted Fair Queuing. Congestion-management algorithm that identifies conversations (in the form of traffic streams), separates packets that belong to each conversation, and ensures that capacity is shared fairly between these individual conversations. WFQ is an automatic way of stabilizing network behavior during congestion and results in increased performance and reduced retransmission.

World Wide Web. See *WWW.*

WWW. Acronym for World Wide Web. Large network of Internet servers that provide hypertext and other services to terminals running client applications, such as a browser.

X.121. ITU-T standard that describes an addressing scheme used in X.25 networks. X.121 addresses are sometimes called IDNs. See also *IDN.*

X.21. ITU-T standard for serial communications over synchronous digital lines. The X.21 protocol is used primarily in Europe and Japan.

X.21bis. ITU-T standard that defines the physical layer protocol for communication between DCE and DTE in an X.25 network. Virtually equivalent to EIA/TIA-232. See also *EIA/TIA-232* and *X.25.*

X.25. ITU-T standard that defines the way connections between DTE and DCE are maintained for remote terminal access and computer communications in PDNs. X.25 specifies LAPB, a data-link layer protocol; and PLP, a network layer protocol. Frame Relay has to some degree superseded X.25.

X.29. ITU-T recommendation that defines the form for control information in the terminal-to-PAD interface used in X.25 networks.

X.3. ITU-T recommendation that defines various PAD parameters used in X.25 networks. See also *PAD* and *X.25.*

xDSL. Group term used to refer to ADSL, HDSL, SDSL and VDSL. All are emerging digital technologies that use the existing copper infrastructure provided by the telephone companies. xDSL is a high-speed alternative to ISDN.

Symbols

Numerics

A

C

E

F

P

S

T

CCIE Professional Development

Routing TCP/IP, Volume I

Jeff Doyle, CCIE

1-57870-041-8 • AVAILABLE NOW

This book takes the reader from a basic understanding of routers and routing protocols through a detailed examination of each of the IP interior routing protocols. Learn techniques for designing networks that maximize the efficiency of the protocol being used. Exercises and review questions provide core study for the CCIE Routing and Switching exam.

Advanced IP Network Design

Alvaro Retana, CCIE; Don Slice, CCIE; and Russ White, CCIE

1-57870-097-3 • AVAILABLE NOW

Network engineers and managers can use these case studies, which highlight various network design goals, to explore issues including protocol choice, network stability, and growth. This book also includes theoretical discussion on advanced design topics.

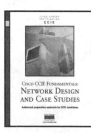

Large-Scale IP Network Solutions

Khalid Raza, CCIE; Salman Asad, CCIE; and Mark Turner

1-57870-084-1 • AVAILABLE NOW

Network engineers can find solutions as their IP networks grow in size and complexity. Examine all the major IP protocols in-depth and learn about scalability, migration planning, network management, and security for large-scale networks.

Cisco CCIE Fundamentals: Network Design and Case Studies, Second Edition

Cisco Systems, Inc.

1-57870-167-8 • AVAILABLE NOW

This two-part reference is a compilation of design tips and configuration examples assembled by Cisco Systems. The design guide portion of this book supports the network administrator who designs and implements routers and switch-based networks, and the case studies supplement the design guide material with real-world configurations. Begin the process of mastering the technologies and protocols necessary to become an effective CCIE.

www.ciscopress.com

Cisco Career Certifications

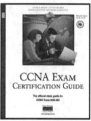

CCNA Exam Certification Guide

Wendell Odom, CCIE

0-7357-0073-7 • AVAILABLE NOW

This book is a comprehensive study tool for CCNA Exam #640-407 and part of a recommended study program from Cisco Systems. *CCNA Exam Certification Guide* helps you understand and master the exam objectives. Instructor-developed elements and techniques maximize your retention and recall of exam topics, and scenario-based exercises help validate your mastery of the exam objectives.

Advanced Cisco Router Configuration

Cisco Systems, Inc., edited by Laura Chappell

1-57870-074-4 • AVAILABLE NOW

Based on the actual Cisco ACRC course, this book provides a thorough treatment of advanced network deployment issues. Learn to apply effective configuration techniques for solid network implementation and management as you prepare for CCNP and CCDP certifications. This book also includes chapter-ending tests for self-assessment.

Introduction to Cisco Router Configuration

Cisco Systems, Inc., edited by Laura Chappell

1-57870-076-0 • AVAILABLE NOW

Based on the actual Cisco ICRC course, this book presents the foundation knowledge necessary to define Cisco router configurations in multiprotocol environments. Examples and chapter-ending tests build a solid framework for understanding internetworking concepts. Prepare for the ICRC course and CCNA certification while mastering the protocols and technologies for router configuration.

Cisco CCNA Preparation Library

Cisco Systems, Inc., Laura Chappell, and Kevin Downes, CCIE

1-57870-125-2 • AVAILABLE NOW • CD-ROM

This boxed set contains two Cisco Press books—*Introduction to Cisco Router Configuration* and *Internetworking Technologies Handbook,* Second Edition—and the *High-Performance Solutions for Desktop Connectivity* CD.

www.ciscopress.com

Cisco Press Solutions

Internetworking SNA with Cisco Solutions

George Sackett and Nancy Sackett

1-57870-083-3 • **AVAILABLE NOW**

This comprehensive guide presents a practical approach to integrating SNA and TCP/IP networks. It provides readers with an understanding of internetworking terms, networking architectures, protocols, and implementations for internetworking SNA with Cisco routers.

Top-Down Network Design

Priscilla Oppenheimer

1-57870-069-8 • **AVAILABLE NOW**

Building reliable, secure, and manageable networks is every network professional's goal. This practical guide teaches you a systematic method for network design that can be applied to campus LANs, remote-access networks, WAN links, and large-scale internetworks. Learn how to analyze business and technical requirements, examine traffic flow and Quality of Service requirements, and select protocols and technologies based on performance goals.

Internetworking Technologies Handbook, Second Edition

Kevin Downes, CCIE, Merilee Ford, H. Kim Lew, Steve Spanier, Tim Stevenson

1-57870-102-3 • **AVAILABLE NOW**

This comprehensive reference provides a foundation for understanding and implementing contemporary internetworking technologies, providing you with the necessary information needed to make rational networking decisions. Master terms, concepts, technologies, and devices that are used in the internetworking industry today. You also learn how to incorporate networking technologies into a LAN/WAN environment, as well as how to apply the OSI reference model to categorize protocols, technologies, and devices.

OSPF Network Design Solutions

Thomas M. Thomas II

1-57870-046-9 • **AVAILABLE NOW**

This comprehensive guide presents a detailed, applied look into the workings of the popular Open Shortest Path First protocol, demonstrating how to dramatically increase network performance and security, and how to most easily maintain large-scale networks. OSPF is thoroughly explained through exhaustive coverage of network design, deployment, management, and troubleshooting.

www.ciscopress.com

Cisco Press Solutions

Internetworking Troubleshooting Handbook

Kevin Downes, CCIE, H. Kim Lew, Spank McCoy,
Tim Stevenson, Kathleen Wallace

1-57870-024-8 • AVAILABLE NOW

Diagnose and resolve specific and potentially problematic issues common to
every network type with this valuable reference. Each section of the book is
devoted to problems common to a specific protocol. Sections are subdivided
into symptoms, descriptions of environments, diagnosing and isolating problem
causes, and problem-solution summaries. This book aims to help you reduce
downtime, improve network performance, and enhance network reliability
using proven troubleshooting solutions.

IP Routing Primer

Robert Wright, CCIE

1-57870-108-2 • AVAILABLE NOW

Learn how IP routing behaves in a Cisco router environment. In addition to
teaching the core fundamentals, this book enhances your ability to troubleshoot
IP routing problems yourself, often eliminating the need to call for additional
technical support. The information is presented in an approachable,
workbook-type format with dozens of detailed illustrations and real-life
scenarios integrated throughout.

Cisco Router Configuration

Allan Leinwand, Bruce Pinsky, Mark Culpepper

1-57870-022-1 • AVAILABLE NOW

An example-oriented and chronological approach helps you implement and
administer your internetworking devices. Starting with the configuration
devices "out of the box," this book moves to configuring Cisco IOS for the
three most popular networking protocols used today: TCP/IP, AppleTalk, and
Novell Interwork Packet Exchange (IPX). You also learn basic administrative
and management configuration, including access control with TACACS+ and
RADIUS, network management with SNMP, logging of messages, and time
control with NTP.

For the latest on Cisco Press resources and Certification and

Training guides, or for information on publishing opportunities, visit

www.ciscopress.com.

**Cisco Press books are available at your local bookstore,
computer store, and online booksellers.**

ISDN Services and Channelized E1 and T1

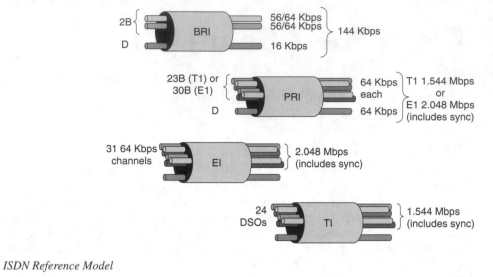

ISDN Reference Model

EIA/TIA-232 Specification

Cisco Press

c i s c o p r e s s . c o m

Committed to being your long-term resource as you grow as a Cisco Networking professional

Help Cisco Press **stay connected** to the issues and challenges you face on a daily basis by registering your product and filling out our brief survey. Complete and mail this form, or better yet ...

Register online and enter to win a FREE book!

Jump to **www.ciscopress.com/register** and register your product online. Each complete entry will be eligible for our monthly drawing to win a FREE book of the winner's choice from the Cisco Press library.

May we contact you via e-mail with information about **new releases, special promotions** and customer benefits?

❑ Yes   ❑ No

E-mail address _____

Name _____

Address _____

City _____ State/Province _____

Country _____ Zip/Post code _____

Where did you buy this product?

❑ Bookstore   ❑ Computer store/electronics store
❑ Online retailer   ❑ Direct from Cisco Press
❑ Mail order   ❑ Class/Seminar
❑ Other_____

When did you buy this product? _____ **Month** _____ **Year**

What price did you pay for this product?

❑ Full retail price   ❑ Discounted price   ❑ Gift

How did you learn about this product?

❑ Friend   ❑ Store personnel   ❑ In-store ad
❑ Cisco Press Catalog   ❑ Postcard in the mail   ❑ Saw it on the shelf
❑ Other Catalog   ❑ Magazine ad   ❑ Article or review
❑ School   ❑ Professional Organization   ❑ Used other products
❑ Other_____

What will this product be used for?

❑ Business use   ❑ School/Education
❑ Other_____

Cisco Press

How many years have you been employed in a computer-related industry?

☐ 2 years or less ☐ 3-5 years ☐ 5+ years

Which best describes your job function?

☐ Corporate Management ☐ Systems Engineering ☐ IS Management
☐ Network Design ☐ Network Support ☐ Webmaster
☐ Marketing/Sales ☐ Consultant ☐ Student
☐ Professor/Teacher ☐ Other _____

What is your formal education background?

☐ High school ☐ Vocational/Technical degree ☐ Some college
☐ College degree ☐ Masters degree ☐ Professional or Doctoral degree

Have you purchased a Cisco Press product before?

☐ Yes ☐ No

On what topics would you like to see more coverage?

_____

_____

Do you have any additional comments or suggestions?

_____

_____

Thank you for completing this survey and registration. Please fold here, seal, and mail to **Cisco Press**.
Building Cisco Remote Access Networks 1-57870-091-4

Indianapolis, IN 46278-8046
P.O. Box #781046
Customer Registration—CP0500227
Cisco Press

ciscopress.com

Indianapolis, IN 46290
201 West 103rd Street
Cisco Press

Place
Stamp
Here

CISCO SYSTEMS

IF YOU'RE USING

CISCO PRODUCTS,

YOU'RE QUALIFIED

TO RECEIVE A

FREE SUBSCRIPTION

TO CISCO'S

PREMIER PUBLICATION,

PACKET™ MAGAZINE.

Packet delivers complete coverage of cutting-edge networking trends and innovations, as well as current product updates. A magazine for technical, hands-on Cisco users, it delivers valuable information for enterprises, service providers, and small and midsized businesses.

Packet is a quarterly publication. To qualify for the upcoming issue, simply click on the URL and follow the prompts to subscribe: www.cisco.com/warp/public/784/packet/subscribe/request.shtml

PACKET

Packet magazine serves as the premier publication linking customers to Cisco Systems, Inc. Delivering complete coverage of cutting-edge networking trends and innovations, *Packet* is a magazine for technical, hands-on users. It delivers industry-specific information for enterprise, service provider, and small and midsized business market segments. A toolchest for planners and decision makers, *Packet* contains a vast array of practical information, boasting sample configurations, real-life customer examples, and tips on getting the most from your Cisco Systems' investments. Simply put, *Packet* magazine is straight talk straight from the worldwide leader in networking for the Internet, Cisco Systems, Inc.

We hope you'll take advantage of this useful resource. I look forward to hearing from you!

Jennifer Biondi
Packet Circulation Manager
packet@cisco.com
www.cisco.com/go/packet

☐ **YES!** I'm requesting a **free** subscription to *Packet* magazine.

☐ No. I'm not interested at this time.

☐ Mr.
☐ Ms.

First Name (Please Print) _____ Last Name _____

Title/Position (Required) _____

Company (Required) _____

Address _____

City _____ State/Province _____

Zip/Postal Code _____ Country _____

Telephone (Include country and area codes) _____ Fax _____

E-mail _____

Signature (Required) _____ Date _____

☐ I would like to receive additional information on Cisco's services and products by e-mail.

1.0 Do you or your company:
A ☐ Use Cisco products   C ☐ Both
B ☐ Resell Cisco products   D ☐ Neither

1. Your organization's relationship to Cisco Systems:
A ☐ Customer/End User   DI ☐ Non-Authorized Reseller   J ☐ Consultant
B ☐ Prospective Customer   E ☐ Integrator   K ☐ Other (specify):
C ☐ Cisco Reseller   G ☐ Cisco Training Partner   _____
D ☐ Cisco Distributor   I ☐ Cisco OEM

2. How would you classify your business?
A ☐ Small/Medium-Sized   B ☐ Enterprise   C ☐ Service Provider

3. Your involvement in network equipment purchases:
A ☐ Recommend   B ☐ Approve   C ☐ Neither

4. Your personal involvement in networking:
A ☐ Entire enterprise at all sites   F ☐ Public network
B ☐ Departments or network segments at more than one site   D ☐ No involvement
C ☐ Single department or network segment   E ☐ Other (specify):
                                                             _____

5. Your Industry:
A ☐ Aerospace   G ☐ a. Education (K–12)   K ☐ Health Care
B ☐ Agriculture/Mining/Construction   ☐ b. Education (College/Univ.) L ☐ Telecommunications
C ☐ Banking/Finance   H ☐ Government—Federal   M ☐ Utilities/Transportation
D ☐ Chemical/Pharmaceutical   I ☐ Government—State   N ☐ Other (specify):
E ☐ Consultant   J ☐ Government—Local   _____
F ☐ Computer/Systems/Electronics